MW01002440

CUBA
ON THE BRINK

ALSO BY JAMES G. BLIGHT AND DAVID A. WELCH

On the Brink:
Americans and Soviets Reexamine the Cuban Missile Crisis

CUBA
ON THE
BRINK

CASTRO, THE MISSILE CRISIS, AND THE SOVIET COLLAPSE

James G. Blight, Bruce J. Allyn, and David A. Welch

*With the Assistance of
David Lewis*

Foreword by Jorge I. Domínguez

PANTHEON BOOKS   NEW YORK

Copyright © 1993 by James G. Blight, Bruce J. Allyn, and David A. Welch
Foreword copyright © 1993 by Jorge I. Domínguez

All rights reserved under International and Pan-American Copyright Conventions.
Published in the United States by Pantheon Books, a division of Random House,
Inc., New York, and simultaneously in Canada by Random House of Canada
Limited, Toronto.

Grateful acknowledgment is made to Russell & Volkening, Inc., for permission to
reprint excerpts from *Memories of Underdevelopment* by Edmundo Desnoes.
Copyright © 1967 by New American Library. Reprinted by permission of Russell
& Volkening, Inc., as agents for the author.

Library of Congress Cataloging-in-Publication Data

Cuba on the brink : Castro, the missile crisis, and the Soviet collapse / James
    G. Blight, Bruce J. Allyn, and David A. Welch.
        p.   cm.
    Includes index.
    ISBN 0-679-42149-1
    1. Cuban Missile Crisis, 1962—Congresses.   2. Cuba—Foreign relations—
Soviet Union—Congresses.   3. Soviet Union—Foreign relations—Cuba—
Congresses.   I. Blight, James G.   II. Allyn, Bruce J.   III. Welch, David A.
E841.C8   1993
972.9106′4—dc20   93-19177

Book design by Glen Edelstein

Manufactured in the United States of America

First Edition

To *janet* and *Melissa,* once more, with feeling;
and to *Asya:* heroines of a revolution

Contents

Foreword

Was Cuba a part of the "Cuban missile crisis"? For many U.S. government decision makers at the time of the crisis in 1962, and for many scholars ever since, the answer has been no. Cuba was just the locale somewhat incidentally related to one of the most important U.S.-Soviet confrontations during the entire history of the Cold War.[1] This invisibility of small countries for U.S. foreign policy making was not unique to Cuba. Arguably, U.S. government decision makers thought of U.S. participation in the Vietnam war mainly as an action to contain the Soviet Union and China; Vietnam, too, was mainly just a locale. Nor was such invisibility limited to the U.S.-Soviet confrontation. In the first U.S. military action after the end of the Cold War, the Bush administration thought of the U.S. intervention in Panama as a response to domestic crises in the United States (drug consumption and traffic as well as the need to define the president's decisiveness); once again, Panama was just a locale.

This fascinating book rests on the premise that Cuba did matter for the Cuban missile crisis. In so demonstrating that premise, *Cuba on the Brink* issues a warning that is highly pertinent for our times: decision makers and scholars will err if they ignore the mighty effect that small countries may have in international affairs.

More specifically, this book also helps to correct the errors of scholars who have worked on the missile crisis and, in the process of revision, the book sheds new light on the crisis and on Cuba's importance to it. Perhaps one way to demonstrate Cuba's importance for the crisis itself, for U.S. foreign policy, and for the world of scholarship is to show how this project has forced me to rethink what I had written about this event.[2]

CUBA'S IMPORTANCE FOR THE CUBAN MISSILE CRISIS

Why did the Soviet Union deploy such military force? U.S. decision makers and scholars have typically thought that the Soviet Union deployed ballistic missiles to Cuba in order to redress the strategic imbalance between the United States and the Soviet Union. This book suggests that the deployment may well have had a significant impact on such imbalance had the USSR been able to retain its strategic weapons in Cuba. But this book also makes clear that a comparably important motivation for the Soviet deployment was the defense of Cuba against U.S. aggression.[3] Cuba mattered to the Cuban missile crisis, above all, because many in the Soviet government, including Nikita Khrushchev, believed that Cuba mattered to them: there might have been no deployment otherwise.

How serious was the likelihood of nuclear war over Cuba? Without underestimating the seriousness of the crisis, many scholars have believed that nuclear war was still somewhat distant because, as General William Smith reports in this book, the U.S. government had not found any nuclear warheads in Cuba. "Nuclear warheads were not identified and were perhaps never deployed to Cuba, although they probably would have been sent later; otherwise the missile launchers would have been pointless," I had written.[4] However, this book shows that nuclear warheads had been delivered to Cuba and that they were intended for installation on both intermediate-range ballistic missiles and shorter-range tactical missiles. The Soviet government contemplated the use of such tactical nuclear weapons in the event of a U.S. invasion of Cuba with conventional military forces; had this occurred, the U.S. government would most likely have retaliated with its own tactical nuclear weapons and perhaps the war might have escalated even further.

Did the actions of Cuban leaders make the outbreak of war more or less probable? One of the most dangerous moments of the entire crisis was the shooting down of a U.S. U-2 reconnaissance airplane. I have argued that "Castro may . . . have given an order that was executed by a Soviet Officer."[5] I was wrong; reality turned out to be more interesting and more dangerous. As this book shows, Castro ordered Cuban anti-aircraft batteries to fire at low-flying U.S. airplanes.[6] There is no evidence that Castro ordered the Soviet officers to fire. Instead, the Soviet officers in Cuba identified so closely with the Cuban government's cause that their field commander gave the order to shoot at the U-2, thinking as an ally supporting comrades in war. Underscoring the importance of this relationship among comrades, Castro reports in this book that "it's possible that our responsibility may have been greater than that of the Soviets" in the shooting down of the U-2. Cuban government actions brought the world much closer to the brink of nuclear warfare.

Did the actions of the Cuban leaders make a peaceful settlement more or less probable? Castro's recommendation to Khrushchev that the Soviet Union should launch a first-strike nuclear attack on the United States in the event that the United States were to launch an invasion of Cuba with conventional military forces clearly frightened the Soviet leadership and contributed to Khrushchev's decision to yield to the United States. In this way, Castro contributed to the settlement even though such was not his intention. This book demonstrates that Castro was ready for war, even for nuclear war, and that he opposed the withdrawal of Soviet missiles and warheads from Cuba on the terms that Khrushchev had accepted.[7] Castro acted to impede the settlement and thus contributed to the risk of renewed confrontation.

DISAGREEMENTS

This book's analysis of Cuba, its relations with the superpowers, and its role during the missile crisis is superb and unmatched in the existing scholarship on this topic. The text conveys in dramatic fashion the mood and feel of the crisis itself and of the January 1992 conference held in Havana, which provides the book's raw material. Nonetheless, there remains room for analytical disagreement. Consider two such disagreements.

Can the leaders of small countries think strategically? This book argues that leaders of small countries matter for the strategies of major powers and for the evolution and the outcome of an event like the missile crisis. And yet, the authors doubt the claims of Fidel Castro and other Cuban officials that their decision to accept the missiles involved truly global strategic thinking, namely, in Castro's words, "that it was imperative to strengthen the socialist camp, and that if we expected the socialist countries to fight for us, we, for simple reasons of image, could not selfishly refuse that cooperation to the socialist camp."[8]

The book's authors claim that Castro was motivated, instead, by his wish to deter a U.S. invasion with such weapons and by his sense of gratification and exultation that the United States would have its nose rubbed in the ground. Castro, the authors claim, has, in effect, made up the strategic explanation because it better serves the subsequent needs to protect Cuban dignity; it would be unseemly to admit to gloating, especially since the crisis ended in a humiliation for Cuba's leaders. The authors present their own cogent reasons for their preferred interpretation.[9] I agree that the factors that they identify were probably among the motivations of Cuba's leaders, but I have no difficulty in accepting President Castro's forthright statement that he did, indeed, think then in global strategic terms. He has certainly thought in such terms ever since. On this important historical point, the authors let their careful textual and contextual analysis overwhelm the larger picture and more important point: Fidel Castro has been a better world strategist throughout his career than most leaders of the major powers.

Can world-class strategists, nonetheless, at times act non-rationally? "Don Quixote's madness and the madness of revolutionaries are similar," Castro told an interviewer; "the spirit is similar . . . that spirit of the knight-errant, of righting wrongs everywhere, of fighting against giants."[10] Willful political action and tactical boldness, Castro has long believed, serve his interests best in the long run, even if there are temporary setbacks. This belief has led him to attempt extraordinary deeds time and again during his career and, often, to succeed at them. Such boldness, such apparent madness, has a strong rational basis evident in many circumstances but especially so during the Cuban missile crisis. It is intended to persuade the United States that the cost of war would be very high; to do so, Castro must seem "mad" in his resolute commitment never to surrender to the United States. And yet, during the missile crisis, this perspective led Castro to behavior that was not rational, namely, to make nuclear war much more probable and thus to risk leading his people to collective suicide. Castro's behavior at a key juncture during the missile crisis no longer served the rational purpose of deterrence.[11]

The book's authors wish to argue that Castro was rational throughout the entire missile crisis episode. The authors claim that Castro was "merely mistaken" in making those decisions that brought his country, and the world, dramatically closer to nuclear war.[12] The authors argue that Castro believed that he and his people faced one and only one rational choice: annihilation with honor or with dishonor. It is not just that this turned out to be false—and that, as Castro would acknowledge years later, the missile crisis settlement contributed to the consolidation of his regime—but that it was false in October 1962. A leader who convinces himself that only collective suicide is possible is not acting rationally; instead, he has allowed non-rational factors to prevent him from thinking rationally and, in so doing, has made it more likely that a non-rational, avoidable outcome would occur.

IMPLICATIONS

The story of the Cuban missile crisis remains pertinent to our times in a great many ways. This books shows, for example, the insufficiencies of U.S. intelligence gathering. The lore of the Cuban missile crisis often praises the great intelligence achievement of discovering the missiles before they became operational. True. But this book shows that U.S. intelligence never discovered that nuclear warheads had been deployed to Cuba at all, much less that they had been deployed for use on both strategic and tactical missiles. Nor did U.S. intelligence come even close to ascertaining the real size of the Soviet deployment of ground troops.

More important, the book shows that small countries can make an enormous difference in world affairs. In the history of the Cold War, only the Koreas and the Vietnams match Cuba's importance. There should no longer be any doubt that Cuba, at least, was not just an object but also a subject in the Cuban missile crisis—just as Armenians, Serbs, Haitians, and, alas, even Cubans are also subjects in the making of the international crises since the end of the Cold War *in Europe*.

This raises a more specific but important implication for the future. The Cold War has not ended in the Caribbean. Cuba's political regime may be a dinosaur, but insofar as its leaders proclaim that they will never surrender to the United States, this dinosaur still attempts to behave as a Tyrannosaurus rex. The United States and Cuba are still managing the debris of the Cold War. As the concluding press conference of the Havana meeting shows (this book's last chapter), even the most rational and clear-thinking U.S. leaders may at times find it difficult to discuss current political topics with Cuban leaders without making things increasingly unmanageable with every word uttered. Even Cuban leaders who have graciously and generously hosted their U.S. interlocutors find such discussions difficult.

Today, as a third of a century ago, it ought to remain a major objective of U.S. and Cuban leaders, and of ordinary citizens in both countries, to accord to each other the respect that the former antagonists who are this book's protagonists accorded to each other during the Havana conference, and to work even harder than they to prevent mere words from getting in the way of their thinking. This is especially important because today, as a third of a century ago, the United States objects to the very nature of the Cuban regime. Today, as a third of a century ago, Fidel Castro and his associates still proclaim that they will defend their version of the homeland even it it means death: "Patria o muerte" ends their speeches. And, if my argument above is correct, Fidel Castro can behave non-rationally in extreme crisis situations. Today, as a third of a century ago, war is still thinkable in U.S.-Cuban relations. That is this splendid book's troubling reminder about the pertinence of the past for the future that Cuba and the United States have and will share.

Jorge I. Domínguez
Harvard University

If they blockade our country they will exalt our nation, because we will resist . . . We are part of humanity and we run the necessary risks, yet, we are not afraid. We must learn how to live in our allotted times and with the dignity with which we know how to live. Everybody, men and women, young and old, we are all one in this moment of danger.

—FIDEL CASTRO,
Radio and Television speech to the Cuban people, 22 October 1962

We're all one, I'll die like everybody else. This island is a trap and the revolution is tragic because we're too small to survive, to come through. Too poor and too few. It's quite an expensive dignity . . . I felt no relief watching the open water. Could see nothing, still, I would feel the battleships, the gray aircraft carriers almost brushing past my face. First they'll certainly bomb us, to soften and destroy us, but the sky was quiet, I was still alive. The safety of that very instant meant nothing, it was an instant without a future. It is the same too right now, this very moment is a moment without a future. Everything can suddenly burst into "roaring flames" and "brilliant luminosity" twenty miles high, as it says in that description of the hydrogen bomb that I just read. Nothing happens, everything is possible.

—EDMUNDO DESNOES,
Memories of Underdevelopment

Dramatis Personae

The participants in the drama that follows are a diverse group of Cuban missile crisis veterans and scholars from the United States, Cuba, and the Russian Federation. Accordingly, we have divided the cast of characters below into former policy makers and academics. As will become obvious, however, the distinction is partly one of convenience, for their memberships often overlap. We also list the former policy makers and scholars from the three delegations who did not participate directly in the conference conversation, but who were present at the conference and instrumental in making it possible.

Veterans

ALEKSEEV, Aleksandr. Soviet ambassador to Cuba, June 1962–January 1968. During the 1950s and early 1960s, Alekseev was posted as a reporter for TASS, the official Soviet news agency, but was in fact a KGB officer (surname: Sh'tov) who served throughout Latin America. Named by Khrushchev to become ambassador to Cuba specifically because of the imminent missile deployment in June 1962, Alekseev played a pivotal role as intermediary between Khrushchev and Castro throughout the crisis. Soviet leader Leonid Brezhnev abruptly recalled Alekseev from his post in January 1968, allegedly for being too pro-Cuban in his sentiments. Alekseev has written many articles for the Russian press containing his own perceptions of the missile crisis.

CASTRO Ruz, Fidel. First secretary of the Central Committee of the Cuban Communist Party, president of the Council of State and the Council of Ministers, and commander-in-chief of the armed forces. Fidel Castro first came to power in Cuba in January 1959, following a successful rebellion against the brutal dictatorship of Fulgencio Batista. In 1962, he was one of six members of the ruling "Secretariat" (which also included Raúl Castro, Emilio Aragonés, Osvaldo Dorticós, Blás Roca, and Ernesto "Che" Guevara). In all significant respects, however, Castro was in charge of Cuban preparations for receipt of the Soviet missiles, of all important contingency planning to repel the expected U.S. invasion of Cuba, and of the negotiations with Soviet representative Anastas I. Mikoyan to establish the conditions under which the missiles would be withdrawn. One of the most charismatic and controversial leaders of the twentieth century, Castro was named head of the Non-Aligned Movement in 1979. He now leads the Cuban austerity program (called the "Special Period in Time of Peace") designed to raise the odds of the survival of socialism in Cuba, following the collapse of the Soviet Union and the end of all forms of Soviet assistance to Cuba.

CLINE, Ray S. Chairman of the United States Global Strategy Council, Washington, D.C. A veteran of service in the Office of Strategic Services (OSS) during World War II, Cline became an analyst with its successor organization, the Central Intelligence Agency (CIA). In his early days with the CIA, Cline had an important role in the development of the American U-2 spy plane. Recalled from service in Asia following the Bay of Pigs fiasco in 1961, Cline was named deputy director (intelligence) of the CIA by the new director, John McCone. During the Cuban missile crisis, Cline supervised the team of analysts from the National Photographic Interpretation Center (NPIC) which discovered the presence of Soviet nuclear missiles in Cuba. Cline left the CIA in 1966 because of disagreement with the Johnson administration's policy in Vietnam.

DARUSENKOV, Oleg. Ambassador of the Russian Federation to Mexico. For nearly thirty years, Darusenkov shuttled back and forth between the Soviet embassy in Havana and the Cuba desk in the International Department of the Central Committee of the Communist Party of the Soviet Union. During the Cuban missile crisis and Anastas Mikoyan's subsequent visit to Cuba in November 1961, he was an aide to ambassador Aleksandr Alekseev in Havana. He assisted in the translation of the crucial Castro-Khrushchev cables between 26 and 31 October.

ESCALANTE Font, Fabian. Division general of the Cuban Ministry of Interior (MININT) and a member of the Central Committee of the Cuban Communist Party. Escalante first joined the Interior Ministry in 1960, rising steadily through its ranks. Just before the missile crisis, Escalante worked for Cuban counterintelligence in Guatemala, reporting to Havana on the training of Cuban exiles who would eventually try to invade at the Bay of Pigs. During the missile crisis, he worked in counterintelligence in Cuba. He was named lieutenant colonel in 1979 and brigadier general in 1984. He first became well known outside Cuba when Fidel Castro named him one of two judges in the military trial of General Arnaldo Ochoa in June 1989, as a result of which Ochoa, Cuba's most decorated war hero and former head of Cuban forces in Angola, was sentenced to death. Escalante has commissioned several studies within MININT of U.S.-backed covert action programs against Cuba in the period of the missile crisis, a subject on which he is Cuba's recognized authority.

GARTHOFF, Raymond L. Senior fellow, Foreign Policy Studies Program, Brookings Institution, Washington, D.C. Garthoff was formerly special assistant for Soviet bloc political/military affairs in the State Department during the Kennedy administration; executive officer of the first Strategic Arms Limitation Talks (SALT I), 1969–73; and ambassador to Bulgaria, 1977–79. He is the author of numerous works on U.S.-Soviet relations. He wrote key memoranda during the Cuban missile crisis analyzing the military significance of the Soviet deployment and the Soviet proposal to withdraw missiles from Cuba in return for the withdrawal of NATO missiles from Turkey. Garthoff participated in all five conferences on the missile crisis as both a scholar and a former policy maker.

GRIBKOV, Gen. Anatoly I. General of the Army of the Russian Federation and general inspector of the Russian Ministry of Defense. A veteran of World War II, Gribkov rose to prominence in 1976 when he was named chief of staff of the Warsaw Treaty Organization (WTO), a position he held until 1989. In 1962, Gribkov helped to plan Operation Anadyr, the secret deployment of men, missiles, and matériel to Cuba, as head of a directorate of the main Operations Directorate of the Soviet General Staff. Gribkov was in Cuba prior to the most intense phase of the crisis and had responsibility for overseeing the Soviet withdrawal from the island, under the terms worked out by President Kennedy and Chairman Khrushchev. Recently, Gribkov has published memoirs on the missile crisis in Russia and in the West.

LECHUGA Hevia, Carlos. Ambassador at large of the Cuban Ministry of External Affairs (MINREX), with special responsibilities at the Geneva Conference on human rights. Originally a journalist, Lechuga was a young writer for *El Mundo* (*The World*) when Fidel Castro came to power in 1959. Lechuga accompanied Castro on his visit to the United States in April 1959, filing daily reports for the Cuban press. Lechuga was Cuban ambassador to the Organization of American States (OAS) in January 1962, when a U.S.-led coalition voted to oust Cuba from the organization. When the Cuban missile crisis broke, Lechuga was serving as ambassador to Mexico. But on 28 October 1962, Fidel Castro recalled him to Havana, met him at the airport, and informed him that he had just been named Cuban ambassador to the United Nations. In New York, he attempted to integrate Cuba into the U.S.-Soviet discussions regarding the terms of the resolution to the crisis. As U.N. ambassador, Lechuga played the role of intermediary in the Kennedy administration's 1963 attempt to move toward more normal relations with Cuba.

McNAMARA, Robert S. Washington, D.C. McNamara was president of the Ford Motor Company, 1960–61; secretary of defense in both the Kennedy and Johnson administrations and a member of the Executive Committee of the National Security Council (ExComm); and president of the World Bank, 1968–81. With the exceptions of President John Kennedy and Attorney General Robert Kennedy, McNamara was perhaps the most important U.S. decision maker in the missile crisis. A dove throughout, McNamara firmly advocated the naval quarantine of Cuba and opposed an air strike and invasion. President Kennedy relied more heavily on McNamara than on anyone else to manage the quarantine and the military, whose leaders uniformly advocated stronger action. McNamara participated in all five conferences on the crisis and was instrumental in preparations for the Havana conference. He is also well known as an articulate spokesman for the view that international crises cannot be "managed," and is, in addition, an advocate of very deep cuts in the nuclear stockpiles of the United States and the republics of the former Soviet Union.

MARTIN, Edwin M. Chair of the executive committee of the Population Crisis Committee, Washington, D.C. A retired foreign service officer, Martin served in many Latin American posts, including U.S. ambassador to Argentina. In 1962, he was assistant secretary of state for inter-American affairs. Martin coordinated U.S. efforts before the missile crisis to isolate Cuba from other governments in the hemisphere. In addition, he was a member of various official and unofficial bodies which oversaw covert U.S. action against Cuba. During the Cuban missile crisis, Martin, who was a member of ExComm, sought and achieved a unanimous OAS vote to condemn the Soviet missile deployment in Cuba and to approve the U.S. "quarantine" (or blockade) of the island.

RISQUET Valdés Saldaña, Jorge. Member, Central Committee of the Cuban Communist Party. As a young man, Risquet was involved in revolutionary movements throughout Latin America, beginning with his joint participation with Ernesto "Che" Guevara in Guatemala in 1954, following the U.S.-backed coup against Jacobo Arbenz Guzmán, who later fled to Cuba. In the 1960s, Risquet was active in African liberation movements, serving on behalf of Cuba from Morocco to Angola. He served briefly as minister of labor in the late 1960s. Beginning in 1975, Risquet became coordinator of all Cuban political-military activities in Africa, with special responsibilities in the two areas of Cuba's heaviest involvement: Angola and the Horn of Africa. In the late 1980s, Risquet was chief Cuban negotiator at the talks which brought an end to the Angolan civil war and which resulted in the independence of Namibia from South African rule. During the missile crisis, Risquet commanded an infantry company stationed in Santiago de Cuba, in the eastern sector of the island, preparing for the expected attack from the nearby U.S. base at Guantánamo Bay.

SCHLESINGER, Arthur M., Jr. Albert Schweitzer Professor of the Humanities, Graduate Center of the City University of New York.

Author of many works on American history, including best-selling biographies of John and Robert Kennedy, and the recipient of two Pulitzer prizes for historical writing, Schlesinger was a White House aide in the Kennedy administration, where his duties included reporting on Latin American affairs. Schlesinger first visited Cuba in 1950. He was the primary author of the presidential White Paper of 3 April 1961 stating the Kennedy administration's brief against the regime of Fidel Castro, and preparing the U.S. public for the invasion at the Bay of Pigs, which occurred two weeks later. During the Kennedy administration, Schlesinger was a primary spokesman in Latin America for Kennedy's "Alliance for Progress," a program designed to prevent the conditions under which other "Cubas" might develop. He has long been an advocate of normalization of relations with Cuba, but has also been a critic of Cuban human rights abuses.

SMITH, Wayne S. Adjunct professor of Latin American studies, Johns Hopkins University, Baltimore, Md. A retired career foreign service officer, Smith began his service as a junior officer on the staff of the U.S. ambassador to Cuba during the waning days of dictator Fulgencio Batista, in 1958. He was present in Havana when the Cuban Revolution triumphed, and remained there until 3 January 1961, when the Eisenhower administration broke relations with the Castro government. In the late 1960s, Smith served in Moscow. During the Carter administration, Smith was centrally involved in opening up relations with Havana, where he served as chief of the U.S. Interests Section from 1979 to 1981, during one of the stormiest periods of U.S.-Cuban relations since the missile crisis. Since retiring from the foreign service, he has authored dozens of books and articles on Cuban politics, history, and culture, and on U.S. policy toward the Castro regime.

SMITH, Gen. William Y. United States Air Force (retired), and President Emeritus of the Institute for Defense Analyses (IDA), Alexandria, Virginia. A career officer in the U.S. Air Force, Smith was a specialist on U.S. nuclear forces. He served several tours of duty in Europe and was twice special assistant to the Chairman of the Joint Chiefs of Staff: under Gen. Maxwell D. Taylor during the Kennedy administration; and under Gen. David Jones during the Carter administration. During the missile crisis, Smith coordinated the Chiefs' activities with respect to the worldwide nuclear alert (which reached, at the height of the crisis, DefCon 2, the highest level of alert ever ordered for U.S. forces) and had oversight, on behalf of General Taylor, of U.S. conventional force preparations in the Caribbean in the event the president ordered an air strike and/or an invasion of Cuba. He has been instrumental in assisting scholars studying the missile crisis to obtain relevant military documents on the U.S. side.

TITOV, Gen. Georgy M. (retired). A veteran of World War II, Titov was stationed in Cuba as a division commander during the missile crisis. He is now one of the leading Russian authorities on Soviet military operations during the crisis. He has published the results of his research in several joint Russian publications with Gen. Anatoly Gribkov, some of which have been translated and published in the West.

TROYANOVSKY, Oleg. Guest scholar, the Kennan Institute of the Woodrow Wilson Center for Scholars, Washington, D.C. Son of the first Soviet ambassador to the United States in 1933, Troyanovsky grew up in Washington, D.C., and attended Swarthmore College. During the period of Nikita Khrushchev's leadership of the Soviet Union, Troyanovsky was his special assistant for international affairs, with special responsibilities vis-à-vis the United States. From 1975 to 1984, Troyanovsky was Soviet ambassador to the United Nations. He retired in 1989 as ambassador to China. During the missile crisis, Troyanovsky played a key role in the drafting of Khrushchev's letters to Kennedy, and in the interpretation of Kennedy's letters to Khrushchev. He also was responsible, at the height of the crisis, for coordinating all information coming to Khrushchev and the Politburo regarding the possibility of a U.S. invasion of Cuba. He is now writing his memoirs.

Scholars

ALLYN, Bruce J. Program Director, Conflict Management Group, Cambridge, Massachusetts, and Adjunct Fellow, John F. Kennedy School of Government. Allyn is a specialist in U.S.–Russian negotiations and conflict management, and has coauthored scholarly works on the Cuban missile crisis.

ARMSTRONG, R. Scott. Codirector, Taxpayers Against Fraud, Washington, D.C. Originally trained in law, Armstrong served on the Senate committee that investigated the activities of President Nixon and his associates during the Watergate scandal. Later he became a reporter for the *Washington Post*. Armstrong founded the National Security Archive in Washington, D.C., the primary source of documentation on the missile crisis and other episodes in the recent history of U.S. foreign policy. He initiated the first Freedom of Information Act (FOIA) requests, in 1977–78, to retrieve classified U.S. documentation on the crisis.

BLIGHT, James G. Senior research fellow and director, U.S.-Russia-Cuba Project, Center for Foreign Policy Development, Thomas J. Watson Jr. Institute for International Studies, Brown University. Trained originally as a psychologist, he is the author of works on the psychology of international affairs and has written several books and articles on the missile crisis.

BRENNER, Philip. Chair, Department of International Politics and Foreign Policy, School of International Service, the American University, Washington, D.C. Brenner is a Cuba specialist who has traveled frequently to the island for over twenty years and is the author of several books on the politics and culture of Cuba. Brenner was also instrumental in obtaining the release of the Kennedy-Khrushchev correspondence from the U.S. State Department just prior to the Havana conference.

DIEZ Acosta, Tomás. Senior researcher, Instituto de Historia de Cuba (Institute of the History of Cuba), Havana. A professional historian, Diez is the supervisor of a large Cuban oral history project dealing with the missile crisis, and is a member of the research team responsible for exhibits at the forthcoming Havana Museum of the October Crisis.

DOMÍNGUEZ, Jorge I. Professor of Government and member of the executive council of the Center for International Affairs, Harvard University. Widely recognized as a leading American scholar of contemporary Cuba, he is the author of standard works on the Cuban economy and Cuban foreign policy. Recently he coordinated the efforts of a team of scholars and former officials, brought together by the Inter-American Dialogue in Washington, D.C., to articulate a new U.S. policy for Cuba after the Cold War.

GUNN, Gillian. Director, Cuba Project, Center for Latin American Studies, Georgetown University. An authority on the Cuban interventions in southern Africa, which she covered as a journalist, Gunn has more recently organized the most important ongoing U.S.-Cuban discussions taking place in the United States. Her "Cuba Study Group" at Georgetown University provides the only important opportunities for scholars, journalists, and officials to interact with U.S. government officials in off-the-record discussions.

HERNÁNDEZ Rodríguez, Rafael. Deputy director, Centro de Estudios sobre America (Center for the Study of the Americas), Havana, Cuba. Cuba's most prolific scholar of the United States, Hernández is also Cuba's best-known student of the Cuban missile crisis, and is the author of many works linking the missile crisis with contemporary U.S.-Cuban relations. A former fellow at both Harvard and Columbia, Hernández has coauthored several important works with scholars from both institutions.

KHRUSHCHEV, Sergei N. Senior research associate, Center for Foreign Policy Development, Thomas J. Watson Jr. Institute for International Studies, Brown University. Originally trained as an engineer with the Soviet Strategic Rocket Forces, Khrushchev was prevented from traveling outside the Soviet bloc from the 1964 ouster of his father, Nikita Khrushchev, until 1989, when he came to the United States to speak about his father's role in the missile crisis. He has since become well known as a biographer and historian of the Soviet leadership during his father's years in power.

KOVALIEV, Felix N. At his retirement in January 1992, Kovaliev was director of the Department of Archival Administration in the Soviet Foreign Ministry. A former Soviet ambassador to several Latin American countries, he was instrumental in obtaining the release of many important Soviet documents on the missile crisis, including records of discussions between Fidel Castro and Anastas Mikoyan in November 1962.

MENDOZA, Jorge Enrique. Director, Instituto de Historia de Cuba (Institute of the History of Cuba), Havana, Cuba. Mendoza served with the rebel army of Fidel Castro in the Sierra Maestra in the late 1950s, where he gained fame in Cuba as the voice of Radio Rebelde (Rebel Radio), the clandestine voice of Castro's "26th of July" movement. For many years, Mendoza was editor of *Granma,* the daily newspaper of the Cuban Communist Party. He remains a close adviser to President Castro on matters of ideology.

MIKOYAN, Sergo A. Senior research associate, Center for Latin American Studies, Georgetown University. For nearly twenty years, Mikoyan was the leading Soviet interpreter of Latin American affairs, while serving as editor in chief of *Latinskaya amerika* (*Latin America*), the leading Soviet journal devoted to Latin American affairs. Mikoyan's current research primarily concerns Russia at the end of the Cold War. During the missile crisis he traveled to Cuba as executive secretary to his father, First Deputy Premier Anastas I. Mikoyan, to participate in the negotiations which brought the crisis to an end.

PASTOR, Robert A. Professor of political science at Emory University and fellow at Emory's Carter Center. Pastor was director of Latin American and Caribbean Affairs on the National Security Council from 1977 to 1981. The author of many works on Latin American politics, he has also organized electoral observation missions in Panama, Nicaragua, Haiti, and Guyana. Pastor has also written several definitive works on the democratization process in Latin America.

WELCH, David A. Assistant professor of political science, University of Toronto. Welch is the author of works on the psychology and philosophy of international relations, on international relations theory, and on the Cuban missile crisis.

Other Participants

ALARCÓN de Quesada, Ricardo. Foreign Minister of Cuba.

AMOSEV, Igor A. Senior historian, Institute of Military History, Moscow.

ARBESÚ Fraga, José Antonio. Head, Americas Department, Central Committee of the Cuban Communist Party.

DEL VALLE Jiménez, Sergio. Former chief of staff of the Cuban army.

KORNBLUH, Peter. Senior analyst, National Security Archive, Washington, D.C.

LANG, janet M. Assistant professor of epidemiology and biostatistics, Boston University School of Public Health.

LEWIS, David. Research assistant, Center for Foreign Policy Development, Thomas J. Watson Jr. Institute for International Studies, Brown University.

MONTERO Rodríguez, Othon. Senior researcher, Instituto de Historia de Cuba, Havana, Cuba.

NEWBERGER, Stuart. Crowell & Moring, Washington, D.C.

POLLO, Jorge. Senior staff officer, Politburo of the Central Committee, Cuban Communist Party.

SAVRANSKAYA, Svetlana. Doctoral candidate, Department of Political Science, Emory University.

SUÁREZ Salazar, Luis. Director, Centro de Estudios sobre America, Havana, Cuba.

WALTER, Sheryl L. General counsel, National Security Archive, Washington, D.C.

WEISS, Thomas G. Deputy director, Thomas J. Watson Jr. Institute for International Studies, Brown University.

CUBA
ON THE BRINK

INTRODUCTION:
TOWARD THE BRINK

Havana is white, yellow; it's whitewashed in pale colors, faded or dirty: green, blue, gray, pink. A motley of buildings. . . . My Havana is the one I see here from my window. It's made up of the poplars of Vedado and crestfallen grimy pines. . . . I can't visualize the city of Havana destroyed, evaporated by a hydrogen bomb. . . . I feel just like one of the cows on our farm when it rained. They would stand motionless, immobile in the middle of the field. Wherever the rain caught them.
—EDMUNDO DESNOES,
Memories of Underdevelopment

THIS BOOK CONTAINS THE BACKGROUND, POLITICAL CONTEXT, PRO-
ceedings, and interpretation of a conference on the Cuban missile crisis of October 1962, held in Havana, Cuba, 9–12 January 1992. Cuban president Fidel Castro hosted and participated fully in each session. Joining him were several other Cuban decision makers in the events of October–November 1962; a U.S. delegation of scholars and former officials from the Kennedy administration led by Kennedy's secretary of defense, Robert McNamara, and by Kennedy White House aide and historian Arthur Schlesinger, Jr.; and a Russian delegation led by Oleg Troyanovsky, former special assistant to Soviet leader Nikita Khrushchev, and Gen. Anatoly I. Gribkov, former head of the Warsaw Pact. There, gathered around one conference table in Havana for the first time (and also, no doubt, for the last), representatives of Cuba's former ally and Cuba's former and current adversary met with Fidel Castro to exchange views and to cross-examine one another on the causes, conduct, and consequences of the most dramatic and dangerous crisis of the nuclear age.

Most people alive today who lived through the Cuban missile crisis of 1962 vividly recall their fear and anxiety as the world seemed to teeter on the brink of nuclear disaster. For six days and nights, the United States and the Soviet Union stared each other down over the deployment of Soviet nuclear missiles to Cuba.* For the young American president, John F. Kennedy, and for his much older adversary, Soviet chairman Nikita Khrushchev, the encounter represented a supreme test both of will and of prudence. Neither desired a direct military confrontation, and both eagerly sought to avoid a third world war. But Kennedy simply could not afford to allow the Soviets to deploy nuclear weapons in America's backyard, because he had warned the Soviets publicly, throughout the summer and early fall of 1962, not to do so. He knew that if he permitted the deployment to stand, the American people, Congress, and the United States' NATO allies would interpret it as a complete unwillingness on his part to defend American interests and commitments. He suspected that friendly regimes around the world would interpret it as a major American defeat. He feared Khrushchev and communists everywhere would interpret it as a sign of weakness, and mount even graver challenges—perhaps in Berlin, the tinderbox of Europe. For his part, Khrushchev could not simply back down in the face of American demands without undermining the Soviet Union's status and prestige as the leader of the socialist community, legitimizing Kennedy's "illegal" blockade of Cuba, and openly surrendering to "imperialism." Thus when Kennedy publicly challenged Khrushchev to remove the missiles in a nationally televised speech on 22 October and announced his intention to impose a "quarantine" on shipments of arms to Cuba, and when Khrushchev defiantly refused the next day to "recognize [the] right of [the] United States to establish control over armaments essential to [the] Republic of Cuba for strengthening its defensive capacity,"[1] few people around the globe could imagine how the superpowers could turn away from the path they had started down and avoid the seemingly inevitable confrontation.

Yet they did. On 28 October, Khrushchev publicly agreed to dismantle, crate, and return to the Soviet Union the weapons the United States considered offensive in exchange for an American pledge not to invade Cuba.[2] At the same time, Kennedy secretly agreed to withdraw American Jupiter missiles from Turkey.[3] Once their passions had

---

*Readers unfamiliar with the events of the Cuban missile crisis should consult the chronology in appendix 1.

cooled, they were able to cut what Khrushchev poignantly called the "knot of war."[4] They did so because they came to appreciate the awesome responsibility they shared for the fate of the Earth; they learned, through a series of shocks and surprises, that they could not fully control the actions of their military establishments; and they came to recognize that their own fallibility—their misjudgments, misperceptions, prejudices, and biases—played a significant role in the genesis of the crisis, and could lead them stumbling into disaster.[5] "[I]f indeed war should break out," Khrushchev wrote Kennedy as the crisis reached its crescendo, "then it would not be in our power to stop it, for such is the logic of war. I have participated in two wars and know that war ends when it has rolled through cities and villages, everywhere sowing death and destruction."[6]

While the world concluded that Khrushchev had conceded more than Kennedy—and thus that the crisis had been a dramatic American victory—Kennedy himself refused to characterize it as such,[7] and it is clear with the benefit of hindsight that the United States and the Soviet Union resolved the crisis on the basis of more or less reciprocal concessions. In Havana, it seemed to Prime Minister Fidel Castro that one of Khrushchev's more significant concessions was Cuba's security. But despite Castro's protestations and his attempts to frustrate the smooth resolution of the crisis (he refused to permit United Nations inspection of Soviet military installations on Cuban territory—Kennedy's sole condition for issuing a non-invasion pledge), Americans took satisfaction in the generally successful resolution of an extremely dangerous encounter. Cuba could demur as much as it liked; the crisis, to Americans, had been a *superpower* confrontation. Cuba may have been the stage, but Castro was not, in any meaningful sense, an actor.[8]

This view was grossly mistaken. The Cuban missile crisis was very much a *Cuban* affair. Fidel Castro played a crucial role at every stage. Only now—thirty years after the event—is this beginning to become clear. And it was only at the Havana conference in 1992 that, for the first time, surviving members of the Kennedy administration began to integrate the missing Cuban dimension of the crisis into the story they had for so long viewed solely through the lens of superpower competition. For them, it was a learning experience of the first order—as it was for their host, Fidel Castro, who, for the first time, confronted his nemeses of yesteryear in a conference room at the Palace of Congresses in Havana to explore together a crisis which, for Cuba, has yet to be satisfactorily resolved.

THE ROAD TO HAVANA

The Havana conference had a distinguished lineage. It was the fifth in a series of conferences on the missile crisis which began in 1987. The purpose of these conferences was to better understand the most dangerous moment of the nuclear age so that we might better avoid another. The opportunity arose because the slowly turning wheels of the U.S. government's declassification procedures began bringing to light documents that called into question the standard version of events— based primarily on the memoirs of American participants in the crisis or on their recollections as told to journalists—that had dominated the scholarship of the event and (more disturbingly) the policy implications that leaders drew from it for more than twenty years. The need arose not only because of the intense superpower rivalry of the 1980s, but also because of the fact that the sands of time were running out on the surviving members of the Kennedy administration.

Our method was to bring together in one room policy makers whose role it was to help President Kennedy weather the storm in 1962, and scholars who had spent a considerable part of their lives studying it, jointly using as their referents newly declassified documents from the period. We hoped that the threefold confrontation between knowledge of the crisis that came from experience (living it forward), knowledge of the crisis that came from books (studying it backward), and the timeless, snapshot record that documents provide would generate a constructive dialectic. *Understanding* would collide with *explanation,* and together, disciplined by documents, they would lead us to newer and more profound insights into the crisis in particular, and into nuclear danger in general. We called our method *critical oral history.*

Critical oral history's crucial methodological advantage is its ability at least partially to correct for the inherent deficiencies of all three sources of knowledge. The weaknesses of memoirs and retrospectives are obvious: human memories are selective, subjective, and unreliable; it is easy to exaggerate one's own role in the retelling of a story; one's present agenda may color one's recollections of an event long past; and recollections tend to be insufficiently self-critical when checked against the facts. Scholars are prone to different kinds of errors: their theories drive their research agendas, and color their interpretations of findings; the questions they ask depend upon the answers they expect; the perspective of hindsight from which they operate leads too easily to hasty backward inferences from (known) effects to earlier causes, exaggerates the sense of inevitability in human affairs, and blinds the analyst to the profound indeterminacy and uncertainty with which policy makers must cope as a matter of course. Finally, documents have their weaknesses as sources of knowledge as well. First and foremost, they do not provide their own context. They can tell us what human beings said and did; they can communicate capabilities and concerns; but they are never self-interpreting, and often provide at best a shaky clue to the innermost thoughts and intentions of national leaders. Our hope was that a properly designed conversation would lead us toward a more accurate picture of the past than would be possible if we relied on recollection or scholarship alone. Our expectation was that the memories of participants would supply the missing context to the documents, and that the documents would supply the facts which human memories are prone to distort or forget. And in concert, different people's memories, and their different ways of understanding an event, would test and correct individual recollections and judgments, reducing the likelihood of gross errors and distortions.

In early March 1987, at Hawk's Cay, Florida, we gave critical oral history its first test.[9] Present were several surviving members of the Kennedy administration (most notably, Secretary of Defense Robert McNamara, former Special Assistant for National Security McGeorge Bundy, and former Special Counsel Theodore Sorensen); several prominent American scholars of the crisis; and, in lieu of knowledgeable Soviets (then impossible to include in the process), several noted American Sovietologists whose job it was to stand in for Nikita Khrushchev. We had no firm intention at the time of taking the exercise further. Most of the participants believed that, while the experiment was worth a try, there wasn't all that much left to learn about the crisis, which even then was the most exhaustively studied event in postwar international politics. But the meeting turned out to be full of surprises. We learned much that was new, began to doubt even more that we thought we had known, and began to appreciate how handicapped we were by attempting to understand what we saw as a *U.S.-Soviet* confrontation without any meaningful Soviet input.[10] In short, while Hawk's Cay altered the history of the Cuban missile crisis, it generated far more questions than answers.

By sheer coincidence, just as we began to realize that the history of the Cuban missile crisis could not progress without Soviet participation, the forces of change in the Soviet Union began to make that participation possible for the very first time. We suspected that the government of Mikhail Gorbachev might see in the critical oral history of an event long past an opportunity both to advance the frontiers of *glasnost* and to promote the "new thinking" *(novoye myshlenie)* in foreign affairs with which he sought to replace the Soviet Union's traditional emphasis on peace through strength. New thinking's stress on confidence-building, crisis avoidance, and the dangers of miscalculation and misperception fit naturally with the picture of the crisis that began to emerge at Hawk's Cay, replacing the simplistic chessboard vision of U.S.-Soviet strategic interaction pervading earlier American accounts.

As a trial balloon, therefore, we held a second conference in October 1987 in Cambridge, Massachusetts—the first in which knowledgeable Soviets participated.[11] It was there for the first time that we became aware of a debate within the *Soviet* academic community on the crucial issue of Khrushchev's motivations for deploying nuclear missiles to Cuba. Fyodor Burlatsky, who, as an aide to Yuri Andropov, had some familiarity with Khrushchev's speeches and correspondence, stressed Khrushchev's desire to rectify the Soviet Union's gross inferiority in deliverable strategic weapons, and to respond to the American deployment of Jupiter missiles in Turkey. But Sergo Mikoyan, the son of First Deputy Premier Anastas Mikoyan (and a Latin Americanist by trade), stressed Khrushchev's desire to deter a seemingly imminent American invasion of Cuba. Western analysts had long assumed that Khrushchev's motives were essentially strategic, dismissing as a face-saving *post hoc* rationalization the claims of Khrushchev, Anatoly Gromyko, and others that the Soviet Union's primary goal was the defense of Cuba.[12] But the mere fact that seemingly knowledgeable *Soviets* disagreed on the point warranted reconsidering the question. The price of reopening the question, however, was potentially enormous: for if Mikoyan was correct, then the Kennedy administration's understanding of the event, and the entire body of literature on the crisis in the West that had ignored the *Cuban* role, were both fatally flawed.

Our appetite whetted, we traveled to Moscow in January 1989 for a larger and more formal conference, attended by former Soviet Foreign Minister Andrei Gromyko, former Ambassador to the United States Anatoly Dobrynin, and many other senior Soviet officials. Also participating for the first time was a Cuban delegation, led by Jorge Risquet, a member of the Cuban Politburo and a longtime colleague of Fidel Castro. It was in Moscow that we began to realize just how intimately Cuba was bound up not only with the genesis and management of the missile crisis, but with the last thirty years of superpower conflict.[13] It was also in Moscow that we began to realize that in the long, intimate, and tangled relationship between the United States and Cuba stretching all the way back into the nineteenth century—a history now essentially forgotten in the United States outside the Cuban-American community and the community of professional historians, but fully alive in Cuba—lay the tectonic forces responsible to some degree for many of these great political upheavals, including the Cuban Revolution itself. Exactly *how* it did so was not as yet clear. But the Cubans at the Moscow conference had a story to tell, and were eager for it to be heard. They issued an invitation to the Americans and Soviets in Moscow to come to Havana to a conference focusing on the Cuban perspective on the crisis.

Risquet's performance at the Moscow conference gave some of the American participants pause, however. While the Soviets had fully embraced glasnost, Cuban officials, it seemed, had difficulty transcending rhetoric and invective. The ongoing hostility between Washington and Havana seemed likely to color or defeat a serious investigation of the historical record. Thus we floated another trial balloon—a conference in Antigua in January 1991—in essence to test the seriousness of Cuban participation and the prospect that a full-scale conference in Havana could contribute meaningfully to rounding out the picture of the crisis.[14] There it became clear that Cuban officials felt constrained not to stray too far from the official line. Some of the issues that we felt had to be addressed to make sense of the Cuban role in the crisis— such as Castro's support for revolutionary movements in Latin America, a cause of great concern to the Kennedy administration—could be addressed only by Castro himself. The real test of Cuban seriousness, in short, could come only in Havana. If we wanted to gauge the Cuban contribution to our process of discovery, we would have to take our chances, and we would have to take the plunge. The results you see here.

What was initially conceived as a heuristic "collision" of veterans, scholars, and documents assumed another dimension in Havana— cross-examination by former adversaries. This had numerous repercussions for those of us attempting to organize and manage the conference. But it also immeasurably increased the potency of the method. In the pages that follow, the reader will bear witness to veterans of the crisis reimmersing themselves in the historical moment; beginning to understand how *their* decisions and actions derived from, and gave rise to, the decisions and actions of former adversaries, in an endless chain stretching much further back than the historical memories of any one of them; and finding themselves surprised by the extent of their own misperceptions and those of others borne of the cultural, political, and ideological contexts in which they inescapably operated.[15]

For the veterans, however, there is more at stake. The Cuban missile crisis is regarded almost universally as the closest call ever to all-out nuclear war. The inadvertent slide to that confrontation is thus their joint responsibility. Together, they put the world at greater risk of nuclear catastrophe than at any time before or since. For the veterans, therefore, the critical oral history process has presented both opportunities and risks, not only for their personal reputations and their places in history, but also for the future political relations of the states and societies they represent. Much of the cross-examination throughout can be seen as attempts to avoid, shift, and finally to assume this burden of nuclear responsibility. This is true in the exchanges, for instance, between American "hawks" and "doves" at Hawk's Cay; between Americans and Soviets in Cambridge and Moscow; and between Americans and Cubans—and even, to an extent, between Soviets and Cubans—in Havana. What began as an exercise in *assigning* responsibility has become a process of *accepting* it mutually. We see this as progress.[16]

Those of us who feared at the outset of this process that there would be little left to learn about the Cuban missile crisis have concluded the process learning much, wondering more, and realizing that certain things will be forever shrouded in mystery. We have been continually astonished at what we have been told, what we have read, and, most of all, by the dawning realization that the world in October 1962 may have come far closer to nuclear catastrophe than anyone at the time thought possible, and by a variety of means almost no one thought plausible. No one wanted such a disaster in 1962; but they came far too close for comfort.

AIDS TO "BEING THERE," HAVANA, JANUARY 1992

Our goal in this book is to greatly enlarge the number of "participants" in the Havana conference by supplying context sufficient for our readers to "be there" vicariously, thereby extending a conversation that the actual participants found both fascinating and important. This is a more ambitious task than simply annotating the conference transcript. For by the time the Havana conference took place, the missile crisis had become far more than a historical curiosity for the members of all three delegations and the countries they represented.[17] For the Russians, the forced withdrawal of missiles from Cuba was a humiliation they still feel viscerally; one, moreover, that seems to have foretold symbolically the outlines of their present, even larger humiliation—their sudden disappearance from the roster of the Great Powers of the world. For the Americans, the conference was a test of Castro's willingness to come clean on Cuba's past anti-American activities, and thus to acknowledge implicitly that the Kennedy administration—and, by implication, all U.S. administrations since Kennedy's—had defensible reasons for at least some of their policies vis-à-vis Cuba. Many members of the U.S. delgation saw Castro's admirable performance on this "test" as a sign of his interest in rapprochement with the United States.

But this was, foremost, Fidel Castro's conference. For the Cuban president, the Havana conference was an experience evidently containing many layers of meaning: "Cuba" was inserted meaningfully, for the first time before a sophisticated group of U.S. interlocutors, into the *Cuban* missile crisis; for the first time, Castro bared his grievances with the Soviets and with Nikita Khrushchev in detail; and for the first time, Castro articulated for a Cuban audience (over half of whom have been born since 1962) the importance that the missile crisis occupies in the life of the nation during his period in power. Castro's evident perplexity at the Americans, his anger and bitterness at the Soviets, and his struggle to extract the larger significance of the missile crisis for Cuba, were also part of "being there" at the conference, and they can hardly be appreciated without having a sense of the emotive penumbra cast by the Cuban leader over the proceedings.

Thus we offer the following aids to "being there:"

• In chapter 1, "Cuba on the Brink, [October] 1962," we confront the "two cultures" problem that has pervaded the study of the crisis in the United States: American scholars who study the missile crisis tend to know little or nothing about Cuba, while "Cubanologists" tend to know little or nothing of the vast research on the crisis. In this short chapter, we introduce the Cuban understanding of their "October crisis," using Cuban and Cubanological materials.

• Chapter 2, "Uses of the Brink," contains the three publicly presented sets of remarks that opened the conference—by Fidel Castro, Robert McNamara, and Oleg Troyanovsky—and an analysis of the relevant subtext. Why did the head of state of a country in crisis devote four days to a discussion of a historical event? Why did Americans, some of whom had already participated in four previous conferences on the missile crisis, participate so eagerly in yet another? And why did the Russians, in a moment of national disintegration, subject themselves to a detailed analysis of a previous, eerily similar humiliation? We provide clues to the answers to such puzzles in our commentary on the uses this vicarious return to the brink had for each of the three groups.

• Chapter 3, "Cuba on the Brink, Then and Now," gives the reader a vicarious seat at the conference table, and access to some of the activity that occurred behind-the-scenes that contributed to much of the drama of the conference. We present in full the transcript of the conference, carefully translated where necessary from the original language audiotapes, lightly edited for style, and, in a few places (marked by ellipses), reorganized in order to maintain the continuity of the discussion. We provide identifying material in footnotes at the bottom of the page, and further discussion or citations in endnotes.

• Chapter 4, "Cuba and the Brink," is a lengthy analytical chapter, concentrating on the relevance of the Cuban context to the crisis itself, and on the relevance of the crisis to Cuba's ongoing (and now acute) geopolitical predicament.

• Finally, chapter 5, "The Legacy of the Brink," is a brief coda in which we assess what critical oral history could and could not accomplish in Havana in January 1992. Tempers flared at a concluding press conference over the issue of human rights in Cuba and its connection to the likelihood of U.S.-Cuban rapprochement; but a fascinating, and more civil exchange, a portion of which we reproduce here, occurred in a private encounter immediately afterward between Fidel Castro and four members of the U.S. delegation.

As a final aid to "being there," we provide epigraphs for the book as a whole, and for each chapter, from the Edmundo Desnoes novel *Memories of Underdevelopment*, first published in Cuba in 1965.[18] The novel, and the film based upon it, are the best-known representatives of their respective genres, and superbly capture the reality of Cuba in the early Castro period. The protagonist is a somewhat ineffectual, middle-class Cuban who cannot decide where he stands with regard to the revolution. In the powerful conclusion, the onset of the missile crisis makes him realize that by virtue of being a Cuban, in Cuba, he has already made his decision, for which he, like virtually all other Cubans, expects to pay the ultimate price. There is, we believe, no more compelling portrayal of "being there" in Cuba in October 1962.

THE COMANDANTE IN HIS LABYRINTH

During the formal negotiations in Cuba leading to the Havana conference, we found ourselves unaccountably on the receiving end of a lecture by a Cuban colleague about the work of Gabriel García Márquez, the Colombian Nobel Prize–winning novelist and a great friend of Fidel Castro, known affectionately in Cuba as "Gabo." Our colleague, departing radically from the agenda we had before us, asked if we had by chance read García Márquez's (then) latest book, a work of historical fiction called *The General in His Labyrinth*. We said we had not. "Ah, of course," he replied, "it is still available only in Spanish."

Inspired by our ignorance, our interlocutor told us the basic outline of the story: the last journey—indeed, the last days—of Simón Bolívar, the great liberator of South America. Dying, unloved, and frustrated by resurgent nationalism that prevented the unification of South America, the old general travels with his handful of remaining followers to his oblivion. The general's dreams have come to nothing. He is exhausted. No one fears him anymore—he who vanquished so many foes. Our colleague went on in this vein for some time before we stopped him to ask, "What does this have to do with our conference?" "*Everything!*" he replied. "Gabo is writing about Fidel. 'The general' is Fidel." We admitted that this was interesting, but hastened back to the more mundane subject of conference logistics.

Some time before the Havana conference, *The General in His Labyrinth* appeared in English translation.[19] Suddenly the discussion came to mind, especially our interlocutor's insistence that the author, who is said to know Castro perhaps better than anyone since Che Guevara, was writing an allegorical ode to Castro. We were struck by the following passage, very near the end:

"We've never had a better opportunity to start over again on the right path," [the general] . . . said. And he concluded with irrefutable conviction: "The day I set foot in the Aragua valley, the entire Venezuelan nation will rise up in my favor."

In a single afternoon he outlined a new military strategy in the presence of the visiting officers, who offered the assistance of their compassionate enthusiasm. Nevertheless, for the rest of the night they had to listen to him declaim in a prophetic tone just how they would rebuild from the beginning, and this time forever, the vast empire of his dreams. Montilla was the only man who dared to dispute the utter disbelief of those who thought they were listening to the ravings of a madman.

"Watch out," he told them. "That's what they thought at Casacoima."

. . . Those who heard him in Casacoima also thought he had lost his mind, and nevertheless it was a prophecy fulfilled in every detail in less than five years.

[The general receives last rites:]

"Damn it," [the general] . . . sighed. "How will I ever get out of this labyrinth!"[20]

The general does *not* get out of his labyrinth. He dies, leaving scarcely a trace of tangible evidence that he had ever lived.

We do not know if, for Gabriel García Márquez, Simón Bolívar "is" Fidel Castro—if the old general "is" the old comandante. But we know of no single metaphor that better captures the experience of the Havana conference. Fidel Castro, once one of the most recognizable, dynamic, resourceful leaders of the century, a hero to millions, a villain to millions of others, was at the Havana conference, so it seemed, struggling to ward off irrelevance. In his vivid characterizations of his efforts to avoid oblivion in October 1962, one sensed that Castro was searching for clues as to how to perform the old magic once again. Absolutely unyielding in his commitment to socialism; utterly alone in a world suddenly without a socialist community of nations; presiding over the rollback, born of economic necessity, of many of the achievements of his revolution; it was impossible not to follow the lead of our Cuban colleague and see the convergence of the old general and the old comandante, and to witness the human drama unfolding in Cuba as a consequence.

Inside the conference room, the tension created by the comandante struggling in *his* labyrinth—then in memory, now in reality—was palpable. Outside the conference room, as we learned, a favorite song among contemporary Cubans, especially young Cubans, is "The Old Man Is Crazy," often sung in repetitive choruses, under cover of darkness in Cuban movie houses, without identifying the "old man" directly. How would it turn out? Time would tell; perhaps not much time at that. This sense of bearing witness to a slice of an epic human drama, of the comandante in his labyrinth, was, without question, the most unusual aspect of "being there."

CUBA ON THE BRINK, 1962:
THE OCTOBER CRISIS

*I remember the precise moment when they interrupted the
song. . . . "Who's that talking?" Noemi had asked, after a while. "It's
Kennedy, President Kennedy, I think. . . ." "What is he saying?" I was
staring fixedly at the parchment light on the dial in the casing of the
radio. "I don't know. . . . He says there are missiles in Cuba." "What
are they, love?" she asked and she embraced me, but I could no longer
feel anything. I was numb. "The atomic bomb?" "Yes, the atomic
bomb," I answered her. "They say they have concrete evidence, photographs. He says . . . I guess the marines will land, they'll bomb Havana. I can't believe it, missiles here, in this beautiful tropical
island. . . . It's all over."*

—EDMUNDO DESNOES,
Memories of Underdevelopment

ON 23 OCTOBER 1962, THE CUBAN NEWSPAPER *HOY* (*TODAY*) PUB-
lished the following summary of the critical event of the previous day:
"At 5:40 p.m., the Prime Minister, Commander in Chief of the armed
forces, ordered the entire Revolutionary Armed Forces to be placed
on combat alert status, taken only in cases of critical danger. This
measure was taken in response to reports coming from the United
States, and to the mobilization of U.S. military forces against our
country. The nation has awakened on a war footing, ready to repel any
attack."[1] Thus did Fidel Castro call Cuba to arms. By the time the issue
of *Hoy* containing the account was published, virtually every able-
bodied man, woman, and child on the island capable of fighting had
taken up weapons at pre-established positions.[2]

Although the timing of the announcement itself was a surprise,
the Cuban leadership—and perhaps most other Cubans as well—considered a full-scale invasion by regular U.S. forces inevitable because
of the U.S. government's palpable hostility toward the Cuban Revolution, illustrated most powerfully by the events of April 1961, when

Cuban forces loyal to and led by Castro overwhelmed a CIA-backed invasion of Cuban exiles at Playa Girón (Girón Beach), on the Bay of Pigs, in south-central Cuba.[3] Girón had demonstrated that it would take much more than a minor invasion of poorly trained and lightly armed exiles to topple Castro; it would take "a direct invasion by the Americans."[4] From the Cuban perspective, it had also telegraphed American intentions. No one doubted *whether* the blow would come; the only question was *when*. Thus the Cubans worked feverishly, with Soviet assistance, to build up their defenses, transforming the island into a fortress against the massive assault that they believed Girón foreshadowed. By 22 October 1962, therefore, Cuba had been preparing for battle, materially and psychologically, for nineteen months.[5]

BACKGROUND TO THE CRISIS: THE SPIRAL OF FEAR AND HOSTILITY

While perhaps the most dramatic illustration of American hostility, Girón was not the first. For more than a year before, Cubans fought a dirty war against counterrevolutionaries who attacked ships bound for Cuba, set fire to crops, assassinated public officials, and even took virtual control of the Escambray hills of central Cuba. In many cases, Castro's security forces could easily trace the threads of conspiracy to the United States. While no doubt overestimating the degree of official support these counterrevolutionary groups enjoyed, the Cuban leadership interpreted Washington's *failure* to disavow and impede them as active complicity.

Matters reached a boiling point on 4 March 1960 when the French ship *La Coubre* exploded while unloading munitions in Havana harbor, causing heavy casualties. Fidel Castro immediately called it sabotage, and the Cuban party daily *Revolución* blamed the United States.[6] This was a turning point in U.S.-Cuban relations, as Castro shed any pretense of seeking an accommodation. He delivered a defiant anti-American speech the day after the explosion, ending with what would become the most sacred slogan of the Cuban Revolution: "patria o muerte!" ("fatherland or death").[7] Castro's speech did nothing to assuage the Eisenhower administration, which had gradually become disillusioned about the prospect of improved relations with Castro and had begun to consider its options. Just two weeks later, Eisenhower approved the plan that would ultimately lead to the Bay of Pigs invasion.[8] The governments of the United States and Cuba had decided simultaneously that there would be no compromise, no accommodation. David and Goliath were both spoiling for a fight.[9]

After the *La Coubre* incident, Cuban-U.S. relations became inexorably more confrontational. Jorge Risquet summarized some of the most important events in this process in his opening remarks at the Moscow conference.[10] His litany included not only the invasion at Playa Girón, but also the steadily increasing CIA-sponsored guerrilla activity in Cuba; U.S. military maneuvers in the Caribbean; and American political initiatives, especially within the Organization of American states (OAS), intended to isolate Castro in Latin America. Another Cuban participant at the Moscow conference, José Antonio Arbesú, read aloud from telling declassified materials relating to Operation Mongoose, the Kennedy administration's secret plan to destabilize and overthrow the Cuban government, which outlined a scenario in which the United States would concoct an excuse for intervening in Cuba, invade the island, and replace the Castro regime with another deemed to be more congenial to American interests.[11] Without any provocation whatsoever, the Cubans at the Moscow conference seemed to argue, the United States set about to regain its imperial fiefdom in Cuba by force. Cuba had no choice but to seek safety under the Soviet defense umbrella, and protect itself against Washington's puppet regimes in Latin America by supporting indigenous revolutionary movements.

Fidel Castro and his colleagues may well have believed throughout the revolutionary period, and particularly during the months leading up to the October crisis, that they were the undeserving victims of U.S. aggression. Yet the historical record will not sustain a claim of Cuban blamelessness. Risquet's narrative at the Moscow conference exemplified the very anger, provocation, and defiance that Eisenhower, and then Kennedy—viewing the world through the prism of East-West conflict—saw as a threat to the peacefulness and stability of the region, and to vital American interests. Cuba frightened Washington every bit as much as Washington frightened Cuba.

The OAS meeting in Punta del Este, Uruguay, in late January 1962, provides a useful illustration of the spiraling dynamic of mutual fear and hostility. At Punta del Este, the OAS expelled Cuba from the organization on the ground that Castro's regime was incompatible with the inter-American system.[12] To this day, Cubans insist that the OAS did so under American pressure. Yet Castro had given all Latin American states pause by escalating his anti-American rhetoric, and by openly declaring his commitment to Marxism-Leninism.[13] It should hardly have been surprising to Castro that the nations of Latin America, in

addition to the United States, would see in this a twofold threat to
the status quo: a threat to orderly domestic affairs (because of the
revolutionary implications of Marxism-Leninism); and a threat to the
global balance (because of the danger that the Soviet Union would
seize the opportunity Castro presented to project its power into the
hemisphere). Castro's response to Cuba's expulsion from the OAS
seemed to justify these fears. In what would become known as the
Second Declaration of Havana, Castro, on 4 February 1962, virtually
declared war on the nations of Latin America. Seething with wrath
and indignation, Castro proclaimed that "an unending torrent of
money flows from Latin America to the United States: some $4,000
per minute, $5 million per day, $2 billion per year, $10 billion every
five years. For each thousand dollars they take from us, they leave us a
corpse. A thousand dollars per corpse: that is the price for what is
known as imperialism! $1,000 per corpse, four times a minute!"[14] The
arithmetic may have been dubious, but the message was unmistakable:
the United States was an evil empire, the source not only of Cuban
woes, but of those of Latin America generally, having stolen and murdered its way to hemispheric domination. "It is the duty of every
revolutionary to make the revolution," Castro declared. "In America
and in the world, it is known that the revolution will be victorious,
but it is improper revolutionary behavior to sit at one's doorstep waiting
for the corpse of imperialism to pass by."[15] Hundreds of thousands of
copies of the declaration were distributed throughout Latin America.
Castro's Cuba had become a lightning rod for the anger and impatience
of 200 million Latin Americans, for Cuba had declared guerrilla war
on their U.S.-backed governments.

Two weeks after the Second Declaration of Havana, on 20 February 1962, Brig. Gen. Edward Lansdale proposed the following
schedule to the high level "5412 group" overseeing Operation
Mongoose:

Phase I: *Action,* March 1962. Start moving in.
Phase II: *Build-up,* April–July 1962. Activating the necessary operations inside Cuba for revolution and concurrently applying the vital
political, economic and military-type support from outside Cuba.
Phase III: *Readiness,* 1 August 1962, check for final policy decision.
Phase IV: *Resistance,* August–September 1962, move into guerrilla
operations.
Phase V: *Revolt,* first two weeks of October 1962. Open revolt and
overthrow of the Communist regime.

Phase VI: *Final,* during month of October 1962. Establishment of new government.[16]

Cuba's extensive intelligence service picked up almost immediately unmistakable signs of U.S. activities related to the plans outlined by Lansdale.[17] "It was under these circumstances," Risquet said in Moscow, "that we informed the Soviet Union that we were concerned about a direct invasion of Cuba by the United States and that we were thinking about how to step up our country's ability to resist an attack."[18]

The Soviets responded generously, no doubt partly for reasons of their own, with the ultimate deterrent—nuclear missiles. Cuban leaders had never dreamed of requesting such weapons, but once Khrushchev made the offer, they quickly and enthusiastically accepted. According to Risquet, they did so primarily because the deployment "assured an improvement in the socialist camp's defense capabilities."[19] But at least some in the Cuban leadership were attracted to the idea largely because it would deter the very American invasion that seemed increasingly inevitable given the United States' program of covert action, its hemispheric diplomacy, and its visible muscle-flexing in the Caribbean.[20]

It is natural for each side to a dispute to see its own actions as a fully justifiable reaction to those of the other. The United States and Cuba certainly blamed each other, in the early 1960s, for their mutual antagonism. But neither side at the time appreciated the many ironies to which the spiral of fear and hostility leading up to the missile crisis gave rise:

- By *assuming* American hostility to the Cuban Revolution, Castro was led to behave in ways that intensified it: openly declaring himself a Marxist-Leninist and aligning himself with the Soviet bloc.
- Castro's association with the Soviet Union and his embrace of Marxism-Leninism contributed to the drift toward military confrontation because they provoked precisely what they sought to deter: a coordinated hemispheric effort to bring down his regime, begun in earnest at Punta del Este.
- By circling the hemispheric wagons, the OAS provoked Castro into issuing the Second Declaration of Havana, intended to deter the governments of Latin America from conspiring with the United States against his regime by holding out the threat of subversion from within. This, in turn, proved that the fears of the OAS had been well founded—if perhaps

self-fulfilling, since Castro managed to maintain civil relations with Mexico, the one country that refused to isolate Castro.

• The United States sought to dissuade Castro from exporting revolution and courting the Soviet Union through a policy of intimidation designed to communicate to Castro his vulnerability. In perhaps the grandest irony of all, this effort helped to provoke the action it was most intended to avoid: a deployment of Soviet nuclear weapons in Cuba.

Thus was the world brought to the brink of nuclear war through an escalating series of steps that appeared fundamentally defensive to all parties concerned.

22–28 OCTOBER 1962: THE CRISIS INSIDE CUBA

It would have been understandable if the prospect of being attacked by the armed forces of a country eighty-seven times larger and vastly superior technologically had led to panic or hysteria in Cuba when news of the crisis broke on 22 October 1962. Yet, by all indications, Cubans reacted calmly and with resolution. Proud of standing their ground, Cubans worked feverishly to prepare for their long-anticipated rendezvous with Armageddon. "[W]hoever wants to investigate Cuba must know that they will have to come in battle fatigues!" Castro declared on 23 October.[21] As the U.S. naval blockade formed around Cuba and American troops and aircraft massed in south Florida, *Revolución* defiantly proclaimed in banner headlines, "The Cuban People Are Prepared to Die for Their Independence."[22]

The calm with which Cubans awaited the storm may be explained by wholesale resignation to their fate. Many Cubans expected the October crisis to culminate in a full-scale air attack and invasion by U.S. military forces. They believed that such an attack would result in a very bloody and protracted war, with hundreds of thousands of Cuban and American casualties. The Cubans expected to lose the initial military contest, and to retreat to the jungles and mountains of Cuba to wage a guerrilla war, just as they had against the Batista government in the late 1950s. They fully expected the Soviet soldiers in Cuba to fight and to die alongside them. And if, as seemed possible—or even likely—Cuba were overwhelmed, or destroyed by nuclear fire, the Cuban leadership believed that the Soviets could be counted upon to redeem the martyrdom of Cuba by using the nuclear weapons deployed on Cuban soil. Under no circumstances would Cuba have surrendered to the United States. "[T]he people had tremendous dignity and were ready to immolate themselves in that kind of struggle if necessary," Sergio del Valle told the Moscow conferees. "[W]e were prepared to fight to the death in the event of an enemy invasion, and . . . we appreciated the fact that our Soviet comrades in their military units in Cuba would do the same."[23]

Viewed from the standpoint of an outsider, and from the distance of several decades, such an attitude must appear suicidal, and hence irrational. But all the evidence suggests that it seemed completely natural to the Cubans, who appear to have faced what they took to be their fate calmly and with considerable courage. Every Cuban citizen who lived through the long week of October 22–28 has a story to tell that confirms del Valle's extravagant claim. One that illustrates the mood on the island as well as any comes from longtime Cuban diplomat Ricardo Alarcón, who recalled one of his humanities professors at the University of Havana—an apolitical man, certainly no friend of Fidel Castro and the revolution—putting on his best suit, gathering several of his learned tomes, and walking slowly and calmly down to the trenches, a ghostly and surreal sight, in order to be with his people at their moment of truth.[24] Maurice Halperin, an American eyewitness in Havana during the crisis who saw many such sights, says plainly that the sort of claims made by del Valle in Moscow are "the simple unvarnished truth."[25]

In retrospect, it is curious but notable that the Cubans expected military support not only from the Soviet *conventional* forces stationed in Cuba, but from the soldiers of the Soviet Strategic Rocket Forces who controlled the nuclear missiles as well. Cuban faith in the Soviet Union was complete.[26] No doubt Defense Minister Raúl Castro believed his menacing threat of 11 September 1962: "You've been warned, imperialists: if you are ready to die at your stations, go ahead, go on with your provocation . . . if you try, imperialism is finished."[27] The Cuban people were told virtually nothing, however, about nuclear launch procedures; had they known, they would have realized that the Soviet strategic nuclear missiles in Cuba were unlikely to survive the initial waves of an American attack.[28] Nor did the Cubans know that Khrushchev had given his commanders in Cuba strict instructions not to use the strategic missiles except on his direct order, or infer from Khrushchev's intense fear of nuclear war that he would never authorize it.[29] Perhaps most importantly—and surprisingly, given the fact that it was public information—the Cubans claim they knew nothing about the nuclear imbalance favoring the United States in 1962. If this is so, they could not have known that any Soviet decision to launch nuclear weapons against the United States would have been an act of national suicide. In reality, Cuba had little reason to expect the Soviet Union to risk nuclear war with the United States for the sake of Cuba.

At the Moscow conference, Sergei Khrushchev was overheard in a corridor conversation saying that his father, Nikita Khrushchev, had received from Castro on the final weekend of October a request to launch Soviet nuclear weapons against the United States.[30] Scott Armstrong put the question squarely to the Soviets and Cubans at the table, who ignored it, and later repudiated it.[31] The letter from Castro to Khrushchev would not be released until much later. But even without the text in hand, it was clear that Khrushchev *believed* he had received a request from Castro to launch Soviet nuclear weapons, and it is at least possible (and in our view likely) that that perception helped convince him to bring the crisis to an immediate and peaceful conclusion.

AFTER THE CRISIS: CUBA FORSAKEN

Determined to fight to the death, confident in the totality of the Soviet commitment to their cause, and convinced of the inevitability and perhaps even the imminence of a U.S. invasion, the Cubans, in their moment of deepest peril, were fully prepared to martyr themselves for socialism. So firm was their conviction that their moment of truth had arrived, and so convinced were they that the outcome, whatever it might be, would be decided in combat, that they reacted at first in stunned incomprehension to the news that Kennedy and Khrushchev had struck a deal, according to which the Soviets would remove their missiles from Cuba in exchange for an American pledge not to invade. As Fidel Castro told Tad Szulc in 1984, "I never considered the withdrawal solution. Perhaps in the revolutionary fervor, passion, fever of those days, we did not consider as conceivable the removal of the missiles once they were established here."[32] But incredulity soon turned to outrage and anger at the Soviets. All over the island, Cubans tore down posters that read "Cuba Is Not Alone."[33] Brigades of Cuban militia were heard spontaneously chanting rhymes deriding Nikita Khrushchev.[34] Maurice Halperin recalls warmly congratulating a Cuban vice-minister on the peaceful resolution of the crisis, only to be met with a chilly response. "You don't understand the Cubans," said Halperin's interlocutor. "Security and material goods are not all that important to us. Honor, dignity, trustworthiness, and independence—without these neither economic growth nor socialism means a damn."[35]

It is impossible to say which was the stronger reaction among the Cubans to the news of the Kennedy-Khrushchev deal: betrayal and humiliation at not having been consulted, or even informed, of the deal (Castro heard about it on the radio); or the insecurity of having suddenly lost their ultimate deterrent in the face of what they took to be an undiminished American threat. Castro set out immediately to restore Cuba's pride and salvage some positive benefit. Hours after hearing of the U.S.-Soviet deal, he broadcast the terms under which *Cuba* would consider the crisis resolved. Castro's "five conditions" included an end to the U.S. economic blockade; cessation of all subversive activities; a halt to all "piratical attacks" against Cuba from U.S. bases; respect for Cuban airspace and territorial waters; and the return to Cuba of the naval base at Guantánamo Bay.[36] The United States ignored Castro's five conditions, much as Cuban leaders expected; but Cuba's pride required a public articulation of dissent and a statement for the record that the superpowers had ignored *Cuban* interests in the settlement of a dispute that ostensibly concerned Cuba.[37] Nor did Castro content himself with a mere rhetorical protest. Castro adamantly refused to allow on-site inspection of any kind to verify the withdrawal of Soviet missiles and bombers, unless Cuba were granted the right to inspect American facilities in south Florida at which the CIA trained anti-Castro exiles.[38]

More than injured pride lay behind Cuban anger at the Soviets for caving in so precipitously, however. Cubans felt genuinely abandoned in their hour of need. Upon hearing of the U.S.-Soviet agreement, Raúl Castro said, "Kennedy gives guarantees that he will not invade the republic of Cuba. Our people do not have a bad memory, and they remember those very same guarantees, given solemnly, just before the mercenary imperialist invasion at Playa Girón."[39] Many Cubans still recall feeling far more at risk *after* the Kennedy-Khrushchev agreement than before.[40] But Cuba had few options. It could neither prevent the Soviets from removing their missiles, nor be as confident in its ability to thwart an American invasion once the Soviets had withdrawn. Castro had to settle for the least of the available evils, and Cuba would clearly be safer if he could salvage *some* security relationship with the Soviet Union than if he indulged Cuba's sense of indignation and burned his bridges with Moscow. "We shall not make the same mistake twice," Castro told a group of irate students at the University of Havana who wished to expel all Soviets from the island; "we shall not break with the Russians after having broken with the Americans."[41] Khrushchev "wounded us," Castro told Italian journalist Gianni Mina in June 1987; "it was sad and painful but we had to acquiesce."[42]

It was at the Moscow conference that high-ranking Cuban officials for the first time publicly expressed directly to the Soviets, in the presence of U.S. officials from the period, their extreme and multifaceted displeasure at the way in which the October crisis was ended. Jorge Risquet excoriated Khrushchev for being unprepared; he attacked the whole of the Soviet leadership, civilian and military, for refusing to listen to the Cubans, who urged the Soviets to go public with the missile agreement in order to avoid a swift and powerful U.S. reaction; and—with palpable passion in his voice—he condemned the Soviets for their failure to consult Cuba on the resolution of the crisis. Cuba had accepted the missiles "knowing that it was gambling with the destiny of an entire people and with the possibility that we would all disappear," Risquet said. "This could not be ignored when the time came to withdraw those missiles. One cannot toy with the sovereignty of a country that way. . . ."[43] But, of course, large and powerful countries *can* and *do* toy with the sovereignty of the small and the weak. This continues to be the ultimate source of Cuban anger both at the United States and at the Soviet Union after all these years. Threatened from the north, abandoned by the east, humiliated before the entire world at their moment of truth, it is no surprise that Cuban voices are filled with emotion when they note, as Jorge Risquet did in Moscow, that "Cuba raised five points, and those five points have not been resolved over the past 27 years."[44]

For Cuba, the October crisis continues.

USES OF THE BRINK:
CUBAN, AMERICAN, AND
RUSSIAN MOTIVES
AT THE HAVANA CONFERENCE

*We're already a modern country, we have twentieth-century weapons,
atomic bombs, we're no longer an insignificant colony, we've already
rushed into history, we have the same weapons that the Russians and
the Americans rattle at each other. Our power of destruction makes us
an equal for a moment to the two great world powers. Still, I'm sure
they'll never accept us on equal terms, they'll take our weapons away,
ignore us, crush this island.*

— EDMUNDO DESNOES,
Memories of Underdevelopment

THE FIRST SESSION OF THE HAVANA CONFERENCE IS TO BE GIVEN
over to opening statements from the leaders of the three delegations:
Cuban president Fidel Castro, former U.S. Secretary of Defense Robert
McNamara, and former Khrushchev aide Oleg Troyanovsky. It is the
only segment of the conference open to the press. The Cuban government has decided not to issue any press visas for the duration of the
conference, fearing inundation by the international press corps and
also, perhaps, fearing that headlines on Cuba's increasingly desperate
domestic situation would displace the missile crisis. Even so, the conference room at the Palace of Congresses is packed with reporters and
camera crews, some from the Cuban press, most from correspondents
representing international news organizations posted and accredited in
Cuba. By special arrangement, a four-man camera crew is present from
the United States, which will videotape the entire conference, as will
one Cuban crew. Each crew has agreed not to release any of its material
until after the conclusion of the conference.[1]

Just before 3:00 P.M., 9 January 1992, all members of the three delegations are present and seated, except for Fidel Castro and Central Committee member Jorge Risquet, Castro's close associate who has supervised the Cuban team that organized the conference. Exactly at 3:00 P.M. Castro, in familiar green fatigues, and Risquet, in a business suit, enter the conference room, accompanied by several aides, an interpreter, and security personnel. Making his way around the large rectangular conference table, Castro first encounters the "Russian" delegation. (It cannot officially be a "Soviet" delegation because, less than two weeks before, the Soviet Union ceased to exist.) Embraces are especially warm and emotional with Aleksandr Alekseev, ambassador in Havana during the missile crisis; with Sergo Mikoyan, who accompanied his father (First Deputy Premier Anastas Mikoyan) to Cuba in early November 1962 to help resolve the crisis; and with Oleg Darusenkov, at the time of the crisis an aide to Alekseev and presently the Russian ambassador to Mexico. Alekseev, who translated and drafted letters between Castro and Soviet leader Nikita Khrushchev on the climactic weekend of the missile crisis (26–28 October 1962), appears to fight back tears as he embraces Castro, with whom he shared the most dangerous and intense experience of his life. Throughout the conference, Castro will always refer to Alekseev as "Alejandro," with the same mixture of respect and affection implied in Alekseev's (and many others') use of "Fidel."

It is a bittersweet reunion for the Russians. As the proceedings of the conference will amply demonstrate, both Castro and Alekseev feel that the Soviet leadership in Moscow caved in to U.S. pressure in October–November 1962, humiliating the Cubans and—as it appeared at the time—leaving Cuba exposed to an American invasion. Many of these men must be grappling with complex feelings at the moment of their encounter with Castro, none more than Gen. Anatoly I. Gribkov, former Warsaw Pact chief of staff, who organized the deployment of men and missiles to Cuba in 1962. They are, in fact, a *Soviet* delegation, logically impossible though that may now be. Indeed, they are in Havana to discuss a time in the early 1960s when the Soviet Union had appeared to many to be ascendant, and they have been invited by one of the few remaining members of the fraternity of communist leaders. Several of us, watching Gribkov, are reminded of Marshal Sergei Akhromeyev, whose suicide note following the August 1991 coup attempt said, poignantly, that with the collapse of the Soviet Union his whole world had been destroyed.[2] So, too, one suspects, with Gribkov, whose demeanor is every inch that of a Soviet military leader, and who has come to Cuba at a moment of what he must certainly consider national humiliation to discuss a previous national humiliation—the missile crisis—with the Cubans the Soviets abandoned, and with the Americans who forced them to do so.

Having finished welcoming the Russians and after briefly greeting his colleagues on the Cuban delegation, Castro moves toward the U.S. contingent, seated across from the Russians and adjacent to the Cubans. Risquet introduces the Cuban president to those whom, Castro will joke throughout the conference, are referred to in Cuban documents from the period as "the imperialists" and "the aggressors." He smiles ironically when he meets Ray Cline, former deputy director (intelligence) of the CIA and the man who supervised the team of photoanalysts who discovered the missiles in Cuba. Castro already knows several of the Americans: former U.S. envoy to Cuba Wayne Smith; historian and Kennedy aide Arthur Schlesinger, Jr.; and Robert Pastor, former head of Latin American Affairs on President Carter's National Security Council. Castro greets each former adversary cordially.

Fidel Castro pauses, however, just as he is about to be introduced to Robert McNamara. Castro knows *of* him, of course. Here is McNamara, whose signature is on countless declassified documents from the period authorizing various sorts of covert operations against Cuba. Here is the man who ran the naval blockade of Cuba during the missile crisis. Here is the man who once was poised to order an air strike and a massive land and sea invasion of Cuba, the goal of which would have been to liquidate the Cuban Revolution and perhaps its commander-in-chief as well. In addition, Castro has no doubt been fully briefed by his Cuban colleagues on McNamara's performance at the Moscow and Antigua conferences, noting especially his passionate intensity (which has reminded some of our Cuban colleagues of Castro himself), his willingness to admit mistakes, but also his relentless pressure on the Cubans to reciprocate. The Cubans have probably guessed (correctly) that McNamara will likely walk out of the conference if, as some of the U.S. delegation fear, it turns into a kangaroo court in which the Kennedy administration is tried for its alleged crimes against Cuba. Castro knows, therefore, that any conference with McNamara present can be neither one-sidedly anti-American nor a mere stroll down memory lane. Castro knows that McNamara will push the Cubans to admit and discuss their share of the responsibility for the crisis of October 1962. And all of us on the U.S. delegation know that this is precisely why he is here.

McNamara introduces himself before Risquet can get in position to do so: "Robert McNamara, sir," he says, and he extends his right hand. Taken by surprise, Castro steps back, stares at McNamara full in the face, and clasps his hands over his belt, priestlike, in what will become a familiar pose. After a moment of silence, during which one could have heard a pin drop in the large and crowded room, a broad smile breaks out over the Cuban leader's face and he, too, extends his right hand. As they shake hands, Castro is heard to say: "So, Mr. McNamara, we meet at last. Welcome to Cuba," followed by more than a smattering of applause from around the room. And thus they did meet: "imperialist" and "subversive"; "capitalist" and "Communist"; representatives of large and small nations; of north and south; of two nations still locked anomalously and dangerously in a tense Cold War. We all hope they are ready to lead the attempt in Havana to understand Cuba's role in producing and surviving the Cold War's most dangerous moment.

CASTRO AND THE CUBANS:

". . . devoid of bitterness or animosity"

Jorge Risquet calls the meeting to order and asks Fidel Castro to offer opening remarks on behalf of the Cuban delegation. Apparently surprised by Risquet's request, Castro explains, unconvincingly to many, that he is a bit unprepared, having discovered the date of the opening of the conference only days before in a news release. This theme will emerge repeatedly throughout the conference: Castro showing deference to those present who have participated in past conferences, who are presumably familiar with the available documents on the crisis and who, in effect, know how critical oral history works in practice. In fact, Castro's contributions to the session on the first day will be modest and often interrogatory, as he becomes acquainted with the process and players.

Even so, Castro's opening remarks offer a good deal of insight into the uses this historical exercise has for the Cubans. First, the Cubans, having been cut out of what they regard as a chance to reach a reasonable resolution to the crisis in 1962, were also excluded from the early phases of the critical oral history of the event as well. As will become clear in the course of the conference, the October crisis was for the Cubans a profoundly bitter experience, utterly different, in many ways, from the experience of Americans and Soviets. Moreover, according to Castro, the reasons Cubans give for their bitterness—

U.S. aggression and Soviet abandonment—need finally to be heard by representatives of both Great Powers and thus to become part of a comprehensive understanding of the events of October 1962. To Castro and the Cubans, this is the overriding reason for their participation in the conference: to put Cuba back into what in the United States has always been known as the *Cuban* missile crisis.

Castro also mentions two somewhat more direct stimuli to his own rekindled interest in the missile crisis, both of which illustrate the pivotal role that declassified documents play in critical oral history. The first of these involves his correspondence with Khrushchev on the climactic weekend of the crisis, 26–28 October 1962.* In September 1990, long-suppressed sections of Khrushchev's memoirs were published in the West. The most sensational story to emerge from these "glasnost tapes," as they were called, derived from Khrushchev's claim that, at the height of the crisis,

> Castro suggested that in order to prevent our nuclear missiles from being destroyed, we should launch a preemptive strike against the United States. He concluded that an attack was unavoidable and that this attack had to be preempted. In other words, we needed to immediately deliver a nuclear missile strike against the United States. When we read this I, and all the others, looked at each other and it became clear to us that Fidel totally failed to understand our purpose.[3]

In his memoirs, Khrushchev also explained what he took to be Castro's intemperate and irresponsible request by saying that "[a]t that time he was a very hot-tempered person . . . he failed to think through the obvious consequences of a proposal that placed the planet on the brink of extinction."[4] Khrushchev recalled that, in ignorance and in anger, Castro had requested of him that he issue an order that would have blown up the world.

Castro had reacted angrily in a speech given just days after the publication of Khrushchev's posthumous accusation. "Perhaps Khrushchev even interpreted it this way," he said; "but in reality it did not happen like that."[5] Turning from Khrushchev's alleged error of interpretation, he then accused unnamed sources in the United States of "stirring this up in order (as always) to provoke hatred and aversion towards Cuba among U.S. public opinion."[6] Castro concluded, still

---

*See appendix 2.

accusingly, that "it would be good, amidst all this rumor-monger-
ing . . . for us to divulge some of these documents."[7] As he says in his
introductory remarks to the conference, the letters in question were
published (in November 1990) and were much discussed during and
after the previous conference in Antigua, in January 1991.[8] Given the
vehemence of Castro's reaction to the controversy initiated by the publication of Khrushchev's memoirs, the members of the U.S. delegation
welcome his stated intention to discuss the crisis "devoid of bitterness
or animosity against anyone." They welcome it, but some wonder
whether the Cuban president is really capable of dispassionate analysis
of such a sensitive subject.

The most immediate stimulus to Castro's interest in the crisis and
the conference, however, is the release, just days before the conference
began, of correspondence between Kennedy and Khrushchev during
the crisis, most of which concerns the nature of the "deal" according
to which the Soviets agreed to withdraw their missiles and bombers
from Cuba. Much of the Kennedy-Khrushchev crisis correspondence
had been published some twenty years before.[9] Upon their release in
the United States, these newly available letters evoked an immediate
controversy, for they seemed to suggest, contrary to what many had
long believed, that the United States had made no firm pledge not to
invade Cuba, as the quid pro quo for removal of Soviet "offensive"
weapons.[10] In fact, several members of the U.S. delegation had already
been sought out in Miami, en route to Havana, to comment on whether
the Kennedy administration had or had not pledged to forgo an invasion of Cuba.[11] Cuban exile organizations began collecting signatures
on petitions urging the Bush administration, on the basis of this putative "discovery," to support Florida-based commando groups bent
on overthrowing the Castro regime by force.[12]

As the proceedings of the conference will make clear, however, the
issue of "the pledge" is of relatively little concern to Castro, who will
in various contexts express his confidence in Cuba's ability to deter a
U.S. invasion by virtue of its demonstrable military capability.[13] Castro
has, of course, long believed that the Soviets caved in to every U.S.
demand as the price for resolving the crisis. Khrushchev eventually
agreed to give up the missiles, bombers, and almost all Soviet troops
in Cuba. At the time, the Cubans believed these concessions placed
their security in jeopardy.

But one suspects that the real bone in the throat of Castro and
the Cubans is the fact that Khrushchev and Kennedy used Cuba as a
bargaining chip to facilitate a successful *U.S.-Soviet* exit from the crisis.

On 27 October 1962, Khrushchev had proposed trading NATO missiles in Turkey for Soviet missiles in Cuba (a proposal which, ultimately, became a secret part of the U.S.-Soviet deal). It was Khrushchev who proposed, as part of such an arrangement, that "the governments of Cuba and Turkey would allow . . . [U.N.] representatives to come to their countries and check fulfillment of this commitment. . . ."14 Khrushchev had not consulted the Cubans on this proposal, which they repudiated as being inimical to their security. In the Cuban view, they were being asked to permit an "invasion" of their territory by others, who would determine whether weapons the Cubans felt were rightfully there had actually been removed. And in one of the newly released letters, Kennedy, on 3 November, appears to "coach" the Soviets on how to get Castro to give up the bombers, as well as the missiles: "[P]erhaps," wrote Kennedy, "the existence of the quarantine can be of assistance to Mr. Mikoyan in his negotiations with Premier Castro."15 Kennedy implicitly authorized Khrushchev to have Mikoyan say that the quarantine would be lifted if Castro relented. As the conferees in Havana will discover, there remains among the Cubans great bitterness toward the Soviets for sacrificing Cuban interests for their own when Cuba courageously accepted the deployment of Soviet missiles knowing that their presence would greatly irritate the Americans and tarnish Cuba's image in Latin America. In that moment of supreme danger, it must have seemed to the Cubans that they had been abandoned and deceived, betrayed by an ally who collaborated with their greatest adversary at Cuba's expense.

JORGE RISQUET: Dear American and Soviet friends, dear Cuban comrades. We now begin the Havana Tripartite Conference on the October crisis, with the words of the president of the Councils of State and of Ministers of Cuba, Commander-in-Chief Fidel Castro.

FIDEL CASTRO: [Taken aback.] Distinguished participants and guests: as you may have noticed, I am a little surprised to be told that I have to open the meeting. Well—I am very grateful for that honor.

Over the last few years we have heard about the efforts being made by a distinguished group of personalities—historians, researchers, politicians, social scientists—to delve deeper into the history of the October crisis. Unfortunately, I personally have not had enough time— or, at least I have not had all the time I would have liked to have had—

to analyze the documents of that period. Moreover, many of those documents have just been published very recently. Barely two days ago, we heard that eighty-five pages of the correspondence between Khrushchev and Kennedy had been released. We had the letters translated as fast as possible. But let me tell you that this meeting caught me somewhat by surprise. With all the work of ending one year and beginning the next, no one reminded me that this meeting started on the 9th. The fact is that on Tuesday I read a news dispatch, and that's when I found out that the meeting would start today. I wish I had been reminded a week before, because now I have been forced to spend the wee hours reviewing documents, letters, refreshing my memory. [Laughter.] The fact is, however, that I have not as yet read these letters, these eighty-five pages, and I think it would be important to familiarize myself with that correspondence before giving any kind of definitive opinion on the issues contained therein as they relate to the October crisis. So, this evening I'm going to have to go over those eighty-five pages. In any case, the material is fascinating, and after a few hours I expect to be much better informed. But since I have not yet done so, I would prefer to defer any presentation of our points of view—or my point of view (I stress *my* point of view, because my comrades who have been participating in this work have their points of view as well). I would prefer to hear the opinions of others, and, when my turn comes up, I will answer a few questions, or make a slightly longer statement. I have plenty of materials to review. But there's no problem with that.

I don't think, however, that I will add anything exceptional, because a great deal is already known about the crisis. Not long ago, we published five letters (or, as they say in political or diplomatic jargon, we "declassified" them)—we declassified several documents, and these five letters were among them. We were forced to declassify them, because rumors were circulating that during the crisis we had suggested to Khrushchev that he launch a preemptive nuclear strike. That kind of statement made it imperative that we publish the correspondence between Khrushchev and myself between the 26th and the 30th of October to set the record straight. It seems to me that rectified things.

When the Soviets and the Americans began to analyze the crisis, we were left out. This was a kind of repetition of the agreements arrived at during the October crisis itself. Not only were we left out from participating in seeking solutions to the crisis, but we were also left out of the historical research and the in-depth analysis of these events later on. It seems to me very fair and reasonable that this situation is being corrected now, and that we are being allowed to participate as well, because, whether one likes it or not, we were a part of the crisis. We lived through the most difficult moments of the crisis, and we can help clarify the facts—serenely, objectively, without any emotionalism.

Our aim is to contribute to the efforts that you have been making, so that the truth—at least in keeping with the available information—will become perfectly clear. I might add that we do not have any material left to declassify; we have nothing against releasing the information that we have, and presenting our points of view as well, so that historians will have complete access to all the evidence. I don't know if the other parties are going to publish more documents, because the letters and messages between Kennedy and Khrushchev—the correspondence between October 30th and the end of December 1962—have now been declassified and published in the United States. But there are more letters dealing with the crisis, there are more messages between Khrushchev and Kennedy. I'm saying this based on my recollections of a visit I had to the Soviet Union during which Khrushchev read me some of them.[16] Of course, to be sure that there were more, I would have to read all these letters that have just been published, but, based on the question I asked one colleague who had already read them, there are some important facts that are not mentioned in those letters. Therefore, these facts must be in later letters, dated after December 1962. Khrushchev read me some of those messages, as I say, in the Soviet Union, and I think they might also shed a bit of light on the subject. So I hope that some of those materials will also be declassified.

Lastly, I'd like to say that we are ready to participate and cooperate without any bitterness or any hard feelings toward any of the parties—not toward those who were our adversaries then, nor toward those who were our allies. Therefore, everything we say here will be completely devoid of bitterness or animosity against anyone. We will try to strictly adhere to the facts.

I'd like to avail myself of this occasion to welcome you on behalf of our country, and to wish you all success. Thank you very much.

McNAMARA AND THE AMERICANS:
"Mongoose . . . did not occur in a vacuum"

When Risquet next asks McNamara to speak on behalf of the U.S. delegation, listeners hear an opening statement almost completely at odds with what they have just heard from Castro. Castro has been brief and self-consciously congenial, while McNamara will offer a lengthy, sustained, confrontational challenge to the Cubans. Castro seemed during the few moments of his remarks to look forward to a shared, detailed analysis of the events of October and November 1962, whereas McNamara hardly mentions the crisis as such, dwelling instead on U.S.-Cuban relations in the late Eisenhower and early Kennedy administrations, with particular attention to what the Kennedy administration found especially intolerable about the Castro regime. Where Castro had begun the discussion with reference to correspondence among the leaders of the countries involved in the missile crisis, McNamara chooses to begin, in part, by reminding those present of what may have appeared to be tangential, but were nonetheless highly explosive issues: Cuba's perceived status at the time as a "puppet" of the Soviet Union; Cuban "subversion" of Latin American governments; overt Cuban hostility to the United States; and what the United States saw as the betrayal of a democratic revolution in Cuba. Thus McNamara, on behalf of the U.S. delegation, begins this long-awaited meeting on the October 1962 missile crisis by, in effect, calling Fidel Castro a "puppet," a terrorist, a troublemaker, and a dictator. At least, he argues, the Cuban leader (who stares directly at him throughout his remarks, while taking voluminous notes) was so viewed by the Kennedy administration.

The peculiar and profound orthogonality between the way the conference is initially framed by Castro and McNamara is deeply ironic. Castro, the Cuban leader who, as he said, had been left on the sidelines by the Americans and Soviets in 1962, focuses on Kennedy and Khrushchev, particularly the fabled "thirteen days" that, for the Americans, have always been synonymous with the crisis.[17] In the heat of the crisis, on 28 October, Castro publicly renounced the Kennedy-Khrushchev deal, demanded an end to the U.S. economic blockade, a halt to "subversion" of Cuba, cessation of "piratical attacks" mounted from bases in Puerto Rico and the United States, an end to violations of Cuban airspace and territorial waters by American forces, and the return of the U.S. naval station at Guantánamo Bay, which had been in U.S. hands for over a half-century. At the time, the United States virtually ignored Castro's attempt, via these "five points," as the Cubans refer to them, to embed the missile crisis in a far broader framework of U.S.-Cuban relations, going back to the nineteenth century, and thus to saddle the United States with the blame for causing the crisis.[18] McNamara, in his opening statement, however, accepts the broad definition of "October crisis," as the Cubans have traditionally understood it, but with a twist: he throws some considerable portion of the burden of responsibility for causing the crisis into the laps of Fidel Castro and his Cuban colleagues.

How has this role reversal come about, and what is its significance at the public opening of the Havana conference? It must be understood, in large part, as the product of the process by which McNamara and many of the other American participants in the critical oral history of the Cuban missile crisis came to appreciate the error of conceiving it solely as a U.S.-Soviet confrontation detached from its Cuban context. This process began abruptly and unexpectedly with the participation of Cubans at the Moscow conference in January 1989.[19] Only after arriving in Moscow did the members of the U.S. delegation learn, first, that the Cubans would be represented at the conference, and, second, that the Cubans very likely had seen U.S. documents (declassified three weeks earlier) on Operation Mongoose, the U.S. effort during the Kennedy years to destabilize and overthrow the Castro regime. Some of the U.S. veterans of the crisis feared they might have been walking into a trap. They were concerned that the Cubans, who had been invited unilaterally by the Soviets to send a delegation, would mount an ambush, hijack the conference, and steer discussion toward what one Kennedy administration veteran referred to sardonically as "Cold War crimes." Even those who had no such fears expressed the view that the presence of Cubans—"bit players" on the great stage of October 1962—was no more than a nuisance, and was obviously motivated by the Soviets' need to appease Castro. McNamara's eloquent and disarming remarks in Moscow on Operation Mongoose, which he cites at length in his opening presentation in Havana, were designed as a preemptive strike, an attempt to put the issue on the table and then to dispense with it, so that the Soviets and Americans could move quickly to a discussion of the nuclear danger they shared in 1962. McNamara understood completely, he said, why the Cubans (and the Soviets) expected a full-scale invasion of Cuba sometime after the Bay of Pigs fiasco in April 1961. However, he said that this was a misperception. The United States, he maintained, had drawn the opposite conclusion: that an invasion of Cuba would be militarily unwise and politically costly. The Kennedy administration simply had no intention of invading Cuba, and that was that.[20] But merely by acknowledging that this misperception was a reasonable one, McNamara gave credence to the Soviet claim—long resisted in American official and academic circles—that the deployment of missiles to Cuba was motivated not solely by a strategic nuclear calculus, but at least in part, and perhaps primarily, to deter an American invasion of Cuba.[21] To appreciate this, it was necessary for McNamara to see the crisis from the Cuban and Soviet perspective: as growing out of a problem in U.S.-Cuban relations, not solely a problem in U.S.-Soviet relations. Thus had McNamara come to adopt the "long view" on the origins of the Cuban missile crisis.

At the Moscow conference, the Cubans were unpersuaded by the disclaimers of McNamara and others on the U.S. delegation. In his very first intervention of the conference, Jorge Risquet asked his colleague José Antonio Arbesú to read into the record the following portion of the declassified documents on Operation Mongoose:

> *ARBESÚ:* [Reading] "Guidelines for Operation Mongoose. (1) Operation Mongoose will evolve according to the following assumptions:
> (a) After executing the overthrow of the government in question, the U.S. will make maximum use of native [Cuban] resources, internal and external, but it recognizes that the final outcome will require the decisive military intervention of the U.S. (b) Its native resources, such as they are developed, will be utilized to prepare for or justify the intervention and therefore facilitate or support it." The document I have read is dated March 14, 1962.[22]

The Cubans in Moscow, who had been on the receiving end of Operation Mongoose, believed they had made their case: the United States was in fact at war with Cuba and did intend ultimately to crush the Cuban Revolution, an accusation most former members of the Kennedy administration denied throughout the conference, and afterward.[23]

Exchanges between Americans and Cubans occurred infrequently at the Moscow conference, which was, after all, primarily a forum for U.S.-Soviet discussion of "their" crisis. Partly because of their dissatisfaction with the U.S.-Soviet focus of the discussion, the Cubans extended an invitation to all present to meet again in Havana to discuss the Cuban side of the story. Some former members of the Kennedy administration were unwilling to take this step (said one privately, "Some of us still have aspirations for high political office"). Others insisted upon a prior demonstration that the Cubans would treat the enterprise seriously and "come clean" on their subversive activities in the region—with documentation—just as the Kennedy administration had come clean on its own, aided by U.S. declassified materials from the period. After all, the Americans insisted, Cuban subversion constituted a threat to the security of the United States and of the hemisphere; it was partly in response to Cuban subversion that the United States mounted its own program of sabotage and destabilization in Cuba.

After a good deal of negotiating, three delegations met again in Antigua in January 1991, without fanfare or media, to explore the U.S.-Cuban background to the crisis. Inauspiciously, the Cubans chose to begin the Antigua conference with a presentation that nearly sent the meeting crashing in flames before it even got off the ground. Gen. Fabian Escalante, vice-minister of the interior, began with a lengthy, well-documented overview of American "acts of war" against Cuba, through Operation Mongoose and other covert adventures. Drawing on material from the files of the Cuban secret police, Escalante identified individual members of various subversive groups, and detailed their interrogations before Escalante and his colleagues. Though the tale had been generally familiar since the publication of the Church Committee hearings in the mid-1970s, the Cuban insistence on telling it again disheartened the U.S. participants.[24] They were hardly surprised by Escalante's conclusion that "between July and October [1962], we did not only have the perception—the suspicion—that we were going to be attacked; we also had proof."[25] But more importantly, they were infuriated by what they took to be the willful and counterproductive attempt by the Cubans, as one participant put it, to "throw Mongoose up in our faces all over again" even in a private, unpublicized setting. Another confided: "Hell, we already admitted we were up to no good. Now this Escalante fellow comes and reads the goon squads' obituaries to us."

To the Cubans, McNamara said at the Antigua conference: "I don't sense that today our Cuban associates, in particular, understand how we looked at the problem then. . . . Mongoose was stupid, I accept that, but it did not occur in a vacuum."[26] But he failed to draw the Cubans out on their own program of covert operations in Latin America in the early 1960s. Instead, the Cuban delegates, led by Jorge Risquet, flatly denied the existence of these activities. This was both ludicrous and frustrating—ludicrous because they were well known, and frustrating to those, like McNamara and Arthur Schlesinger, who hoped the critical oral history process might be used to explore the possibilities for U.S.-Cuban rapprochement. Cuban "stonewalling," as they called it, seemed to indicate that high-level Cuban officials were still unable or unwilling to hold open and honest discussions with Americans about issues which divided them. If the Cubans could not discuss the past openly, then it was impossible, they believed, to be sanguine about the present and future.

For U.S. scholars seeking to unravel the twisted fabric of inter-active decision making leading to and through the missile crisis, Antigua appeared to be a dead end. As one remarked, "It's like hearing only one end of a telephone conversation." Perhaps, some speculated, we would have to await the passing of the Castro regime before Americans and Cubans could candidly discuss the issues to which McNamara and Escalante alluded in Antigua. Or perhaps, as several Cubans hinted as they left Antigua, only Fidel Castro could respond to the kinds of questions the U.S. delegates were posing. We should come to Havana, they said, and see for ourselves.

We spent a good deal of time in the year between the Antigua and Havana conferences exploring what is known, in the open litera-ture, regarding the "concerns" McNamara mentions in his opening presentation to the Havana conference. Indeed, McNamara's four points correspond roughly to those in a presidential white paper, *Cuba,* released by the Kennedy administration on 3 April 1961, just before the invasion attempt at the Bay of Pigs. Its table of contents neatly summarizes the Kennedy administration's case against Castro's Cuba:

I. The Betrayal of the Cuban Revolution.
II. The Establishment of the Communist Bridgehead.
III. The Delivery of the Revolution to the Sino-Soviet Bloc.
IV. The Assault on the Hemisphere.
V. Conclusion.[27]

The "Conclusion" of the 3 April 1961 white paper anticipated the events that would occur two weeks later at the Bay of Pigs:

> We call once again on the Castro regime to sever its links with the international Communist movement. . . . If this call is unheeded, we are confident that the Cuban people, with their passion for liberty, will continue to strive for a free Cuba . . . in the spirit of José Martí.[28]

Two of the primary authors of that 1961 broadside against the Cuban Revolution—Arthur Schlesinger (in the White House) and Wayne Smith (in the State Department)—are members of the U.S. delegation to the Havana conference.

McNamara had said in Antigua that the U.S. actions against Cuba did not occur in a vacuum. In the months leading up to the Havana

conference, Schlesinger, Smith, and their colleagues helped us to transform the putative "vacuum" of Cuban actions into a very thick notebook
of primary and secondary documentation on just those Cuban actions
to which the former U.S. policy makers believed they were responding
during the period leading up to the missile crisis.[29] We gave the Cubans
copies of these materials well in advance of the meeting. McNamara's
opening remarks are therefore roughly equivalent, in what they imply,
to those of Arbesú in Moscow and Escalante in Antigua. McNamara,
in other words, is asking the Cubans to admit and explain their actions.
But there is little optimism that they will. In Havana, half our number
are specialists on Cuban and Latin American affairs: as the conference
gets under way, not one of them is willing to bet that Fidel Castro and
his colleagues will respond positively to McNamara's challenge.
McNamara himself is skeptical that Castro is ready to exchange accusation for revelation, hostility for collaboration, rhetoric for understanding, and rumor for declassified, real-time documents. But he will
try. He will step into Castro's shoes—by defining the missile crisis
principally as a derivative of U.S.-Cuban hostility—on the hope that
Castro will then step into his. If he does not, McNamara is prepared
to walk out of the conference.

RISQUET: We invite Mr. Robert McNamara to take the floor on
behalf of the American participants.

ROBERT McNAMARA: Mr. President, we are all very grateful to you
for hosting this meeting, and we are even more grateful to you for
your personal presence here.

As we heard yesterday at the missile site,* and, I think, as we all
know, the actions of the Soviet Union, Cuba, and the United States
in October 1962 brought our nations to the verge of military conflict,
and brought the world to the brink of nuclear disaster. No one of us

---

*The day before the conference, all three delegations visited the newest monument in Ha-
vana: a Soviet SS-4 medium-range ballistic missile, erected on the coast facing the United
States ninety miles away, commemorating the missile crisis. There one member of each
delegation gave a brief speech recalling the crisis, and the danger it posed to humankind.
The monument is thrice ironic: a gift from Moscow, it was intended to signify Soviet-
Cuban solidarity even as the USSR collapsed and abandoned Cuba, economically and militarily, to her fate; a sign of friendship, it recalls the single historical moment in which
Cuba felt most betrayed by Moscow; and standing defiantly against American "imperialism," the missile itself is disarmed, inoperable, and—like Cuba—exposed.

intended by our actions to create such risks. To understand, therefore, what caused the crisis and how to avoid such events in the future, the parties have met together in a series of meetings. As you know, this is the fifth of those meetings. As I look around the room, I see that perhaps ninety percent of the persons present have not attended any one of the previous discussions. Therefore, I'm going to begin my remarks by referring briefly to those meetings.

By the conclusion of the meeting in Moscow three years ago, it had become clear that the decisions of each of the three participating nations and their leaders, immediately before and during the crisis, had been distorted by misinformation, miscalculation, and mispercep- tions. I'll cite only four of what I think were many examples. First, before the Soviet missiles were introduced into Cuba in the summer of 1962, the Soviet Union and Cuba believed that the United States intended to invade this island and to destroy its government. As I'll state more fully in a moment, we had no such intention. Second, the United States believed the Soviets would not move nuclear warheads off the soil of the Soviet Union, since they never had. But they did. In Moscow, we were told that by October 24, 1962, twenty Soviet nuclear warheads had been delivered to Cuba and their missiles were targeted—or were to be targeted—on cities in the United States. Third, the Soviets believed that the missiles could be introduced secretly into Cuba, without detection, and that when their presence was disclosed, the U.S. would not respond. Here, too, they were in error. Fourth, and finally, and perhaps most importantly, those who urged President Kennedy to destroy the missiles by a U.S. air attack, which in all likelihood would have been followed by a sea and a land invasion, were almost certainly mistaken in their belief that the Soviets would not respond with military action. At that time, the CIA had reported to us that there were 10,000 Soviet troops in Cuba.[30] We learned in Moscow that there were 43,000, along with 270,000 well-armed Cuban troops, and both forces, in the words of their commanders, were determined to "fight to the death." The Cuban officials estimated they would have suffered 100,000 casualties and the Soviets expressed utter disbelief that we would have thought that, in the face of such a catastrophic defeat, they would not have responded militarily some- where in the world. The result, of course, would have been a high probability of uncontrollable escalation.

By the end of our meeting in Moscow, I believe we had agreed that we could draw two conclusions, two major lessons from our dis- cussions. First, in this age of high-technology weapons, crisis management is dangerous, difficult, and uncertain. It is not possible to predict with confidence the consequences of military action between the Great Powers and their allies, because of misjudgment, misinformation, and miscalculation of the kind I have referred to. Therefore, we must direct our attention to crisis avoidance. At a minimum, crisis avoidance requires that potential adversaries take great care to try to understand how their actions will be interpreted by the other party. I think we all performed poorly in this respect during the missile crisis. Let me illustrate my point by referring to an exchange which took place at the opening of the Moscow meeting. In the chair was Georgy Shakhnazarov, who was to be present today and unfortunately could not be, and he asked me as one of the U.S. participants who had been a member of the Executive Committee during the crisis, to put the first question. I said, "My question is a very obvious one: what was the purpose of the deployment of the nuclear-tipped missiles into Cuba by the Soviet Union?" And Georgy asked, "Who wants to answer?" Andrei Gromyko, the foreign minister of the Soviet Union in 1962, responded—these were his words, and I quote—"I can answer that question with a few words. This action was intended to strengthen the defensive capability of Cuba. To avert the threats against it. I repeat, to strengthen the defensive capability of Cuba. That is all." End of quote.

I then replied in these words:

> Mr. Chairman, that leads me to make two comments. [. . .] My first comment is stimulated by the implication of Mr. Gromyko's answer, the implication being that the U.S. intended prior to the emplacement of the missiles to invade Cuba. Now, I want to make two points with respect to that implication. The first is that if I had been a Cuban, I think I might have thought that. I want to be very frank in saying that.

These are the words I said in Moscow, but I also repeat them today. I want to be very frank. If I'd been a Cuban, I would have thought exactly what I think you thought.

> . . . [O]ne of the most important lessons of this event is that we must look at ourselves from the point of view of others. And as I say I want to state quite frankly that with hindsight, if I had been a Cuban leader, I think I might have expected a U.S. invasion. Why? Because the U.S. had carried out what I have referred to publicly as a deba-

cle—the Bay of Pigs invasion—we'd carried it out in the sense that we had supported it. We did not support it militarily and I think this should be recognized and emphasized, as it was specifically the decision of President Kennedy *not* to support it with the use of U.S. military force—but in any event, we'd carried it out, and after the debacle, there were many voices in the United States that said the error was not in approving the Bay of Pigs operation; the error was in the failure to support it with military force, the implication being that at some point in the future, force would be applied.

Secondly, there were covert operations. The Cubans knew that. There were covert operations extending over a long period of time. [. . . My] recollection is that they extended from the late 1950s into the period we're discussing, the summer and fall of 1962.

And thirdly, there were important voices in the United States— important leaders of our Senate, important leaders of our House— who were calling for the invasion of Cuba. [. . .] So I state quite frankly again that if I had been a Cuban leader at that time, I might well have concluded that there was a great risk of U.S. invasion. And I should say, as well, if I had been a Soviet leader at the time, I might have come to the same conclusion.

And I continued in Moscow with these words:

The second point I want to make—and I think it shows the degree of misperception that can exist and can influence both parties to a dispute [. . . —is that] I can state unequivocally we had *absolutely no intention* of invading Cuba. Now, I don't want to suggest there weren't contingency plans; all of you—certainly our Cuban friends and our Soviet friends—are familiar with contingency plans. All of our militaries—Soviet, Cuban and U.S.—have contingency plans covering a wide range of contingencies. [. . . But] I state again, we had absolutely no intention of invading Cuba, and therefore, the Soviet action to install missiles with that as its objective was, I think, based on a misconception—a clearly understandable one, and one that we, in part, were responsible for. I accept that.[31]

Now, that ends my quotation of my statement in Moscow. By that statement we took the first step toward trying to put ourselves in your shoes. We hoped it would lead you to try to put yourselves in our place, lead you to an effort to understand why the U.S. president and U.S. officials in at least two administrations, both before and after the missile crisis, behaved in ways hostile to the Cuban government. But neither in Moscow nor later in Antigua did such a discussion take place.

Let me begin it here. I do so not to antagonize and certainly not to embarrass the Cuban or Soviet participants, but rather to suggest that if our three peoples wish in the future to move away from relations based on fear and hostility, we must try to understand what brought about that fear and hostility in the past. We can then consider whether conditions have so changed, or whether conditions can be so changed, as to shift the basis for our relations in the future.

Put very briefly—and I'll elaborate on this point in a moment—but put very briefly, every U.S. administration, Republican and Democratic alike, has viewed Cuba, first, as an agent of the Soviet Union in pursuit of its Cold War aims and, therefore, as a direct threat to the security of the United States; and second, as a violator of accepted norms of international behavior, particularly in the field of political freedom and civil rights. In our previous meetings, the U.S. and Soviet participants were extremely candid, and, as a result, I think we now better understand each other's perceptions and miscalculations. This meeting in Havana offers the U.S. and Cuban participants an opportunity to replicate that experience, to improve our understanding of each other's motives as a first step toward narrowing our differences.

Perhaps a good place to begin is to acknowledge that our shared history is viewed very differently by both countries and that this divergence contributed both to the sharp break in relations between our nations thirty-one years ago, and to the attitudes with which we viewed the missile crisis. Let me give four illustrations of these differences of view. First, Americans have been taught that the U.S. liberated Cuba from Spain, while Cubans learn that it was the result of their long struggle for independence. Second, Americans view themselves as idealistic and selfless in not annexing Cuba after the end of the Spanish-American war, whereas Cubans think the U.S. used every chance to dominate their nation. Third, Americans think they used the Platt Amendment to mediate and resolve internal disputes in Cuba, whereas Cubans tend to think that the amendment was designed to permit the U.S. to intervene in Cuban affairs for its own selfish purposes; and finally, Americans tend to think that their investments in Cuba contributed to the nation's development, whereas the Cuban government has tended to look at the economic relationship as exploitative.[32]

Because of these different points of historical departure, the U.S. was ill-prepared to understand the basis for a fundamental revolution that you led, which was fervently nationalistic. Nonetheless, the Eisenhower administration decided to try to work with that new regime, despite suspicions of radicalism, Marxism, and anti-Americanism. In its view, its efforts were rebuffed. Now, we are very aware that the Cuban perception of the break in relations with the United States is that it occurred because the U.S. would not accept major elements of the revolution, in particular land reform and other actions to achieve social justice. But the Kennedy administration did not view the problem in those terms. Indeed, the Alliance for Progress was the administration's commitment to achieving those same economic and social ends throughout the hemisphere. I don't doubt there was an emotional dimension to the break in 1959, and this stemmed from history and the U.S. fear that a neighbor ninety miles away could become an outpost for what was then our principal adversary. But our four major concerns, which I am going to summarize, represented a calculation of U.S. interest that, as I said, has reflected U.S. views in every administration from Eisenhower through to the Bush administration:

- Our principal concern was Cuba's military relationship with the Soviet Union. It's significant, I think, that Eisenhower's initial decision in March of 1960 to have the CIA train Cuban exiles was not made after the agrarian reform, but rather after the visit of a high-ranking Soviet leader to Havana.*
- Our second concern was Cuba's support for armed groups whose goal was to overthrow many, if not all, of the governments in Latin America and the Caribbean.
- Our third concern was the constant, hostile rhetoric directed at the United States and other governments in the hemisphere. Now, words, of course, don't break bones, but they do have consequences, and the hostility of Cuban rhetoric, in the opinion of many in the United States, made it difficult for any U.S. administration to take steps that could be interpreted as conciliatory to Cuba. Many in the American public felt that way. It's true that the U.S. also engaged—and still does engage—in considerable propaganda directed at Cuba, but, rightly or wrongly, we viewed our efforts as reacting to, not precipitating, Cuba's.

---

*Soviet First Deputy Prime Minister Anastas I. Mikoyan. While in Cuba (4–13 February 1960), Mikoyan negotiated economic and trade agreements with Castro.

• Our fourth concern was that the Cuban government betrayed its promises of a free election and began to establish a dictatorship that violated the civil and political liberties of the Cuban people. We are aware that we have many failings—that U.S. support, for example, for democracy in the hemisphere has not always been consistent—but that does not make the defense of democracy by the U.S. either hypocritical or insincere. It's a fundamental interest of the American people, and those rights are embedded as well in the Universal Declaration of Human Rights of the entire international community.

I think President Kennedy summarized these concerns well in one of his last speeches. It was given to the Inter-American Press Association shortly before he died, on November 18, 1963. In that speech he stated, in his words, that our objection was to subversion, to dictatorship, to a Soviet satellite, not the "genuine Cuban revolution, a revolution against the tyranny and corruption of the past." And Kennedy concluded by saying, "Once this barrier is removed, we will be ready and anxious to work with the Cuban people in pursuit of those progressive goals which a few short years ago stirred their hopes . . . and we'll be willing as well to extend the hand of friendship and assistance."[33]

Now, it was those concerns which led President Kennedy to support the Bay of Pigs invasion, to launch Operation Mongoose, and to declare the installation of Soviet missiles as unacceptable. We've reviewed the extensive documentation which you have—and which we have—on Mongoose. We discussed it in detail in Antigua. I view the operation as regrettable. As a matter of fact, in Antigua I characterized it—and I think the word was correctly chosen—I characterized it as stupid. I don't think it would be productive to discuss any further what we did. It would be much more useful to discuss why we did it and to consider whether our four concerns and perceptions were well-founded at the time, and if so, whether there are grounds for similar concerns today.

I've tried to explain our motives and our actions. We need to know more about yours, in particular about the subversive movements launched against many governments in Latin America—not just against dictatorships, but against democracies such as Venezuela. And we need to know what Cuba did or intended to do to implement the comment that was made—or reported, I should say—in Tad Szulc's book published recently. It was a comment attributed to you, Mr. President, made, it is said, in 1958, that after overthrowing Batista, "a much bigger and greater war will start for me, a war I shall launch against them [the United States]. I realize that this will be my true destiny."[34] I don't know whether that is accurate or not, and I don't dwell on that except as illustrative of the kinds of language—and we both used it—which affected our leaders and our peoples.

We need to know how you expect us to react toward your policies. For us to understand each other better, we need to know how your policies—especially as related to Cuba's support for subversion—have evolved over time, and what lessons you have drawn from these experiences.

I hope, as you indicated, that our discussions will eschew the hostile rhetoric that has sometimes characterized the past exchanges between our two governments. I hope that we can approach these issues with detachment and with the purpose of trying to extract the lessons from thirty years that might permit us to stop repeating the past and begin to shape a more productive and a very much different future.

The end of the Cold War has eliminated the principal threat to the hemisphere and to U.S security. Our other concerns—denial of political freedom and violation of internationally accepted norms of civil rights, whether they are justified or not—remain. But Cuba is not the only nation with which the United States has disagreement on these issues. And the United States is not the only nation that criticizes Cuba's conduct in these respects. Surely, therefore, the United States and Cuba should be able to address these remaining issues through normal diplomatic channels, and do so without the overriding fear and hostility exemplified by the missile crisis—without the overriding fear, without the hostility that has dominated our relationship for over three decades. We've each feared—and I think with some justification—that the security of our nation was at risk during that period of time. If it ever was, it no longer is.

Thank you very much, sir.

TROYANOVSKY AND THE RUSSIANS:

". . . a further contribution to the normalization of the situation . . ."

Risquet now asks Oleg Troyanovsky to give the opening presentation "on behalf of the Soviet participants." Troyanovsky, former aide to

Khrushchev and recently retired from his post as ambassador to China, focuses on what he calls the "political importance" of the conference which, he points out, is largely due to "the active participation of Comrade Fidel Castro." After a brief reference to lessons of the crisis, Troyanovsky concludes his opening remarks with "the hope that our meeting will be a further contribution to the normalization of the situation in this important part of the world." It is a friendly greeting, modest in length and its stated expectations for the conference. This seems altogether appropriate at the outset of a conference whose primary fault lines are bound to follow fissures in U.S.-Cuban relations.

Those few of us on the U.S. delegation who have participated in all five conferences on the missile crisis cannot but notice that the *political* significance of Russian participation has come nearly full circle: from irrelevance to centrality to (in Havana) near complete irrelevance once again. At the Hawk's Cay conference, planned in 1986 and held in March 1987, no Soviets were present.[35] Gorbachev was still not widely viewed in the West as a serious reformer; the concept of "glasnost," just beginning to appear popularly, was generally thought to be mere window dressing on the edifice of Soviet Communism. Khrushchev, the last previous reformer, had not been mentioned in the Soviet press since his one-sentence obituary in 1971.[36] The Hawk's Cay conference, then, was not about the Soviets (or the Cubans), but about using knowledge of U.S. management of the missile crisis to help American officials stay away from the brink of nuclear war.

The Cambridge conference later that year proved, to those of us who participated, that glasnost was for real and that Gorbachev's "new thinking"—emphasizing mutual, or common security—was now being applied by the Soviets to the conduct of Soviet-American relations. By the time of the Moscow conference in January 1989, glasnost, *perestroika* and "new thinking" were in full flower, and proof of their having come of age was the presence at the conference of former long-time foreign minister Andrei Gromyko and former long-time ambassador to Washington Anatoly Dobrynin, who for more than a generation had been on the front lines of Soviet policy toward the United States. The Soviets named as co-chairs two of Gorbachev's most intimate advisers, Georgy Shakhnazarov and Yevgeny Primakov.[37] The U.S.-Soviet political significance of the Moscow conference was acknowledged in messages sent to the conference participants by Presidents Gorbachev and Bush.[38] Gorbachev remarked that the timing of the conference was prescient and that therefore the crisis "has not lost its topicality, especially in conditions when new political thinking is finding an ever-widening response."[39] In a similar gesture, President Bush, who had been inaugurated just days earlier, said, "I applaud this latest example of the new openness of the Soviet Union under President Gorbachev. . . ."[40] In keeping with the intensely political and over-whelmingly U.S.-Soviet orientation of the conference, the word "Cuba" never appeared in Bush's message (it was expunged from an earlier draft) and Fidel Castro was not invited to send a message to the conference.[41] The conference, to the Soviets who hosted it, was to be "about" U.S.-Soviet rapprochement.

The "Research Agenda" drafted for the Moscow conference under Shakhnazarov's supervision was a veritable manifesto of the Gorbachev/ Shevardnadze revolution in foreign policy at its high-water mark. Shakhnazarov joked privately about having to tolerate what he called "the detective story"—testimony about the crisis of 1962—as a convenient platform from which to dive into the Gorbachev agenda. The agenda of "Lessons for the Future" developed by Shakhnazarov were:

1. The need to prevent crises.
2. The necessity of negotiation and mutual compromise.
3. The need for communication.
4. The importance of seeking to understand each other's interests.
5. The danger of the uncontrollable.
6. The time factor in crisis.
7. The nature of strategic parity and nuclear deterrence.
8. Preparing leaders to deal with crises.[42]

The previous year Gorbachev had written a book, with Shakhnazarov's assistance, emphasizing just these factors as cornerstones of Soviet foreign policy.[43] In fact, in his closing remarks to the Moscow conference, Shakhnazarov commented that the discussion had been, by his lights, too apolitical and too historical. But he pronounced it a success anyway, even though "the percentage of time drawing lessons was not equal to the percentage of time spent understanding the events."[44]

After the Moscow conference, the Soviets became progressively less relevant to the critical oral history of the missile crisis, for two interacting reasons: first, we pursued the previously unknown (and largely unconsidered) Cuban story of the crisis with increasing vigor; and second, during the exploration of the Cuban story, the Soviet government began obviously and pervasively to distance itself politically from Cuba. The Soviets did this for several reasons: to cut their financial outlay; to appease radical, pro-democracy reformers; and to begin to respond to U.S. pressure to reduce aid to Cuba.[45] Thus, by the time of the Antigua conference in January 1991, the purpose of Soviet participation was largely symbolic—to re-create the trilateral nature of the crisis under investigation—and also facilitative—to explore this way of bringing influential Cubans and Americans together to try to resolve their differences. For by this time the Soviet government had decided that their abnormal and unsatisfactory relationship with Cuba could be solved only if the *Americans* resolved *their* abnormal relations with their island neighbor. In the case of U.S.-Cuban rapprochement the Cubans, the Soviets believed, would release them honorably from old, suddenly unwanted obligations, many deriving from the Soviet-Cuban attempt to manage the debris of the missile crisis.[46] Oleg Darusenkov began speaking openly of the study of the missile crisis as a "marvelous pretext" for helping to bring about the normalization of U.S.-Cuban relations.

According to a plan agreed to in Moscow in June 1991 by U.S. and Soviet organizers, the Soviet delegation to the Havana conference was to be led by Shakhnazarov, still a senior aide to President Gorbachev, and Marshal Dimitry Yazov, Soviet minister of defense. The delegation would also include Anatoly Dobrynin.[47] Shakhnazarov was to be there as a symbol of Gorbachev's wish for the normalization of U.S.-Cuban relations and as encouragement to the United States to end its Cold War with Cuba. Yazov, himself a veteran of service in Cuba during the missile crisis and long a hard-line supporter of Cuba's interests, was expected to convey, symbolically and literally, a complementary message: that the Soviets would *never* abandon Cuba under U.S. pressure. Shakhnazarov would come with a carrot for the United States; Yazov would brandish a stick.[48]

The "Soviets" never did abandon Cuba. The "Soviets" simply ceased to exist in the months following the failed coup attempt in August 1991. As Troyanovsky speaks his words of greeting to the Havana conference, therefore, the "Soviet" absentees are very much on the minds of those in the U.S. delegation: Yazov, who has been imprisoned by the Russian government of Boris Yeltsin for his role in the coup; and Dobrynin who, as a senior official in the (suddenly) *Russian* Foreign Ministry, has decided that it would be less than prudent for him to come to Communist Cuba during his first few days as a minister of non-Communist Russia.

Finally, Shakhnazarov, the virtual father of senior Soviet involvement in the critical oral history of the missile crisis, and a man who had dealt with Cuba for over twenty-five years while working in the Central Committee, has canceled at the eleventh hour. His reason: he is now but an aide to a man, Gorbachev, who represents only the memory of a country. Under such circumstances, Shakhnazarov thinks it inappropriate to lead a delegation when, as a matter of fact, he had nothing to do with the missile crisis, and now he has nothing to do with the government of the country in which he lives. Georgy is missed. McNamara has referred to his unfortunate absence in his opening remarks. It is a bitter, sad termination of a fruitful collaboration.

Troyanovsky's expressed hope that the Havana conference will contribute to the normalization of U.S.-Cuban relations, therefore, has little or nothing to do with the political wishes of the Russian government. Cuba now has almost no political significance for Russia, whose aid to Cuba has ceased and whose trade with Cuba is on a strictly hard-currency basis.[49] It is the *United States* to which Cuba remains politically connected through the missile crisis. The situation is nicely illustrated by a comparison of the Gorbachev-Bush messages to the Moscow conference in January 1989 and the forewords to the complete Kennedy-Khrushchev correspondence by Russian Foreign Minister Andrei Kozyrev and U.S. Secretary of State James Baker in April 1992. Kozyrev's only mention of the third player in the crisis comes when he notes that "Soviet nuclear missiles had been stationed in Cuba." To Kozyrev, the joint publication simply shows what is possible "with the transformation of Russia into a democratic, normal, but non-Communist great power. . . ."[50] Baker, too, says that the joint publication of the letters "marks another step, a symbolic one, down our path of partnership and friendship." But it is also Baker who mentions Cuba in a political context: "[W]e hope," he says, "that democracy will come to Cuba as it has come to Central and Eastern Europe and the former Soviet Union."[51] Such sentiments are anathema to the Cuban leadership, which regards Cuba's internal political arrangements as Cuba's sovereign concern. The significance lay not only in Baker's having mentioned Cuba, but also in Kozyrev's agreeing to a joint publication in which Baker's remark appears.

Thus, when Jorge Risquet asks Oleg Troyanovsky "to take the floor on behalf of the Soviet participants," Troyanovsky does exactly that. His expressed hope for normalization of U.S.-Cuban relations is a *Soviet* wish from days gone by. Moreover, this will be the last time many on the U.S. side will hear present and former Russian officials refer to one another, and to the Cubans, with the prefix "Comrade."

Several Russians, including Troyanovsky, will have interesting things to say during the conference about the missile crisis. But their remarks will be politically insignificant. We cannot but recall a time, less than a half-dozen years before, when meaningful Soviet participation in a discussion of the Cuban missile crisis was still an unrealizable dream. Now, at the beginning of this conference, more than one U.S. participant has confided privately a preference for having somehow or other excluded all the Russians, no matter who they are, in order to facilitate the achievement of the two principal objectives of the meeting: learning more about Cuba in the missile crisis; and exploring avenues for normalizing U.S.-Cuban relations.

RISQUET: Thank you, Mr. McNamara, for your words. We invite Mr. Troyanovsky to take the floor on behalf of the Soviet participants.

OLEG TROYANOVSKY: Thank you very much.

Esteemed President Fidel Castro; ladies and gentlemen; colleagues: In his statement, Mr. McNamara referred to a great many issues, issues that are to be the object of study of this meeting, and we will have an opportunity to discuss all of them. We will be able to ask each other questions. But at this moment, our delegation would like to focus on more specific questions. First of all, we would like to say on behalf of the Soviet delegation how thankful we are to the Cuban government for having hosted this meeting to study what has been called the Caribbean crisis, the Cuban crisis, the missile crisis, or the October crisis, depending on the terminology used in different countries. We are thankful for the welcome, and for all the attention we have received, and we are particularly thankful for the active participation of Comrade Fidel Castro—the fact that he is present confers special importance on this meeting: political importance. We are all also pleased to see that the U.S. delegation includes such very important personalities as Mr. McNamara, who was personally in the epicenter of the crisis to be discussed. Of course, we cannot but express our appreciation to our colleagues from Brown University who have done a great job in conceiving of and organizing this series of discussions or round tables aimed at leaving a clear and precise chronicle of the crisis of October 1962. This is very important for the history of humankind. Mr. Schlesinger, as a historian, I'm sure, could confirm or deny this; but I think it might be rather difficult to find some other period in history that has been studied in all its facets and in all its details.

I must say that this period deserves to be studied, because never before in the history of humanity had the world come so close to a worldwide catastrophe. I recall that Mr. John Foster Dulles, then secretary of state, once said in a spirit of Cold War rhetoric that to carry out an effective foreign policy it was indispensable to have no fear of reaching the final brink and looking into the abyss.[52] However, the leaders of the early sixties were a lot wiser, and when the moment came to approach the brink of war, they were able to take a step back. And this, of course, is a paramount lesson for our generation and for future generations. It is a lesson that should be studied in depth.

In conclusion, I should like to say that we are living in a rapidly changing world, and we should like to express the hope that our meeting will be a further contribution to the normalization of the situation in this important part of the world, because without a normalization in this region it is difficult to seriously state that a new era has begun for humankind. Thank you very much, Mr. President.

RISQUET: We thank Mr. Troyanovsky for his statement.

The aim of this first session was to hear of the greetings of the representatives of the three countries. The substantive issues that have been contained in these statements will not be debated now, but in the next sessions. Consequently, we have come to the end of our first session, and we would like to propose a half-hour break. At ten minutes past four, we will begin the second session with the statements of the representatives of the Soviet delegation. We shall resume our work then. But now, a break for refreshments.

CUBA ON THE BRINK, THEN AND NOW: THE HAVANA CONFERENCE ON THE CUBAN MISSILE CRISIS

I got into bed and put the light out: but I couldn't sleep. The missiles are there, in Pinar del Rio, Santa Clara, in Oriente. . . . The island seems to be covered with missiles all over. They'll brush us away, put us out, they're going to sink this alligator island into the bottom of the Caribbean. Then the battleships will sail over us and say: "This is where Cuba used to be." And the waves, the tides, will sweep over the island that had sunk into the bottom of the sea.

The Pentagon must already have a plan to destroy us. They'll crush us with the sheer weight of their arms and men. And if the Russians fire their missiles the earth might split in two. All because of Cuba. Never have we been more important nor more miserable.

—EDMUNDO DESNOES,
Memories of Underdevelopment

DURING A HALF-HOUR BREAK FOLLOWING TROYANOVSKY'S OPENING remarks, the conference room is cleared of journalists and camera crews, except for the two specially designated teams, one from Cuba and one from the United States. During the break an aide to Fidel Castro informs us that the president is downstairs in the corridor and would like to chat informally with the members of both the U.S. and Russian delegations. In a scene that will occur many times before the conference concludes, dozens of people surround Castro, jostling for position, trying to hear the conversation, all the while attempting to move close enough to enter into it. Castro towers over his stocky security agents, and most others as well, and when he speaks he gesticulates furiously with both hands, creating what little space there is between him and the throng of actual and would-be interlocutors. He is assisted by Ms. Juanita Vera García, his Spanish-English interpreter, who is justly renowned not only for the speed and accuracy of her translation, but also for her ability to reproduce exactly the verbal emphases, even the hand gestures, of the president.

Notable among the conversations in this raucous hallway is an encounter between Castro and Ray Cline, former CIA deputy director for intelligence, who supervised the analysis of the U-2 photographs that confirmed the presence of missiles in Cuba in 1962. As was later reported, they meet "beard to beard," though Castro is nearly a foot taller than Cline (to whom many would accurately refer throughout the conference as "the man who resembles Hemingway").[1] Castro opens by saying, "So, you found us out, eh, Mr. Cline?" to which Cline responds, "Well, yes, I guess I did." Cline then remarks that he is grateful for having been issued a visa to attend the conference. Castro retreats a step, and a look of mock horror comes over his face. "Why, Mr. Cline," he replied, "it is our pleasure. Allow me to say how grateful we are that—*this* time—you *asked* for one!" The two, together with all who hear the exchange, fall into a fit of laughter, and Castro good-naturedly smacks the shorter Cline on the shoulder.

These and other conversations, including one between Castro and McNamara, prove to be time well spent, particularly for the Americans. McNamara's opening statement has been tough, but Castro seems to indicate in the corridor that the subject McNamara has raised is fair game. Many of us return to the conference room breathing a bit easier. We now begin the Havana conference in earnest, behind closed doors.

OPERATION ANADYR:

". . . on the brink of a nuclear holocaust"

By prior agreement, the Russians make the first set of presentations, followed by questions and comments from the Cuban and American sides. There are several reasons to favor this arrangement. First, Russian military officers who played a role in the crisis have not participated in previous conferences. In addition, the leader of the present Russian military contingent, Gen. Anatoly I. Gribkov, had participated in the planning of Operation Anadyr, as the Soviet deployment of men and missiles had been known to those who carried it out. The details of the deployment, particularly regarding the nuclear weapons, are of great interest to U.S. participants, who in 1962 made estimates based on very little hard information, and to the Cubans, who knew very little about the details of the Soviet nuclear command structure. Having the Russians go first also emphasizes the participation of Oleg Troyanovsky, regarded by many as the only man alive who "knows everything" (as

Sergei Khrushchev once said) about the discussions and decisions that occurred in Khrushchev's inner circle of advisers. Finally, such an arrangement will, we hope, permit Fidel Castro to ease into the conversation, as he becomes acquainted with the way critical oral history works and with the veterans from the U.S. and Russian delegations. The Cuban organizers have confided to us privately that Castro feels a bit sheepish about entering directly into a discussion with veterans and scholars who have spent years becoming familiar with the details of the crisis. As a Cuban official put it, "Fidel doesn't want to embarrass himself in front of people who may *know* more about his actions than he *remembers*." This turns out not to be a problem. By the time Castro enters fully into the discussion on the second day, he has reviewed a host of documents, and he will restrict his remarks for the most part to topics that he alone can address credibly.

A member of the U.S. delegation jokes that General Gribkov "looks like a guy who is taking down names to be used against people next time, when the coup attempt *works*." Although he is not in uniform, he looks every inch a Soviet military officer. Thickly set, stern-faced, deliberate, sincere to a fault, and utterly devoid of humor, Gribkov reminds us of Marshal Zhukov, Marshal Malinovsky, and the now-disgraced Marshal Yazov, standing stone-faced in Red Square on May Day, as the Soviet legions and their weapons parade by. We learn that his memoir of Operation Anadyr will be published soon in Germany, and that he thus comes to Havana having spent a good deal of time reviewing documents from the period, and having conversed with his former colleagues.[2]

Gribkov electrifies the members of the U.S. delegation with his claims: that the Soviets had tactical nuclear weapons in Cuba during the crisis, and that, in the event of a U.S. invasion and the expected loss of secure communication with Moscow, Khrushchev had delegated the authority to use the weapons to Gen. Issa Pliyev, commander-in-chief of all Soviet forces in Cuba. This Pliyev would almost certainly have done. Gribkov's claims may not be entirely accurate, as we discuss in chapter 4; but there has been no single moment quite as dramatic as this in any of the previous conferences. During Gribkov's presentation, McNamara grimaces in astonishment and fumbles with his earphone, striving to hear the translation more clearly. McNamara realizes that if the United States had invaded Cuba, as many felt would be necessary had Khrushchev not agreed to remove the missiles, thousands of American soldiers might have been killed on Cuban beaches by Soviet tactical nuclear weapons. An American nuclear reprisal conceivably could have led to a wider U.S.-Soviet war, and, ultimately, nuclear holocaust.[3] The Americans grill Gribkov, who at first interprets their bewilderment as doubt. Feeling his veracity questioned, Gribkov responds testily to McNamara, Gen. William Y. Smith, and Raymond Garthoff.[4] For the first time we begin to suspect that there was nuclear danger *in* Cuba in October 1962, not merely *because of* Cuba.

Troyanovsky then takes the floor. A retired career diplomat who actually grew up in the United States (his father was the first Soviet ambassador to Washington in 1933), and who went to Swarthmore College, he is as carefully indirect and respectful as Gribkov is blunt and unapologetic. Troyanovsky provides interesting firsthand insight into Soviet decision making before and during the crisis, painting a more detailed picture than we had heard before.

This portion of the discussion concludes with Fidel Castro's first significant intervention. He makes two points that will arise repeatedly in his contributions to the conference: first, that the Cubans accepted the missiles not for the defense of Cuba, but to provide assistance to the Soviets, and to the socialist community generally, in achieving a more favorable balance of nuclear forces with the West (a claim of which we are skeptical); and second, that from the outset, the Cubans wanted to go public with the agreement to deploy the missiles, but were rebuffed by Khrushchev. This is the opening wedge of a series of criticisms that Castro directs at the Soviets' handling of the deployment and of the crisis. The discussion is cut short by Jorge Risquet, who announces, loyally but (as subsequent discussion will show) prematurely, "I think that this has been clarified totally."

RISQUET: Dear friends; we are now going to begin our second work session. The president of the Institute of History [Jorge E. Mendoza], who was supposed to chair this session, has asked me to take his place. According to the agenda we are going to hear the presentation by the Soviet delegation, and discuss their statements. I invite our Soviet friends to take the floor.

GENERAL ANATOLY GRIBKOV: Dear Comrade Fidel Castro; ladies and gentlemen; comrades all: I would like first of all to thank our Cuban comrades for inviting the military delegation of my country to this meeting. Since in previous meetings the military were not present, I am participating in such a significant meeting for the first time. Thus,

I would like to introduce myself. In 1962, I was the head of a bureau of the Main Operations Directorate of the Soviet General Staff. At present, I am a general of the army, and a general inspector of the Defense Ministry.

Allow me to present an overview of the military part of the crisis that we are studying. The political situation has been exhaustively examined in previous meetings. Consequently, in my presentation, I would like to turn your attention to the military aspects of that time.

As you are all well aware, according to our military assessments, a critical situation had developed after the events at Playa Girón, or the Bay of Pigs [17–19 April 1961]. Our problem was to determine how we could help Cuba defend its liberty and its sovereignty. The Soviet government decided to provide Cuba with military assistance, and instructed the High Command, in the middle of May 1962, to prepare a proposal on an operational plan and a force structure to assist the Cuban military in securing the defense of Cuban territory. At this time it was also decided to draft a formal agreement between the Soviet Union and Cuba in this regard. Allow me to give you the name of this agreement. We had three options, and we chose one upon consultation with the leaders, that is, Comrade Fidel Castro and Nikita Sergeievich Khrushchev. The agreement—or rather, the draft—was called an "Agreement Between the Government of the Republic of Cuba and the Government of the USSR on Military Co-operation for the Defense of the National Territory of Cuba in the Event of Aggression."[5] In the preamble of the agreement, it said—and I would like you to pay attention—"It is necessary and has been decided to take the necessary steps for the joint defense of the legitimate rights of the people of Cuba and the Soviet Union, taking into account the urgent need to adopt measures to guarantee mutual security, in view of the possibility of an imminent attack against the Republic of Cuba and the Soviet Union."[6] As you can see in this draft agreement, there was mention of the defense of the interest of the Soviet Union. This agreement was drafted and examined by the governments of both states. The necessary amendments were made, and the agreement, owing to circumstance, was initialled but not signed by the representatives of Cuba and the Soviet Union.*

We presented our government with a proposed plan to deploy

---

*The first draft of the agreement was initialed by Cuban minister of defense Raúl Castro and Soviet minister of defense Rodion Ya. Malinovsky in July 1962, but the revised draft agreed upon in August was never signed by Castro, Khrushchev, or their representatives.

troops and equipment in Cuba, but we had to consider how we were going to represent the operation. Our cover was that we were going to carry out a strategic exercise through the deployment of Soviet troops in the north. The troops themselves were later told that they were going to go to Cuba to defend the island's independence. The name of the operation was "Anadyr." That is the name of a river in the northern region of our country, in a very cold region. Well, this story, I would say, allowed us to prepare the troops to be deployed in Cuba.

What was the force that we would have to train in our country in a very short span of time and transport to the other side of the ocean? This was its composition:

> • A medium-range missile division. We saw this unit as a means to prevent aggression; I repeat, as a means to deter aggression. This division was made up of five regiments. Three were R-12 [NATO designation SS-4] regiments, with missiles whose range was 2,500 km (24 launchers with a complement of 1½ missiles for each launcher). Two were R-14 [SS-5] missile regiments (sixteen launchers, also 1½ missiles per launcher). Forty launchers were foreseen in all, together with the appropriate number of missiles [sixty]. I would like to add that at the beginning of the crisis—that is, on October 22nd—three R-12 regiments were already in Cuba, and two regiment sites were already laid out in their deployment areas. The third regiment site was under construction. The two R-14 regiments were still en route at sea, and in accordance with the instructions of the Soviet government, returned to the Soviet Union.
> • Two air defense missile divisions comprised of twenty-four missile sites: 144 S-75 [NATO designation SA-2] launchers. The Americans are probably familiar with these data, but I can repeat their range (65 km) and altitude (100 m to 30 km).
> • Four motorized rifle regiments, reinforced by three tactical nuclear missile batteries—six launchers for *Luna* [NATO designation FROG*] missiles with a 60 km range. We initially considered calling these units brigades, but then we changed our minds and decided to call them regiments that we were going to deploy there to defend the shores and the missile sites, jointly with the Cuban troops.

---

*Free Rocket Over Ground.

• The Air Force had a regiment of forty MiG-21 aircraft in Cuba; thirty[-three] tactical aircraft (Il-28s); and a separate naval squadron of nine Il-28 aircraft. At the onset of the crisis, only six planes had been assembled, and only a few flights had been made.

• Two regiments of tactical cruise missiles were also provided. In each regiment there were ten launchers: one for training, and nine for combat. There were eighteen combat launchers in all. Range: 150 km. We brought over eighty conventional cruise missiles for these two regiments.

• We also had an Mi-8 transport helicopter regiment, and a transport air squadron with nine already-obsolete Li-2 planes.

• Now the Navy. We planned to deploy two squadrons to Cuba: one squadron of surface ships, comprising two cruisers and two destroyers; and a squadron of submarines, comprising eleven submarines. These two squadrons never went to Cuba. They were scheduled to be sent out later.

• A missile regiment for coastal defense, with the *Sopka* missile, had eight launchers at four sites on the coast. Thirty-two cruise missiles were brought for these eight launchers. The range of the missiles against targets at sea was 80 km. The Americans are familiar with these data; that's why I merely mention them.

• Finally, there was a brigade of twelve missile-launching [*Komar*] patrol boats, with two P-15 missiles each, with a range of 40 km.

These were the military units that were to be sent to Cuba. Aside from these military units, there was a communications unit, and support services.

As you can see, this was a very significant group of forces. Much has been written about the missiles, but if you analyze the military structure of what we sent to Cuba, the missile unit was brought only to deter aggression, and that was the only one that was deployed for that purpose. The others—jointly with the Cuban armed forces—were to defend the island of Cuba from attack by air, by land, and by sea.

Before the crisis, we had foreseen bringing in 45,000 men. By the time of the crisis, we had brought in 42,000. Never before in the history of the Soviet Armed Forces and in the history of Russia had we transported so many troops to the other side of the ocean. Consequently, when we were entrusted by the government with the planning of this operation, we said that there were many issues and unknowns to be taken into account. We devoted day and night to these preparations. We made all the necessary calculations, but these had to be done in absolute secrecy. To transport these troops, we had to use eighty-five ships from our merchant marine, and to assemble in secrecy ships of various kinds scattered all over the seas. They had to be equipped with special technology and with the necessary crew, a special crew. Consequently, the merchant marine had to make great efforts to accomplish this task.

The Navy got the necessary ships, and 185 trips were made with these ships transporting the forces. The ships were distributed among seven ports in the White Sea, the Barents Sea, the Baltic Sea, the Black Sea, and so forth.[7] Aside from the plan for transporting the troops, we also prepared a plan to cover these operations, replete with the necessary diversionary tactics and disinformation, as is done by all armed forces. The steps that we took in this regard were generally successful.

Simultaneously, we prepared the command structure. We had to establish a command structure for such a complex military force. We began with the staff of a Missile Army, and appointed as its commander General [Pavel B.] Dankevich. We then reached the conclusion that this group should be under the command of an experienced and multiservice commander. We analyzed all the proposals that were made, and General Issa Alexandrovich Pliyev was appointed overall commander. He had actively participated in the Second World War and was twice named a Hero of the Soviet Union. We modified the staff of the Missile Army to add deputy commanders for the Air Force, Navy, and Air Defense forces, to support General Pliyev, who was known in Cuba as Ivan Alexandrovich Pavlov.

To identify the area for the deployment of troops in Cuba, in keeping with the agreement, we sent a group to Cuba headed by Pliyev. Each service was represented. We sent them by plane, and, jointly with Cubans, they selected the sites for the deployment of forces.

When the essential planning was completed by the General Staff, and when most of the troops were already aboard the ships and on their way, some units were already being deployed in Cuba. It was then that I was instructed to leave for Cuba by plane, with some other admirals and generals, as a representative of Minister of Defense Malinovsky, to check on the status of the operation. I would like to quote Malinovsky when he gave me the order to convey Khrushchev's and the defense minister's instructions to Pliyev: "The missile forces will fire only if authorized by Nikita Sergeievich Khrushchev"—it was repeated—"only if instructed by the Supreme Commander-in-Chief himself." Comrade Pliyev was to remember that the missile division had been sent to Cuba to deter aggression. The tactical nuclear forces—the six *Luna* launchers I've mentioned—could be employed with nuclear weapons during a direct invasion by the aggressor. It was said that before arriving at a decision on employing the tactical missiles, the situation had to be very thoroughly and carefully assessed, and, in case of extreme need only, then could the decision be made. That was my mission when I was sent to Cuba.

On October 22nd, the day when Kennedy spoke on the radio and on television, we already had 42,000 troops in Cuba and three missile regiments (one division). The sites were ready for two regiments (not yet for the third). None of the missiles was placed in combat readiness. They had not yet been fueled, nor supplied with oxidating agents. The warheads were some 250 or 300 kilometers from the launch sites, and had not yet been released for use.

All the units—all the necessary units, that is—were in their combat positions covering the missile sites. These units were deployed throughout the territory of Cuba. They were to cover the whole island, together, that is, with the air defense units and the air force, which would work jointly with the Cuban Air Force. The fighter planes were ready for combat. All the planes—forty MiG-21s—had been assembled and were ready for combat. But despite this, no one fired on the American planes that were flying over Cuba. These included high-altitude U-2s, and other low-level reconnaissance planes that flew so low that, in some cases, we could even see the pilots. We later learned that negotiations were taking place between Khrushchev and Kennedy. But, while they were in Cuba, the commanders of our troops were not informed of these secret negotiations.

Now everything is clear. We all know a lot about the Cuban crisis. We know what the situation was like then. But at that time there were many dangers, many things we knew nothing about—not just the Soviets, but also the Cubans. And there were many things that the American command did not know about.

Intelligence provided data on the preparations being made in the United States—that is, strikes that were being prepared. There was the possibility of landings in Cuba. Together with the General Staff of the Cuban Revolutionary Armed Forces, we devised a plan to repel aggression. It was foreseen that if the aggressor were to cut the Cuban territory into sections, we would then have to use fall-back operational command centers in different parts of the country—west, central, and east. That is, the troops stationed in Cuba should be ready to fight in order to thwart aggression against Cuba. I must say that the fighting spirit of the Cuban Revolutionary Armed Forces and of the Cuban people, and the fighting spirit of the Soviet troops in Cuba, was high. We were all ready and willing to fight to the very last man. We didn't just plan an initial resistance. We even decided that if it proved necessary—if large tracts of the island were occupied—we would form guerrilla units in order to continue defending the interests of revolutionary Cuba. I'm using the very words that we used in 1962. That's the way we were then. We did not have anywhere to withdraw to. No retreat was possible. Our Soviet soldiers were willing to give their all to defend Cuba, and we are very grateful to the Cuban people, to the Cuban armed forces, and to you, dear Comrade Fidel Castro, for your appreciation of our soldiers who were stationed in Cuba then.

Many things have come into the open here, as at previous meetings. A lot of information has been published on the Cuban crisis. But many people who were far from this reality have also written. Allow me to say that, considering all the possible options in the event of an attack against Cuba, the aggressor would have suffered great losses, either in the event of an air attack with a subsequent landing, or in a direct assault. An air attack would not have destroyed all the missiles. Even if the three intermediate-range missile regiments had been destroyed, leaving only the six *Luna* launchers (which were very hard to destroy), they would have been made ready with nuclear weapons, and we are all perfectly aware of the fact that losses would have been tremendous.

Allow me to say that the wisdom and common sense of the three leaders—Fidel Castro, Kennedy, and Khrushchev—prevented a catastrophe. But the world was on the brink of a nuclear holocaust. It is evident that this should be a useful lesson to all the leaders of nuclear countries. We must be very careful with these weapons. This is not a time for swords. I believe that the present rulers of the countries with nuclear weapons will learn from the bitter experience of 1962.

When the order to withdraw the troops from Cuba was issued, our soldiers did all they had to do to obey it. They did what they were told as regards the missiles and the matériel. They were also instructed to train Cuban troops; our men did their utmost to train the Cuban military in all aspects.

I am a military man who fought hard in 1939 and 1940. I was in a tank during the Second World War. I was a lieutenant. I had to fight. I know the bitterness of retreat, and we had victories. But during my long military career—in the fifty-four years that I have served as a military man—my most humiliating experience was the inspection of our ships at sea. You know what I am talking about. I believe that Fidel Castro did right when he refused to allow Cuban territory to be inspected, the ports and the territorial waters of Cuba; but our ships were inspected on the high seas. At that time, we had to tell the Americans the number of missiles that the ships were to carry, and then the American ships and helicopters came, inspected the ships, and said okay. I, as a military man, must say that we did everything that was requested of us, from the political and military point of view. We did as we had been told to do.

Much more could be said on this military aspect of the crisis but I would not like to elaborate, because you are familiar with most of this. During the meeting we can go further into details. Thank you very much for your attention.

RISQUET: I want to thank the General for his very moving statement, and I would like to ask Mr. Troyanovsky to please address the meeting.

TROYANOVSKY: Mr. Chairman, do you think this is the best way to proceed, or do you think perhaps it might be better for questions to be addressed to the speaker who already spoke?

RISQUET: That's a very good idea. Let's open the floor to questions and debate on the General's statement, and then we will hear from Troyanovsky. Would anyone like to take the floor? General Smith?

GENERAL WILLIAM Y. SMITH: Some of the questions that have been foremost in the minds of the United States since the time of the crisis were the number of nuclear warheads that were actually in place in Cuba between October 22 and October 30, 1962; where they were located in Cuba; and at what point—and by what means—were they removed from Cuba at the end of the crisis? I wonder if there's any information about that that you could give us. I say that because we watched very carefully as Soviet forces were leaving Cuba for indications that they took nuclear weapons. To my knowledge—and I personally watched this very closely—we never had conclusive evidence that any nuclear weapons left Cuba. For that matter, we never had conclusive evidence that nuclear weapons ever reached Cuba. You have told us before they were in Cuba, so my question is: how many, where were they, when did they leave, and how?

RISQUET: Would you like to answer, General, sir?

GRIBKOV: As I said, we brought over twenty-four R-12 launchers, and thirty-six missiles. Another six R-12 missiles were for training purposes. They were deployed in two regions: one region was San Cristóbal, and the second—I don't remember the town nearby, but it was in the western part of Cuba.* General [Igor D.] Statsenko, the commander of the missile units, was ordered to report frankly to the U.N. deputy secretary general on the progress of the withdrawal, without hiding any information. Forgive me, I'm referring to U Thant, who was acting secretary general. General Statsenko reported to U Thant, in the presence of Comrade Alekseev, who is present here. When U Thant asked when the missiles were going to be withdrawn, the answer the commander gave him was, "As soon as the necessary ships arrive, we will withdraw the launchers and the rockets." On November 1st everything was ready to be loaded in the ports, and by November 20th it was reported that there were no more missile forces in Cuba.

GENERAL SMITH: I am drawing a distinction between the missiles that were capable of delivering nuclear warheads and the nuclear warheads themselves.

GRIBKOV: At the same time we also withdrew the warheads. This was not written up anywhere, but one ship bringing over additional warheads was not unloaded. This ship spent a few days during the crisis in port, and left for the Soviet Union as it had arrived, without unloading the warheads. These warheads were for the R-14 missiles.

RISQUET: Thank you, General.

RAYMOND GARTHOFF: We have just learned for the first time that it was intended to supply tactical nuclear weapons to the Group of Forces in Cuba. You mentioned six short-range *Luna* tactical launchers. Did that mean there would be six nuclear warheads supplied? And had those warheads yet reached Cuba at the time of the crisis?

GRIBKOV: There's something I'd like to correct in your question right off. Were you saying that tactical weapons had been brought for the *Cuban* forces? No, there were no tactical nuclear weapons brought

---

*The San Cristóbal MRBM complex (four sites), in Pinar del Río Province, was the westernmost. The second MRBM complex (two sites) near Sagua la Grande, in Las Villas Province, was in central Cuba. See Central Intelligence Agency Memorandum, "The Crisis, USSR/Cuba," 28 October 1962, in McAuliffe, *CIA Documents on the Cuban Missile Crisis,* p. 344.

for Cuban forces. For all our medium-range launchers we had 1½ missiles. Then there were six tactical launchers. These were under the command of Soviet regiment commanders. Three regiments had two launchers each, and one of them had none—that one was in Holguin, under Yazov. All of these were withdrawn at the same time.

GARTHOFF: So they were actually in Cuba at the time of the crisis, those six warheads? Armed? And were we correctly informed on an earlier occasion that there were twenty warheads in all, or twenty warheads for the strategic missiles actually in Cuba?

GRIBKOV: Please, do not get confused between the number of missiles and the number of launchers. I've read the U.S. materials and the Soviet materials, and there is a confusion there. We brought to Cuba twenty-four R-12 launchers, and, for each one, 1.5 missile loadings. In addition, there were six *Luna* launchers, with 1.5 missile loadings each, with nuclear warheads. That is, for six launchers there were nine tactical nuclear rockets. By November 20th, I repeat, there wasn't a single nuclear warhead left on Cuban territory.

RISQUET: There may be some translation problems, but I think the answer is clear. All of these missiles were in the hands of the Soviet forces. I think a translator made a mistake and said that the Cuban forces had them.

GRIBKOV: All Soviet missile troops—and not only the missile troops, but also the rest of the Soviet troops—were subordinated to the Soviet command. None were subordinated to the Cuban command, and Commander-in-Chief Fidel Castro can confirm that.

GARTHOFF: Thank you very much. I don't want to extend this; I just wanted to clarify matters, because we had understood that there were the thirty-six R-12 missiles, the twenty-four launchers, but we have been told that a total of only twenty warheads had actually reached Cuba at the time of the quarantine. That was apparently an error. If I understood you correctly now, you said that all of those R-12 missiles had warheads here.

RISQUET: I'd like to remind us all, please, that we should ask for the floor before deciding to speak on our own. Mr. McNamara, I think, was asking for the floor. I'm going to give the floor to Mr. McNamara.

McNAMARA: Mr. Chairman, this is a very interesting, very important, and to me a very confusing discussion of the number of nuclear warheads in Cuba on October 20, or between October 20 and October 30. May I suggest that, rather than try to clarify the issue now, we agree that General Smith and Ambassador Garthoff meet with General Gribkov at his convenience and discuss the matter further?

CASTRO: I wonder why only the American general and the general of the armed forces of the former Soviet Union should meet? I think if we are going to clarify these things, at least a Cuban general or a civilian should be at the meeting.

RISQUET: It seems that there is a certain persistence here of the superpowers' past tendency to ignore other parties. I think we should accept Mr. McNamara's suggestion, as amended by the Commander-in-Chief.

GRIBKOV: The question that has been brought up, I think, touches an important point. It happens sometimes that when two parties leave a third party on the margin, you get polemic. Now, when the question of the withdrawal of the missiles from Cuba was being discussed, no one asked Fidel Castro's opinion. When it was decided to bring them to Cuba, he was consulted. That decision was adopted jointly; there was a draft agreement that was discussed and negotiated. But when the missiles were to be withdrawn from Cuba, that was decided behind Fidel Castro's back. Nikita Sergeievich Khrushchev decided that together with John F. Kennedy. So I can well understand Fidel Castro's position, and I can well understand that he felt offended at the time.

Furthermore, when in 1979 the United States brought up the question of the motorized rifle brigade,[8] there was an agreement between the USSR and Cuba on the stationing of this unit in Cuba, and I should like to say here, in a kind of self-criticism, that we on the Soviet side did not act correctly at the time. We had a different leader, Mr. Brezhnev, who immediately—together with the Foreign Ministry—denied the existence of the brigade, and insisted that it was a training center. This, too, was done without consulting Comrade Fidel Castro. Later on, when Mr. Gorbachev was our leader, Mr. Baker met with Mr. Gorbachev, and they agreed that the brigade would be withdrawn from Cuba—again without consulting Fidel Castro.

This, of course, is quite incorrect. It is incorrect from the international legal standpoint, and from a simple human point of view. We had a joint decision to bring the troops over, but then there was a unilateral decision to withdraw them. I quite agree with Comrade Fidel

Castro that one cannot solve such important issues unilaterally. This is just a small digression.

RISQUET: There was a question left on the table. The question was how many warheads there were. There was a proposal by Mr. Mc-Namara, amended by Commander Fidel Castro, to the effect that this could be clarified in a smaller meeting and then brought to the plenary. But I would like to ask the General if he agreed with this suggestion, or if we might continue discussing it here in the plenary session?

GRIBKOV: I can answer you now so as not to leave you hanging.

RISQUET: Please do so, sir.

GRIBKOV: I'll repeat again. The R-12 launchers had thirty-six combat missiles and their warheads; and the *Luna* launchers—the tactical weapons—had nine missiles and their corresponding warheads. The R-14s were aboard ship, and they returned to the Soviet Union—I think the name of the ship they were on was the *Indigirka*. It came by a northern port. It did not unload its warheads. I visited the ship, and when it was agreed that the ship should return, it did so without unloading the warheads.

RISQUET: I think the answer is perfectly clear, then. Are there any other questions?

CASTRO: I think the answer to that question is extremely precise and clear. I wanted to know those details, because rumors have been circulating. I can well appreciate the courage with which the question has been answered by General Gribkov. I have no doubts about the clarity and sincerity of that answer.

He also said something about the chain of command, and whether the troops were commanded by Soviets, or if any units were commanded by Cubans. This was governed by Article 10 of the Agreement. Article 10 said—it says, because it's right here—"Both parties agree that the military units of each State will be under the command of their respective governments and they will, in coordination, determine the use of their corresponding forces to repel a foreign aggression and to restore peace." So here we had two armies and two commands. Of course, we Cubans had no warheads or launchers of any sort. I think we should go on record historically on that. I think this article explains the way the command of the troops was agreed. We could give no orders to the Soviet troops in any kind of combat action, nor could they give us any orders. Each had its own command, and that's the way it worked, although there was very close contact and a high degree of coordination.

When the time comes, more details can be given on some aspects of the question because we, too, made decisions. There were some occasions on which we were obliged to make decisions, and we did so, such as the decision to fire on the planes that were overflying Cuba—especially on the low-flying planes, because we did not have the capability to shoot at aircraft flying at 20,000 meters. What I'm talking about is airplanes flying at 100 to 300 meters. At a certain moment, we gave the order to fire on those aircraft.* We ordered our antiaircraft batteries to fire upon them. Later on we can give you more details; but the conventional antiaircraft forces were in our hands. The Soviets had the antiair missiles. We had 57 mm cannon— cannon of various calibers that had a range of 7,000 or 8,000 meters; perhaps up to 10,000 meters. They were in our hands. And at a given moment we decided that we could not tolerate these low-level flights, because these low flights were a precursor to a surprise attack through which to destroy our equipment and our troops. So, at a given moment, we decided not to tolerate them, because they were in fact more dangerous than the U-2 overflights. The U-2s had already taken pictures of everything they felt like photographing anyway, and it wasn't an attack craft; it wasn't a danger, whereas the low-flying craft were combat aircraft, and, as we saw it, could not be tolerated. This was a sovereign decision made by the command of our forces to fire on low-flying aircraft. The exact moment when the order was given I can give you later; I don't want to take up any more of your time. Thank you.

RISQUET: Mr. McNamara.

McNAMARA: Mr. Chairman: I don't want to extend the discussion of nuclear warheads. It's a footnote to history now. In a sense it's of little importance for the future, but it is an important footnote to history.

I think we—at least, I—in the U.S. may have misunderstood. I simply want to state my understanding. I don't wish to discuss it, but I would like General Gribkov to listen to what I say, and if I misstate what he has said, I would like him to correct me before I leave on Sunday.

---

*Castro ordered Cuban antiaircraft artillery to open fire on American aircraft on 26 October.

In the U.S. at the time, the CIA reported uncertainty as to whether there were any nuclear warheads on the soil of Cuba. They believed there were not. They stated they had considerable evidence that twenty warheads were on the high seas aboard a ship named the *Poltava*. When we were in Moscow three years ago, we made such a statement, and a Soviet general—whose name I believe was Volkogonov*—stated, "The CIA was correct. There were twenty warheads on the *Poltava* on the high seas." But he said the CIA was in error in believing there were no warheads on the soil of Cuba. He said that his records indicated— and that he was authorized to state, by his government—that there were twenty nuclear warheads on the soil of Cuba between October 20 and roughly October 30.[9]

If I understood the statements made here today correctly, General Volkogonov was in error. There were some warheads on the high seas for the R-14 missiles, perhaps on a different ship, but I understand— and, as I said, I don't want to discuss this now, but I would like to be corrected if my understanding is wrong before I leave—I understand that instead of twenty nuclear warheads on the soil of Cuba there were at that time thirty-six for the R-12s, and nine for the *Lunas,* for a total of forty-five. My understanding may be incorrect; please correct me before I leave if it is.

RISQUET: All right, Mr. McNamara. The figures are quite clear from my point of view. A request has been made for clarification, and before you leave I'm sure that this clarification will be given to you, in private or in public. For us it's quite clear, the figures are quite clear. [To Gribkov:] Would you like to make this clarification now, or before Mr. McNamara leaves? He is asking whether it is correct to say that there were thirty-six warheads for the R-12s and nine for the *Lunas,* for a total of forty-five.

GRIBKOV: Mr. McNamara, in full respect, I would like to say that you were a very young and energetic minister. We thought then that the United States had made a good choice for the Department of Defense. You did much for the U.S. armed forces. As an old official of the General Staff I'm quite aware of all these things.

What Volkogonov said to you is something that was said by someone who was not in close contact with the troops. I was an official on

---

*Gen. Dimitry Volkogonov, then head of the Soviet Ministry of Defense Institute of Military History.

the General Staff and head of an operational section. I planned the operation with my own hands. I can tell you in detail how we loaded the ships. Minister of the Maritime Fleet Karamzin* was present with the plans for each ship, for example the *Poltava*. I was responsible for the matériel and the weapons, and in my office we were in charge of loading these ships and maintaining secrecy. So who is in a better position to know about this—Volkogonov or Gribkov? You have to decide. Volkogonov is a Doctor in Philosophical Sciences, in Historical Sciences, but I am a military man with fifty-four years of experience, a true military man. [Laughter.]

McNamara: I'm completely satisfied. The answer is forty-five. [Laughter.]

Risquet: I think that Volkogonov has written about twenty books on psychology, or so he told me in Moscow.

Gribkov: I don't think we should now debate whether there were twenty warheads, or twenty-one. That's not important. We can discuss the figures, or even write a thesis on this; but at that time, we—the military—were in charge of these matters. You know what your army did, we know what our army did. That's why—well, let's trust one another.

McNamara: Mr. Chairman, the issue of nuclear warheads and the dangers that the human race—not just our three countries—but the dangers that the human race faces so long as there are such huge numbers on the face of the Earth today, are extremely important. I think I'm correct roughly in saying that there are 50,000 nuclear warheads on the planet. I have felt this is an extraordinarily dangerous situation for humanity. I take it that the General very much agrees, and therefore I want to pursue this just one small point further: not the numbers, but rather his statement—and I may have misunderstood it—but with respect to the question of the authority to use the nuclear warheads, which is very, very important, and which is going to be a problem with the human race as long as nuclear warheads are on this Earth.

If I understood him correctly, he said authority lay in two different

---

*Yevgeny V. Karamzin, Deputy Minister of the Merchant Marine.

categories. The authority to use—to launch—the R-12 warheads rested with Khrushchev and all the Politburo*—the Supreme Command, in effect. I quite understand that that's exactly what we thought at the time. But I understood him to say that the authority to launch the *Luna* warheads depended upon—I think the translator used the word "variant"—anyway, I interpreted the answer to mean that the authority to use the *Luna* warheads depended upon the local commander's decision in the face of a potential U.S. attack. I see the General nods. That was exactly my impression. I don't wish to argue whether that was a wise delegation of authority or not. That's not my point at all. My point is to emphasize to all of us what I think some of us felt at the time, and what the three heads of state felt—the comandante, Khrushchev, and Kennedy: that this was an extraordinarily dangerous situation. I mention this not because of the past, I mention it because of the future. These dangers will exist as long as we have thousands of warheads.

RISQUET: All right; are there any other questions for General Gribkov, or can we move to our friend Troyanovsky? I think that General Gribkov has been quite thorough. Troyanovsky has the floor.

TROYANOVSKY: Since I did not participate in previous meetings on this issue, and since in the previous meetings a wide variety of aspects of the 1962 crisis were discussed and published, I would like to refer only to my personal impressions, my recollections, particularly on that specific week. I was then one of Khrushchev's aides for foreign policy affairs. Khrushchev had quite a limited cabinet made up of four advisers. One, the recently deceased [Grigory T.] Shuisky was the head adviser, the senior adviser, and he dealt with national affairs, economic affairs, political affairs. Another adviser was [Vladimir S.] Lebedev, who dealt with ideological matters. The third, [Andrei S.] Shevchenko, dealt with economic matters. I was in charge of foreign policy issues. Khrushchev also had an adviser for receptions at the Central Committee and the Council of Ministers, and he had two or three stenographers. That was Khrushchev's personal team.

Before the onset of the crisis, we received an enormous amount of information on the intentions of the United States to launch a second attack on Cuba. We have heard from Mr. McNamara that there were

---

*In 1962, the leadership of the Communist Party of the Soviet Union was called the Presidium.

no such intentions. However, the plans did exist. That's evident. These plans in one way or another were made known to us. Although there was some disinformation, we formed quite a realistic impression of an imminent attack. Consequently, it was logical for Khrushchev to think of ways to protect Cuba in the event of such an attack.

Even though I was familiar with all the information that Khrushchev received on foreign policy, I did not immediately find out his intention to deploy nuclear missiles to Cuba. I recall perfectly well the day when another adviser called me—that is, the recently deceased Mr. Lebedev—and he said the following. He told me that we were contemplating the idea of deploying nuclear missiles in Cuba if the Cuban leadership agreed. I was definitely taken aback with this information, because being somewhat knowledgeable of U.S. affairs, and realizing the importance of such a step, I knew this would entail serious consequences. I was then faced with the dilemma of discussing this with Khrushchev or not, although my colleagues in the Secretariat told me that there was no sense in discussing this because the decision had been made and a change in the decision would be impossible. However, I was doing this just to calm my own conscience, and when I found the appropriate time I talked to Khrushchev. He said that he was aware that this was a very serious decision, but why should we not do what the Americans had been doing all along? Why couldn't we deploy missiles in Cuba when we were surrounded by U.S. military bases and U.S. missiles? He even said that the Americans appealed to the Monroe Doctrine every so often, but that the Monroe Doctrine did not just call for the non-intervention of European states in U.S. affairs, but also the non-intervention of the U.S. in European affairs. The United States had already discarded this doctrine.[10] Against this logic, what was I to say, especially since I really did not expect a change in the decision that had been made? That was the end of our discussion.

The second time I discussed it with Khrushchev was in October. I was alone in Khrushchev's office, and he said, "Yes, the missiles will be deployed soon, and there's going to be a storm around all this." I then said, "Nikita Sergeievich, I hope we will not founder." He said, "Let us hope so." But it was too late to change anything, and I had the feeling that he was perfectly aware of the seriousness of the possible consequences.

Later, on October 22nd, we learned that Kennedy was to speak on a very important problem, as it was then called. We all realized that it had to do with the Soviet missiles in Cuba. A session of the Presidium of the Central Committee was convened—it was not called the Politburo then, but the Presidium of the Central Committee of the Communist Party. This meeting lasted well into the night. We received a message from Kennedy an hour before he spoke. We received the message through the U.S. Embassy in Moscow. It was already past midnight. I remember that I read the message at the session. I would say that the first reaction was quite calm, because what was talked about was a quarantine. The quarantine was something abstract. There was no real threat of aggression, or of strikes against Cuba, etc. I also remember that Khrushchev dictated the main points of reply to that message, and the officials of the Ministry of Foreign Affairs responded as they should. I have to say that what Khrushchev dictated sometimes had to be polished, and the final text presented to him. At the end of the session, Khrushchev recommended to the participants in the meeting that they spend the night at the Kremlin, so that U.S. correspondents, watching for our reactions, should not get the feeling that we were nervous, that we were holding night meetings, and so forth.

Afterwards, as you all know, there was an exchange of messages, an almost daily exchange of messages. Because of the different times in the United States and the Soviet Union, we could send a message and it would be received in Washington that same day.[11] The first message from Khrushchev was quite harsh, although they softened, as did the tone of Kennedy's messages, quite a bit later on.[12]

Let me tell you something that happened then. I recall that in the early days, at the beginning of the crisis, [Vasily V.] Kuznetsov, who was the first deputy minister of foreign affairs—evidently [Foreign Minister Andrei] Gromyko had not yet returned from the United States—Kuznetsov said to Khrushchev that, in response to the pressure exerted by the Americans around Cuba, we had to respond by exerting pressure in some other place, preferably around Berlin. Khrushchev replied quite harshly, saying that we did not need that kind of advice. I had the feeling then that he did not intend to expand the scope of confrontation.

Gradually, however, tensions mounted, and I would say that the highest point of tension came on Saturday the 27th. We received a communiqué that a U-2 had been shot down over Cuba, and this generated some disquiet because we did not know how the Americans would react. But later on, at dawn, we received a message from Comrade Fidel Castro, a message you all know. I can't say that this message generated the feeling that was later referred to in the Western press—namely, that it was a call for preemptive war. That was not the case. But I can say that it did generate some nervousness. The message said that an attack was to take place in twenty-four to seventy-two hours. Later, in the *dacha,* Khrushchev convened a meeting of the Presidium of the Central Committee. By then we had already received a message from President Kennedy proposing the withdrawal of the missiles in exchange for guarantees, or a commitment, not to attack Cuba. All this was known during the session of the 28th. Moreover, I remember that during this session I was called to the phone. It was the adviser to the minister of foreign affairs, Gromyko, who said that a telegram had just been received from Ambassador [Anatoly] Dobrynin, regarding an interview with Robert Kennedy which had been held on October 27th. He read the message to me; I made the necessary notes, and I read the message to the participants in the Presidium meeting. The telegram was quite alarming, and although Robert Kennedy said at the end that it was not an ultimatum, it said that the answer to the Kennedy message had to come in less than twenty-four hours, that we should not delay, and that we should give a very precise answer. As Dobrynin said, there were many hotheads in Washington who were demanding an attack against Cuba, and it was quite understandable that it was going to be difficult for the president to keep everything under control.

This, of course, created a state of alarm during the session, and this was compounded by another circumstance which has been so far unknown. Army General Semyon Ivanov, I think, was called to the phone, and when he came back he said that a message had been received saying that Kennedy would once again speak at 1700 hours, Moscow time. Everyone agreed that Kennedy intended to declare war, to launch an attack. A telegram was sent to the embassy in Washington to verify this. We did not know whether the previous day's appearance was going to be broadcast again. We had the feeling then that there was very little time to unravel what was taking place. That's why we drafted a message to Kennedy. [Leonid F.] Ilychev, secretary of the Central Committee, was told to broadcast this text over the radio, an open text, before 1700 hours Moscow time, before Kennedy's appearance. Of course, we realized that with this haste we were creating a very difficult situation for our Cuban comrades. That's why we sent a telegram to Comrade Fidel Castro informing him of the decision, and telling him, as a partial justification for not consulting with him, that we did not have time to do so.

Allow me to say that Khrushchev was not at all pleased about the way the situation unfolded with regard to Cuba. He suffered great anguish over these things, and then decided to send Mikoyan to Cuba to see whether we could set the situation straight. I was present at the session of the Presidium where Mikoyan reported on his trip to Cuba, and I recall that Khrushchev highly appreciated what Mikoyan had done, finding a solution to this very, very unpleasant situation. I remember he said that no one besides Mikoyan could have been able to carry out such a mission.

Of course, such hasty actions led to important omissions. In Khrushchev's message there was no direct reference to rockets, but rather to "the weapons that you, Mr. President, call offensive."[13] This made it possible for our adversaries later to demand the withdrawal not just of the missiles but also of the bombers—the Il-28s, if I'm not mistaken.

That is more or less what I wanted to tell you, so that you know how things were done.

RISQUET: Thank you very much, Comrade Troyanovsky. We are going to have a half an hour recess. At 6:30 we shall resume.

*   *   *

RISQUET: Esteemed friends; we can continue now with the debate on item 2 on the agenda, on the political and civilian side of the crisis, on the basis of the statement made by Mr. Troyanovsky. Mr. Wayne Smith?

WAYNE SMITH: This was brought up in the Moscow meeting, and again at Antigua; but I don't think a satisfactory answer has ever been given. Perhaps there is none. The question I have is, how did the Soviet side expect to get the weapons in—to get the missiles in—undiscovered? If they were putting them in because they believed that Cuba was likely to be invaded, certainly between the day that the missiles started to arrive and the time that they were operative, Cuba was even more vulnerable to invasion. That practically was an invitation to the United States to react militarily. How did they believe they could install the missiles without being discovered? Given the difficulties, would it not have been better to try to do it openly?

RISQUET: The question has some military and some political aspects. Who would like to answer? It is a political question, but the General explained that the 40,000 troops arrived before the missiles.

GRIBKOV: I can answer briefly. Any military operation has to be prepared, even if you are going to do it in the Persian Gulf. We did this secretly—we prepared the plans secretly—and we prepared a program for disinformation. As a matter of fact, U.S. intelligence was ignorant of a great deal that was going on. I'm not being critical of the former intelligence people involved. I am looking at my colleague here [Ray Cline], who very much resembles Hemingway [laughter]. We prepared all of this secretly. And we had to go according to a plan. Thus, between the 25th and the 27th of November we were supposed to have everything ready, and this was all agreed upon by Soviet and Cuban leaders. At that time both states were going to disclose this information. There was going to be a report saying that certain military units had been brought to Cuba, but things didn't turn out that way because on the 22nd, Kennedy spoke, revealing the deployment. In any case, even under those circumstances, we were ultimately successful in protecting Cuba's security and independence. Mr. Kennedy then said, "If you take out the missiles, we give you our word that we will not intervene in Cuba, and furthermore, we are going to keep our allies from doing so." We believed his word, and we withdrew the missiles.

You also deployed Jupiter missiles in Italy and Turkey secretly.* Then you deployed [cruise] missiles in Sicily. Did you announce this to the world? No. You also deployed missiles in West Germany.† Why were they being deployed so close to the Soviet Union? The flight time of these missiles would be five to six minutes from those points to the Soviet Union. This is much shorter than the time it would take from the United States. We military men are always counting minutes and seconds in this way. [Wayne Smith signals for the floor.] I understood the question and I am attempting to answer it. Why did we do it secretly? We also considered the possibility of discovery.

RISQUET: Let's let the General finish, and then we'll recognize some other comrade. Did he finish? General, did you finish?

GRIBKOV: You asked if we considered whether or not the American side would discover the plan. We, of course, considered the possibility of U.S. intelligence discovering what we were doing. And the fact was

---

*Gribkov is incorrect on this. The United States deployed Jupiter missiles in Turkey and Italy openly, under the rubric of NATO.
†Gribkov appears to be referring to the deployment of Pershing II missiles in the early 1980s.

that on the 14th, when the sites were photographed because we had not been able to hide them, you saw all these things on the photographs. The launch pads were made of concrete, and we had to install these white concrete slabs which could be very easily detected from the air. It was very difficult to camouflage them. Some of our comrades came to their own conclusions when they visited Cuba, important administrators. They said that you could place the missiles in such a way that they would be indistinguishable from palm trees.[14] But this was a rather stupid conclusion, because one has to prepare the entire site. One has to prepare all of the command facilities. You've got to lay cables, communications. You've got to create all the foundations for the launching platforms. It's very complicated in general and, of course, intelligence did discover what was going on because of this. But the fact is that intelligence discovered it rather late.

RISQUET: Thank you very much, General. Alekseev.

ALEKSANDR ALEKSEEV: I had a rather direct involvement in the situation, not on the military side, but I had a great deal to do with the negotiations. Around May 1st or 2nd I was called to Moscow—I was working here in the embassy—and I spoke to Khrushchev. He said, "You have been working in Cuba for some time now, for about two years; you have good relations with the Cuban leaders, and we have decided to name you ambassador, to appoint you to the embassy." I was also told that I was going to be called again when members of the Political Bureau were there. Some days later I was called to the Kremlin, and in Khrushchev's office I found [Frol R.] Kozlov, Gromyko, Malinovsky, [Sharaf] Rashidov (who was an alternate Presidium member), and Marshal Biryuzov. Comrade Mikoyan was also there. I don't recall if Ivanov was there; he might have been.

Then the conversation began all over again. I spoke to them about Fidel, about Che Guevara, about Cuba—and Khrushchev was very emotional when he talked about Cuba. We all listened to him, and then out of nowhere he asked me, "You are the ambassador, and you should know we"—meaning either the government or someone—"have decided to send missiles to Cuba because there is no other way to protect Cuba's revolution despite our interventions in the U.N. We have not been able to stop the United States." He said that he did have some information that seemed to indicate that.

I, too, was shocked, and I didn't exactly know how to react. Except for Mikoyan, I only knew the others there from photographs. I didn't know how to react. I was in a rather difficult position. But they asked me, "How will Fidel Castro react to this decision?" And I answered their question. I told Khrushchev, "I don't think Fidel Castro is going to agree." Why? Because the first line of defense of the Cuban Revolution was above all the solidarity of Latin America and the progressive countries, and if we installed missiles, I thought this would provoke a rejection of the Cuban Revolution from the rest of the hemisphere.

Malinovsky reacted negatively. "How can the Cuban Revolution give up this opportunity?" he asked. "Spain was a bourgeois country, and yet it received our weapons."

There was discussion of sending a delegation to hold talks with the Cuban government. It was decided to send Rashidov (who had been to Cuba before), Marshal Biryuzov (the commander of the Strategic Rocket Forces), and myself.

Before leaving for Cuba, Khrushchev called us again to the country house—most of the members of the Political Bureau were present—and Khrushchev said that in Alekseev's opinion Fidel Castro would not agree. In view of that, he said our delegation would have to argue that there was no other alternative for the effective defense of Cuba, and see how Fidel Castro reacted to that.

So we came here to Cuba. I had an interview with Raúl Castro. I told him a delegation would arrive, and he said, "What for?" I said that in our delegation we had a certain Engineer Petrov, who was actually Marshal Biryuzov, and that Biryuzov wanted to speak to Fidel Castro. Some hours later the meeting was held, and a conversation ensued. As I recall, when we explained the situation to Fidel, he did not give us an immediate answer. He thought about it and later he asked, "Is this in the interest of the socialist camp?" And we said, "No, this is in the interest of the Cuban Revolution." This is what Khrushchev had said. But, subsequently, the Cuban government got together, they discussed the matter, and they understood that there was a serious intention by the Soviet government to defend the Cuban Revolution. Thus, the Cuban leadership agreed to the negotiations.

After that, we met with Raúl Castro, and we drew up the draft agreement in almost complete isolation. Malinovsky, Ivanov, and the General here present [Gribkov]—as well as Khrushchev, of course—knew about this. No one else did. I, with my very poor Spanish, had to translate the agreement. By that time I was ambassador. I brought the draft to Fidel Castro, and he studied it. There were a great many technical provisions; the political aspects were rather thin, and Fidel Castro introduced the necessary corrections, and some time later, in August, Che Guevara was sent to Moscow where he met with Khrushchev. At that moment, the agreement was initialed by Malinovsky and by Raúl Castro.*

Khrushchev was firmly convinced that the operation could be carried out secretly and that the Americans would not find out. The only thing he advised was, "Do not rush. Do everything in such a way that U.S. public opinion will not be aware of this until November 4th or after November 4th. After that there won't be any great difficulties. The Americans are going to have to swallow this the same way we have had to swallow the pill of the missiles in Turkey. We are two sovereign states, and when everything is ready in November, I will travel to Cuba and we will tell the world about this operation." Khrushchev was convinced that the operation would not be discovered until it was complete. So he insisted. He said, "We can do the same thing the Americans do. We can use the same methods."

In July, the transportation of equipment and troops began, and from then until October 14th we were able to transport a great deal, and the United States may have received a lot of information because they had a great many volunteer agents here. Why were there so many troops, they wondered? Why so many weapons coming into Cuba? Why were Soviet troops here? They were dressed as civilians, but you could tell that they were Soviets. Anyone could deduce that something was going on. It was mentioned that the missiles themselves were not photographed, but the sites were. All of this was perfectly visible from the air, and this is the way things unfolded. Everything else is rather well known.

It is rather difficult to understand the way in which the missiles were withdrawn. Things went wrong. As ambassador, I did not know what to say. There were reports that the missiles were going to be withdrawn, and that this was an extraordinary circumstance. I don't think it is true that there was no time to consult Fidel Castro. Khrushchev knew him. He knew what he was like. He knew that he was a true leader, and, very simply, when Khrushchev realized that the Americans were not going to swallow the pill, he decided to proceed as he did, hoping to explain everything later. It was, of course, understood that the Cuban cause was a just one. I think his actions can be explained by the fact that, at the last moment, Nikita simply did not consider the need for consultation. This was a mistake, and I think the big mistake was things didn't happen, so to speak, above the board. Our

---

*Contrary to Alekseev's implication, the agreement was initialed not in August, but in July, during Raúl Castro's visit to Moscow (2–17 July 1962).

Cuban colleagues had proposed arriving at an agreement. But for Khrushchev, the deal with Kennedy was a way to defend Cuba and the interests of the socialist camp.

These all occurred in a Cold War context. We did not think the way we do today, and we simply arrived at a mistaken conclusion. I must say that there was one individual who was very meticulous and careful. Gromyko said that he was afraid that the operation would turn into an adventure because it could be discovered at any time. Gromyko told me this a bit imprecisely, but, in any case, he did say it. So we cannot say that there was total unanimity on this at the time.

I would like to add that Khrushchev's conviction that the operation would not be discovered was very firm. He actually believed that.

RISQUET: Have you finished, sir? Thank you very much, Alekseev. Mikoyan has the floor.

SERGO MIKOYAN: I'd like to say that I was very impressed by the statement made by General Gribkov. Not only was I impressed, but it actually shed new light on the crisis for me. We've been discussing this crisis over a number of meetings, and it is clear that not everything has been said. Now, however, we are seeing the statement made by Dean Rusk in another light—that an opportunity was lost by the U.S. to destroy the revolution in Cuba.[15] It was widely thought that the Cuban Revolution could have been destroyed if it had been attacked on Monday, and the rest of the world would not have been greatly affected. However, judging from the statements made by General Gribkov, we see that there might have been a nuclear war, and that losses on the U.S. side would have been greater than casualties in the Second World War. We also understand that Soviet and Cuban casualties would have been even greater. In any case, all of these facts underscore the immense danger that existed at the time.

It is wrong to think that the decision arrived at by Khrushchev and Kennedy was arrived at too quickly and showed weakness. I believe it freed us from the first nuclear war in the world, and this would have been a war of completely unpredictable consequences.

RISQUET: Thank you, Comrade Mikoyan. General Gribkov has the floor.

GRIBKOV: I'd like to elaborate at this point what Comrade Alekseev has said. When the question of deploying the missiles was discussed on the second occasion, it was necessary for the members of the Political Bureau to sign to indicate their concurrence. (The Political Bureau was then referred to as the Presidium.) Semyon Pavlovich Ivanov, a colonel general, was secretary of the National Defense Council. He had to get the signatures of all the members of the leadership. But not all signed. Not all of the secretaries of the Central Committee signed, and Mikoyan, as member of the Political Bureau, did not sign either. In our country we had the following norm: if you agreed with a certain document, you would write down that you were in favor. Not all were in favor, but a great many did sign.

Ivanov reported to Khrushchev that a number of comrades did not want to sign—some secretaries of the Central Committee—because they maintained that they were not members of the Political Bureau. Khrushchev then said, "Go see them and see if they'll sign." When Ivanov approached them with Khrushchev's mandate, then everyone signed. So there was no real unanimity on the Soviet side either, despite the fact that there is a signed document. That's what I wanted to add.

RISQUET: Thank you very much. Are there any questions? Jorge Domínguez.

JORGE DOMÍNGUEZ: On the question of the clandestine deployment of weapons to Cuba, at the Antigua meeting it was reported that there was a difference of opinion between Cuba and the Soviet Union: that Cuba preferred to make the deployment public, among other reasons because it considered it a sovereign right to invite its Soviet allies to send those weapons to Cuba. The question is, what did Moscow think about that opinion of the Cuban national leadership, and why was it decided not to accept the proposal presented by Comandante Ernesto Guevara?

RISQUET: You have asked a question, but you can get an answer from either the Cuban side or from the Soviet side. I would, of course, at some time like to have an answer from the Cuban side; but for now, I will direct the question to the Soviet side. Of course, the Cuban side reserves the right to speak to this point.

ALEKSEEV: With respect to the withdrawal of the missiles, our Cuban comrades may have well imagined the magnitude of the operation, involving 40,000 men. That is why that issue was not considered.

Now, on the question of whether it was too early or too late when Che Guevara got to Moscow, Raúl also had the impression that the deployment could not be carried out secretly, and that it was preferable to do it openly. In September, the Cubans suggested that the operation had to be brought out into the open, and the signing of the agreement made public. This was the proposal made by Che Guevara and [Emilio] Aragonés. Khrushchev said that nothing was going to happen. If they began to get nervous, Khrushchev said, we could send the Baltic fleet.[16] After that, nothing else was said. That is all that was known. Does that answer the question?

DOMÍNGUEZ: I confess that it did not answer my question. My impression is that the Cuban national leadership made a proposal which apparently was not accepted. Cuba did not have a casual opinion on this, but one that had to do with its sovereignty, and it had to do with the nature of its relations with the Soviet Union. The information I've gotten back seems to me incomplete. Something must have been discussed in detail previous to arriving at the conclusion that the transfer of the men and matériel had to be secret. That's why I have this lingering doubt.

CASTRO: I think this question brought up by Wayne [Smith] on the period between the actual agreement and the final deployment of the weapons is very interesting. This was a dangerous period. I, of course, do not have the experience of this outstanding Soviet general; but, in any case, I have some familiarity with military activities, not only because of personal experience, but from all that I have read throughout my life. And I did have my opinions on all of these questions.

All military operations have a critical period. When we stormed the Moncada on the 26th of July [1953], this was after a long period of covert and clandestine operations. Well, not clandestine; they were legal. Really, we organized the attack on Moncada in a perfectly legal way. But it was a long period of planning an operation which was, I think, a lot more difficult than bringing in these weapons brought in by the Soviets in 1962. Things often depend on a thread, a detail, an accident, anything. With Girón, when the Bay of Pigs operation was organized against us, there was also a lot of movement, recruitment, training, transfers of personnel to Guatemala, Nicaragua, people going to Puerto Cabezas, to Nicaragua—a great many operations. It was practically public knowledge that something was going on. Of course, we had no details. But we could see what was going on, and the fact is that the operation did not surprise us. So we do have some experience in this type of matter. All operations historically do have a critical period.

Now, then. We were very confident in the experience of the Soviet Union. We had practically just won against the Batista army—it was just two years after the end of our war. The Soviets, on the other hand, had decades of experience in diplomatic, international, and military matters. The Soviets were our very powerful ally. You simply could not compare our power with theirs. I'm referring specifically to this point brought up by you [indicating Wayne Smith], and then recapped by Domínguez. We had unlimited confidence in them. When we had an opinion on something, we expressed it; but always on the basis of the idea that they had more experience than we did, and that they knew how to do things better.

Secondly, we also based our position on the fact that only they knew what the correlation of forces was between them and the United States. You've got to go back to these times, the months before those days. The conquest of space—don't you remember [Yuri] Gagarin's flight? Don't you remember the great Soviet might, when they first put a man in space with colossal rockets? Don't you remember when Nikita said that the Soviet Union had missiles that could hit a fly in the air? I'll never forget that statement. But what we did not know was how many missiles the Soviets had, how many the Americans had, how many planes, how many bombs on each side and so on, because in Nikita's public rhetoric you could see—you could detect—confidence, certainty, and strength. You've got to go back to those times to be able to understand this.

So, then. In any case, Raúl traveled to Moscow in July. Alejandro [Alekseev] mentioned the date; Alejandro talked about a great many things. He talked about the conversations over there, when Raúl went to the Soviet Union. I've got the materials here. I've got some papers. I'm not going to read them; I don't want to frighten you. Among the many things I have here with me, however, is a report presented in 1968, six years later—not thirty years later, but six years after the event; thoughts and experiences were a lot fresher at the time—a report to the recently created Central Committee of the Party. At the time of the October crisis, the new Central Committee did not exist. This report touched a great many topics, but I did dwell on the question of the October crisis, and there was an interruption where Raúl recalled correctly and explained that when he traveled to the USSR I had told him that I wanted him to ask Khrushchev a single question: what would happen if the operation were discovered while it was in progress? This was the single question I wanted him to ask. There was no friction, and Khrushchev gave exactly the answer that Alekseev quoted: "There is nothing to worry about. Don't worry about this. If there is any difficulty, we'll send out the Baltic fleet as a show of support." But we did not think that it was the Baltic fleet that would solve the problem. What we were thinking about was Soviet will and determination, about Soviet strength. And we got the statement of the top leader of the Soviet Union that there was nothing to worry about, that he would not allow it. So what was really protecting us was the global strategic might of the USSR, not the rockets here. You know perfectly well that if a country says it's not going to tolerate something, it can follow up. I don't want to go into this too far, but there are a great many contemporary examples. Before Cuba there were problems in Berlin—very serious problems in Berlin—and on more than one occasion, one country or another expressed a certain determination. So here we were talking about the prestige, the honor of a country, and if a given country was determined to protect us during that interim period, they could do it.

But I repeat: I wanted one question asked: that one—the one you asked—and the answer was the same one that they gave Guevara and Aragonés.

Guevara and Aragonés took with them the final draft, the final wording of the agreement. There was a previous draft that had been initialed, and it's the one the Soviet general mentioned—forgive me, I find it easier to say "General" than to say "Gribkov." So they took this document with them. This was written by me, by hand, and, as Alejandro said, when I received the initial document, I found that there were gaps and loopholes in the treatment of the political context. In my opinion, the question was essentially political: the decision was political, the will had to be political, and everything depended upon the political context. I said, "This agreement has to be clear, precise, and concrete, because no one should forget for one second that we are not outlaws, we are not violating any moral principle. We are acting within the principles of international law—within moral principles—and we have an absolute right to do what we are doing." We had no reason to fear asserting those rights. I sent this. Notice that it was written by me, because when it comes to doing things secretly, we have some experience.

There is a long history here. There is a long history because you've got to see everything that happens in those three or four months, from the moment the weapons began to arrive to what happened later, as a single piece. There are a great many anecdotes, but we are not discussing anecdotes here. We are discussing essentials. It was not easy to keep the secret, because such a large movement of troops and matériel was difficult to camouflage. But I observed the unfolding of events, and trusted in the Soviets.

So Che Guevara and Aragonés traveled to the USSR [27 August–2 September 1962], and since I was observing things, I said, "If our conduct is legal, if it is moral, if it is correct, why should we do something that may give rise to a scandal? Why should it seem that we are doing something secretly, covertly, as if we were doing something wrong, something to which we have no right?" I said, "Why not publish the military agreement? Of course, this agreement doesn't mention any specific weapons or missiles. It refers to units, armed forces, all of those things." Of course, we could have published this treaty. It could have been made public—completely public. As I say, I was watching the unfolding of events. I argued that we were giving the adversary the initiative. Well, actually, that's not the word we used. What we actually said is, "We're giving *imperialism* the initiative, we're giving *the enemy* the initiative," and all of those things. But now since we're speaking in a more elegant forum, I will say "the adversary"—I've translated it into more elegant language. [Laughter.] What I told Khrushchev was that we were giving the United States the initiative by continuing along that line. I then suggested that we should publish the agreement, and I also said, "In any case, the final decision in this matter is yours." And I repeat why we said this: because they were better aware of the global situation, they were better aware of the correlation of forces between the Soviet Union and the United States. We didn't know anything else. The Soviet leadership—specifically Nikita—was perfectly aware of the situation, and had more information than I did. It was his final decision. And he, in fact, decided to continue the way he started off: that is, not to publish the agreement, to make no reference to it. He might have been influenced by the November 4th [U.S. congressional] elections. I think this was an idea that he always had in his head—to avoid a scandal about all of this—but that was the decision, and he answered again that if there was a crisis if the operation was discovered, what they were going to discover was something legal. It's as if a man and his girlfriend go to the movies; they may not tell anyone, but it's not illegal. Or maybe a couple goes to the beach and rents a room in a hotel; they are not betraying anyone, they are not committing any crime. What we were doing was something legal.

So I said, "Let Nikita make the final decision." We said nothing more about this, because we simply did not have enough information to press the argument. Besides, we trusted them a great deal, because the Soviets had much more experience than we did in all of these areas.

So this is why the operation continued as it did. On the question of secrecy, there is a lot to be said, because the missiles might not have been discovered. I'm certain that they might not have been discovered. Those aircraft might have been shot down. The missiles would not have been discovered if all the U-2s that were flying overhead had been shot down. But now we are into a different issue, because one of the questions we might ask here is, why were the surface-to-air missiles here? What were they doing here? Why deploy surface-to-air missiles and then allow the U-2s to fly by? I think that in this case there was a clear political mistake. I don't blame the military for that. I agree with what the General said regarding the efficiency, capability, and spirit of the Soviet military. But they, of course, have very strict orders, and among other things, they most certainly had the order not to shoot, not to fire on the U-2s. This, too, was a political question, but it is inconceivable to me that they deployed surface-to-air missiles and then let the planes fly. Those U-2s should not have been allowed to fly over Cuba. Otherwise, why were the antiaircraft missiles there? They weren't there just in case of war. So, in my judgment, there were political mistakes, there was excessive caution.[17] On the one hand, Khrushchev had great audacity. This is undeniable, and I do not deny it. I'm far from feeling any animosity for Khrushchev; I rather feel gratitude for his solidarity with our country, the cooperation we received, the many things he did for us. Far be it from me to have any adverse attitude toward Khrushchev. Quite the contrary. I really like him, in spite of all the things that may have happened. But that's not what I'm here to analyze. We've got to analyze other things.

I will give my opinion, my point of view, on how we saw the proposal to send the missiles. We have our position on that. Without a doubt, the decision to send these forces was audacious. But alongside that audacity there was hesitation. I ask, "What would have happened if there had been no U-2s? What would have happened if the U-2s were shot down and there were no pictures?" If *we* had had the surface-to-air missiles, you can rest assured that the U-2s would not have gotten through. That is certain. The other stance is simply not understandable.

Forgive me for taking so much time, but this information could help clarify this point, which might be important for the historians. I think all of us together have helped clarify these things, and I am confirming many other things that Alejandro said about the Baltic fleet. The important thing for us was not the Baltic fleet; we know how many ships they had. The important thing for us was the global strategic might of the Soviet Union. We saw that it was Soviet will, Soviet determination, Soviet global might, that protected us. This was the only thing that could stop a strike or an invasion against Cuba in the middle of the operation that was being mounted.

Undoubtedly, the order of the deployment was logical: first, the support personnel, and so on. But the operation might have been discovered—perhaps with infiltrators, people coming in and taking the pictures on land—but they were discovered by the U-2s. I am not going to discuss this matter further. There are many other points of interest. What I am trying to do, since you invited me to this meeting, is to contribute to having all of the facts here. I feel no animosity toward anyone, I don't even have complaints against anyone. But if we're meeting, it must be so that truth may come out.

RISQUET: I think that this has been clarified totally.

THE NOVEMBER CRISIS:
"Mikoyan . . . was an extraordinary man"

To Americans who recall living through the crisis, and to most American students of it, the crisis as such came to an abrupt end on 28 October 1962 with an exchange of radio messages between Kennedy and Khrushchev. The Soviets would withdraw their missiles; the United States would pledge not to invade Cuba (and would, as part of a secret arrangement with the Soviets, withdraw NATO missiles from Turkey within six months). Yet though the sense of extreme nuclear danger did subside, the crisis was far from over on 28 October. American forces, poised to invade Cuba, remained on nuclear alert worldwide. The naval blockade remained in place. Militarily, nothing changed on 28 October.

The diplomatic scene, however, shifted from Washington and Moscow to New York and Havana. In New York, an American team led by U.N. Ambassador Adlai Stevenson and Special Negotiator John J. McCloy, together with a Soviet group led by U.N. Ambassador Valerian Zorin and Deputy Foreign Minister Vasily Kuznetsov, worked on the details of the Kennedy-Khrushchev agreement: what, exactly, was an "offensive" weapon? Did this include Il-28 bombers and *Komar* torpedo boats, in addition to the ballistic missiles? How was Soviet withdrawal to be verified, since the Cubans had refused to submit to on-site inspection? Ultimately, the Soviets agreed to withdraw the Il-28 bombers as well as the nuclear missiles. Khrushchev sent First Deputy Premier Anastas Mikoyan to Cuba with a team that included his son, Sergo, to smooth over relations with Fidel Castro while the terms of the U.S.-Soviet agreement were being worked out in New York without direct Cuban participation (the United States refused to allow Cuba to participate when the Soviets proposed it).

Philip Brenner opens a discussion of the "November crisis" by asking both the Soviets and Cubans about their perceptions of the process by which the United States forced withdrawal of the Il-28 bombers as well as the strategic missiles. The Russians—Gribkov, former ambassador to Cuba Aleksandr Alekseev, and Sergo Mikoyan— still evince bitterness thirty years later at what they took at the time to be their gratuitous humiliation at the hands of the United States. To them, it was perfectly clear that the Il-28s were not "offensive" weapons. Raymond Garthoff, who advised the U.S. participants in the New York negotiations, explains the American view at the time.

The response by Fidel Castro illustrates recurring features of his interventions. First, his most bitter remarks are directed at the Russians, for caving in under U.S. pressure. Second, into his comments about the Il-28s, he inserts an energetic rebuttal of an accusation made in the opening public sessions by McNamara (and obviously unrelated to the issue of the Il-28s). He fills in the context of a remark he made in 1958, quoted by biographer Tad Szulc, in which he vowed to take his guerrilla war to the United States itself.[18] This is characteristic of Castro's conversation: words, ideas, and answers to questions are interspersed with material pertinent to previous questions, and the whole effect is akin to a cascading waterfall of verbiage, splashing upon the listener. Often, therefore, his "answers" turn out to be much more nuanced and interesting than the "questions" which stimulated them. Third, Castro's remarks are often refreshingly personal, sometimes funny or ironic and anecdotal, relatively free of the kind of ideological disputations for which he is well known. Thus, in a single intervention, he can express tremendous disappointment with the Soviets' cave-in to the Americans and deeply felt affection for Mikoyan, an "extraordinary man."

The pathos of Mikoyan's mission to Havana is marvelously rendered in an anecdote told by a former close associate of Castro, Carlos Franqui, who edited the daily *Revolución* in the early days of the revolution (but who later broke with Castro and now lives in Italy):

Mikoyan and Fidel finally settled their differences and together made a visit down to the Zapata swamps, the scene of the Bay of Pigs war. Fidel had always loved the swamp for some reason or other and kept his picturesque crocodiles well fed. A photo in the family album shows Fidel, Mikoyan and the crocodiles. It has no caption, but a version of it was circulated by Fidel himself. It's called "The Crocodile and the Sardine" and the story goes like this: Mikoyan examines the crocodiles for a while and then notices some little fish swimming in the same water. "Comandante, why are these little fish here?" "Mr. Vice-Prime Minister, those little fish are there so that the crocodiles can eat them." And that is exactly what the missile crisis was: two great powers fooling around at the expense of a small one. The Cuban people realized they were alone in the world.[19]

It was the task of Mikoyan to rescue the fragile peace by convincing Fidel Castro's Cuba to submit to being partially "devoured" by the United States and the Soviet Union. In this he was successful; that he retained Castro's affection demonstrates that he truly was a remarkable man.

RISQUET: . . . Are there any other questions? One over here, one back there.

PHILIP BRENNER: Thank you. That was an extraordinary answer.

As President Castro said in his opening address, the letters that were released this week between President Kennedy and Chairman Khrushchev will be very important to this conference, and in addition he also said that we now know from previous conferences how important it was that Cuba was in this crisis. We cannot understand the crisis without understanding Cuba. This leads to some questions for our Soviet colleagues about the period between October 28th and November 20th, when in fact Cuba was very prominent in that crisis because of the Il-28 light bombers. The Il-28 light bombers were very important to the United States, and President Castro spoke very strongly about not returning the Il-28 bombers to the Soviet Union as the United States had demanded. There are several questions about that that I would like to ask you.

First, can you tell us when the decision was made to send Il-28 bombers to Cuba? Chairman Khrushchev said in one letter to President Kennedy that the decision was made only after President Kennedy had ordered the call-up of U.S. military reserves.[20] Is that the case? Was the decision made after President Kennedy's decision, or was this part of the July agreement? Why were Il-28s chosen? They were twelve-year-old bombers, seemingly obsolete. Why did you not give Cuba better equipment? Why did you give Cuba equipment that might have been able to carry nuclear bombs, and thus might have frightened the United States? In fact, *did* you give the Il-28s to Cuba? Was there a formal agreement to turn over the Il-28s to Cuban possession, such that when the decision was made to return them to the Soviet Union, this violated an agreement with Cuba? And last, what was your intention for the Il-28s? Did you ever intend to put nuclear bombs on the Il-28s?

RISQUET: Who would like to answer?

GRIBKOV: I'll answer. Bringing the Il-28s to Cuba—as I said in my first presentation—was foreseen from the very beginning. The operational plan called for a regiment of Il-28s consisting of thirty-three planes. An additional squadron of nine planes would be subordinated to the Navy. The regiment never arrived, but the nine planes did. Out of these nine planes, six were assembled, but they did not fly—that is, we could not test them in the air.

There were no nuclear weapons for them. These were tactical planes with an operational radius of 520 kilometers. Although the U.S. considered them offensive, that opinion was incorrect. The Americans knew the technical description of the plane, in the same way that we knew the kinds of planes that the United States had and what they could do, because we watched one another. The American claim that these were strategic planes intended to launch a nuclear strike against the United States was incorrect. Are you satisfied?

RISQUET: I would like to remind Philip Brenner that, during the Antigua conference, our friend McNamara explained that U.S. demands for the withdrawal of the Il-28s was a political issue. The president was addressing a political and not a military issue. These planes were obsolete. The MiG-21s in Cuba were more dangerous for the United States than the Il-28s, which did not have nuclear warheads. They could only be used to bomb CIA spy ships. I remembered that this was discussed in Antigua, and that it was made very clear. Comrade Kovaliev.

FELIX KOVALIEV: I would like to add the following to what Gribkov said in response to the questions about the Il-28 bombers and the reservists in the United States, who the planes belonged to, and so forth. I'm going to answer these questions. I can't answer the others.

In a letter from President Khrushchev to the Council of Ministers, it was said that the Il-28s should be withdrawn from the Soviet armed forces. This was before President Kennedy's decision to call up the 150,000 U.S. military reservists. Had this decision not been taken, these planes would have been withdrawn and destroyed, and they would not have been supplied to Cuba. That is the answer to the first question. As to the question of whom the planes belonged to, I think that is quite a clear question. They, like the rest of the Soviet troops and war matériel, were under Soviet command, and only the Soviet command could operate them. The problem of transferring these planes to the Cubans—well, this was never considered. Thank you.

RISQUET: Are you satisfied by the answer, Professor Brenner?

BRENNER: Yes, the second answer was especially clear. Then I have a question for our Cuban colleagues. Why did you think the Il-28s were yours if the Soviets thought that they had never transferred them to you?

CASTRO: We never said that the Il-28s were ours. We never said that. They came with the rest of the military equipment for the Soviet units, and we were against the withdrawal of the Il-28s. Not much is known about this. But with Mikoyan, whom I remember fondly, we discussed this question of the Il-28s—bitterly, I would say. The [withdrawal of the] Il-28s was an ulterior demand made by the Americans. I beg the Soviets' indulgence. I've always believed—or at least I believed then—that we knew the Americans better than the Soviets: their psychology, their actions, what they do, their history.[21] We were closer to them here. We have learned to guess what they are doing, to interpret them. Often we know what they are doing not through intelligence, but through intuition. We guess what they are thinking, what they are planning, what they're scheming. And we don't have those ferocious anti-American feelings that McNamara referred to. I hope that someone will be able to answer that famous phrase about the war, because that is an incomplete sentence—as incomplete as that alleged biography, because you can't write a biography without talking to the subject, and when the author came to Cuba it had been agreed that we were going to have long interviews so that I could give my viewpoints. And he never heard my viewpoints. This is not an honest, a 100 percent honest biography. And he is not a 100 percent honest writer. If any of the writers here decided to do that and agreed on this, and then wrote a book, a book that was never completed because of various reasons that I won't mention here—well, he never completed his task. He left earlier than planned. He wrote the biography without speaking to me. That statement is part of a letter. Let me tell you about it. Let me make this clear so that nobody else will have to speak on this. This was part of a letter that says—and I remember it by heart; Mendoza, who is an historian, knows this because he has learned it by heart— "When I saw the bombs that the planes are dropping on Sariol's house"—and then I repeat, I quote: "When I saw the missiles that they dropped on Mario's house, I swore that the Americans were going to pay dearly for what they were doing."[22] That is to say, you can't quote that sentence in isolation—that we are going to have a war with the Americans, as if my vocation were war, or what I aspired to was war, or all I wanted was war. That is very far from reality. But the Americans from the base at Guantánamo had supplied these bombs, and they were bombing a family home—they were bombing civilians with American bombs!—it was then that I wrote this message. I was on a mountain, watching the bombing of Mario Sariol's house. That's when I wrote this note. And I expressed this feeling of irritation. So— it is not legitimate to take a phrase out of its context and quote it in isolation and pass it off as said by someone who is crazy, who loves war, and who hates the United States, who wants to exterminate the United States. It is a sentence written by a person who was watching the bombs fall, bombs that had been supplied from the base at Guantánamo.[23]

I said that I hoped that some other comrades, historians, who are more knowledgeable than I am—perhaps I have a better knowledge of strategic ideas—well, maybe they will be able to answer. But, you see, there was a story behind all this.

Now, the story as regards my position on the Il-28s. We said we were against withdrawing them. Mikoyan said originally that the Il-28s were not included. It was very hard for Mikoyan, and Khrushchev said quite rightly that no one could have done the job better than Mikoyan. He was an extraordinary man. He was a wonderful man. Mikoyan said that the Il-28s would not be withdrawn. When we asked him what we'd do if the Americans then demanded the withdrawal of the Il-28s, Mikoyan said, "To hell with the Americans! To hell with the Americans!" A few days later, they demanded the withdrawal of the Il-28s. The Soviets acceded to the demand for the withdrawal of the Il-28s, and Mikoyan was forced to explain to us that the Il-28s were to be withdrawn.[24] You can imagine how we felt, particularly after the promise that they would remain. After that I sent a letter to U Thant, because the Il-28s were being taken away. They had taken away the rockets, so what difference did it make if they took the Il-28s? It wasn't worth straining relations, making relations more tense between the USSR and us over the Il-28s. So we cooperated. We told U Thant that we would not hamper the withdrawal of the Il-28s. We sent him a letter to that effect. We didn't *agree* with the demand—it was not just, it was not reasonable—but we would contribute by facilitating the withdrawal of the Il-28s. This is in a letter written to U Thant. I wrote it. It was dated November 19th. It was not yet a month after the crisis, but it was a long time after the missile issue had been resolved that the demand of the withdrawal of the Il-28s came up. So I wrote a letter to U Thant saying that we would not hamper it, although we didn't agree, and weren't very happy about the withdrawal of the Il-28s. We simply said we were not going to hamper the withdrawal, even though we were totally against the withdrawal of the Il-28s. Next time *you* speak, Mendoza, please; work, all of you! Don't leave all the work to me. I'll have to retire. I'll have to withdraw just like the Il-28s. [Laughter.]

RISQUET: Alekseev.

ALEKSEEV: The problem of the Il-28s was really an artificial one. When it was agreed that the rockets would be withdrawn and when Mikoyan arrived, it became necessary to normalize relations—not with the United States, but with Cuba. We had offended Cuba so much that Mikoyan had to improve relations with the Cuban leadership. When there was talk of inspection, we thought that the Americans had been so frightened by the crisis that they were not going to insist on too much. That is, we would allow them to inspect our ships and that would be enough. But Fidel was against all inspections. He said, "You don't know the Americans. After the inspection they are going to formulate all sorts of demands. And," he predicted, "they are going to demand that you withdraw the Il-28s." But then we said, "Oh no, they are going to be satisfied with the withdrawal of the missiles." He also said they were going to demand the withdrawal of the torpedo boats, called Mosquitos; and Fidel said, "Ultimately, they are going to demand that we include in the government the exiles in Miami. If we are going to make concessions they will go as far as that." And I must admit that Mikoyan and I said, "Fidel, oh no, how can you think that? There's going to be no problem." But, in a matter of two weeks they demanded the withdrawal of the Il-28s. We were going to leave them to the Cubans, but we had not yet discussed this, so in this situation Mikoyan summoned up all his eloquence to convince Fidel. He said, "They are obsolete planes. The best thing we can do is just take them away," and, well, Fidel had to agree.

A few days elapsed, and there was still talk of the torpedo boats and the missiles. Mikoyan stayed here in Cuba negotiating over three weeks. It was necessary to convince the Cubans to agree, and the Cubans *had* to agree, because there was no other way out. And ultimately we left a brigade. We started a sort of game of secrecy. Gromyko later [in 1979] thought to change the description of the brigade, and to call it a training unit or a training center. That's how the brigade came to stay here. Fidel Castro showed us an article on the subject, and he said, "This is no training unit or training center. This is a motorized rifle brigade!" But—well, the brigade remained behind.

Anyway, Mikoyan and Fidel's negotiations ended happily, since the Americans did not insist on demanding that Miami exiles be included in the government. This has nothing to do with military problems. [Laughter.]

RISQUET: Order, please, order. It is 1950 hours. I see some signs of tiredness in the not-so-young. We can continue and finish with this today, or we can postpone it for tomorrow. Are there many more questions? I don't want to cut the debate short, but I know that many people are tired, and there's still dinner. Somebody over there; Mikoyan? Would you like to speak?

MIKOYAN: I wanted to add that the issue of the Il-28s and the torpedo boats started on November 1st, and probably in the State Department, because Stevenson in negotiations with Mikoyan in New York did not mention this. But when Mikoyan went to the airport to catch the plane for Cuba, he said that he supported Fidel Castro's five points, and at that time Vasily Vasilich Kuznetsov brought a letter from Stevenson—this was aside from the negotiations—and in that letter, there were additional demands. This was very strange, and not very serious, and it was evident that Fidel Castro was right: the U.S. administration, after winning concessions, was beginning to demand more concessions.

Later these demands were conveyed to Moscow, through diplomatic channels.

I believe that this was a great mistake. Instead of this, I think that it would have been desirable to insist on the return of Guantánamo Bay. We should not have allowed the Americans to pressure us. We should have pressured the United States, and insisted on the withdrawal of the troops stationed at Guantánamo as a condition for the withdrawal of the missiles.

RISQUET: Thank you, Mikoyan.

GARTHOFF: Mr. Chairman, there are a couple of things I would like to briefly say about the Il-28s; but I would agree to put it off until tomorrow if you prefer.

RISQUET: I think that if we still have several questions pending, the wisest thing would be to adjourn now and resume tomorrow at nine o'clock. We would continue the debate, finish it, and then move on to item three. Is there a consensus for adjournment? All right, the session is adjourned with a not yet concluded debate on this topic. Everyone should be here at nine o'clock tomorrow.

*   *   *

[The following conversation occurred late the following day but is inserted here for editorial continuity.]
GARTHOFF: . . . I'm going to speak briefly about some developments in connection with the Il-28 continuation of the Cuban crisis— in part, to briefly answer a couple of questions and comments that were made earlier, but mainly to clarify American policy in the later stages of the resolution of the Cuban missile crisis.

The question of our insistence that the Il-28 bombers also be removed from Cuba was a central point in that phase of the negotiations. First, I would just say that it was of course understood by American specialists in these matters that the Il-28 was an obsolescent airplane, as General Gribkov correctly advised us, and that it did not in that sense represent a serious strategic threat.[25] Indeed, we also were aware that most of the Il-28s had been withdrawn from service in the Soviet Air Force in the first half of 1960, and that some had been supplied by the Soviet Union to other countries. Nonetheless, the airplane was officially listed as being nuclear-capable and, incidentally, our information—which may not have been correct—attributed a somewhat greater range to the airplane than we were told yesterday: 600 nautical miles with a 6,000-pound bomb, and a little more with a smaller bomb.

Because of its limited capabilities, the United States was, in fact, ready to accept the Il-28s in Cuba, although our assumptions were, first of all, that it was being provided to the Cubans, since we did not know about the fact that a Soviet Group of Forces was being established there. Second, if the Il-28s represented *all* that was being supplied, it didn't necessarily indicate the same kind of Soviet intention which we attributed when we discovered nuclear missiles. As a result, on October 14—just one day before the missiles were observed for the first time—McGeorge Bundy, the special assistant to the president for national security affairs, stated in a public speech that "[s]o far, everything that has been delivered to Cuba falls within the categories of aid which the Soviet Union has provided, for example, to neutral states like Egypt or Indonesia, and I should not be surprised to see additional military assistance of this sort."[26] Now, he didn't mention the Il-28s, the first of which were in crates we had photographed on the decks of a Soviet ship headed for Cuba on September 28th. But his reference to Egypt and Indonesia was in a sense a signal, because those two countries had received Il-28s. (Incidentally, it was because we had observed the delivery of those aircraft to those countries that the intelligence experts immediately recognized the crates as containing Il-28 airplanes. This led to comments within the American intelligence community on a new science called "crateology.")

The second important aspect, as far as the Il-28s and the reason for the change in American position is concerned, was that it took on a different light when we saw the missiles. The president made this clear with his proclamation of the quarantine, which included specific reference not only to missiles, and their equipment, but also to bombers. And there were a couple other references in President Kennedy's exchanges with Chairman Khrushchev to the missile weapons "*and* other offensive weapons" in Cuba. The result was that when Chairman Khrushchev then agreed in his message on October 28th to "withdraw the weapons that you consider offensive," we felt it was appropriate to make clear that we considered bombers as well as missiles "offensive," and that in addition to the missiles, the Il-28s should also be removed.

Now, this argument went on, then, from the 30th or so of October to the 20th of November. Reference was made to the memorandum that Ambassador Stevenson and Mr. McCloy gave to First Deputy Prime Minister Mikoyan on the 2nd of November, which listed for the first time comprehensively what we regarded as "offensive weapons"— weapons that we expected to be removed. It included missiles and associated equipment, and warheads, bombers and associated equipment, and the short-range missile-carrying *Komar* motor torpedo boats. The reason for the inclusion of the last was that we considered all surface-to-surface missiles to be, in a sense, offensive. We were aware of the *Luna* missile, which it now turns out was nuclear-capable; but we did not include that in the list, because of its limited range and it was on land in Cuba. But the patrol boats conceivably could have been sent to fire on ports in the southern United States, or on some other country in the Caribbean.

The delivery of that message to Mr. Mikoyan as he was about to board the plane for Cuba was the result of an odd accident. The instructions from Washington to our representatives in New York had been sent out the day before, and Mr. McCloy and Ambassador Stevenson were supposed to have presented this list to Mr. Mikoyan at a dinner meeting that they had on the 1st of November, and that would have provided some opportunity for any reaction and discussion. But they forgot to give it to him. And as a result it was submitted to him by messenger the next morning under a brief letter from Ambassador Stevenson, saying that "in the discussion, which of course concerned a number of other matters as well, we neglected to give you this list of the weapons that we consider offensive and which we presume you intend to remove." Well, that discussion, of course, went on until the 6th and 7th of November, when we reaffirmed the need for withdrawal of the Il-28s, but dropped our proposal that the patrol boats also be included. And I might also say that there were different views within the United States government throughout this period on whether we should press for the withdrawal of the Il-28s. President Kennedy himself hesitated at a couple of points. There were some who felt we should interpret the language more broadly and press for removal of *all* Soviet military equipment and personnel from Cuba. There were some who felt that the missiles had been the main thing, and now that that had been agreed and was being done, we should not ask for anything more. But the view which prevailed was, of course, the one that you are aware of and I've been talking about: the Il-28s should be removed.

Well, after the 20th of November we were informed that the crated planes—most of the planes were still in crates, only a few had been assembled—would be taken out. Forty-two Il-28s were declared and were observed departing, and that ended that element of the crisis.

The last comment I want to make in this connection is simply that we did not know at that time at all that a Soviet Group of Forces had been dispatched to Cuba. We were aware of most of the elements, the visible elements. For example, we assumed that the four reinforced regiments were there for local protection of the missile sites and some other objects. We thought that the coastal defense and air defense elements were to be, or were being, transferred to the Cubans. We did not realize that there were nearly as many Soviet forces there as there were. I think it's been remarked already that we thought in October that there were 10,000 Soviet troops in Cuba. By the middle of November, our estimate was 16,000 and, even after the crisis—in 1963— our final estimate in retrospect was that there had been 22,000 Soviet military personnel in Cuba. So we underestimated by half the size of the force; but, more important, we did not realize that it was a Soviet combat force—a conventional force—in addition to the missiles. If we had, I think there would have been very strong pressure in the United States to have pressed for the removal of the whole force.[27] So what we didn't know, in this case, may have helped to prevent the crisis from becoming sharper than it was.

But in any event, I wanted to explain this because it was not a question of the United States government arbitrarily trying to squeeze as much out as we could. We did feel that there was a legitimate basis for asking for the withdrawal of the Il-28 bombers, and even raising the question of the patrol boats. And the fact that Khrushchev had agreed to removal of "the weapons *you*"—that is, we—"consider offensive" did provide a basis for advancing this position. Thank you.

MIKOYAN: I have some questions, and possibly some objections in connection with some of the statements made by our American colleagues. . . .

This to Garthoff. We have had an ongoing polemic on this question, sir. It is not at all convincing that this letter was simply forgotten by Stevenson and McCloy. I was there, but I wasn't present at the Mikoyan-Stevenson-McCloy interviews. However, every night [my father] told us what happened, and there were so many details, so many things were discussed, and McCloy spoke so often with Kennedy— about which he later told Mikoyan—they even talked about the question of inspection. In fact, McCloy suggested an inspection, not on

Cuban soil, but of the ships. Mikoyan had informed him that the USSR supported the Cuban rejection of inspections on Cuban soil. McCloy then said, "We can then check for missiles aboard the ships." What I mean to say is that these negotiations dealt with a great many details which were settled, and thus when the memorandum was brought to the airport, Mikoyan was simply shocked. He did not see it as a continuation of the negotiations—not as something in line with the negotiations—but as a kind of rider attached. He didn't understand why he had been given that letter, and what he said was, "I consider that I have not even received it. I refuse to accept it. The administration is firing grapeshot. You in the State Department were doing your work effectively and efficiently, and that is to your credit; but this is irresponsible." I would like to hear your remarks on this because I have the impression that Kennedy and McCloy did not talk about this. . . .

GARTHOFF: There were different views within the American government as to whether and how firmly we should press the question of the Il-28s, and perhaps other systems as well. And it is true that I wrote a memorandum which was sent up to New York on October 29th from the State Department saying, "It is clear that the weapons systems which must be removed are the 1,000 nautical mile and 2,200 nautical mile surface-to-surface missiles, Il-28 jet light bombers, and the warheads and support equipment for these systems." And then I went on to say, "We cannot reasonably insist that the MiG fighters"—which a lot of people wanted to include—"surface-to-air missiles, or non-missile ground force weapons be removed," and so on.[28] Of these, the missile-carrying patrol boats were most susceptible of offensive deployment.

But the instruction that was sent up to Stevenson and McCloy on the first was not a State Department position; it was an instruction from the president, and there was no question about it. There had been an instruction to Stevenson on October 31 to provide to the Soviets the list of weapons deemed offensive by the United States, including bomber aircraft, and air-to-surface missiles, guided missiles, and the patrol boats. After, on the morning of November 2nd, when he sent the list over—I can read it, because it is only three sentences long; the full letter from Ambassador Stevenson reads as follows: "One thing that Mr. McCloy and I neglected to discuss with you last night was the list of items that the United States considers in the category of offensive weapons within the meaning of the exchange between

President Kennedy and Chairman Khrushchev. Such a list is appended to this letter. We trust that the weapons you plan to remove include all those on this list." We became aware of that in Washington. There were some little remarks about people forgetting to say something that was this important, but there was no real conflict over this, and I'm quite sure that neither Stevenson nor McCloy intentionally withheld it or passed over it—among other reasons because they did not that night ask for any change in their instructions. They clearly recognized they had the instructions, and they fulfilled them belatedly.

EDWIN MARTIN: . . . Just following up on this comment about the relations between Washington and the negotiators in the United Nations, I—and I think others who were sitting in Washington reviewing their proposals and issuing instructions—got the general feeling that McCloy and Stevenson were anxious to reach a settlement which would promote the value of the United Nations and its place in history. And rather often they made proposals which were too soft, in our view, in dealing with the Soviet Union and they had to be revised and strengthened. This was a rather standard conflict, so to speak, between the groups. They both did come down and sit with us in Washington, from time to time, but there was a concessionary attitude there which I have a very definite feeling of. . . .

TOMÁS DIEZ: I'd like to return to the topic of the Il-28s. We heard that on September 28 the U.S. intelligence services learned of the presence of this aircraft in Cuba. And we didn't see the same thing that happened when they found out about the missiles. However, when we had confirmation of the withdrawal of the missiles from Cuba early in November, the question of the Il-28s suddenly became a huge problem, an enormous strategic problem. We know from U.S. publications that the Executive Committee of the National Security Council met on November 19 to consider ways to exert pressure for the withdrawal of these aircraft. There was even talk of an air strike against Cuba. There were draft letters written to allies in Europe—France, West Germany, Great Britain—and I ask myself, at a time when the danger of war had already decreased, was this not merely complicating the situation?[29]

And there is another matter. The end of the naval blockade was made conditional on the withdrawal of the Il-28s. Take, for example, the low-level overflights: if you consider the number of flights that took place between October 22nd and October 28th, when Khrushchev answered Kennedy, and if you study the number of low-level overflights that took place after that, you will see that there was an *increase* in flights after the actual period of danger had ceased. I ask, wasn't this further complicating the situation? I'd like to have some feedback from the U.S. side on this question.

THE U-2 SHOOT-DOWN:
"Why should we repent?"

Nothing better illustrates the incommensurabilities between the Great Powers' view of the missile crisis, and that of Cuba, than their reactions to the shoot-down of the American U-2 reconnaissance plane on the morning of 27 October. As the discussion makes clear, Khrushchev was very disturbed by the shoot-down, which he obviously knew he did not order and which he may have feared would be interpreted by the United States as a deliberate Soviet escalation, perhaps even as evidence that the Soviets had decided to risk all-out war over their missiles in Cuba. That Khrushchev may have been mistaken regarding who shot it down—Soviets or Cubans—is much less important than that it signified to him that events were spiraling out of control on the ground in Cuba.

In his memoirs, Robert Kennedy wrote that the shoot-down would "change the course of events and alter history."[30] Shortly after news of the shoot-down reached the White House, Robert Kennedy met with Ambassador Anatoly Dobrynin, and reported the following conversation:

> He [Dobrynin] said the Cubans resented the fact that we were violating Cuban air space. I replied that if we had not violated Cuban air space, we would still be believing what Khrushchev had said—that there would be no missiles placed in Cuba. In any case, I said, this matter was far more serious than the air space of Cuba—it involved the peoples of both our countries and, in fact, people all over the globe.[31]

On this, the Americans and Russians could not have been in more complete agreement: the crisis, at its most dangerous moment, had little or nothing to do with Cuban airspace, or anything else specifically "Cuban." The crisis had become a global confrontation.

But the inverse seemed true in Cuba: the rise in the temperature of the crisis to a boiling point had *everything* to do with U.S. overflights, both low-level reconnaissance and the very high-altitude missions of the U-2s. On previous research trips to Cuba we had begun to understand what the overflights—and the shoot-down—meant to Cubans and Russians on the ground in Cuba. In May 1989, we first visited Havana's Museum of the Revolution. Its penultimate exhibit is the burnt, mangled fuselage of the U-2 in question.[32] As we stepped back and out of line to obtain a better angle from which to take a photograph, a teacher and her class of what appeared to be junior high school students stopped in front of it. After the teacher gave a short lecture on the missile crisis and shoot-down, she turned toward the wreckage as she and the entire class threw their right fists into the air shouting: *"Patria o muerte. Venceremos!"* ("Fatherland or death. We shall overcome!"). There had been no indication whatever that this display was for our personal edification. The U-2 shoot-down, while important in October 1962, had become, for us, a footnote in history. Yet it was to these Cuban schoolchildren and their teacher part of a living legend of their vulnerability, but also of their capacity and will to defend themselves.

In August 1990, we became the first Americans to visit the reconstructed surface-to-air (SAM) site near Banes, in eastern Cuba, from which the missile was fired that brought down the U-2. There, on an unbearably hot August day, in the midst of endless, flat, green fields of sugarcane, we had been met by various dignitaries from Banes, including the mayor. Beneath the tip of a SAM launcher, overlooking a piece of wreckage said to be from the U-2, the mayor of Banes told his story of the crisis, the details of the Soviet base nearby, and so forth. But when he reached the point in the story concerning the low-level U.S. overflights, he ducked down low, as if to avoid a flying object, and without the slightest apparent awareness of doing so. What is more, all the Banes town fathers, each of whom had served "in the trenches" in October 1962, did likewise. When they ducked, their eyes widened and a look approaching outright terror swept over each of their faces. One of us mentioned this to our hosts: that they were reacting as if the events in question had occurred only yesterday. One replied: "During each overflight we had to assume we would be killed, that the bombing would begin, that we would never see our families again. We cannot forget that. Never."

Some of us, therefore, are not surprised when a somewhat technical, highly circumscribed question regarding the various claims made about the shoot-down leads Fidel Castro to make a lengthy and energetic set of comments. Castro wants to elaborate on several points he regards as central. First, his order to the *Cubans* on 26 October to fire at low-level overflights greatly influenced the *Soviets* who, inspired by their Cuban comrades, fired their SAMs at the U-2. Second, the order to shoot was based on the belief that all U.S. overflights were preliminary to a U.S. air attack against the missile sites. Third, there is an important connection between the order to shoot at overflights and his letter to Khrushchev on the night of 26/27 October urging the Soviet leader to launch a nuclear strike against the United States if American forces invaded the island. Both were predicated on the belief that an attack was imminent and that any war would immediately go nuclear (because the Soviets would launch their tactical and strategic nuclear weapons in Cuba). Cuba would go down fighting; it would have been up to the Soviets to redeem the martyrdom of Cuba. The order Castro gave to fire at the low-level reconnaissance aircraft was meant, in large part, to boost morale, to encourage the feeling that the Cubans could act constructively to protect themselves. The letter to Khrushchev, according to Castro, was meant to bolster Khrushchev's resolve, to convince him that he should under no circumstances cave in on *Cuba*'s behalf, and to make clear that Cuba would stay the course—all the way to annihilation, if necessary.

The discussion ends with a "clarification" from Castro: that he gladly accepts the majority of responsibility for the shoot-down of the U-2. "It was," he says, "totally correct. . . . What are we to regret? Why should we repent?" This is consistent with the Cuban legend of the crisis and of the role of the shoot-down of the U-2: that Cuba *can* protect itself against a U.S. invasion and that the wreckage of the U-2—in Havana, in Banes, and elsewhere—symbolizes this belief in supreme self-reliance. The Soviets may have pushed the button, but they were awakened to their plight and responsibilities by the Cubans. And since 1964, Cubans are quick to add, SAMs in Cuba have been manned by *Cubans*.[33]

RISQUET: Good morning, dear friends. We shall now resume and finish what is left of the second session, which was interrupted last night. As you all remember, we began with the statement of General Gribkov of the Soviet Union. Would anyone like to take the floor now?

BRUCE ALLYN: This is just a follow-up question to General Gribkov about the U-2 shoot-down on the 27th of October. There's one small puzzle that remains about it which you didn't cover yesterday in your presentation. There was a rumor that it was shot down by the Cubans, and this was certainly not possible because the Soviets were in control of the SAM sites. As President Castro said yesterday, he would quite happily have shot down the U-2s had Cubans had control of the SAMs. It's somewhat interesting that General Statsenko reportedly told U Thant after the crisis that it *had* been shot down by the Cubans. There was also an unfortunate mistake in the American version of Khrushchev's memoirs, which reported that it was shot down by the Cubans.

This is an interesting puzzle, and I wonder if the Soviet military representatives can help us clarify how the rumor may have been propagated. We know (at least from the Moscow meeting) that Marshal Malinovsky apparently sent a strong letter of rebuke to the Soviet commander in Cuba, complaining that the U-2 had been shot down without authorization from Moscow. This whole question of whether it could have been shot down without authorization from Moscow became even more interesting yesterday, when we learned that the authority to use the tactical nuclear weapons may have been vested in the local commander in Cuba. Perhaps the military didn't want to admit that the U-2 had been shot down by the Soviet side.

When we learned the story of how the U-2 was shot down as the result of the decision of two Soviet generals in Cuba, that did clarify the basic question.[34] But I wonder if you could help us understand how the rumor persisted that the plane had been shot down by the Cubans. The rumor was propagated by one book published in the United States, which said that Mr. Castro himself had taken command of a SAM site and pressed the button that shot down the U-2.[35] We know this is incorrect. But there's been a lot of fantasy and mythology about it. Can you help us clarify how that rumor was propagated? That might be useful.

RISQUET: Actually there's not so much confusion. I think perhaps this confusion has been perfectly cleared up. But I would like to give the floor to a representative of the Soviet delegation so that he can reclarify what has already been perfectly clarified. I'm going to ask Blight and Brenner, who visited the responsible Soviet general at the Frank País Hospital, to give us their impressions on this.

GRIBKOV: I think that this is something that was clarified a long time ago. The U-2 manned by Major [Rudolf] Anderson was shot down with a Soviet missile under Soviet command. The order was issued by General Pliyev's deputy, General [Stepan Naumovich] Grechko. The order reached those under their command, and at 10:21 the plane was shot down. There were no orders from Moscow. It is also totally incorrect that the commander-in-chief of the Cuban Revolutionary Armed Forces, our dear Comrade Fidel Castro, pressed the button to shoot down the U-2. From the very beginning we said that the Soviet troops were commanded by Soviets, and there was no order issued by Commander Fidel Castro. He can corroborate here.

What Statsenko said was incorrect. Perhaps he didn't have the correct information. He was the commander of a missile division, and maybe he heard something and misconstrued it. That's my official answer.

RISQUET: Mr. Blight, would you like to give your views of the interview you had with the Soviet general in Havana, the one who executed the order?

JAMES BLIGHT: I will speak briefly. I must say I was not close to the situation in which this occurred.

Last spring we had an opportunity to interview here in Cuba General Georgy Voronkov, who was in Havana for medical treatment. I think the only thing I would add is a piece of—I wouldn't call it information, but a piece of context. As I recall, he was very firm in stating that the Cuban and Soviet forces, while separate, were highly coordinated, and—he was very insistent about this—the Soviet armed forces believed that they were here to protect Cuba, and that at a given point the overflights—both the low-level overflights and the high-level overflights—combined with the increasing tension due to the onrush of events and the apparent imminence of attack and war, caused the situation, as it were, to bubble over. So when this U-2 appeared on the radar screen, as he put it, he gave the order to shoot it down. Events had reached such a point that he believed war had either broken out or was about to break out, and the point he kept emphasizing to us was that the situation on the ground with these overflights had simply become intolerable.

RISQUET: Are you satisfied?

ALLYN: I want to re-emphasize that the facts of the shoot-down were made quite clear at the last meeting; but it is very interesting that the confusion about who shot down the U-2 remained long afterwards, and appeared in memoirs and other sources many years later.[36] It is interesting that this wasn't clarified right away. But we have now talked to the actual individual who fired the missile, and so the facts of the shoot-down are very clear. Thank you.

CASTRO: I could add a few more points which I think are necessary for a full understanding of the problem. The antiaircraft missiles were in the hands of the Soviet troops and the Soviet command, but they did not have conventional artillery. We, on the other hand, had a large number of conventional antiaircraft batteries of different calibers. Already in 1961 we had had them, and later we received various other types. We used them at the Bay of Pigs. So, we had hundreds of pieces of conventional antiaircraft artillery. When we declared general mobilization, we also mobilized the people who were going to man the artillery. They were quite inexperienced, but they were familiar with the techniques.

So then we were faced with a practical military problem: the antiaircraft missiles could only fire at targets higher than 1,000 meters. When the crisis erupted, we started having low-level overflights. On the 23rd or the 24th, I think, I visited a Soviet antiaircraft missile battery east of Havana, and I saw that that unit was very vulnerable because the planes were flying overhead at a very low level—well under 1,000 meters. The only antiaircraft battery at that site was a two-barrel piece. I felt that that was a very dangerous situation, and that these antiaircraft weapons were in a very vulnerable position. So we immediately deployed some fifty Cuban antiaircraft batteries around the antiaircraft missile sites and around the strategic medium-range missiles, because we were very worried by the risk those units would be under in the event of a surprise air attack.

It should be said that a surprise air strike was a threat that was hanging over us from the very beginning. Documents from that time tell us that one of the options under consideration was a surprise air strike to destroy the missile sites, and we—I would say with that guerrilla instinct—analyzed what we should do, and what we did was that we used almost all our conventional antiaircraft artillery to defend these units against low-level overflights. And in a relatively short time we deployed these units around these missile sites to protect them against a surprise air strike.

Now, then: the situation grew increasingly tense, and low-level overflights more frequent, and we became convinced that it was extremely dangerous to allow low-level overflights. That was our conviction. It was our territory. We considered that we had the right to take whatever steps we deemed pertinent using our weapons in our territory, and we contacted the Soviet command, that is, the head of all the Soviet troops, General Pliyev. He had his command post here, southwest of the capital. We had a long meeting with him and his staff, and I told them that we had decided to fire against the low-level flights—those were the only ones we could reach. Yesterday I said that we were not so worried about the high-altitude aircraft flying at 20,000 meters, because those were not war planes. The danger was posed by the planes which overflew us every day at a low level. Those were flying not just for observation, but also to demoralize our troops. These planes were, in effect, training daily on how they could destroy our weapons. I told them that we had decided to shoot down low-flying planes, that we felt it was our duty, I told them we had reached this decision: we cannot tolerate these low-level overflights under these conditions, because any day at dawn they're going to destroy all these units.

It was a longer conversation, of course. It included other aspects of the situation—perhaps they will come up here later—but the essential thing about the meeting was to inform him of this decision to fire, a decision taken on the afternoon and evening of the 26th of October.

So, the next day, in the morning, when the planes started to come all over the place—they flew over San Cristóbal—our batteries opened fire. All our batteries fired on all low-level flights on the morning of the 27th when the planes appeared at their usual time. So the order was fulfilled. Now, we didn't have ground-to-air missiles. I explained to the Soviet commander the seriousness of these overflights, and I explained our point of view, to persuade them that our order had been correct. We could say that the war started in Cuba on October the 27th in the morning. Of course, those fast-flying jet planes, as soon as they heard the first shots, went higher to evade our artillery. Our artillerymen were not experts; the planes were flying at an altitude of 100 or 150 meters. I saw them more than once. I saw them flying over; the planes seemed quite vulnerable, but we couldn't shoot down any of the low-flying planes. But we demonstrated our resistance.

The U-2 planes overflew us almost every day. It's still a mystery what led the Soviet commander and the commander of that battery to issue the order to open fire. Obviously, we couldn't give them any orders, but we cannot say that they were solely responsible. And we were in total agreement with their firing against the U-2, because even though they did not pose the same danger from the military standpoint, the principle was the same. I said yesterday that we should not have tolerated the flight of the U-2s.

But, I agree with the Soviet officer that the order was not issued by Moscow. Now, what is my interpretation? These soldiers were all together. They had a common enemy. The firing started and, in a basic spirit of solidarity, the Soviets decided to fire as well. That is my interpretation. Our batteries opened fire that morning. When the planes started overflying from the west, sometime later a plane was shot down overflying Oriente. Prior to that, the radars usually were not operating; one of the issues that we had discussed with the Soviets on the evening of the 26th was that we had to activate the radars. We couldn't leave them off. We had to have time to be warned of the planes' approach. That was what happened. We met on the night before, started firing in the morning, and later in the day heard the news that the Soviet battery had fired against a U-2 in Oriente and had shot it down.

I can add that Khrushchev for some time believed that we had shot down the plane. I don't know whether he blamed us for shooting down the plane directly, or whether he thought that the accident had occurred as a result of the Cuban decision to fire against low-level overflights. But he sincerely believed this. I have letters here, written on those days, which were published. He said, "You shot down a plane. You shot down a plane and you didn't do that before."[37] That is really what he said; he was pointing the finger at us. He said we had shot it down, because, you see, there were two major confusions around this. One, on the part of Khrushchev, was a sincere confusion, confusion about how the U-2 had been brought down. And then there was confusion surrounding my October 26 letter—that is, Khrushchev's interpretation of that letter. This confusion of Khrushchev's regarding my letter, in which he thought that I was proposing a preemptive strike, lasted for quite a long time in Khrushchev's mind. He not only told us that in the letter, but also several weeks later in a conversation with Carlos Rafael [Rodríguez]. He again referred to the suggestion that we'd made to launch a preemptive first strike. He really believed this; he didn't invent it.

Now, to know why this confusion around my letter of the 26th started, we should recall the way the letter was dictated. The letter was written and dictated at the Soviet embassy and sent from there. We almost didn't have translators. I'd write and dictate it, and then I'd revise it again. I'd say, for example, "Delete this word, add this, change that." This was in the wee hours of the morning of the 27th, the night between the 26th and the 27th. It was almost dawn when we finished. I did that after my meeting with the Soviets. I asked myself, "After almost five days of intensive work, what is there still left to do? We've done everything in terms of military preparation. Well, the only thing that remains to do is to send a letter to Khrushchev." To understand this, we have to keep in mind that on that night of the 26th, we saw no possible solution. We couldn't see a way out. Under the threat of an invasion, of an attack, with enormous propaganda using all the mass media, and an international campaign talking about this very serious problem, we really couldn't see any solution. We in Cuba had taken all the steps that were humanly possible. We had talked with the Soviet General Staff, we explained our views. There were other things I said that may come up sometime later. And when we finished all that, I asked myself, "What is still to be done? What remains to be done? What can I do? What is the last thing I can do?" And I dared to write a letter to Nikita, a letter aimed at encouraging him. That was my intention. The aim was to strengthen him morally, because I knew that he had to be suffering greatly, intensely. I thought I knew him well. I thought I knew what he was thinking and that he must have been at that time very anxious over the situation.

So I decided to write that letter—a letter, as I said, aimed at encouraging him. You see, I had other fears, really: I was afraid that there'd be mistakes, hesitations, because I was already seeing that mistakes were being made, and there were signs of hesitation. I proposed some ideas as to what should be done in the event, not of an air strike, but of an invasion of Cuba in an attempt to occupy it. That is in my letter of the night between the 26th and 27th, written and sent from the embassy. And that letter has been used at times to explain why there was a quick [Soviet] response [to President Kennedy's letter to Khrushchev, and to Robert Kennedy's verbal message to Dobrynin, of 27 October] without consultation, and it has been used to support the theory that I suggested a preemptive strike. Actually, I was recalling the events of the Second World War and what had happened during the Second World War.[38] As you all know, during the Second World War, Soviet troops were taken by surprise. As you know, there was a lot of information, there were a lot of intelligence reports in the USSR about preparations for a Nazi invasion. Three million men had been mobilized, hundreds and thousands of planes had been made ready. Even a blind man would have been able to realize that the Soviet Union was going to be attacked. We were all aware of [Richard] Sorge's* story about an attack on the Soviet Union, but Stalin had this fixed idea that that was a provocation, that they wanted to lead him into war, and that it would be inconceivable for them to make the mistake of attacking the Soviet Union, of launching a war on two fronts. I have my views on that moment, but the fact is that the Soviet soldiers were on leave—everybody was, you know, taking it easy. The planes were concentrated at the frontline airports, and this facilitated the Nazi attack. I am sure that if the Soviet army had been mobilized, the Nazis would not have reached Leningrad; they wouldn't have reached Moscow; they wouldn't have reached Volgograd [Stalingrad]. This was proven later when the Soviets managed to regroup their troops, when they recovered from the first strike, when they managed the great feat of moving entire industries eastwards, when Leningrad resisted for 900 days—an almost unprecedented event. The battles near Moscow were terrible. And then Volgograd. I believe that if subjective views had not prevailed—blind views, I would say—and if Stalin had not been obsessed about the provocation, the Soviet army would have been mobilized. Everyone here present, soldier or not, knows that forces taken by surprise, forces not mobilized, are extremely weak. That weakness cost the Soviets millions of men, almost all their air force, their mechanized units, enormous retreats—all because of a misconception!

Throughout our revolutionary history, any time that we have smelled danger, we've taken the necessary steps. And we would rather make the mistake of taking excessive precautions than be taken by surprise because of carelessness.

These are things you can well imagine. For example, when our planes were attacked at the Bay of Pigs, we had realized forty-eight hours before that, without a doubt, there was going to be a landing. We were already mobilized when the air strike hit our air bases. We had already dispersed our planes, and we were able to respond immediately. There's an enormous difference between a mobilized force—a mobilized people—and a people that is taken by surprise. I was very much concerned that history would repeat itself, that the events of the Second World War would be repeated. And yesterday the Soviet general

---

*Richard Sorge was a Soviet spy who reported precise information from sources within the Japanese government about the impending German attack on the Soviet Union in 1941. He was executed by the Japanese in 1944. See Mikhail Heller and Aleksandr M. Nekrich, *Utopia in Power: The History of the Soviet Union from 1917 to the Present*, trans. Phyllis B. Carlos (New York: Summit, 1986), p. 361.

told us his views. I think that there is no one better than he to talk about this, because of the role he played in those events. He said that if an attack were to take place, it would have been a very harsh and bloody war. And he told us about the presence of tactical nuclear weapons, not just strategic nuclear weapons. Now, if the commanders were authorized to use tactical nuclear weapons, it goes without saying that in the event of an invasion we would have had nuclear war. What is a unit going to do if the country is being invaded and they have the tactical weapons? So I was convinced that an invasion would become a thermonuclear war. And that is why in my letter I laid out two possibilities: that is, an air strike, or an invasion. I thought that the invasion was less likely. I thought the most likely event would be the air strike to destroy the sites. But if there was an invasion, and if war erupted, I thought that then the mistakes of the Second World War should not be repeated. I was very much concerned that, for either political or subjective reasons, the same mistake that they had made during the Second World War would be repeated. And this is what inspired my letter. I wanted to say, "If this happens, there shouldn't be any hesitation. We should not allow for a repetition of the events of the Second World War." That is the letter I wrote on the 26th— the same day after I returned from my meeting with the Soviet military command.

To finish up, I must say that at that meeting with the Soviet command, where I analyzed these problems—not this problem of the nuclear weapons, but that of the low-level overflights; that it was impossible to continue tolerating these overflights—the Soviet military commander spoke to the commanders of the various units. They presented a report, and he said, "Motorized mechanized units in combat readiness, the air force regiment in combat readiness, antiaircraft units ready, naval units ready, missile units ready." That is exactly what he said: "Missile units ready for combat." Then, each commander stood up and reported on their units. I do not have precise technical information on the equipment or the warheads. I did expect to visit the bases later. But at that time they were under construction, they were getting ready, they were dealing with other things, and I did not have technical information on details. But I did receive reports that all units were ready for combat. I had this information, and I suggested to the Soviet military commander not to leave all the missiles in the same sites; he should act as if the missiles were going to be attacked by surprise, so that if an attack occurred part of the missiles would not be destroyed. I concretely suggested—I insisted (and it seems that everybody agreed on this)—"please don't keep all these missiles in the same sites. Deploy them in relatively distant sites, and preserve them from surprise air attacks, so that in the event of a surprise air attack, not all the missiles will be destroyed." I went as far as to suggest all that on the basis of the possibility of a surprise attack. A surprise attack is successful if it destroys all the missiles. But a surprise attack is not successful if at least one-third of the missiles survive. As an elementary precaution, I suggested these things to the Soviet commander.

I think that all these things are linked, because they are associated with these events: the meeting with the Soviet commanders when we decided to resist and to shoot at low-level overflights with our artillery; the U-2 issue; and, finally, the letter that I sent to Khrushchev. Alejandro is here; he was the ambassador then. We had close relations and contacts with him then, and he will recall the meeting at his home—the drafting of the letter, when it was sent, and at what time it was received, because that's a very important element regarding the influence of the letter. The letter was actually sent early in the morning of the 27th, when it was almost the night of the 27th in Moscow. By then the formula for solving the crisis was already well developed, since Khrushchev proposed the basic terms for a solution on the 26th. It's possible that while I was meeting with the Soviet command here in Cuba discussing these problems, Khrushchev was sending his message with the promise to withdraw the missiles in return for guarantees. On the 27th there was another letter from Khrushchev, according to all indications.* On the 27th there was also a letter from Kennedy answering him. And it was on the 28th when Moscow said the last word. But we can say that on October 28th the solution of the problem emerged, resulting from Khrushchev's messages on the 26th and 27th—the difference being that, on the 26th, there was no mention of the missiles in Turkey, whereas, on the 27th, the Soviet message referred to the missiles in Turkey. So the United States got two messages: one—the first—without Turkey, on the 26th; and another with Turkey on the 27th. It appears that my famous letter arrived in the early hours of the 28th. I explain all these things chronologically because this actually determines whether or not my letter had any influ-

---

*On 26 October, Khrushchev offered to withdraw Soviet missiles from Cuba in return for an American pledge not to invade the island. Before Kennedy answered, Khrushchev proposed on 27 October, in a letter broadcast by Radio Moscow, to withdraw Soviet missiles from Cuba in return for the American withdrawal of NATO Jupiter missiles from Turkey. The texts of both letters may be found in *Problems of Communism* 41, special issue (Spring 1992), pp. 37–45 and 45–50, respectively.

ence. From my point of view it could not have had any influence because the solution had already been worked out.

Now, we didn't know that Khrushchev had sent that message to Kennedy on the 26th, broaching the possibility of withdrawing the missiles in exchange for guarantees. We didn't know that the solution was already taking shape. When he sent the letter to Kennedy, he could have sent us a copy saying, "I've sent this letter to Kennedy." And then we would have at least been informed; if not consulted, at least informed. I believe that on the 27th, when he sent the Turkish letter, as I call it, he could have sent us a copy, and we would have been informed that Turkey was part of this negotiation. We didn't know anything about this. He knew what he had sent to Kennedy. He knew of Kennedy's answer. So when my letter arrived, the decision had already been made. And I think that my letter cannot have had any influence on that decision.[39] If we want to reconstruct history as it was, we should keep in mind all these factors. The linkage among all these events is what actually explains what happened.

The legend that I pressed the button arose from the fact that Cuba had made the decision to fire against low-level overflights. But we didn't have any buttons. What we had were triggers; antiaircraft weapons have triggers. Consequently, we actually did not know how the U-2 was shot down. We didn't know. It took a long time for us to learn to man those ground-to-air missiles. But there may have been direct influence between the actions that Cubans were taking and the actions of the Soviets, between the meeting with the high command and what happened on the next day. Because I told them: "Turn on the radars; you can't stay blind! Turn on the radars!" The situation was very tense. And an air strike was perfectly possible under those circumstances. Perhaps an invasion would have required more time to carry out. That, in my view, is the explanation of the legend about the situation. For me, the events are clear. I don't know whether this information that I've given you will help you clarify the situation in your minds.

GRIBKOV: In reply to the question—

RISQUET: Yes, sir, of course.

GRIBKOV: When Anderson's airplane was shot down, we wrote a report to the minister of defense, Marshal of the Soviet Union Malinovsky. We explained how the airplane was shot down by our antiaircraft batteries. [Gen. Georgy] Titov and I wrote the report. Titov was head of the operational department of the troops in Cuba. When our report was received in Moscow—signed by Comrade Pliyev—we received a brief and severe reply signed by Malinovsky. It said, more or less, "You were hasty in shooting down the American U-2 while the talks were under way successfully with the American side." We were expecting to be punished for having shot down the plane, so the reply was actually light. But even before that, we had requested authorization to open fire from the minister of defense—and, of course, through him, from the political leadership. We had warned them that American planes were making low-level and high-level overflights, and we requested authorization to open fire. They, however, refused that authorization. However, when Commander-in-Chief Fidel Castro ordered his troops—his antiaircraft batteries—to fire, our commander also issued the order to be in a state of maximum alert. He ordered that our batteries be ready, that our radars be operational. The order to shoot down the plane was given by General Stepan Naumovich Grechko at the regiment commander's headquarters. From there it was transferred to the regiments, and then to the battery commander. Immediately after the information arrived, the aircraft was shot down.

Elsewhere, also, there has been talk of Fidel Castro having pushed the button.[40] I would, however, once again like to refer to the document mentioned by Comrade Fidel Castro, because there is some sort of misunderstanding here. Khrushchev sent Fidel a message on the 28th (Moscow time) saying the following: "Yesterday you shot down an aircraft and you had never done that before when they flew over your territory. This step will be used by the aggressor for his own ends."[41] Khrushchev was underscoring the fact that there were Soviet troops here, together with the Cuban troops; there was a critique addressed to us for shooting down that plane.

Later, on the 30th, in another letter from Khrushchev to Fidel Castro, he said the following: "The shooting down of a U.S. plane over Cuba turned out to be a useful measure because this operation ended without complications. Let it be a lesson for the imperialists."[42] Whatever Voronkov, the battery commander, might have said, the order was issued at the command post and was sent down from the regiment. That is all I wanted to add.

RISQUET: Thank you very much. Blight, you had something else?

BLIGHT: I think we all owe a debt of gratitude to President Castro and General Gribkov for clarifying this. As you know, in the U.S., those of us who study this event have reason to believe that the shooting down of the U-2 was one of the fundamental events of this crisis. It was certainly perceived in Washington, as far as I understand it, as signalling that the crisis had entered a very serious and wholly new situation. The question I would like to put would be to the Russian delegation, particularly to Ambassador Troyanovsky and to Sergei Khrushchev, regarding what President Castro said about his letter on the 26th and the probable lack of influence that it had on the decision-making process in Moscow that led to the resolution of the crisis. Particularly, I am interested in the question of the timing of the resolution of the crisis. That would be the first question. A second question would be, Do you have any insights on the way that the letter was received at the time? Did Chairman Khrushchev understand—or, to what extent did he understand—President Castro's motives as he has explained them to us today in great and illuminating detail? Those would be my two questions.

RISQUET: Are our Soviet colleagues prepared to answer that?

TROYANOVSKY: Yesterday I said that, as I see it, what particularly worried the leadership in the Soviet Union in the letter from Fidel Castro was the information that there might be a landing within the next twenty-four hours. This jibed with other reports and, also, bore some relation to the talks between Robert Kennedy and Dobrynin, where we were informed that the United States required an answer within twenty-four hours. There were a number of reports then co-inciding, which helped accelerate the final decision to accept the Kennedy proposal. This proposal, to a large degree, coincided with the proposals made in the Khrushchev letters of the 26th and the 27th. All of this sped up the answer sent to Washington on the 28th. I cannot assert that the Fidel Castro letter was considered a call for a preemptive strike.

The letter was received, I think, very early in the morning of the 28th. There was, subsequently, a meeting of the Presidium in the morning of the 28th, immediately after that. They were familiar with that letter already at the meeting, and a bit later in the meeting, as I said, the Dobrynin telegram came in about his interview with Robert Kennedy. That's all I can tell you about your question.

RISQUET: Sergei Khrushchev, go ahead.

SERGEI KHRUSHCHEV: I should like to add a bit perhaps, not facts, but psychological considerations. You must understand that Khrushchev could not conceive of starting another war, because, as he understood it, this would be the end of humanity. Psychologically, as you know, he was prepared to withdraw the missiles. The exchange of letters had already begun, and the process was approaching a conclusion. I think the news of the U-2 shoot-down—particularly considering the fact that the troops had been forbidden to shoot down any aircraft—increased the nervousness in Moscow, and we can suppose, as Troyanovsky said, that the letter was read to Khrushchev over the telephone. Troyanovsky read the letter received before dawn from Cuba. This information, and these nuances, did lead to a certain amount of confusion. Where the letter says, "You can adopt this decision on your own," it might have been interpreted as referring to the launching of missiles. Perhaps Troyanovsky could tell us if Khrushchev had read the letter, or if his understanding was based solely on the information he received over the telephone. This would be perhaps helpful in clearing this up. Thank you.

OLEG DARUSENKOV: I wanted to add a small detail so as to clarify the picture just a little bit further.

As far as I understand, there is no Spanish version of the letter. When doubts arose, Alekseev called me to his office and he gave me a page with two or three phrases in Spanish that had been written by Comrade Fidel Castro. It was not then possible to reproduce precisely the ideas contained in these phrases, because evidently what we had here was more or less an outline of an idea. It seems the letter was written in Russian on the basis of what Comrade Fidel was dictating in Spanish. At this time it was quite late. We had spent a few days of maddening work, and in such conditions, a number of small details might have cropped up that were, subsequently, very important.

TROYANOVSKY: Sergei Khrushchev asked whether or not his father had subsequently seen the letter received from Havana. This letter was read to Khrushchev over the telephone and was circulated to the Politburo members. Thus, at the meeting, everyone had the letter before him. It was not read at the meeting, but I have no doubt that all of the participants, Khrushchev included, must have read the letter. It is quite difficult to conceive that the confusion was in any way related to the fact that the letter was first read to Khrushchev over the telephone.

RISQUET: Alekseev, please.

ALEKSEEV: On the question of the shooting down of the aircraft: I was ambassador here, and up until 1978, I was convinced that the

Cubans had shot down the aircraft. There have been many reports saying that it was the Cubans that shot down the aircraft. In any case, in the early '70s, even Khrushchev's memoirs had said that the plane had been shot down by the Cubans. Now Sergei Khrushchev has taken something out which says that the Russians had shot down the plane; but in the '70s it was understood that the Cubans had shot it down. Later, Statsenko explained that he had shot down the aircraft, and that was the first time that I had heard that the plane had been shot down by the Soviets. Later, I heard from Fidel Castro himself that the Cubans did not have these weapons at all.

Other than Statsenko—who did not present a very exact explanation—I had the situation explained to me by General [Leonid S.] Garbuz, who was Pliyev's second deputy, and who spoke about this with Grechko at the command post. When the radars detected the approach of the aircraft, they began to consider their course of action. The situation was very tense. They tried to get through to Pliyev, but he wasn't there. Therefore, Grechko assumed the responsibility, because he was the commander of the air defense forces, and gave the order to fire three missiles. Two missiles brought the plane down. After that, the telegram was sent off to Malinovsky; Malinovsky said that it had been hasty, but in the final analysis, there were no overly great complications.

I don't understand why our Cuban comrades, and Fidel Castro, were not concerned by the fact that they were being saddled with the responsibility for having done something that they did not do. I never actually talked about this personally with Khrushchev, but I have considered this. I think the most important thing is that this episode illustrates how a war can arise between two countries when the leaders don't even know what's going on. I don't understand how Khrushchev could have said that the Cubans shot it down when it was the Soviet military command that had given the order. Kennedy did not believe Khrushchev's assertions, because he knew the orders must have come from the Soviet government, although they actually came from the military. I don't remember having heard at Statsenko's meeting with U Thant that the Cubans had shot down the U-2.

At that time, [Cuban president Osvaldo] Dorticós had met with Fidel to discuss a number of important issues. It was on the 27th, at 2:00 A.M. Fidel was quite concerned about the situation, and one of the first things said was that they were expecting an imminent air strike or a landing within seventy-two hours; that is when they decided to send a letter to Khrushchev describing the critical nature of the situation and calling for the appropriate measures. We spoke and thought for a long time. There were two of us there—[Constantin] Manakhov and I were there, and Darusenkov was around somewhere—as Fidel was dictating and we were writing. We did not have a perfect mastery of the language, and if we had, I think Khrushchev would not have been so concerned about the possibility of the letter containing a request for a preemptive strike. But as I was saying, while Fidel was dictating, we were translating and writing. Darusenkov was translating. The letter was two or three pages long, and I must say that I recall that Fidel was choosing his words very precisely, because this was an immense responsibility. At that time I decided to send a brief advance telegram, because writing the whole letter would have taken hours, perhaps. I telegraphed that Fidel was meeting with us, that he was drafting a letter, and that there was danger of an imminent air strike or invasion from the United States. The telegram, of course, got there sooner than the letter, at 2:00 P.M. on the 27th, while Fidel's letter got to Moscow at 1:00 A.M. on the 28th. I agree with Comrade Fidel that his letter had no impact on the adoption of the agreement, which had already been arrived at, so to speak.

This meeting in Moscow we've been talking about was a formal one, because meetings at the time had a role, although it was Khrushchev who made the final decisions. He personally decided to withdraw the missiles. He was a responsible individual. He knew, of course, that a nuclear war would be horrible. But I don't understand why he understood that Fidel was calling for a preemptive strike. When Mikoyan arrived, he asked the same question that Khrushchev did, and as I had asked Fidel Castro earlier. Mikoyan asked Fidel if he had called for a preemptive strike, and Fidel said, "No! Alejandro made a mistake in the letter." We have this telegram. We have the draft of the telegram, and it was subsequently published in the daily, *Granma*. I must repeat here that the government's decision was adopted before the arrival of the letter.[43]

The inclusion of the Turkish missiles in the negotiations, of course, concerned Fidel, because this crucial issue concerned Cuban security, and all of a sudden you had the dismantling of missile bases in Turkey brought into the negotiations.

It seems to me that the letter might have had some importance. When Fidel traveled to Moscow, Khrushchev told him that the letter had had an influence on the decision. But the fact is that Khrushchev's appraisal of the situation was that it was extremely tense and it was also his opinion that he had made a mistake. Khrushchev had said to

Fidel Castro that he hadn't had time to consult with him, but it wasn't that Khrushchev didn't have the time to consult so much as the fact that he knew that asking Castro's opinion would have drawn things out, and it was too late to ask him. But the shooting down of the aircraft was an expression of the solidarity of our troops with the Cubans. At the time we were ready to do anything for the Cuban Revolution, and to support Fidel—all of us who were here. That's all I wanted to add.

RISQUET: Khrushchev, please.

KHRUSHCHEV: I wanted to speak about [Nikita] Khrushchev's memoirs. The three volumes published in the United States contain a number of mistakes. They were written without consultations with the Soviet Union; that is why they contain the mistake about the Cubans having shot down the aircraft. There are mistakes, particularly, in the chapter on the Cuban crisis. There is a simple statement that the Cubans had shot down the aircraft together with the Soviet troops that were there, and in a more detailed explanation it says that the aircraft was shot down by the Soviet troops. This is the kind of confusion that historians have to unravel. The complete text of Khrushchev's memoirs will probably be much larger, it will be edited in Moscow, and all of the original texts are available to anyone who really wants to unearth what happened there. It is all down in black and white.

I would like to tell Alekseev that, on the basis of the chronology of the dramatic events of the 28th, when we received the information on the letter, I believe that the decision was adopted at the very last moment. There had to be an answer to Kennedy to avoid a confrontation. That is why the meeting was called and the vote was taken with Khrushchev present. I think, actually, they were not very certain about what had to be done at that moment; but the decision was made nonetheless.

RISQUET: General Titov.

GENERAL GEORGY TITOV: I would like to shed a little light on the question of the shooting down of the aircraft, to close the topic. One has to understand the situation at the time. I recall that on the 25th, 26th, and 27th, we were expecting a strike by the U.S. armed forces. We were at the command posts, and we felt that we were about to launch into military operations, because U.S. aircraft were flying over Cuban territory and inspecting it indiscriminately. Our troops were in defensive positions then, and we could not allow a total discovery of our defensive dispositions. This was a definite possibility, because we were being watched by these aircraft that were flying over Cuba constantly. On a number of occasions we requested authorization to fire on these aircraft, because they had in fact already begun what we considered to be military operations. While we were awaiting a decision from Moscow, our commander, Pliyev, made the decision to shoot down the U-2. The order was given by Grechko, as Grechko said he was the general commanding the troops in Cuba. There's nothing else involved here. I could, if required, sign an affidavit for the U.S. delegation.

RISQUET: Comrade Fidel.

CASTRO: I wanted to clarify this question of the shoot-down of the plane. My aim was to give a detailed explanation of the things that actually happened.

I don't want to deny our responsibility in the shooting down of the plane. On the contrary, it's possible that our responsibility may have been greater than that of the Soviets. So we are not trying to blame the Soviets for having brought down the plane.

I was in full agreement with the shooting down of the plane. I considered it totally correct for them to shoot down the plane. I think that this was the only consistent thing that we did in those days. When you are expecting a surprise attack, when the adversary has the initiative and when they can decide when that surprise attack is going to be launched, I think that the only correct thing, militarily and defensively, was to be ready to prevent a surprise attack at all cost. So I think that what was done was totally right.

I don't think that the United States would have allowed Soviet planes to overfly Florida, Marathon Key, or any other place without shooting it down immediately. I wonder whether the United States would have allowed a single plane flying over its military bases, its troop concentration sites? No! They would have brought it down, and they would have considered the act of sending such a plane a very serious action. We, however, were forced to allow overflights all over our territory and simply remain idle. So I assume full historical responsibility for the shooting down of the plane.

I think that the Soviet government later realized this, because, even though at that point they were criticizing us—we have the letters here, where we were accused of shooting down a plane—my understanding when they said that was that both of us were being blamed—that is, the Soviet troops and the Cuban troops—when Khrushchev said, "You shot down a plane yesterday and you hadn't before."

Neither we nor the Soviet soldiers were aware of the messages sent by Khrushchev on the 26th and the 27th. You see, I think that Khrushchev was far more informed than we were. He was already proposing a solution, and we knew nothing. Kennedy immediately accepted Khrushchev's proposal of the 26th, because it was exactly what he was demanding. And all that in exchange for only a guarantee, for the commitment to give a guarantee. No one knew that here. On the 27th, we knew nothing of there being a second letter. We first heard of Turkey on the 28th, in the morning.[44] We woke up to the news that mention was being made of Turkey, and that there was an arrangement. We still hadn't heard of the proposal of the withdrawal of the missiles in exchange for a guarantee; nor had we heard anything about what had happened on the 27th; and we knew nothing of Kennedy's reply. We were in a situation of maximum alert, of maximum tension, and under those conditions we acted according to our judgment. It was totally correct.

What's more, if this whole operation had been carried out with the same resolution, the outcome would have been different, and it would not have been war. The fact is that often it's hesitation that can lead to war, not firmness. The Soviet government realized this, and eventually they decorated the soldier, the officer, who brought down the plane [Voronkov].[45] They recognized and decorated this man, and I think that the Soviet soldiers were proud of the action carried out by this man. So we are not making a moral assessment of this event. What are we to regret? Why should we repent? How can you prove that what was done was wrong? On what grounds?

I believe it was fair to give that soldier recognition, a decoration. This was done subsequently, and the soldier deserved it. We were in a situation of war. We had not heard of the messages, and judging by the letter Nikita sent me on the 23rd, I didn't see the slightest indication that he would solve the problem simply by caving in to American demands.

I think that a solution might have been found, but in a different way—a more honorable solution. I'm certain of this. But I am not going to elaborate on this.

Perhaps we should move on to other topics and other reflections. We are not making a moral judgment. We are making a historical assessment of what happened, of what everyone did, of the incidents. It is true that all of this happened very quickly, in a few hours and under exceptional conditions. At the time we didn't have official translators; we didn't have anything. We didn't even have anyone who spoke Russian. The Soviet embassy had some people who spoke Spanish. [Pointing to Darusenkov:] You were there, but you were not a translator. You were *serving* as a translator. Who translated what I was dictating? I drafted things and I dictated, and more than once I came back on different points. Who was jotting down what I was dictating? It was Manakhov. You weren't there? [Darunsenkov shakes his head.] No. It was Constantin Manakhov, the tall one.

That's what happened. It was not like now; we didn't have the certainty that we have now. Normally, all the notes that I wrote by hand, I then recopied. I would keep the originals. We have the other letters that followed, where I explained carefully what I had said to Khrushchev, and exactly what I mean; but under the conditions at that time, in the midst of that tension, we'd have to see if you have copies or anything written regarding this message that I wrote on the 26th.

In these letters that were published by the Americans, between October 30th and December, there are paragraphs that are missing, there are messages that have been lost; at times they had to ask the Soviet embassy for assistance to see if they could provide materials on this topic, even though the United States was much better organized. It seems that some messages, however, were lost, or were misplaced in files, or somebody kept them in their pockets, and perhaps they ended up at the dry cleaners. [Laughter.] Many things at that time were written by hand. So anything could have happened. But what I do want to stress is that we are not seeking to avoid any responsibility. What we are interested in is explaining what actually happened through our personal contributions, so as to avoid confusions which may give rise to all kinds of stories.

RISQUET: General Gribkov.

GRIBKOV: It seems to me that this issue has been fully clarified. Let's put an end to it, because there is enough evidence, and the conclusions are similar. The plane was brought down on the orders issued by the Soviet Command, and by Soviet missiles. Thank you.

RISQUET: First of all, it's time for recess; secondly, I think that the issue has been sufficiently debated, and I think it would be better that when we reconvene we move on to the next item. General Smith has requested the floor. You have it, sir; but I propose, if we all agree, to conclude with this issue.

GENERAL SMITH: One brief comment.

As interesting and as informative as our previous discussion has been, the one thing that I have drawn from this discussion is that we were much closer to a nuclear war than any of us thought—or at least than I thought—and that reinforces to me the wisdom of the decision that President Kennedy and Premier Khrushchev made at that time to bring this crisis to an end before all of us suffered much more unnecessary damage.

RISQUET: Thank you, General. Do we then agree that we have come to the conclusion of this item, and that after the recess we shall move on to the next item? Okay. It's 10:40; at ten past eleven we should move to the third item. Our friend Troyanovsky will chair that session.

THE CIA'S EVIDENCE:

" . . . to change . . . the 'correlation of forces' . . . "

Ray Cline's presence on the U.S. delegation is of great interest to the Cubans. As Cline informs the conference in his prepared remarks, he did not serve in that branch of the CIA—Clandestine Services—that was of such concern to the Cubans after 1960. Rather, Cline emphasizes, he was recalled from Asia *after* the Bay of Pigs fiasco to head the "intelligence" unit, a large component of which was responsible for assessing the strategic nuclear capabilities of the Soviet Union.[46] It was natural that virtually everyone working on the assessment of Soviet nuclear forces would attribute the missile deployment not, as Khrushchev claimed, to a wish to defend Cuba, but rather—as Fidel Castro and the Cubans always suspected—to bolster Soviet nuclear capability. Thus, in an odd twist, neither Ray Cline from the CIA nor Fidel Castro believed General Gribkov when he proclaimed, as had Khrushchev and, more recently, former Foreign Minister Andrei Gromyko, that the Soviet deployment was undertaken to defend Cuba.[47] As Cline says, he has no doubt that the principal purpose of the missiles was "to change the correlation of forces," a remark which draws a nod of agreement from Castro.[48]

Yet as novel as Cline's participation is to the Cubans, his presence is also something of a controversial novelty to some of the other members of the U.S. delegation. Cline's former boss, CIA director John McCone, had a bitter feud with McNamara following the missile crisis. McCone claimed to have predicted the Soviet missile deployment to Cuba, only to have been ignored by McNamara's Defense Department.[49] Cline himself had taken up the cudgels following the Moscow conference in January 1989, claiming, first, that there had been no danger of nuclear war in October 1962 because Khrushchev, aware of his nuclear inferiority, would never have initiated war; and second, that because of Gorbachev's "topspin of *glasnost*," Gromyko and others at the conference had simply been spouting the line most congenial to the current Soviet foreign policy agenda—that the defense of Cuba was the *only* motive for the Soviet deployment.[50] Cline strongly implied that McNamara and the others on the U.S. delegation had been fooled by "historical revisionism serving Moscow's interests."[51] As McNamara notes in his reply to Fidel Castro's question about the nature of the nuclear balance, the differences between Cline and McNamara are as wide as ever.

In yet another curious twist, it is Gribkov, the Russian in charge of organizing the deployment to Cuba, who makes the strongest case in opposition to the view that Cline represents (commonly known as the "hawks' " view).[52] Gribkov notes that there would have been no reason to deploy 42,000 troops and tactical nuclear weapons to Cuba if there had been no intention to defend against an American attack, nor would it have made sense to plan to retreat to the interior of the island and to fight a guerrilla war if the defense faltered. Given that intention, how could there have been no risk of nuclear war in the event of an American invasion?

Cline's presentation seems curiously impervious to these aspects of Gribkov's remarks, as indeed do Castro's views. Neither the man from the CIA "who resembles Hemingway" nor the Cuban revolutionary seems to want to absorb the force of what Gribkov has said: *because* the Soviets were determined to defend Cuba, *therein* lay the seeds of nuclear danger, if the United States had attacked and invaded the island. Perhaps Cline, who no doubt knew the details of the nuclear imbalance far better than Khrushchev, cannot, even in retrospect, appreciate how much Khrushchev was willing to risk to save the Cuban Revolution. Perhaps Castro, whose revolution Khrushchev (in Castro's view) abandoned in the missile crisis, cannot, even in retrospect, take seriously Khrushchev's claim that while in Bulgaria in April 1962, "one thought kept hammering away at my brain: what will happen if we lose Cuba?"[53]

TROYANOVSKY: I think we should begin. As I understand, it is the United States' turn now to speak. . . . Who will be our next speaker on the U.S. side? Mr. Cline, please.

RAY CLINE: I've never been able to engage in any of these conferences before—I'm not sure they wanted me to [laughter]—but I do want to make a confession to my Russian friends and my Cuban friends: that I was working in the CIA as the deputy director for research and analysis—we called it "intelligence"—and I managed the National Photo Interpretation Center, which did indeed find the pictures of the missile sites at San Cristóbal. We found a lot of other sites later, but the first evidence firmly indicating that Khrushchev had sent nuclear-armed missiles to Cuba was on the 14th of October 1962. Now, I had evidence from my research staff that we did have an indication that missiles were being sent to San Cristóbal, and we finally decided that we had to make a U-2 overflight in order to discover whether these missiles were actually there. Fortunately, we did find them and I sent the photographs from the U-2 plane to [Special Assistant for National Security] McGeorge Bundy, [Attorney General] Bobby Kennedy, and Jack Kennedy on the morning of the 16th of October. So I am the villain, I guess, in finding these extraordinary pictures which changed the mind of President Kennedy. I can tell you—and I talked to President Kennedy most of that summer about the evidence we found—that he did not anticipate that Khrushchev would put the missiles in Cuba. He didn't think it was true. They had some rather preliminary exchanges of letters. President Kennedy anticipated that any conflict with the Soviet Union over Cuba would be conducted on the diplomatic level, and that he would not be forced to deal with the presence of a nuclear missile system in the Western Hemisphere.

I briefed these issues extensively, and reported what was happening when much of the Soviet military hardware went to Cuba all through the summer, until finally we did find conclusive evidence. My boss, John McCone, had a strong feeling that Soviet missiles would be put in Cuba. He said it was just a hunch; he didn't have any evidence any more than we did. But he said he wanted to make sure that we searched as thoroughly as necessary to find evidence of missile installations. Well, John McCone went to France on a honeymoon; he married a second wife, and he went to the Riviera [23 August–23 September 1962].

He was so frustrated that he kept firing me messages from the Riviera on his honeymoon all the time saying, "You've got to do something more about this. Get this evidence out and tell President Kennedy what to say." So I ended up being a principal proponent of this operation. And I think we succeeded in influencing the course of events.

Incidentally, I want to tell you that I was serving as a CIA station chief in Asia during the Bay of Pigs operation. That was a wonderful thing for me, because I was not responsible for the Bay of Pigs. [Laughter.] And I probably would not have become deputy director if I had been out there dealing with the Bay of Pigs. [Laughter.] The Bay of Pigs was a total fiasco. Every strategic disaster occurred. I knew about it, but I didn't like it, and I was delighted that I was able to manage the missile crisis in a more constructive way.

We had to get the evidence—that's what intelligence is all about—and we had to keep the president and his advisers informed. And eventually we took the pictures up to the United Nations to brief [U.S. Ambassador to the United Nations] Adlai Stevenson and many of the foreign observers in the United Nations, to explain what was happening in the Soviet Union. I thought Khrushchev was a pretty sensible fellow, but I think he did take a serious risk in making the decision to put the missiles in Cuba.

Another point that I wanted to mention was that I briefed Kennedy on the CIA satellite reconnaissance system. At that time it was totally secret; nobody knew about orbiting satellite systems. They went around the Earth every ninety minutes, and you could map huge areas of the Soviet Union or any other part of the world. I revealed that the Soviet Union was boasting about enormous missile superiority—we called it the missile gap at that time. But when we managed to get all the photographs from the National Photo Interpretation Center, I found that they had many fewer missiles than the United States had; it was about four to one. And that was very hard for us to believe, because many of the military people were confident that Khrushchev had created a superior missile system. In fact, it turned out that, since we started up our missile production very efficiently and very promptly, we ended up with four times the number of Soviet missiles.

I wanted to mention this to you because the ratio, in addition to the hundreds of intercontinental bombers which could have been used, meant that if we were firm we could force Khrushchev to retreat. I talked to Kennedy about that. I said, "Look, we have real intercontinental strategic superiority, and they will not use it against us. They would be crazy to use it against us. We don't want a war; we don't want a military conflict. But if the missiles are in Cuba, then we have to respond in a firm and strategic way." And we did. We forced Khrushchev to retreat, and I think that was wise. I think the Kennedy-Khrushchev agreement was one of the things that saved our strategic interests and prevented war from coming in the Soviet Union. I didn't think it could possibly be nuclear war, but I did think there might be a direct military conflict. Nobody wanted a nuclear war, neither the USSR nor the United States, and once we discovered the evidence of the missile sites, we had to win in a diplomatic and political way.

I just want to make a couple of more points. I want to get into the broader perspective of what we were trying to do in the United States. I was an adviser to the National Security Council—not a member, but an adviser, because we tried to get them all the intelligence—and I felt that something was misunderstood. After all, we had a cold war with the Soviet Union beginning in the Stalin days that had nothing to do with Cuba. President Fidel Castro came along in 1959, and he was not the primary actor in this situation. It was a very direct conflict between Moscow and Washington. So I felt that the priority for the Soviet Union was to change the balance of strategic military power—what Russians always called the "correlation of forces"—and I believe that was their major goal. Now, this is speculative; I cannot prove any of these things. But this is what we thought in the CIA.

I thought the Soviets' second priority was to force the United States military out of Berlin. This was an issue for many years, and Khrushchev was very anxious to somehow force—particularly Kennedy—to retreat from Berlin. And while we would have tried to solve the Cuban crisis by diplomatic and political measures, President Kennedy insisted that we couldn't get out of Berlin.

In my view—contrary to what I think many people here believe—the defense of Cuba was only the third Soviet priority. There was indeed an intent to create a nuclear missile force, but I am not sure—and I hope my Russian colleagues can tell me—but I think that Khrushchev was indeed trying to squeeze Berlin, and that he thought if a nuclear force was put in Cuba the Americans would be so much on the defensive and would be concentrating so completely on the Caribbean, and not on Europe, that they might be able to squeeze us out of Berlin.[54] I don't think that was ever realistic, but I do believe that we should recognize that these were very broad issues.

Now, the last thing that I want to say to you—and I'll try to be brief—is this: I think everybody probably now knows about a National Security Council paper called NSC-68, written in April 1950.* And if any of you haven't read that, I think you ought to take a look at it, because to me it was very prophetic. The reason that that strategic policy was adopted was that Stalin and Kim Il Sung and Mao Zedong attacked South Korea, and we felt that we had to respond to that. Many Americans didn't expect to respond to it, but they did. At any rate, I just want to read you quickly a few paragraphs from this NSC-68 document, because I think it puts the missile crisis in the correct perspective—that it was indeed a conflict with the Soviet Union that had little to do with Cuba. Cuba became an incident in this episode. I am sorry to tell President Castro that he probably was the third priority in the exercise.

At any rate, let me just read you a few paragraphs: "The gravest threat to the security of the United States within the foreseeable future stems from the hostile designs and formidable power of the USSR and from the nature of the Soviet system. Even though"—I'm just skipping now various paragraphs—"Even though present estimates indicate that the Soviet leaders probably do not intend deliberate armed action involving the United States at this time, the possibility of such deliberate resort to war cannot be ruled out." And, of course, that's why the Cuban missile crisis became a military confrontation. But the remarkable thing is that what we said was, "Our current security programs and strategic plans are based upon these objectives, aims and measures: to reduce the power and influence of the USSR to limits which no longer constitute a threat to the peace, national independence, and stability of the world family of nations; to bring about a basic change in the conduct of international relations by the government in power in Russia to conform with the purposes and principles set forth in the U.N. Charter"; and then, finally, we said: "We should endeavor to achieve our general objectives by methods short of war through the pursuit of the following aims: to encourage and promote the gradual retraction of undue Russian power and influence from the present perimeter areas around traditional Russian boundaries"—we meant Eastern Europe—"and the emergence of the satellite countries as en-

---

*NSC-68 formalized the Truman administration's doctrine of "Containment." In what follows, Cline quotes selectively from the document. For the published text, see U.S. Department of State, *Foreign Relations of the United States: 1950*, vol. 1 (Washington, D.C.: Government Printing Office, 1977), pp. 234–92.

tities independent of the USSR." Of course that's what happened in 1989, whatever the reasons. The last part of the paragraph is "to encourage the development among the Russian peoples of attitudes which may help to modify current Soviet behavior and permit a revival of the national life of groups, evidencing the ability and determination to achieve and maintain national independence."

Well, as I say, I think some of this language is still rather prophetic, because when you talk about the Commonwealth of Independent States, that really was our goal. We wanted not to have a Soviet empire, but a Commonwealth of States.

So I wanted to call this to your attention. It was only declassified a number of years ago, and most people don't know about it. I helped contribute to writing it when I was in the CIA. Paul Nitze was the chairman, and he did a remarkable job, so if anybody wants a copy of this document, I'll be glad to send it to you. Thank you very much.

TROYANOVSKY: Thank you very much. Who will be our next speaker from the U.S. side?

DAVID WELCH: I wonder if I can persuade Ray Cline to say a few words about whether he thought the deployment of Soviet missiles to Cuba *did* significantly alter the strategic nuclear balance? And then I wonder if, perhaps, General Gribkov could answer the same question.

I would also be interested to know from Mr. Troyanovsky if Mr. Khrushchev ever spoke of that rationale for the deployment; and I would like to hear from the Cubans if Marshal Biryuzov ever spoke of that rationale when he was in Cuba in May and June.

TROYANOVSKY: . . . Please, Mr. Cline.

CLINE: Well, I believe that Khrushchev did refer to the balance of power in a very big way, and, of course, during all that correspondence, emphasized that what they were doing was defending Cuba. So I must say that governments tend to have different priorities, different bureaucracies have different priorities, and I am sure there was an interest in saving the Cuban commonwealth, the Cuban system. But I felt that the primary objective was to develop the new balance of power, because the Russians were falling behind in intercontinental missiles. So I felt— and this was my judgment, but I think the CIA people generally agreed with it—that if he put missiles in Cuba, it would indeed change the balance of power, because we thought there would probably end up being about eighty-four missiles. Of course, originally it was only forty-two, but we thought that if the missiles got established in Cuba, they would build them up, and it would be a real hazard for the United States. Now, one of the reasons was that we had set up a defense system which was all oriented toward the Soviet Union, the northern Atlantic, and the northern Pacific. We had very little in the way of defenses in the southern part of the United States. I think that's why those missiles were significant. In my view, they were not intended for a military firing of any kind, but they would have a political effect on the balance of power that would be much more favorable to the Soviet Union than they would otherwise have had. If there was a danger to the United States, it was that these missiles would shift the focus much more on Western Hemisphere issues, and preoccupy us with Cuba—which we *did* get preoccupied with—and we would begin to lose our interest in NATO and the defense of Berlin.

So I believe that if the missiles finally had stayed there in Cuba, they would have built them up, and eventually they might have changed the balance of power.

TROYANOVSKY: . . . I give the floor to Sergei Khrushchev.

KHRUSHCHEV: Thank you. This is an old question. I've posed it many times, but finally I'm going to address it to Mr. Cline. He said that with the aid of satellites it was discovered that the Soviet Union had many fewer missiles than the United States supposed. This is a very important point, in my view, since we know that as of the beginning of the Cold War, the Soviet Union lived under the threat of a U.S. nuclear strike, and the Soviet Union was always looking for a chance to respond to this strike. And this led to the development of missiles in our country, although, in view of the events of the October crisis, we overestimated our potential.

The United States learned that we did not have as many missiles as they thought. At one point, Khrushchev said that we built missiles like sausages. I said then, "How can you say that, since we only have two or three?" He said, "The important thing is to make the Americans believe that. And that way we prevent an attack." And on these grounds our entire policy was based. We threatened with missiles we didn't have. That happened in the case of the Suez crisis, and the Iraqi crisis.[55] But it happened that in 1962 the United States discovered the real balance of forces in terms of missiles.

I think that this can be traced to Penkovsky.* Penkovsky was the one who obtained this intelligence. After this, the Americans started their reconnaissance flights in outer space. And I've always thought that it was impossible in 1962 to take pictures of the whole territory of the Soviet Union and determine the exact number of missiles that we had. That is, the system was not fully operational. We found film capsules from these reconnaissance satellites which would crash in Kazakhstan. So my question is: how did your intelligence activity correlate to Penkovsky's activity, and what was the role of surveillance from outer space? . . .

TROYANOVSKY: Mr. Cline, please.

CLINE: I believe that Penkovsky was a very important source of information for the intelligence services in Washington. He gave us hundreds and hundreds of documents. He was not a current operations officer, but he did manage to provide the CIA with literally thousands of pages of documents about the structure of the military system. However, while we were getting those documents, we didn't know at that time—and I'm talking about 1960 and 1961—what the actual current data were. And the Pentagon in particular—it was the Air Force primarily—were absolutely convinced that the Soviet Union had hundreds of missiles.

Well, in August 1961, as I recall, we did fly the first effective reconnaissance satellite mission. And I remind you that this is an extraordinary achievement. The satellite flew ninety miles above the Earth, and still took useful photographs. And it also, as I recall, circled the Earth every ninety minutes. Of course, as the world turns, you could move across the Soviet Union, and cover an enormous area of the country. Actually, that's why we put the satellites up—because there were eleven time zones in the Soviet Union, and we were able to cut across them. So, what I want to say is that the actual photography from satellites was the key, and what made the United States feel that it had confidence in protecting ourselves. As I recall in the fall of 1961, we covered nearly all of the railroad systems and the major highways

---

*Col. Oleg Penkovsky, an officer in Soviet military intelligence, worked for British and American intelligence until his arrest during the missile crisis. Jerrold L. Schecter and Peter S. Deriabin, *The Spy Who Saved the World: How a Soviet Colonel Changed the Course of the Cold War* (New York: Charles Scribner's Sons, 1992), is an engaging if somewhat hyperbolic account of Penkovsky's activities.

and the cities, and decided that the Soviet Union had only twenty-five missiles at that time. That was the end of 1961. We were not even sure exactly how many they had, but we knew there were no more than twenty-five. By 1962, and the approach of the Cuban missile crisis in October, we thought there were, I believe, perhaps fifty. I'm not absolutely sure of what the number was. But the Minuteman in America was being produced very quickly. We had thought we were so far behind the Soviet Union that we really went all out to build the Minuteman missiles. And in September and October '62, we circled the Earth and found that we had four times as many Minuteman missiles as the Soviet Union had. And in some cases, some of those Soviet missiles were not even very operable. They were still on sites that were not intended for firing, they were intended only for testing. It was only at that time that we learned what was happening.

Now, I've mentioned to you earlier, I think, that once we persuaded President Kennedy that he had the superior balance of power in the intercontinental missile business, he never expected Khrushchev to put the missiles in Cuba; he thought that would be a mistake. And I must tell you that when we talked to him all that summer, he was very dubious about it. He thought that we should accept Khrushchev's word. He was being very cordial to us. You know that Khrushchev said that he was going to help Kennedy in the congressional elections in the fall of '62.[56] So, I was quite sure that President Kennedy thought that there was little chance of the missiles being deployed in Cuba. But he did say, as I recall, on September 12th, that if offensive weapons came into Cuba, there would be a grave crisis.[57] I'm not sure I have the exact language, but he did say publicly that there would be a real confrontation if the missiles came to Cuba. I still don't understand why Nikita Khrushchev decided to do that. It's very hard for me to understand why he took this risk. And, of course, to me it was a mistake. He was a very clever man; he had a lot of dynamism, and he had a lot of political ideas. But I believe that, somehow—perhaps because he wanted to help defend Cuba, and perhaps because he wanted to shore up a communist state in the Caribbean—he overreached.

I was absolutely sure that if Khrushchev and Kennedy could treat each other reasonably, in a friendly fashion, that the missiles would have to be withdrawn from Cuba. I never doubted that. Once, President Kennedy said that he felt he had been deceived, particularly by Gromyko. Gromyko came to the White House in the middle of that first week of the crisis, and he clearly lied about the deployment.[58] But I was confident that if Kennedy and Khrushchev could be reasonably friendly—which they were before the crisis occurred—we would get the missiles out of Cuba.

Now, that was a speculation, not a certainty. And intelligence is not a policy maker. Intelligence just tells you what the facts are. And that's all we did. But anyway, I felt that that was one of the major mistakes that Nikita Khrushchev made. Thank you.

TROYANOVSKY: Thank you. Mr. Garthoff wanted to add something.

GARTHOFF: I want briefly to add a little to what Ray Cline has said answering this question. First, I need to say that I went to the Department of State in September 1961, and I was there during the Cuban missile crisis. But in preceding years, I had been working on Soviet affairs for Ray Cline's predecessor at the [Central Intelligence] Agency. So I was there, for example, during the Penkovsky period, and for most of it—the earlier part—I was probably one of the few people who read all those hundreds of pages, the hundreds of documents he provided. It was very valuable information. But some of the material he provided was things he had picked up, gossip picked up around the Ministry of Defense and elsewhere. Some of it was very interesting and probably true. Some of it was interesting and probably not true, and it was sometimes very difficult to tell. So much depended on the kind of information, and the source. But he did, for example, provide us with the full characteristics of, and other data with respect to, the R-12 and R-14 systems. We even learned those designations from him for the first time. (Incidentally, those Russian designations for what we called the SS-4 and SS-5 missiles were never publicly cited until, actually, the first edition of my book on the missile crisis in October 1987,[59] and then, officially in December 1987, in connection with the INF* Treaty.)

But to go back to the point, Colonel Penkovsky did not tell us— he did not learn, at least in time to tell us anything—about the missiles going to Cuba. He did give us information, some of which was helpful and some of which was not, with respect to intentions during the Berlin crisis in 1961. He had begun reporting in April 1961, and this lasted until shortly before he was arrested on the 22nd of October 1962. But if I may slightly amend what Ray Cline said, the first successful space reconnaissance mission was in August 1960, not August

---

*Intermediate-range Nuclear Force.

1961, and we began to get useful information in early 1961 which permitted Secretary McNamara, when he first came in office in February, to make a statement—perhaps politically prematurely—to the effect that there wasn't any missile gap, right after President Kennedy had just won an election running on the theme that there *was* one. But in any case, during the course of 1961 there were several successful missions making it more and more clear and certain that there were, in fact, at that time only four Soviet ICBM launching pads operational in Plesetsk, with the first operational system—what we call the SS-6 (the Soviet term was the *Semiorka*, the R-7). But, in 1961, they were of course already constructing sites for the second system, which we call the SS-7.

As Ray Cline has correctly recalled, our estimate at the time of the Cuban missile crisis was that there were fifty to seventy-five probably operational. Later, looking back on it, we revised that down to forty-four. General Volkogonov said there were twenty or so, which I interpreted to mean twenty-four, if that was correct.[60] That would not be very different from what we had thought, because these missiles were coming in in groups of ten. We did not know, of course, precisely when each complex was operational. When the construction was all completed, and everything was there that we could observe that would be needed to fire the missile, we counted it as operational. So perhaps there were only twenty-four when we thought, looking back, that there were forty-four. But the point is that the number was quite small then, and not growing rapidly.

At that same time, in October 1962, we rushed some of our missiles along which were being deployed, and by October 31st we had 172 operational ICBMs on alert—on station—and 144 Polaris missiles at sea on station. I say nothing, of course, of the discrepancy in bombers, where we had 1,450 strategic bombers on alert status, with a total initial salvo of 2,952 weapons on the strategic bombers and intercontinental missiles. So the discrepancy between actual operational American and Soviet intercontinental strategic forces was very great, and in that sense, an addition of (let's say) twenty-four R-12s in Cuba doubled, perhaps, the Soviet force if they were fired first, and could have taken under fire additional soft targets—lucrative targets in the United States, such as SAC* bases, for which there were not enough ICBMs in the Soviet Union at that time. So in that sense, the Soviet

---

*Strategic Air Command.

deployment added a lot. It changed the strategic balance. But, of course, in every meaningful way, it didn't really affect the strategic balance at all, because even if a larger portion of the American force was destroyed, most of it could still be launched, and there would still have been a disproportion between the capability of the two sides.

On the general point that Ray mentioned—that in the end it was our strong judgment that Khrushchev would not, could not, and should not deploy missiles in Cuba—in an estimate published on September 19th, 1962, the intelligence community concluded that on balance, weighing pros and cons, they believed that the Soviet Union would not deploy missiles in Cuba.[61] Even after that estimate proved to be an error, one of the chief CIA estimators still insisted we weren't wrong; it was *Khrushchev* who was wrong, and who had made the mistake.

TROYANOVSKY: Mr. McNamara wanted to add something.

McNAMARA: Mr. Chairman, I know we all want to leave, but I want to end this session on a humorous note. I think we've had an extraordinarily interesting and important statement from the president, and I'm very grateful to him for taking the time to sit in these meetings and then respond as he did. And I'm very much looking forward to his further statement tomorrow. But on a humorous note, and as a partial answer to Sergei, Ray Garthoff is absolutely correct in his recollection of when we realized there *was* a missile gap, but that it was in the reverse direction. The political campaign that culminated in President Kennedy's election in November 1960 was fought in part on the missile gap. So, when I became secretary of defense on the 20th of January, I thought that my first job was to appraise that missile gap and eliminate it. So my deputy and I spent, I'd say, fifty percent of our time for the first three weeks on the missile gap, and we discovered that there was indeed a gap, but the U.S. had superiority and the Soviets were inferior—quite the opposite of what had been contended during the campaign. Well, this was both good and bad news, in one sense. It was good in the sense that we were stronger. It was bad in the sense that we had a hell of a lot of explaining to do if anybody ever found out about it. So three weeks after I'd been inaugurated, my public affairs officer, Arthur Sylvester, came to me, and he said, "Bob, you haven't met the Pentagon press." I said, "I'm not ready to, Arthur; my God, I come from the auto industry. I don't know a damn thing about this place." "No, no," he said, "they are great people; you come and meet them." So we met them in a room like this, about half this size, with the door closed, at 1:30 in the afternoon. I understood this was all off the record. The first question was, "Mr. Secretary, you've been secretary three weeks; what have you learned about the missile gap?" "Oh," I said, "I've learned there isn't any, or if there is, it's in our favor." They beat down the door! The room emptied right away! [Laughter.] And I'm not exaggerating: the late afternoon edition of *The Washington Star* said, "McNamara declares no missile gap." The next day, Senator Dirksen,* at the Senate, asked for President Kennedy's resignation on the grounds that he won the election on false pretenses. So I went to see Kennedy, and I said, "My God, Mr. President, you brought me down here. I came down here to help you, and all I've done is to destroy the foundation of your election. I will resign." He said, "Hell, Bob, we all make mistakes; goodbye." [Laughter.] So that was the end of the missile gap, roughly in mid-February 1961.

TROYANOVSKY: Thank you, would you like to add anything else? I think that we still have time.

CASTRO: No, no, just a question. Mr. McNamara, when was the nuclear balance achieved—the nuclear balance that has been so much discussed in recent years in the negotiations between the United States and the USSR?

McNAMARA: Mr. President, some time I hope you and I can talk about this at greater length. It's a very important question. I discussed it with several Soviets roughly in 1983, and I said this in reply—we were defining parity, deterrence, sufficiency and so on; "balance"—and I said to them in response to one of them who asked me that exact question: "I can't tell you when nuclear balance was achieved, if by 'balance' you mean the term 'parity,' if you will. But I can tell you when it existed"—in this respect, I differ somewhat from Ray Cline's views expressed this morning; and for those of you who weren't present at previous meetings, we've had long debates about this. But I said this, Mr. President: that I believed parity existed in October 1962, in the following sense—and this is why I have never felt that the movement of the missiles into Cuba changed the strategic balance, because parity existed before the missiles were put into Cuba. There was a gross imbalance in numbers. We estimated—I think probably we overesti-

---

*Sen. Everett Dirksen (R-Illinois).

mated the total number of Soviet strategic nuclear warheads—but we estimated that we had roughly 5,000 to the Soviets' 300. How can I possibly say parity existed? Because we in the U.S., contrary to what the Soviets believed—and they had reason for their belief, but they were in error—contrary to what they believed, we did not believe we had a first strike capability. We did not believe prior to the missile crisis or during the missile crisis, when it was a question that had to be considered—Kennedy and I did not believe—that we could launch our 5,000 warheads against the Soviet Union and destroy a sufficient number of what we thought were 300 (perhaps less) so that the number remaining could not inflict unacceptable damage on us. And, therefore, neither Kennedy nor I believed before the missiles were emplaced in Cuba that we had a first strike capability. Now, the Soviets might have thought we did, and if they thought that, they might have acted to try to change our thinking. But we did not have a first strike capability before the missiles were placed in Cuba.

We did not have a first strike capability, but we had confidence in our deterrent. We believed that our 5,000 warheads would deter the Soviets from ever initiating the use of their 300 in a first strike. So we believed we were deterring them. After they put the missiles in Cuba, we certainly didn't have a first strike capability. We hadn't had it before; we clearly didn't have it afterwards. But after the missiles were emplaced in Cuba, we continued to have complete confidence that we were deterring a Soviet nuclear first strike, because of the tremendous imbalance. I know how absurd this sounds, in a sense. It sounds absurd to say that we had a "balance" in October '62 when we had 5,000 and they had 300. But in terms of strategic theory, in terms of strategic deterrence, a balance did exist. Thank you, sir.

TROYANOVSKY: Thank you. . . .

DIRTY WARS:
"What, are we living in 1962, or 1992?"

To this point, discussion in the conference has been about issues which are mainly of historical interest: details of the Soviet deployment, the U-2 shoot-down, the November 1962 negotiations related to removal of the Il-28 bombers, and what the CIA knew, and when they knew it, about Soviet nuclear capability. For the most part, therefore, the participants, including Fidel Castro, have discussed the topics with self-conscious objectivity and detachment that is notable, considering the political tensions that now exist between the Russians and Cubans, as well as between the Cubans and Americans. If anyone has appeared thus far to be carrying a chip on his shoulder, it has been General Gribkov, who at times seems to some of the Americans to be a bit too enthusiastic to prove his undying loyalty to the Cuban Revolution and his universal skepticism toward anything said by the Americans, and General Titov, who seems more interested in swearing affidavits than in having a frank historical discussion. For the most part, however, the veterans have conducted themselves not much differently from the scholars, probing politely, answering generously, without any obvious attempt to discredit the questioner or presenter. Much of the time it has seemed as friendly an exercise as a game of "three-cornered catch."

All this will now change, as the discussion is moved by the American side—chiefly by Edwin Martin, the Kennedy State Department's assistant secretary for inter-American affairs—to specifically U.S.-Cuban issues that ignited the crisis, many of which remain unresolved. The interventions will slide precipitously to the frontier of incivility, as the discussion moves to the heart of what radically divides the United States and Cuba. These issues include U.S. hostility to Cuba (considered "defensive" by the United States); Cuba's support for revolutionary governments and insurgencies in Latin America (which the United States calls "subversion"); and the internal Cuban situation with regard to human rights (which the United States maintains violates Cubans' civil rights on a massive scale).

As we begin to discuss these perennially divisive U.S.-Cuban bilateral issues, it is difficult to escape the impression that, whereas in a discussion of the triangular U.S.-Soviet-Cuban dimensions of the crisis, in which history is being used in various ways by representatives of the three countries, in a discussion of U.S.-Cuban bilateral issues history is, in a sense, using the participants. The "history" is still very much with them. Only with considerable effort can they escape its clutches sufficiently to put it to use. We have entered a time warp. Thus Fidel Castro will say, when at last he can no longer listen to the discussion with equanimity, "I've listened to interventions such as the one by Mr. Martin, and I say, 'What, are we living in 1962, or 1992?' "

Recent events have conspired to transform the conference room into a hothouse of Cuban resentment on just the issues to which Martin will refer. The remaining Kennedy-Khrushchev crisis letters have just been released, and they seem to suggest that, in the absence of Cuban acquiescence to on-site inspection, the Kennedy administration's pledge not to invade Cuba never came into force.[62] Furthermore, just a few weeks earlier, the State Department released the so-called New York documents, which show decisively that President Kennedy's negotiating instructions to the New York team, led by Adlai Stevenson and John McCloy, required adequate inspection guarantees as a quid pro quo for the U.S. non-invasion pledge.[63]

As soon as the content of these documents became known, hundreds of Cuban exiles lined up at the Washington, D.C., headquarters of Radio Martí (the U.S. Information Agency's anti-Castro station broadcast to Cuba) to sign a petition requesting assistance from the Bush administration for "an invasion of Cuba."[64] The Cuban government's response has been predictably twofold: they asserted that there *was* a firm pledge not to invade Cuba, but, in any case, they would fight "to the last drop of blood" to defend Cuba from a U.S. (or U.S.-backed) invasion.[65] We on the U.S. delegation thus began to understand what the Cubans mean when they say, as they often do, that the October crisis is unresolved.

On 8 January, the day before the first official session of the conference, three Cuban exiles from South Florida stood on trial before a "People's Court" in Havana.[66] Cuban police had captured them with over a thousand pounds of *plastique* explosives as they tried to land in a rubber raft on the north coast of Cuba. This was precisely the kind of "invasion" of Cuba the exiles had pressured the Bush administration to sanction, and though the State Department disavowed the landing, it did so in a manner guaranteed to infuriate the Cubans: by attaching to their condemnation of the "invasion" a demand that the Cubans treat the invaders humanely.[67] Cuba executed one of the three infiltrators and gave the other two thirty-year prison sentences.

Finally, on 9 January, just before the first session of the conference was to begin, a family attempting to steal a boat with which to escape to Florida murdered four guards in a Havana marina. The next day, over 100,000 Cubans gathered in Revolution Square to mourn the victims. Fidel Castro did not attend, choosing instead to participate in the conference. But his brother, Defense Minister Raúl Castro, gave a speech blaming the murders on groups in Cuba and the United States. He warned that these "counterrevolutionaries" would not "have better luck than that of their predecessors in the 1960s."[68] He also threatened to reinstate the revolutionary tribunals by which the triumphant revolutionaries had sentenced many of their enemies to death in the 1960s. The headline on 10 January in *Granma,* the Communist Party daily, read, in bold red letters, "DEATH WILL BE MET WITH DEATH."

Such is the context in which Edwin Martin introduces into the discussion—and seeks to *justify*—various attempts during the Kennedy administration to limit Cuban influence and to destroy the Castro regime. Ed Martin seems to us to be the ideal man to recount the efforts of the Kennedy administration to isolate Cuba in the Organization of American States (OAS), to combat Cuban "subversion" in the hemisphere, and to build hemispheric solidarity in favor of the administration's response to the discovery of Soviet missiles in Cuba. Mild-mannered, a speaker of fluent Spanish with broad experience in Latin America, Martin presents his summary of U.S.-Cuban issues related to the missile crisis quite matter-of-factly, devoid of smugness or defensiveness of any kind. He has been asked, in effect, to step back into the flow of events in 1961–62 and tell it as it was, a task made easier and more accurate by his having a book in progress titled *Kennedy and Latin America.* So it is that Martin explains to our Cuban colleagues the various ways in which the United States tried to make good its intention to do as much damage as possible to Cuba, diplomatically and economically.

While Martin aims simply to remind the participants of a few facts, we soon discover that the "facts" he presents are vigorously disputed by the Cubans, who deeply resent his presentation. We joke afterwards with him about his being the "Mr. Magoo" of the U.S. delegation, after the cartoon character of a generation ago who often left in his wake a good deal of turmoil, of which he meant to produce none, and of which he was often serenely unaware.

During a long private meeting the evening before, the members of the American delegation gathered together at McNamara's villa in an attempt to anticipate the Cuban reaction to Martin's forthcoming statement. We had two clues: Fidel Castro's temperate, informed discussion in the conference thus far; and Raúl Castro's blood-curdling, saber-rattling speech. We were reminded of President Kennedy's comment, ending the U.S. discussion of the missile crisis late in the evening on "Black Saturday," 27 October 1962. "Now," he said, "it can go either way."[69] We agreed at the conclusion of our meeting that one way will lead us quickly and decisively to walk out of the conference. We would not submit to a harangue from Castro about the sins of the Kennedy administration. We called that "Raúl's Way."[70] The other— "Fidel's Way," in the lexicon of the moment—would, we believed, yield a deeper mutual comprehension of U.S.-Cuban decision making leading to the missile crisis and (to the considerable extent to which those issues remain salient) to a clearer notion of the present obstacles to U.S.-Cuban rapprochement.

TROYANOVSKY: . . . It was suggested that the question-and-answer period come after the general presentation, not after each speaker. If no one objects, I think this is the way we are going to do it. I believe the first speaker on the U.S. side is going to be General Smith, am I right? [Edwin Martin raises his hand.] Mr. Martin, you have the floor, sir.

MARTIN: Thank you, Mr. Chairman. Commander Castro, and others here who have been very much involved in the Cuban missile crisis: I was at that time the assistant secretary of state for Latin America, and a participant in the ExComm. I have not been at the previous conferences for various reasons, so I'm not sure how much of what I will say is brand-new. But I do have two general comments that I would like to make.

There is, of course, a lot of controversy, I believe, over what the U.S. intentions were which might have justified the Soviet movement of forces into Cuba on a large scale in the latter part of 1962. I think I was fairly close to U.S. thinking in this matter and, regularly, President Kennedy and Secretary of State Rusk expressed the view that our policy had two purposes. One was to do as much damage as we could by trade restrictions to the Cuban economy, preventing trade with Cuba by our friends, thereby increasing the cost to the Soviet Union, and to some extent the other bloc countries in Eastern Europe, of supporting Castro and his regime in Cuba. At the same time, we were doing everything we could to diminish and curtail the impact of Cuba and its Soviet friend in the Latin American countries in their efforts to increase the power of the communist parties and other various elements which would like to upset the governments in the other countries, and make them additional allies of the Soviet Union in the Western Hemisphere. We felt that if we could be successful on those two paths, the Soviets would be forced to calculate that their assistance and support for Cuba wasn't worth its cost, and they would cut off their support and relations with Cuba. The basis for our policy subsequent to the missile crisis in dealing with our relations with Cuba and the Soviet Union in this hemisphere was nonmilitary and essentially economic.

The second general point I would like to make was mentioned yesterday. I found that there was a great deal of importance attached in the United States to our militarily weak position in West Berlin, and we had a considerable controversy at the time with the Soviet Union over our relations with West Berlin. West Berlin was not just ninety miles away from the U.S., as Cuba was, but was surrounded directly by Soviet, or Soviet allied, forces. We were very vulnerable there, if there was a desire to retaliate or to make threats that would persuade us not to take action against Cuba. I think that needs to be kept in mind, because it did come up rather often in our considerations of what action to take against Cuba, and was certainly a deterrent to the military option at the time we were making our choices in that first week of ExComm.

Now, I've been asked to talk broadly about how we managed to get unanimous support from the countries of Latin America for the quarantine on the Tuesday [23 October 1962], when the OAS Council met on this subject, following Kennedy's speech the night before and his presentation of the pictures of the missile locations in Cuba. The historical background to this is important. There is a long tradition in many of the Latin American countries—and a very strong one in the U.S.—to prevent further European influence and infiltration into the Western Hemisphere. The people came from there, but they'd declared their independence, often by military action. There were some actions taken in the latter part of the nineteenth century and into the twentieth century by European countries to whom other countries owed money, and for other reasons, and the U.S. took military actions on a small scale to prevent further European influence.[71] So that was a background which became important in the Cuba situation, when the close Soviet-Cuban connections were clear, and it was something that influenced the views of many of the Latin American countries as well as the people and government of the United States.

Furthermore, there was in most of the Latin American countries, although not all, a very strong opposition to Soviet communism. The Soviet Union had made clear publicly that their intention and expectation was to convert the world to communism, and that they would be pushing for that everywhere. And they certainly were in a number of continents, not just here. But when Cuba became clearly an agent of the Soviet Union in doing this, this increased greatly the concern of Latin America about a communist regime in Cuba.

This started in '60–'61 and led to a meeting, in January of 1962, of the OAS foreign ministers in Punta del Este, to consider what action to take to restrict the capacity of Cuba as a Soviet agent to influence the political control of the countries of Latin America. At that meeting there were a number of countries which did not feel as concerned as others, but we were able to get fourteen votes—the two-thirds majority—to pass resolutions requesting countries—not *insisting*, but *requesting* countries—to cut off diplomatic relations with Cuba, and to institute trade restrictions with Cuba. There were a number of countries, including large ones like Mexico and Brazil, which were still rather leftist-oriented, and not so worried about communist regimes, and they were not willing to accept this. Usually on the various resolutions they abstained rather than voting "no," but some did vote "no."

Then, in the summer of 1962, as has been described here, the Soviets started putting in a large volume of munitions and war equipment into Cuba. This aroused a very substantive alarm as to what capacity that might give Cuba to intervene militarily. They had done so on a modest scale in the Dominican Republic and Venezuela, and we were concerned that this would give them the capacity to do it on a much larger scale. We were also concerned that it might permit them to train, as they were doing, very many of the young communists, often university students from Latin America—as Commander Castro had been—on the importance and value of communism in solving their domestic problems, and also allow Cuba to provide them with some types of equipment to help them create disorder in their countries and arouse more support for their activities. So, that was a problem which that meeting addressed. But when we saw the much larger amount of equipment that was being sent here, it seemed to us that we could not be sure that it would be defensive only, and—if not against the U.S.—it might be used offensively against other Latin American countries, of which there were a number with fairly weak military power surrounding the Caribbean and close to Cuba.

Therefore, President Kennedy gave a speech pointing out these problems, and indicating what the U.S. would not stand for.[72] And at the annual meeting of the General Assembly of the United Nations in the latter part of September, attended usually by foreign ministers, Secretary Rusk—and I was with him—had three meetings with groups of Latin American countries to discuss this problem, on a very informal basis. They agreed to continue the discussion on a somewhat more formal basis by having an informal meeting of the OAS Council, with the ministers attending who were in the United States for the U.N. meeting, on October 2nd and 3rd.

They met in Washington, chaired by Secretary Rusk. They had lunch with President Kennedy, and they issued a press release describing their concern about the buildup of military power in Cuba, which was going on with the help of the Soviet Union, and the increased activity of the Soviet Union in their countries which this might cause.[73] The vote for that press release was unanimous; there was no dissent at all. And several paragraphs from that press release, justifying their alarm at what was going on, were copied in the press release issued after the OAS meeting.

Now, the president, as you know, had made his speech on Monday night [22 October 1962], and showed pictures of what was going on in Cuba. In advance of that, we had notified our ambassadors early Sunday of our position, and told them what we were going to ask them to do when they got a cable that said "go." They were to present a copy of the speech that the president was going to make to the foreign minister, or the top official in the foreign ministry, and to ask for an appointment in the latter part of the afternoon of Monday with the president of the country, or the top chief executive who was in town. So these other countries were prepared at home, as well as in Washington, for what was going to come up.

At seven o'clock, the president made his speech, and all the ambassadors were there. After the speech, I met with the ambassadors to talk about the meeting the next day of the OAS Council—which couldn't be a meeting of ministers on such short notice—and the action we were calling on them to take. We found that they were on the whole very sympathetic, in light of the evidence that we had presented of the movement of equipment into Cuba.

We met the next morning. Secretary Rusk made a very good speech about our purposes and efforts, and there was considerable discussion back and forth, so that the vote was not taken till after a noon adjournment. During the noon break we were a little concerned about the two big countries that had been hesitant at the January meeting: Brazil and Mexico. In the case of Mexico, the president was touring the Far East, but we finally got our material to him—half of it in Manila as he was getting on a plane, and the other half in Hawaii as he was getting off. It was presented to him by the general commanding the U.S. Pacific forces in Hawaii. And when we took a vote in the latter part of the afternoon, we had a favorable vote on the resolution that we had proposed, except for two countries. The problem there was largely a communications one, because secure telephone conversations were not easily available in several of the countries. However, after the vote had been taken, the representative, the ambassador from Peru, got his instructions to vote "yes." The ambassador of Bolivia did not, but he voted "yes" anyway, and we tried to see that he wasn't punished for voting without instructions—and he was not. It was just a communications problem, not a policy question, that forced him to vote without instructions. But, as a result, we had unanimous support from the OAS to take the actions that involved the quarantine. This support was rather unusual for us, but the real basis for it, I think, was that we were not voting against Cuba; we were voting against the Soviet Union. That is quite a different story in the Western Hemisphere, which has a certain degree of solidarity among its countries, but is very much alienated from the European scene. This brought political respect.

The resolution also called for subsequent action, and I had an informal meeting with the OAS ambassadors in Washington on the 19th of November to consider having a ministerial meeting on very short notice to extend our action beyond the quarantine, because of the failure to reach agreement with the Soviet Union on the demands contained in our letter. It was only when we got the letter on the 20th, accepting the removal of the [Il-28] airplanes, that we were able to cancel that meeting. But we were prepared and did still have, I believe— I'm sure—unanimous support for further action if that became necessary. The action which was taken, of course, was a modest quarantine, not involving firing guns or weapons of any sort. But what should have happened later on is hard to say.

Anyway, that's the basic pattern of our collaboration with the Latin American countries, which was, I think, helpful in securing a peaceful solution to what could have been a very difficult problem.

Now, of course, it didn't end Cuban subversive activities in Latin America, which continued on a very substantial scale, including unloading a large amount of weapons on the coast of Venezuela the next year, and other steps which required a reaction. But at least we did not have a U.S.-Soviet confrontation to deal with subsequently. . . .

In looking back at mistakes that were made in handling this problem, it occurred to me that on that Monday night, I delivered a speech to the annual dinner of the Washington Newspaper Correspondents Association, on the Cuba situation. It was cleared carefully with Defense, CIA, and State, and my theme was that there was no chance that the Soviets would take the risks involved in placing nuclear weapons in Cuba. They had not done so in the adjacent Eastern European countries, which were both close and had long-standing fellow communist regimes, so they wouldn't take any chance with doing it as far away as Cuba. I also addressed the question of the Turkey analogy, and pointed out some basic differences in case they were put there.

After the speech we had a question-and-answer period, and about half-way through that, I was told that there was a phone call that I had to take. The phone message was: "We have seen those things. Come to a meeting in the president's office at ten o'clock tomorrow morning." And I had to go back and answer on the basis of my speech, not my telephone call.

TROYANOVSKY: . . . Who else would like to speak, address a question? Go ahead, please.

MIKOYAN: . . . I think that what Mr. Martin had said on the causes and consequences was somewhat confused chronologically. He said that the increase of Soviet armed forces in Cuba in the summer of 1962 and other actions had alarmed the Americans, and they began to organize and mobilize themselves and the OAS as a result. I think it was quite the other way around. In January 1962, Cuba was excluded from the OAS at the Punta del Este meeting. This action was assessed by Cuba and by the USSR as a diplomatic preparation for a forthcoming invasion or aggression, and this in turn led to the increased Soviet military presence in Cuba. . . .

MARTIN: . . . On the question of why the Soviets put the weapons into Cuba in '62, I can understand that they might feel that the action of the OAS in trade-related matters might be the start of a harsher approach to Cuba that would involve military action. However, our feeling was that the trade and other economic and political isolation measures were designed primarily to *avoid* the necessity, later on, of military action. And we saw them in those terms. We just did not see a justification for this additional Soviet military force. I think it's not uncommon in the world in general to have difficulty in deciding whether a military force is intended to be used offensively or defensively. There is a considerable amount of ambiguity in that matter, and one has to be sure one can protect adequately one's own interests, if the intentions should, for some reason, sometimes change from defensive to offensive. Thank you.

THE HAVANA CONFERENCE • 147

CUBA AT WAR
"[T]he intention of the United States . . . was the total annihilation of Cuba"

Ed Martin's overall theme was that there existed a "basic pattern of collaboration" between the United States and Latin American countries, a contention that is thoroughly repudiated by Carlos Lechuga, who was Cuba's ambassador to the OAS during part of the Kennedy period. There was no "collaboration," according to Lechuga. Instead, he recalls, the United States bullied its Latin American neighbors and, when necessary, bought the votes it needed to push through anti-Castro resolutions. The Alliance for Progress, much touted by the Kennedy administration as a plan for the reconstruction of Latin America, was, according to Lechuga, in reality nothing more than bribery money with which to keep poor Latin American countries anti-communist and (thus) anti-Cuban.

Martin denies this. Martin also accuses the Cubans of having initiated such a substantial program of subverting Latin American governments that the United States simply had to respond, as a responsible member of the hemispheric community. Jorge Risquet joins his colleague Lechuga in implying that Martin's remarks are rubbish. "The OAS," says Risquet, was the U.S. "Ministry of Colonies." The Cubans thus say, in effect, that Martin has lied when he denied that the United States bribed and threatened Latin American countries. The temperature of the discussion has risen suddenly and dramatically.

It reaches the boiling point with the response to Martin by Gen. Fabian Escalante, vice-minister of the interior. Seeming to the U.S. participants to assume the role of prosecuting attorney, Escalante, with ostentatious numerical virtuosity, reels off the sins against Cuba by the Kennedy administration: "5,780 acts of sabotage in Cuba"; "716 occasions . . . " and so on. As he did at the previous conference in Antigua, Escalante concludes by asserting that Operation Mongoose, far from being the minor irritant the Kennedy administration would like everyone to believe it was, actually constituted "a call for generalized war," the goal of which "went far beyond economic strangulation: it was the total annihilation of Cuba."

Escalante's self-righteous performance reminds several of us of a visit we paid in May 1989 to the newly built Museum of State Security in Havana, an institution consisting of room after room of relics putatively captured from CIA-backed infiltrators. During our tour the director, enumerating the gory details of each event depicted in the many exhibits, worked himself up into a frenzy of anti-American rhetoric, and finally blurted out, "So, how does it make you feel to know that your country is guilty of such terrible crimes against Cuba?" In truth, we felt somewhat embarrassed—for the United States, which significantly aggravated human suffering in Cuba through a shortsighted and ill-informed policy of subversion; and for Cuba, for whom the hostility of the CIA was so psychologically and politically valuable that if legitimate relics could not be found to fill the museum, obvious fakes would do.* We simply thanked the director for his hospitality and walked away; after all, the director had accused us, *personally*, of nothing. But on 10 January 1992, Lechuga, Risquet, and Escalante did, in effect, point their fingers at the veterans of the U.S. delegation and pronounce them "guilty as charged," without showing the slightest interest in discussing Cuba's analogous activities, to which (as Martin's presentation made clear) the United States believed it was responding.

TROYANOVSKY: Thank you. Mr. Lechuga, from the Cuban delegation, has the floor.

CARLOS LECHUGA: I wanted to remark on the comment made by Mr. Martin. His comments give the impression that the whole movement of the OAS and the Latin American governments against Cuba during those years was the result of a tradition in Latin America to avoid European intervention. History is different.

I was a witness to this, because I was ambassador in the OAS at the time, and I know that many of these countries in Latin America moved against Cuba at OAS meetings as a result of different pressures from the United States—economic pressures, friendly pressures, political pressures, and of course we don't deny that there were governments who needed no pressure at all because they were for various reasons enemies of the Cuban Revolution. However, at the Santiago de Chile meeting, during the Eisenhower administration [August 1959], as well as at the Costa Rica meeting [August 1960],[74] and then

---

*Among the more obvious and comical forgeries we encountered was a "captured CIA operative's photo identity card" with the words "SECRET AGENT" emblazoned across the top in bold letters; and a "New York City Police Department Report" on the activities of a member of the Cuban exile group Alpha 66 clearly written by a native Spanish speaker but signed with an Irish name.

the last meeting at Punta del Este, when Cuba was expelled from the OAS—all this movement was essentially due to the diplomatic and general pressures of the United States. It was not a spontaneous action to avoid a European infiltration into Latin America or anything of the sort.

At the Antigua meeting, I quoted the letters from [Sen.] Wayne Morse [D-Oregon] and from [Sen. Bourke B.] Hickenlooper [R-Iowa] who were at the [Punta del Este] meeting. They sent a report to the Senate Foreign Relations Committee, and these two senators openly stated in their report that the meeting was closely linked to the Alliance for Progress; in other words, the money that the Latin American governments were being offered to vote against Cuba was money that would come through the Alliance for Progress. This was in addition to a scandal at the conference when the Haitian vote was openly bought. They were part of a group of countries that included Brazil, Mexico, Argentina, Chile, Bolivia and Ecuador that did not agree with the U.S. petition to punish Cuba, and the U.S. managed to get Haiti out of this group by buying the Haitian ambassador. This was done openly; everybody knew about it.

I simply wanted to be objective. It is not a question of a tradition against European infiltration; it was due to the maneuvers of the United States. I'm not saying anything new, but I would like to be precise on historic truth.

And by the way, when I heard that Mr. Martin was coming to this meeting, I looked and found something very curious in a book referring to a speech by Edwin Martin in Los Angeles in 1963, where he said that in eighteen months as under secretary, his staff devoted one-third of their time to Cuba, and they were surprised that they were devoting so much time "to a small island of seven million people, when the responsibility of his office was to make and implement policy for twenty-two countries in one of the most important strategic areas of the world for the United States with a population of 200 million inhabitants." That is, Mr. Martin's office was very much concerned—much more than normal—with Cuba, and this was reflected, before and after, in the attitude of many Latin American governments. I simply wanted to make that clarification, to shed light on how the process worked in general. Thank you very much.

TROYANOVSKY: Thank you very much, sir. . . . Mr. Martin, please.

MARTIN: I've been asked two questions. One was, "Didn't the money for the Alliance for Progress have a great deal to do with getting the votes at the January meeting in Punta del Este on Cuba?" I can't say that the Alliance for Progress and its generosity didn't make countries friendly to us, but after the meeting, several countries—a group of countries in Central America—sent us a very strong protest, because we'd made no reduction in our aid to the countries that *didn't* vote with us. In other words, no country was penalized for not voting with us at Punta del Este, and no country was rewarded for voting for us. We did not change the Alliance for Progress on the basis of any country's attitude toward action against Cuba.

Second, Ambassador Lechuga referred to my spending a large portion of my time on Cuba while I was assistant secretary. I would say that it had to be defined broadly. It was Cuba's activities in the countries of Latin America—which were nearly all of them—which we called the "Cold War Program," and which occupied our time. We devoted most of our effort to dealing with that, not to what happened in Cuba itself. Cuba did have very extensive programs for destabilizing other countries. Several thousand student-level people were, at any one time, being trained in Cuba in how to go home and carry out activities against the government on behalf of communists and the communist party in their countries. They were also supplied funds, and sometimes weapons, so that we had a major effort on our hands in trying to build up support among the people of the Latin American countries for a democratic system that would be friendly to the United States and to the majority of the countries of the hemisphere. Except for Cuba and, briefly, much later on, Chile, none of the countries was, in fact, communist. What they were doing was trying to take power in those countries on behalf of the communists and, in effect, through Cuba, enhance the Soviet world power position. It was not just Cuba as such, but the whole communist threat in Latin America, that concerned us.

RISQUET: I will say a few words about Mr. Martin's comments, to conclude with this item regarding the OAS. I am not a career diplomat like Comrade Lechuga, so I'm going to say things straightforwardly.

For many years, the OAS was the Ministry of Colonies of the United States. That is a historical reality. And—not necessarily as Martin said—the United States got unusual support from Latin American countries, with the honorable exception of Mexico. I would like to recall that in 1954 there was a meeting of the OAS in Caracas, convened by the United States, to place Guatemala in the dock. Guatemala's was not a communist regime, but a democratic regime; but it had committed the enormous crime of implementing an agrarian reform program, which affected the lands of the powerful United Fruit Company. After the Cuban Revolution, the OAS also sanctioned the criminal action of the United States against the Dominican Republic, although theirs was not a communist regime, or a regime under European influence.

I would also like to remind you that if they had been so consistent with the Monroe Doctrine, preventing foreign influence or extracontinental influence in Latin America, the United States should have supported Argentina against the British in their just claims over the Malvinas Islands.[75]

Thank you. That was my comment.

TROYANOVSKY: I have on my list many requests for the floor. Perhaps we should now give the floor to Comrade Escalante, and then have a recess.

FABIAN ESCALANTE: Actually, I wanted to make a number of comments. This morning Mr. Martin has twice referred to U.S. intentions in early 1962 with regard to Cuba. He summarized his ideas by saying that the strategy contained two major objectives: doing as much harm as possible to the Cuban economy, and preventing the reverberation of the Cuban Revolution in Latin America. He also said that the military option had been virtually discarded. If that is so, we would have to then consider that all the steps that Cuba took during 1962, and which it had taken in the end of 1961—including the Cuban-Soviet agreement to deploy missiles in Cuba—were practically warmongering actions. We were provoking a global confrontation when the United States did not harbor these intentions. If those intentions existed before the Bay of Pigs—which everybody agrees was a great mistake—then it has been claimed here that the United States had abandoned these intentions afterwards. Well, many things have been said about this, but I would like to make a few observations and provide some information.

At the Antigua meeting, we provided some data—I'm not going to repeat them, of course—but I would like to refer to one in particular. From January to August 1962, there were 5,780 acts of sabotage in Cuba—terrorist and subversive actions—of which, on 716 occasions, there was damage done to important economic and social objectives. All of this, of course, was done with U.S.-supplied matériel and bombs, and by infiltration teams trained in the United States. These were acts of supreme hostility. Here I have a detailed chronology [waves booklet]—we explained this in Antigua. We could provide many details of how Cuban security bodies perceived the U.S. attitude. We thought that this was not merely a war of attrition, but that this war of attrition was part of a strategy that had been adopted, the first stage in a process intended to deal the revolution a final fatal blow.

I said that I have a chronology here, based on information published in the United States, and documents that you all know. The first document produced by Operation Mongoose, dated January 18, states that its objective was to overthrow the Cuban government.[76] As you all know, Mongoose was the product of the Special Group (Augmented) of the National Security Council that was set up in November 1961. On January 19th, there was a meeting in Attorney General Robert Kennedy's office. This meeting was attended by Richard Helms, second-in-command at the CIA. His aide [George McManus] took some notes which were later published. They said, "Conclusion overthrow of Castro is possible. . . . a solution to the Cuban problem today carried top priority in U.S. Gov[ernment]. No time, money, effort—or manpower is to be spared. Yesterday . . . the president indicated to [Robert Kennedy] that the final chapter had not been written—it's got to be done and will be done."[77]

You see, Mongoose was not merely a CIA endeavor. That would be false. It was an effort backed by the U.S. administration, in which all U.S. agencies participated. Of course, the CIA played a role, as did the Department of Defense.[78]

In the final document, adopted by President Kennedy on March 16th—that is, the "Guidelines for Operation Mongoose"—there are two very important points: "(a) In undertaking to cause the overthrow of the Castro government, the U.S. will make maximum use of indigenous resources, internal and external, but recognizes that final success will require decisive U.S. military intervention. (b) Such indigenous resources as are developed will be used to prepare for and justify this intervention, and thereafter to facilitate and support it."[79] This was a call for generalized war.

In April of that year, as has been published in several studies carried out in the United States, a special group was to be dispatched to Cuba in order to orchestrate Fidel Castro's murder. In July there was a contingency plan prepared because "serious" information had been received that in Cuba a popular uprising was being generated without the aid of the United States, and they had to be ready so that if that popular rebellion developed the United States could send over troops and deal the final blow. This idea, this conception, this view, is based on a doctrine prepared by the Special Group (Augmented) of the

National Security Council. At the Bay of Pigs, the United States sought to overthrow the Cuban government by landing a mercenary brigade in Cuba, ignoring the elements that they had here. But in 1962 the doctrine was different: it was to foster an internal uprising through acts of sabotage, in order to create the subjective and objective conditions which would facilitate collective intervention or direct U.S. intervention (that is, with or without American allies). Mongoose continued.

I would like to make two other comments, because I know that you are familiar with all these facts. The first comment is that during the October crisis—I'm not referring to the Alpha 66 raid on Caibarién, which as a matter of fact was subsidized by the CIA—on October 14th, a ship from the CIA departed for Cuba carrying an infiltration team headed by the chief of the group for infiltration operations at CIA, Miguel Orozco. They landed in Pinar del Río, with the mission of blowing up the Matahambre mines. Later on this team was arrested. In his statement, Miguel Orozco said many things. Of course, when a person is under arrest, he might say anything. But I would like to draw your attention to a particular statement. Miguel Orozco said that, at that moment, the CIA had undertaken a plan which required the recruitment of Cubans. It had two purposes: first, occupying Cayo Romano, on the northern coast of Cuba, in order to establish a provisional counterrevolutionary government—the Miró Cardona government; and, second, to launch an attack, using counterrevolutionary Cuban troops, against Puerto Cabezas, to create the pretext that the revolutionary government was taking revenge on [Nicaraguan president Luis] Somoza [Debayle] for the assistance that he had lent to the Bay of Pigs invasion. In the very midst of the missile crisis, this plan was under way.

Mongoose was suspended, according to a document that we read, in January 1963.[80] But, as you know, for over thirty years U.S. hostility—concrete material hostility; tangible hostility which has cost hundreds and thousands of lives; even bacteriological warfare—has continued. We can provide many, many examples, although we're not going to do that, of course. That is why I wanted to voice my view that the intentions of the United States in 1962—in early 1962— went beyond economic strangulation. That in itself, of course, is terrible, and doesn't just harm the government and the authorities, but the whole people. But the intention of the United States went far beyond economic strangulation: it was the total annihilation of Cuba.

McNAMARA'S CHALLENGE:
"We haven't had one word on that subject"

The anger that the Lechuga-Risquet-Escalante intervention engendered in many U.S. participants can scarcely be exaggerated. This seemed to those of us who had participated in the Antigua conference to be just more of the same stonewalling we had encountered there; more portrayals of Cuba the helpless, blameless victim of mindless U.S. aggression. Several of us on the U.S. delegation, including McNamara, had been aware that this might happen and that he, especially, might be harangued in a kind of mock trial, the spectacle thence being used for domestic political purposes in the Cuban media. In fact, the document cited by Escalante, the U.S. Defense Department's manifesto for Operation Mongoose, was the same document that the Cubans had read aloud to begin their participation in the Moscow conference three years earlier.[81]

McNamara now lays down the gauntlet: Mongoose may have been ill conceived, but the United States felt it had to respond somehow to Cuban dirty wars, Cuban subversion of other governments, and Cuban assaults on the vital interests of the United States. "We haven't had one word on that subject." We then break for lunch, which proves to be a raucous affair. Someone comments about the utter absurdity of the Cuban delegates "playing Little Red Riding Hood and making us out to be the Big Bad Wolf." In Antigua, Cuban stonewalling on these issues had caught us by surprise. We had been unprepared to follow up with detailed questions about Cuban "subversion" in Latin America. But all of us in Havana carried with us a large notebook titled, "Cuban Support for Revolutionary Movements, 1959–1963." It was filled with evidence of Cuban "subversive" activities. None, perhaps, was more striking than the handwritten dedication from Fidel Castro to American journalist Lee Lockwood, for his book of interviews conducted with the Cuban leader in 1965. It reads: *"El deter de todo revolucionario es hacer la Revolución"* ("the duty of the revolutionary is to make revolution").[82] "Castro has been *proud* of Cuba's involvement in this stuff," one of the senior U.S. participants notes at lunch; "this denial is absurd."

We break from lunch having agreed—not all of us enthusiastically, it must be said—to terminate our participation in the conference if the "trial" atmosphere does not end. We will ask Castro pointedly how he discharged his duty as a revolutionary—how, exactly, he and Cuba sought to "make the revolution." As we leave, many of our younger members struggle to keep pace with McNamara, our eldest, back to the conference room.

TROYANOVSKY: We wanted to have a recess, but Mr. McNamara is asking for the floor.

MCNAMARA: Mr. Chairman, I ask your permission for a thirty- or sixty-second intervention in relation to what Minister Escalante has said. As I indicated in my opening statement, I believe Mongoose was reprehensible. I said in Antigua it was stupid. I don't think there is any purpose in going over it today, and I don't wish to try to argue the issue. I want to make only two points. First, it's incorrect for Minister Escalante to say that President Kennedy ever approved the potential use of military force in connection with Mongoose. He never did. Nor did the Chiefs. Nor, I think, did the Special Group [(Augmented)] ever mean to. That does not make Mongoose other than reprehensible, stupid, and I would say irresponsible.

However, the purpose of this meeting, in part, was to understand why otherwise intelligent people—leave me out of it—but otherwise intelligent people engaged in such actions. In a sense, Eisenhower, Jack Kennedy, Robert Kennedy, Dean Rusk, and McGeorge Bundy were all associated with a series of operations which included the Bay of Pigs, Mongoose, and many other equally stupid, reprehensible, and apparently irresponsible actions. Why did a group of intelligent, responsible leaders engage in it? We haven't had one word on that subject. I urge we do so before we break. Thank you.

TROYANOVSKY: Thank you very much. I think we will have our recess now, and we'll meet again at 3:00. Excuse me, ladies and gentlemen, 2:30. Reconvene at 2:30.

U.S. PLANS AND INTENTIONS:
". . . deeper into the military aspects . . ."

So charged do the U.S. participants feel the atmosphere to be that they appear to overreact to the initial request of the session, posed by General Gribkov, "to go a bit deeper into the military aspects." This leads initially to declarations on the part of McNamara, Schlesinger, and General Smith that, while the United States had contingency plans for attacking Cuba, President Kennedy never intended to execute them.

This issue—plans versus intentions—has come up in all five conferences. The documents seem to suggest rather powerfully a concerted U.S. readiness to attack and invade Cuba. Yet oral testimony, together with recently available documentation, leads to no firm conclusion in the matter.[83] But Gribkov, not having been present at previous conferences and thus being relatively unfamiliar with all the heat the issue has generated, turns out to be asking a rather more straightforward question about the military details of the plans. When these are supplied, principally by Garthoff, the general seems satisfied. It also seems likely, however, that Gribkov remains as convinced as ever that the United States intended to invade Cuba, despite the strenuous assertions of McNamara and the other U.S. participants that Kennedy had no such intention.

There follows a lengthy, rather curious intervention by Jorge Enrique Mendoza, director of the Institute of the History of Cuba, and an old associate of Castro's from their days in the Sierra Maestra.[84] Tracing U.S. hostility toward Cuba to roots in the nineteenth century, Mendoza focuses on bombings against civilians carried out during the waning days of the Eisenhower administration. Seated at the far end of the conference room from most of the U.S. delegation, he holds up photographs (which none of us can see) that, he claims, prove his contention. Wayne Smith, who was serving in the U.S. embassy in Havana at the time as a young ambassador's aide, responds with a balanced analysis of the U.S.–Cuba "chicken and egg" problem. It is fruitless, he contends, to try to prove that U.S. (or Cuban) hostility came first and is thus the "cause" of the other's "response."

As Smith is concluding, McNamara is seen writing a note, which he sends down the line of U.S. participants. Some of us are apprehensive, because McNamara was initially skeptical about Wayne Smith's participation owing to his reputation, in some quarters, for being a bit too inclined to see things from the Cuban point of view. Perhaps, we fear, McNamara has just drafted our instructions to walk out. Perhaps Mendoza's meandering, one-sided tirade has put "Maximum Bob" over the edge.[85] But the note reads: "You were right about Wayne. He's excellent." By this time we notice Fidel Castro signaling that he wishes to intervene.

———————————————

TROYANOVSKY: I think we might get on with our meeting. Next on my list I have General Gribkov, to whom I'm going to give the floor.

GRIBKOV: I would like to address a question to the U.S. side. So far, we've been talking about general questions. I am interested in the military side. I fully agree with what McNamara said when he remarked that Mongoose was absurd. But I would like someone from the U.S. side to go a bit deeper into the military aspects.

A great deal has been said. A great deal has been written. It has been said that six months after the Bay of Pigs, in October of 1961, President Kennedy issued secret orders to a group that had been put together for an invasion of Cuba, and that the White House assumed responsibility that this action against Cuba did not exclude military action. As a soldier, I would like to have some further information on those plans. When I spoke, I put all my cards on the table so that there would be no misunderstanding. I hid nothing, and I would ask the U.S. side to give us some of the details on the military angles after the Bay of Pigs—including Mongoose—right up to the crisis; that is, up to October '62. We'd like to hear how the military forces were organized, and how they pursued their military tasks.

TROYANOVSKY: Mr. McNamara?

MCNAMARA: Mr. Chairman, I'm going to ask General Smith in just a second to answer that question. But I wanted to introduce his answer with a statement that addresses one of the words General Gribkov used, and a thought that has been expressed in publications relating to the Cuban missile crisis and some other things: namely, that either President Kennedy issued secret orders to a small group—a group that excluded the secretary of defense and the Chiefs—or, alternatively, that the president and I did not know what the hell was going on in the Defense Department, and that the Defense Department had secret plans to invade, or something or other.

Now, let me tell you, we made lots of mistakes—we as a nation have. We as a nation, in military operations, have made lots of mistakes, and I want to tell you just one thing. No secretary of defense—and certainly not I—can exclude himself from responsibility for those errors. There's nothing—and I mean literally *nothing*—involving any significant military action that did not occur as a result of the decision of the president, through the secretary of defense. I just want to make that clear.

Bill, you go ahead and respond. Oh, Arthur, you wanted to say something first? Okay.

ARTHUR SCHLESINGER: If I may, I'd like to respond directly to General Gribkov's very reasonable questions. What happened was that at the end of November 1961, President Kennedy issued an instruction—not an order—not to the Department of Defense, but to the CIA.

McNAMARA: '61 or '62?

SCHLESINGER: '61. And I quote from that instruction: "to use our available assets to help Cuba overthrow the Communist regime." This was the birth of what became known as Operation Mongoose. Operation Mongoose was put in the hands of a man well known to our friends from the Defense Department: [Brigadier] General [Edward] Lansdale. General Lansdale had been an imaginative and, at one point in his career, an effective kind of covert actions specialist, first in the Philippines, later in Vietnam. He was a man of soaring imagination given to melodramatic fantasies of one sort or another, and he was made head of Operation Mongoose. He came up with a whole collection of ideas in January of 1962, and he presented them to a review group in the intelligence community called the Special Group (Augmented). General Escalante this morning quoted from the meeting held in the attorney general's office in January '62, in which it was said that no time, money, effort or manpower was to be spared to help Operation Mongoose. But the follow-up was the submission of these plans to the Special Group (Augmented), and the Special Group (Augmented) rejected most of the plans. They directed Lansdale instead to make the collection of intelligence a priority. The phrase used was this (and this is a quote): "the immediate collection of intelligence, the immediate priority objectives of U.S. efforts in the coming months."[86] While the Special Group was willing to permit a little concurrent sabotage, the acts there, it told Lansdale, must be inconspicuous and on a scale—and again I quote—"short of those reasonably calculated to inspire a revolt." The Special Group (Augmented) further insisted that sensitive operations—sabotage, for example—would have to be presented in more detail on a case-by-case basis.

In spite of the restraint of the Special Group, Operation Mongoose did a lot of very foolish things. I think the word "stupid" used by Secretary McNamara is perhaps almost an understatement. Nonetheless, this was not a major effort. The idea was that in time maybe this would stir up an internal revolt in Cuba. The documents which have been disclosed by the U.S. government through the Church Committee and elsewhere make clear that this was a marginal operation of the U.S. government, regarded by some people with great dubiety. I would say that my friend Robert Kennedy, the attorney general, in one of his less uncritical moments, let Mongoose get somewhat out of hand. He had a very busy year in 1962 fighting for civil rights and racial justice here and there; so what attention he gave to Operation Mongoose was not very effective, and not very useful, since it was mostly devoted to telling them to do more. But they didn't do very much, and at no point was a military invasion contemplated. The whole theory—Lansdale's whole theory—in Operation Mongoose was to stir up an internal revolt inside Cuba.

McNamara: Yes, that's exactly correct. Now, let me just ask General Smith to comment on the military aspects, because this is a very, very important element—not just for you, General Gribkov, but also, I think, for the comandante. What were Kennedy's instructions, relating to military operations with respect to Cuba?

General Smith: I do not recall after the crisis any specific instructions from President Kennedy, or Secretary McNamara, or anyone, to prepare a specific plan for the invasion of Cuba. I will say that my principal duties lay elsewhere after the crisis. Once the crisis was over in the middle of December of 1962, I personally turned my attention to other things. But I will tell you that the military—the U.S. military—developed contingency plans for an attack on Cuba should that become necessary. As you know, General, we in the military make our living by doing contingency planning. We had contingency plans for the defense of Berlin, we had contingency plans for the defense of Western Europe, we had contingency plans for the defense of the Panama Canal, we had contingency plans for operations against Cuba. If there was a necessity, and we were directed to do so, the military had to be prepared to conduct an air attack, and if necessary, a land attack against Cuba. But that was one of a series of contingency plans with no more attention given to it than others—indeed, *less* than to some other crises. Some of the other possibilities seemed far more likely.

McNamara: May I add just one final word? I can say unequivocally that President Kennedy never expressed to me this belief that the U.S. should invade Cuba—excepting only during the crisis. But except for that period from October 15 to October 28 or shortly thereafter—excepting for that period—President Kennedy never, never, never talked to me about his belief that under certain circumstances we should invade Cuba. The point I began with, and the point I want to end with, is, whatever you may think about civilian control—and Bill will doubly acknowledge this—there was no possibility that there would have been any military operations without my direction or the president's direction. Thank you, sir.

Schlesinger: I might add one more thing, if I may; and that is that if President Kennedy had wanted to invade Cuba, the emplacement of nuclear missiles in Cuba by the Soviet Union would have provided the perfect pretext. In fact, he—President Kennedy—rejected the idea of an invasion of Cuba, even with that pretext, which the world would have held as a perfect justification. Even when that pretext was available to him, he rejected it.

Troyanovsky: You would like to add something, General Gribkov?

Gribkov: I did not get a complete answer to my question. Even in your magazine *Look* there was an outstanding, well-known journalist who quoted the following words: "Six months after the Bay of Pigs in October 1961"—that is, one year before the Cuban crisis—"President Kennedy, still not free of the impact of that crisis, issued a secret order to the Joint Chiefs of Staff to prepare an invasion plan"—I repeat, a plan of invasion—"against Cuba, and that the White House assumed responsibility for using any means to fight against the Cuban people, including militarily."[87] So what I wanted was someone on the U.S. side to deny or tell us about this plan that had been hatched to invade Cuba as far back as October 1961, when the reserves were mobilized and all the infantry troops were ready, and air and naval forces were concentrated. I would like someone to address this military aspect after the Bay of Pigs, and including the Bay of Pigs. I want the purely military aspects. I am not a diplomat. I am not interested in that. I am interested in the military aspects, please.

General Smith: I will tell you quite simply, in October of 1962, as soon as possible after the discovery of Soviet missiles in Cuba, the

United States military was preparing to invade Cuba, because at that point they saw possibly no other alternative but to attack Cuba and to invade. So, if your question was, did the United States military prepare to invade Cuba during the Cuban missile crisis, I can answer that question simply. They were doing everything possible to become ready so they could attack if they were directed by civilian authority. Is that the answer you want?

SCHLESINGER: I think the General is referring to the events of October 1961.

GENERAL SMITH: No, no, he is—

SCHLESINGER: General Gribkov is talking about October '61.

GRIBKOV: Yes, October '61. Beginning from October '61 up until the Cuban crisis.

SCHLESINGER: I don't know what General Gribkov is quoting. But I think that journalist based his belief on that instruction which I read a few moments ago about using all the available effort to overthrow the government of Cuba. This did not contemplate a military invasion, this was covert action. There was no plan, no secret plan. As far as I knew—and I was involved in Latin American affairs in the White House at this period—there was not in October 1961, or at any point, a secret plan for the invasion of Cuba as distinct from contingency plans for an invasion of anything. But there was Operation Mongoose which I've described, and which, I might add, came to an end when, during the Cuban missile crisis, it was discovered that under Operation Mongoose sabotage teams were being sent into Cuba. This was seen to be so irresponsible that Operation Mongoose was brought to an end, though sabotage efforts against the Cuban society continued in 1963.

GRIBKOV: Again, either my question is not clear, or someone is dodging it. In October 1962, in the U.S. administration the talk was not of groups, but of troops—tank divisions, landing troops, infantry, and air troops. This was according to the data we had. And the Chiefs of Staff had been given orders to follow events closely. There were seven divisions ready; some 150,000 reserve troops were mobilized; some 500 aircraft were mobilized; nearly 100 warships. I say, I am a soldier and I understand that this number of ships, aircraft and divisions is not for a diversion; this is for a large military operation. As you were observing us, we also were watching you. We had our intelligence people working on this. There was a very big buildup, and in October that force was assembled. I told you everything I knew about our deployment. I told you what kinds of weapons we had, and even of things that you knew nothing about. So, I would like you to give me those details on the military aspects on your side.

McNamara: Let me make two or three comments. First, the General is absolutely correct about the force buildup. There was an immense force buildup, at least as large as—I would say a little larger than—what he just referred to. But there had been no presidential decision to use that force. Arthur Schlesinger said that if there was ever a time in the past thirty years when we would have been justified in our eyes, and perhaps in the eyes of the world, to invade Cuba, it would have been then. President Kennedy specifically and consciously—and, I think, responsibly—refused to make that decision. You were not present at the first conference in a place called Hawk's Cay about four years ago—we discussed this in Antigua, but more fully at that first meeting, where there were no Soviet or Cuban participants—but we U.S. participants had a heck of an argument amongst ourselves about what President Kennedy would have done had not Khrushchev, on Sunday the 28th, sent the message by radio that he was withdrawing the missiles. I think that's a very interesting question, and it relates indirectly to what you were talking about, General, because not only did President Kennedy not issue an order in October 1961 to prepare a secret plan to use military force against Cuba—that is absolutely incorrect—not only did he not do that, but when we had built up this force, we built it up without drawing up a contingency plan. We called up reserves, we moved people. There was no question that you knew what was going on. Anybody with any brains at all would have understood what was going on. We called people from all over the United States into the southeastern part of the United States: ships, aircraft, men, a tremendous force. But the president had *not* made the decision to use it, and the question became, after the fact—you know, thirty years or so after the fact—what would he have done if Khrushchev had not announced the withdrawal on Sunday?

Now, I am speculating, but I am speculating on my intimate knowledge of his thought process, and it relates to your question. Did he give secret orders? Did he have an intention of invading Cuba? I want to tell you that I am *absolutely convinced* that had Khrushchev not taken those missiles out on Sunday—or announced he was taking them out—Kennedy would not have invaded soon. I don't want to say he never would have invaded. He would not have invaded soon. He and I would have done what I call "tightening the screw on the quarantine." And, sir—I say this without any disrespect, without any hostility—but in a sense what I'm saying is that Kennedy did not want to invade Cuba. He didn't want to invade it on Sunday the 28th, he didn't want to invade it on Monday the 29th, he didn't want to invade it ever, if he could avoid it. And I think—this is all a response to your question— I think we would have tightened the screw on the quarantine. Quite frankly, I think there would have been a repackaging, or a different packaging, of the Jupiter missile withdrawal deal—all designed to try to avoid the invasion of Cuba. That would have been a disastrous thing, not just from the point of view of Cuba, but from the point of view of history, and of the history of the United States.

GARTHOFF: In 1961, a series of military contingency plans of the kind that General Smith and Secretary McNamara were talking about for possible military action against Cuba were prepared. OPLAN 312 was for an air strike; OPLAN 314 was for a subsequent land invasion; later, OPLAN 316 was a variant of 314, based on a shorter time for preparing an invasion force, and so on.[88] Elements of these contingency plans were included in, or taken into account in, arranging some of the normal training exercises which took place during the spring, summer, and fall of 1962. But this is exactly, as has been said, similar to preparing contingency plans, and conducting exercises in accordance with them, of the kind that are carried out by all armies, and covering a wide variety of possible actions, most of which never occur.

In the period after the large Soviet military supply buildup in Cuba had been observed in the summer of 1962, shortly before the missiles were discovered, actions were taken to begin to increase readiness for possible resort to some of these contingency plans for Cuba. After the missiles were discovered, as Secretary McNamara and General Smith have said, there was, of course, a very active effort then undertaken to prepare fully for the possible implementation of those plans. The buildup at that time included one Marine and five U.S. Army divisions—of which two were Airborne. It included a paratroop force larger than the one that had landed in Normandy. The force totalled 100,000 Army and 40,000 Marine combat troops. The Air Force and Navy—the tactical air forces—had 579 combat aircraft ready for action in the immediate area. The Navy had 183 ships, including 8 aircraft carriers on station. The air strike plan called for 1,190 strike sorties on the first day, and potential casualties were estimated at some 18,500 in ten days of combat.

MCNAMARA: U.S. casualties?

GARTHOFF: Yes.

Now, the buildup continued until after the withdrawal of the missiles, and peaked on November 15, just before the resolution of the Il-28 question. But the forces then began standing down and returning to normal station, and so forth. So there's no question: the United States assembled very efficiently a very substantial invasion force in a short time at a moment when it suddenly appeared that the unlikely event of implementing these particular contingency plans might actually arise. But there are two entirely different questions here: the whole question of the contingency plans before and after October 1962, and the actual preparation for implementing variants of those plans during the missile crisis itself.

TROYANOVSKY: [Jorge] Mendoza, please. Oh, excuse me.

CASTRO: Could you please repeat the number of missions on the first day? I couldn't hear you correctly.

GARTHOFF: 1,190.

CASTRO: Translate that. [Pause.] Oh, I thought I had heard 119,000. I thought that a bit exaggerated. [Laughter.] I'm more at ease now.

TROYANOVSKY: Mendoza, please.

JORGE ENRIQUE MENDOZA: After speaking about the October crisis for several hours, one might get the impression that all the historical problems between Cuba and the United States are only those related to this crisis. It would be interesting to explain that problems with the U.S. government were already evident in the period of the Sierra Maestra—that is, before the Cuban Revolution had come into power. We could spend a few minutes explaining this.

However, in fact, these differences between Cuba and the U.S. date back to the nineteenth century, to the theory of the "ripe fruit"—that is, the theory propounded by the U.S. administration of the time which held that Cuba should fall under U.S. domination.[89] It is not by accident that José Martí publicly stated—in a newspaper article—the following: "And once the United States is in Cuba, who will drive it out?"[90] Martí's position is also well known as established in a letter sent to his friend Manuel Mercado in May 1895, in defense of Cuba's independence and sovereignty, for which the Cuban people had been struggling for several decades. Martí expressed his hope to "prevent, by the independence of Cuba, the United States from spreading over the West Indies and falling, with that added weight, upon other lands of our America."[91]

At the beginning of this century, the Platt Amendment was imposed on Cuba. That irritated the most clear-sighted Cubans of ninety years ago. For example, in his diary—in the last entry, dated January 8th, 1899, referring to the intervention of the U.S. Army in Cuba— the commander of Cuba's Liberation Army, Maximo Gomez, wrote that, "because of the U.S. invasion, Cuba is now faced with a terrible situation of poverty and humiliation, because its sovereignty has been curtailed and violated. The day this bizarre situation comes to an end, the Americans will probably leave behind not one iota of friendly feeling." That's what the head of the Cuban Liberation Army wrote.

We—our generation—lived through the events of the Sierra Maestra, while the Batista army received supplies from the United States, and even through the Guantánamo naval base. In May 1958, a secret cell of the 26th of July Movement formed by Cuban workers in the Guantánamo naval base took some pictures of Batista's war planes taking on bombs of all kinds—including napalm bombs. [Waving photograph:] This picture was taken at that time. This is an original picture I have here. It was published by the 26th of July Movement. I would like to read what the 26th of July Movement wrote above this picture. This is the way it was sold in order to collect funds for the movement. It reads, "Planes of the Batista army loading bombs and ammunition at the Caimanera Naval Base in Cuba, bombs that are used to kill Cuban peasants and the people at large. The 26th of July Movement has no other option but to denounce before the people and the world the support of the Washington administration for the dictatorship of Batista and others in America acting behind the backs of the democratic feelings of the admirable U.S people, thereby earning for themselves the already visible repudiation of the peoples of Latin America who love freedom and democracy."

This is another picture taken at the base. Here you see the seal which reads, "The United States." These bombings were quite frequent, particularly in the summer of 1958. Even before the letter written by Commander Fidel Castro which was mentioned yesterday by Mr. McNamara, the bombings were stepped up in May and early June. The first time that Commander-in-Chief Fidel Castro addressed all Cuba through Radio Rebelde in the Sierra Maestra, he denounced the delivery of these weapons to Batista's army. I have a photocopy of the original document drafted by Fidel for his speech. These bombings killed a child, among the many people that they killed. The child's name was Orestes Gutiérrez Peña, and when Commander Fidel described what was happening there, he immediately added, "The United States can see here the use that its friends—the dictators of America—make of the weapons that it supplies for the defense of the continent." This was a speech in April 1958, when Fidel denounced before Latin American public opinion, and that of the whole world—including that of the United States—the supplies and support that were being given to the Batista tyranny.

I would like to refer only to the most salient problems at the time. In the month of May—or, rather, July—U.S. troops left the base and took over the water supply system in Guantánamo. In August, Commander-in-Chief Fidel Castro made a public declaration, read over Radio Rebelde, on the occupation of Cuban soil by the U.S. Navy. There were several points in the speech; I'm just going to mention the first. It read: "The area of the Guantánamo aqueduct is Cuban territory, and should be immediately vacated by U.S. troops." Fortunately, this incident was solved adequately after a few days, and U.S. troops withdrew from the Guantánamo aqueduct and returned to the naval base. But in October, there were other incidents—very serious incidents—of political aggression against the nascent Cuban Revolution. Under the pretext of an incident when two U.S. technicians from Texaco were briefly detained by some guerrillas of the Rebel Army under the command of Captain Fernando Vecino, now the minister of higher education, the State Department convened a press conference of all the journalists accredited in Washington, and the spokesman then, Lincoln White, made very serious accusations against the Rebel Army, against the 26th of July Movement, and against Comrade Fidel. He accused all of them of being kidnappers and of not respecting the civilized laws of war. His words represented a threat to our sovereignty.[92] We heard that on the evening of October 23, 1958, and this provoked a reply by the Rebel Command of the revolutionary movement. An explanation of the events was made, and it was conclusively proved that they had not been kidnapped; that nobody had gone and seized these technicians at home; that there was no demand for their exchange; that they were immediately released; that there was no danger for the troops and for the technicians; and, particularly, that nothing was demanded in exchange. After explaining the situation in Cuba and the incident, the Radio Rebelde editorial concluded by saying, "It is good to warn that Cuba is a free and sovereign country. We want to maintain the best relations of friendship between Cuba and the United States. We would not like to have a conflict erupt between Cuba and the United States, a conflict that could not be solved within reason and within the rights of the people. But if the U.S. State Department continues to allow itself to be dragged into the intrigues of Mr. [Earl T.] Smith"—the ambassador in Havana then—"and Batista, it will make the unjustifiable mistake of leading its country into an act of aggression against Cuba and our sovereignty, and we will defend our sovereignty with honor. There are duties toward our country that we cannot but fulfill. A big and powerful country like the United States is not honored by the words and threats contained in the recent statements by the State Department. Threats are worthy of a cowardly and submissive people, but not for men who are willing to die defending their people."

Of course, the Cuban Revolution during the guerrilla war did not have difficulties only with the U.S. administration. We recall the time when England sold tanks and planes to Batista's army. At the time it was necessary to issue—to pass a law against those sales. I have here what Fidel drafted. I have a photocopy of this law, "Law No. 4 of the Sierra Maestra, on the English aggression against the people of Cuba." So the Cuban Revolution, from very early on, when it had not yet come to power, had to use its legitimate rights to defend the independence and sovereignty of the country in the face of the U.S. administration and other governments that had followed that example.

I wanted to recall these events among others in an effort to clarify in this meeting that the incidents that are being discussed around the October crisis have historical antecedents that date back over a century. Thank you.

TROYANOVSKY: Thank you very much. Mr. Wayne Smith, would you like to answer?

WAYNE SMITH: I was in the embassy. I was not the Smith that Mr. Mendoza has referred to, but I was in the embassy, and I say the following not to excuse or defend some U.S. actions, but simply to explain.

I'm glad that Mr. Mendoza has raised these issues and put them in historical context, because I think we are to some extent talking about the chicken and the egg—namely, whose hostility came first. In fact, the relationship—something of an adversarial relationship—between the two countries goes all the way back to the earliest days of our republic, when we saw Cuba as the most strategically important piece of territory outside the limits of the United States. The Gulf of Mexico was vital to the United States. The interior of the United States emptied out through the Mississippi River and the port of New Orleans. We had to have control of the Gulf, and there was Cuba, like a cork in the bottle of the Gulf of Mexico. It was felt that so long as Spain controlled Cuba—Spain being a weak nation in Europe—it was tolerable, but that no other country could control Cuba. Thus the no-transfer resolution of 1825. As for this attitude, it was quite inevitable that Cuban leaders, of course, would seek to be as free and independent as they possibly could. They would not accept U.S. control, as it were, of Cuba. So it goes back a long way.[93]

As for the arms that were picked up at the Guantánamo naval base: as you know, the United States had declared an arms embargo against Cuba, because the arms that were being furnished to the Batista army under the military assistance agreement were obviously being used against the Cuban people. In a typical bureaucratic fashion, there were some in the U.S. government who did not wish to have an arms embargo against Cuba. There were others who insisted that there must be one, so an arms embargo was declared. But we—something Mr. Mendoza didn't mention—we left our military mission in Cuba training Batista's troops, and I recall the graduating ceremonies of one of the consignments, one of (I suppose) the yearly training sessions of recruits as they graduated and marched off down to the Sierra Maestra, in the spring of 1958, to fight the 26th of July. On the reviewing stand were all the officers of the U.S. military mission. The arms embargo had been declared, but the Cuban government came to us and said that they had already paid. (I was not in the embassy at that point; I don't know this firsthand. This is on the basis of memos I read subsequently.) The Cuban government had come to us and said that they had already paid for certain bombs and rockets and other equipment and ammunition, and it had not been delivered. It was decided to deliver it at the Guantánamo naval base—a most unfortunate, a most unhappy decision since that was bound to come to the attention of the 26th of July. Here you had Cuban Air Force planes at the Guantánamo naval base being loaded with bombs and rockets, and subsequently used against the Cuban population. It was a terrible mistake that was made, but it was part of the arms embargo that the United States had declared against the Batista government.[94]

There were actions of this kind on the part of the United States which clearly caused the new Cuban government to be suspicious as it came to power. I would insist, however, that as the revolutionary government came to power there was a decision in the United States government to try to reach some rapport, and Ambassador Earl T.

Smith was withdrawn—or left—and Ambassador Philip Bonsal arrived with instructions to do his best to establish some rapport with the new Cuban government. This, I think, we will get to in some greater detail on the Cuban side later. I just wanted to point out that there was rhetoric—I was here sitting at the embassy those two years—on the part of the Cuban government, and some actions on the part of the Cuban government, which caused great concern within the United States government. They, in turn, may have followed from previous actions or attitudes of the U.S. government. But we cannot ignore the chain of causes and effects. It goes a long way back. Cause and effect begins, and it carries on, and there is no gap, and there is no one point at which the United States is not reacting to something on the Cuban side, or the Cuban side reacting to something on ours.

We need to get more into the cause and effect, and especially that two-year period between the time the revolutionary government comes to power in 1959 and the time that we break relations and there is really virtually open hostility between us—partly because the Bay of Pigs follows very soon after that. I was someone who was here during those two years, and I was open, I must say, to the ideas of the revolution to bring about a more just society, to end some of the ills, the corruption of the previous governments, especially of the Batista dictatorship. At the same time, I was sensitive to the rhetoric, the attitudes, and some of the actions of the Cuban government which did cause concern within my own government, and I know we will get to those issues at a future point in the conference. That is all I have to say. Thank you.

TROYANOVSKY: [To Rafael Hernández:] Did you want to address this point or some other point?

RAFAEL HERNÁNDEZ: I have a question. Among the pieces missing from this puzzle, there is one that hasn't been explained here or in Antigua, and I think it is important for the reconstruction of history—not because of its anecdotal value, but because it would help us to understand the logic of events and of policies. The question is the following: When did CIA covert operations against the Cuban Revolution begin? The most famous, perhaps, of those operations—the Bay of Pigs—was approved by the president in March of 1960, but we also know that the CIA had been working on that operation and had been recruiting counterrevolutionaries for many months before then. There is evidence indicating that these actions did not begin with the recruitment of the Bay of Pigs mercenaries. This isn't what Wayne called "the chicken and egg problem"; the CIA was in Cuba before the revolution. When did operations begin aimed at affecting the revolutionary process itself, undermining it? I would like to hear some member of the U.S. group speak to this. Ray Cline said that he was in Asia; I imagine he wasn't doing anything related to Vietnam [laughter]—but, in any case, he or some other member of the U.S. delegation might help us understand better what happened—the logic of this process. Can he give us some information on how and when the CIA began to operate against the revolution, whose idea it was, and who gave the instructions? That is the question.

TROYANOVSKY: Is there someone in the U.S. delegation who would like to address this question?

WAYNE SMITH: I can give Rafael my impressions. Please remember I was the third secretary in the embassy. No one told me much of anything. But, I was also the ambassador's aide, and did see a lot of documents.

I would say that our impression in the United States embassy in Havana, at that point, was that there was no concerted effort until after March 1960. Now, that is not to say that the CIA might not have been trying to recruit agents. I think that is an eternal effort. But, in terms of a concerted effort, including a series of sabotage operations, planning for the Bay of Pigs, and so forth, our impression was that that did not begin until March of 1960. We have discussed that in the coffee breaks here.

In some measure I contributed, I suppose, to that decision, on the basis of what I would now regard as mistaken conclusions. You recall that Ambassador Bonsal was recalled to the United States, I believe, in December of 1959, for consultations, and while there, he convinced President Eisenhower and Secretary of State [Christian] Herter that we should make one last effort to negotiate, to reach some accommodation with Cuba. And so, the approach was made to the Cuban side indicating that the United States wished to negotiate the differences between us. And the response from the Cuban government was positive: yes, the Cuban government also wished to negotiate the differences between us, and would shortly name a delegation. That was in January of 1960. But then in February came the visit of Anastas Mikoyan—it has been fascinating to compare notes with Sergo Mikoyan over the past few years. On the basis of that visit and the warmth of the speeches, the warmth of the reception, the agreements signed and so forth, we at the American embassy reached the conclusion that the die was cast, that Cuba had made its decision to associate itself with the Soviet Union. Therefore, when the Cuban government came back to us shortly after the visit and indicated that it was now ready to name the delegation and was ready to begin the talks, the United States government had decided that it was no longer interested and placed some conditions on the talks which, in effect, ruled them out.[95] It was not by chance at all that, in March of 1960, President Eisenhower signed the finding which authorized CIA activities that eventually led to the Bay of Pigs, because of the conclusion on the part of the United States government that Cuba had made its decision to associate itself with the Soviet Union.

Now, that is not to say, Rafael, that there may not have been CIA operatives in Miami who—anticipating the day when something like this might be decided upon—were going around talking to Cuban exiles there, and beginning to recruit people. But it was our very firm impression in the embassy that no such operations began until after March of 1960. Thank you.

SCHLESINGER: I have a brief addendum to Wayne Smith's statement. In 1964, Richard Nixon said: "I have been the strongest and most persistent advocate for setting up and supporting such a program"— that is, the CIA program of covert action against Cuba. Phil Bonsal, in his excellent book about Castro and Cuba, called Richard Nixon the father of the operations here. Brigadier General Robert Cushman, Nixon's military aide and later his deputy director of the CIA, described Nixon to Howard Hunt, in 1960, as the "the project's action officer in the White House." This was the Bay of Pigs project. As H. R. Haldemann, who was Nixon's top aide when Nixon became president, wrote, "Nixon knew more about the genesis of the Bay of Pigs than almost anyone."[96]

CASTRO'S RESPONSE:
"If the idea is to put Cuba on trial, then Cuba will accept that trial"

McNamara had said, in response to several previous Cuban interventions, that we had yet to hear "one word" about Cuban activities to which U.S. policy makers felt they were responding in the period before the missile crisis. Castro must have realized by now that, in the minds of the U.S. participants, Cuba was indeed on trial. Not in the same sense that some of the Cubans seemed to be attempting to put the United States on trial: for past crimes of *commission*. Rather, Castro and his colleagues are being held accountable for errors of *omission*, regarded by the U.S. participants as sufficiently grievous to warrant a premature termination of the conference. Informed of this fact at the lunch break, a Cuban organizer had listened and then disappeared to carry the message to the Cuban delegation. Returning, he reported: "It is up to Fidel. He knows."

After asserting (not quite convincingly) that such matters as we have been discussing are barely relevant to the October crisis, Castro agrees to take up the challenge: "If the idea is to put Cuba on trial, then Cuba will accept that trial." Castro's following intervention is, to some, the outstanding event of the conference. When at last Fidel Castro chooses to address the issue, we are witnesses to thousands upon thousands of words in response to McNamara's challenge. For those of us who are new to Fidel Castro, it now seems almost as if a dam has broken. The words come out in a torrent, covering the issues raised by McNamara and Martin, and much more besides.

A bravura performance, it covers virtually every aspect of U.S.-Cuban hostility: Cuban support for Marxist opponents of U.S.-backed governments in Latin America in the early 1960s; the Cubans' understanding of their historical relationship to the United States (that, in the early 1960s, they were responding to two hundred years of *U.S.* intervention in Cuban affairs); and human rights in Cuba today—an issue that we on the U.S. delegation had de-emphasized as being too sensitive to admit of productive discussion. His method of entering into these questions is not lost on the leader of the U.S. delegation: Castro, in the role of a professor criticizing the main points of a student's thesis, goes through McNamara's opening statement, point by point, explaining, rebutting, elaborating, sometimes entertaining, often illuminating.

In so doing, he stuns everyone on the U.S. delegation, even those personally familiar with him. Later, some of our Cuba specialists will say that with this statement, Castro has enunciated a new Cuban foreign policy.[97] For he easily exceeds the requirements set out by McNamara; he not only discusses in detail Cuba's involvement in "subversion," he swears off it. In phrases that will be often cited after the conference, he admits:

> There's a new situation in Latin America. Have we changed? Yes, we've changed. The world has changed and Latin America has

changed. And, therefore, that kind of activity by Cuba no longer
exists.

In responding to McNamara's challenge, chiefly via a creative con-
cordance to McNamara's remarks, the Cuban leader transforms what
was fast becoming a "trial" of mutual accusation and recrimination
into one of the single most productive moments of the conference.

By the time Fidel Castro delivers his remarks in our conference
room, Raúl Castro has already given his anti-imperialist speech at the
funeral service downtown for the four murdered marina guards. Later,
a member of the U.S. delegation will remark to Fidel Castro about the
discrepancy, inquiring as to how he can make the two performances,
the two apparently antithetical "speeches," the two points of view,
coincide. Castro says this in response:

> There is no "contradiction," as you call it. We in the conference room
> are playing by the new rules. We are discussing our differences in a
> civilized fashion. But those who murdered the guards, and those who
> continue to infiltrate Cuba from Florida in the hope of destroying
> us—they are playing by the old rules. For those who play that way,
> by the old rules, we must respond in kind, especially now, when we
> face our greatest challenge since the October crisis.[98]

Someone at that point raised a glass "to the new rules," and Castro
did likewise.

TROYANOVSKY: Now I would like to—please, Commander-in-Chief
Castro?

CASTRO: I had not wanted to take part in the debate at this point,
but it seems to me that we are somehow getting beyond our subject.
Right now I am not too sure of what it would be most interesting to
discuss here when my turn comes around: these things we are now
discussing, or the October crisis. I think we are out on the margins of
the question. But, I think this is because of some of the things that
have been said today, and some yesterday.

At certain times, listening to the representatives of the United
States, I've felt rather amazed, because I get the impression that we
have been living in a fantasy world. Yesterday and today—and my

colleagues have been telling me also in Antigua—when the focus has been on the behavior of Cuba, attempts are made to justify American policy in terms of those actions. If the idea is to put Cuba on trial, then Cuba will accept that trial—but it won't confine the trial simply to the October crisis. It must be a trial of Cuba before and after— everything that happened before and everything that happened afterwards. At one point here I thought I was hearing the old rhetoric of the Cold War—the old arguments of the Cold War: Cuba as a Soviet base, Cuba as a Soviet agent, Cuba as an organizer of subversion of Latin America—the causes that gave rise to all of the actions and policies of the different U.S. administrations against Cuba. And I ask myself if anyone can be so ignorant of history, as if there were no history of relations between the United States and Cuba and the United States and Latin America, going back almost two hundred years, long before Cuba existed and long before the Cuban Revolution existed. I ask myself the following—and I don't want to enter into a polemic; I am just trying to reflect on these questions—how many interventions were there in the Caribbean before the Cuban Revolution—U.S. interventions? How many actions were undertaken against the interests of Latin America throughout history? How can we forget, for example, that the United States emerged as a very powerful nation? There was a small group of states that became independent, the first ones in this hemisphere, into whose territory the United States started to expand. The United States seized almost half of Mexico's territory. How can we forget what happened in Central America—the expeditions to Central America—what happened in Panama, the means they used to take over Panama? How can we forget the methods used to intervene in almost all the countries of Central America and Latin America? How can we forget the interventions in Nicaragua, Haiti, the Dominican Republic, and several times in Cuba? How can we forget the situation of Puerto Rico—a Latin American country, completely Latin American, as Latin American as Cuba? Puerto Rico was occupied by the United States and is still today a country that belongs to—that is under the domination of—the United States. How can we forget all this history, before and since, in these relations? How can we forget the interventions of all kinds? If we had been interventionists, it might have been because we had great teachers: the United States. No other country has intervened more in Latin America than the United States.

So, then; we are accused, and people want to condemn us, and they want to send us into the seventh circle of hell for helping the revolutions in Latin America. I ask myself: which circle would we have to send the United States to? And I ask myself: if this is one of the causes, why was there so much action and hostility against Cuba, and attempts to crush Cuba and liquidate all of us? Where is the morality of using those arguments, and trying to seek justifications in this?

I've listened to interventions such as the one made by Mr. Martin, and I say, "What, are we living in 1962, or 1992?" In fact, the statement made by his very outstanding and capable colleague yesterday, Mr. McNamara, was very elegant. It was a very hard statement against us— very hard. In fact, I had to explain yesterday that I was not a ferocious enemy of the United States, and I had to explain the question of the letter used by Tad Szulc and referred to by McNamara in his statement.[99] I think no one can accuse us of having sown the seeds of hate against the people of the United States, and the best proof of it is that in no country of Latin America—not even in those countries that are most friendly to the United States; not even those countries that eat out of the hands of the United States (some of them survive on that)—not even there will you find U.S. citizens treated as respectfully as they are in Cuba. Nowhere do they receive the hospitality and consideration they receive in Cuba, and we feel proud of the fact that U.S. citizens are treated this way. In sports, nowhere are U.S. athletes applauded as much as they are here, and they are our main rivals. We have tried to instill in the people, not fanaticism, not hatred, but a political culture. The first thing we are taught is that all nations are equal, that all nations are brothers—the feeling of solidarity among peoples. But yesterday we received very strong accusations, in very elegant language.

I don't want to go into other subjects, but, at some point, since I know there is interest in analyzing these questions, Cuba will of course be expected to say something. To briefly touch one, McNamara yesterday raised the question of Cuba having been a direct threat to the United States. He said that there was the perception that Cuba was "a direct threat to the security of the United States," and "a violator of accepted norms of international behavior"; he added, "particularly in the field of political freedom and civil rights." I've referred to this. Let's make a catalogue and see who has violated more international standards.

I listened, and I made notes of the different perceptions of us. In the United States, Americans are taught that they gave Cuba its independence. I think that this teaching is wrong. The people of the United States should not be taught that, because although the United States did intervene at the end of our war of independence, we have our own opinions on that situation, our own assessments. We believe that Spain was defeated, Spain could not continue the war against Cuba. There was a ten-year war, then the 1895 war. Spain was completely exhausted, and that is when the U.S. intervention came. They occupied the country for a number of years; simultaneously, they occupied Puerto Rico and kept it; simultaneously they occupied the Philippines and kept it. In fact, McNamara was saying that some Americans feel that the United States was too generous because it did not keep Cuba. Cuba had great support in world public opinion; Cuba had fought heroically; and despite that, four years later, the United States imposed a government on us, and imposed the Platt Amendment. You know the Platt Amendment was an imposition. We were told: either you accept the Platt Amendment, or there is no independence. No country in the world would accept that kind of amendment in its constitution, because it gives the right to another country to intervene to establish peace.[100] The Platt Amendment is very much repudiated in our country.

I think Americans would be offended if they were told that their independence was given to them by Spaniards and Frenchmen—by Miranda* and Lafayette†—and it would be unfair to say that. The Spanish and the French helped, but the weight of the main struggle was borne by the people of the United States. No one has ever attempted to say anything like that, and I think one of the things that would have to be done—since there are contradictory perceptions— is to give Americans a proper education, and tell them the historical truth, instead of shaping their opinions on the basis of false premises.

He [McNamara] mentioned four points: one on the role of the United States in establishing Cuban independence; one about the criticism for not having kept Cuba—there are different perceptions there on both sides; the question of the Platt Amendment; and then, lastly he said something that I thought about when I jotted it down. The United States believed that its investments here contributed to the development of the country. One cannot deny that, economically and technically, U.S. investments did help economic growth, economic development. This is undeniable. But at a certain point, all of that got bogged down. What you say was true of the early decades, when a

---

*Francisco de Miranda (1750–1816), a Venezuelan, served in the American revolution as a Spanish officer, and received the British surrender at Pensacola.
†Marie Joseph Paul Yves Roch Gilbert du Motier, Marquis de Lafayette, was a French soldier and statesman who served as a major general on the staff of Gen. George Washington. He fought in the campaigns of 1777–78 and at Yorktown in 1781, and also persuaded Louis XVI to support the American revolutionaries with French forces.

great many sugar mills were built; but from a certain point on, the economic development of Cuba got stuck. I agree that there are different perceptions, and I think we should begin by checking to see what the different perceptions are on these questions; but I believe in any case what we've got to do is get to work, to see to it that the objective historical truth prevails.

He spoke about the main concerns. The military relations between Cuba and the Soviet Union were one of the three main concerns. He mentioned Eisenhower's decision after Mikoyan came to Cuba. So now it turns out that Mikoyan is to blame for everything, because when our friend's father [indicating Sergo Mikoyan] decided to visit us in the name of the Soviet Union, this immediately justified an order to organize the overthrow of the Cuban Revolution. If they had known what a noble individual Mikoyan was, if they had not acted on the basis of prejudice, they would not have done this.

Mikoyan almost freed the United States of Castro, because he brought a newly designed Soviet helicopter, and we took a trip around the country to show him tourist centers and beaches. We went to some beaches on the southern coast of Cuba. We took Mikoyan to Cayo Largo, where no one went; he took a dip in the Caribbean, got dressed again, and left. We had no protocol, no organization, we had nothing. We practically took a trip all around Cuba in a gesture of friendship and hospitality toward him at the time, and it's a miracle that we didn't get killed in that helicopter. The Soviets had just conquered space, they had sent a man into space, and this Soviet pilot wanted to go east and we were running out of gasoline and I told him, "If you go east we'll go into the ocean. You've got to go north, and do it now, because we've got twenty minutes of fuel." This was the first time there was a hijacking in this area, and I did it. I almost performed the courtesy of drowning. [Laughter.] I had to hijack this helicopter. I persuaded Mikoyan, "If I'm mistaken the worst that can happen is we will get to land, but if I'm right and he's wrong, we're going to fall into the sea, and that will be that." I convinced Mikoyan, fortunately. About twenty years later the Soviets sent us a recommendation: that leaders should not fly in helicopters, because helicopters are very dangerous. They told us this twenty years later—twenty years after Mikoyan and I took the trip. [Laughter.]

So Mikoyan, with his pilot and his helicopter and his Soviet maps that weren't very precise—and they had no navigational experience around the island—Mikoyan almost freed the United States of Castro, although Castro was not the essential, unique, or exclusive factor in this revolution. The Americans said "Castro," and they thought by eliminating Castro, in one fell swoop they would eliminate the revolution. As they say in Cuba, "If you kill the dog, there's no more rabies." This is one way to see revolutions: as symbolized and personified by individuals. I think, in fact, the argument that Mikoyan's visit was a justification for American policy cannot be defended.

Before the military activities, economic actions had begun—hostility of all sorts had begun way before March of 1960. The economic blockade began before; various economic measures began before; the United States suppressed all credits long before that. The campaigns against Cuba were very earnest from the very beginning, simply because we were doing to the war criminals of Batista what the United States did in Nuremberg. But there's a difference: when the United States tried the war criminals in Nuremberg, there was no precedent. But Mendoza can report to you that in the Sierra Maestra the revolutionary movement did draft and decree an entire penal code on the basis of which to sanction anyone who committed war crimes. That was the object of a very strong campaign.

I remember when I visited the United States. There was no ill will against the United States; in fact, we had a great many friends. But the fact is that we were practically impotent against this great campaign over there against Cuba, as the positions of the revolutionary government became clear. But I went to Washington.[101] I was invited by the press, and I didn't mind—sincerely. But the president of the United States didn't even invite me for a cup of coffee, because I wasn't worthy of a cup of coffee with the president of the United States. They sent me Nixon, in fact. It's not a question of it being a dishonor to have Nixon, since Nixon was vice president. But in any case, when I visited in April—I think it was April—I was received at the Capitol in a little office. He talked to me, he let me talk. He doesn't speak much. He asked a few things and let me talk. I explained the social and economic situation in Cuba, the poverty, the inequality, the hundreds of thousands of unemployed, the landless peasants, the measures that we had to adopt to solve the situation—and Nixon listened, said nothing, and made no remarks.[102] But when the interview concluded, it's well known that he sent a memo to Eisenhower saying, "Castro is a communist and the revolutionary government has to be overthrown." He said it right there. He suggested this to the president as early as April 1959. Not Mikoyan, not a single Soviet had visited this country.[103]

Now, you may say, "Nixon was right. He was clairvoyant; he was a prophet." Well, no, he wasn't clairvoyant, and he wasn't a prophet, because our program was not a socialist program: it was the Moncada program, the one that we mentioned at the trial. It was an advanced social program, but it was not a socialist program. It was not a communist program.[104] At the time, because of our political culture and our political base, we believed that it was not the time to propose the building of socialism in Cuba. But at that time American economic pressures of all types began. They became stronger and stronger.

I could also say quite honestly that we had two problems: two administrations that had no experience—the Cuban one and the American one. How is this possible, you might ask? Because the United States had no experience in dealing with revolutions. When something happened in Guatemala, the CIA worked efficiently and quickly and liquidated the [Jacobo] Arbenz [Guzmán] government following the agrarian reform [1954]. McNamara said yesterday that a revolution promoting social justice, agrarian reform and others would have found the understanding and support of Kennedy. But McNamara didn't say that if Kennedy had said this, that if he had told Nixon this in 1959, Nixon would have accused Kennedy of being a communist. Anyone who spoke of agrarian reform was accused of being a communist. Anyone who spoke about helping the people, of social reform, was accused of being communist and was not allowed into the United States.

Why did the Alliance for Progress emerge? I ask myself if that program would have existed without the Cuban Revolution. Perhaps the Cuban Revolution made a big impression on politicians in the United States. Might it not have been at the bottom of the idea of the Alliance for Progress, which emerged after the Bay of Pigs invasion? The Alliance for Progress was the U.S. administration's reply to the fear of a revolutionary epidemic in the hemisphere, because the administration was aware of the terrible poverty that existed in Latin America, and they were afraid that the objective conditions would lead to revolutionary changes. It was a brilliant idea, I say, to launch the Alliance for Progress. But the Alliance for Progress came after the Cuban Revolution, and as a result of the Cuban Revolution.

We must not forget that they took from us our sugar quota, which was four million tons.[105] This is something that had existed in a century of trade relations between Cuba and the United States, since we were a colony. It was taken from us overnight, and they shared it among the countries of Latin America. There was candy for everyone except for Cuba. Cuba was deprived of its sugar quota, and it was distributed among the rest of the governments of Latin America. What for? To create hunger here. Why our gratitude to the USSR, gentlemen? This gratitude is understandable and logical. When we were deprived of the sugar quota, the USSR turned up and said it was ready to buy Cuban sugar. When they suspended oil shipments and left us without fuel, the USSR turned up and said it was ready to supply us with oil. At that time, with a ton of sugar we could buy seven tons of oil. After oil rose to monopoly prices—after the events in the Middle East [in 1973]—with a ton of sugar you could buy a maximum of almost two— 1.8—tons of oil. This is perhaps one of the most difficult problems Cuba has today: the change in the relative prices of sugar and oil. But every time the United States took some measure against us, we had someone there to help us. There was someone there making great efforts on our behalf.[106] I have to admit that this proved Nikita's audacity and courage. At that time we consumed 4 million tons of oil, and Soviet production was just over 100 million. With Soviet ships they were able to supply the fuel we needed. We began to receive support from the Soviet Union under very difficult circumstances, just as the United States adopted blockade measures against us. What could Cuba have done without that? Well, you can ask that now. What is Cuba going to do now, blockaded by the United States, and the USSR no longer exists? These are the kinds of problems that we have to solve today, and not even that kind of problem discourages us. But it was very important for us; we can't forget these things. It wasn't just CIA operations; there were political measures, economic measures, that complicated life in this country. This was the foundation of our relations with the USSR.

For practically a year we had no diplomatic relations with the USSR. In fact, we did not buy our first weapons from a socialist country, in order to avoid having that used as a pretext. We bought them in Italy and Belgium. What happened? When the second ship that arrived in Cuba from Belgium with weapons was being unloaded, they picked up one of the crates and the ship exploded. There were two explosions; they killed more than a hundred workers and soldiers who were unloading those weapons. Without a doubt that ship was sabotaged from abroad.[107] Since then, after that, thousands of ships have been unloaded in Cuba, and there hasn't been a single explosion since. Perhaps in a hundred years reports will be declassified and our great-great-great grandchildren will know how the *La Coubre* was sabotaged, causing so much loss of life.

We bought six cannons from Italy, and the necessary ammunition; we received ammunition for three and half. We were not able to buy weapons in the West. I recall that was when we bought the first weapons from Czechoslovakia and the USSR. Czechoslovakia sent us World War II weapons, on credit, but they were weapons that had been left there by the Nazis. The Soviets gave us a credit, but they gave us new weapons.

People say we have promoted revolution. Not a word is said about the fact that the United States organized all the countries of Latin America, aligned them, gave them Cuba's sugar quota, gave them the Alliance for Progress, and got them all together to blockade and destroy Cuba. Not a word is said about that. We can admit that we would have liked to see revolution in the rest of these countries, because we despaired of having constructive relations with them when they co-operated in the United States' actions against us. "What can we expect of these governments?" we wondered. But there was one government that was not hostile to Cuba and never broke relations with Cuba, and with that government—a Latin American capitalist government: Mexico—we had the best of relations throughout this period. If the other countries in Latin America had been respectful toward us, if they had not been in favor of destroying the Cuban Revolution, they would not have encouraged Cuban desires for revolutionary changes.

Has anyone mentioned the Dominican Republic? Yes, we helped organize an expedition to the Dominican Republic. This was an old commitment. When I was a student, I was enrolled in an expedition—it was after World War II, in 1947—to overthrow [Rafael Leónidas] Trujillo [Molina]. I was close to the cause of the Dominican Republic when I was a law student, when I was in my second year of law school. There was supposed to be an expedition to liberate the Dominican Republic. Many things happened, and that expedition never took place. I was not heading it, but I had already won some sort of rank while training for it. I spent time on a virtual desert island—a very uncomfortable place—training for it.[108] But there are other illustrious personalities in Latin America that cooperated with us in the organization of that expedition against Trujillo. Trujillo was seen as a symbol of the worst in this hemisphere, and Trujillo was the product of a U.S. intervention. He had the support of one of the armies created by the United States. Yes, we made an attempt.

Democratic governments have been mentioned. But some so-called democratic governments joined the United States in attempts to destroy the Cuban Revolution. We base ourselves on the principle that revolutions cannot be exported, because if you have a clear idea of what a revolution is, you know that it is objective domestic conditions that shape a revolution. What we did was support revolutions. We didn't export revolution, because the concept of exporting revolution is impossible. In any case, of course, in dealing with us, other countries observed no laws or standards, so as far as we were concerned, we felt that we had the right to support revolutionary movements in the rest of the countries of Latin America which were supporting the counterrevolutionary movement against Cuba. Where did the Bay of Pigs invasion come from? Guatemala, Nicaragua. Where did the pirate attacks come from? From Costa Rica and other countries in the Caribbean—from the Dominican Republic. No one has mentioned the pirate attacks. They existed before and after the October crisis.

So what is the question, then? Did we support the revolutionary movements? Do we admit it? Yes, we admit it. We supported the revolutionary movements.[109] And I believe very simply that a country attacked and harassed as Cuba was then had every right to act the way it did. If you ask me if that is Cuba's policy today, I'd tell you no, because there have been great changes in Latin America. We have friendly and respectful relations with almost all the countries in Latin America. There's a new situation in Latin America. Have we changed? Yes, we've changed. The world has changed, and Latin America has changed. And, therefore, that kind of activity by Cuba no longer exists. On the contrary, wherever we have been able to help find a peaceful solution, we have done so—and not simply to build up credits.

Now, we hear a lot about the question of political and civil rights. This has been treated in a very dogmatic, very superficial way, and there is a complete ignorance of the political system in our country. They talk about free elections. We had a period of de facto government. But we institutionalized the country. We drafted a constitution, we established an electoral system. All this is ignored, but the fact that you ignore it does not mean that it doesn't exist. They talk about civil rights, and I ask myself: is there anywhere in the world where more has been done for humankind than in Cuba? The infant mortality in Cuba is 10.7 per thousand, whereas in some other countries it is more than a hundred, and the average in Latin America is 55 per thousand live born. I ask myself: What country has saved more infant lives than Cuba? Children who grow up healthy and with an education? Mr. McNamara knows this, because he was president of the World Bank, and no one has more precise information than he does about the tragedy of starvation, malnutrition, lack of health services that exist in the world. We have calculated that we have saved hundreds of thousands of lives, lives of children who would have died without our health programs.[110] We have carried education to levels that do not exist in any other country. We have provided employment for everyone. We have no undernourished children, no children abandoned in the streets, no barefoot children or child beggars. There is no country in the Third World, or in Latin America, that has done for people what we have done. We did away with racial discrimination. Isn't racial discrimination a gross violation of human and civil rights? Discrimination against women, isn't that a blatant violation of those rights? Prostitution as a way of life for many women, as used to be the case in Cuba—isn't that a gross violation of human rights? Unemployment or underemployment of 30 and 40 percent of the population—isn't that a gross violation of human rights? Death from starvation or from curable diseases—isn't that a violation of human rights? And isn't that what is happening in all of Latin America, and in the Third World, clearly, visibly, every day? How many die? The director of UNICEF told me that 700,000 children died in Latin America that could have been saved if they had had Cuba's health system. So then, the social system of Latin America is murdering 700,000 children every year that could have lived. And are we to take these countries as a model of democracy, then, or of respect for human rights?

I'm not going to refer to the slanders about Cuba, as regards tortures and those kinds of thing. These are just disgusting lies that have been repeated tens of times; but there isn't a single case in our country. And there isn't a single case of people disappearing in our country, whereas this is something frequent in the rest of Latin America, with one kind of government or another. In our country there isn't a single case of the police or the army firing against students, firing against workers, firing against peasants, against protestors. We see that even in England. We see horses trampling the people of England when they go to protest against some sort of tax, for instance.[111] You don't see the spectacle of the fire engines—the kind of thing you see in South Korea all the time. You don't see this in Cuba, this daily repression that you see in South Korea. This has never been seen in Cuba. Nothing of the sort.

Furthermore, the people in Cuba are armed, because our armed forces are made up not of a professional army, but of the entire nation—workers, peasants, students—organized, trained, and armed. They are our forces. If in Latin America they gave weapons to the people, many governments would not last at all, because there is a permanent contradiction and conflict between the people and the government.

Now, if human rights are the foundation of U.S. foreign policy, why does the U.S. have such a close relationship with the government of South Korea? Why such close friendships with governments like the [Augusto] Pinochet government [of Chile], where so many people disappeared? Why such close friendship with the Argentine government, where between 10,000 and 30,000 people disappeared? The United States had excellent relations with that government. They used Battalion 401 of Argentine Intelligence to organize the dirty war in Nicaragua. The Argentines launched the action against the Falkland Islands because they felt that the United States would support them, because they were supporting the United States in their dirty wars. The U.S. lent these governments dozens of billions of dollars. There was no blockade against them; but there was a blockade against Cuba. There was no blockade against the military government in Argentina; but there was a blockade against Cuba. There was no blockade against South Africa, there was no cessation of investments, while our soldiers were fighting in Angola to fight for their liberation, to help destroy apartheid. Ask [Nelson] Mandela, the leader of the black South Africans, his opinion of Cuba. Ask him his assessment of Cuba, and how much he appreciates the blood shed by Cuba over there. He said this to our people: that Cuba's contribution was very important in the struggle against apartheid.

So, then; you can't talk about morality or about a political philosophy when you have two sets of laws, two sets of principles, two standards. Was there a blockade against [Nicaraguan president Anastasio] Somoza [Debayle]? What blockade was there against the Salvadorean military, who have murdered dozens of thousands of people? A hundred thousand people have disappeared in a small country like Guatemala. We've never heard about a blockade by the United States against those countries, nor have they organized expeditions.

So the criticism that Cuba does not respect human and political rights is ahistorical, parochial, and unfair. As I was saying to a group of religious leaders recently here in Havana, let us meet in the world and let us get to the bottom of what civil and human rights mean, in all areas. Analyze our election system. Who nominates delegates in Cuba in each district? Who nominates them and who elects them? The people, not the Party. We've developed mechanisms that are ignored by others, but they are there and they are a reality, and they are progressive.

We have our ideas, we have our conceptions, but in the light of truth, with full honesty and frankness, we are ready to discuss all problems, and we are not afraid to hear these criticisms; but I think it is my duty to maintain in this civilized forum here—in this unusual meeting that we have here—that some of the arguments employed to justify the actions taken against Cuba are inconsistent, for all of the various reasons that I have explained.

There are other things which we could go into. I think we'll talk about the October crisis again, unless you want to go on with the trial against Cuba. We are ready to go on sitting here in the docket, the accused; but I think there are other things worth talking about. Is this going to be the last meeting or is this going to go on in the future? I was under the impression that this was one of the last meetings to get all the information. I'm ready to give you all the evidence necessary so that we can have a fair interpretation of things, of events, as truthful an interpretation as possible, one as objective as possible. There are things on which I might agree with the Americans. Why not? I am friends with almost all of the Soviets here. I have a great deal of respect for them. But this doesn't mean that all of my points of view coincide with their points of view on the October crisis.

I understood that at a certain point it would be my turn to make my statement and presentation. What I've been saying, by the way, will free me and you of my having to make a rather long statement, so, when my turn comes, I am going to refer to the essential elements of the crisis—how it originated, how it was generated, the first contacts, and so on. I will discuss my perceptions, and my interpretation of motivations. It's not that I've just thought of them; I have had them on paper for many years. I have my points of view, and I can explain them. Broaching some of these things I have just discussed, covering some of these issues, reduces the amount that I would have had to say of value vis-à-vis the essential subject of this meeting.

You have the floor now for any questions you may have. If the chairman allows, and the U.S. side has any questions, I'm ready to go into the question-and-answer period right now, or after a recess. I'm not afraid of the subject.

RISQUET: There is a 6:30 reception at the Interests Section, Comandante.

CASTRO: The chairman of the meeting has the floor. Let him decide.

TROYANOVSKY: . . . I think we have time for only one question, and General Gribkov would like to ask it.

GRIBKOV: We received information in October 1962 that, among the six or seven divisions that were getting ready to attack Cuba, there were Argentine forces, Venezuelan forces, and forces from the Dominican Republic, and military support was ready to come from Ecuador, Colombia, Costa Rica, Peru, Honduras, Haiti, Guatemala, and Nicaragua. These countries did not send their forces, but they were ready to. I would like to hear whether this information, this intelligence that we received, was accurate or not.

TROYANOVSKY: Who could answer, please? Please, General William Smith.

GENERAL SMITH: Certainly at the time we wanted to have as much support throughout the Alliance for Progress group as we could, as Ambassador Martin had said. But we had, to my knowledge, no intention of having those forces engaged in combat, if for no other reason than that it would be too complex. You know, it was hard enough within the time that we had to get the U.S. forces ready to the point that they could cooperate together and fight effectively. There was neither any need to have other forces involved, nor was there the time to get them organized so they could participate meaningfully.

GARTHOFF: It's my recollection that there was at least discussion and planning, and it may have led to a commitment of some Argentine, Dominican, and perhaps some other naval ships to supplement the quarantine force in a symbolic way; but there was never any consideration given to the use of army—of ground forces—or air forces of any other country. It was, as I said, simply symbolic, as far as those were concerned.[112]

While I have the floor, I would like to take just one minute to make a statement on another subject. The Department of State has just released a few weeks ago the latest volume in the series, *Foreign Relations of the United States.* It's over 1,200 pages of formerly classified, secret documentation on all aspects of American foreign relations with Cuba through the years 1958, 1959, and 1960. It includes the texts—in some cases with some deletions—but it includes the texts of National Security Council meetings, and of the meeting in March 1960 of which we were speaking, in which they discussed the setting up of a force using Cuban émigrés. It also includes information on recruitment and training programs under way. While it may not include everything, it includes a great deal of previously secret information about all aspects of American policy and relations with respect to Cuba, and I will be happy to give this to the Cuban delegation at the end of the conference. It is planned—I've spoken with the historian's office in the State Department—they plan to issue two volumes on United States policy toward Cuba in the years 1961, '62, and '63. One will cover the period to the missile crisis; the second, the missile crisis; and thereafter to the end of 1963. But those volumes will not be published until 1993. But there is material here which I mentioned now because it is, of course, quite relevant to the discussion we were having earlier this afternoon, and which I think will be of interest, in view of our desire to move forward in clarifying the record by making available information which had been secret, but which can now help us to understand history. Thank you.

TROYANOVSKY: Thank you very much. I think that we should adjourn. I remind you that at 6:30 there's a reception at the U.S. Interests Section. I have been requested to inform you that you are all invited, whether you have received a written invitation or not. Tomorrow we shall resume at nine o'clock in the morning.

THE OCTOBER CRISIS:
"... the road to peace is not the road of sacrificing the rights of peoples ..."

The U.S. participants arrive the next morning with considerable anticipation of Fidel Castro's scheduled major presentation, with accompanying declassified documents (we have been told) on the October crisis. Castro's forthcoming presentation had been the principal topic of speculation at a reception for all three delegations at the residence of the chief of the U.S. Interests Section the previous evening.* The hosts of the event were Alan Flanigan, U.S. chief of section (who is attending all conference sessions and events as an observer), and his wife, Beverly.

On the ride over to the U.S. residence, we were regaled with tales of its colorful past by a former occupant, U.S. delegation member Wayne Smith, who served in Cuba during the waning days of the

---

*Both the Cuban mission in Washington, D.C., and the U.S. mission in Havana are called "interests sections," rather than embassies, and each is headed by a "chief," rather than an ambassador. The two countries adopted this nomenclature when they partially reestablished relations in 1977.

Batista regime in 1958, and during the early Castro period, 1959–60, before returning to Cuba during the Carter period to become U.S. chief of section. Nothing Wayne could say, however, fully prepared those who had not seen the residence before for its size and opulence. One conference participant said it reminded him of the Taj Mahal. Another joked that he finally understood why there was a Cuban Revolution. Still another recalled an anecdote told by former Cuban foreign minister Raúl Roa, who said that before the revolution, the foreign minister's job was to wait for the telephone to ring, pick it up, and get his instructions *in English*.[113] Wayne Smith responded, "And not only the foreign minister."

Alan Flanigan remarked during the reception that the assembled delegations constituted, without question, one of the most unusual groups to visit the residence in years, probably in decades. Here were former Kennedy administration officials who, in the conference and elsewhere, had been implicated in various policies, plots, and plans whose ultimate goal was to destroy the Castro regime. Here, too, were the highest-ranking Cuban Communist Party officials ever to appear there, including Jorge Risquet, veteran of countless guerrilla wars in Latin America and Africa; and Gen. Fabian Escalante, known in some U.S. circles as "the Hangman of Havana" for having sentenced (as one of the two judges) Cuban general Arnaldo Ochoa to death in a controversial 1989 trial.[114] No less striking, in its way, was the presence in the U.S. residence of General Gribkov, former commander-in-chief of the Warsaw Pact, and navy captain Igor Amosev, who was, as far as he knew (he said with a wink) still *persona non grata* in the United States, having been removed many years before for alleged "spying." For a few of us on the U.S. delegation, no less remarkable was the presence of *both* Robert McNamara and Ray Cline, whose views during the missile crisis, and ever since, have been, according to both, utterly incompatible.[115] This cornucopia of political contradiction had come together, united that evening only by a common interest in the great events of October 1962 and by a thirst only the tropics can induce.

Toward the end of the reception an intense discussion developed about what Castro (who had absented himself from the reception to tend to state business) would say on the following morning about the crisis. McNamara put the question to a group that included some of the Cuban conference organizers from the Central Committee and Foreign Ministry, via Wayne Smith, who was pressed into service as an interpreter. A Cuban official responded:

It will be very difficult, in my opinion, to say what must be said. Fidel must speak of Kennedy with you and other close Kennedy associates present. But he must speak of Khrushchev and Mikoyan with their sons present. And remember, Mr. McNamara, history has yet to record whether Cuba has suffered more from U.S. hostility or Soviet friendship. We Cubans began asking ourselves this question privately for the first time during the October crisis.

All the Cubans involved in this conversation implied that Castro would, in effect, address that question publicly, for the first time, on the following morning.

This is precisely what Castro now does, more tactfully than perhaps was expected. He will quote himself saying to U Thant during the crisis that "the road to peace is not the road of sacrificing the rights of peoples," and he will meditate at length on the degrees to which both Khrushchev and Kennedy—the Soviet friend and the American enemy—sacrificed the rights of Cuba on the altar of superpower expedience.

KHRUSHCHEV AND KENNEDY:
". . . two people for whom I feel great respect"

Castro begins by discussing his views on Khrushchev and Kennedy. Nothing could be clearer than that Castro remains supremely ambivalent about Khrushchev. On the one hand, as Castro narrates his reactions to Khrushchev's behavior in the missile crisis, he portrays Khrushchev as a great friend of Cuba. Having been asked by the Cubans for assistance, he sent nuclear weapons. He embraced Castro (literally as well as figuratively) and Cuban socialism as early as the fall of 1960, while others in the Soviet leadership were still deeply skeptical about making such a commitment.[116] Moreover, even after the near rupture in Cuban-Soviet relations following the missile crisis, Khrushchev took the lead in bringing the Cubans back into the fold, a process capped by Castro's long visit to the Soviet Union in April–May 1963.

Yet even in January 1992, in Castro's mature judgment, Khrushchev cannot be forgiven what could easily have been catastrophic blunders in 1962. He refused to listen to Cuban requests to go public with the deployment; he backed down in the face of U.S. demands; he terminated the crisis without the slightest apparent concern for

Cuban apprehensions about their security; and he betrayed and insulted Cuba by treating the missiles deployed in Cuba and Turkey as bargaining chips. Indeed, we suspect that Castro's balanced, judicious appraisal of Khrushchev in 1992 bears little relation to the prevailing view of the Soviet leader after the missile crisis, when for a time he was arguably the most hated man in Cuba. In a January 1968 "secret speech" to the Cuban Central Committee, Castro, even a half-dozen years later, seethed with bitter resentment against Khrushchev. After reading his colleagues a passage from one of Khrushchev's letters, in which the Soviet leader celebrates the fact that "Cuba was saved," and "Cuba lives," Castro exploded:

> That episode was an evident defeat for the socialist community and for the revolutionary movement. . . . "Cuba was saved. Cuba lives." But Cuba had been alive and Cuba had been living, and Cuba did not want to live at the expense of humiliation or surrender; for that, you do not have to be a revolutionary. Revolutionaries are not just concerned with living, but with how one lives, living most of all with dignity, living with a cause, living for a cause.[117]

What was prudence to the old Bolshevik was cowardice to the young Caribbean firebrand.

In December 1962 a Cuban delegation visited Moscow and discussed their differences with Khrushchev. The delegation was led by Carlos Rafael Rodríguez, the only member of the prerevolutionary Communist Party to rise to the highest ranks of Castro's inner circle. According to Rodríguez, Khrushchev said to him during that visit, "Tell me, why is Fidel so angry with me? Doesn't he know that I love him like a son?" Rodríguez reports that he replied to Khrushchev, "That's just the problem, Nikita, he's *not* your son. He's the leader of a sovereign country, in spite of what you people did to us in the October crisis."[118] As Castro begins speaking about Khrushchev in January 1992, he is still younger now than Khrushchev was during the missile crisis.[119]

In his speech to the United Nations in September 1960 (during the trip on which he met Khrushchev for the first time), Castro had referred to Kennedy as an "illiterate and ignorant millionaire."[120] Even in July 1963, after the missile crisis and upon returning from his long visit with Khrushchev in the Soviet Union, Castro offered the Cuban people a long litany of "how this ruffian Kennedy acts"—chiefly a list of the continuing sabotage operations against Cuba—even as Kennedy was extending an olive branch to the Soviet Union.[121] That Kennedy had *withheld* the use of direct military force during both the Bay of Pigs invasion and the missile crisis was at the time wholly obscured by the fact that Kennedy had *authorized* the Bay of Pigs operation and that he had *threatened* an invasion of Cuba. Cubans at the time were also convinced that Kennedy was working hand-in-glove with the Cuban exile community. When Kennedy greeted the ransomed veterans of the Bay of Pigs in the Orange Bowl, receiving their colors and promising them that their banner would one day fly "in a free Havana,"[122] *Revolución* reported the story with the headline, "Kennedy and Jacqueline inspect their worms."[123]

Kennedy's assassination, however, profoundly and forever changed the Cuban view of the man who was their hated adversary during the momentous events of the early 1960s. Some of us listening to Castro's remarks about Kennedy recall an evening spent in eastern Cuba over a year earlier discussing Kennedy with a group of Cuban officials and scholars. One explained why, in spite of the bitterness of the early 1960s, Kennedy is by far the most respected—even loved—U.S. president since the triumph of the revolution in 1959:

> You see, by *not* attacking Cuba in April 1961 and October 1962, we believe Kennedy's anti-Cuban machinery turned against him, like Frankenstein's monster. Those forces—the Mafia, the radical Cuban exiles, and the CIA—afterwards conspired successfully to assassinate *him*, because he prevented them from assassinating Fidel and destroying the Cuban Revolution. In a strange way, we believe, Kennedy had to die so that the Cuban Revolution could live.[124]

Whether or not there is anything to this conspiracy theory, we have never discussed Kennedy with a Cuban who does not profess to believe it. Thus when Castro discusses Khrushchev and Kennedy—"two people for whom I feel a great deal of respect"—one senses that the respect is highly qualified with respect to his old friend Khrushchev, but uncomplicated and sincere regarding his old enemy, Kennedy.

TROYANOVSKY: As I understand, it is the U.S. delegation's turn to chair. So, if you are ready, we are ready also.

McNAMARA: Mr. President; Mr. Ambassador; I believe the chair this morning will be Mr. Blight. Jim, you're in the chair.

BLIGHT: Thank you. I'd like to begin with a big "thank you" to our Cuban hosts, especially because of their willingness to improvise as the conference has progressed. They have really managed to improve it, and to make it even more effective than I think any of us dreamed it would be.

Now, my understanding is that today we are to have the privilege of hearing, for the first time, a comprehensive and complete—as complete as possible—presentation by President Castro on something that has remained a great mystery to all of us on the U.S. side who have studied this: that is, the Cuban perspective, the Cuban point of view, the Cuban reality during what we've always called in the United States the "Cuban" missile crisis—somewhat ironically, I might add. Cuba, from our point of view, has been left out of the Cuban missile crisis. And this process in which our three countries have participated in Moscow and Antigua and here has sought to redress an imbalance of many decades. And so, as the chair, I would like to invite our host, President Castro, to begin.

CASTRO: [Taken aback.] All right; another surprise. I thought that this morning we were going to discuss an item brought up by the American delegation yesterday. I thought perhaps my presentation would be in the afternoon. In any case, I think I can make the effort. If you prefer, I'll start with the presentation. Perhaps I'll need some help, some documentation. I think that I have the essential points in mind to speak right now. If I don't elaborate a lot, don't think that it is because I am trying to withhold information; it's because I don't want to make a traditional two-and-a-half-hour or three-hour speech, but rather to summarize my thoughts as much as possible, and concentrate on the essential things. I will also try to bear in mind everything that has been discussed in the past two days; I don't want to repeat what has been said here.

In my view, many things have been clarified here. I think, actually, that this meeting has been very, very rich in content—at least for me, since I was not able to participate in the previous meetings, and I don't know each and every one of the things that had been said earlier. I have a general idea, and that is why I think that I should confine myself to those things which, because of their nature, have not been reported in other meetings.

Let me start by saying that in analyzing a period such as this one, we must also analyze or review the participation of several personalities in it. Two of them are two very important personalities of our time:

Khrushchev and Kennedy. They were two people for whom I feel great respect. In the case of Khrushchev, for the gestures of friendship he had for our country in very difficult times, I've always regarded him with affection. I met him personally. I remember when, immediately after a meeting of heads of state in the United Nations, he went to visit me at the Theresa Hotel, where I had virtually been confined at the time due to the enormous hostility directed at me there.* I was practically ejected from my original hotel. I had two options: either to go and set up a tent on the United Nations patio, or to go to the Theresa Hotel. There I was welcomed, and I received the visits of many heads of state, Khrushchev among them. That was a great honor; he behaved toward us extremely well. Anytime or every time that we requested anything from him, he did everything possible to try to meet our requests. I had the feeling that I was rather dealing with a peasant— a very wise peasant—but, more than that, an intelligent man—a very intelligent man—an audacious man, and a courageous man. Those were my personal impressions of Khrushchev.

I also have my own assessment of Kennedy's personal qualities, independent of the conflicts that emerged between his administration and mine. I think he was a talented man, a courageous man, a man with the necessary qualifications to rule his country. He made mistakes, but he also had great successes. He was the main figure in the United States during the October crisis, a man with new ideas. Some of them were brilliant, or at least very intelligent, such as the Alliance for Progress. Also, in my view, because of the boost in the authority that he got after the October crisis, when his leadership was consolidated in the United States, he might have been one of the presidents—or perhaps the president best able—to rectify American policy toward Cuba.

I had proof of this precisely the day he died [22 November 1963]. That morning I was talking to a French journalist, Jean Daniel, who had had a long interview with Kennedy. Kennedy had requested Daniel to come to Cuba and talk to me and convey a message to me. While we were talking, the radio announced the assassination of President Kennedy in Dallas. You can see how many coincidences there have been. On the basis of what the journalist said, I realized that Kennedy was thinking about the possibility of having an exchange and trying to find a solution to the problems with Cuba, since he started by requesting Daniel to talk to me about how we had all been on the

---

*The two met on 20 September 1960.

brink of a nuclear war, and to find out if I was aware of this. He wanted to hold an exchange of views. We were talking about this when we received the news of his death. I think he was an able man, because of his authority, because of his talent, and because he was ready to rectify some aspects of U.S. policy toward Cuba.

I tell you this very sincerely to substantiate why I feel this respect toward these historical personalities. It is not my intention to hurt anyone or to offend the memory of anyone.

As to the most immediate antecedents of the problem that was to emerge later, we have the Bay of Pigs.[125] However, I do not blame Kennedy for the Bay of Pigs; actually, Kennedy inherited this from the previous administration. The decisions had already been made; everything had been made ready. Kennedy had just come into office, and he was faced with a very difficult problem. To a certain extent he had made some commitments regarding Cuba in some speeches during the election campaign. But in my view, he was not at all pleased with that operation. It is true that he had sufficient constitutional authority to have put an end to it, to have stopped it; but constitutional authority is not enough sometimes to solve some problems. You need moral authority as well—political authority; great political authority, which is not common in administrations during their first weeks after coming into power, and sometimes not even during the first presidential term. Sometimes it is said that a president cannot solve a certain problem during his first term, because he must stand for reelection and can only solve it in a second term. So I don't blame him for Playa Girón, for the Bay of Pigs invasion. And, to a certain extent, we have to recognize that he acted quite calmly during the event itself.

As was said here, that was a political catastrophe of the first magnitude. It cannot be compared as a military disaster with other military disasters; but, from the military standpoint—given the scale of the fighting—it was, in a sense, a disaster, or a catastrophe. It was a hard test for Kennedy, and I would say that at that time he proved himself to be courageous. I remember what he said when he assumed full responsibility for the event: that victory had many fathers, but that defeat was an orphan.[126] He could have taken the decision to order U.S. troops, ships, and planes to participate. The fighting in Girón was waged in sight of the aircraft carriers and ships, which were three miles away from our shores. I saw that personally when we went into Girón on the evening of April 19th, 1961. There, you could see the Navy. There were no lights on the ships; they were in combat readiness; and they witnessed what was happening. They were ready to fight. As a matter of fact, the Bay of Pigs plan even called for the intervention of military forces, because the aim was to establish a government, recognize it, and then to support it with troops. So, the Girón plan already contained the premises for the use of military force against our country. It called for intervention and occupation of the country. The troops that landed had no support from our people. They would not have been able to do anything but occupy a small tract of land and create in Cuba a sort of Taiwan, or something. But we know that the plan provided for recognition of that government, and intervention. So, if Kennedy had not been calm and courageous then, if he had not been fully aware of the mistake that that operation implied—militarily and politically—he might have committed American forces.

Of course, Kennedy was greatly concerned with Latin American public opinion. He didn't want to inaugurate his administration with such an event. So he decided not to issue the order to the U.S. troops to intervene. If he had, that would have been a very bloody war. For our part, I don't know whether the number of casualties would have been as high as if we had had an intervention during the crisis of October '62. I imagine that that would have been a different kind of war, with unforeseeable consequences. But in spite of this, we did estimate the number of victims. By then, in our country, we had hundreds of thousands of men and women under arms; weapons had been distributed throughout the country, in the mountains, in the plains, in the cities. There would have been an enormous resistance on the part of the population. They had the necessary weapons. And we had just come out of a war; the guerrilla traditions were still fresh in our minds. Our people had to face a well-equipped army with 80,000 men in arms, and when the war ended, we only had 3,000 or more weapons. And at that time, we could count on some 300,000 men and women to be armed—or able to get weapons—and, to a certain extent, organized and trained. We had cannons, artillery, tanks—a few—and the troops that manned them had received accelerated training. I asked the first advisers at that time—some specialists were teaching us how to use the weapons from Czechoslovakia, and from the USSR; we had a lot of cannons and antiaircraft artillery—I asked them whether they could train all the personnel needed. They provided that training in a matter of weeks. What our soldiers learned in the mornings, they taught to the rest of our comrades in the various camps that we organized. And there was great enthusiasm among the population. Perhaps we'd still be fighting today had there been an intervention in 1962. This would have meant for our country perhaps a toll of thousands or hundreds of thousands of deaths, enormous losses, and a prolonged struggle against those who came to occupy our territory. That's why I say that we should recognize in Kennedy the common sense and the wisdom not to have ordered the intervention of U.S. troops at that time.

I know that there would have been presidents who would not have hesitated for a minute to issue the order for U.S. troops to intervene. I'm telling you this so that you can understand why we assessed Kennedy's conduct at the time so highly. But Girón, the Bay of Pigs, was undoubtedly the prelude to the October crisis, because, for Kennedy, this was a severe political blow. He was very saddened and embittered by these events, and as of then, the Cuban issue had a different, special connotation for him. This was reflected in the relations between our two countries.

I'm not going to talk about clandestine or covert operations, sabotage, and so on, which were continuous throughout that period. I'm not going to refer to the plans, the assassination attempts which, in one way or another, took place at the time. That is not the aim of our analysis. Indeed, there was great bitterness in Kennedy as a result, that is true. The idea was that in one way or another he had to put an end to the revolutionary process in Cuba. He also used strategic and political methods—I mentioned the example of the Alliance for Progress for changing the objective conditions, because he knew that the objective conditions in Latin America were, as they still are today, conducive to social outbursts. And he wanted to tackle the problem from that angle.

Now, then; we should remember that after the Bay of Pigs crisis, there was a meeting between Kennedy and Khrushchev at Vienna [3–4 June 1961]. According to the news that we got, Khrushchev was very concerned by Kennedy's statements with regard to Cuba. Perhaps some people who are present here could provide details of the meeting, and confirm or correct the story we heard that, when the discussion turned to Hungary, Kennedy said that while the Soviets had solved the problem in Hungary, the United States had not yet been able to solve the problem of Cuba.[127] I don't know if that was actually broached at the Vienna summit; I don't have the means to say whether it was true or not. [Darusenkov nods.] Darusenkov believes that it was discussed in Vienna. But afterwards, we heard the story that, in a conversation with [Aleksei] Adzhubei, Khrushchev's son-in-law and the editor of *Izvestia*—I apologize if I'm not pronouncing his last name correctly—Kennedy mentioned Hungary and the problems that yet had to be solved with Cuba. The Soviets perceived this as an affirmation, as a sort of promise, that the problem of Cuba was going to be solved. I do remember that Adzhubei came to visit us, although I don't remember the exact date—I don't know if this was after the trip to Washington; perhaps Oleg Troyanovsky will remember this. We would have to identify the exact date, and in which of the two conversations— or both—the question of Hungary came up. But I do know of Khrushchev's great concern regarding those conversations. This was a frequent topic of conversation long before he even considered the idea of deploying the missiles.

Of course, we were requesting more weapons. We were ready to defend ourselves. We requested more weapons, and we signed some agreements for supplies to be given to our armed forces. That was the situation up to the month of May 1962. Earlier here we heard some of the details about Soviet decision making. Alejandro Alekseev, who was the ambassador in our country for many years—he was already the ambassador here during the crisis—he and other members of the Soviet delegation have told us here details of the conversations about the missiles long before we heard of the idea.

We were informed of [Sharaf] Rashidov's visit; he was a party leader in Uzbekistan. He had visited us earlier and had spent several months in Cuba dealing with agricultural matters and irrigation. He came with a Marshal [S. S.] Biryuzov.* I don't speak English well at all, but I'm even worse at Russian. Petrov was his *nom de guerre*. Well, Petrov—Biryuzov—was a very lively, very energetic man. He later died in an air accident, I think in Yugoslavia. He came with Rashidov, and he was the one who brought up the missile issue. He did not start with the missile issue. We received him immediately. But he did not start, as I said, by speaking about the missiles. He started discussing international affairs, Cuba, the risks for Cuba, and at a certain point he asked, "What would be necessary to prevent a U.S. invasion?" And I immediately replied, "Well, if the United States knows that an invasion of Cuba would imply war with the Soviet Union, then, in my view, that would be the best way to prevent an invasion of Cuba." That was my answer. To corroborate this with documents, if you wish, you can see the version that I gave six years later in a report to the Central Committee in 1968. I said, "And at that time a delegation of Soviet military came, headed by a marshal, who asked how we considered

---

*Biryuzov was commander-in-chief of the Soviet Strategic Rocket Forces. His delegation traveled to Cuba in late May 1962.

that an invasion could be prevented. And we said by taking measures which would clearly tell imperialism"—I apologize for using this term, but that's the way I said it [laughter]—"that any aggression against Cuba would entail a war not just with Cuba. But the man already had ideas in mind. He said, 'But, concretely, how? We have to take concrete steps that would indicate this.' He had already been given the mission of proposing the deployment of strategic missiles, and perhaps he was afraid we would not accept."[128]

Now, the deployment of the missiles here might have served as a basis for campaigns against the revolution throughout the rest of Latin America. But we had no doubts. In the first place, when we were told about the missiles, we believed that this was something that would buttress the defensive power of the entire socialist camp. We believed that it would contribute to this end. We didn't want to think only about our particular problems then. Secondarily, the missiles would contribute to our own defense. But our leadership met to analyze this proposal, and to reach a decision. And how was this problem posed? In our view, it strengthened the socialist camp; and if we thought that the socialist camp should be ready to go to war for any socialist country, we had no right to base our decision on narrow self-interest. I continued: "We saw the problem of propaganda, but also the actual danger of any crisis that could emerge. Without any kind of hesitation, and honestly—with a true internationalist feeling—all the comrades agreed to reply immediately and affirmatively, and with enormous confidence in a country which had great experience in many spheres, in international affairs, and even war."

We told them that we would like to sign a military agreement. Then they sent a draft agreement; this I've already discussed. Here I have a verbatim record of what I explained in a personal talk in 1968 about the prelude to the October crisis. To summarize, we, from the very first, saw this as a strategic operation. I'm going to tell the truth about how we thought. In reality, we didn't really like the missiles. If it had been a matter only of our own defense, we would not have accepted the deployment of the missiles here. But don't think that this was because we were afraid of the dangers that might follow the deployment of the missiles here; rather, it was because this would damage the image of the revolution, and we were very zealous in protecting the image of the revolution throughout the rest of Latin America. The presence of the missiles would in fact turn us into a Soviet military base, and that entailed a high political cost for the image of our country, an image we so highly valued. So, if it had been just for our own defense, I think that, in full honesty—and Alejandro knows this—we would not have accepted the deployment of the missiles. But indeed, we regarded the deployment of the missiles as something that would strengthen the socialist camp—something that, to a certain extent, would help to improve the so-called balance of power.

That's the way we perceived it then. We did not start discussing this. It seemed logical, if we had started discussing whether it was a good idea or not, we would have reached the conclusion that they should not be deployed. We would have refused to accept the missiles. Naturally, their deployment was not presented in this way, with these objectives. But that's what we perceived immediately. Afterwards, we asked questions: What kind of missiles? How many? We had no practical knowledge about this, and we were told that we would be getting forty-two missiles. That's what has been said here. It seems that thirty-six were operational, and six were for instruction. But he [Biryuzov] said forty-two missiles. We said that we had to convene a meeting of the leadership, that we needed time to tell them about this before we reached a decision, but that we'd be quick. Immediately after the meeting with the Soviets was over, we convened a meeting of the leadership and we analyzed this issue along the lines that I have explained. "Gentlemen, the presence of the missiles implies this and this and this." We didn't ignore the fact—this was clear to us—that the presence of the missiles would generate enormous political tensions. That was clear. But we approached this from the point of view of our moral duties, our political duties, our internationalist duties, as well as we understood them.

There had been plenty of talk about missiles, but in another sense. After the Girón invasion, there had been talk of missiles. You would have to read the declarations by Nikita. More than once he insinuated that, if there was an invasion of Cuba, he would retaliate, even with missiles.[129] He insinuated that publicly more than once—so much so that people here talked about Soviet missiles before the crisis—after the Bay of Pigs—as if the missiles were here. Many comrades in their speeches talked about the missiles. I, however, refrained from talking about the missiles, because I did not consider it correct for people to pin their hopes for defense on foreign support. For me, our population had to be totally ready, as we are today—and today more than ever— to develop self-confidence and the capacity to struggle and resist without foreign support. So, in none of my speeches—and there were a great many during this period—did I mention Soviet missiles as a possible aid, but Nikita encouraged this idea with his public declarations.[130]

As was discussed here yesterday, even the United States thought that there was a strategic missile gap, and Kennedy said so during his campaigns. Throughout the world there was this perception of a missile gap. It was known that the United States had a very powerful air force, but that the Soviet Union had advanced greatly in the sphere of missiles. At the time, the Soviets had made spectacular technical events, such as in space flights. The first space flight was by a Soviet pilot in a Soviet space ship. That had an enormous impact on world public opinion, and even in the United States itself. It is not surprising, then, that we thought the fighting capacity of each of the two big powers in the nuclear sphere was quite similar. But be that as it may, and even supposing that the Soviet Union had had many more missiles than they actually had, we perceived that the presence of these missiles in Cuba would mean a modification or change in the balance of power. I wouldn't say *change;* you can't talk about a change in the balance of power, but rather a considerable *improvement* in the balance of power in favor of the socialist countries—the ones we regarded as our allies, our friends, our brothers, as sharing a common ideology.

Of course, we never regarded the missiles as something that would one day be used against the United States, in an attack against the United States, in an unjustified first strike. I recall that Nikita insisted that they would never launch a nuclear first strike. This idea was an obsession with him.[131] He was constantly talking about this, constantly talking about peace, constantly talking about negotiations with the United States, trying to do away with the Cold War, with the arms race, and so on.

So, in order to assess the mood of the time, you have to know what the prevailing ideas were about the capabilities of the two powers. We saw that this would improve the position of the socialist camp, and we regarded the issue of Cuba's defense as the secondary issue, for the reasons I already gave you. That is how we perceived things then, and we have maintained these perceptions throughout these years. That is why I read to you from this speech I gave twenty-four years ago. Had we known then what we know now about the balance of power, we'd have realized the practical importance—the military importance—of these forty-two missiles, because, by being deployed in Cuba, they were transformed from medium-range missiles into strategic missiles.

When we left our meeting and returned to the marshal and Rashidov, I gave them this reply. Unfortunately, that was not recorded. It should have been, but recordings then were quite underdeveloped; you didn't have those small recorders that you can carry in your pocket. Now you can record anything. You can record this meeting; this meeting *is* being recorded. Sometimes we have visits by heads of state, the most recent one, by Gorbachev, and we told him—we agreed that everything that we were going to discuss was going to be recorded. Of course, you ask for your interlocutor's agreement, as a rule. There are some who are more in favor of being recorded than others. The meetings with U Thant were recorded by mutual accord, for the sake of posterity. But, in any case, we replied that if this deployment was to strengthen the socialist camp, and at the same time—and I ranked this second—if this would contribute to the defense of Cuba, then we would be ready to receive all the missiles that were necessary.[132] To be more exact, we would be ready to receive even 1,000 missiles if they wanted to send them. I said 1,000. That was the decision. *Alea iacta est,** as a Roman general said; I think it was Julius Caesar. If the decision is made, the decision is made. But this decision was taken in this spirit, and with that purpose.

This may help explain why we were so indignant about the course of events that followed, why we adopted a defiant and almost intransigent attitude in the wake of the crisis. The deployment followed the agreement, a process that was so clearly explained by the Soviet general. The Soviets organized, actually in a very few months, the deployment of forces and weapons. From a logistic point of view, it was a perfect operation. We appreciated and admired this, and not merely from the viewpoint of military theory.

We, too, have been forced to dispatch troops abroad, as we did in Angola. I remember the first time, when we sent 36,000 men with most of their weapons in a few weeks.[133] I also remember what we did after Cuito Cuanavale,† when we raised our force level to 53,000 men. We have some experience in the transportation of troops using our own ships. There were no Soviet ships. We transported troops and

---

*"The die is cast."

†The battle of Cuito Cuanavale was, from the Cuban perspective, the Stalingrad of the Angolan war. In early 1988, South African forces inflicted terrible losses on MPLA forces at Mavinga, in southeastern Angola, and pursued them to Cuito Cuanavale, 300 miles north of the border with Namibia. The Cubans rushed forces to the front and held the line in February 1988. The South Africans then withdrew back into Namibia, their protectorate. From the Cuban perspective, Cuito Cuanavale signaled the beginning of the end of apartheid. See Weiss and Blight, *The Suffering Grass*, pp. 160–61.

weapons on our ships, and in Cuito Cuanavale, by ourselves. That was the way the Angola operation was carried out in 1975. We acted on our own decision. The Soviet Union expressed only concerns in 1975. But that was a free and sovereign decision made by our country. In Cuito Cuanavale, a crisis situation emerged which forced us to send an enormous amount of forces, and we did this resolutely. You have to be resolute, or else you will be defeated. If you need 20,000 troops and you send 10,000, the most likely thing is that you will be defeated. We had the South Africans right there. They were powerful. They manufactured good weapons, they had good training, good planes, and we made ready to fight them. When they launched an offensive, they included 1,000 antiaircraft weapons, since they had quite a large superiority. So we have some experience in the transportation of troops, and we know what an operation of this sort entails. Of course, we didn't send missiles, but we did send heavy weaponry of all kinds.

Now, the deployment of the missiles was an operation that the Soviets carried out with great efficiency and in a very short time. They did what they had to do, and assumed full responsibility.

We have yet to explain our understanding of the motivations. There are various opinions on this question, particularly from the Soviet side, and they have mirrored what has been said in the Soviet Union about this. They have also used the arguments that Nikita always used. I said he was very wise. The way that he presented the issue to the other leaders of the Soviet Party and the way he actually thought are two different issues. There might have been other Soviet leaders familiar with the intimate motivations of Nikita Khrushchev.

In the light of what we know today about the real balance of power, or correlation of forces, it is evident that repairing it was an imperative. I don't criticize Khrushchev for the fact that he tried to improve the balance of forces. I think this is something legal, something legitimate in terms of international law, and absolutely moral: that is, to try to improve the balance of forces between the socialist camp and the United States. And if what they really had was fifty or sixty ICBMs, it is clear that the presence of those forty-two missiles almost doubled their effective capacity. We haven't talked about the submarines, but certainly someone must know how many missiles they had aboard submarines and their capability for deterrent strikes. I know they had submarines with nuclear missiles; they haven't been mentioned here; at least, we haven't heard how many they had at the time. But, undoubtedly, these land-based missiles would have doubled the number.[134]

If we had known about that balance of power, which we ignored—I repeat, if the conversation had been framed in terms of improving the balance of power—we might have advised them to be prudent. Because I think if you've got fifty, you've got to be more prudent than if you've got three hundred. This is clear, of course. If we had been familiar with that information, and if it had been put to us in strategic terms, we would have advised prudence. As I say, and I repeat, the defense of the country was not our concern. Otherwise, how would we be today, when we're not receiving missiles—when we are receiving practically nothing? Here you see us all peaceful and calm. The United States is much more powerful than we are. They have smart weapons—all kinds of conventional weapons—and here you see us peaceful and calm. We have confidence in ourselves. We trust our own combat capability, and we are proud of that capability. Obviously, it is difficult to divine Nikita's intimate thoughts; but that's the way we perceived it, and it seems that's the way the rest of the Soviet delegation perceived it.

He was very astute. He was capable of talking about an issue in one set of terms, while thinking about it in other terms. But I could find no other explanation, and even today I can find no other explanation. Of course, it's true that Nikita loved Cuba very much. He especially cherished Cuba. He had a weakness for Cuba, you might say—emotionally, and so on—because he was a man of political conviction, a man with a political doctrine, a political theory, and he was consistent with that doctrine. He thought in terms of capitalism versus socialism. He had very firm convictions. He thought, perhaps in a kind of mistaken conception, that socialism would, in peaceful competition, overcome capitalism. I say that this was perhaps an erroneous conception, because I don't think that the objective of a socialist society should be consumerism. I don't think that the countries of the Third World have to imitate capitalism and its consumerism. I ask myself what would happen if each Chinese family had a car, and if each Indian family had a car as well? And each family in Bangladesh, and Pakistan? If they had such success in their development, how far would the oil go? How far would the fuel go? How much more poisoning will the atmosphere tolerate? How much other damage? So, as I said, I think there was a mistaken conception of the role of socialism. Socialism is intended for the basic problems of humankind: education, health, culture, housing, food, nutrition—all of the essential material needs. Socialism is not about everyone having an automobile, or a lot of consumer goods.

People should have what the environment will tolerate. We have quite different conceptions of socialism. But he was a man with very deep-seated political convictions.

I don't think Nikita wanted war. I think nothing could have been further from his mind than a nuclear war. He was very much aware of what a nuclear war meant for the Soviet Union. He was obsessed by the idea of achieving a certain parity. I think the reasoning expressed yesterday by Mr. McNamara was excellent, when he said that parity existed any time each side had a retaliatory capacity that could cause immense damage. But even if one country were hit by all the nuclear weapons of the other, the world would be destroyed anyway, because the fall-out, and problems of all sorts, would be so great. If you used only 10,000 of the 50,000 warheads that exist, that would be the end of the world—even if you dropped them all on the same place. I think McNamara's reasoning about when parity actually exists is wise, because parity exists from the very moment when you have the capacity to inflict intolerable damage to the extent that it would be inconceivable to launch a first nuclear strike.[135]

I tried to find out how that had been discussed in the leadership of the Soviet Party and government when I traveled to the USSR in 1963. The fact is that I was never able to get to the bottom of that. I asked many questions of all the Politburo members: [Soviet Deputy Premier Aleksei N.] Kosygin, Gromyko—I don't remember if he was a member.* I asked all of them, one by one, "How was this decision made? Which were the arguments used?" And I wasn't able to get a single word. They often simply didn't reply to my questions. And, of course, you can't be impertinent and say, "Hey, answer my question." Despite all the questions I asked, I never got a clear answer on the role of the strategic argument in the Soviet deliberations. So I want to make clear that this was our perception of the motivation. I've got to say that.

THE SECRET DECEPTIVE DEPLOYMENT:
". . . a very big mistake"

Fidel Castro has no difficulty whatsoever understanding Kennedy's outrage at Khrushchev's dissembling about missiles in Cuba; for he,

---

*Foreign Minister Andrei Gromyko joined the Politburo in 1973.

Castro, also found it offensive, albeit for different reasons. In his speech, on 22 October 1962, announcing the crisis, Kennedy denounced ". . . this secret, swift, and extraordinary buildup of Communist missiles" and "this clandestine, reckless and provocative threat to world peace."[136] This was the trump card the Cubans wanted to deny the United States in late August when, sensing a crisis brewing, they urged Khrushchev unsuccessfully to go public with the deployment.

American officials have said at previous conferences that Castro may well have been right. A public deployment of missiles to Cuba would have greatly constrained American options. The following exchange took place at the Cambridge conference in October 1987:

[SERGO] MIKOYAN: If we had declared officially in September in the U.N. that we intended to defend Cuba with missiles, what would have been the American reaction?

[McGEORGE] BUNDY: Well, it would have been a totally different situation. It's very hard to say.

MIKOYAN: Might it have made it harder for you and easier for us?

BUNDY: That may very well be.

[THEODORE] SORENSEN: I think it certainly would have made it more difficult for us.[137]

The deception, Castro contends, was "a very big mistake," because without it the Soviet Union might have succeeded in deploying missiles to Cuba without precipitating a crisis. Soviet officials in 1962, however, dismissed the suggestion out of hand.[138] Years later, Andrei Gromyko continued to do so. "If this measure were not carried out in secrecy, it just would not have worked," Gromyko insisted at the Moscow conference in 1989. "I think that all present will have to agree."[139]

CASTRO: [Continuing.] The agreement began being implemented almost immediately—that is, this verbal agreement. It had yet to be formalized, but the agreement was already practically operational. In the USSR, they produced the draft to which Alejandro referred. The draft was sent to Cuba. It was politically vague, in the sense that it had no clear political justification. There was no talk of strategic weapons.

But based on some of the points in the draft—the wherefores and therefores—I drafted the political justification for the articles of the agreement: "The Soviet Union will send to the Republic of Cuba armed forces to reinforce its defense against the danger of a foreign aggression, and thus contribute to the preservation of world peace. The type of Soviet troops, and their areas of deployment in the Republic of Cuba, will be established by the representatives named pursuant to Article 11." Article 11 refers to the representatives of both sides. There was no mention of strategic weapons, and this agreement could have been made public. No one could have objected to the legality or morality of this agreement.[140]

Of course, it was not indispensable to have missiles here to defend Cuba. I forgot to mention that argument. We could have had a military treaty with the USSR saying that an attack on Cuba would be the equivalent to an aggression against the USSR. The United States has many of these pacts throughout the world, and they are respected, because the word of a state is respected. There is a risk to ignoring treaties, and they are taken into consideration.

So that's what I was saying: that the Americans should know this. The USSR could have stated that an aggression against Cuba was the equivalent of an aggression against the USSR. We could have signed a military agreement, and we would have been able to achieve the objective of Cuba's defense without missiles. I am absolutely convinced of that. This is one of the things that reaffirms the conviction that we had at the time, and which we have maintained today—although there isn't a single word on record of a different argument being used. And that is why our colleagues on the Soviet delegation—I know I can't say "Soviet" anymore, now that it's the Commonwealth of Independent States—but what I mean is, those who participated have answered—in my opinion with absolute honesty—any questions about the conditions prevailing then in the Soviet Union.

We made a considerable effort during the time when the missiles were deployed to accommodate and facilitate the operation. People lived in those sites. There were farms and facilities that we had to clear out. We appointed one of the Party and government leaders to devote himself exclusively to the task of negotiating the acquisition of land for the missile installations. It was a considerable amount of land. I don't have the numbers, but hundreds of families had to be relocated. We had to negotiate with them, give them land, give them advantages—and all of this secretly, because we couldn't explain what this was for.

There were all sorts of leaks. We had to adopt the following method: anyone who knew anything was considered to be in isolation. And many officers would come and say, "Listen, I've found out about this, and I've come to stay here because in such and such a place, in talking to such and such Soviet officer—." You can just imagine, 42,000 men; they'd establish relations and talk to one another. Others would see something. So, we adopted the method that you adopt in severe epidemics: that is, to isolate everyone who is infected. If you knew something, you were infected, so you were in quarantine. There was a process for this. There were large troop movements, and there was talk of offensive weapons, of missiles. Furthermore, when the missiles began to arrive, they were huge. I think the current ones may be more modern; maybe you can carry them in a suitcase. I don't know what the technology is like in that area now. Other people know more about this than I. But those were enormous things: twenty-five, thirty meters, a block long. When these huge objects were unloaded, no matter how much you tried to mask this when you transported them, people would notice. This, I would say, was the best-kept secret in history, because several million Cubans knew about it. This was something that you simply could not hide.

I think the CIA must have received news of the missiles, because we have spontaneous informants here—people who don't support the revolution and sympathize with the United States. But no one had any certain information. There was no proof. This was an extremely complicated operation, and an infinity of details had to be seen to to keep this secret.[141]

A great many other things happened that I'm not going to repeat: Raúl's trip to Moscow [2–17 July 1962]; the trip by Che and Aragonés to the Soviet Union [27 August–2 September 1962], when they took with them the final draft of the agreement, which was accepted. Our draft was accepted just as it was, without changing a comma. I also talked about that.

We've got to recall that a certain atmosphere was brewing which seemed rather negative to us, and that is why we felt that we should go public with the law and publish this military agreement, just like that. Secrecy put us at a disadvantage; both at a political disadvantage, and at a practical disadvantage. But we've got to distinguish between secrets—many military operations have to be secret; the details of the operation, at any rate, if not necessarily the essentials—and what Khrushchev said about it. I think this is an important point, and here there was a big mistake, a very big mistake. Not only was it a mistake to deploy the missiles secretly, which was damaging to us, but it was a mistake to give Kennedy false information, having gotten into the game of the character of the weapons: whether they were offensive or defensive. No, in none of the Cuban statements was there ever any participation in this game of the character of the weapons. We refused to play that game, and in the public statements of the government, and then at the U.N., we always said that Cuba considered that it had the sovereign right to have the kind of weapons it considered convenient, and that no one had any right to establish what kind of weapons our country could or could not have. We never denied the strategic character of the weapons. We did not want to play that game; we did not agree with that approach. So, we never denied or affirmed the character of the weapons, but rather we reaffirmed our right to have the kind of weapons we considered convenient for our defense.

On the other hand, you've got to admit this, given that Khrushchev did get into the game of categorizing the weapons: his basis for categorizing the weapons was the intention behind their deployment. Since he did not have the intention of using the weapons in an offensive operation, he considered them defensive. The intention defined the character of the weapons. But it became clear that Kennedy didn't understand it that way. He did not understand this question of intentions. He was looking at the *kind* of weapons—whether or not they were strategic weapons. That was the issue. And it's perfectly clear that Kennedy was convinced that strategic weapons were not going to be transferred to Cuba. So I would say that he saw more than just cunning in this; he saw deception. The secret of the military agreement, and the deception, were two realities that were very damaging. I think that there should have been a different approach, not this attempt at deception. This was very damaging because Kennedy had a lot at stake. He had already had the Bay of Pigs setback. He was going into his second year. There were going to be elections. Khrushchev didn't want to affect these elections. Perhaps this was one of the things Khrushchev considered in not publishing the agreement; he didn't want to do anything to damage Kennedy in those elections. But he did the worst possible thing, given that what was being done could be discovered.

Kennedy believed what he was told, in my opinion. This is obvious in his public statements. He was kind of relieved. "Well, they're filling that country with tanks, cannons, and so on; but at least there are no strategic weapons." He calculated on a logical basis. This did not give him a legal objection to the missiles when the crisis broke out, but it gave him the opportunity to present himself to the world as having been deceived. He could say, "I was told—they repeated this frequently—that they would not deploy these missiles." So before world public opinion, Kennedy gained in moral stature, if not in legal stature. He said, "I was assured this, and this other has turned out." He was put in a difficult personal situation—something that Khrushchev would not have wanted, but which happened. He was the man who had been deceived. He had been told one thing, and the truth was something else. This was one of the advantages that he derived, not only from secrecy, but from the deception.

What other advantage was there? When the deployment was finally discovered on the 14th, the United States had an immense advantage, because they had the secret in their hands. They could then take the initiative. The initiative in the military field was then in the hands of the United States, because they knew what was going on. And they could afford to adopt one option or another: a political response, the quarantine, or a surprise air strike against those installations. I think that that was a very dangerous moment from the military point of view. A surprise attack would have been illegal, arbitrary, and unfair from all points of view; even immoral, as a matter of fact, because one must comply with international law, and no one has a right to attack any country, to invade another country.[142] But in any case, Kennedy had the option. He could have ordered a surprise attack when no one was expecting it.

Of course, the Soviet general explained something here that was very important: the warheads were not at the missile sites. The warheads were a considerable distance away, which is the way it should be. For the same reason, I told the Soviet commander on the 26th of October—in the middle of the crisis—that he shouldn't concentrate all the missiles, so that they would not all be destroyed. A certain capacity had to be reserved. This is an elementary measure, which undoubtedly the Soviets adopted; but I'm afraid that a large part—almost all the surface-to-surface missiles, and all the visible facilities—could have been destroyed in a total surprise attack, because those antiaircraft missiles could only be fired against aircraft flying above 1,000 meters. Those facilities lacked defenses. They were defended against low flights when we mobilized all our conventional batteries and devoted them to their protection; but up until that moment they were very vulnerable.

Afterwards, things changed, of course. The situation improved, but the United States had eight days—or, rather, six days; they found out on the sixteenth—before making the information they had public. They had six days to act, and it was a very dangerous moment. So from the political and military point of view, the way this was managed in these two aspects, in my opinion, had negative consequences. But this was the way in which it was managed. I've explained our attitude. We had our opinion. I don't know anything beyond that.

THE CRISIS AND AFTERMATH:
". . . like talking about rope in the house of a hanged man"

At the Antigua conference in January 1991, our Cuban colleagues presented us with a token of their appreciation for having organized the meeting: a chunk of steel reinforcement, taken from a concrete piling at the former Soviet missile site at Remedios, on Cuba's north coast, mounted on a carved and polished wooden base. The steel had characteristic Soviet markings; on the base, written in Spanish in a scroll-like hand, were these words: "In memory of the sad and luminous days of the October crisis." They were written by Che Guevara in 1965 in his "farewell letter" to Fidel Castro.[143]

As Castro begins to speak now about the epicenter of the crisis, of the danger and disappointment—the sadness and luminosity—we are reminded of the vast difference between the memento containing Che Guevara's words, and the plaques given by President Kennedy after the crisis to his closest associates: small, mounted metal calendars of October 1962, with the 16th through the 28th—the famous thirteen days—in dark boldface. Guevara's words express deep, indelible regret, along with a sense of being left hanging, of there being no proper conclusion to the events. The Kennedy plaque, on the other hand, symbolizes an equally indelible, fully and successfully concluded set of events. As Castro speaks, he appears to look directly at McNamara, who returns his gaze, as if both are seeking to discover points of contact between the former's bitter luminosity and the latter's fear.

The details come cascading forth in a flurry of commentaries on several documents, some of which Castro "declassifies" as he cites them and comments on them: Khrushchev's letter to him of 23 October, expressing firm resolve; the military agreement, which is consistent with the letter; his own letter to U Thant of 28 October, listing the "Five Points" upon which Castro made Cuban agreement to the resolution of the crisis contingent;[144] the bitter discussions with U Thant in Cuba regarding Cuba's refusal to permit on-site inspection; and finally, a long "poetic" letter from Khrushchev on 31 January 1963, followed by extensive remarks about his trip to the Soviet Union in April–May 1963, during which Khrushchev inadvertently confirmed what Castro had suspected all along: that the Americans and Soviets had used Cuba and Turkey as bargaining chips—a slip Castro likened to "talking about rope in the house of a hanged man." Khrushchev let this slip, no less, on the "glorious" trip the intent of which was to smooth over relations between Cuba and the Soviet Union.

Fidel Castro, at any rate, makes amends for some bizarrely distorted history for which he has been partially responsible. On the 1963 trip, for example, Castro gave a speech describing the missile crisis in these terms: "The Soviet Union . . . did not hesitate to risk a harsh war in defense of our little country. History does not know of a similar act of solidarity. That is internationalism, that is Communism."[145] This, Castro now informs us in word and manner, is rubbish. With some apparent "sadness," evident especially when looking at his Soviet friend "Alejandro" Alekseev, with whom he personally shared these momentous events, but also with a good deal of "luminosity," Castro brings us much nearer than we have ever been before to the bitter Cuban experience of October 1962.

CASTRO: [Continuing.] The crisis broke out on the 22nd, but that morning we had put our troops on a combat alert. When we saw all the movements, the meetings in Washington, all the facts that were already public, we realized that it had to be the missiles. We didn't waste any time and placed all our forces on maximum alert. So that morning, before Kennedy spoke, we had already mobilized our forces. *Our* forces. We also advised the Soviets of the situation. After the crisis became public on the night of the 22nd, from that moment on, measures for our defense occupied almost all of our time. We worked feverishly, night and day, on the things that I've explained: the mobilization of our forces, support for the surface-to-surface missiles— for the medium-range rockets. We gave the Soviet installations practically all our antiaircraft batteries. We felt that the most important objectives to defend, when the crisis erupted, were those sites.

Now, what was Khrushchev's mood? He was in a very combative and determined mood, and on the 23rd he sent a letter that reads as follows. I'm declassifying here. Does "declassification" have anything to do with the class struggle? [Laughter.] Well, anyway, it says here:

Dear Comrade Castro:

The Soviet Government just received from the President of the United States, Mr. Kennedy, the following document, copy of which is hereto attached.

We consider this statement of the Government of the United States, and Kennedy's statement on October 22nd, to be an exceptional interference in the affairs of the Republic of Cuba, a violation of the norms of international law and of the fundamental rules that govern relations among States, and as a blatant act of provocation against the Soviet Union.

The Republic of Cuba has the same rights as any other sovereign State to defend its country and to select its allies as it wishes.

We reject the brazen demands of the U.S. Government to control the sending of weapons to Cuba, and their aspiration to determine what kind of weapons the Republic of Cuba may possess. The Government of the United States is perfectly aware of the fact that no sovereign State would allow interference in its relations with other States, and would not report on measures aimed at strengthening the defense of their country.

In reply to Kennedy's statement, the Soviet Government has expressed the most determined protest against the piratical actions of the United States Government, denouncing them as perfidious and aggressive—these are pirate-like, perfidious, and aggressive actions against sovereign States—and declares its determination to fight actively against such nations.

We have issued orders to our representatives in the Security Council to urgently present the question of the violation by the United States of standards of international law and of the United Nations Charter at the Security Council, and to issue a clear protest against the aggressive and perfidious actions of U.S. imperialism.

Because of the situation, we have issued instructions to our military personnel in Cuba on the need to adopt the necessary measures to be completely ready for combat. We are certain that the actions undertaken by U.S. imperialism and aimed at depriving the Republic of Cuba of its legitimate right to strengthen its defensive capability and the defense of its country will provoke a protest by all peace-loving peoples—

In fact, there were no great protests, to tell the truth, because there were adverse political conditions created by the procedures followed.

But in any case this is in parenthesis, this is not a quote. I'm saying this now.

> . . . will provoke angry protests by all peace-loving peoples and a movement by the masses in defense of the just cause of revolutionary Cuba.

This might have been partially achieved if we had done things openly. All this is true, of course, because we had every right to do what we were doing, and if we had the right to do so, why should we have acted in a way that implied that we didn't have the right, that we were doing something wrong? This should have been analyzed in ethical, political, and legal terms, not in terms of forces, military balances, and so on.

> We are sending you, Comrade Castro, and all of your comrades-in-arms, our warm greetings, and we express our firm certainty that the aggressive plans of American imperialism will fail.

The rest was the U.S. statement.

This is the letter we received on the 23rd, nothing else. In it is a clear and firm determination to fight against the "piratical, perfidious, aggressive" actions of the United States. And what I said was, "Well, it looks like war. I cannot conceive of any retreat." This idea of retreating never entered my mind. We never thought it was possible. And Khrushchev, who knew how many missiles and nuclear weapons we had, sent us this letter on the 23rd. We said, "Well, things are clear; things are clear." And we went to do our own job.

Then, the moment came when I drafted the letter [dated 26 October 1962]. When we had adopted every humanly possible measure, I met with the Soviet military command. They reported that everything was ready. All of the weapons mentioned here by the Soviet general were ready, and morale was high. There was—how should I say it?—this strange situation among the Soviet troops, in that they were faced by a great danger, and they were at the same time very serene. The Cuban military and the Soviet military were all very calm. The Cuban population was totally calm as well. If you had surveyed the Cuban population and you asked them, "Do you want the rockets to be sent back?" ninety percent would have said, "No." The population was serene and intransigent on this. They did not want the rockets taken back.

On the 26th we explained to the Soviet military that these low-level flights were intolerable—intolerable—and therefore our batteries were going to fire. We wanted them to know that. According to the agreement, there were two armies and two commands. We commanded our army in our country, and we said, "We can't tolerate this any further, it's very dangerous." I've already mentioned this, and I'm not going to repeat it. On the 27th, at dawn, when the airplanes came—this was every day, very early—they ran into our antiaircraft fire. The Soviet antiaircraft missile battery shot down the U-2, and that, of course, was a very tense moment. But for us everything was very clear since the moment that we met on the 26th.

While we were talking to the Soviet military command, while we were sending this message to Khrushchev, Khrushchev had already sent a message to Kennedy—you know this—and this message contained the foundations for the solution: that is, the withdrawal of the missiles in exchange for guarantees not to attack Cuba.[146] Then, on the following day, there was another message, and from what I have been told, on the second day the message contained, aside from guarantees for Cuba, the issue of the missiles in Turkey.[147] Of course, when this news reached us—it arrived here on the 28th—it produced great indignation, because we had felt that we had become some kind of bargaining chip. Not only was this a decision taken without *consulting* us, several steps were taken without *informing* us. They could have informed us of the messages of the 26th and the 27th. There was time to do that. We heard over the radio on the 28th that there had been an agreement. So we were humiliated. I understand the Soviet general when he said that one of the bitterest things he had to suffer in his life was the inspection of the ships at sea. On the 28th we found out about the agreement. A message came in one or two hours later through the [Soviet] embassy, and the reaction of our nation was of profound indignation, not relief; all of the people, all of our cadres.

So the political decision we adopted was to launch our five-point list of demands, five very simple points:

• First: An end to the economic blockade and all economic and trade pressure measures throughout the world by the United States against our country.

• Second: An end to all subversive activities, drops of weapons and explosives by air and by sea, organization of mercenary invasions, infiltration of spies and saboteurs—actions all carried out from U.S. territory and from some accomplice countries.

• Third: An end to pirate attacks from bases in the United States and Puerto Rico.
• Fourth: An end to all violations of our sea and airspace by American aircraft and naval craft.
• Fifth: Withdrawal from the naval base in Guantánamo, and return of the territory occupied by the United States.

Those were our five points on the 28th.

We would not have been against a solution. If there was a danger of war, if we had known that Nikita was ready to withdraw the missiles and find a solution on a dignified basis, it would have made no sense to insist on blocking a solution. There had to be a solution—but an *acceptable* solution. The simple solution of withdrawing the missiles because the United States was giving its word that it wasn't going to attack us was incongruent with everything that had been done, and it was incongruent with the circumstances in our country that had to be overcome.

It would have been enough for Nikita to say, "We agree to withdraw the missiles if you give satisfactory guarantees for Cuba." Cuba would not have blocked this; it would have helped in that negotiation. But the minimum guarantees we wanted were these five—not just a guarantee of not invading. And I think the world would have been relieved by such a beginning to the solution of the crisis. Nikita's admitting that they were ready to withdraw the missiles would have been a relief; people would have felt that it was reasonable to reach an agreement on the basis of issues having to do with Cuba.

If the motive for the missiles was really Cuba, they should have thought about Cuba then, and not the missiles in Turkey. It's evident that the missiles in Turkey were present in their minds. Khrushchev was thinking about the missiles in Turkey. They talked about the missiles on the Black Sea.[148] At the end there is also mention of the missiles in Turkey, for whatever reason, perhaps because someone said they should be included. But from the international political point of view—for the honest, peace-loving people in the world; people who supported socialism in Cuba, or independence, or anything—it made no sense to exchange missiles in Cuba for missiles in Turkey. If the cause was Cuba, what did Turkey have to do with the defense of Cuba? Nothing at all! And these five points proposed by Cuba were absolutely reasonable. We could have had a worthwhile negotiation, and the missiles could have been withdrawn, if that was what was necessary to preserve the peace. Peace was endangered. I think the procedures used favored those actions that endangered peace. I've explained that. But there we were. It was the 28th. There was nothing to be done. The commitment had been made. Cuba had been ignored. Turkey had been mentioned. So we proposed our five points.

We've talked about U Thant's trip. The Soviet government asked us to stop firing on American planes. We agreed. We said, "Okay; but only as long as negotiations go on." Exclusively during the negotiations, we gave the order to cease fire. These aircraft were flying very low. There were no low overflights late on the 27th. They didn't fly in the afternoon. There were no low overflights late on the 27th or on the 28th. But then, when our batteries ceased firing, they began their low-level overflights again, during the entire time of the negotiation. It was very humiliating to our population to see those aircraft flying at 100 meters. This demoralized our antiaircraft gunners. One has to understand the personality, the character of the Cuban people, to understand how this can harm their morale.

Then U Thant came [30 October 1962]. I explained our positions, and particularly our categorical opposition to inspection. We didn't accept it. The USSR is sovereign, and so are we. No one can authorize an inspection of our territory if we don't authorize it. So we said: No inspection. That was one of our reactions, because we didn't agree with the outcome of the crisis. When U Thant came, I explained our positions, as I said, and our key broad proposals. He proposed that we accept a group of U.N. representatives, and all of that—U.N. aerial reconnaissance, aircraft manned by persons acceptable to the Cuban, Russian, and American governments. We were in no mood for aerial surveillance at that point. Here is the record of our conversation. U Thant said, "The United States has told me that as soon as the inspection system is implemented, they'll make a public statement—at the Security Council if necesssary—declaring that they will not maintain aggressive intentions against the Cuban government, and that they will guarantee the territorial integrity of the nation." [To Chomy:*] Where is my reply? [Pause.] Here it is. I said, "We do not understand why we are being asked to do this, because we have not violated any law. We haven't carried out any aggression against anyone. All of our actions have been based on international law. We have been the victims,

*Dr. José M. Miyar Barrueco, Castro's personal secretary, who is better known by his nickname, "Chomy," is sitting slightly behind Castro and to his left, feeding him documents. According to Tad Szulc, Chomy "must be the most overworked individual in Cuba." *Fidel,* p. 70.

first of all of a blockade—an illegal act. Secondly, it is pretentious for another country to determine what we have the right to do in our country. Cuba is a sovereign state." I'm reading the essentials here. "The United States has repeatedly been violating our airspace without any right to do so. We can accept anything that is within the law, that does not harm our status as a sovereign state, anything that does not diminish our condition as a sovereign state. I understand that this inspection idea is another attempt to humiliate our country. Therefore we do not accept it. This demand for inspections is to validate their pretension to violate our right to act with complete freedom within our own borders—to decide what we can or cannot do within our borders. The threat to attack us directly if Cuba achieves a certain level of military strength that the United States will determine is absurd. We have no intention of reporting to, or consulting, the Senate or the House [of Representatives] of the United States on the question of what weapons we may consider advisable to acquire, and the measures we may take to defend our country fully. We have not given, and have no intention of giving, the U.S. Congress any of our sovereign prerogatives. We can negotiate honestly and sincerely. We would not be honest if we accepted that the sovereign right of our country was negotiable."

Then, U Thant explained that "any U.N. actions in Cuba can only be undertaken with the consent of the government and people of Cuba." But here, in essence, are other points made by U Thant; very interesting ones. "My colleagues and I," he says—this is the second meeting—

CHOMY: This is the first one that continues here.

CASTRO: What I said was, "First of all, my government has no doubts regarding the honesty, interest, and disinterestedness with which the present Secretary General of the United Nations is working. We have no doubts about your intentions, your good faith, of your extraordinary interest in finding a solution to the problem. I understand the interest that we must all have in peace. But the road to peace is not the road of sacrificing the rights of peoples, not the violations of the rights of peoples, because that is the road that leads to war. The road to peace is the road to guarantees of the rights of peoples, and the readiness of peoples to resist in the defense of those rights. The road to the last World War passed through the desolation of Czechoslovakia, the annexation of Austria—all tolerated. They tolerated German imperialism, and this led to war. That is why it is difficult to understand why there can be talk of immediate solutions independently of future solutions.

What is more important is not paying any price for peace now, but guaranteeing peace, lasting peace. Cuba is not Austria, nor are we the Sudetenland, nor is Cuba the Congo. We have a firm intention to defend our rights at any risk." I hope Chomy hasn't underlined anything else here; otherwise this is going to be very long. [Laughter.]

Here I said, "It should have been sufficient for them to receive the decision by the Soviet government to withdraw the missiles brought here for the defense of the Republic of Cuba. Cuba has not hampered the withdrawal of those weapons. If what the United States wants, in addition to this, is to humiliate our country, they will not be successful. We have never hesitated for a minute in our determination to defend our rights." And I added, "We are equally opposed to inspections in our ports. If the Soviet Union authorizes inspections on the high seas, why would it then be necessary to inspect them again in Cuban ports? What I want to say is in the first place that the United States has no right to invade Cuba, and that one cannot negotiate on the basis of a promise not to commit a crime—with a simple promise not to commit a crime. And in the face of that danger, we trust more in our determination to defend ourselves than we do in the words of the government of the United States." And I say, "Why not place equal value on the public commitment made in the United Nations by the Soviet Union to withdraw the strategic weapons sent for the defense of the Republic of Cuba?" These were essentially the points I made to U Thant.

And he said interesting things. He said, "My colleagues and I"—I'm reading the essentials—"are of the opinion that the blockade is illegal. No state can tolerate a military or even an economic blockade. This is the imposition of force by a Great Power against a small country." He also said that it was illegal and inadmissible to continue the aerial reconnaissance of Cuba. These three things—economic blockade, military blockade, and aerial reconnaissance—are all illegal. Here it says, "In the United States there are three forces: the Pentagon, the Central Intelligence Agency, and the State Department." The man who looks like Hemingway isn't going to like this very much. [Laughter.] "In my opinion," he says, "the Pentagon and the CIA have more power than the State Department." I think Martin is the one who isn't going to like this. [Laughter.] "If the CIA and the Pentagon continue having this power, I see the future of the world in a very bad light." U Thant said this, the secretary general. I hope that you don't have any monuments to U Thant in the United States, or if you do, that you won't take them away with a crane. [Laughter.] He said he told the United States that "if they did something drastic, I would not only report it to the Security Council, I would accuse the United States openly at the Security Council. And although the United States has the votes and the veto, there would be a moral sanction. I also told them that I would resign if the United Nations cannot stop a Great Power from attacking a small country. Under those circumstances, then I do not want to be the secretary general. And I warned them not to commit any aggression against Cuba, because that would be the end of the United Nations. My intention is to achieve peace and the defense of the United Nations." These are the statements of U Thant. "I'm considering the first proposal Khrushchev made on the dismantling and inspection accepted by the Soviet Union. Since Your Excellency considers that the Soviet Union was referring to inspection outside of Cuba, I consider that this might create some division and misunderstandings between the Soviet Union and Cuba," he said. There are other things here of course, but I think the most interesting things here are the things U Thant said.

This was the 31st of October. There were two meetings on the 30th and on the 31st. Then came Mikoyan's visit, two or three days after U Thant. [To Chomy:] Do you remember the date? [Pause.] He arrived here on November 2nd. Then came the long talks with Mikoyan on the basis of our two countries' positions. These negotiations were very difficult because first there was talk of the missiles, then there was the question of the Il-28s, then other things—it was endless. I already referred to that, so I shouldn't repeat it.

There was a very unpleasant event when the conversations with Mikoyan started: it was the news that his wife had died. We even gave him the option to return to Moscow, and he made a very generous gesture. Theirs was a long-standing marriage. They were very close. We saw Mikoyan cry. But he decided to stay here in Cuba and continue with the talks rather than go back to the USSR. It was very hard for us to receive the news at a time when we were beginning very thorny negotiations. He stayed here for three weeks, more or less. And we held discussions all the time.

As you have now learned—perhaps some of us were familiar with this before—the correspondence with Khrushchev has been published. Chomy, please help me find the letters. I had them here. [Pause.] Oh, here they are. These are the translated letters. I did my homework on the first day and read the eighty-five pages. That is why I was a bit sleepy yesterday here in the meeting. They are very interesting, actually. Here you can see when the Il-28 problem appeared in the discussion. In all honesty, I must say that I see a difference here between Kennedy's conduct and Khrushchev's conduct in these letters. It must be said that Khrushchev acted with great dignity, very honorably. You can see that he was anxious, not just to solve these problems, but many other problems as well. I can see here a very noble, reflective, capable, intelligent Khrushchev, who uses very profound arguments, not just about the crisis, but about world peace. However, we also see a very hard Kennedy. Kennedy does not evince in these letters the same nobility.[149] You can see that he was turning the screw on Khrushchev again and again, and the further away the missiles got, the more he turned the screw. That is what I see in these letters. It's not the same thing to negotiate while the missiles are right there as it is when the missiles have been withdrawn. So Kennedy's language became harsher and harsher as the ships sailed for the Soviet Union. New demands were made; he talked about verification, about continuing guarantees—he insisted on that. He was reluctant to formalize the commitments that he had made to Khrushchev. He used very subtle language; he said things one way here, and tried to tone them down another way there. You see Khrushchev fighting to have Kennedy's commitments formalized and implemented. Undoubtedly, Khrushchev's position from the objective standpoint was much weaker by then, particularly after November 20th, once the missiles were withdrawn.

We knew nothing of these letters, of course. We had no information on this. But we did have one problem pending. Days went by, and the planes kept on flying. That was intolerable. We told Mikoyan that we would have no other option but to fire on low-flying planes. We issued the necessary orders. I knew there would be a U.S. counterattack, and since I was responsible for issuing these orders, I went to one of our air bases and I spent the morning there—that was on the next day, I think, on November 16th. I had the moral duty, since there were going to be reprisals. Two planes usually overflew that base at ten o'clock in the morning, and I thought it was my moral duty—not to commit suicide there—but to be there with the troops that were going to shoot. They were going to fire all over the place, in many places. We told Mikoyan this twenty-four hours before—twenty-four or forty-eight hours, I'm not sure—so that he would inform the Soviets. And that morning we were left there waiting for the planes, and fortunately they didn't show up. That was the best thing that could have happened: that the planes did not fly, because they would have been shot down. There was such an enormous amount of antiaircraft weaponry there that it was impossible not to hit them, no matter how inexperienced our gunners were. They were flying very low and slowly at some hundred meters. I was there but they didn't come.

I know that in one of the letters on November 15th, Kennedy told Khrushchev that Castro was the bad guy, that he wanted war.[150] You see, he mentioned me quite often, always trying to provoke some friction with the Soviets, to see if they would punish us in some way, creating frictions between the Soviets and us. He said he had news that the low overflying planes were going to be fired at. I imagine that Mikoyan somehow conveyed to him that we had decided to fire. I thought that it was not very intelligent on the part of the United States to continue with the overflights. There was no reason to complicate matters further by doing something that was senseless at the time, whose only purpose was to humiliate.

CHOMY: Here is a letter to U Thant.

CASTRO: U Thant? Where? What day was that? The 15th—November 15th—a letter from the prime minister to Acting Secretary General U Thant, informing him that Cuba "will not tolerate further overflights over the island because they serve U.S. military plans against the Revolution and our national defense. We affirm that sabotage and subversion groups are being introduced into Cuba, which proves the military utility to the United States of these overflights." So we also informed U Thant on November 15th, 1962, that we would open fire on U.S. planes.

I think the attitude adopted by the administration not to provoke a conflict was wise. They realized that it was unnecessary and unwise— that our reaction was a logical one. Further conflict could have interrupted the withdrawal of the missiles, or something else. It could have complicated matters. So, there were no overflights. They didn't continue with the overflights. Later, along the coasts they came closer. There was a lot of firing. Some came too close and, when they were close, the antiaircraft batteries fired. But there were no other overflights as of mid-November. There was, of course, the U-2. But the people didn't see the U-2s. We did not agree with the U-2 flights, but there was nothing we could do. In the end, the Soviets gave us the antiaircraft weapons, and our people learned how to use them. That was a long process. We had to take people out of the university and train the graduates to use the antiaircraft weapons. But when they gave them to us, the Soviets said that it was under the condition that we could not fire on the U-2s, so we were faced with a dilemma of either having no antiaircraft batteries or committing ourselves not to fire on U-2s. That was quite a long time afterwards, after we got the missiles. That is the only thing I can say of any importance on Cuba during those days. There is reference to that in these letters.

In December, things got a bit better at the end. Now were these the only letters? You are giving me more papers, Chomy! [Pause.] Yes, that was the Il-28 thing, but we've discussed that already. [Pause.] I think that these are very revealing letters. At that moment, circumstances had changed. Khrushchev prior to the crisis was one person, and, after the crisis, a different one. Kennedy also before the crisis was one person, and after the crisis a different one. If before the crisis Kennedy was very noble and very trusting, and if Khrushchev nourished the deception—by playing the semantic game about offensive and defensive weapons—afterwards, at a later stage, you see a very noble, very open, very sincere Khrushchev, and a harder Kennedy, who is pressuring him, to use a very precise term. But it is admirable to see the efforts made by Khrushchev then. He acted very elegantly. He made no concessions with regards to Cuba, except when he referred to "the Spanish nature"—but he was not being insulting, of course.[151] In addition, he made a not very elegant reference to [West German Chancellor Konrad] Adenauer. That is the only part of the letter that I didn't like too much. It is not that I sympathized with Adenauer— far be it from me, ideologically. But the phrase that he used—"an old man, with a foot in the grave, should not complicate plans"—well, I don't think this is very elegant.[152] I don't think that he couched that in very elegant terms. Kennedy, of course, defended Adenauer. He said, "Well, after all, these problems are not related."

But, in any case, these letters have enriched public knowledge. Now we should ask the State Department to continue declassifying more letters, because we're still missing the letters from 1963, which could reveal things of interest, as I seem to recall.

[To Chomy:] Let me see the letter.

Now, three months elapsed, and on January 31—almost four months: November, December, January; yes, three months and a bit— on January 31, 1963, Khrushchev wrote me a long letter, a wonderful letter, as a matter of fact. It is so long that it is thirty-one pages. Of course, I'm not going to read it, but I can lend it to anyone. It was a beautiful, elegant, friendly letter—a very friendly letter, almost poetic in some of the paragraphs—inviting me to visit the Soviet Union. He was traveling from a congress in Berlin to Moscow by train. He wrote a very persuasive letter. He knew how to express himself very well. He was wonderful at writing letters. Things had cooled down a bit; tempers had calmed a bit. It had been pretty hot for a while. I accepted the invitation.*

It was a miracle I got there. I had to fly in a Tu-114 for sixteen hours. That was based on one of the bombers they had. We reached Murmansk, after a direct flight from Havana, in sixteen hours. The plane had four engines that vibrated, and we had to make a blind landing. Fortunately, Khrushchev, who was very careful about details, sent the best pilot that they had in the Soviet Union. Only that man could have managed to land flying amidst the mountains in Murmansk with a fog so thick that you couldn't see more than five meters. On the third attempt, we finally landed. Mikoyan was waiting for me with a delegation in Murmansk. I spoke with Khrushchev on the telephone, a little while later. That was the first time I visited the Soviet Union and perhaps my role in this entire matter might have ended that day when we were trying to land there in Murmansk. I told my staff, well, if we crash we are not even going to realize it. I was sitting with the pilots, watching them. And suddenly I said, "Let me get out of here, because instead of helping I might complicate matters." Finally, that monster landed. It was enormous. That's the way I came to visit the USSR.

It was an excellent letter. That's why I'm telling you that I know Khrushchev well. He had wonderful feelings for Cuba. I was very grateful to him for this letter. So, this is the way I got the invitation to visit the USSR.

We talked in the USSR. I had my own ideas about the crisis, but I wanted to find out what the objective had been, what had been said, and so on. Neither he nor the others ever deviated from his explanation as a rule. And I was unable to clarify the issue. Now, he did read many messages to me, for hours: messages sent by President Kennedy, through Robert Kennedy, or through [Llewellyn] Thompson—I think that's the name. There was a translator, and Khrushchev read and read all his correspondence. I devoted great interest to this to see if any of the topics were dealt with in this quarter—probably the first quarter of '63: the first four months, rather—January, February, March, April. You see, I traveled to the Soviet Union at the end of April. We were

---

*Castro and his entourage toured the Soviet Union 27 April–23 May 1963.

sitting in a hunting preserve somewhere. He worked very hard, but he liked hunting. It was almost spring, and we were wearing enormous, very thick coats. That's the only way you can sit outside when it's spring. And he read the messages—the various exchanges. They were still discussing Cuban security.

There was a moment—two moments, rather—two interesting moments for me. There was a moment when, while Khrushchev was reading and the other one was translating, where Kennedy used a phrase suggesting that something was going to happen in reference to Cuba. And then when Khrushchev read the reply, he said—this was not recorded, but I have not forgotten it—"something is going to happen; something unbelievable." That was the word that Khrushchev used in his reply. It seems that at a certain point the mood became somber again when he said that something was going to happen with Cuba, something unbelievable. Probably he meant that there was going to be a war. He was usually elegant, very honorable in his expressions; but I never forgot that phrase. And Khrushchev continued to read and read. I think at one point he said something he didn't want me to hear. Well, maybe, he made a mistake. Anybody can make a mistake. Nobody had underlined the essential parts. And at a certain moment he said—the message, that is—"we have fulfilled all our commitments." Listen to these words. "And we have withdrawn, or we are withdrawing, or we're going to withdraw the missiles from Turkey and Italy." I remember very well: that he didn't mention just Turkey. He also mentioned Italy. That was imprinted in my mind.[153]

Once I asked the Soviets—I even asked Gromyko—if, in the document, the Americans had agreed to withdraw their missiles from Italy. We were going to receive several MiG-23 aircraft, and they were always asking whether the 1962 agreements were being violated. Well, in any case, the reply was, "Turkey, yes, but not Italy." But in that message that Nikita was reading and the translator was translating, it said, "we have withdrawn, will withdraw, are withdrawing"—that is, it referred to the withdrawal of the missiles from Turkey and Italy. I said, "Well, well: there's been no public mention of this. This must have been some kind of present, or concession." Perhaps it was Kennedy helping Khrushchev. You see, at times, Khrushchev wanted to help Kennedy; sometimes he wanted to hamper Kennedy or hurt Kennedy, even unwillingly. But at other times Kennedy helped Khrushchev. The only thing I know is that I remember that phrase.

When I heard that, I imagine that Nikita realized that that was the last sentence I wanted to hear. He knew how I thought, and how we were totally against being used as a bargaining chip. That ran counter to the theory that the missiles had been sent to defend Cuba. You do not defend Cuba by withdrawing missiles from Turkey. That was very clear. That was elementary logic. Defending Cuba would have been accomplished by insisting that the United States withdraw from the base at Guantánamo, stop the pirate attacks, and end the blockade. But withdrawing missiles from Turkey completely contradicted the theory that the main objective of the deployment had been defending Cuba. So, when that cropped up—when it was read there—I looked at him, and I said, "Come again, please? Please, repeat that part." And he read it again. And he said, "the missiles in Turkey and Italy." And I said, "Ah." And he laughed with that mischievous smile that he had. But I'm certain that the information on Italy slipped out by mistake. Because it was like talking about rope in the house of a hanged man. These are two interesting points. I'm alerting researchers that they should look into that. We will await with interest its declassification, now that we are declassifying—now that we are de-ideologizing international relations. I think that all these things should be brought to light—I mean the papers, the documents—once and for all.

There were efforts on both sides—and we also made our efforts—to overcome that incident, to try to save relations with the Soviet Union, to prevent them from becoming even more embittered. However, these 1962 incidents did influence relations between the Soviet Union and Cuba for several years. These documents are available to historians here. If not, we can have copies made. [Pause; discussion with Chomy.] This one too? This agreement? I think that the text of the agreement has never been published—the one we adopted. I don't know whether historians are interested in it. We can photocopy it. We can copy it for the historians. It is totally declassified. Maybe you would rather have it in your hands. I also have this letter, the one that was sent on the 23rd. It may be of interest.

I can't remember anything else which in my view would be of specific interest to the studies that you are doing. If we find any other documents—anything else, anything of interest—we can give it to you. We have nothing to hide—nothing at all—with regard to the October crisis, if it might be useful, if it can contribute to clarifying events, and to drawing the relevant conclusions.

I'm not going to reach any conclusions here. I think that there is a lot of material that has to be reflected on, meditated upon, which stems from the fruitful effort of bringing things to light. As one of the Soviet representatives here said, never has a problem been so thoroughly discussed as this one. It is an issue from which many important lessons may be learned. Thank you very much.

They tell me that I have spoken for two hours and fifteen minutes, and in fact I went beyond the time I had planned. I beg your indulgence.

These documents are declassified. How do you manage the records of these meetings?

RISQUET: Each person who speaks is sent a copy so they can rectify it, and then it is published in book form. After each one has revised what he said, anything can be corrected.

CASTRO: So far I don't think I have to revise anything.

BLIGHT: Thank you very much, Mr. President. We have an expression in the U.S.—you may also use it here in Cuba—and that is, "drinking champagne from a fire hose." [Puzzled looks all around.] Let me explain. I feel the richness, the flavor, the reality, the quality are a little overwhelming when taken in the quantity that you just have given us. So if there's no objection, I recommend a short break before we return and spend considerably more time asking you about that champagne than it took you to present it. If that's all right with you, and if it's all right with the other delegates, we will break for twenty minutes. At about ten minutes to twelve we return and resume.

HISTORICAL PUZZLES:
". . . trying to reconstruct the past"

From the moment that dates had been established for the Havana conference and Fidel Castro's participation promised by the Cuban organizers, the former Kennedy administration officials on the U.S. delegation had begun to doubt the wisdom of going to Havana. In addition to fears of being "set up"—brought to Havana under the pretense of Cuban interest in serious discussion only to be subjected to a tirade or a trial—many felt that Fidel Castro was simply not a man with whom one could engage productively in critical oral history. Arthur Schlesinger, for example, doubted that Castro had any serious interest in history as such. At least, Schlesinger reported, Castro had seemed uninterested in discussing the early 1960s in 1985, when Castro and Schlesinger had last met.

At the very least, everyone on the U.S. delegation thought it likely that Castro, the most loquacious leader of modern times, would subject us to a peripatetic monologue of the kind for which he is justly famous. Our apprehension had begun with remarks by Cuban officials familiar with Castro's ways. Smiling knowingly, they suggested that their commander-in-chief might attend the conference, or he might meet us at the airport, cancel the conference, and take us to a mountain hideaway (or on a tour of the island). He might, we were told, do anything. In any case, he would do what he wanted to do. The only prediction all the Cubans made in common was that, despite the traditional format of the conference (morning and afternoon sessions, with breaks and lunch), the really important conversations would undoubtedly occur in unexpected places, probably in the middle of the night.

Although the organizers of the conference reported none of these conversations back to the already skeptical former members of the Kennedy administration, they had their own sources, and thus their own fears of possibilities similar to those raised by our Cuban colleagues. When the Cubans discussed Castro's idiosyncratic approach to discussion, they often did so with a chuckle and a wink. To our senior U.S. participants, however, this was not a laughing matter. As one put it shortly before the conference: "I want a serious discussion and I don't see how that's possible when we are exhausted or bouncing around in a Soviet jeep."

Concern became near panic shortly before the conference when several members of our delegation learned of the publication of a book called *An Encounter with Fidel*, by the Italian journalist Gianni Mina. It consisted of the edited transcript of an uninterrupted, *fifteen-hour* interview with Castro,[154] a length that positively horrified those no longer young on our delegation whom Schlesinger called "relics of the Kennedy administration."[155] It also struck terror into the hearts of those of us who, though much younger, found the prospect of such loquacity impossible to contemplate with equanimity. Nor were our prospective delegates encouraged or amused by the novelist Gabriel García Márquez's foreword to the Mina book, which contains a bizarrely admiring recollection of Castro's seven-hour speech upon assuming power in Cuba in January 1959 ("It must be a world record"), and this dubious reassurance: "That is how it is: weary of talking, he rests by talking."[156] This mode of operation, indeed, did not appear to comport well, if at all, with the requirements of critical oral history: familiarity with documents, cross-questioning by people with diverse viewpoints, and, above all, an orderly and collective search for historical truth.

Following Fidel Castro's major intervention on the October crisis, we are ready to begin the question-and-answer phase. (Castro, conscious of the fears of the U.S. participants, had apologized for speaking too long at the end of that intervention, which the Americans universally felt was judicious, informative, and even a bit too brief!) We all feel Castro has earned the compliment made by Schlesinger, before he asks the first question: that if other heads of state were as attentive to the importance and nature of historical inquiry as Castro has been today, "it would enormously facilitate the job of the historian in trying to reconstruct the past." Castro had *not* talked for fifteen hours straight; he had *not* acted as judge and jury at a mock trial; he *had*, with grace and subtlety, given a nuanced picture of Cuban decision making in the missile crisis. Castro returns early to the question-and-answer phase. As the meeting is called to order, the chair is bombarded with written messages and hand-signals from those seeking the floor to ask Castro a question.

VENEZUELA:
". . . the Castro way and the Betancourt way"

Arthur Schlesinger begins by asking Castro about covert action programs meant to destabilize the democratically elected government of Rómulo Betancourt of Venezuela. This has considerable historical significance because, as Schlesinger says, Kennedy tended to see the fundamental U.S. policy choice in Latin America as a choice between "the Castro way and the Betancourt way"—between, as Kennedy viewed it, Marxist authoritarianism and freely elected social democracy. Castro had during the early 1960s referred to Betancourt by such sobriquets as "the Venezuelan puppet" and "Made in U.S.A.," and he heavily subsidized anti-Betancourt rebels.[157]

Schlesinger's question thus goes to the heart of a particular set of Castro's actions that made him a pariah to the Kennedy administration. Schlesinger is also no doubt eager to discover whether Castro will pursue the sensitive issue of subversion of democratically elected governments, an inquiry on which both Schlesinger and McNamara met a stone wall of Cuban denial at the Antigua conference, particularly from Jorge Risquet, the leader of the Cuban delegation.[158] Castro's response is altogether more satisfactory than Risquet's, a fact that prompts a member of the U.S. delegation to compare Risquet and Castro, both of whom are bearded: "So," he concluded, "Castro is *not* just a taller version of Risquet, is he?"

BLIGHT: A logistical point to begin with: our Cuban hosts have asked that we break for lunch around two o'clock, and that's what we'll do. First of all, I'd simply like to say on behalf of the U.S. delegation once again, thank you very much for an extraordinary presentation— and also, Mr. President, for the generous and extraordinarily useful act of declassifying this material and offering it to us.

For some of us who've been following this event in these conferences for many, many years, it is an unusual experience to sit through a presentation more than two hours long and have virtually all of it be new, interesting, and important. And I speak here for all of us.

I'd like to begin with an attempt to symbolically reciprocate. Our documents on the U.S. side have been declassified over many, many years through a very arduous and sometimes difficult process of fighting tooth and nail with the State Department. The National Security Archive in Washington, D.C., has led this charge, and this process would have been absolutely impossible without it. The Archive was founded by Mr. Scott Armstrong, and I'd like to ask Ms. Sheryl Walter, the legal counsel of the National Security Archive, to present you several thousand pages of declassified material. [Laughter and applause.] I should say that we're prepared on the flight back to the U.S. to pay the extra charge it will take to fill all the suitcases we're expecting to take back full of Cuban documents. [Laughter.]

Well, the floor is open for questions and for comments. I recognize Arthur Schlesinger.

SCHLESINGER: I'd like to express, as a professional historian—I'm sure I speak for the community of historians—our gratitude to President Castro for his talk, his discussion, his analysis, his disclosures, and his remarks this morning. I hope he will set an example for all heads of state. It would enormously facilitate the job of the historian in trying to reconstruct the past.

As part of that reconstruction, I wonder whether President Castro would tell us something about one problem which he touched on yesterday. His remarks yesterday explain in part why Cuba undertook the policies that it did. I think more detail on the character of those policies might be helpful; I'm speaking about the campaigns, the covert action programs, undertaken by the government of Cuba, particularly with relation to Venezuela.[159]

Let me say a word in explanation. I was in the White House in the Kennedy years. President Kennedy shared with President Castro a belief that the time had come for social change in Latin America, and the Alliance for Progress, as President Castro has said, was one instrument by which he hoped to move that social revolution in democratic directions. In doing this, he tangled with the oligarchs of Latin America. Indeed, President Castro at one time predicted that the oligarchs' opposition to the Alliance for Progress would doom it. As allies in this course we saw the progressive democratic regimes of Latin America—not many of them in that period—and, particularly, Rómulo Betancourt in Venezuela. To put it in oversimplified terms, the social revolutions in Latin America seemed to be a choice between the Castro way and the Betancourt way. President Kennedy once told a meeting of Latin American ambassadors, making the case for reform—he said, "Those who make peaceful revolution impossible make violent revolution inevitable."[160]

Therefore, Betancourt was of particular interest both symbolically and practically to the Kennedy administration. And indeed, what appeared to us to be the efforts on the part of the Cuban government to arm guerrillas against Betancourt, and efforts to overthrow the Betancourt regime, seemed particularly crucial in shaping the Kennedy administration's policy toward Cuba. I think we'd all appreciate it if Dr. Castro could make some observations about the nature of the covert action campaigns against Venezuela.

CASTRO: I can answer that question with pleasure.

Let me say that if *we* are going to be accused of being subversive, you would have to accuse Rómulo Betancourt of being subversive, because Rómulo Betancourt—together with [José] Figueres* and a number of political leaders all over Latin America—were working to aid revolutionary movements in Latin America when I was a student in the university.[161] They were working for the overthrow of Trujillo, for example, and they were working for the overthrow of Somoza, and other similar causes. They had relations with the [Carlos] Prío [So-

---

*President of Costa Rica, 1952–58.

carrás] government in Cuba [1948–52], which was the government in power before the March 10 coup d'état in Cuba. Prío's was not a paragon of honest government. There were thieves of all sorts. It was a very corrupt government.[162] But they did have relations with some of the political personalities that we've just mentioned. Before we'd had the Grau* government, and then the Prío government.

During the Grau administration—before Prío—all of these democratic forces in Latin America were participating in the struggle to overthrow Trujillo. I was a student in my second year of law school when, with the cooperation of all these democratic forces, an expedition was organized in Cuba to overthrow Trujillo. It was organized at Confites Key, just north of Cuba. At that time I was president of the Committee for Democracy in the Dominican Republic, and despite the fact that I had very little to do with the people who were in that— because I was in the opposition to the Cuban government—it was the Cuban government I was helping to organize the expedition. You can probably find that in the archives of the State Department. I immediately signed up in that expedition against Trujillo.[163]

That expedition ended in betrayal. Some of those corrupt elements turned on us. They gave orders here to stop the boats. Imagine what the plans were of that democratic group! From the beginning, they had problems in Cuba. Only a part of the expedition left Cuba. I was in the part that went on. I had risen rapidly: I began as a lieutenant, and I'd been made a captain. We were going to invade Santo Domingo in the name of democracy, not in the name of Marxism-Leninism. All of these political leaders were participating in this, and I recall we were stopped by a government frigate. They told us to return. We thought it was Trujillo's, then we found out it wasn't, and we had to return. I refused to become a prisoner. At the entrance to Nipe Bay, I escaped with some of the weapons. The captain of the ship was helping me, and they said, "They're going to give you everything back." I said, "They're not going to give you anything; they're going to stop the expedition." So I got away from them. The rest were brought over, taken in cattle rail cars to Havana, and I returned disguised as a peasant or something. But everybody recognized me, because it was always very difficult for me to disguise myself. So, all of those leaders were involved in that—the thing in the Dominican Republic—and this has to do with Venezuela.

---

*Ramón Grau San Martín, provisional president of Cuba briefly in 1933, and again 1944–48.

In our struggle in the Sierra Maestra, we had some Dominicans participating, and we were committed to helping them. This was a long-standing thing. Trujillo was an ally of Batista's. He sent him weapons. And we promised to help them, and we did—we kept our word to them. But there was this democratic movement, and the Venezuelans were in it. They were together with us in undertaking a liberation effort in Santo Domingo. I'll go even further: the Venezuelan government was involved. Trujillo also disliked Rómulo Betancourt very much.

For whatever reason, Rómulo Betancourt never sympathized much with our revolutionary movement, although it is said that in his youth Rómulo Betancourt had been a communist. The historians will have to figure that out. He was a man of the left; he fought against military regimes. The first president was Rómulo Gallegos [1947–48]; he was overthrown.

I visited Venezuela in 1959. An immense, impressive multitude turned out. They had just had elections. The forces were divided. There was an opposition from the left against Rómulo Betancourt. There was a strong communist party, because it had fought against the military government of [Gen. Marcos] Pérez Jiménez.* And there were many leftists in that junta that overthrew him. In Caracas they did win the majority against Rómulo Betancourt, but Rómulo Betancourt was elected president. Relations were not good, for whatever reason. We just didn't get along. It's not that I didn't get along with *him;* he didn't get along with *me.* There are people who interpreted that with a certain amount of jealousy, because of the immense welcome I had been given in Caracas. And while there, I had to manage things carefully, because people began to shout things against Rómulo—an immense multitude, maybe 400,000 people. And I had to go against the multitude, and say that I had not gone there to meet with them so that people could use the occasion to attack political personalities. I had to defend Rómulo.

But then Rómulo later became one of the most active enemies of the Cuban Revolution, whatever his origins and his history.[164] Rómulo Betancourt faced in his country very strong opposition from the left—even military opposition—because there were two big

---

*A three-man junta ruled Venezuela from 1948 to 1952. When the leader of the junta, Carlos Delgado, was assassinated, a fraudulent election was held, and Pérez Jiménez, one of the three, was sworn in as president on 1 January 1953. Betancourt replaced him in 1958.

and bloody military uprisings against Rómulo in Venezuela. The left was against him—the Communist Party and many other forces of the left. So we did not create the opposition, because we could not create it. The opposition there rose against Rómulo spontaneously.

They broke relations with us; they joined the blockade; they supported the United States actively against the Cuban Revolution, and he had ceased to be a friend or an associate of Cuba in the struggles for liberation in Latin America. He was then an enemy, and without a doubt we did help the leftist forces in Venezuela. We helped the Communist Party, and all the other leftist organizations, and some of the military and people who were not communists in various sectors. I must say that there was strong repression in Venezuela. The hand of the Rómulo Betancourt government in acting against the revolutionaries was not at all soft. They did all kinds of things; we don't have to stop to talk about them. We really were not organizing the opposition to Rómulo Betancourt. What we did was support the opposition against Rómulo Betancourt. That is absolutely true, and these are the factors that gave rise to that.

Neither will I deny that the ideological factor had an influence. I am not going to say that it was just a practical question of fighting against people who wanted to destroy us. There was also the ideological element, and the desire for revolutionary change. That's what I can tell you about the background to, and the reasons behind, our support for that movement. We definitely supported that movement. But Cuba was not the only one that supported that movement.

I'm not going to go into the activities of the United States now—I'm going to leave that aside. I mentioned that yesterday. But, many leaders who are not communists—many leaders in Latin America who are not communists—helped the revolutionary movement. We might say for example that Panama, during the Torrijos government*—a government that did not have bad relations with the United States; they had cordial relations—helped a great deal in the struggle against Somoza in Nicaragua. Venezuela helped a lot in the struggle against Somoza. We might say that in Costa Rica, one of the super-democratic presidents they had over there, as the Costa Rican presidents are wont to be as a rule, helped in the fight against Somoza in association with us.

---

*Gen. Omar Torrijos was president of Panama from 1968 to 1981.

So, what I want to say is that we are not the only ones who have at various times helped revolutionary movements in one way or another in Latin America. Very honorable, very respectable political leaders that are very well thought of by the United States participated together with us in some of these liberation crusades when we had already been a socialist government for a long time—one with a Marxist-Leninist doctrine.

You cannot forget that we in Latin America are a family. We see these things somehow as within the family. Although, of course, I believe that even if we are a family, as long as states exist, the best practice and the best philosophy is respect for the sovereignty of each independent state until the time, if we are able, when we integrate into a great community of Latin-American states, as the Europeans have done after so many centuries of war.

In Latin America there is a tradition of helping revolutionary movements. Throughout history, and in the independence wars, they helped each other against the Spanish colonialists. Even the Americans sometimes helped; they sent a ship or two with provisions, weapons. Everyone helped in one way or another in the peoples' struggles for independence. The United States was also helped. I mentioned that yesterday. Even we Cubans helped in the independence of the United States. We weren't independent then, but a certain number of men who had been born here participated in the independence struggles of the United States together with Spaniards and Frenchmen. Later, in Latin America, all of these nations helped each other in their struggle for independence. We are not the inventors of helping and supporting revolutionary movements.

Now, we would agree, and we do agree—and in fact, this is today the policy of the government of Cuba—to comply with international laws and standards. But there has to be reciprocity. Laws cannot be valid for one and not for another, I think. Laws are for everyone.

We believe that the most practical political thing is for us in Latin America to be a family: a family hoping to unite. But as long as we are not united, as long as there are independent states in Latin America, they must be respected. This is my point of view, based on the experience of history. I do not deny, nor do I intend to deny, the activities we carried out.

We wanted changes, of course. We had a political position; we had an ideological position. We wanted revolutionary change. We still do. This doesn't mean that we are going to help anybody to do it. I think we've got to practice a policy of mutual respect between all the countries of Latin America, including Cuba. Today we follow a different path in our relations with the countries of Latin America, whatever the social regime.

But what I can tell you is that the only country that did not join in the blockade, and in the activities directed against Cuba, was Mexico. And our policy toward Mexico is accordingly unblemished. We could have followed the same policy—and, in fact, did maintain the same policy—with all those who had a similar policy with respect to Cuba. But, when they joined the U.S. blockade and joined the fight against us, they gave us the moral freedom—I would say the legitimate freedom—to support the revolutionary movements for change in Latin America.

SCHLESINGER: I think we all welcome the changes that President Castro has described in Cuban policy, and I appreciate very much the frankness with which he discussed the Venezuelan situation. And, of course, he is quite right historically that Latin Americans have a tradition of helping revolutionary movements. The only concluding observation I would make is that I hope that a distinction is drawn—a distinction which has not always been observed in the United States—between helping revolutionary movements against undemocratic regimes, and helping revolutionary movements against democratic regimes.

THE KENNEDY "OPENING":
". . . a kind of bridge, some sort of communication"

The floor is given to Oleg Troyanovsky, who asks Castro to elaborate on his earlier remark about the visit to Havana of French journalist Jean Daniel, who had been sent by Kennedy to explore with Castro the possibility for U.S.-Cuban rapprochement. The general outline of the story is well known.[165] Yet many on the U.S. side are intrigued by Castro's characterization of the instructions he, Castro, believes Kennedy gave to Daniel. Of particular interest is Castro's conviction that with the Daniel mission, Kennedy wished to learn if Castro understood the gravity of the missile crisis at its most dangerous moments. Castro seems convinced of two things: first, that in exploring this, "a kind of bridge, some sort of communication," Kennedy showed unusual acumen in linking Castro and Cuba with the missile crisis; and second, Kennedy was motivated by the danger of the missile crisis not only to move toward détente with the Soviet Union, but also, in time, with Cuba.

BLIGHT: Please, Mr. Troyanovsky.

TROYANOVSKY: Before asking a question, I would like on behalf of our delegation to thank Comrade Fidel Castro for his statement, which, in our opinion, has produced a very deep impression on everyone here, because of its content, and because of the way in which he expressed the facts and his impressions.

This is the third time that I have been present at a statement by Fidel Castro. The first time was in New York, in the General Assembly, in the '60s; the second time was again in the General Assembly toward the end of the '70s, I think; and today is the third time. On each occasion, it has produced an unforgettable impression. Thank you, very much.

Now I have a short question. You recalled in your statement your conversation with a French journalist who transmitted to you something from President Kennedy. For the majority of us this is a new fact. Perhaps you might shed a little bit of light on what the conversation was about?

CASTRO: A journalist turned up in our country—a well-known French journalist—who had just had a meeting with Kennedy. He was very much impressed with Kennedy; he said he was very meticulous, that he had everything organized. He was staying in a hotel here in Havana, and as soon as I got the news I said I would meet with him. He said he had a message from Kennedy. To be able to have more time to talk to him, I said, "Okay, I'll pick you up and we'll go to Varadero," to create a relaxed environment in which he could relate the message he brought.

Now, this was not a message in the formal sense of the word. The idea was that Kennedy wanted him to come. There was a lot of talk about the crisis; of the immense danger of a war breaking out, practically in the same terms we've used here; and the consequences of that war. He told me that Kennedy wanted him to speak to me, to analyze these questions, and to ask me if I was fully aware of the immensity of that danger. The essence of the message was to have a long talk with me on all of these questions, and then to return to the United States, to Washington, to report on his talk with me.

This was interpreted as a gesture, as an indication of a desire to establish contact, to explore what our thinking was on all of this—and, furthermore, to establish a certain kind of communication. So Kennedy said, "Go over there, have these talks, analyze these issues, and come back." I can tell you that, as a matter of fact, he didn't even get through everything he had to explain to me, because it was rather early that Kennedy was shot—about eleven o'clock Dallas time. I think it was before noon; I don't remember the exact time.[166] We hadn't had lunch, anyway, so I don't think it could have been two o'clock in the afternoon. But in any case, while we were in our conversation, in the middle of our talks, the news came over the radio of the assassination attempt against John F. Kennedy. What a coincidence!

I interpreted that as a gesture. We needed a kind of bridge, some sort of communication. Since Kennedy had such great authority in his own country after the crisis, he could have done things that he had not done before. In my view, he had the courage to do them. You had to have courage to defy the state of opinion on all these questions. You can't forget that that was around the time that he gave that famous speech at a U.S. university in which he praised the Soviet Union, in which he recalled the struggle of the Soviet Union—the enormous destruction suffered by the Soviet Union—and he compared it to what it would have meant in the United States if the U.S. had suffered an equivalent level of destruction. I think at the time no one had given a more promising speech than that one—a speech favoring a real opening, real peaceful coexistence, and a policy of peace. That speech was received by all progressive people in the world as something really very positive.[167] No one had ever expressed that kind of recognition, and it is precisely at that moment that they killed him.

But I'll tell you something else. At the very moment I was talking to Jean Daniel, someone—I don't know if it was in Madrid; [pause] no, I'm corrected, it was in Paris—someone was turning over a pen with a poison dart to kill me.[168] So you can see the paradoxes, the contradictions, the way things happen by chance. I don't want to attack anyone here; I am not going to interrogate Cline on that. [Laughter.] We are talking about the October crisis, and some day this will be published. Maybe it was Cline's people. No, he had nothing to do with that. But, in any case, someone was giving someone a pen with a poison dart to kill me, exactly on the same day and at the same time that Jean Daniel was talking to me about this message, this communication from

Kennedy. So you see how many strange things—paradoxes—have taken place on this Earth.

I can't give you very much more information, because in essence, as I said, it wasn't a written message, and it wasn't a precise verbal message saying, "We want to improve relations." But Kennedy did speak respectfully about me to Jean Daniel. He talked about that a long time. He asked him to come and see me, and then return to Washington and brief him. That's what I can tell you. Maybe Jean Daniel can be located. [To Chomy:] Has he died? No, I don't think so. As far as I know, he hasn't. He's written several articles. Does he provide any additional data? If you can get those articles and send them, that might be interesting if they want further information on that.

TROYANOVSKY: Thank you very much, sir.

BLIGHT: Professor Schlesinger has a comment.

SCHLESINGER: Jean Daniel has written about this meeting with President Castro in his memoirs, and also in some articles published at the time, or shortly after Kennedy's death, in *The New Republic*.[169] I might add, to supplement what President Castro has been saying, that this was only part of President Kennedy's exploration toward the normalization of relations with Cuba. We had then as ambassadors—one of Kennedy's ambassadors—a journalist named William Attwood who was editor of *Look* magazine. In 1959 he had come to Havana to interview Dr. Castro. Bill Attwood was seconded to the United Nations to work with Adlai Stevenson in the General Assembly in the autumn of 1963. He then had conversations with Dr. Carlos Lechuga, who is with us here today, about the possibility of exploring a rapprochement. On September 18, he sent the State Department a memorandum on Cuba in which he asked authority to pursue these negotiations. The memorandum went to Averell Harriman, who favored the plan and told him that, because of its domestic political implications, we should discuss it with Robert Kennedy. Robert Kennedy said he was in favor of the plan, but told him to get in touch with McGeorge Bundy. Bundy said he was in favor of the plan, and reported back to Attwood that the president—that is, Kennedy—was in favor of pushing toward an opening to Cuba, to take Castro out of the Soviet fold, perhaps wiping out the Bay of Pigs, and maybe getting back to normal. This was the authorization that Attwood had.

Arrangements, I believe, were made—or, at least, I understood that they were made—for Attwood to fly to Havana in late November and talk with Cuban officials—I don't know if he was to talk with President Castro, or with the foreign minister, or other people in the Foreign Ministry—to see what could be done, as Robert Kennedy said the next year, to effect the normalization of relations. So Jean Daniel was not the only channel. Perhaps Dr. Lechuga would like to supplement my remarks about the Attwood situation.

BLIGHT: Ambassador Lechuga?

LECHUGA: In point of fact, those talks with Attwood—who was part of the U.S. delegation to the United Nations in 1963—did take place. Attwood came to see me. He made an appointment with a television journalist, Lisa Howard, to suggest the possibility of talks with Cuba aiming at a normalization of relations. As Attwood has said in his book,[170] and as Schlesinger said in the book on Robert Kennedy,[171] Attwood brought this up to Averell Harriman, who was under secretary of state for political affairs. Harriman recommended a memorandum on the question. Then you had these procedures through the State Department, and ultimately it came to Robert Kennedy, who accepted the idea of exploring relations with Cuba. Attwood says in his book that President Kennedy immediately accepted those explorations vis-à-vis Cuba. Jean Daniel's visit, as Attwood says in his book, came about because during those talks with me in New York, he found out that Jean Daniel—a friend of his—was in town, and he thought it might be convenient, more helpful, for Daniel to talk to Kennedy. Attwood then called Ben Bradley, of *The Washington Post,* who was a mutual friend, and Bradley—who was a friend of Kennedy's—arranged the meeting between Jean Daniel and Kennedy. [To Castro:] That is when Daniel came to Cuba to speak to you, sir.

CASTRO: That was in November?

LECHUGA: That was in November, early in November, because we met on a few occasions, and the last interview was two or three days before Kennedy's assassination. Kennedy had agreed with Attwood that, when he returned from Dallas, they would talk about the results of the talks with me—and, of course, about the visit by Daniel to Cuba. That was the way it happened.

SOVIET MISSILES AND U.S. INSPECTIONS:
"We weren't against a peaceful solution"

Robert Pastor then asks Castro two related questions regarding the Cuban decision to accept the missiles and the Cuban decision to refuse absolutely the inspection of Cuban territory, as demanded by the United States, and as agreed to in New York by U.S. and Soviet negotiators. Castro's response, fairly lengthy and at times very energetic, is an elaboration of points made earlier. First, according to Castro, the reason the opinion of Latin American governments counted for so little in the Cuban decision to accept the missiles was that most were already pro-U.S. (and anti-Cuban). In that case, he implies, it made sense to accept the missiles as a gesture of solidarity with Cuba's new "family," the socialist bloc. Second, on the question of refusing inspection, Castro implies that this was the one means by which Cuba could insert itself into the U.S.-Soviet resolution, an outcome that it found inimical to its interests and insulting to its pride. It could refuse unilaterally to have its territory "violated," and it did.

In the midst of responding to Pastor's second query, Castro suddenly launches into a discussion of two decisive battles of the Angolan war. His point seems to be that while Cuba was excluded from the negotiating process in 1962, it proved to be a faithful negotiator in the process that included the United States and Soviet Union, and which led to a peaceful settlement of the war by 1989.[172] Listening to Castro move from the missile crisis to the Angolan war and back again, we wonder if he is aware of a peculiar conjunction of these events that nearly scuttled this collaborative process. In January 1989, the U.S. embassy in Moscow had planned a reception for participants in the Moscow conference at Spasso House, the residence of the U.S. ambassador. At the last minute, the site of the reception was shifted to a Moscow hotel, to give the (false) impression that the reception was hosted by the Soviets. As we later learned from a U.S. official at the Moscow embassy, the Bush administration, in office a little more than a week, "did not want to send the signal that U.S. policy toward Cuba had changed in any way" from the hard-line approach of the Reagan administration. Fearing the press would notice and report the presence of high-level Cuban officials at Spasso House, Washington ordered the embassy to cancel the reception. The Cubans were not told of this distant early warning of renewed U.S. hostility. Typically, the Soviets cooperated fully in the charade.

We wondered then, and we wonder now, whether in fact Castro decided (as we were told) to send a delegation to the Moscow conference on the chance that Cuba's participation in the Angolan negotiations might pay dividends in improved relations with the new, ostensibly more pragmatic administration of George Bush. It did not. The snub in Moscow was but the opening salvo in a renewed U.S. offensive against Cuba. Castro's remarks to the Havana conference suggest that he harbors continued bitterness over the failure of constructive Cuban participation in the Angolan accords to yield improvement in U.S.-Cuban relations.

BLIGHT: Please, Professor Pastor.

ROBERT PASTOR: Thank you, Jim. President Castro, I am wondering if I can pursue two separate subjects that you have mentioned. Two days ago, Ambassador Alekseev said that when Khrushchev first told him that missiles would be installed in Cuba, he said that he personally felt that you would not accept them because that could provoke solidarity in a negative reaction to Cuba. Yesterday we heard Edwin Martin say that in Punta del Este, in early 1962, fourteen Latin American nations joined the United States to isolate Cuba, but that Brazil and Mexico were opposed, and that there were some reservations. However, after the missiles were installed, the reservations of Brazil and Mexico and the others evaporated. And Latin America did do as Ambassador Alekseev thought they would: unite in a condemnation of the action. You have said that you considered in your decision the possible negative effects on the revolutionary image of Cuba, but you didn't mention the Latin American dimension—whether you had felt this would be a cost with Latin America, or whether you had already felt that Latin America had taken such a hostile position toward Cuba that it would not make a difference.

The second question relates to your conversations with U Thant. I would be interested to hear some further elaboration as to whether alternative ideas were discussed about ways to close the agreement between Kennedy and Khrushchev. The two conditions that precluded closure related to U.N. inspection, but the question is whether U Thant considered—or whether you considered—perhaps expanding the definition of inspection, so that if Cuba were to accept U.N. inspection, the United States would be required to cease its overflights and its subversive activities against Cuba as part of the agreement on the non-invasion pledge.

CASTRO: I think I explained in my statement the things that worried us regarding Cuba's image. When I spoke of Cuba's image, I was thinking *primarily* of Latin America; the rest of the world as well, but mainly Latin America. For us it was perfectly clear. I think I put it this way: that becoming a military base would imply a very high political cost and, therefore, if the issue had been the defense of Cuba, we would have preferred not to have the missiles. Alejandro was right when he said what he did when he was informed of the intention. He said that we would not accept it because it was presented to us as being for the defense of Cuba. But as we immediately perceived it, the purpose was strategic, even though they emphasized the argument of defending Cuba. This is the way we interpreted it right away, I and my colleagues. Then we met. We analyzed the issue, and all of us had the same interpretation: that the real issue was strategic; that it was imperative to strengthen the socialist camp; and that if we expected the socialist countries to fight for us, we, for simple reasons of image, could not selfishly refuse that cooperation to the socialist camp.

This was the argument we used in our meeting where we unanimously agreed to accept the missiles, in spite of all the inconveniences that we felt they would entail. But, we weren't very concerned with the image of Cuba in the eyes of other governments, because these governments were rather managed by the influence, and the political and economic power, of the United States. Not all of them; but there was always a number of governments who immediately joined in— Central American governments. There were other governments with a greater sense of dignity, liberty, and independence who did not bend to the policies of the United States toward Cuba. One example is Mexico. But Chile withstood for a while; Ecuador for a while; Bolivia; Brazil; Uruguay—six or seven countries withstood all those pressures. But all the rightist governments, all the military governments, without exception, supported U.S. policy. And these other governments were against us. There is one that simply sold out. The Haitian government always sold its vote whenever one of these things came up. They assumed a kind of a neutral position, and then they had to be given something for them to vote in one direction or another at the time.

So we were primarily interested in public opinion. We did not want to convey the image of becoming a Soviet military base, or having Soviet military bases in our country. You can rest assured that that was our position. Those were the reasons why we accepted the missiles, and in this connection Alejandro was right. He, however, perceived it in one way, and we in another. This didn't take a split second, and we immediately realized—we immediately came to the conclusion—that this was in fact a strategic operation. And I think we were being realistic about that. Today, when all of the facts are out, we find that so much altruism would be impossible in connection with such a risky venture. Later events seem to prove this, in my opinion. However, we were aware of that, and primarily concerned about Latin America.

As regards U Thant, I would have to review my materials. As I said, I haven't had the time to make an exhaustive review. But what I've got here are the essentials. As you can probably see, we have a shorthand version. Perhaps with a more careful review, I might be able to add further data, although I think the essence was there in what they [Chomy and his staff] underlined for me. I didn't even do the underlining. I asked them to bring out the materials that might be of interest, and Comrade Miyar prepared the notes. I said, in fact, that I thought I was going to speak in the afternoon, not this morning. I had a few things to talk over with them. I had to review the materials, and make sure they were in order.

Now, U Thant came on a peace mission. He came to mediate, to use the U.N. to find some way to deal with the crisis. The problem is that we could not accept inspection. We could not. I think that would have diminished our sovereignty. The withdrawal of the missiles had already diminished our sovereignty, because the commitment never to reintroduce these weapons meant that we could not have them. That was a commitment we did not make. But the only country that could supply us those weapons was the Soviet Union; so, in fact, certain kinds of weapons were prohibited to us. We couldn't agree with that because we have a strong sense of sovereignty, a very deep-rooted sense; this is evident in all our materials and documents throughout our history, even those that are not public knowledge. We saw inspection as a humiliation of the country, because it wasn't necessary, in fact. We were the first ones who should have made an inspection, and we had nothing to inspect. We were certain that they would take them out the same way they had brought them in, and we didn't hamper that. We made no attempt to do so. An absurd situation would have arisen if we had opposed the withdrawal of the missiles. We would have come into conflict with the Soviets. We would have had to come into conflict with our friends, our brothers, with the military personnel that had been here together with us, and had been ready to die. I saw a great many Soviets crying on the 28th—Soviet military commanders actually crying at the news of the withdrawal of the missiles! I can never forget that. Those people had excellent relations with us. Alejandro had ex-cellent relations with us. They were all very much afflicted. So what could we do? Employ force and violence against the Soviets? We couldn't say, "No, you can't take them with you." That would be madness, total madness. We had no other alternative, moral or political, other than simply to allow the missiles to be withdrawn. Nothing else made sense. What could we do with them? We wouldn't even know how to use them. I had hopes of eventually learning something about missiles after they were deployed, and on a number of things the Soviets might have given me some information. As a matter of fact, when I visited the USSR, I asked Khrushchev to take me out to see an ICBM base. Let me tell you he did take me out to see an ICBM base. This has been published. So, in the Soviet Union I was able to see what they were like, and I'm not going to give you any more information on that because it hasn't been declassified. But I'm sure you know anyway, because of the satellite pictures, and because you must have more people cooperating over there, more collaborators. I think any-thing you want to find out over there you probably can. But, in any case, I am not going to give any more data on the ICBM base I saw in the '60s. I imagine they're a bit more modern today. But, in point of fact, we had no alternative. We had to let them go.

We weren't against a peaceful solution. What we didn't agree with was the way things were done, and the essence of what was done. The essential interest of our country had not been taken into account, and we could not be asked to trust the Americans. We were going to have to depend on their word. That was very flimsy, as we saw it. We didn't agree with that. But we had no alternative. What we *could* do was to stand firm on questions of sovereignty—on whether there would be inspections or not. We didn't agree with the solution; why should we agree to inspections? Why should we have to cooperate with that?

Furthermore, this would have been beyond the comprehension of our population. In fact, we had to make a statement about the Il-28s, because they had already left. They agreed to take them. I explained already that Mikoyan, when I mentioned the likelihood of the demand, said, "No, impossible." Mikoyan said, "To hell with the Americans!" No, I'll be more precise: "To hell with the imperialists!" He didn't say "the Americans." I think it's more elegant to say "imperialists" than it is to say "the Americans." Well, these were the words he used: "The hell with the imperialists if they want us to take the Il-28s away." And a few days later he had to come and explain that they were going to take them. So I said: "Okay, take the Il-28s."[173] How was I going to explain this to the people? I had to make a statement: "We accepted this because they're obsolete planes," and all that sort of thing. The people didn't like it at all. The role we had to play was not pleasant at all—that is, trying to explain that we agreed to their withdrawal. But what we wanted was to avoid any further accumulation of bitterness in the relations between the Soviets and us.

We also have to consider that we had very close economic relations with the Soviets. The entire life of the country, the energy of the country, depended on the Soviets. Who else was going to supply us? At the time, the national oil companies that exist today did not exist. At the time, a few multinational oil companies dominated all of the oil market. The USSR supplied the oil, they supplied the weapons. After the October crisis, we did have one victory, which was weapons free of charge. Before that, they were sold to us on credit. But because of the crisis—well, first, the weapons that were left here, we got those free. And then after that, for almost thirty years, we received our weapons and arms free from the Soviet Union. This was one of the positive aspects of the October crisis. So, we didn't want to make relations bitter. Who could profit from that? No one was going to profit from that. We simply had to control that anger. Our people would never have accepted the idea of inspections. But this wasn't even really a question of public opinion. We simply didn't accept the idea of the inspection.

I think we could have reached an agreement on anything because, in fact—and history bears this out—we have been very serious in all our international commitments. Where we have made a commitment, we have fulfilled it. Take, for example, the recent commitment in Angola. Why was there peace in Angola? Because of the immense effort that Cuba made during a tremendous crisis for Angola, at a time when the main troops were surrounded in Cuito Cuanavale—a battle which we had nothing to do with, and in a military operation with which we did not agree. A tremendous crisis arose. So at that time we had to make this effort to save the situation. We said we would do it, and we did it. And then we moved on the Namibian border. We threatened vital points. We sent 40,000 men in a single direction. They had a thousand antiaircraft weapons, and hundreds of tanks. I think it was a respectable force, the one that advanced there. We didn't want war. We were in a position to make very effective strikes, but if they were going to cost thousands or hundreds of thousands of lives, we wanted a solution other than that one. We were ready to fight if there was no alternative. We would have moved into Namibian territory if we had to, if we were attacked from there. But it was not our intention to cross the border. At a certain point they began to hit us with their long-range artillery—about forty-kilometer range—the South African 140mm cannon. So what did we do? We hit Calueque. This is a reservoir in Angolan territory. We mounted a very precise low-level attack, a tremendous blow. It was a very precise strike against South African units. They stopped firing. Our intention was not to cross the border. For political reasons we weren't going to cross the border. But we were threatening vital points. And one of them was the water, which was on the Angolan side. We expected a counterattack. If they had counterattacked, the war might have become generalized. We could have hit their bases.

You've got to tell the truth; the truth is the truth. At that time, no socialist country wanted to supply us with additional tanks, because they were afraid that we would cross the border. We said, "We have no intention of crossing the border." So what did we do? We built an airfield in a few weeks, right next to the border. We pushed our lines up 250 kilometers. We moved our lines forward. All of the South African bases were within reach of our aviation. If they hit us, we would hit them. All of our aircraft were dispersed and underground. There were all kinds of defenses for them: twenty-kilometer range rockets, and hand-held rockets that could fire against low-flying aircraft. We did shoot down a number of South African aircraft that came in low on Cuito Cuanavale. We had tremendous forces. But we didn't want war. What we wanted was for them to withdraw from Angola; so we negotiated.

The Americans are firsthand witnesses to our role in those negotiations, and of the formal way, the serious way, in which we kept our word. We've always been concerned with that, and there can be no other policy, because the policy of lies pays no dividends. The policy of violating agreements pays no dividends.

We would have been ready to reach agreements without these humiliations. We might have said, "We are going to go inspect the United States." There was a time when we accepted observers—you'll find this in the letters—observers in the United States, Cuba, and I don't know where else in the Caribbean.[174] But the United States was included. This seemed to us to be more equitable. But the United States did not want observers on their territory, and they replied to Nikita that then there would have to be observers in the Black Sea and in the ports where the weapons were shipped to Cuba.[175] The United States refused to accept observers; you'll find that there in the letters.

And the special determination to get the Il-28s out of here was also clear. After the October crisis, bases were created for pirate attacks: bases in Central America—Costa Rica and Nicaragua—and in Puerto Rico. Bases were set up to carry out pirate attacks against Cuba. Without a doubt, those Il-28s would have given us greater range in conventional war. Range is very important in conventional warfare. One of the difficulties we had with our planes in Angola was that they had less range than the South African aircraft. And when we wanted the additional fuel tanks, no one gave us additional fuel tanks. We went country by country, and we asked the Soviet Union, and no one wanted to give us more fuel tanks. The few we had we sent over. We had a few additional fuel tanks that doubled the operational range of our aircraft. With the Il-28s, we would have had greater range. But those Il-28s could not have reached Costa Rica. They couldn't reach Costa Rica, but they did give us a bit more leeway to hit the pirate ships, the identified mother ships. That was the only advantage. It was a tactical advantage; there was nothing strategic involved, and it wasn't essential. But I must note that the pirate attacks continued after the October crisis. They no longer sailed from U.S. bases, but they had set up bases in Central America, and the mother ships came from there. They launched speed boats and hit economic targets in Cuba.

So, regarding our readiness to make commitments: yes, we could have made commitments at the time, commitments that were fair. I saw no logic behind inspecting us. It would have had to be bilateral. We would have had to be allowed to inspect possible bases for pirate attacks in the United States. On a reciprocal basis, we might have accepted some sort of observation. But it wasn't necessary, because the most important thing is the seriousness of states when you enter into commitments. Does that answer your question, sir?

THE LUNAS:
". . . the most dangerous element . . ."

It is difficult to exaggerate the extent to which the Cubans resented having been omitted from the critical oral history of the Cuban missile crisis. This resentment has manifested itself at peculiar times and in

unexpected situations. Once, in 1989, for example, our Cuban interpreter refused to work until we explained to her why Cuba had been
omitted from the first two conferences. (She had been part of a team
that had translated the first edition of *On the Brink*, which was finished
just in time for the members of the Cuban delegation to read en route
to the Moscow conference.) After several elaborate, increasingly self-
abnegating *mea culpas*, she at last relented, having done her patriotic
duty in the presence of this new but (to an interpreter) sinister form
of Yankee imperialism.

On another occasion, in April 1990, over lunch in Havana's China-
town, we met with two Cuban colleagues to discuss the idea that
eventually became the Antigua conference in January 1991. Our Cuban
interlocutors, one from the Central Committee and one from the Foreign Ministry, turned the conversation to a passage of McNamara's in
On the Brink that, both were convinced, would be proved wrong if and
when we turned our attention fully to the Cuban side of the crisis.
This was the passage:

> There was just too damned much fear in the missile crisis. If you just
> keep piling it on, well, people may crack. You do not want to reduce
> your leaders to quivering, panicky, irrational people, do
> you? . . . There was, I assure you, plenty of fear to go around in Oc-
> tober 1962. . . . You see, if a President doesn't believe he's got much
> time, he may—I don't think he will, but the risk goes up that he
> may—act impulsively, thinking that by striking first, he will limit
> damage. And this is precisely why huge arsenals and short fuses are
> destabilizing—they both lead to surplus fear, which may lead people
> to act irrationally in a crisis. . . . So, the question posed by the missile
> crisis for today is . . . How do we keep the peace, just as we kept the
> peace in October 1962, but with less reliance on fear?[176]

In Cuba, according to our Cuban colleagues, there was *no* fear. One
of our interlocutors remembered digging trenches by day and dancing
at the Tropicana by night, even during the height of the crisis. The
other recalled being given responsibility that week by the Cuban Foreign Ministry for reading pirated editions of U.S. Army publications
on the likely effects of nuclear explosions, especially in urban areas. He
said he read them for a few hours, then drafted a one-sentence memo
to his superiors: "In the event that nuclear weapons are used in or near
Havana City, it and we shall all be destroyed." Asked if in the prepa-

ration of his truncated "report" he didn't feel the kind of fear Mc-
Namara was talking about, he replied, "No, not really. I do recall feeling
sadness at the prospect of the death of my wife and children. But no
fear. I mean: we *knew* we were going to die."

This conversation comes immediately to mind as McNamara and
Castro now engage in what many feel is the single most provocative
exchange of the conference. McNamara, who in October 1962 and
ever since, has worried about the debilitating effect of nuclear fear, asks
Castro what he would have done and what he thinks would have happened if the United States had invaded Cuba. Castro's answer is shock-
ing to McNamara, in part because Castro bluntly admits that he would
have espoused the use of nuclear weapons by the Soviets in Cuba, but
also because it draws on what Castro calls "the very singular experience"
of Cubans in the crisis: an experience not shared by McNamara, nor
any of us on the U.S. delegation. Castro says he knew of the *Lunas*;
he was confident that they would be used; he knew the United States
would respond if they were; he knew Cuba "would disappear."
McNamara registers his horror at Castro's view of what would probably
have happened in the event of an invasion and the initiation of nuclear
war by the use of Soviet *Lunas*—"the most dangerous element of the
entire episode." Yet McNamara also seems to grasp what lay at the core
of Castro's thinking: not fear, as was true for McNamara and, in fact,
for many Americans and Soviets—a fear rooted in uncertainty concerning one's ability to control the crisis; but resignation, rooted in
the absolute certainty of nuclear doom and his complete inability to
prevent it. This seems to McNamara (and others) to suggest that the
missile crisis was even more dangerous than he had imagined.

Thus Fidel Castro, having studied McNamara's "surplus fear" hypothesis in *On the Brink,* explains to McNamara why, in his view, "the
danger of nuclear war . . . cannot be prevented on the basis of fear of
nuclear weapons." Why? Because in the "singular" Cuban experience,
there was no fear, at the moment of truth. Was this irrational, as
McNamara's previous statement in *On the Brink* might suggest? No,
implies Castro. It was the rational choice between two options: annihilation with the honor of going down fighting, or annihilation as
cowards.[177] McNamara and Castro thus arrive at equal enthusiasm for
radical nuclear disarmament, based on their individual experiences of
October 1962, even though their experiences were dissimilar.

Gribkov provides a coda to this exchange, reconfirming the defensive intentions of the Soviet Group of Forces in Cuba. But he also

reemphasizes Soviet pre-delegation of authority for use of the *Lunas* to General Pliyev which, in its way, highlights all that McNamara and Castro have just said.

BLIGHT: Mr. McNamara.

McNAMARA: Mr. President, that was an extraordinary statement this morning, and I, as one of the participants in the crisis, want to congratulate you on the candor and thoughtfulness with which you expressed your understanding of events as they evolved. It is with particular reference to one of those circumstances, which I was unaware of until this meeting, that I wish to put a question.

I think the most extraordinary statement I have heard here—at least with respect to the military aspects of the crisis—was that of General Gribkov, who, if I understood him correctly, stated that the Soviet Union anticipated the possibility of a large-scale U.S. invasion of the type that we were equipped for by October 27. I think Ray Garthoff summarized it. Some of you were not in the room. Let me just repeat it very quickly: something on the order of 1,190 air sorties the first day, five army divisions, three marine divisions, 140,000 U.S. ground troops. The Soviet Union, as I understand it, to some degree anticipated that, and equipped their forces here—the 42,000 Soviet troops—with six what they call *Luna* launchers—we call them FROGs—and nine tactical nuclear warheads. Later, perhaps, we should extend the discussion of the implications of that for the future of a nuclear world. It strikes me in one sense as the most dangerous element of the entire episode. But, my question to you, sir, is this: Were you aware that the Soviet forces (a) were equipped with six *Luna* launchers and nine nuclear warheads; and (b)—something I never could have conceived of—that because the Soviets were concerned about the ability of the Soviet troops and the Cuban troops to repel the possible U.S. invasion using conventional arms, the Soviets authorized the field commanders in Cuba, without further consultation with the Soviet Union—which of course would have been very difficult because of communication problems—to utilize those nuclear launchers and nuclear warheads?;* (a) Were you aware of it? (b) What was your inter-

---

*For a discussion of the subsequent controversy surrounding this latter issue, see chapter 4, pp. 352–56, below.

pretation or expectation of the possible effect on Cuba? How did you think the U.S. would respond, and what might the implications have been for your nation and the world?

CASTRO: Well, I actually thought that there were *more* tactical nuclear weapons. There was mention of tactical nuclear weapons in the report of the Soviet Command. There was mention of the *Luna* missiles. I don't know whether the naval forces had them, too. There was mention of the tactical nuclear weapons, and the motorized, or mechanized, regiments.

In the first place, I think that there were very few. Had the Americans carried out this kind of operation, they would have carried more than just nine tactical nuclear weapons.[178] Nine was not a very logical number. If I had been consulted, I would have said that there was need for more tactical nuclear weapons. I think that you have to analyze things from the military standpoint. We had already made the political decision to deploy nuclear weapons, and the political decision entailed the risks of our involvement in a nuclear war. Of course, we always thought that in the event of a nuclear war—with Soviet nuclear arms here or not—we would have been involved. Logic indicates that if two big powers clash in a nuclear war, they are not going to start mincing their steps in selecting objectives that they believe have to be neutralized or destroyed. We've always thought that in a nuclear war, the whole world would be included in it, and it would affect everyone. But I was really surprised by the number of nuclear arms. Compared to the forty-two strategic weapons, that's very few tactical. I imagine that in the Soviet Union there were many more tactical weapons than strategic weapons. I also think that if it was a matter of defending Cuba without creating an international problem, the presence of tactical weapons would not have created the same problem that the strategic weapons did. It couldn't have been said that tactical nuclear weapons in Cuba represented a threat to the United States. It might even have been considered an appropriate formula. If the intent was simply to defend Cuba, a number of tactical weapons for the mechanized units would have been more practical.

Now, we started from the assumption that if there was an invasion of Cuba, nuclear war would erupt. We were certain of that. If the invasion took place in the situation that had been created, nuclear war would have been the result. Everybody here was simply resigned to the fate that we would be forced to pay the price, that we would disappear. We saw that danger—I'm saying it frankly—and the conclusion, Mr. McNamara, that we might derive is that if we were going to rely on fear, we would never be able to prevent a nuclear war. The danger of nuclear war has to be eliminated by other means; it cannot be prevented on the basis of fear of nuclear weapons, or that human beings are going to be deterred by the fear of nuclear weapons. We have lived through the very singular experience of becoming practically the first target of those nuclear weapons: no one lost their equanimity or their calm in the face of such a danger, despite the fact that the self-preservation instinct is supposed to have been more powerful. That's why 50,000 warheads are simply madness. You see, humans have been doing mad things with technology, which is more highly developed than their abilities to organize and make policy. It is not surprising that we are very much concerned about the problems in the Soviet Union. Everyone is worried about the possibility of some of the re-publics having nuclear weapons, because all this entails enormous dangers.

You want me to give you my opinion in the event of an invasion with all the troops, with 1,190 sorties? Would I have been ready to use nuclear weapons? Yes, I would have agreed to the use of nuclear weapons. Because, in any case, we took it for granted that it would become a nuclear war anyway, and that we were going to disappear. Before having the country occupied—totally occupied—we were ready to die in the defense of our country. I would have agreed, in the event of the invasion that you are talking about, with the use of tactical nuclear weapons. You've asked me to speak frankly and, in all frankness, I must say that I would have had that opinion. If Mr. McNamara or Mr. Kennedy had been in our place, and had their country been in-vaded, or if their country was going to be occupied—given an enor-mous concentration of conventional forces—they would have used tactical nuclear weapons. And after the experience of what happened, do you want me to tell you something? I am glad that the military here had the authority, and that they did not have to consult. That facilitated an agreement between Soviet and Cuban military men. It was an advantage for all of us.

I wish we had had the tactical nuclear weapons. It would have been wonderful. We wouldn't have rushed to use them, you can be sure of that. The closer to Cuba the decision of using a weapon effective against a landing, the better. Of course, after we had used ours, they would have replied with, say, 400 tactical weapons—we don't know how many would have been fired at us. In any case, we were resigned to our fate. So, the idea of withdrawing the weapons simply didn't cross our minds.

I read you Khrushchev's letter of the 23rd. In that letter, there is a total political determination, full determination. Khrushchev had all the information. He knew the number of arms, the correlation of forces, and—well, in my message to Khrushchev, I tried to avoid any sign or symptom of concern. In my letter to Khrushchev, I expressed two concerns: one, not using language which would clash with his great anxiety for peace, with his psychology. I didn't want to use terms which would be too strong and would clash with his mentality, his idiosyncrasy. I imagine that he must have suffered greatly during those days, because he was not a man who wanted war. He was a man who sincerely desired peace. So when, as a result of all this, it looked like what was going to come was war, he must have suffered enormously. So, in my message I aimed at two things: first, not saying anything that would hurt him; but, also, not saying anything that could be interpreted as meaning that we, the Cubans, were worried or afraid. I was careful in my choice of words in some of the sentences. I said, "You have been and continue to be a tireless defender of peace and I realize how bitter these hours must be, when the outcome of your superhuman efforts is so seriously threatened. However, up to the last moment we will maintain the hope that peace will be safeguarded and we are willing to contribute to this as much as we can. But at the same time, we are ready to calmly confront a situation which we view as quite real and quite close."[179] I even thanked him; I reiterated my gratitude, and our people's infinite gratitude, to the Soviet people for their generosity and fraternal feelings.

I had these two concerns because it was a very sensitive message, and I reviewed it very carefully. As I said on a previous occasion, I was afraid of hesitations, because hesitations—and you historians know this very well—have caused many defeats throughout history. Behind a defeat—behind any defeat—there is hesitation, there are mistakes. If there are hesitations, I said, we may have a defeat. Because I also know the Americans. The Americans always do their best not to make mistakes. They may make mistakes, of course; they aren't infallible. But, in general, they like to foresee, to plan and plan. Why did they have 5,000 warheads? That seemed to be too many. And later they continued manufacturing them. The manufacture of all these weapons is incomprehensible, because they're unnecessary. It seems the Americans built so many warheads because they thought the Soviets had so many. But—

[to Cline:] well, you had the satellites. Perhaps you should have told us the number of missiles the Soviets had. That would have been very good. If the satellites that you placed in orbit had photographed the missiles that the Soviets had, you could have told us. You would have done well. But, well, you had your reasons for withholding that information. You had your reasons. We didn't know any better, and it seems that Kennedy didn't know any better when he was campaigning, according to what we have heard here. And after he was elected, he found out, when they gave him the—well, you know—the briefcase, and the codes, and the report on what the Soviets had. We didn't know. I thought that the Soviets had several hundred intercontinental missiles. Later it was said that they had reached 800 or 1,000—this was said publicly in many conversations. Later, the Soviets accelerated production of the missiles. But the figures that were read out here yesterday—forty, fifty, sixty—those are low figures, actually. We imagined thousands, even more, because that was the impression that was created.[180] And if Kennedy, who had been a senator—who was in the upper circles—believed that there was a missile gap, is it surprising that the rest of us, in the rest of the world, had erroneous information? That's why I said that if I'd known this information, and we had discussed the deployment on the basis of the strategic issues—I continue to believe that this was what was at the bottom of the issue—I would have counseled prudence, since for us there was no anxiety, no fear, in the thought that we were going to be invaded, and that they were going to crush us. After all, we had developed the mentality of fighters, of patriots ready to fight. We were not afraid of fighting. Imagine what would be the situation now, at this point in time, if we were afraid! Yet we are calm. I'm not boasting. It is a philosophy. It is a way of thinking. If we had known that this was the correlation of forces, we would have advised prudence. "Don't bring that kind of missile," I would have said, "because under these conditions you can't do that. You shouldn't do that. That's what I think." As a friend, as a true friend of the Soviets—as a brother—I would have said, "Don't do that."

So, we had our view. But as I explained here, we had unlimited faith in the Soviets, and we had a different impression in general of their capability. We didn't believe that it was greater than that of the United States. We knew it wasn't, globally speaking, when you considered all the military bases around the Soviet Union, and the bombers—the U.S. bombers. But, in the case of the missiles, we believed what Kennedy believed before the elections: that there was a favorable situation for the USSR.

I have to add two things: we don't have satellites that take pictures of U.S. territory, and neither have we contingency plans to invade the United States. None.

RISQUET: Nor the intention.

McNAMARA: One small footnote to history, particularly for the Cuban and Soviet participants who may not be aware of it, is that on October 29th, 1962, at 10:00 P.M. in the evening, Admiral Dennison, who was CINCLANT—the commander-in-chief of our Atlantic forces—and who would have been the commander in the event of an invasion of Cuba, cabled the Joint Chiefs and said, "I have information that the Soviet forces in Cuba are equipped with (what we called) FROG launchers"—which was our term for the Soviet *Luna* launchers—"with nuclear warheads, and, therefore, I in effect request authority to equip U.S. invasion forces with *Honest John*, which are dual capable—conventional and nuclear-capable—artillery; and nuclear warheads."[181] The Chiefs considered the matter, discussed it with me, and we said, "No." And our invasion force, had it invaded, would *not* have been equipped with tactical nuclear weapons. Now, I don't wish by that statement to imply—I don't think we need discuss this matter—but I don't wish by that statement to imply that had the invasion occurred, had it been met with nuclear fire from the *Luna* launchers, that the U.S. would not have, very quickly, made available tactical nuclear warheads to its forces. But I simply want to come back to the point that I think you have emphasized: that this was an added element of danger which some of us—I take it you, and certainly I; and, I think, the Chiefs—(a) had not anticipated, and (b) would have been horrified to think of the consequences of. And I go back to my initial statement, which perhaps we can talk about later if we wish. This is simply another example that human beings are incapable of fully controlling such complex situations as military conflict among nations today. Now, that is dangerous in a world equipped with conventional weapons. It is absolutely potentially disastrous in a world that has as many nuclear weapons as we have today. It horrifies me to think what would have happened in the event of an invasion of Cuba! But it frightens me to think that the world may continue for decades with this risk! And the conclusion I draw is that we must join together in trying—quickly—to reduce the number of nuclear warheads in the world. Thank you, sir.

CASTRO: If you allow me, I agree with what you've said. I believe that the decision not to authorize the commanders of the expeditionary forces to carry nuclear weapons was wise, because the situation was very different on the American side than on the Cuban side. We would not have rushed into using nuclear weapons from the very beginning if we had been in your shoes. But for us, perhaps an enormous naval flotilla, impossible to stop, might have posed the problem. For the United States, giving these weapons to the troops was not a necessity, since they had those thousands of planes, which could immediately be equipped with nuclear weapons of any kind without posing additional risks to the troops using them or being equipped to use them—if in a matter of minutes there could have been an air retaliation using nuclear weapons, from the military and political point of view, it was wise and correct not to equip American forces with nuclear weapons at the outset. That simply would have increased the risks. The use of nuclear weapons is a desperate act; and while the defenders might have been in a desperate situation, U.S. troops would not, since there was always the possibility of a nuclear counterattack if these weapons were used against them.

BLIGHT: Ambassador Martin.

MARTIN: This has been a most important and very illuminating conversation. I have two rather small corrections I would like to make.

One: Professor Pastor had said that we reached unanimity after we saw the nuclear weapons in Cuba. Actually, at the October 2nd and 3rd meeting of all the countries of Latin America, we reached unanimity on the need for strong action if this buildup of military capacity should continue. So it was not just the nuclear weapons that led to a unanimous view, but it was the general buildup of Soviet equipment in Cuba.

The second is that it's been suggested that we got unanimous action in both cases by the use of our economic weapons. It is true that in the case of the January [1962] meeting, we did agree for one country to study again two projects we had turned down. We did study them, but we turned them down again—so they didn't get a penny out of it. There was no use of economic weapons of any kind at the meeting which adopted the quarantine policy.

BLIGHT: I recognize Gillian Gunn.

GILLIAN GUNN: I understand that you have said that if you had understood—if you had known—the real correlation of forces between the Soviet Union and the United States—if you had known what we now know about the United States having a far greater number of nuclear warheads than the Soviet Union—you would have urged prudence when you were approached in May 1962 about the deployment of missiles on Cuban soil. And yet, if I understand correctly, Mr. McNamara had told us that he inadvertently gave this information to the U.S. press when he thought he was speaking off the record, and ended up finding he was speaking *on* the record in a January 1961 discussion, shortly after the Kennedy administration took office. So we have a period of one year and five months when, apparently, there was a statement on the public record by the United States that the correlation of forces was quite different from what the Soviet Union had been claiming, and yet this information did not seem to be utilized in Cuba. So my questions are: were you unaware of the statement by Mr. McNamara in January 1961? Or were you aware of the statement and yet did not believe it? And if you were aware of the statement, did you make any attempt to clarify this matter with the Soviet Union? And did they give you any reassurances which neutralized the impact of McNamara's statement?

CASTRO: Actually, I didn't say that I ignored the correlation of forces in terms of warheads. We always knew that the United States had many more warheads. We are talking about ballistic launchers—the number of missiles, rather—which were the most fearsome weapons because of the speed and accuracy with which they can reach their targets. I said that I supposed that they were in a better situation, or that they had a better correlation, in terms of ballistic missiles. That is what I said, because it is the only thing I could say. I had the same feeling that Kennedy had, I imagine, that in matters of intercontinental ballistic missiles, the Soviets were in a better situation—not in terms of total global arms. The United States started manufacturing nuclear warheads before, and the U.S. has manufactured an endless number of nuclear warheads—this is something well known by everyone—as well as all kinds of weapons. But quantity does not make for quality. There comes a time when quality surpasses actual needs. There are different systems—the submarines, the missiles, the air force—to guarantee survival in the event of a surprise attack from the other side. This has always existed—that is, the variety of weapons systems. Until very recently, there was talk of anti-ballistic means as the last resort amid the crazed arms race. I want to clear this up.

And secondly, we were hearing declarations every day on nuclear issues. I didn't read all the statements that the U.S. leaders made every day. I don't even know when he made the statement; in January 1961? In January 1961, we were occupied with other things. We were not thinking about missiles or anything of the sort. We were thinking about the invasion that was being organized against us. We were concentrating on that. It was not a nuclear threat. It was a conventional threat, and it didn't even cross our minds to think about nuclear weapons and missiles.

I explained here how the missile issue cropped up. Actually, we were not reading much about all these details. Rather, we guided ourselves by Soviet declarations, and by facts such as demonstrations of technical prowess in space. And we know that to launch a man into outer space you need a rocket, a rocket as big as an intercontinental missile.

I actually don't remember that. We did not keep abreast of all these statements, and it was not logical for us to follow these details so closely as to what one part said and the other part said. Of course, you'd have to assume that we had total trust in Mr. McNamara, and at that time we didn't trust McNamara completely.

McNAMARA: Touché! [Laughter.]

BLIGHT: Please, General Gribkov.

GRIBKOV: I wanted to go into a brief exercise here, because there have been a great many questions addressed to Fidel Castro, and I would like to give him a rest. So I would like to make a clarification. So far, the U.S. delegation has been saying that they did not know of the existence of the *Luna* tactical weapons in Cuba. Today it became clear from Mr. McNamara's question that they knew there were *Lunas* in Cuba and, therefore, they included this in their deliberations. We know that in Western Europe, in each division there are similar weapons, and, as regards the use of nuclear weapons, the commander of each army corps in Western Europe, for instance, is authorized, in the case of a Soviet or Warsaw Pact attack, to use tactical weapons. Is that not true? This is in the records, in your standing orders. And since you equipped the seven divisions earmarked for operations against Cuba with the launchers for these missiles, it was very easy to include the weapons, the *Honest Johns,* especially considering what Fidel Castro said: that is, that the U.S. had ballistic delivery systems which made it easy to deliver the warheads.

I repeat: everything that was brought—all the Soviet weapons brought to Cuba—were in no way intended as offensive weapons. There are many present here who have a perfect understanding of the fact that the troops of the Cuban armed forces, and the Soviet troops that were stationed here, were not capable of launching an offensive against the United States from Cuba. This would simply have been completely absurd. Everything that was brought was for the defense of the achievements of the Cuban people.

In my first statement, I said that these mid-range missiles were intended to deter, and the intention of striking a blow at the United States was never considered. I repeat that the composition of the Soviet Group of Forces was suited only for defense. If you analyze it, this is clear: there was one defensive division, two antiaircraft divisions, four mechanized regiments, and one *Sopka* coastal missile unit. I explained this on the first day. The Il-28 aircraft that were mentioned here, and the other forces—the rocket-launching patrol boats—all of this was brought over to defend Cuba.

And—I repeat—when Pliyev received orders from Khrushchev, he told him on leaving Moscow that the medium-range missile forces could be used exclusively—I repeat, exclusively—with the authorization of the commander-in-chief, Khrushchev. "The order has to come from Moscow whatever happens." Even when the crisis broke, the order never arrived from Moscow to activate the R-12 warheads. I want to repeat this so you can hear this directly from us.

Now, as regards the tactical *Luna* rockets: the commanders were authorized, in case of an evident landing by the adversary on Cuba, to analyze the situation under the circumstances, because communication with Moscow would have taken a long time. So Pliyev was authorized to order the regimental commanders to use those tactical weapons.

When I traveled to Cuba, I received the instructions of Defense Minister Malinovsky. I want to repeat the order literally. He said, "Tell Pliyev the view of the High Command. The Statsenko missile division must only go into action"—we have this Russian saying, "let it go into action"—"only on an authorization from the commander-in-chief to use the tactical weapons.* If you use the tactical weapons, it must be in the face of an invasion, that is, a penetration into Cuban territory."

---

*Gribkov evidently means "strategic" here, not "tactical." Gen. Igor Statsenko, attached to the Strategic Rocket Forces, commanded strategic missiles in Cuba, not tactical *Lunas*.

I want to mention an example in Western Europe. We are not going to play "cat and mouse." We watched you, you watched us. We know that in your defense plans you included the order that as soon as our troops penetrated so far into the territory of West Germany, you would use tactical weapons. That was in your plans.

I wanted to explain something here. Someone had asked Fidel Castro about the countries in Latin America. I'd like to corroborate that when the blockade was set up around Cuba, Argentina, Venezuela, and the Dominican Republic had already chosen their troops: Argentina, a brigade of marines, and two naval ships, 5,000 people all together; Venezuela had already appointed two ships of the usual kind—frigates—employed in these actions; and the Dominican Republic had also promised four ships. Argentina had assigned five aircraft: three transport craft to carry the troops, and two patrol craft, as well as infantry troops. Argentina promised 3,000 and Venezuela 5,000. The governments of Ecuador, Colombia, Costa Rica, Peru, Honduras, Haiti, Guatemala, and Nicaragua expressed their readiness to assign men and matériel, and to put them under U.S. command. They also agreed to make available their air fields, ports, and so on, for the use of U.S. troops. We know that Adenauer gave his approval for these actions, as did De Gaulle, and others. Even in Africa a number of governments were attracted to the side of the United States. I will tell you that we sent Commander Pliyev and another group through Conakry—

BLIGHT: General, please, sir. I beg your pardon. I've been asked by our Cuban hosts to keep in mind the people downstairs who are preparing lunch, and I wonder if we could resolve this by having you conclude your question, or your presentation, and having a very quick response from General Smith and Ambassador Ray Garthoff about the issues that you have raised. Then we can break for lunch. Thank you.

GRIBKOV: Just a minute. That's all I need. We sent this group through Conakry to choose, along with the help of our Cuban friends, deployment sites for our missile weapons and personnel. And although we built the Conakry airport, they closed it down under pressure from the United States. When we traveled to Cuba with my staff, before arriving in Conakry, we were told that it was closed to Soviets. So, we had to use a different air field. When we got out of Dakar, they closed Dakar to us also, so that the breadth of pressures and influences involved in the Cuban situation was immense. Thank you very much.

BLIGHT: Thank you very much, General Gribkov. Quick responses are now in order from General Smith and Ambassador Garthoff, and then we'll break for lunch.

GENERAL SMITH: Mr. President, I know that you and Secretary McNamara have both heard more military discussions than you can remember, or care to; but I ask your indulgence for one brief one. The U.S. forces for the invasion of Cuba had forces that were nuclear *capable.* That means, like the land weapons and the aircraft, that they could use nuclear weapons. We knew that there were *Lunas* in Cuba; but to our knowledge, those *Lunas* had no nuclear warheads. At the time of the October crisis we had no evidence that there were any nuclear weapons in Cuba. So our forces were prepared to conduct any invasion that was ordered by the president with conventional forces. When Admiral Dennison heard that the *Lunas* were there, he said, "We may not know they have nuclear weapons, but they are nuclear *capable;* I would like authority to use nuclear weapons if necessary," and, as Secretary McNamara reported, the answer to that was "no," because there was no evidence any nuclear weapons were there.

Secondly, with respect to the use of the weapons in Cuba, as military men, you will understand that military people think in terms of capabilities, not intentions, and the R-12 rockets had the *capability* of hitting the United States. The offensive weapons from Cuba had the capability of endangering U.S. facilities and equipment, and ships, and therefore, we demanded the removal of those offensive weapons because of their *capabilities,* not because we were making judgments at that time about Soviet *intentions.*

Thirdly, the United States was trying to mobilize as much support as possible in the world for its position at the time. You mentioned to me yesterday about other nations being involved in the invasion of Cuba had it occurred. I do not know of that, but when I return, I'm going to look into that more deeply, and you will get an answer from me as to what I can find out about any other participation that was involved. I don't think there was any in the invasion itself, but I will look.

The final point is the most important point that I want to make. The United States forces in Europe, as you know, were prepared to use nuclear weapons. And there were plans, as you said, at a certain point, that they would remove those weapons from storage sites, so that they would become mobile. But no nuclear weapon in the United States can be fired at any time without direct authorization of the president at that time. And in fact, in the NATO Alliance, that is further complicated because no nuclear weapon can be fired in Europe without consultation with the other allies. But the decision to make those weapons available to NATO must come from the United States, and no U.S. military commander in the field has any authority to use nuclear weapons in the absence of that authority from the president at the time.

McNamara: Mr. Chairman, thirty seconds. That is absolutely correct. But, in addition, neither in late '61 nor early '62—and certainly not after the Cuban situation—could I personally conceive of any situation in which the U.S. would benefit from ever initiating the use of nuclear weapons. Quite contrary to then accepted NATO policy, I met privately, first, with President Kennedy before his death, and later with President Johnson, and I said this to them: "Mr. President: number one, no nuclear weapon could ever be fired without your personal authority. Number two, there may be a time when you are asked to grant the authority to initiate—not respond to, but initiate—the use of nuclear weapons. I tell you I cannot conceive of a situation in which an initiator—and I would apply this to the Soviets as well as the U.S.— could ever benefit itself by initiating the use of nuclear weapons." I could not conceive one then, and I cannot conceive one today.

Blight: Thank you very much. Thanks to all of you. Thank you, especially, President Castro. Let's break for lunch. We'll resume here at 4:00 P.M.

CUBA'S FUTURE:
". . . to see to it that our revolution survives"

Even before the Antigua conference in January 1991, one of the scholarly advisers to the U.S. organizers began urging us to consider the likelihood and possible consequences of what he called the "Cuba poof!" hypothesis: the chance that Castro's Cuba would be history before we could convene a conference at which to examine a portion of its history. We were aware that the tendency to consign Castro and his regime prematurely to the dust bin of history has a long tradition. For example, Paul Nitze, in a memorandum dated 6 December 1962, endorsed the view that "the missile crisis weakened Castro" to such an extent that "now Castro is at the end of the line."[182] But of course, Castro had not gone "poof" after the missile crisis. In fact, by early

1989, when we first encountered Cubans in the critical oral history process, Castro had already ruled Cuba for thirty years. At the Antigua conference there was no discussion whatsoever, during the formal proceedings or otherwise, of the possible imminent demise of Castro. As it happened, we were almost completely focused at that time on the U.S.-Soviet dimensions of the crisis.

Yet by that moment Fidel Castro had already raised the issue with the Cuban people and had settled upon a strategy for Cuba's survival. By 1988, Castro had begun to see the handwriting on the wall for socialism: the Soviet Union and, with it, the entire socialist world, was in crisis, economically and psychologically. In the Eastern bloc, experiments in reform were under way, experiments which would shortly explode into a full-fledged revolution, ending communist rule first in the external Soviet empire in Eastern Europe and, by January 1992, in the Soviet Union itself.[183]

Cuba under Fidel Castro would have none of that. In Cuba there would be no experiments with multiparty democracy, no movement toward a market economy, and, above all, no compromise or surrender to "the imperialists." Castro made all of this clear as early as July 1988, in his annual report to the Cuban people, given on the anniversary of the first armed attack by his rebel group against the Batista government in 1953. "Our party knows it cannot make mistakes that will weaken it ideologically," Castro said. "[T]herefore, . . . the party's role must not be weakened; it must be strengthened. . . . Lenin, likewise, did not need more than one party to carry out the October Revolution." He dismissed out of hand any thought of market reforms: "I hope that when we celebrate the 70th anniversary and centennial [of the Cuban Revolution], history will prove that we do not need Capitalist political formulas. They are complete garbage, they are worthless, they constitute unending political deceit." And on the American threat, Castro said, "[T]he concept of the war of all the people makes us very strong. . . . If imperialism opportunistically had wanted to take advantage of the situation [Cuba's aid to Angola] for an attack on our country, it would have encountered our people and would have experienced a Bay of Pigs, 2 Bays of Pigs, 3 Bays of Pigs, 100 Bays of Pigs, I am sure."[184] If it came to that, Cuba would remain the last bastion of socialism on Earth—"Socialism on One Island," as one observer put it.[185] One party would rule; Cuba would perfect socialism, not replace it; and Cuba would circle the wagons, committing national suicide before caving in to the United States.[186]

These were brave socialist sentiments in mid-1988. But in 1989–

90, the roof had begun to fall in on Cuba. The Soviet collapse was well under way, and with it eighty-five percent of Cuba's trade. In December 1989, the United States invaded Panama and captured strongman Manuel Noriega. Cuba went on military alert, fearing it might be the next American target. In February 1990, Nicaraguan voters rejected Cuba's allies and protégés, the Sandinistas, and their leader, Daniel Ortega, voluntarily relinquished power. By the summer of 1990, the Cuban exile community in the United States had worked itself into a frenzy. In Miami's "Little Havana," bumper stickers proclaimed, "First Manuel, then Daniel, next Fidel" and "Christmas in Havana," as the exiles sensed that the end of Castro's rule might be near.

Castro's response was once again complete defiance—this time of both the (former) Eastern bloc and the United States. On 7 March 1990, he announced in a speech in Havana that Cuba had entered a "Special Period in time of peace," a period that would be the most severe test of the revolution since the missile crisis:

> The Yankees know this; they know that there is this thorn that is stuck. Well, those who want to collapse over there will collapse, but here there will be no collapse. . . . Once again, underestimation; all the time underestimation; underestimation with the [pirate] bands; underestimation with the blockade when they wanted to destroy us economically; underestimation at the time of Girón; underestimation during the October crisis. They are always underestimating us because of their arrogance, because their pretensions blind them to understanding.[187]

During the spring of 1990 articles proliferated in the U.S. press about the presumed imminence of Castro's "fall."[188]

Did Castro's Cuba have a future? Or was it, one way or another, about to go "poof"? By January 1992, when our delegation arrived in Havana, these issues were very much on everyone's mind. Castro himself would reiterate in various ways throughout the conference that the goal of the Cuban people had become "to see to it that the revolution survives." But would it be possible, in the midst of this struggle for survival, many wondered, for Castro to conduct a serious inquiry into the missile crisis with "the imperialists"?

CUBAN FOREIGN POLICY:
"Times have changed; we have changed"

Wayne Smith begins the discussion of Cuba's future by inviting Fidel Castro to say formally what he has appeared to imply throughout the conference: that despite its history of involvement with revolutionary insurgencies, Cuba will henceforth abide by the principles of the U.N. charter and respect the sovereignty of all other countries. Castro immediately responds affirmatively: "Times have changed; we have changed." He concludes a long answer to a short question by stating his—and Cuba's—agreement to uphold "international norms" regarding sovereignty.

Yet on the way from his analysis of the changing times to his confirmation of Cuba's conformity with these new requirements, Castro politely but firmly condemns the United States for violating the very principles which, at Wayne Smith's invitation, he has espoused. His examples, tellingly, are Latin American examples: the U.S. invasion of Panama; the Contra war against Nicaragua; ignoring the plight of the democratically elected government of Jean-Bertrand Aristide in Haiti, until it was too late to prevent the military coup that ousted him. In answering the question, therefore, Castro turns the question back on the United States, and he does not appear to be sanguine about the prospects for U.S. conformity to "international norms."

BLIGHT: Before we begin, I'm authorized by our Cuban hosts to announce that we've been invited by the president to attend a reception at the Presidential Palace tonight at 8:45. Those of us who are staying in the protocol area here should be ready to leave at 8:15 sharp. Also, this afternoon, beginning now and going until approximately 5:00 or so, we'll continue with questions and answers about the October crisis, directly following which President Castro will offer some concluding remarks and observations, and synthesis about the October crisis. Following that, we will break up and leave to prepare to go to the reception. Jorge Risquet?

RISQUET: I wanted to refer to the statement by Mr. McNamara that we all applauded, where he called for the elimination of nuclear weapons because of the risk of a catastrophe that we all experienced thirty years ago. Since there are many here who were not present at the previous conferences in Moscow and Antigua, I would like, in supporting this idea for the elimination of all nuclear weapons, chemical weapons, and weapons of mass destruction, to add that in the past, when these weapons of mass destruction did not exist, three-quarters of the world was colonized by the Great Powers with conventional weapons. So, to this very fair appeal, I would add the need to respect the independence and self-determination of all nations, big and small, so that they may live in peace, free of all foreign interference, and build their own destinies and choose whatever path to economic, social, and political development that they wish. I think this would complete the recommendation.

This would be another vital lesson to draw from the crisis. The October crisis became a nuclear crisis, but the causes leading to it were, we might say, conventional: aggression by a large country against a small country.

I would also like to recall what Mr. McNamara said himself when he became president of the World Bank: that the real atom bomb was in the Third World, whose population was experiencing rampant growth along with rampant growth in poverty and backwardness. This situation that he mentioned is becoming increasingly difficult, and this could lead to immense social outbreaks of unforeseeable consequences. If the world were free of all these weapons of mass destruction, this could help free the Third World of underdevelopment.

I think these three points might be drawn from what we have discussed, so that in the future we might have a world of peace and progress for all the men and women of the Earth. That is all I wanted to add to the statement made by McNamara.

BLIGHT: Thank you. Mr. McNamara, would you like to respond to that or not? [McNamara shakes his head.] Okay. Now, if I call on you and you have forgotten what you meant to ask before lunch, you have two choices: one is to pass, the other is to invent a new question. With that warning in mind, I'd like to call on Wayne Smith.

WAYNE SMITH: Mr. President, you have acknowledged that Cuba supported revolutionary groups during the early '60s. You also said that that is not Cuba's policy now. I'd like to follow up on that statement of yours and look to the future, as it were.

I think all of us around the table here would acknowledge that our governments have made mistakes in the past. The United States also has overthrown a few governments and tried to overthrow a few others. The Soviet government has done the same in the past. More recently, the United States government was condemned by the World Court for giving aid to the Contras in their war against the government of Nicaragua. At that time, that provoked something of a debate in the United States, and there were a series of essays published by the Council on Foreign Relations in which the issue of international law was raised.[189] I remember at the time Jeane Kirkpatrick argued that the United States, for its part, would commit itself to live within the Charter of the United Nations, to conduct its foreign policy entirely within the Charter of the United Nations and within the parameters of international law, if only the Soviets would do the same. Well, I think the world has changed dramatically since that point, and we are now talking of a new world order, or a new system—a new international system—and, for its part, the Soviet government under President Gorbachev had committed itself to live within the U.N. charter. Various Cuban officials have subscribed to the concept that what we must all now do is to commit ourselves fully to respect the sovereignty of other countries, living within—conducting our relations within—the charter of the U.N. We are not an official delegation here, so we cannot commit *our* government to that; but we can certainly all work for it. I would simply invite you, following on your early statements, to comment on that, and to indicate whether indeed the Cuban government does subscribe to that.

CASTRO: I can say I'm at a disadvantage here, because you can make any statement you like without committing your government, whereas whatever I say here does constitute a commitment. But I have no objections to answering your question, or to reflecting on the subject.

As I said here, we have a policy that differs from the one we had at a certain point in time. Times have changed; we have changed. Our country, our leaders, are more mature. We have more experience, more realism, without forsaking our principles or our idealism. We do have more experience. Latin America changed, and we changed also. They changed vis-à-vis us, and we changed vis-à-vis them.

Of course, our policies have an implicit commitment. You can't support a revolutionary movement one day and then the next day say, "To hell with them; to hell with revolutionaries, let's forget about them," just because it is convenient for the state. I think that we have fulfilled our word up until the end. We helped the Nicaraguans, that's well known. There's a new situation there, which is not easy to understand, because there are Contras, Contra-Contras, Compas, Compas-

Compas, and who knows what else. And we have nothing to do with that. What we've got over there is doctors, a relatively large number of doctors, helping out in Nicaragua's health programs. We've helped the Salvadoreans, and we were consistent. We helped them to a certain point, when the prospects for peace became apparent. And we have supported those prospects for peace. The war was no longer the main objective; peace became the objective, and many of us cooperated with that. We consider the El Salvador problem to be solved. But for some time, apart from political support—as of the moment these prospects for peace appeared and the revolutionaries began to negotiate and find solutions by mutual agreement among the parties—we abstained from any type of activity in support of military actions in El Salvador. This was some time ago.

We also had a commitment with the revolutionaries in Chile, and we supported the Chilean revolutionaries against Pinochet. There, too, there was a political process. Pinochet is still there, but he is no longer the government. There is a civilian government, the result of agreements there—of elections—and we have accepted that situation strictly. We've explained to the Chilean revolutionaries how far our commitment went: as long as there was a military regime, or a regime of force there. And all activities related to our cooperation in the area of weapons and training and so on ceased. We have respected that situation. We have viewed it positively, and we are—I might say—free of commitments. You can't walk away from commitments; that would be dishonorable. So we followed through on our commitments, and the evolution of events freed us of them.

As regards the international situation, considering the changes in the world and based on our own experience, we also freed ourselves of commitments in other areas. I explained here how peace was achieved in Angola, and what our contribution was to that peace. We were in Angola for fourteen years. We participated at two very important moments. The first time was when the South Africans invaded Angola, and later when they invaded again. I already said that our last effort was undertaken because of the Cuito Cuanavale situation, which was very difficult. There we made our last effort. We achieved peace, and we withdrew our forces from Angola. We fulfilled the timetable for withdrawal fifteen days ahead of time. We strictly fulfilled all of our commitments. Before that, we had been withdrawing our troops from Ethiopia, troops that had gone there when Somalia invaded Ethiopia.[190] This was a struggle that we had tried to avoid. I participated in meetings between Ethiopia and Somalia. We had meetings with both. We advised them not to go to war. We supported the changes in Ethiopia, because they had an emperor and slavery. We looked favorably on the revolutionary movement, and, in that war, we supported them also.

On those occasions when we have given military support, we have tried to avoid participating in internal conflicts. So, in Angola, in general, we did not participate in actions between UNITA* and the MPLA,† except when we were attacked or when there was a certain degree of danger. But, as a general rule, we did everything possible— and we succeeded—in avoiding involvement in internal conflicts. Our problem was with the South Africans. Our troops were on a line to protect the country from South African penetration. We also know a bit about the correlation of forces. There was a time when the correlation of forces was very favorable, but not at first: not in 1975, when we began to withdraw the troops. Then the South Africans got militarily very strong; they began aggression again, and in the end we were forced to make an enormous effort to find a solution to the problem without risking a defeat at the hands of the South Africans. We have avoided getting involved in domestic conflicts in these countries, as a policy. I think that's the worst deal you can make: that is, getting involved in domestic conflicts with troops over there.

This is different from support—cooperation in the military field. Once upon a time the so-called subversive wars, as the West calls them, were always attributed to the socialists. But then the United States also adopted policies in this field, and began to organize their own irregular wars. They supported that a great deal in Afghanistan, when the Soviets were there; they supported UNITA a great deal in Angola. The United States, which was a mediator in the conflict, avoided making any commitment to supply weapons to the Angolans, but up until the last moment they supplied weapons to UNITA. The history of the war against the Sandinistas in Nicaragua is well known: the war was strongly supported by the United States. So what at one time was the tactic of the revolutionary—the irregular war—also became a tactic of the United States.[191] This, I think, is something that we have to admit; I think it's fair and correct.

These internationalist operations with our own troops, as far as we are concerned, is a stage that is finished. The world has changed. There is a new situation. We would like to help; we have good inten-

---

*União Nacional para a Independência Total de Angola (National Union for the Total Independence of Angola).
†Movimento Popular de Libertação de Angola (Angolan Popular Liberation Movement).

tions. But those kinds of military operations are not realistic, and we have said that internationalism has to begin with ourselves. The most important internationalist mission is to see to it that our revolution survives. Therefore, our essential task, in all directions, is centered here, domestically. If we believe in our ideas and principles, let us defend them here. Let us solve *our* problems. That is the policy that we are following. So, both aiding revolutionary movements and providing military aid outside of our borders we consider to be something of the past. This kind of policy is no longer realistic, and we've got enough work here to keep us busy at present.

You've also seen what happened in Haiti, with the overthrow of the Aristide government. We had a good opinion of the process that was taking place in Haiti. Then a military coup was staged. There was an explosion of emigration, and a large number of Haitians wound up here in Cuba, because they left Haiti on boats and were shipwrecked. As a rule, when they run out of gasoline, we give them gasoline and let them go on. If their boats break down, we fix them and let them go on. If the vessel is destroyed, as often happens, then, with the United Nations and with other organizations, we try to get them to return to their country. We've never tried to force them to return. These are issues we have discussed with the United Nations. This has implications for us, including sanitary ones. Unfortunately, there are many diseases rampant there which we have under control, or which are non-existent in our country. Some of these immigrants are carriers of these diseases. And there are other diseases, for instance, AIDS. There's very little AIDS in Cuba. There are not only material difficulties and expenditures involved in dealing with Haitian refugees, but also health difficulties. However, we do give them the attention they need. We give them what we can, awaiting the moment when some international agency takes charge. Haiti is a neighboring country.

If we were to opt for the U.S. policy, we could send a small or a large expedition—some sort of madness like that—and go over there to reestablish the democratic government in Haiti. But we are against that. We are against our doing it, and we are against anyone else doing it, because we are very much concerned about respect for sovereignty. I think sovereignty is very important. I don't know if some day the entire world will be a single family, a single state, or if the United Nations will become a federation of states, and there will be a world government. I've read some fiction books about world government, one in which people voted by interactive television. They didn't have to go anywhere to vote. But, sovereignty for us is something very important, and I think it's very important for many countries in the world.

The events that have taken place in the Soviet Union are proof of the strength of nationalist feelings. They are very important. Once upon a time, Marxists felt that nationalist feelings would weaken over time. At one point in time, the nation was seen as something progressive over feudalism or tribalism, and nationalist feelings were seen as a very positive force. As internationalists, we analyzed the positive and negative aspects of nationalism. Nationalism has immense strength. Just like religion, it is immensely strong. Some had thought that with development and the emergence of science, the conquest of space, the atom, biology, microbiology—with all of these things, religious feelings would be weakened. But, in fact, religious feelings have become stronger in the world, and this is obvious in all continents everywhere. Religious feelings are very strong. These are two things over which theoreticians and revolutionaries who thought that the development of socialism would overcome different stages were generally mistaken. Of course, we've never had any kind of nationalistic conflicts, nor any kind of religious conflicts. We haven't had that. But we have seen the immense strength of religious and nationalist movements.

However, I don't think the time has come to do away with the principle of sovereignty—much less when we see an upsurge of hegemony, like the hegemony of the United States, with the disappearance of bipolarity. We now have unipolarity. These are realities. The influence of U.S. power in the world is something that worries a great many of us, or all of us. Are we going to move from a bipolar world to a unipolar world under the baton of the United States? We don't want to be under anybody's baton. But this is a real and tangible force. Perhaps the United States will have time to meditate on all of this.

I recall when I used to talk to senators, and to visitors who came to our country. They used to say that the Soviets wanted to take over the world, and I said, "Do you really believe that?" I was seeing the great efforts being made in the Soviet Union to solve their own problems, and to develop. And I couldn't perceive any intention to take over the world, despite the fact that they were pleased when they saw any revolution take place, because this meant a triumph of their ideas. They were appreciative of that; but actually promoting them, that's something quite different.

A lot has been said here about when we helped the revolutionaries in Venezuela. I can add a bit more, since we have been speaking so frankly here. You can't imagine the reprimand the Soviets sent us be-

cause of our aid to the revolutionary movement in Venezuela. They
were completely against our support for the revolutionary movement,
and we were doing nothing on behalf of the Soviets. The Soviets had
nothing to do with our aid for the revolutionary movement in Nicaragua, nor did they have anything to do with the force we sent to
Angola in 1975. All we got from the Soviet Union was concern. On
one occasion, they said we had sent a division, and what I said was,
"There's a whole lot more than a division there. That's not news."
What we were sending there were regiments and more regiments,
because after we were in the conflict with the South Africans—after
we were there helping the Angolans toward the end of the colonial
period—the South Africans came in and they penetrated about a thousand kilometers. That's when the first Cubans were killed there. They
were helping the Angolans. We couldn't evade that problem. It wasn't
just a question of helping the Angolans, it was a question of saving
the Cubans there. But the Soviets were not at all sympathetic to the
transportation of our troops to Angola. It's true they had a certain
commitment with the MPLA, just as they had with FRELIMO* in
Mozambique. They sent them weapons. A great many people sent
weapons to the liberation movements in Africa—a great many people
in the world. But, in any case, there were a number of commitments,
and some weapons arrived. Later, they did coordinate with us to some
extent. We asked them, "Please see if you can send some weapons,"
when we were already there and the situation was rather tense. We
asked them to send some of the weapons that they were going to send
the Angolans anyway, and some of the ones they were going to send
us. But the idea that the Soviets were using us to establish their global
hegemony is nonsense. Sincerely. What there was was a great deal of
discord, a great deal of criticism by the Soviets in connection with the
activities we were carrying out.

But when I used to meet with these politicians from the United
States, I'd ask them, "Do you really think the Soviets want to take over
the world? Do you think that anybody is mad enough to want to take
over the world? Why don't we give it to them? The world is a giant
mountain of problems. Who wants to receive those problems as a
present?" I think the United States also is going to discover that the
world is a mountain of problems. And Haiti is one lesson, right here
in the Caribbean, right nearby. There are terrible social problems in
Haiti.

*Frente para a Libertação de Moçambique (Front for the Liberation of Mozambique).

I began to think about this: how can the United States act the way they do? They feel they've got to do away with Noriega in Panama, so they go and do that; they get Noriega, and they don't even have evidence against him. And then they don't help the country after they invade it. They make war in Nicaragua, and finally they achieve their political objectives: the opposition won, the Sandinistas are out of power. But then they stop spending money on Nicaragua! They don't have it or they won't spend it. Maybe if they saved some of the money on weapons that Risquet was talking about, they could send some more money to the Nicaraguans, and maybe a bit more money to the Panamanians, and maybe a bit more money to the Haitians. They carry out these military operations, and after the military operations, they're not in a position to help, or there isn't a real will to help.

The world is full of problems. The statistics are familiar to Mr. McNamara from the World Bank reports. In the letters here between Khrushchev and Kennedy, it says that there were 650 million Chinese.[192] Now there are 1.14 billion Chinese! It's incredible! The figure practically doubled in just thirty years. In these letters you can read that there were 600 million. The population of India has doubled, and in Pakistan, in Bangladesh, and in Latin America, the population has also doubled. There are very serious problems in the world, and the United States is going to discover those problems.

There is a certain euphoria in the United States over what is happening in the USSR, and over the Gulf war, and so on. There is this euphoria. But the world is a very hard and difficult reality, and I think the Americans are going to discover that. We already know that the Soviets don't want it, and I was suggesting that we give it as a present to anyone who did want it, in fact.

Yes, we agree to living in a world of peace, in a world governed by international norms, as a principle, as a policy, and as a reality, on the basis of the maturity of our political process, and on the basis of our experience.

THE CUBAN REVOLUTION:
"... a monument to the Special Period"

Having transformed a question about Cuba's respect for national sovereignty into a condemnation of American foreign policy, Castro now converts a question about Cuban threat assessment in October 1962 into an analysis of the problems and prospects of the Cuban Revolution. Scott Armstrong asks him to elaborate on why, exactly, the Cubans were so convinced of the inevitability of a U.S. invasion. Armstrong notes that, even in January 1992, Cuba takes the threat of a U.S. invasion seriously. Castro has in this case little to say about 1962, but a great deal to say about 1992, especially the factors that, as he sees it, threaten the survival of the Cuban Revolution. Then, in a kind of double transformation of the original question, he proclaims the virtues of the multifaceted and, by some estimates, desperate conditions in Cuba brought on by the "Special Period." After a generation of unfortunate but necessary dependence on Soviet assistance, Castro seems to relish Cuba's opportunity to stand on its own. "In the end," he says hopefully, "we will have to erect a monument to the Special Period."

During his peroration on Cuba's "good fortune" to be going through a period of severe economic hardship, one of the scholars in our delegation recalls the picture of Castro that Lee Lockwood chose for the cover of his superb 1967 book containing his several-days-long interview with Castro in 1965. It shows the Cuban president in his customary fatigues, but wearing baseball shoes, fingers taped (presumably) to combat blisters from the bat, and with a look of total exasperation on his face. Inside the book, the same picture has beneath it the caption, "As in everything else he does, Fidel plays baseball to win and complains loudly to the umpire upon losing a close call."[193]

Castro's friend, the novelist Gabriel García Márquez, has explained that Castro's competitiveness is of a special kind. He does not merely seek victory; rather, "his attitude in the face of defeat, even in the slightest events of daily life, seems to obey a private logic: he will not even admit it, and he does not have a moment's peace until he manages to invert the terms and turn it into a victory."[194] But as Castro ruminates on the Special Period as an opportunity for moral heroism in the comfortable splendor of our conference room, Cubans from all walks of life in the city around us endure unfamiliar shortages of basic necessities with no immediate prospect of relief. We wonder whether they, too, relish the Special Period.

———————————————

BLIGHT: Thank you. Mr. Armstrong.

ARMSTRONG: Mr. President, you've given us an insightful view of the evolution of your thinking during 1962; but I would like to see if we can get you to elaborate on the evolution of your assessment of the threat of a United States invasion during that period. We've talked about how the United States forces built up during 1962. In Moscow, I believe General Smith acknowledged that part of the purpose of building up forces prior to the crisis was to give the impression that the United States might invade—perception management, if you will. Ray Garthoff has given you the figures of what that force would have been during the crisis, and I'm interested in particular in what type of invasion you anticipated, and how you saw the resolve of the American military and its political leadership. I think we're interested, because we accept the fact that the threat of an invasion is not one that you consider to be so remote. Thirty years later, as I understand it, the Committees for the National Defense are still building facilities, and in the Special Period, when you have very little concrete, some of it is being spent even today to strengthen them.

Since this will be the only question I'll get to ask, I want to add an overlay to it. I realize the question may be longer than the answer most people would give, but I assume that won't be true in your case. [Laughter.] The overlay is this: to a large extent, you are the embodiment of the revolution in Cuba, and while we've had very candid assessments from the *compañeros* on the panel there, and others, we do not have the benefit of Che's thinking, nor do we have Raúl here today with us. There are others: [Emilio] Aragonés was with us in Moscow; we have not seen him since then—I know that's not because of differences over the Cuban missile crisis. But I'm interested if you can tell us, or help us to understand, the differences of opinion that may have existed—different assessments of the United States, different assessments of the Soviet Union. Where did your colleagues not share your views? And how were those differences ironed out in the decisions themselves? At any rate, it's a long enough question; we would like to hear the answer. Thank you.

CASTRO: Yes, it has almost nothing to do with the October crisis. It was a long question; there are about five or six questions in it. It's impossible for me to be briefer than you. I shall try nevertheless.

At the time, obviously, we were always perceiving dangers. During the October crisis—and after as well—there were many covert actions. So we were always perceiving dangers. But we didn't lose sleep over it. What we did in the face of these dangers was to see how we could prepare better, how we could train the people to wage the kind of war the situation called for.

We expanded our efforts when the Reagan administration came to power. It was Reagan's threats in the Santa Fe document that led us to delve deeper into what later developed into the concept of the War of All the People.[195] It's not conventional warfare, like Iraq or anything. It is our conception, and it was born of our own revolutionary origins, and of the history of Cuba.

Cuba fought against Spain when that country was one of the mightiest powers in the world. All the Latin American nations had already attained independence from Spain; Cuba had to wage its struggle alone in the middle of the past century. Cuba had to fight and fight for a very long time, totally alone. We, as revolutionaries, draw inspiration not just from the past or from Marxist ideas, but also from the ideas of Martí, and from the revolutionary experience of our people in their long struggle against Spain.[196] So, all these elements influenced our thinking in the struggle for power, in the underground struggle, and particularly in the struggle in the mountains.

I told you that the discrepancy between Batista's forces and ours was enormous in favor of Batista. When we won the war, there were about twenty-five armed men in the Batista army for every one of us. Of course, our success gave us a lot of confidence and experience. We have developed these ideas, particularly because we perceived Reagan's policy as being a very aggressive policy toward Cuba.

We have been preparing, let's say, for some twelve years in the event that Cuba is invaded—what would we do, how would we retaliate, how would we resist; all these things. We have developed these ideas a lot. I'm not trying to impress anyone with this; I'm just answering your question. We lose no sleep over that. We are ready to face any kind of danger that might develop for our country's security. We have lived that way for a long time. Our lives have been lived in that way, in that insecurity. You in the United States have no idea of the insecurities that we have known. If you were worried about the number of missiles despite your 5,000 warheads—if you perceived anything as a threat to your security given your military strength—imagine what it is to be the neighbor and the adversary of a country like that ninety miles away! And in our case, our enemy—the United States—has a naval base right in our territory! We have had to adapt our thinking to this situation. People have an enormous capacity for adaptation.

I can tell you that we have team leadership, despite the fact that some comrades may have a lot of influence, while others might not have so much. Of course, the historical leaders are more influential; but in any case, we have always had a team, a leadership team. Each of us has his own sphere, and this has been the way over the years. When the proposal for the deployment of the missiles came up, there were no differences. When the denouement of the crisis took place, and we adopted certain positions here, there were no discrepancies among us. There have been none. There may be nuances from time to time; but in these affairs that I've mentioned, there weren't even nuances. Throughout the history of the revolution, of course, there may have been nuances. Some were more influenced by the Soviets, others were not as influenced by the Soviets—I declare that I have felt throughout great affection for the Soviets, and of course, for example, when I see them here, I feel affection and friendship toward them. If for you it was surprising to hear some of the things here, imagine our surprise in the light of events that have taken place in the Soviet Union! For us this was even worse than the October crisis. What is the October crisis compared to the situation we are in after the disintegration of the Soviet Union? It's a very serious event. But we haven't lost our equanimity, or our confidence, or our security over that.

Many of us studied in the Soviet Union. Some were more or less influenced, and there were nuances regarding economic ideas; but discrepancies? Serious, principled discrepancies? No. We've never had that within the leadership team, I would say, and these minor contradictions, these minor nuances—well, they've always been solved by talking, discussing, and we have managed to maintain unity as something sacred. At particularly difficult moments—in moments of danger—that unity has been even greater within the Party and within the leadership.

Do not believe that the revolution is a single man. Heaven forbid! We've tried to train new cadres. There are a lot of new cadres here in the leadership of the country now; there are many young people. We are trying to renew the revolution. You might ask, Why don't they renew me? Well, I think it would be wonderful if they could! But in these difficult times, if it crossed my mind to resign, or if I proposed to find a substitute to take on my duties, they would probably say that I was the greatest traitor in the world, because now we face difficult challenges.

Well, you were asking about invasion plans. You have contingency plans; McNamara talked about them. A big nation can have those things. But a small nation can't—well, except for ourselves, for our defense, of course; but we can't have contingency plans, much less for invasion. But at this moment, I don't think that the United States is considering any invasion. This, of course, does not mean that if we have any serious internal problems—serious internal conflicts—something that they have longed for in order to be able to intervene with armed force—well, that danger is obvious. We have to adapt our minds for that, and figure out what to do if that occurred, and how to maintain our purpose to fight to the end. But, at present, given the events in the Soviet Union, and the enormous economic difficulties we have had to face all of a sudden, I tend to think that the Americans are probably confident that the revolution will deteriorate, that it will lose popular support, and that it will not be able to survive the enormous economic obstacles implicit in the disappearance of the socialist bloc, and the loss of the Soviet Union. So now, despite being historical figures involved in this for many years, we're now in a position in which none of us can think of retiring. No one is going to pay us a pension; no one is even going to allow it. We would be considered traitors. So we have to go on as long as we have the necessary strength, as long as we have life, the mental capacity. We have no option. Life has imposed these realities. But there are a lot of new people. We are trying to renew our cadre with the hope that we will always have a team that will be able to carry the torch with the same spirit. I think that we are actually succeeding. I don't even want to ask any of the scholars beside us here if he or she is planning to retire. McNamara has not retired. He's still there, active in his scholarly, historical, and even political activities. What he does is high politics—outside the government, that is, but it's still high politics. And as all the historians here know, historians don't retire. I don't think politicians ever retire on their own. Rather, they are, as a rule, retired by others. I think I'll always be a politician. I think it was Aristotle who said that man was a political animal, and political animals will always be political animals. Scientists are always going to be scientists, and historians will always be historians, and politicians will always be politicians, influencing events in one way or another, directly or indirectly. But it's not a matter of power or hunger for power because, in fact, the problems that we have to face every day—the tasks that we have to carry out—are so difficult that I'd really say it's heroic. To head Belgium, Luxembourg, the Netherlands or any other developed European country—even the United States, I would say, with all the difficulties and problems you may have, of one kind or another—would be much simpler: twenty, thirty, forty times simpler than ruling a country in Cuba's condition.

So, political work becomes something heroic, and that is the way we regard our political duties. It's duty, not ambition. I would like to be an academic. I would like to be a historian. I would like to do many of the things that you do. But if that idea ever crossed my mind, why, I'm sure I would never be allowed to do it. I hope that one day, when all this has passed and we show that we can resist—it still has to be proven; we are facing the most terrible test—if we survive the problems in the Soviet Union, if our revolution survives these problems—and this is not a commitment, of course—but whenever it's possible, I would like to do something else. I honestly tell you this, because I do not enjoy that which you call power. I'm not in love with power, and we've always regarded the state as an instrument to implement ideas or purposes which in our view are fair, are human, and humane as we see them.

But to conclude, I repeat: I don't think that the United States is contemplating a normal invasion. In special circumstances, it might happen—in fact, it would be very likely. But as long as we are united—cohesive—then it is more difficult. Their hopes are placed in the revolution not surviving the challenges it is facing, the problems it is facing, based on the fact that we are receiving not even one-third of the fuel that we need, that we are receiving far fewer imports than before. That's why we are now in a situation that we call the "Special Period." But perhaps one day we will be thankful for this Special Period, because of the effort that our people are making now—the scientists, the workers, the engineers, by the thousands—to try to solve our enormous economic problems. These are admirable people. Recently, there was a forum of technicians and innovators where 34,000 papers were presented with 40,000 solutions to problems—how to save fuel here, how to use magnetizers and emulsifiers in order to increase the efficient use of fuel by 8 or 10 percent. The number of inventions that our people are producing is incredible. Hundreds of thousands of people are working on the search for solutions to our fuel shortage. We have returned to the ox, the noble ox, because we have less and less fuel for agriculture. Before that, oxen had disappeared, and we only had tractors. But if the earth is wet, tractors can't work, while oxen can. This increases productivity thirteen or fourteen times. We have come back to the bicycle. Maybe the United States will go back to the bicycle, not because they don't have fuel, but because they will discover that it is more healthy than having one car per family, or per citizen. We didn't even think of bicycles before. We hardly ever used the bicycle here. But last year we distributed hundreds of thousands of bicycles. In 1992, we will distribute one million more. We only use half the trips in urban buses that we used before. Never in our wildest dreams did we imagine what we could do. We've tried to make the people understand, and cooperate with us in this struggle, because it is important that everyone contribute. We have no fertilizers, so we are developing biofertilization. The ideal, the aspiration, of the developed countries is not to use chemical fertilizers. Take pesticides. We are developing new varieties of crops that are more resistant to disease, with higher yields. We are pursuing tissue culture. From a cell we get a new plant. We are working on producing more food without fertilizers, without animal feed. We are pursuing innovations in raising cattle. We are using sugarcane as cattle feed; we are innovating in rational grazing, using electrified fences. We are developing legume banks as protein sources. We are using saccharin. The number of things that we are doing is incredible! And we would never have done this had we not been forced to by the straits that we are in today.

So, if we work as we should work—as we must work—in the end we will have to erect a monument to the Special Period. I'll never say I am happy about what has happened in the Soviet Union. We will always feel sad. We hope that in some way or another they will maintain some unity, that they will maintain the common economic space that they created through the decades, and that they will maintain a common defense. They will have to, if they don't want to be treated as Third World countries. We certainly hope that they will maintain their unity, in the interest of all, of world peace. I don't think that anyone wishes to see the Soviet Union torn asunder into twenty different pieces. No one stands to profit; on the contrary, it would sharpen the economic problems that the world is going through. I've elaborated these considerations, because today our task is to survive. I thought it appropriate to say a few words about how we intend to survive. We have a foothold in science. This is one of the largest investments in the country. We have invested in man's intelligence. Food programs are a priority. We don't know whether we will be able to change our shirts for a while; we may have to mend old clothes. But the food program we have implemented, and some other plans, such as tourism, are the essentials with which we intend to survive. We are resorting to our fundamental resources, particularly brainpower, that have been developed throughout these years.

Now, the United States is betting that we won't survive, and we are betting that we will. That's the gamble. This is not being analyzed in military terms, although, of course, we are not neglecting this aspect, much less now when we know that the Americans have so many sophisticated and super-modern weapons. In a different forum, perhaps I wouldn't be as elegant; but I have said I harbor no hostile feelings toward the American people, or individual Americans. We've had political problems, but it is not a problem of hatred. Our ideology is not based on that. It's not like other ideologies, such as fascism. Fascism had no ideology; it was very reactionary. It was based on hatred, doctrines of racial superiority, anti-Semitism, etc. Our political programs are based on ideas, not on feelings of hatred, revenge, or whatever. Life has taught us that ideas are stronger than those feelings, or man's basest passions.

Have I answered all your questions? Yes or no?

ARMSTRONG: I could ask your colleagues if they disagreed, but I don't think it would be productive.

CASTRO: These colleagues? Let's ask them. Or do you think that they'll be shot for whatever they say, or kicked out of here, or what? You are the ones who have made me speak. And I'm telling them that they have to participate. They announced that I was to make a summary. I shouldn't. I think—and I beg of you, who are chairing now—when we conclude the session, you should give the floor to the president of the Institute of History here. Because I'm a guest here, don't forget that. I was invited. You invited me, and they invited me, so I spoke because they've given me the floor. I've been almost compelled to speak. So I am asking you, Mr. Chairman, when the time comes for the conclusions, to let Mr. Mendoza, who is the head of the Institute of History, take the floor. He says he would be very brief. Most certainly briefer than I will. And I think we all stand to profit from that.

LOOSE ENDS:
"You cannot abandon a country"

The conferees are increasingly conscious of the clock. Although we have been sitting in the conference room for two and a half days and have not had time to digest all that we have heard, we are hungry for more—hungry, yet tired; except Fidel Castro, that is, whose stamina seemingly knows no bounds. He looks as fresh as the minute he walked into the room on the very first day of the conference.

The first item of business is the schedule. Castro extends the session with a simple "I'm not in a hurry," and we move on with questions and answers. Raymond Garthoff, a man legendary for his analytical mind and his eye for detail (traits largely responsible for a highly successful career first as an intelligence analyst and then as a scholar of U.S.-Soviet relations), cannot resist the temptation to complete and correct the record on a few minor points; to ask Castro whether he had considered alternatives to the missile deployment to bolster Cuban security in 1962; and to inquire about the Soviet brigade that remained in Cuba after the withdrawal of the missiles, only to be "discovered" during the Carter presidency, triggering a brief diplomatic crisis.[197] Castro answers each of Garthoff's questions concisely, but in the course of doing so ranges widely over larger and more profoundly political issues, demonstrating the sweep and agility of his hyperactive mind. Castro ruminates on the role the crisis played in Khrushchev's ouster; on the subsequent development of U.S.-Soviet relations; on the hollowness and illusion of the West's Cold War "victory"; and on Cuba's faithful discharge of its commitment to Angola. We are finally made aware that this last theme, which has surfaced repeatedly throughout the conference, constitutes a vital subtext, when Castro, ostensibly addressing Garthoff, permits his gaze to fix on the Russian delegation as he proclaims, "You cannot abandon a country."

There can be no doubt that the collapse of communism in Eastern Europe brought Cuba's close relationship with the Soviet Union to an abrupt (and, from the Cuban perspective, untimely) end. To Castro, clearly, it grates like an unresolved cadence. He cannot and does not blame the Russians sitting with him at the table, all of whom share his grief and anger at the Soviet Union's demise. But there is no mistaking his quiet rage, a rage which recalls his sense of abandonment and humiliation during the missile crisis itself, which Garthoff's comments on the U.S.-Soviet missile trade no doubt enkindled anew.

Having made his point, Castro sits back in his chair with his hands folded on his stomach, and listens politely as Sergo Mikoyan eagerly steers the discussion back in the direction of American intentions toward Cuba in 1962.

BLIGHT: I'd like to ask some counsel here from my good friend Jorge Risquet, from whom I've been taking orders. I'm actually a puppet chairman. As I understand, at five o'clock—and it is now one minute to five o'clock—at five o'clock we should move into the summary, synthesis, integration, and conclusion that the president just referred to. Is that correct? Is that where we should move now?

CASTRO: No. I'm not in a hurry. There are a few people here who want to say something.

BLIGHT: Very well. I'm glad to hear you say that, because I've got a list here half as long as my left arm. Next on my list is Ambassador Garthoff.

GARTHOFF: Thank you, Mr. Chairman. Mr. President, you noted the strange coincidence in time of President Kennedy's positive message to you through Mr. Daniel and the provision of a poison device— actually, it was a fake pen—to Rolando Cubela Secades. There were contradictory strands in U.S. policy toward Cuba in 1963, but also, perhaps, it was one of those cases where the right hand did not know what the far-right hand was doing.

I thought you might be interested in one such case that is particularly relevant. As I mentioned, I was in the Central Intelligence Agency in the late 1950s, in intelligence analysis and in estimates. Soon after your victory in Cuba, in early 1959, a friend of mine from our clandestine services told me very confidentially that CIA had provided some of the arms to the July 26 Movement. He wouldn't tell me how, or how much, or when, but after your success it was clear that he thought CIA would not want this information known, even in the rest of the United States government, much less publicly at that time. I mention it now because I think sufficient time has passed, and it might be of interest to you.

There is one point that you raised today, concerning withdrawal of U.S. missiles from Italy as well as Turkey, that I would like to briefly clarify. This was not the result of any later negotiation or agreement. Robert Kennedy had introduced the subject of our missiles in Italy, as well as Turkey, in a talk with Ambassador Dobrynin as early as October 24 or 25, and again in the oral understanding of October 27—because, as he said, the United States was in fact planning to withdraw its missiles from both Turkey and Italy. When asked how soon, he replied he didn't know, but he thought about four or five months. The day after the exchange of letters—that is, on October 29—Ambassador Dobrynin again saw him, and asked for a written commitment on the withdrawal of American missiles from Turkey. The next day he was called in and his draft message was returned to him. He was told that the United States would not provide any written commitment, and that if the Soviet Union made any public reference to such a deal, we would change our plans and keep the missiles in Turkey and Italy.[198] Nothing further was done about it in terms of exchanges. The last of the missiles was out of Turkey and Italy on April 25, 1963, exactly six months after the exchange had taken place. At that time, I believe, President Kennedy sent an oral message to Chairman Khrushchev confirming that the missiles were now all out of Turkey and Italy, as we had projected was our intention, assuming the situation remained normal.

SCHLESINGER: Italy? There was nothing about Italy in Robert Kennedy's memorandum of the conversation.

GARTHOFF: Yes, well—

SCHLESINGER: Of course, it is your error to have mentioned Italy.

GARTHOFF: We will have to look into that later. That is my understanding.

The two very brief specific questions I wanted to ask in closing were these: first, as you noted, there were alternatives to the action that was taken. Did Cuba ever suggest joining the Warsaw Pact, or concluding a formal military alliance with the Soviet Union? Second, when did Cuba ask that one brigade of Soviet ground troops remain here? Thank you.

CASTRO: You've got four points here. You remarked on the rumors about the CIA supplying weapons to the 26th of July. I really have never heard a word about that, but I think they would have been right to give weapons to the 26th of July Movement. They would have been defending a just cause. So if they didn't, I'm very sorry about that, and if they did, well, I would like to take this occasion to thank them. [Laughter.]

Now, about Italy and Turkey. I am happy to have heard that explanation, because as I see it, it coincides with what I recall Khrushchev saying. You know, diplomats are diplomats, and politicians are politicians. I surmised that certain things had been done, some pretexts had been used, and various things were going to be exchanged. I am sure that the Kennedy administration did not ignore the fact that it would benefit Khrushchev if he were able to present himself to his own staff, to his own government, as saying that he had obtained something in return. A good diplomat would not have said that those missiles were being withdrawn because they were obsolete, but as a show of goodwill, to encourage feelings of goodwill, and to assuage the Soviet Union's concern for peace. Khrushchev needed some cooperation, some support, because Khrushchev's role as leader of the Soviet Union came to an end as a result of the October crisis.[199] This is my opinion. The situation wound up costing him his position as general secretary of the Communist Party of the Soviet Union. When you read his letters, and when you know his attitude, you understand that, for the United States—and for Kennedy himself—it was better to try to carry on with Khrushchev than to have to deal with a new, unfamiliar leadership. It cannot be doubted that the new leadership that replaced Khrushchev did a lot of work in the area of missiles, of rocketry. It is difficult to imagine what they must have invested. But the October crisis was traumatic for the Soviets, and they began to work desperately to reach what was called nuclear "balance," or "parity"—which, as I said here, is something relative. There is no doubt but that the Soviet Union did come to possess a very considerable strategic force. This is evident in the agreements arrived at by the Soviet Union and the United States. But the Soviets have not explained what those agreements are, how many missiles of one type or another are to be destroyed. The SS-20s, for instance, didn't exist at the time of the October crisis, but they deployed between 300 and 400 in Europe, and I understand that they were destroyed. There is no doubt but that the leadership that replaced Khrushchev launched itself headlong into the development of rocketry and nuclear weaponry. This is a fact. I think that served no one's interests—not the interests of the United States, nor those of the Soviet Union. Perhaps some of the problems that developed later in the USSR were a result of the excessive expenditure on weapons, and those consequences are also being paid by the United States. If you analyze the ten-trillion-dollar debt, adding up the public and private debt, you need a rocket to reach that debt. Consider the economic problems of the United States: the low savings rates, the low profitability rates, patterns of investment in housing, and so on. If you analyze the economy of the United States objectively, you realize that, while the Germans, Japanese, and others were investing in technology to make their economies more competitive and their industries more competitive, the United States was investing colossal sums on weapons. Look at the budget deficits, which are expected to be higher this year, and they are already astronomical. Look at the trade deficit, something which has been going on for about fifteen years. There is no economy that can withstand that. Someone told me that the USSR went bankrupt in the arms race, and I said, "Not only the USSR; you did also." Perhaps a Khrushchev, with his attitude, would have undertaken negotiations on weapons and on peace, and they could have saved those infinite sums

of money that were spent on weapons. Perhaps if this kind of understanding that was arrived at with Gorbachev had been reached in the
Khrushchev era, everyone would have been better off. So, if you analyze
the history of what might have been and wasn't, I think that anything
that helped Khrushchev was beneficial to U.S. policy. That is what I
thought.[200]

You mentioned an oral message. In the published letters, there
isn't a single word on the Turkey and Italy missiles. I think there were
oral messages, and from what Nikita read me—and Thompson was
involved; I didn't know whether this Thompson was an assumed name,
but apparently not, since there was a Thompson in the administration*—it is clear that, aside from the written messages, there were oral
messages—verbal messages and exchanges. Of course, they can't be
declassified. Only someone who knew what happened could say. If this
Thompson participated in this, you might wait for him to quit being
ambassador and retire, so you can ask him about his role at that time.[201]
I'm not saying this or that was the case in particular; I simply recall
what I remember to give the historians a clue so they can delve into
this. What happened with the missiles in Turkey and Italy? Were they
to be withdrawn? Was that withdrawal advanced? Was this offered to
Khrushchev as a quid pro quo to provide his government with some
stability? Investigate that. Diplomats are diplomats. It doesn't mean
that they aren't honest, but they can present something that had already
been decided as a concession. What I think is that, perhaps, Kennedy
did not want to enter into public commitments, but could, on the
other hand, make secret, private concessions without a written record.
He was very sensitive about the idea of making concessions that would
show him as weak.

Just for your information, I mentioned what I was told personally,
and how it happened, because it might be worthwhile to go into this
aspect. It is part of history to find out if something was said, if a
promise was made, if an attempt was made to help him. There was, at
least, this verbatim statement. I may not remember the exact tense—
"we're withdrawing," or "we have withdrawn" the missiles from Turkey
and Italy. Someone said it was on April 25th. I had this talk with
Khrushchev in mid-May, so maybe the phrase he used was, "we have

---

*Llewellyn Thompson, a former U.S. ambassador to the Soviet Union, played a crucial
role in the management of the crisis as a member of the ExComm. See, e.g., Welch and
Blight, "The Eleventh Hour of the Cuban Missile Crisis," pp. 18–19.

withdrawn." This was in April. I traveled in April, just before May Day, which is an important commemoration, and these talks must have been in May—well into May.

There was something else; what was it? Oh, yes; the Warsaw Pact alternative. That never crossed our minds. It never occurred to us to say, "Hey, let us into the Warsaw Pact." First of all, we didn't like that Pact too much, to tell you the truth. Secondly, they wouldn't have let us in. So, it never crossed our minds to ask for membership—and we were right, since we would have no Warsaw Pact now, anyway.[202] So we were never in it. We never requested it.[203]

On the brigade, this was all part of our resistance to the withdrawal of what had been brought in. They decided to leave the antiaircraft missiles, but we didn't want them to take the brigades, either. Because if the defense of Cuba was the cause, someone's word is good, but someone's word with four brigades is even better, even without tactical missiles.

We spent fourteen years in Angola, and we're a micro-country. If you analyze the effort that you had to make in Vietnam—you had about half a million men in Vietnam at one point—and you are a country with at least twenty times more people than Cuba, it's as if you had had over a million men in some other country abroad. In the USSR, people say they had—I don't remember how many men in Afghanistan. I did the calculation, and the number of men that we had in Angola was many, many times greater, in per capita terms. I want you to know that although it appears to be closer on the map, Luanda is further away than Moscow. And Afghanistan is right next to the Soviet Union. On the map you always see this very broad north, and so on; but on an aircraft, you take two hours longer to get to Luanda via Sal Island. So it was further away than Moscow. And we spent fourteen years there because of a question of honor, because we had made a commitment. Everybody here knows that it was often said that we were being paid for our soldiers. This was never true, and for a long time they never even paid for the doctors or the teachers. We had, and do have, a great many doctors, technicians, teachers abroad. This nonmilitary cooperation is going to continue as long as we are able to do it. The countries that receive it pay for their stay there, their small stipends, but we pay the salaries. And for a great many years we gave our civilian aid completely free: technicians, teachers, and so on. We were there for fourteen years because we were loyal, because we had made a commitment. What were we going to do? Were we going to say, "We're leaving; we're going to abandon you"? It might have been convenient for us, but you can't always do things when it's convenient for you. As I was saying about commitments, one has to fulfill commitments. This is a principle. You cannot abandon a country. It is unethical, immoral, against honor, and against principle. And we have kept our principles with revolutionary movements. We have fulfilled our duties to other countries.

Well, the four brigades, I say, might have remained here. In the final analysis, as a result of our negotiations with Mikoyan, the agreement was to leave one regiment. It was something—at least a hair off the dog. No *Lunas,* no tactical rockets, no strategic rockets; in this case, a hair off the camel, a hair off the dog, or off the wolf. At least one hair. We had one brigade. It was something; better to have something than nothing. So, one brigade remained. As Alejandro or someone explained, there was a U.S. senator—Church*—who began agitating as if this were some kind of discovery. Everybody knew it was there. It never got any publicity to avoid problems, but the brigade remained there. In 1979, in the middle of a Non-Aligned conference, a message arrived from the Soviets. That time we were consulted. "Should we say that the brigade was a training center?" we were asked. And when we were drafting a telegram saying that we didn't agree with this name change, saying that it was a training center, the news was published in Moscow that what we had here was Training Center Number 12. Just imagine the mess that that got us into! So then the newspapers asked, "What is it? That which you call a brigade, and which they are calling a training center, is a fully prepared unit with full combat readiness." What I did was treat the problem ironically. I let everyone understand that it was a brigade, but I didn't want to make the Soviets out to be liars over there and create a new conflict because it was no longer called a brigade but a training center. We never agreed with that kind of thing, I'm telling you. They consulted us, but they never awaited our answer. That's what you can say about the brigade, and that's the truth. So, they changed the name, that's all. That's it.

BLIGHT: Thank you. Sergo Mikoyan?

MIKOYAN: I think I should protest to the U.S. chairman because the floor is being given exclusively to the U.S. side. I wouldn't want to

---

*Sen. Frank Church (D-Idaho), chairman of the Senate Foreign Relations Committee.

have asked my question so late, because it's not only a historical question.

Robert McNamara, the question is for you, sir. You said that on the 14th of October the United States had no intention of attacking Cuba. I think it would be interesting to hear you substantiate that, because we would then be able to have some idea of whether or not there was a threat of the United States attacking Cuba, and it would also help us understand whether the United States poses a threat to Cuba today. We are studying the history of this crisis, after all, but with a view to the future. Thank you, sir.

McNamara: That's a very good question, and a very basic one, and I will try to answer it. If any of my associates disagree, I'd be happy to have them correct me.

There are two parts to the question, really. First—if I understood you correctly—what substantiation do I have for my statement that, up until October 14, 1962, the U.S. had no intent to invade? I can only speak of the Kennedy administration—that is to say, from January 20, 1961, to October 14, 1962. But during that period I was the secretary of defense. I did have close relations with President Kennedy, as I suggested in a comment to General Gribkov. I don't believe there was any conceivable possibility of any significant military action other than at the direction of the president, and through me. So I think I knew what the president was thinking of.

I think Arthur Schlesinger also had knowledge of it, and I believe General Smith had close relations with the chairman of the Joint Chiefs of Staff, General Taylor. I think they can corroborate what I'm about to say, which is that I am *absolutely positive* that President Kennedy never, at any time during that period—January 20, 1961 to October 14, 1962—had any intention whatsoever to invade Cuba.

Now, the second part of the question, if I understood it correctly—perhaps in a sense the more important part—is, why was that the case? All of the evidence—the physical evidence, the political evidence—would point to a likely decision to invade. I say there wasn't any, and had we just continued on that course in the future, I don't believe there would have been any. Why? There are three major reasons in my opinion. The first is that there was no security threat to the United States from Cuba sufficient to justify the high human cost to both the United States and Cuba that would have been associated with an invasion, and therefore the president was unwilling to undertake an action that would have carried that cost.

Secondly, without an accepted and visible threat to the security of the United States—which there was not—the political cost would have been very, very high within the hemisphere and in Western Europe, and the dissension, the criticism that would have developed in Western Europe would have been so divisive, in my opinion—and I think in the president's as well—as to weaken NATO and weaken what we considered a necessary deterrent to possible Soviet or Warsaw Pact action against Western Europe. The third reason—and this has been referred to in some publications—you may put very little emphasis on. If you do put little emphasis on it, I think you're wrong. Even in the face of the known presence of the missiles—which we *did* consider a security threat, particularly because of their political implications— and even in view of the problem of deceit, and of accepting what some thought would be a significant shift in the military balance, many American leaders believed that an invasion of Cuba by the U.S.—the invasion by a large country of a small country, and the destruction that would result—was so contrary to our history as to be totally unacceptable. That argument was put forward particularly by Robert Kennedy. It was very persuasive. For example, Douglas Dillon, who was then secretary of the treasury, favored the invasion up to the time that argument was put forward.[204] This I think you all know. The members of the Executive Committee were split into two camps right up to the last: those who favored an air attack, which they were honest enough to state almost surely would have been followed by a sea and land invasion; and those who opposed it in favor of the quarantine. Up to the time Robert Kennedy made the statement I've just suggested he made, Doug Dillon, the secretary of the treasury, was strongly in favor of the attack. Robert Kennedy's argument persuaded him to shift his support, which he did.

Those are the three major reasons. Thank you.

GENERAL SMITH: I'd just like to add one sentence. During those years—from '58 on—Khrushchev was placing tremendous pressure on the United States in Berlin. And all our military emphasis was on resisting that threat. We did not have the resources to divert to serious planning for an invasion of Cuba.

SCHLESINGER: I would like, if I may, to add one sentence, and that is to elaborate on Bob McNamara's third point. Had Kennedy wished to invade Cuba, the emplacement of nuclear missiles in Cuba would have provided the perfect reason to do so. And obviously, he did not. Even then, he did not do it.

U.S.-CUBAN RELATIONS:
". . . is there any way out of the thirty-year-old conflict . . . ?"

An American familiar with Fidel Castro's pattern of interacting with American dignitaries remarks toward the end of the conference that he has never seen the Cuban president so *disciplined.* There has been much discussion of issues which are known to produce in him marathon flights of patriotic Cuban fury, such as U.S. covert actions against Cuba, American complaints about Cuba's "export of revolution," and Cuban dependence on the Soviets. These, taken together, have constituted for more than thirty years the U.S. "brief" against Castro's Cuba. Moreover, our American interlocutor marvels, these discussions here have taken place with some of the very "culprits" who were responsible for hostile actions against Cuba which have achieved almost mythic status in the rhetoric of the Cuban Revolution. In spite of what would otherwise have been circumstances virtually guaranteed to produce the usual fury in Castro, he has kept himself on a tight rein. There have been few overlong interventions; he has lightened particularly sensitive discussion with humor; and he has taken what has seemed to all participants to be an evident delight in the process of reconstructing the missile crisis, of learning as well as instructing. Many judge, therefore, that Castro has consciously decided to use this conference in every way possible to persuade the influential former officials on the U.S. delegation that he does indeed seek rapprochement with the United States, as a matter of principle and as a matter of necessity in the post–Cold War world.

Finally, the issue of repairing U.S.-Cuban relations is brought into the open by Oleg Darusenkov, Russian ambassador to Mexico and, for many years, a key figure in the conduct of Soviet policy toward Cuba. He asks, "[I]s there any way out of the thirty-year-old conflict?" In so doing, Darusenkov refers to a document prepared by the U.S. organizers and distributed to all conference participants a month before the conference: "The Legacy of October 1962." In it, the mutual concerns of the three countries, over the thirty-year period, are summarized. The question posed at its conclusion, which Darusenkov now puts before the conference in propositional form, is this: U.S.-Cuban hostility has, for thirty years, centered on Soviet influence *in* Cuba and Soviet influence *via* Cuba, to other parts of the world; Soviet influence no longer exists either *in* Cuba or *via* Cuba; therefore, U.S.-Cuban hostility should now come to an end. According to Darusenkov, "[T]he only thing that is needed to solve the Cuban problem is sufficient political will." In his view, it is *American* political will that is lacking, not Cuban. Darusenkov wishes to have this discussed openly.

As the subsequent discussion shows, Darusenkov has raised an issue which strains Fidel Castro's powers of self-discipline almost to the breaking point. He agrees to devote two hours to the subject on the following afternoon, so that he may presently take several more questions on the missile crisis, which is the subject on the table. But when Philip Brenner asks a question about Cuban perceptions of U.S. decision making in the early 1960s, Castro has little to say in answer to it, but a great deal to say about the virtual impossibility, as he sees it, of giving an affirmative answer to the question posed by Darusenkov. Warming to this subject and becoming visibly agitated, Castro asserts that whenever Cuba has, for various reasons, conformed to U.S. requirements for improved relations, the United States has thrown up another obstacle. "So," he says, "break links with the USSR; leave Angola; leave Nicaragua; now, the latest one is democratic reforms . . . and the question of human rights. . . . I don't want to go into that." But he cannot help himself. Time and again he begins to discuss some contentious U.S.-Cuban issue, only to pull back by saying he won't go into *that*. Castro plays Hamlet: to attack American policy, or not to attack American policy? To delve into the issue, or not to delve into the issue? This meditation occupies all the remaining time in the session.

The following day, McNamara begins by raising the subject of U.S.-Cuban hostility, expressing his conviction, based on what he has learned at the conference, that "these are differences that ought to be handled bilaterally, through normal diplomatic channels." Wayne Smith supports this with a call for Cuba's reentry into the OAS.

But now Castro turns the tables. Having been asked to speak about U.S.-Cuban issues, and having agreed to do so the day before, he excuses himself. He is worried, he says, about the lack of time, the lack of continuity with the previous discussion, and the difficulty of avoiding rhetorical outbursts. Yet he cannot resist addressing the issue of human rights at the very end. "I can prove," he says, "that in no other Third World country are there the guarantees, the security, and the possibilities that we have in Cuba." As he starts to try to "prove" it, he pulls back yet again, and turns to his old friend Darusenkov with a supremely ironic grin to express his hope that the human rights situation in the former republics of the Soviet Union will not be as bad as it is in most of the Third World.

BLIGHT: Ambassador Darusenkov.

DARUSENKOV: Mr. Chairman, we are coming to the end of some very interesting and fruitful meetings. Great credit is due to President Fidel Castro and, in general, to the brilliant trio made up by Fidel, McNamara, and Gribkov, who have presented a wonderful interplay. However, I would be leaving without feeling fully satisfied if we did not refer to a very interesting item on our agenda. That is, is there any way out of the thirty-year-old conflict between Cuba and the United States and the USSR? We are not studying history for the sake of history, but to be able to understand the present better, and to foresee the future. Since the October crisis, twenty-eight years have elapsed— almost twenty-nine, if we count the months. Since then, we have not gotten any younger. We can only show what is left of our hair. The world has changed, particularly in the past two years, and these changes may be compared to the changes that took place in our country in 1917 and after. Unfortunately, something has remained the same. Practically all the conflicts have been solved, or are about to be solved, but there is something to which we have not yet found a solution, and that is the Cuban problem. This, I would say, bucks the trend of world developments. Meanwhile, existing objective conditions—perhaps for the first time—offer the most realistic chance for succeeding in this task.

So, let us try to recall what brought about the Caribbean crisis, and, in general, tensions in relations between Cuba, the United States, and the Soviet Union. If we abstract from details—even substantial details, in many cases—the main issue of concern for the United States was twofold: the close military relationship between Cuba and the Soviet Union, which was interpreted as a threat to the United States, to its territory; and the so-called subversive Cuban activity in Latin America, which greatly irritated Washington. If we take an objective look at the present situation, these two factors have ceased to exist.

At present, the United States is posing an additional demand which has to do with human rights in Cuba—democracy, and so forth.

First of all, this problem—if indeed it exists—does not pose a threat to the United States. In any case, it is not a vital issue for the United States. Even if there were grounds to talk about this, the situation in Cuba in this sphere is far from the way it is being depicted. I believe that in the world you could find dozens of countries where the situation in this regard is much more alarming.

Let us examine the presentation made by Comrade Fidel Castro. You can go out into the streets here in Cuba, see Cuban realities for yourself, and you will see that dozens of countries would wish to have the social rights existing in Cuba. There may be formal grounds to talk about civil rights—or rather, pretexts—but let us look at it from another standpoint. In which besieged fortress—and Cuba has been a besieged fortress—would civil rights have been respected so fully? That fortress would never have withstood these onslaughts. It seems to me that the first thing that you have to do is lift the siege and *then* begin discussing limitations on civil rights, and see whether this is indeed a problem.

From my own point of view, at present, the only thing that is needed to solve the Cuban problem is sufficient political will. As regards Cuba, I believe that that political will exists. It has been manifested more than once. Let us recall recent history: the Angolan problem. To a certain extent thanks to Cuba's political will, this international conflict of considerable magnitude has been resolved. It would have seemed that there were some opportunities there to try to solve the situation with the United States. But when the gun-fire ceased, U.S.-Cuban relations worsened once again. Of course, this is a bad omen for the future.

I think that now there is an excellent possibility to put an end to the negative course of events in this region of the world. What is needed is to meet without any precondition, and tackle the roadblocks to reestablishing normal relations, so as to keep U.S.-Cuban relations in step with the development of contemporary events worldwide. Those of us meeting here, in particular the Soviet delegation—and perhaps it is also true to some extent of the American delegation—are not trying to shape the policy of our countries. Our powers to do that are very limited. But I do believe that we should dedicate some time at this meeting to the analysis of such a beguiling problem as this. I think that this would be a good contribution, a valuable contribution, to a very just and correct cause. Thank you for your attention.

BLIGHT: Thank you, Ambassador Darusenkov. The chairman has a question. It seems to me that Ambassador Darusenkov has raised a large and extremely important set of issues, and if I'm not mistaken, the gist of his comments are directed at the U.S. delegation. As we all know, each of these three delegations representing the three perspectives of the three countries has some things to say to the other about what exactly is required to emerge from this thirty-year entanglement that Ambassador Darusenkov spoke of.

I'd like to suggest that this set of issues is really too large to stuff in at the tail end of the day today. [To Darusenkov:] I wonder if you agree with me, since you've raised it. I would like to suggest that we devote at least a couple of hours tomorrow to seeing intellectually whether we can try to figure our way out of this entanglement. I put that proposal on the table. Can we find a couple of hours tomorrow to deal with this set of issues that Ambassador Darusenkov has raised? How about one o'clock till three o'clock tomorrow—or whenever the president would find it convenient, *if* he would find it convenient?

CASTRO: Well, we can't refuse. We had hoped that this was going to be over today, but if you want to continue, for my part, I have no objections. Ask the rest of the members; but I think their families, their plans, whatever they were going to do tomorrow, could accommodate a special session of this historic forum to this issue. You can do one of two things: either devote two hours tomorrow, or a whole session, to the topic. I have no objections; whatever you decide is all right with me. Tomorrow is Sunday. For us it's a working day anyway, so we're not going to sacrifice anything, and it's very pleasant to be here talking to you.

BLIGHT: Mr. President, I wonder if, in Cuba—which, like the United States, loves baseball—you use the expression, "expect the fastball but look for the curve." [Puzzled looks all around.] What I mean by that is, don't be too rigidly attached to your preconceived agenda, or preconceived ideas about what pitch is going to be thrown to you. [Laughter.] I just want you to know that we have thrown you a curve ball, and you have hit a home-run. [Laughter.]

RISQUET: Let's take a look at the schedule. Tomorrow morning we have a visit to the Hemingway Museum, isn't that so? How much time would that take? From 9:00 to 12:00? Is that okay? We have a press conference at 2:00. I think we should go to the Hemingway Museum, have lunch, and after lunch—let's say at around 2:00—we will have this debate, and postpone the press conference until 4:00. That doesn't involve so many people; it's a press conference with a few members from each of the three delegations. Let's have the press conference at four o'clock. In the morning, let's go to the Hemingway Museum, have lunch, and then meet.

BLIGHT: We accept.

CASTRO: Are the conclusions tomorrow? The conclusions are going to be tomorrow, then? Let's have somebody who speaks English and another one who speaks Russian, because I'm not getting anything over this [the translation has ceased through his earphone].

BLIGHT: You ask about the summary?

CASTRO: So then the conclusions are going to be tomorrow?

BLIGHT: Shall we continue? Would you be willing to continue with a few more questions about the October crisis, Mr. President?

CASTRO: It depends on the time you need to take a shower before going to the reception. I'll go on. I think that we're going to award you with the medal of Hero of Labor. Maybe the Soviets and I will agree and award you the medal of the Hero of Labor. I don't aspire to that medal, but, well, I'd be willing to answer a reasonable number of additional questions—as I said, a reasonable number, because it's almost six o'clock.

BLIGHT: Would three be a reasonable number?

CASTRO: That depends on what the three questions are. [Laughter.]

BLIGHT: I'd like to call on Professor Brenner.

BRENNER: Thank you, Chairman. Mr. President, I think I speak once again for all the scholars in thanking you for your willingness to share with us the documents from the Cuban side on the October crisis. This will make an extraordinary contribution to our understanding of this history.

As you know, in the United States we have made an effort to obtain documents. You received this morning an index to some of these documents; I have before me the information about the documents we are still trying to receive, and I'm pleased to see that you have an easier time releasing information here than our State Department sometimes has. In fact, we would like to make a present to you of this set of court documents that request information from the United States government.

But documents don't always tell us what we need to know. It is wonderful to have you here to learn about your perceptions. Let me ask you about two very concrete perceptions:

On September 4, 1962, President Kennedy made a speech in which he thought he was conveying a very clear message to both the Soviet and Cuban governments about the United States' intentions if there were missiles deployed in Cuba.[205] The first question then is, What was your perception of that speech? Did you get the message?

The second question is about your perception after the October crisis. You said at the time that a conflict was avoided, but peace was not achieved, and by that you meant that there was a continuing war with the United States; that the conditions that led to the crisis did not end. I'd like to understand, then, why the Cuban government persisted in aiding revolutionaries in Latin America, and how you understood the United States would react to that. What was your perception of the United States' reaction to Cuban support for revolutionary activities in Latin America after the crisis?

CASTRO: Now, on your first question; there were a number of speeches. What I perceived from all of these speeches was that a crisis was afoot. I explained my opinion that the agreement should have been published; I explained that we suggested that to the Soviets; and I explained the results of that suggestion. After that, we just waited for events to develop. As I said, we had confidence in the experience of the Soviets. We did not know what the correlation of forces was between the two countries, but I remember the message. I imagine that there were many public statements from all sources, counting senators, political leaders, leaders of the House, and administration officials. There were a great many statements, and I don't really remember this specific one that you mentioned. But I got the message.

The phrase you mentioned was correct: an international conflict was avoided, but peace had not been achieved. For our country, there was no peace. In fact, I already explained how after the October crisis, military activities against Cuba continued, through these mother ships, these pirate attacks. They just went on. Throughout those years, activities against Cuba continued, if not militarily, then at least economically. The blockade became tighter—the economic blockade;

counterrevolutionary activities did not cease to be supported by the United States; economic sabotage did not cease. So, one cannot say that we had peace.

We had a slight breathing space as a result of the Vietnam war. The United States was seriously committed in the Vietnam war. For several years, they had to send half a million men out there. They were involved in that war, and this was what you might call a breathing space for our country, because it was no longer the main objective of U.S. foreign policy. Our activities in Latin America developed—our cooperation with these revolutionary movements was very active. It was essentially, although not exclusively, political cooperation. But it was intense. Even so, I think it has been blown out of proportion. Conditions are not easy in all countries, yet not all countries have revolutionary movements. We could cooperate with a revolutionary movement where it existed, but not where it didn't exist. Where no such movement existed, we did not attempt to create one. So I think it's a little bit blown out of proportion.[206]

Changes took place. We would have to check more precisely when it was that the countries in the Caribbean basin began to change—new countries that became independent; Torrijos and others took the initiative to begin to reestablish diplomatic relations with Cuba; and today Cuba has diplomatic relations with the majority of the countries in Latin America. And we have considerable relations with other countries. In those where we have no diplomatic or consular relations, we have contacts through different channels, as a rule. This does not mean that 100 percent of these governments are friendly. Some make hostile statements about us, and we know that they are under pressure from the United States. So it is not an ideal or a perfect situation. But there has been a big, substantial change in the situation.

The United States is always inventing something new in connection with Cuba. For a long time they said that as long as we had links with the Soviet Union, relations couldn't improve. So suddenly one day, the Soviet Union disappeared.

For a long time they said that as long as we had troops in Angola, relations with Cuba could not improve. The moment came when that war was over. It ended successfully. Not only did we help consolidate the independence of Angola, but we also helped to assure compliance with the U.N. resolution on Namibian independence. Not only that, but the war also made a considerable contribution to the struggle against apartheid, and to the far-reaching changes that have taken place in South Africa. If you listen to what [Nelson] Mandela said—the leader of the ANC [African National Congress]—he is highly appreciative of the efforts of the Cubans supporting Angola and fighting against the South Africans. He believes that this was a decisive factor in accelerating the struggle against apartheid, which is one of the most rejected and condemned systems in the world. So we did our duty there. And then, when everything there was done and there was no point to being there, we withdrew. The Americans must know that it's easy to send troops, and hard to get them out. It's much easier to send them than to withdraw them, because interests are created.

We could have withdrawn our troops from Ethiopia. We had withdrawn a great many, but there was one unit in particular that it wasn't easy to withdraw. We managed finally to withdraw it as the result of a major political and diplomatic effort to obtain the Ethiopian government's approval.

We had a small detachment in the Congo, which was a kind of support point for the forces in Cabinda, where we had been defending the Gulf Oil Company's interests for about fourteen years. I don't know why, but that's one of the paradoxes of life: we were defending U.S. oil interests in that region. Of course, we weren't defending Gulf Oil's interests; we were defending the Angolans' oil. That was an interest of the Angolans. But automatically we were also defending the oil, and I think we did it very efficiently. There was practically not a single act of sabotage. On one occasion, South Africans tried to sabotage the installations, and we captured them. A commando unit went to blow up the wells—friends of yours; you always had relations with South Africa. But we were there defending the interests of a U.S. multinational from the South Africans, and we discharged our duties effectively.[207]

Then you said that we had to get out of Nicaragua. When the political changes took place in Nicaragua, we withdrew our military advisers. There was no longer any Cuban personnel there.

Then the question was subversion. The subversion issue changed. Our policy evolved in line with the changes in Latin America. We evolved, and relations changed, and our "subversion" came to an end.

So: "Break links with the USSR; leave Angola; leave Nicaragua"— there was always a reason. Now, the latest one is democratic reforms— I imagine along the lines of the United States—and the question of human rights.[208] I'm not going to talk about that. I already dwelt on civil rights, or human rights, whatever you want to call it. I don't want to go into that. Part of this relates to what you want to discuss tomorrow. Our relations never improve, and the U.S. invents new reasons again and again not to improve relations. You never know what the next reason is going to be. But these new issues are linked to the internal affairs of our country—to the sovereignty of our country. And I don't think this is a solid argument. I think it can be defeated. We have a good arsenal of arguments to discuss all of these issues linked to civil or human rights.

Everything has changed, but the United States has not changed its policy toward us. Well, there were moments—I don't mean to imply that the United States has always behaved the same. There was a period when relations improved. That was during the Carter administration. I must say that might have been a constructive period, but there were certain obstacles that hampered that process. But there were some positive steps taken. The U.S. Interests Section was opened. First the Swiss embassy handled American interests, then the Interests Section opened with U.S. diplomatic personnel. We arrived at some agreements in various fields. So there was a period of progress. I think we are all a little bit at fault for the fact that more progress was not made during that period. That's my opinion. There have been ups and downs. Then, as you know, the Reagan administration had a very ideological, very doctrinaire position. They were very hard on that. But even with the Reagan administration, we did arrive at some agreements—migratory agreements.[209] But problems and incidents cropped up. Their main complaint against us was losing force—that is, our support for the revolutionary movements—because our relations were normalizing with countries in Latin America. But there were some thorny areas. There was the Nicaragua situation and El Salvador, where you had the most acute problems—problems that today no longer exist. All of these events might have had negative influences on each other, because relations got very bad. There was no confidence, there was mistrust, that kind of thing—all of that had an influence. But throughout this period, when relations were getting worse and worse because we were helping revolutionary movements, the United States was doing the opposite. It's not necessary to go into details; everyone knows that during the period of the military governments in Latin America, the United States supported them. The United States even provided support for opposition forces against some governments—military cooperation, security cooperation. A great deal of the experience obtained in Vietnam was transferred to the security forces of Latin America. I do not intend to make accusations, but those military schools in the United States trained the best leaders of the military governments in Latin America. They all studied in U.S. schools. We are accused of helping revolutionary movements, but the United States trained all of these military leaders, even Torrijos. But Torrijos at a certain point rebelled and improved relations with Cuba. Take [Gen. Juan] Velasco Alvarado* in Peru. There was a group of generals who staged, not a leftist coup, but perhaps a progressive coup, since they wanted to help the people. They were military men, many of them trained in the United States. I know a few Latin American generals that have assumed good positions. I think Mengistu† studied in the United States. He took military courses in the United States and he told me that when he was in the United States, he had seen things that he did not like—the civil rights situation, problems with the black population. This had a great influence on his political thinking. There were soldiers who became revolutionaries in the United States, Latin American soldiers.

But, as a rule, the position of the United States was ideological. It had nothing to do with civil rights. You can prove historically—and history is very long—that the United States has supported military governments, governments of force. For a long time they preferred such governments, you might say—certainly over a period which includes a large part of the revolutionary period in Cuba. We know what happened in Chile.‡ The United States suspended all aid to the Allende government, but they never suspended their relations with the military government, and they kept up their technical and military aid. In fact, the United States' relations with rightist military governments in Latin America were very strong, although there were ups and downs.

As a rule, those military governments—governments of force—received support, weapons, and training from the United States. There are books and films and documentaries that reveal that many of those heads of security departments were trained in the United States. And I can assure you that they behaved with incredible cruelty. Not even the Nazis behaved like that. We've all read about the barbaric crimes of the Nazis. Even they did not achieve the refinement of the torturers in Chile and Argentina and in other countries. They did incredible

---

*In 1968, Velasco Alvarado instituted a program of social reform, suspended Peru's constitution, and seized American-owned corporations. He was overthrown in a 1975 coup led by Francisco Morales Bermudez.

†Lt. Gen. Mengistu Haile Mariam was one of the leaders of the coup that deposed Ethiopian emperor Haile Selassie in 1974. He became chairman of the Provisional Military Administrative Council, or Dirgue, in 1977, and head of the newly formed Ethiopian Communist Party in 1984. He ruled Ethiopia until 1991.

‡Salvador Allende, Marxist founder of the Chilean Socialist Party, became president of Chile in 1970, and subsequently instituted a radical reform program. The Chilean military overthrew Allende—with Washington's blessing—on 11 September 1973.

things, like taking a child from a mother and threatening to drop it from a ten-story window, and cutting off someone's hand in front of others. The torturers were highly refined. They were the result of science. Not even Batista equalled them, and Batista was cruel. Batista's were vulgar torturers. Torture became a science in Latin America during those military governments.

The disappeared, or missing persons, is a new category. There are many people in Chile who are looking for relatives who have disappeared. And in Argentina there are thousands upon thousands of families that are looking for relatives who have disappeared. This was incredible; it was macabre. In Guatemala, tens of thousands of people disappeared, after Castillo de Armas's government was installed with U.S. assistance.* I have met families of these people who have disappeared. It's horrible, because the families still hold out hope that they are alive. They were deceived, lied to, and given false hope. Years went by, and they thought that a husband, a father, or a son was still alive; years! Perhaps one of the most atrocious phenomena of all are these disappearances. And all this became fashionable in Latin America in the last thirty years—after the October crisis, after the Bay of Pigs—because not all governments had an Alliance for Progress, a policy with a content, with a social direction. Truly horrible things took place in Latin America.

Of course, we would like our position, the positive evolution in our thinking—to which we were led by reality and life—to be the evolution of the United States as well. I've already said you can't be idealistic and run around dreaming things. I said that the United States, I was sure, would learn what this world was like. They would learn how complicated this world is. And no one knows what will happen in Latin America, because the situation in Latin America is such that there are continuous explosions, continuous problems. No one knows what may happen. The fact that the USSR disappeared does not mean that the causes that give rise to changes, revolutions, social outbreaks—whatever you call them—have disappeared. The situation is desperate in many countries in Latin America, and in the rest of the world. In Latin America alone, there are hundreds of thousands of doctors, engineers, and professionals—highly trained individuals—who were accustomed to a certain standard of living, and who had certain aspirations that have not been realized.

---

*Col. Carlos Castillo de Armas succeeded Jacobo Arbenz Guzmán in June 1954.

Sometimes we host here in Cuba meetings of teachers from Latin America. Every two years there is a large meeting. Hundreds of people come from Latin America, and what they say about schools and classrooms and teachers is terrible. If you could just look at that from the people's perspective, you would imagine that they were all radical revolutionary communists. Nobody knows what a communist is any more, but before they used to hang the sign of communist around anyone's neck. I said the other day that it's a miracle they didn't call Kennedy a communist when he proposed the Alliance for Progress. I've seen meetings of doctors, and it's incredible what they say. At meetings of all kinds, sometimes sponsored by international associations, they refer to the problems in these countries—and it's terrible what they say! The pressures are there for violent unrest, latent. I think this relative stability in Latin America today really has nothing to do with the social situation in the hemisphere, which is not improving. It is getting worse, as a rule. And problems exist even in countries where there is a great deal of money. In Venezuela, there have been serious disturbances—serious outbreaks—and Venezuela is one of the richest countries in Latin America. It has the highest revenue in hard currency, the highest standard of living.

The situation is explosive. The conditions of the masses are practically intolerable. An increase in gasoline prices, an increase in food prices—anything can produce very serious problems. At the moment, there's a neo-liberal wave. It's in fashion. They're privatizing everything. They're selling everything. They're even selling the parks, the streets, the highways—everything. So there's a liberal wave. I think this is going to be the flow, and then we are going to get an ebb. But it is true that there is a very serious situation, and one cannot really forecast how long this relative stability is going to last.

If those countries become destabilized, we are not going to get involved. We are not going to promote destabilization. We are not going to take advantage of the objective conditions to promote anything. This is a policy of a different era. Our relations are based on different standards. Now I'm invited to inaugurations. I can't go to all of them. I'm invited to international meetings, and the attitude toward Cuba has changed radically among Latin American governments. So this is not a problem today. But the reaction of the United States is. They're accustomed to supporting rightist governments and governments of force.

I've gotten into some of the issues that are going to be discussed tomorrow, but I think they were linked. We've got two more questions.

BLIGHT: Thank you very much, Mr. President. I believe that Professor Brenner asked more than one question, and I thank you very much for giving far more than one answer.

CASTRO: Well, I'll answer the other two questions. I'm willing.

BLIGHT: If there are no strenuous objections, I would like to use the chair's prerogative to substitute for the last couple of questions a presentation on behalf of the U.S. delegation, at the end of the session which has been our great pleasure and honor to chair. Would you be amenable to accepting a presentation at this time, Mr. President?

CASTRO: What presentation?

BLIGHT: This lovely young lady—janet Lang—will present this. I'll describe it. This is an official American League baseball, autographed by the members of the Kennedy administration present. When I say that it is an American League baseball, I mean for it to be interpreted as the official baseball of the Western Hemisphere. [Laughter.]

CASTRO: I'll receive it in full confidence. I'm not going to imagine even for a minute that it has a bomb inside. [Laughter and applause.]

BLIGHT: Meeting adjourned.

*　　*　　*

BLIGHT: Welcome back. I'd like now to turn the chair of the meeting over to Ambassador Troyanovsky, from the Russian delegation.

TROYANOVSKY: I am ready, of course, to assume the chair, if there is no objection from any of the three sides. If there isn't any, I'd like to say that today our time is limited, since, if I'm not mistaken, we have a press conference at four o'clock. I also understand that the subject of our debate this afternoon should focus on the subject introduced by Ambassador Darusenkov yesterday; that is, prospects for the normalization of the situation in this region of the world. If this is the general understanding, then I will now recognize anyone who would like to speak first. I recognize Mr. McNamara.

McNAMARA: Mr. Chairman, as we all know—and I think one of your colleagues stated it very clearly when we went to see the missile when we first arrived—the actions of your country, and mine, and Cuba, in October 1962, and in some of the months prior to that time, brought our nations to the verge of military conflict, and brought the world to the verge of nuclear disaster. And although some of us—many of you, and the president and I and my associates—were very sensitive to the great danger that our nations faced, and that the world faced in October '62, I think during this meeting we've learned that the danger was even greater than we thought.

The purpose of these meetings has been to understand what caused that crisis, and in particular to consider how to avoid future crises of that kind; not only crises between our nations, but crises with other nations in this post–Cold War world. My understanding of the causes of the crisis, and my understanding of the way in which the Cuban leaders and the Cuban people in particular viewed their relations with the U.S., have advanced tremendously during these meetings.

I thought yesterday and the afternoon of the day before was one of the most productive periods in my association with geopolitics. I've learned a tremendous amount. I'm deeply grateful to the president, a head of state, for his willingness to spend two-and-a-half days with us examining these things. And it has led me to conclude that the hostile relationships of the past were based primarily on fears which may have been justified at the time on each of our parts—yours and ours—but which are no longer justified.

We feared for our security. Now, the comandante has expressed the spirit of self-reliance and of determination of a very small nation to protect itself against a potential military strike by a nation, as I think he said, twenty times larger. I admire immensely the courage with which he has led his nation to defend itself, to prepare to defend itself against such a strike. I don't think such a strike was ever probable in the last thirty years, excepting only during the missile crisis. But he had ample reason for believing what he did. We feared—and I know it's almost impossible for the Cubans and the Russians—the Soviets—present to believe this—we feared our security was endangered by Cuba's actions, and particularly by the relationship between Cuba and the Soviet Union. But whether those fears of the past were ever justified, I am certain that they underlay the Cuban missile crisis. I am certain they underlay the hostility that has characterized our relations for thirty years.

But whether they were ever justified or not, they are not justified today. The threats to security no longer exist. Hence, while I think the U.S. and Cuba, particularly, are left with remaining differences—I mentioned political freedoms and civil rights; I don't wish to debate those—the major obstacle to improved relations has been removed.

Let me digress just one moment, Mr. President, if I may, to say that while I know you would characterize me otherwise, I consider myself a revolutionary. [Laughter.] Now, let me tell you why I do. In our country, we customarily equate human rights with civil rights; we consider those terms synonymous. You do not—and I am with you every step of the way. The most basic human right is the right to live, the right to live a productive life. That is the most basic one; you have to have it before you get to civil rights. You've got to have the right to live a productive life. To live a productive life, you need a foundation of health and education, and to my sadness and embarrassment, I must tell you all that I think Cuba is leading the Third World in health and education. I'll give you an illustration. I think—correct me if I'm wrong—I think Cuba's infant mortality rate today, as measured by WHO [World Health Organization], is on the order of 10.7 per 1,000 live births. I believe Brazil's is on the order of 60, and Brazil's income per capita is far higher than Cuba's. That is a tremendous accomplishment! I spent thirteen years at the World Bank—that's why I think I'm a revolutionary, sir—trying to make similar progress among developing nations elsewhere in the world, and I failed. You far exceeded anything I did.

Now, the thing that embarrasses me is not that your infant mortality rate is 10.7 and Brazil's is 59. If I were a Brazilian I'd be embarrassed by that. The thing that really embarrasses me is that I read in *The Washington Post* a few weeks ago—and I believe it's correct—that Cuba's infant mortality rate is lower than that of the capital of the richest country in the world, Washington, D.C. I think yours is 10.7, and I believe Washington's—the District of Columbia's—is on the order of 19. That is an absolute disgrace. So, in that sense, in terms of human rights, you've made great advances. And you and I may disagree—and I think we do—on political freedoms and civil rights; but I admire immensely what you've done in these basic human rights of health and education.

Now, I come back to my point, which is that I think the foundation of the hostility that has existed between our nations for thirty years—I'm speaking now of Cuba and the U.S.—is gone. The threats to our security, as I suggest—whether we ever appraised them correctly—no longer exist. We're left with differences, and some rather profound differences—political freedoms, civil rights, economic embargoes, Guantánamo—but these are the kinds of differences that exist among all nations. We're not the only nation that criticizes Cuba in some of these respects, and Cuba is not the only nation with whom we have these differences. But these are differences that ought to be handled bilaterally, through normal diplomatic channels, and I hope they will be. I hope, therefore, that the relationship during the next thirty years—the bilateral relationship—will be conducted on a totally different foundation than it has been in the past. And if it is, sir, I think you can take great credit for this meeting having contributed to that. Thank you very much.

TROYANOVSKY: Thank you very much, sir. Is there anyone else who would like to address the meeting? Yes sir, Mr. Smith.

WAYNE SMITH: There's really very little that I can add to the eloquent statement Mr. McNamara has just made. I would simply like to call attention to one additional detail: that is, that Cuba's membership in the Organization of American States was suspended in January 1962 because of the conclusion by the Organization of American States that Cuba's adoption of the Marxist-Leninist system, and the consequent international implications of that, made its membership in the OAS inconvenient and inconsistent with its charter. But I emphasize that it was the *international* implications that prompted that decision. Colombia, the country that called for the meeting at Punta del Este, or that called for the meeting of foreign ministers, emphasized that the Colombian proposal focused entirely on international matters. It did not touch internal questions at all. Internal matters were left up to each nation to decide; each nation had to decide for itself the political and economic system which it considered most convenient, which best suited its particular conditions. But Cuba's association with the Sino-Soviet bloc, which seemed determined to bring about world revolution, and so forth and so on—I apologize for some of the terms that we used, as the president has apologized for some of the terms that were used in the Cuban and Soviet correspondence—but the aggressive Sino-Soviet bloc that was bent on world revolution made Cuba's association with that bloc a danger to the hemisphere. In other words, the focus was on the international consequences of Cuba's association with the Sino-Soviet bloc.

Secretary of State Rusk made the same point in his speech. If, therefore, the emphasis was on Cuba's ties with the Soviet Union, because of the international consequences, then certainly, the reasons for Cuba's suspension from the Organization of American States, if they had not become irrelevant years ago, most certainly have become irrelevant by this point. There may be political issues to be dealt with, but the basic juridical obstacle to Cuba's membership has long since become irrelevant. Thank you.

TROYANOVSKY: Thank you very much. I would like, however, to introduce a small correction. In 1962, there was no Sino-Soviet bloc. At that time we had already parted.

WAYNE SMITH: We might have insisted in 1962 that there was. But if there wasn't—whether there was or not in 1962—I think that the idea that there is one now is laughable.

TROYANOVSKY: Is there anyone else who would like to address this issue? Comrade President, would you like to address the meeting at this point?

CASTRO: I'm always taken by surprise on this question of addressing the meeting. Right now I really don't know what I'm going to do, because I've listened to what McNamara has said, and what Wayne Smith has said, and I've heard the opinions of different personalities here present who have expressed their concern that a meeting as excellent as this one, with such excellent results, should conclude on a sensitive and delicate issue that might give rise to polemics, and might somehow detract from the success that we have had so far. I understood from McNamara's statement that he felt that what we had done here in Havana was an important step toward broaching the question of relations between Cuba and the United States in the same spirit, and also the possibility of bilateral talks. We are not against anyone who wants to contribute to that, if they are so inclined. But I do realize that, although we agreed yesterday to meet to discuss these things for two hours, there's a press conference immediately after, and then bilateral talks. We agreed because we were ready to discuss any topic, to cooperate fully. I didn't want to begrudge you a single moment. But if we analyze it correctly, I mean, two hours is not enough to go into this issue in depth—and it's no longer two hours, but about an hour and a half.

Second, this is an issue that should be thought about. I don't think it should be the object of improvisations.

Third, I think we should avoid the risk of doing something unusual—that is, beginning to discuss relations between Cuba and the United States at an international meeting where things that we say here might at a certain point have an influence on the approach to this through other channels.

Fourth, my situation here is a bit unique, because, as I said yesterday, I was at a disadvantage in my double capacity as guest and also as a government official. I cannot sit here and discuss things like a scholar. A scholar is much freer than I am to debate these topics, and anything that I say here, no matter how much I insist on the fact that it was a personal opinion, in some way is representative of the position of the government. That is why I think what Mr. McNamara suggested was very wise.

I think the different concerns that we have heard in connection with this meeting, or the subject on the agenda here this afternoon, can be discussed. I think we can discuss these issues. We have a great many arguments with which to explain our policies, and to explain what we do. We have a great deal of information to share on the way that our government operates. All of this requires very extensive substantiation, and requires historical analysis—even contemporary historical analysis—on the great diversity of systems that exist in the world, and even the need to try to have a pluralistic world. We cannot have a world that is forced into a single mold, because that doesn't exist, and because there are great differences between Europe and the United States as regards forms and systems of government. I know that you are republicans. I'm not saying this in a partisan way. I say "republican" as a system of government; you do not have monarchies. And yet, there are quite a few monarchies left in the world, and I imagine they will continue to exist because some people have been able to thrive on the monarchical system. The Japanese, for example, have an emperor. This is not the system you might have in Canada or Latin America.*

This problem was discussed at the time of the war for independence—that is, what type of government the Latin Americans were going to have. [Simón] Bolívar† had his opinions. He was a republican. They even considered lifelong presidencies and senates, but not monarchies; these were republican ideas. San Martín‡ was for the monarchy. He wanted to find a French prince to rule over the republic of southern South America. He disagreed with Bolívar on this. There's a famous Guayaquil meeting in which he argued that the diversity of countries could not be ruled other than through a monarchy. I, of course, agree

---

*As is the case in Japan, Canada's head of state is a monarch (the reigning king or queen of Britain). Both countries are democracies, however, whose heads of government (their respective prime ministers) occupy the highest de facto political office.

†Simón Bolívar (1783–1830) liberated his native Venezuela from Spanish rule in 1821, and Peru in 1824. He formed the republic of Bolivia from Upper Peru the following year. Bolívar's dream was to unite all of South America, but he was unable to overcome regionalism and parochialism and lived to witness the political disintegration of the territories he liberated.

‡José de San Martín (1778–1850) was an Argentinean general who, along with Bolívar, liberated most of Chile and Peru from Spanish rule.

to a great extent with Bolívar. I think that he was right. But this kind of thing was being debated.

The Spanish Civil War [1936–39], for instance, was a war between defenders of the republic and those who defended a different kind of government, including the monarchy. There's a monarchy in England; in Sweden; I think in Belgium; Holland, I think, also has a monarchy. Some have presidents elected directly, others have presidents elected by the parliament, as in Italy. In Spain, for instance, you have a monarchy, and on the other hand, a government elected by the parliament, and the ones that go to parliament are elected by the party, because they have a list of candidates; they calculate how many votes each party has, and they establish lists, and the parties select the names of those on the lists, and it is they who elect the head of government. There are countries like China, where there's another system. I don't know if we should be trying to change China.

What I fear, and what we are very sensitive to, is that the debate might become a debate on problems in Cuba—domestic issues in Cuba. We are really very sensitive to these questions that have to do with sovereignty and the internal affairs of the country. That debate then would oblige us to make a comparative analysis with very solid arguments, and also to explain our system: how the government is elected here; how our National Assembly works; what its powers are; who elects the National Assembly; who nominates the candidates to the position of district delegates, who then elect the National Assembly. I would have to explain what happened in our Party Congress, what new things we did. I would have to explain the decision to have direct elections of the members of the National Assembly—the members are not nominated by the Party, but by the people, which is an essential principle. I would have to explain how, while our system works with a leading party with specific functions in the area of electing the bodies of power and seeing to it that all the principles are complied with, it is the people who nominate, and the people who elect.

So, if we get into a debate of this type, we would have to pass judgment on many other systems, and on many other governments. We would have to analyze what goes on in China, a huge country with which the U.S. has excellent relations. China is a socialist country with a leading party, a country that has its own system of government. We would have to analyze what is happening in the USSR—what happened before, and what happens. I'm saying all this just to give you an idea of the depth that an academic debate would have here, and this despite the fact that I'm not a scholar. I am disadvantaged in two senses: in the sense of my professional capacity, and in the sense of my political responsibilities.

It seems to me that we could do this at a conference someday; but it seems to me that this is not the most appropriate moment. It would get us involved in this type of discussion. I mentioned these things just to give you an idea of the dozens of contradictions that would arise if there is any attempt to make our relations with the United States conditional on domestic issues in our country. This is the risk we run. We are learning how to be wise, particularly after discussing all of these things related to the October crisis. Those are the problems we would have if we did get into this debate.

I was very much amused by what McNamara said. He said he was a revolutionary "although you might think otherwise." You have no right to assume how I think, because there are two or three McNamaras—in particular, there is a McNamara of once-upon-a-time, and a McNamara of today. He said that he is a revolutionary, and I say, what he is doing *is* revolutionary. I believe that the contribution he has made to the analysis of the October crisis—together with the rest of the U.S. delegation—is extremely useful, extremely positive, and, I would say, something revolutionary. But this suspicion that McNamara might be a revolutionary is one that I have harbored for some time now, since he was president of the World Bank, when he published reports and statistics of what was happening in the world, and of the realities of those things. It seemed to me that those were revolutionary reports, because on the basis of those reports you can draw a great many conclusions about the problems that we have in the world. That is essentially the reason why I share McNamara's opinion.

I must say with absolute sincerity that I have learned a great deal at this meeting. I have learned things that I did not know, things that I believe are very important when we analyze facts and behaviors connected to the October crisis. I believe that the spirit with which we have discussed this here has been excellent—the respect for each other's opinions, the sincerity, the honesty. I think I have been witness to a method that is very suited to debating very complex and difficult issues.

I am very familiar with the Soviets. Many of those here present are old friends. This is difficult—not friends who are old, but friends of long standing. [Laughter.] Some were ambassadors, some worked here, some I met at one time or another in our lives. It is not easy to analyze the conduct of historical personalities, particularly in the presence of relatives of those historical personalities. It was our duty to speak clearly, to explain our perceptions of each other's behavior, the way they acted—on some occasions critically. But it was not difficult to do this, because the images we have of those people are lofty, and it was our honorable duty to recognize those brilliant qualities of those personalities whose actions we've had to judge. When one is honest, one speaks the truth without prejudice. I said some things about Kennedy, who was our adversary, but this is not the first time that I've said them. In various interviews with the press, I have mentioned some of the things which I reiterated here. Thanks to that, it was easier for us to get over the difficulty of analyzing and passing judgment upon the conduct of personalities of those times.

But I was saying that I have friendly relations with almost all the Soviets; I know them all. I couldn't say the same about the U.S. delegation, although I did have the honor of meeting some of the participants. Wayne Smith was here in Cuba as head of the Interests Section for some time [1979–82], and we think very highly of him. He is not nominated for anything now, so I'm not campaigning in his favor. [Laughter.] With Arthur Schlesinger—I apologize if I'm not pronouncing your name correctly—I've had conversations. But, for the rest, well, we have never before had the honor of meeting. The man who was here described as resembling Hemingway, Mr. Cline—well, perhaps he expected that we harbored some hard feelings toward him. Perhaps he had been told that we would. He even told me that he thought that we were not going to grant him a visa. Imagine what kind of resentment—what volcano of resentment—would have been necessary to refuse a visa to a high intelligence official, simply because he discovered the presence of strategic missiles here! The fact is that, despite the fact that he worked for intelligence organizations for a long time, he had no information as to what Cuba is like, and what Cubans are like. It seems that even after you retire you can still make mistakes. On the other hand it was a great pleasure for us to meet with him, to find out who the person was who found us out. We recognize our deficiencies, our failings, and there's no resentment. If you knew Cuba better, you would have had a different idea of what Cubans are like, how we treat people, friends and adversaries alike.

We have been discussing history, and for us it is a privilege to meet personalities that played a role in that history. And I say this because I have a very good impression of the U.S. delegation. That I have a very good impression of the Soviet delegation is nothing new. While I wouldn't say that it is totally new to have an excellent impression of the U.S. delegation, I would say that it is something that is very constructive, which helps to create an atmosphere of confidence, to eliminate our qualms—because even if we may think that we have no reservations, we may have some. Once upon a time, harsher terms were used; but, fortunately, we overcame these stumbling blocks, because our aim was that this meeting be a forum for serene, calm analysis, in an atmosphere of détente. I think that that is the path toward the solution of the problems between us.

I think that everybody is saddled with enormous problems, and I knew that McNamara was aware of this. Now that the Cold War has come to an end, there are other dangers. We are faced with other dangers; environmental phenomena, for example. Those are very serious problems. We have started to experience these things here— climatic changes, which increase the violence of cyclones and prolong droughts. There are phenomena that warm the atmosphere, increase plagues and pests, and affect rainfall. We are faced with many problems related to development, to population growth, to the emergence of new diseases which affect human beings and plants. Humanity has made many mistakes, not just in the manufacture of weapons; there is desertification, deforestation—even a small country such as Haiti creates problems for all of us, problems that are not easy to solve for those of us who do not have an immediate answer.

I'm for peace; and I say this very candidly, as candidly as I've said other things. I'm for international cooperation. I mentioned—not to be self-righteous—our cooperation with other countries in the sphere of public health. We have doctors in over thirty countries working totally free of charge. We pay them their salaries here in Cuba, and the host country provides them with food and lodging and a small per diem of around thirty dollars or so—sometimes a bit more, sometimes a bit less. A European doctor in any African country would cost $75,000 or $80,000, according to WHO. We have over 1,000 doctors working abroad. We expect by the year 2000 to have 10,000 doctors serving on the basis of cooperation in other countries. Our doctors go to the countryside, and they go to the mountains; they don't go there to live in the cities. Ten to twelve doctors live together in a house, so they are very economical. They have enormous experience, particularly in tropical medicine and in diseases prevalent in large parts of the world—diseases that we don't even have here. And we are ready to continue along this path of cooperation. We have scant resources, but we have proven here in Cuba that with scant resources we can cooperate with other countries.

Yesterday I said that we did not intend to send soldiers abroad. Militarily, we focus our internationalist spirit in our country, on self-defense. Yesterday I talked about how our foreign policy gradually developed. But I should add that we are sending doctors abroad, and I've always said that it's always better to send doctors and teachers abroad than soldiers. We are ready to cooperate in any health programs sponsored by the United Nations, the church—we have even offered the various churches cooperation if they want to help a given country in the sphere of medicine. We are ready to cooperate with any country and undertake joint programs to promote health, education, technology, and agriculture, because we have the men and women who are ready and willing to go to these places. And sometimes this is the most difficult aspect. In the United States, the Peace Corps was organized once, and they asked for volunteers. I'm telling you now that we have thousands of volunteers—hundreds of thousands of volunteers—to carry out cooperative work in the sphere of peace.

I believe that the idea that peace must prevail regardless of social systems is something that predominates in the world. I gave you the example of China, because with its socialism and with its political system—similar in certain respects to ours—China has broad relations with the West, and with the United States. I don't think anyone would question China's international conduct, its policy of opening economically, and its policy of peace. Quite often with very scant resources you can do much.

We are honored by Mr. McNamara's statement when he referred to the infant mortality rate in our country. In 1991 it was 10.7. It is still 10.7. Actually, in 1990, it was 10.74, and in 1991 it was 10.66. It was reduced by eight-hundredths in a year of great economic difficulties, when we had difficulties with hygiene resources—shortages of soap, detergent, and so on. And even under these conditions, we've managed to cut down our infant mortality rate by eight-hundredths.

Despite our difficult conditions, all the children in the country have teachers and schools. There's not one single hospital that has been closed down, not a single school that has been closed down. We give employment to all university graduates, and that is automatic. We give a subsidy to all those who graduate from the polytechnic schools as skilled workers, automatically, whether we have employment opportunities or not. I've said that with billions of dollars less income, the country is making ends meet—with less than half of the fuel that we had traditionally received. We have not resorted to shock policies. Shock policies are merciless. Anyone might defend the idea that a shock policy is a violation of human rights, because pensioners starve, those in low-income brackets starve. In the USSR now, we are seeing some of these phenomena. There are cases of people who have a pension of 500 rubles. Once upon a time that was a lot of money. You could live on 500 rubles. But when a kilogram of meat costs 120 rubles, then 500 rubles is nothing, or next to nothing. In Latin America we have many examples of that kind of policy; schools are shut down, hospitals are shut down, everything. What we do is we share what we have. We distribute it. Nobody is left destitute. I can assure you that any Latin American society would have blown up into pieces if they had had to face the kind of difficulties that Cuba is now facing. That's why I say— and I repeat—that you can do much with little if the people are aware of the nature of the problems, and if the people cooperate—if the people have a cause to fight for, a cause that will help them withstand privations. This is achieved when there is patriotism, when there's political culture. Perhaps this does not comprise the whole of the population, but I would say that it does comprise the majority—the most active, the most hard-working part of the population. That's why, even under these conditions—and perhaps in more difficult conditions which we are expecting to have—perhaps we will have less electric power. In our country, TV sets are turned on only for a few hours every night. How many things have we had to give up? How many things have we had to grant top priority to, while sacrificing others in order to survive? But the unity of our people, the cooperation of the people, is what explains why our society has not exploded. Other societies are not as inured to these things as we are. We are because of our convictions. That is why we have achieved these successes, such as the success in the field of health that McNamara was talking about. This remark is very, very encouraging, because most of the time what we get are snide remarks.

I heard yesterday that the situation of human rights—civil rights, rather—was better than in other places; it was not as bad as in other places. Actually, I didn't agree with that. And that's the kind of debate we would have been led into today. I can prove—and I say that; I can *prove*—that in no other Third World country are there the guarantees, the security, and the possibilities that we have here in Cuba. We might talk about our electoral system. We have eradicated prostitution, for example. I think that freeing a society from prostitution is highly commendable. In a society, eliminating beggars is highly commendable. That doesn't mean that we don't have any people who have an incli- nation for prostitution. But this is not a vital need in our country; no woman is forced into prostitution, unemployment, destitution. We have eliminated racial discrimination. This has been an educational task. You can't eliminate it by decree. Racism is eliminated only by education. You have to use persuasive means. In our country you don't see enormous inequalities: people sleeping in the streets without a home, without food, and then people with enormous wealth. In our country, there's a maximum distribution of wealth. We don't have a communist system; this is a socialist system, so it's not perfect. But we can defend what we've achieved, and we have enough arguments to substantiate this, to prove what things really are like in our country. One more point—I'm taking this opportunity because I didn't want to keep these things bottled up. There are places where things are even worse. After all, Comrade Oleg Darusenkov, let's see what happens in the former republics of the Soviet Union. Let's see the level of social justice that they are going to have. I certainly hope that it will be good, and that it will not be as bad as the Third World. Honestly, that is my hope.

I don't think there's anything else to add.

I would like to thank you all for your kindness. I would like to thank you for your attention, for your patience, with my many interventions—sometimes quite long, like yesterday's, when I promised that I would speak only two or three hours. Technically, I kept my word; I only spoke two hours and a quarter. I did not speak for two and a half hours, or three hours. But I will leave here with a very deep impression, with a great hope, with the satisfaction of having had the opportunity to participate in something as constructive, as noble, as positive as what has taken place here. And I express Cuba's readiness to continue cooperating in this direction, and to continue working with you in clearing up historical events—these and others—and in any other lofty enterprise that you wish to undertake.

Thank you very much. [Applause.]

TROYANOVSKY: I think this general applause is expressive of our thanks and appreciation to President Castro for his concluding remarks, as well as for his active participation in our discussion.

I am convinced that we can all leave the room with a feeling of satisfaction, and a feeling that we have done something useful—not only because we have shed light on some additional aspects of the 1962 crisis, but because of the constructive atmosphere—I would even say friendly atmosphere; an atmosphere of mutual understanding—in which all of this has taken place.

I would like to express the hope that our meeting—perhaps not in a direct sense, but in an indirect sense—will contribute to the improvement of the atmosphere in this part of the world, as well as in other parts of our world.

If there is no one else who wishes to address the meeting, I think we can consider our work concluded with a feeling of general satisfaction. [Applause.]

C   H   A   P   T   E   R   F   O   U   R

CUBA AND THE BRINK:
FIDEL CASTRO v. HISTORY

"Los ex-ter-mi-na-re-mos," Fidel declared just a while ago. Most
likely the Pentagon will exterminate us. But he's assumed the responsi-
bility, whatever that is. He grabbed the bull by the horns. Ready for
anything. He's mad. For a moment I felt, as he talked, that he was
speaking from the only position we can take. We're on the summit of
the world and not in the depths of underdevelopment.
                                            —EDMUNDO DESNOES,
                                      Memories of Underdevelopment

As FIDEL CASTRO TOLD THE HAVANA CONFEREES, THE DAY AFTER
President Kennedy announced the discovery of the missiles and his
intention to impose a naval quarantine of Cuba he received a letter
from Nikita Khrushchev expressing "a clear and firm determination to
fight" against the "piratical, perfidious, aggressive" actions of the
United States. "Well, it looks like war," Castro recalls telling his comrades. "I cannot conceive of any retreat. . . . We said, 'Well, things are
clear; things are clear.' And we want to do our own job."[1] "It calms us
to know that the aggressors will be exterminated," Castro said on 23
October 1962. "It calms us to know this."[2]

How could an educated and highly intelligent man view with such
equanimity the destruction of Cuba, let alone global nuclear catastrophe? How is it possible that, with millions of lives hanging in the
balance—not only American lives and Soviet lives, but *Cuban* lives—
Fidel Castro would fatalistically accept annihilation rather than strive
to do whatever he could to save his country and the world? What
twisted ends or logic would lead a man to devote his entire attention

at the climax of the crisis to crafting a message intended to *prevent* compromise or concession as Khrushchev, staring down the gun barrel of nuclear war, began to weaken and waver? Why, when the slightest incident could spark a military confrontation, did Castro instruct his forces to open fire on American reconnaissance planes? And why, when he received word of the Kennedy-Khrushchev deal on 28 October, was his only reaction shock and horror—without the slightest sense of relief?

Is Fidel Castro insane?

If there is an article of faith about human behavior in politics and social science, it is the assumption that human beings value survival above all else, or that the highest end of the state is self-preservation. Nothing frightens statesmen—or confuses scholars—more than someone whose behavior suggests a preference for death over life. Suicides, martyrs, and fanatics are notoriously difficult to understand, to predict, to persuade, and to deter. Consequently, they are frightening. The United States vastly prefers the pedestrian megalomania of Saddam Hussein—even after the Gulf war—to the fundamentalist zealotry of the mullahs.[3] And this, more than anything else, explains why the United States felt so helpless in its war against terrorism in Europe and the Middle East during the 1980s. Suicide bombers do not listen to reason.

Is Fidel Castro a suicide, a martyr, or a fanatic? Certainly not a suicide. The United States would have been delighted if he were, for they would have been spared the great effort and embarrassment of attempting to kill him.[4] Nor was he a fanatic, although his entourage included some who were. Che Guevara, for instance, in an editorial written during the crisis (but published only after his death), defiantly proclaimed his willingness to "walk by the path of liberation even when it may cost millions of atomic victims, because in the struggle to the death between two systems the only thing that can be considered is the definitive victory of socialism or its retrogression under the nuclear victory of imperialist aggression."[5] Che was fully willing to give his life for socialism—and ultimately did so in the mountains of Bolivia. But scholars continue to debate the strength of Castro's ideological commitments and tend on balance to see his profession of Marxism-Leninism as instrumental to his Cuban nationalism, his Latin-Americanism, and his dedication to some rather vague notion of social justice. Offhand, it is difficult to see how any of these ends could have been advanced by fighting the first battle of World War III on Cuban soil in 1962.

Was he—or did he hope to be—a martyr? In a sense, Castro's life would have been easier and more complete if he had been. No doubt José Martí would be less revered in Cuba today had he lived out his life grappling with the mundane exigencies of governing an independent Cuba rather than having died in battle fighting for one. The lustre of Camelot would no doubt have faded to some degree, too, if John F. Kennedy had lived to preside over the domestic turmoil of the 1960s. Ideals are more durable and more radiant than idealists, and nothing seizes and holds the public imagination like the tragedy of an idealist felled in the pursuit of a noble cause. Castro's misfortune has been to outlive the glory of the revolution he wrought and to preside over a country tired of noble causes and in want of bread and electricity. Martyrdom was almost his in October 1962, and one senses that, if it had come, Fidel Castro would have been content with that fate.

Nevertheless, Fidel Castro sought neither death nor martyrdom in 1962. He simply could not see any way in which he could avoid either. So convinced was he of the United States' unrelenting hostility to the Cuban Revolution that he persuaded himself that death would come sooner or later, and his overwhelming concern at the time was to ensure that when it came, it came with dignity, honor, and drama. He saw himself very much a tragic hero, engaged in mortal battle against the evil foe for a just and righteous cause—a battle in which he would win a decisive moral victory even as he suffered the inevitable material defeat. His anguish and fury at what he saw as Khrushchev's capitulation to imperialism robbed him of his chance to go down in a blaze of glory. William Manchester captures the sentiment perfectly in the following passage describing the anguish of the Japanese soldiers on the island of New Britain when Gen. Douglas MacArthur chose to bypass rather than assault their fortress of Rabaul:

> The Americans never came. *They never came.* Month after month the
> embattled garrison awaited a blow in vain. Word reached its men of
> tremendous battles elsewhere—marines were storming ashore in the
> Gilberts, the Marshalls, and the Marianas, and MacArthur's drives
> elsewhere were accelerating as his amphibious operations succeeded
> one another with breathtaking speed—but no ships were sighted off
> Rabaul. The emperor's infantrymen soured, embittered by their unre-
> quited hostility. By early 1944 even the B-17s and B-24s stopped
> raiding them. Truk was being devastated by Nimitz's carrier planes,
> but the sky over Rabaul was serene, and sentinels posted to sound the
> alarm when the allied patrols approached overland from Cape

Gloucester and Arawe stared out at a mocking green silence. All they wanted was an opportunity to sell their lives dearly before they were killed or eviscerated themselves in honorable seppuku. They believed they were entitled to a Nipponese götterdämmerung, and MacArthur was denying them it, and they were experiencing a kind of psychological hernia.[6]

Castro was not insane in 1962; he was merely mistaken. The inevitable blow would not come. It has not come these thirty-odd years. And while his romantic and Manichean streaks are still evident, he professes to have changed his mind about the prospects of the Cuban Revolution. He now believes, he says, that it will survive. In the comfort of an air-conditioned Havana conference hall, he tells us that Cuba is confident of its ability to weather the Special Period and defend against any conceivable aggression. But he also clearly remains convinced of the United States' unrelenting hostility, and has battened down the hatches. He senses that the storm may soon come. And, ironically, if it does, he will have the missile crisis to thank that it did not come sooner.

FIDEL CASTRO v. JOHN QUINCY ADAMS AND WILLIAM McKINLEY
"[W]e've got . . . to see to it that the objective historical truth prevails"

In pursuit of their interests, leaders must constantly estimate threats, gauge the intentions and assess the goals of other states, and predict their likely behavior. These are all processes that are susceptible to a number of biases and errors, because the goals, intentions, and calculations of others are rarely obvious, and must be inferred. Such inferences involve *interpretations,* often based on ambiguous or confusing evidence. Interpretation is a difficult business; as philosophers have long been aware, it is only possible to interpret the behavior of others on the basis of some prior understanding of their behavior, a process that courts infinite regress.[7]

Psychologists have suggested that people invoke a number of shorthands or surrogates to compensate for the difficulties of interpretation. One of these, the "availability heuristic," suggests that we interpret the actions of others in the light of our own concerns, needs, and values, because these are readily available to us.[8] Another source of misperception is the "evoked set." When ambiguous information may be interpreted in a number of different ways, we tend to interpret it in accordance with whatever is in the forefront of our minds at that moment. Someone who hears a bump in the night while reading a crime novel will naturally imagine that someone has broken into the house; but if she is reading a ghost story, she is more likely to leap to the conclusion that the house is haunted.[9]

These two notions—the availability heuristic and the evoked set—help us to understand why the Kennedy administration and American historians understood the Cuban missile crisis for so long strictly as a superpower confrontation involving essentially strategic stakes. For fifteen years, the United States had been preoccupied with the struggle against communism both at home (epitomized by the gross excesses of the McCarthy era) and abroad (in the epic battle against what seemed then still to be a monolithic "Sino-Soviet bloc"). More immediately, the Kennedy administration had recently been preoccupied with fending off Khrushchev in Berlin. To do so, they deliberately exploded the "missile gap" myth upon which Khrushchev had based his policy of nuclear bluff and bluster.[10] Thus when Khrushchev attempted to sneak strategic nuclear weapons into Cuba, American policy makers—and American analysts—were naturally inclined to interpret the move either as a gambit intended ultimately to increase Soviet leverage in Berlin, or as an attempt to shore up the Soviet Union's recently exposed nuclear inferiority.[11] These were the things foremost in their own minds. Not intending to invade Cuba, American policy makers, understandably, did not—or could not—imagine that Khrushchev intended the deployment to serve defensive or deterrent purposes.[12] And Khrushchev, convinced as he was of both the legality of the deployment and its essential similarity to the American deployment of Jupiter missiles in Turkey and Italy, grossly overestimated the weight that considerations of legality or reciprocity would carry should the United States prematurely discover, or later object to, the presence of Soviet missiles in Cuba. Such misperceptions and misjudgments are the natural and unavoidable consequences of the ways in which human beings try to make sense of the world around them.

Though understandable, it is nevertheless erroneous to see the Cuban missile crisis strictly as a superpower confrontation involving nothing more than strategic stakes, and it is a mistake to see Cuba merely as a stage upon which the superpowers played out their drama. The Cuban missile crisis cannot be understood apart from the long history of relations between the United States and its smaller neighbor.

for it was this history, more than anything else, that brought Fidel Castro onto the world stage and made him what he was. It was this history that he was struggling to overcome, and it is this history which even now preoccupies him. "At one point here I thought I was hearing the old rhetoric of the Cold War," Castro told the Havana conferees— "the old arguments of the Cold War: Cuba as a Soviet base, Cuba as a Soviet agent, Cuba as an organizer of subversion in Latin America— the causes that gave rise to all of the actions and policies of the different U.S. administrations against Cuba. And I ask myself if anyone can be so ignorant of history, as if there were no history of relations between the United States and Cuba and the United States and Latin America, going back almost 200 years, long before Cuba existed and long before the Cuban Revolution existed."[13]

Castro sees himself as part of a historical process—the liberation of Cuba, first from Spanish colonialism and then from American imperialism—which has yet to be completed since the United States refuses to accept Cuba as a fully sovereign state and to treat it with the respect and dignity it deserves. He also clearly sees the October crisis as a crucial event in that process. His entire understanding of the event is shaped by it, because the long and difficult history of U.S.-Cuban relations was and is in the forefront of *his* mind. He was certain at the time that Kennedy seized upon the Soviet deployment as an opportunity to destroy the Cuban Revolution. He continues to believe that the crisis was the product primarily of American imperialism and hostility. Castro is still wrestling with the ghosts of John Quincy Adams and William McKinley.

Early American Policy

Geography alone would suffice to ensure that the fate of Cuba would somehow be bound up inextricably with that of the United States.[14] In 1823, Secretary of State John Quincy Adams expressed it thus:

> Cuba, almost in sight of our shores, from a multitude of considerations has become an object of transcendent importance to the political and commercial interests of our Union. Its commanding position, with reference to the Gulf of Mexico, and the West India seas; the character of its population; its situation midway between our Southern Coast, and the Island of St. Domingo; its safe and capacious harbor of Havanna fronting a long line of our shores destitute of the same advantage; the nature of its productions, and of its wants fur-

nishing the supplies and needing the returns of a commerce immensely profitable, and mutually beneficial, give it an importance in the sum of our national interests with which that of no other foreign Territory can be compared, and little inferior to that which binds the different members of this Union together.

Such indeed are, between the interests of that Island and of this country, the geographical, commercial, moral, and political relations formed by nature, gathering in the process of time, and even now verging to maturity that in looking forward to the probable course of events for the short period of half a century, it is scarcely possible to resist the conviction, that the annexation of Cuba to our federal Republic will be indispensable to the continuance and integrity of the Union itself.[15]

The "laws of political gravitation," Adams pronounced, would inevitably bring Cuba into the United States.[16]

The slavery issue provided a check on the laws of political gravitation for a time. Cuba had more slaves per capita than anywhere in the world, and as the United States expanded, slavery became an explosive political issue. Wealthy Cuban planters looked to annexation as a means of protecting the institution of slavery on the island, fearing that independence or political instability under prolonged Spanish rule might result in a catastrophic slave revolt, as had happened already in neighboring Santo Domingo.[17] Their natural allies in the United States were southern pro-slavery expansionists who sought to protect or improve their position in Congress vis-à-vis the largely antislavery north. But it was precisely the strength of those who sought to contain or abolish slavery that prevented the annexation of Cuba from becoming a widely popular political program in the United States, and no president would pursue the idea with any vigor until the explosiveness of the slavery issue had already reached a point that doomed annexation. As long as Cuba remained in Spanish hands, therefore, successive American administrations were content to leave it alone. Spain's days as a great military and economic power were numbered, and Spain posed no real threat to the safety and well-being of a growing United States.

American presidents periodically worried, however, that Cuba would fall into French or English hands,[18] and this was the chief external impetus behind President James Monroe's message to Congress of 2 December 1823, articulating the doctrine which would later bear his name, in which he warned Europe against future efforts to colonize the Americas, or to interfere with the newly won independence of American republics.[19] Cuban independence was not at the time considered a serious option in the United States. When John Quincy Adams became president, his secretary of state, Henry Clay, bluntly told Alexander H. Everett, American minister to Spain, that Cuba's population was "incompetent, at present, from its composition and amount, to maintain self government."[20]

What was it about Cuba that distinguished it from Mexico, Bolivia, Argentina, or Chile, which the United States had already recognized as independent? Why, according to Clay, were its people "incompetent" to maintain self-government? Primarily, it seems, because of its racial composition.[21] The Spanish population in Cuba differed little in culture, education, or socioeconomic class from that of other Latin American countries, but the island's distinguishing feature was its proportion of slaves. But if Cuba could not govern itself, could not be transferred to another power, and seemed unlikely to remain forever under Spanish control, what did fate hold for it?

According to journalist John L. O'Sullivan, creator of the phrase "Manifest Destiny," the answer was annexation. On 23 July 1847, an editorial in the *New York Sun* presented O'Sullivan's plan to purchase Cuba under the headline, "Cuba under the flag of the United States." "Cuba by geographical position, necessity and right belongs to the United States, it may and must be ours," the *Sun* proclaimed. "The moment has arrived to place it in our hands and under our flag. Cuba is in the market for sale, and we are authorized by parties eminently able to fulfil what they propose, to say that if the United States will offer the Spanish government one hundred million dollars Cuba is ours, and that within one week's notice, the whole amount will be raised and paid over by the inhabitants of the island."[22] O'Sullivan had the ear of President James K. Polk, who leaned toward acquiring the island because of information he had received, through O'Sullivan and others, that Cuba would soon rise up in open rebellion against Spanish rule. If the United States were not in a position to prevent it, Britain or France might step into the vacuum. This was a prospect Polk could not bear because of Cuba's rising strategic importance. Polk's recent war against Mexico gave the United States unchallenged control of California and spurred interest in an Isthmian canal linking the Atlantic and Pacific; Britain and France were both possible rivals for control of such a canal, and if either of them possessed Cuba, they stood to command access to it. In 1848, therefore, Polk ordered his minister in Madrid to negotiate the purchase of the island.

If Spain had not vehemently rejected the sale, opposition in the United States might have derailed it in any case. Expansion was popular in 1848, but even some of the most ardent expansionists felt sated with California and New Mexico. Only the southern slaveholding faction was strongly in favor, and O'Sullivan had prepared no contingency plan for defusing the slavery issue. The acquisition therefore lay fallow, the anticipated rebellion failed to dislodge the Spanish, and the United States turned its attention inward.

Polk's immediate successors, Zachary Taylor and Millard Fillmore, did not pursue the acquisition of Cuba and enforced the neutrality laws, which forbade American assistance to Cuban rebels, as best they could. Franklin Pierce, pro-expansion Democratic president from 1853 to 1857, once again attempted to negotiate a purchase, toyed with the idea of seizing the island (using as a pretext the confiscation of the cargo of an American steamer, the *Black Warrior*, that had violated Spanish customs restrictions in Havana), and commissioned a study of the Cuban question by three senior American diplomats. The result, the "Ostend Manifesto" of 1854, made the argument that the United States would be justified in occupying the island for the purpose of self-defense if Spain refused to sell it and if conditions there threatened the "internal peace and the existence" of the Union.[23] But the slavery issue was even more of an impediment to Pierce's plans than it had been to Polk's, and the long, slow slide into civil war prevented the acquisition of Cuba from receiving the full attention of the government and the nation.

The Civil War left the United States in no position to expand, and though a major revolt on the island of Cuba in 1868 drew the interest and sympathy of the American public, the United States had neither the moral reserves nor the navy to intervene.[24] The most that Andrew Johnson and Ulysses S. Grant were willing to do was assert the no-transfer principle and locate it explicitly in the Monroe Doctrine. Grant, in his message of 1869, even explicitly disclaimed any intention to intervene in relations between Spain and her colonies, and once again invoked neutrality laws.[25] But Reconstruction and the political consolidation of the continental United States did not put an end to American interest in Cuba; they merely forced a hiatus. By the end of the century, American armed forces would be in physical possession of the island.

American Intervention, 1898

In February 1895, Cuban insurgents rose up in arms once again to throw off the yoke of an oppressive and corrupt Spanish colonial rule. Initially the insurgents did remarkably well, and set up a provisional republican government in the eastern part of the island. But most of Cuba remained under Spanish control, and the insurgents resorted to a scorched-earth policy, hoping to render the island worthless to Spain.

Spain reciprocated with the iron fist, reaching new depths of barbarity in an innovative policy known as "reconcentration." In February 1896, the newly appointed captain general, Valeriano Weyler, ordered the populations of entire districts into villages and towns, dug trenches around them, put up barbed-wire fences, built guardhouses at regular intervals, and proclaimed that anyone found outside the camps would be considered an insurgent and shot on sight. The camps themselves were unable to support the numbers herded into them, and hundreds of thousands died of starvation or disease. The American press—especially (but not exclusively) the "yellow press," led by William Randolph Hearst's *New York Journal* and Joseph Pulitzer's *New York World*—competed eagerly for the most gruesome stories of Spanish atrocities, largely ignoring the insurgents' own. The rebel junta in New York very effectively fanned the flames of humanitarian outrage, and actively campaigned for American funds and supplies. Before long, American public opinion began to favor an activist, interventionist policy.[26]

The United States was interested in the conflict for more than just its barbarity, however. It greatly disrupted a lucrative trade, and it jeopardized millions of dollars' worth of American property in Cuba.[27] The war was expensive in other respects as well: investigations and representations on behalf of American citizens injured by the conflict cost a good deal of money; the government had to pay for coastal patrols to enforce neutrality and prevent filibusters; and customs receipts on Cuban trade fell off dramatically at a time when the federal budget was very precariously balanced.[28] Congress demanded that President Grover Cleveland pursue a more active Cuban policy in an attempt to bring the conflict to an end. Instead, Cleveland proclaimed neutrality and set about enforcing the appropriate laws designed to prevent aid from reaching the insurgents.[29] In a message to Congress on 2 December 1895, he called for Americans to remain impartial and to observe the neutrality legislation.[30] But Congress increased the pressure, passing resolutions in 1896 calling on the president to grant belligerent rights to the Cuban insurgents and to take steps toward securing Cuban independence, through forcible intervention if necessary.[31]

Cleveland was of two minds on the issue. As late as 1896, he had been toying with the idea of trying once again to purchase the island. But he felt that "incorporating" Cuba somehow into the United States "would be entering upon dangerous ground." At the same time, the president thought it "absurd" for the United States to buy the island and permit the Cubans to manage their own affairs.[32] He therefore decided against the idea.[33] Granting the insurgents belligerent rights posed additional problems, for it would have freed Spain from its responsibility to protect American property.[34] Cleveland resolved to do what he could to ease the pain and suffering on the island without direct intervention.

On 4 April 1896, Secretary of State Richard Olney urged Spain not to abandon the island, in order to avoid a "war of races." To deflect Spanish charges that the United States was interfering in its domestic affairs, Olney listed four considerations justifying American interest in the conflict: first, Americans favored the struggle for "freer political institutions" anywhere; second, the war had reached unacceptable levels of inhumanity; third, the United States desired to avoid a prolonged interruption of trade; and fourth, the "wholesale destruction of property" was "utterly destroying American investments."[35] Olney offered the president's help in bringing the conflict to a negotiated end that respected Spanish sovereignty over the island but that also gave the inhabitants "all such rights and powers of self-government as they can reasonably ask."[36] Spain declined on the ground that American mediation would be an affront to Spanish sovereignty.

There was little else Cleveland could do; his term of office would expire before a settlement to the conflict could be reached. In an interesting historical irony, one of the president's last initiatives was to propose sending a cruiser to Havana harbor to demonstrate concern for American lives and property. The cabinet approved the idea on 8 December 1896, but the secretary of the navy succeeded in convincing Cleveland "that an accident might befall the American warship and so exacerbate America's relations with Spain."[37]

Cuba was not much of an issue during the 1896 election. Democratic candidate William Jennings Bryan and his free silver platform were themselves the dominant concerns.[38] But the new Republican president, William McKinley, inherited Cleveland's Cuban predicament, and was no better prepared to deal with it. His inaugural address was circumspect and pacific: "It will be our aim to pursue a firm and dignified foreign policy," McKinley stated, "which shall be just, impartial, ever watchful of our national honor, and always insisting upon the enforcement of the lawful rights of American citizens everywhere. Our diplomacy should seek nothing more and nothing less than is due us. We want no wars of conquest; we must avoid the temptation of territorial aggression. Wars should never be entered upon until every agency of peace has failed; peace is preferable to war in almost every contingency."[39] Within two years he had conquered Cuba and the Philippines.

McKinley, like so many of his predecessors, flirted with the idea of purchasing the island early in his term.[40] But he settled on a policy of prodding Spain into resolving the conflict quickly and humanely, however it could do so, and periodically threatened, implicitly or explicitly, to intervene with military force. Initially, he met with no success. On 8 June 1897, he sent a confidential note to the Spanish government objecting to Weyler's reconcentration policy.[41] Spain was unmoved. But in early autumn, he issued a virtual ultimatum that led Spain to promise reforms, recall General Weyler, abandon reconcentration, and create an elected Cuban legislature. McKinley was satisfied. The insurgents were not; they would accept nothing short of complete independence.[42] The war dragged on.

Riots broke out in Havana on 12 January 1898, when soldiers loyal to Weyler ransacked the offices of three newspapers that had openly criticized the general. The American consul general, Fitzhugh Lee, interpreted the riots as the beginning of anarchy. Though they quickly subsided, McKinley once again brandished the specter of intervention.[43] He sent one of the navy's newest vessels to Havana, the armored cruiser *Maine*—ostensibly on a courtesy call to resume friendly port visits, but in reality to signal American concern.[44] On 15 February, the ship exploded and sank with heavy loss of life. Two reports by the U.S. naval board of examiners—one shortly after the incident, another thirteen years later—found that plates from the bottom of the ship had been blown inward and upward by an external explosion, triggering a second blast in the ship's forward magazine.[45]

The destruction of the *Maine* actually made many American jingoes think twice about military involvement, and some of the more interventionist journals initially called for restraint. But the public outcry swelled to a crescendo that the administration simply could not resist.[46] If economic and humanitarian motives had not been strong enough to push the nation into war, the demand for vengeance tipped the balance.[47] Of course, there was no proof that the Spanish had been responsible for the incident. It is certainly difficult to imagine what Spain stood to gain by destroying an American ship and killing 266 American sailors. But few Americans paused to consider the question; they had simply had enough.

On 27 March, the president issued his final demand: Spain would abandon reconcentration at once, grant an armistice until October, and enter into negotiations with the rebels with American mediation. The next day, in a separate telegram, he added that the only satisfactory outcome of the negotiations would be Cuban independence.[48] Spain essentially complied with the first two planks of McKinley's proposal, but tacitly rejected the demand for independence.

On 11 April, McKinley asked Congress for permission to intervene. A week later, the House and Senate passed resolutions recognizing Cuban independence, demanding that Spain withdraw from the island, and authorizing the president to use the armed forces of the United States to enforce the demand. Sen. Henry M. Teller of Colorado proposed a resolution, accepted by both houses without dissent or a recorded vote, designed to blunt European criticism of the American action:

> [Resolved:] That the United States hereby disclaims any disposition or intention to exercise sovereignty, jurisdiction, or control over the said island except for the pacification thereof, and asserts its determination, when that is accomplished, to leave the government and control of the island to its people.[49]

Spain severed diplomatic relations with Washington and, on 24 April, declared war. Congress, not to be outdone, declared war the following day, retroactive to 21 April. By the middle of the summer, the United States found itself in control of most of the Spanish empire.

Historians continue to debate whether McKinley led or followed public opinion into war, and whether the United States fought the war primarily for economic or humanitarian reasons.[50] In his April message to Congress, McKinley himself justified intervention first by appealing to humanitarianism, the need "to put an end to the barbarities, bloodshed, starvation, and horrible miseries" in Cuba; second, to protect American lives and property; third, to redress "the very serious injury to the commerce, trade, and business of our people . . . and the wanton destruction of property and devastation of the island"; and fourth, what McKinley called "of the utmost importance," to end the "menace to our peace" and the "enormous expense" incurred by the American government as a result of the unrest.[51] Notably absent from this list was concern for the wishes of the Cuban people. "The right of the Cubans to control their own affairs does not seem to have been seriously considered by American statesmen," write John Grenville and George Berkeley Young. "Many knowledgeable Americans doubted whether the Cubans were really ready for self-government and feared that immediate independence would create fresh problems for the United States. McKinley shared these fears and inclined to the view that the Cubans would first have to pass through a period of American tutelage before they could be trusted to make wise use of a representative government."[52]

The president, Congress, and the American people were all firmly convinced that intervention had been undertaken with the noblest purposes in mind. The United States had liberated the island from Spanish oppression. Now it would do Cuba another favor: it would govern Cuba until the Cubans themselves were ready to take control of their own destiny, and would always be there to help. The United States had "assumed before the world a grave responsibility for the future good government of Cuba," McKinley stated in his annual message of 5 December 1899. "The new Cuba . . . must needs be bound to us by ties of singular intimacy and strength if its enduring welfare is to be assured."[53] He ordered the new military governor of Cuba, Leonard Wood, "to go down there to get the people ready for a republican form of government . . . and to get out of the island as soon as we safely can."[54]

From the Platt Amendment to Punta del Este

In March 1901, Congress passed the Platt Amendment, an attachment to the Army Appropriations Bill, authorizing the president to terminate the occupation of Cuba as soon as a Cuban government was organized under a constitution that (1) never permitted a "foreign power" to gain a foothold on Cuban soil; (2) restricted its foreign debt; (3) permitted American intervention to preserve Cuban independence or to maintain a government "adequate for the protection of life, property, and individual liberty"; and (4) leased or sold lands for American coaling stations or naval bases at points to be determined.[55] The armed forces of the United States did not evacuate Cuba until 1902. They did so only after it became apparent to Cuban leaders, who initially rejected the Platt Amendment soundly, that the occupation force was in no hurry to leave. The United States gave Cuba assurances that it would

exercise its right to intervene only in the event of a serious foreign
threat or domestic disturbance, but insisted upon appending the Platt
Amendment to the Cuban constitution and embodying it in the Permanent Treaty of 1903 between the United States and the Republic
of Cuba.[56]

Under President Theodore Roosevelt, intervention became the
cornerstone of the United States' Latin American policy as a whole.
In his annual message of 1905, Roosevelt declared that "[c]hronic
wrong-doing, or an impotence which results in a general loosening of
the ties of civilized society, may in America, as elsewhere, ultimately
require intervention by some civilized nation, and in the western hemisphere the adherence of the United States to the Monroe Doctrine
may force the United States, however reluctantly, in flagrant cases of
such wrong-doing or impotence, to the exercise of an international
police power."[57] The Roosevelt corollary to the Monroe Doctrine essentially declared that it was better for the United States to enforce
contractual obligations than for other powers to do so, and from the
American point of view, this was undeniably true. But, as Dexter
Perkins observes, "By a development as interesting as it appeared continuous, even inexorable, the Roosevelt corollary had led directly to
the coercion of the very states it was intended to protect. The Monroe
Doctrine, aimed to prevent the intervention of European powers, had
become a justification for the intervention of the United States."[58]
Before long, the United States would establish protectorates in Nicaragua, Haiti, and the Dominican Republic.

American intervention in Latin America undoubtedly improved
the financial conditions of the governments in question, but it had no
appreciable effect on political attitudes or practices.[59] Most significantly,
Latin America deeply resented it, repeatedly condemned it, and sought
its formal renunciation. In the early 1920s, Charles Evans Hughes,
secretary of state under Presidents Warren G. Harding and Calvin
Coolidge, began the process of stepping back from the Roosevelt corollary and started to dismantle the edifice of American interventionism.
But he did not renounce treaties expressly authorizing intervention in
Cuba, Panama, the Dominican Republic, and Haiti.[60] In 1928, Under
Secretary of State J. Reuben Clark's *Memorandum on the Monroe Doctrine* effectively overturned the Roosevelt corollary by declaring that
"[t]he doctrine states a case of United States *vs.* Europe, not of United
States *vs.* Latin America"; but the Clark memorandum did not repu-
diate the right to intervene in the domestic affairs of other states when
American interests were threatened—it merely refused to locate that

right in the Monroe Doctrine.[61] Coolidge, however, terminated the most egregious American meddling in Cuba's domestic affairs, leaving the Cuban government, as Julius Pratt puts it, "free to develop into the type of corrupt dictatorship that was seemingly indigenous to the soil."[62]

The election of Franklin Delano Roosevelt in 1932 heralded an important change in U.S.-Latin American relations. Roosevelt repudiated unilateral intervention in the internal affairs of other nations. "In the field of world policy," Roosevelt declared, "I would dedicate this Nation to the policy of the Good Neighbor—the neighbor who resolutely respects himself, and, because he does so, respects the rights of others—the neighbor who respects his obligations and respects the sanctity of agreements in and with a world of neighbors."[63] In Montevideo in 1933, Roosevelt's secretary of state, Cordell Hull, delivered the first major installment of the "Good Neighbor" policy by signing a Convention on the Rights and Duties of States that declared, *inter alia*, "No state has the right to intervene in the internal or external affairs of another." But Hull made an explicit exception of Cuba, owing to the existing treaty.[64]

Roosevelt finally abrogated the Permanent Treaty in May 1934, explicitly giving up the United States' right of intervention, lifting restrictions on Cuba's ability to negotiate treaties with others, and leaving Cuba free to borrow money wherever she liked. But the U.S. Navy retained the lease of Guantánamo Bay, and the agreement abrogating the Platt Amendment retroactively validated all of the actions of the American military during its various interventions.[65] A reciprocal trade agreement signed in 1934 replaced the old commercial treaty, and it succeeded in stimulating the Cuban economy; but it bound Cuba even more tightly to the United States and made her vulnerable to unilateral changes in American policy.[66]

Despite the disavowal of military intervention, the U.S. ambassador in Havana continued to exert tremendous influence on Cuban affairs, and the United States quickly found that Cuban political decisions were easily influenced through economic action.[67] Moreover, Roosevelt's one serious deviation from his Latin American policy of non-interference occurred in Cuba. In the first year of his presidency, he helped topple the reformist government of Dr. Ramón Grau San Martín by withholding recognition and ominously stationing American warships in Cuban waters. For this he would tacitly apologize in 1944, by welcoming Grau to Washington as president of Cuba.[68] But it was difficult for Cubans to undertand how Roosevelt could uphold his relations with Cuba as a model of his Good Neighbor Policy when the United States continued to meddle directly in Cuban politics.

Latin America virtually disappeared from the American agenda during the Second World War, for obvious reasons. The United States emerged from the war vastly more powerful but feeling less secure than it had entered, with unfortunate and paradoxical effects on its hemispheric relations. The communist threat quickly supplanted the fascist threat as the primary bogey of American foreign policy, consuming the nation's attention and its diplomatic resources. U.S. Latin American policy concentrated on preventing the spread of communism and on enlisting the support of Latin American governments in the battle. A series of international meetings laid the groundwork for a pan-American system of resistance to communism: the ninth International Conference of American States at Bogotá in 1948 condemned "the political activity of international communism" as a system "tending to suppress political rights and liberties"; a foreign ministers' meeting in 1951 charged the Inter-American Defense Board with planning measures for the common defense; and the tenth Inter-American Conference in March 1954 declared that "the domination or control of the political institutions of any American state by the international communist movement, extending to this Hemisphere the political system of an extracontinental power, would constitute a threat to the sovereignty and political independence of the American states."[69] These diplomatic initiatives made it possible to respond to a communist threat in the region on grounds of collective security and self-defense.

With its attention thus so firmly focused on containing communism, the United States poured billions of dollars' worth of Marshall Plan aid into rebuilding Western Europe—the first line of defense against Soviet communism. This had three unfortunate effects on Latin America: first, it created competition for the fledgling Latin American industries that had sprung up during the war; second, it inflated the prices of their imports; and third, it generated profound resentment. During the war itself, as part of the effort to rally Latin America to the Allied cause, American officials had made several public statements that generated expectations of substantial material rewards for cooperation against the Axis powers. With most of the available aid being channeled into Europe, the expected rewards never materialized. Although the United States had tacitly assumed responsibility for the welfare and prosperity of the non-Soviet world, it was clearly demonstrating its priorities by channeling its resources elsewhere.[70]

The United States was instrumental in the drafting of the charter of the Organization of American States at Bogotá, Article 15 of which unqualifiedly asserted the principle of non-intervention:

No State, or group of States has the right to intervene directly or in-directly, for any reason whatever, in the internal or external affairs of any other State. The foregoing principle prohibits not only the armed force but also any other form of interference or attempted threat against the personality of the State or against its political, economic, or cultural elements.[71]

By 1951, the charter had been ratified and put into effect by its members. Just three years later, however—on 2 July 1954—the Central Intelligence Agency succeeded in bringing down the government of Jacobo Arbenz Guzmán in Guatemala, a sovereign Latin American state. Arbenz had committed the fatal error of land reform, and the United States felt fully justified in toppling him to contain the spread of communism. Indeed, the March 1954 declaration had been designed with Guatemala in mind. The action clearly demonstrated that the United States considered the war on communism more important than its obligations under Article 15 of the OAS charter, and thus that the U.S. commitment to non-intervention was seriously qualified.

Fidel Castro can be credited with finally bringing Cuba itself to the top of the American agenda after a sixty-year absence. In the months before he and his rag-tag band of revolutionaries finally succeeded in driving Fulgencio Batista from the country (on New Year's Day, 1959), Castro had enjoyed a fair measure of sympathy and support in the United States. He was a romantic figure engaged in the pursuit of a worthy goal: the overthrow of a corrupt and unpopular dictator. Although several of Castro's co-conspirators had openly communist sym-pathies, Castro himself had given no indication that his was anything other than a purely nationalist revolution. Indeed, in the early years, he was openly hostile to the Cuban Communist Party. The Eisenhower administration, therefore, chose to adopt a hands-off policy and to let the Cuban Revolution run its course. In March 1958, the president even froze arms shipments to Batista because of Castro's growing strength and popularity.[72] But once in power, the new regime's eco-nomic and foreign policies quickly alienated the United States.

The economic blow was a far-reaching program of nationalization without compensation that affected approximately a billion dollars' worth of American assets, most of it in sugar, tobacco, oil refining, utilities, tourism, and real estate. The foreign policy blow was a declaration on 19 December 1960 openly aligning Cuba with the Sino-Soviet bloc. President Eisenhower imposed limited economic sanctions and cut off diplomatic relations. His successor, President Kennedy, went even further, eliminating the sugar quota that had guaranteed Cuba access to the American market. Castro's nationalization program, in retrospect, was ill conceived and counterproductive. Well-placed Cubans today openly voice their regrets about the way in which it was done. But the American attempt to punish Cuba economically for its actions had the unfortunate effect of driving Cuba even further into the Soviet camp. Nikita Khrushchev was only too happy to step in and fill the economic void created by American sanctions.

The damage that Castro had done to American interests was considerable, and by flirting with the Soviet Union he threatened to upset a hemispheric anti-communist status quo. American opinion, both in the government and in the country at large, gradually turned to the conclusion that he had to go.

Enter the CIA.

The CIA's most serious attempt to overthrow Castro was the Bay of Pigs invasion, 17–19 April 1961. The scheme, hatched during the Eisenhower administration, called for training and equipping a force of Cuban exiles in Central America that would land, with American air support, on the southern coast of the island near the Escambray mountains, move into the hills, and rally the Cuban people against their new dictator. As Peter Wyden puts it, "The 'Guatemala Model' was on everybody's mind."[73] But Cuba was not Guatemala, and Castro was not Arbenz. The CIA grossly underestimated Castro's popularity, and the size, equipment, and training of the invasion force were wholly inadequate to the task at hand. Moreover, the CIA tinkered with the plan right up until the day of the invasion itself, in the process virtually guaranteeing that it would fail. They moved the landing site westward from Trinidad to Playa Girón, a flat, swampy area far away from the Escambray mountains affording no cover and no escape; they scaled back the number of bombing runs authorized for the small, poorly equipped exile air force to the point where it failed to knock out Castro's air power; and at the last minute, President Kennedy decided to hold back the American air support needed to cover the landing. At the eleventh hour, sensing disaster, the two principal subcommanders threatened to quit because of the changes. Richard Bissell, the CIA's deputy director for planning who supervised the operation, managed to talk them out of it only after a long and emotional appeal.[74] The invasion was a dismal failure.

While history has judged Kennedy harshly for the Bay of Pigs fiasco, Kennedy had, in fact, been pinned on the horns of a dilemma that he had inherited from the Eisenhower administration. He was reluctant to use American military force directly against Castro because of the ill will this would generate in Latin America. He knew that overt intervention in Cuba would undermine the improvement he sought in U.S. relations with Latin America through the Alliance for Progress. But as CIA director Allen Dulles argued vehemently, it would be difficult to turn back once preparations for an exile invasion were under way in Central America. If the invaders were pulled out and brought back to the United States, or if they were otherwise dispersed, they would blow the cover on the operation and alienate the right (who would conclude that Kennedy lacked nerve), the left (who would be appalled at the idea in the first place), and the Latin Americans (who would question the president's commitment to non-intervention). Perhaps most importantly, Khrushchev would conclude that Kennedy was soft on communism. Dulles feared that canceling the operation would therefore trigger communist takeovers throughout the hemisphere. Moreover, Dulles noted, it was also entirely possible that the exiles would resist being disarmed.[75]

The plan met strong opposition from many of the administration's Latin American specialists and top military advisers. Sen. J. William Fulbright wrote a detailed memorandum to the president leveling a full broadside against the scheme on legal, political, and moral grounds. "To give this activity even covert support is of a piece with the hypocrisy and cynicism for which the United States is constantly denouncing the Soviet Union in the United Nations and elsewhere," Fulbright wrote. "The point will not be lost on the rest of the world—nor on our own consciences."[76] But Kennedy decided that the landing should go ahead, with the United States keeping itself as far away from it as possible. He would later take full public responsibility for the fiasco, but he would thereafter harbor serious doubts about the competence of the CIA.

Covert operations against Castro continued, though apparently with little expectation of success on the part of senior policy makers. Operation Mongoose began in February 1962, and provided an outlet for the government's hostility toward the Castro regime—a "psychological salve for inaction," as Special Assistant for National Security McGeorge Bundy would later describe it.[77] But having been burned once by a large-scale attempt to unseat Castro, Kennedy was loath to try a frontal assault a second time. He settled on a policy of harassment, saber-rattling, and diplomatic isolation intended to keep Castro off balance and to contain him. The harassment included running operatives back and forth between Cuba and Florida, blowing up factories, and staging hit-and-run attacks against the Cuban coast. The saber-rattling included bolstering the deployment of American troops in the region, buzzing Cuban air fields, flying high-altitude reconnaissance missions over the island, and staging threatening exercises (including one called PHIBRIGLEX-62, in which marines invaded the mythical Republic of Vieques to unseat a mythical dictator called "Ortsac"— Castro spelled backward). Kennedy completed Cuba's diplomatic isolation at Punta del Este in January 1962, when the OAS declared Castro's government incompatible with the inter-American system, excluded Cuba from the OAS, and imposed an arms embargo.

American "Imperialism": Two Perspectives

Such were the depths to which U.S.-Cuban relations had fallen on the eve of the Cuban missile crisis. Rarely, during the previous century and a half, had those relations been better than cordial; never had they been bilaterally friendly. Curiously, though, no matter what the state of relations at any given time, they always appeared to be better from the American perspective than from the Cuban. The United States generally felt that it had exercised forbearance throughout the colonial phase of Cuba's history; it was convinced it had done Cuba an important service in the Spanish-American war; it sincerely believed that it had treated Cuba with patience and equanimity ever since; and it resented—because it did not understand—Castro's anti-Americanism.

The American occupation of Spain's former colonies was undoubtedly an imperialism of sorts. But the dominant contemporary view in American historiography was that it was a "benevolent imperialism," "an imperialism against imperialism. It did not last long and it was not really bad."[78] Had voice been given to the perception common in Cuba today that the United States waited just until Cuban insurgents had brought Spain to her knees and then opportunistically snatched victory from the hands of the patriots, only to supplant one foreign rule with another, the sentiment would have been dismissed in the United States as at least ungrateful, and probably delusional. By the same token, few in Cuba would have credited the claim of Professor Bemis that Cubans "hoped for the intervention of their great friend and neighbor, the republic of the mainland, to free them from their monarchial mistress in the Old World."[79] There were those in Cuba who had indeed hoped for American help in defeating the Spanish; but it was difficult for them not to be suspicious of the United States' timing given the professed humanitarian motive. After all, reconcentration had begun two years before American troops intervened. It was also difficult not to be suspicious of the sinking of the *Maine,* which seemed to serve American interests (as a *casus belli*) much more efficiently than it served any conceivable Spanish interest. It was also difficult (especially for Spain and other European powers) to reconcile American intervention with the Monroe Doctrine: "With the existing colonies or dependencies of any European power," Monroe had said, "we have not interfered, and shall not interfere." Dexter Perkins's contention that the Monroe Doctrine could not have been interpreted as self-denying with respect to Cuba, because those who formulated it also favored annexation, would only have reinforced the impression that the United States interprets its principles selectively and applies them at its convenience.[80]

Even more puzzling was American behavior after the war. Senator Teller's resolution had stated "[t]hat the United States hereby disclaims any disposition or intention to exercise sovereignty, jurisdiction, or control over the said island except for the pacification thereof, and asserts its determination, when that is accomplished, to leave the government and control of the island to its people." Professor Bemis maintains that "[t]hese words sounded hollow to a cynical Europe and Asia hardened to a contrary practice. They have been made good."[81] This was an evaluation that would not have been understood outside the United States. As if the contradictions between the Platt Amendment and Teller's resolution were not difficult enough to resolve, the first and fourth provisions of the Platt Amendment itself were completely incongruous: what else was the American base at Guantánamo but a foreign foothold on Cuban territory?

Bemis goes on at length about the "forbearance" of the United States in the exercise of its Platt Amendment rights. "If ever there were an emblem of pride on the escutcheon of American idealism," he writes, "it is the attitude in our century of the Continental Republic toward Cuba. The urge to annex was there, no doubt, for a century, but it was bridled, curbed, and halted by a great and historic self-denial, checked by the common people of the United States and their opposition to imperialism."[82] This was an observation that only an American could have made. From the Cuban perspective, the Platt Amendment was as blatant an affront to Cuban sovereignty as could possibly be imagined. What Bemis considered to be "forbearance"—more than thirty years of direct or indirect control of Cuban affairs—was deeply resented in Cuba as humiliating paternalism.

The fact that Cuban politics never closely approximated the American ideal meant that the United States felt justified in repeatedly intervening to try to set things right. From time to time, the intervention would be overt, as it was between 1906 and 1909, and between 1916 and 1921.[83] The rest of the time, it was understood that Cuban governments would rarely take any serious initiatives without first consulting Washington. It was unfortunate for the later development of U.S.-Cuban relations that a paternalistic interventionist pattern developed so early and so strongly, however, and that Cuba essentially dropped out of the American political consciousness; for the pattern might not have set so firmly if it had been subject to the kind of domestic criticism and reevaluation that attends issues in the public spotlight. A high degree of American influence in Cuba came to be taken so much for granted that when Fidel Castro stopped playing by the rules in the early 1960s, the dominant American reaction was righteous indignation. What the United States had failed to understand was that Cubans did not share the American perspective. Their resentment—indeed, their anti-Americanism—was itself a reaction to what *they* saw as the main lines of American policy since Jefferson: the paternalism; the unilateralism; the apparent contradictions between principles and behavior; the opportunism; the exploitation. U.S. policy put a very high value on Cuba's geographic position and economic potential, but a very low value on its pride. That policy helped Castro come to power, and that policy helped create the international conditions that led to the deployment of Soviet missiles.

The Illusion of Historical Objectivity

Castro's belief that the missile crisis was primarily the product of American imperialism and hostility is clearly understandable. But Kennedy—and Americans generally—did not share Castro's perspective on the crisis, in part because they had long forgotten (if they had ever known) the details of U.S.-Cuban relations over the centuries. But even if they had remembered the details, they would have disagreed with Castro over their interpretation and significance. Such disagreements were evident at the Havana conference every time a historical issue arose. McNamara anticipated this and shrewdly attempted in his opening statement to transform the fact of historical disagreement into a basis for mutually exploring the role and significance of misperceptions:

Perhaps a good place to begin is to acknowledge that our shared history is viewed very differently by both countries and that this divergence contributed both to the sharp break in relations between our nations thirty-one years ago, and to the attitudes with which we viewed the missile crisis. Let me give four illustrations of these differences of view. First, Americans have been taught that the U.S. liberated Cuba from Spain, while Cubans learn that it was the result of their long struggle for independence. Second, Americans view themselves as idealistic and selfless in not annexing Cuba after the end of the Spanish-American war, whereas Cubans think the U.S. used every chance to dominate their nation. Third, Americans think they used the Platt Amendment to mediate and resolve internal disputes in Cuba, whereas Cubans tend to think that the amendment was designed to permit the U.S. to intervene in Cuban affairs for its own selfish purposes; and finally, Americans tend to think that their investments in Cuba contributed to the nation's development, whereas the Cuban government has tended to look at the economic relationship as exploitative.[84]

But Castro would not take the bait. Later in the conference, he replied:

In the United States, Americans are taught that they gave Cuba its independence. I think that this teaching is wrong. The people of the United States should not be taught that, because although the United States did intervene at the end of our war of independence, we have our own opinions on that situation, our own assessments. We believe that Spain was defeated, Spain could not continue the war against Cuba. There was a ten-year war, then the 1895 war. Spain was completely exhausted, and that is when the U.S. intervention came. They occupied the country for a number of years; simultaneously, they occupied Puerto Rico and kept it; simultaneously they occupied the Philippines and kept it. In fact, McNamara was saying that some Americans feel that the United States was too generous because it did not keep Cuba. Cuba had great support in world public opinion; Cuba had fought heroically; and despite that, four years later, the United States imposed a government on us, and imposed the Platt Amendment. You know the Platt Amendment was an imposition. We were told: either you accept the Platt Amendment, or there is no independence. No country in the world would accept that kind of amendment in its constitution, because it gives the right to another country to intervene to establish peace. . . . I agree that there are different perceptions, and I think we should begin by checking to see what the different perceptions are on these questions; but I believe in any case what we've got to do is get to work, to see to it that the objective historical truth prevails.[85]

There is, of course, no such thing as "objective historical truth" on matters of interpretation, which always have an irreducibly subjective element.[86] What seems generous and benevolent to a large and powerful country is almost bound to seem meddling and paternalistic to a small and weak neighbor, particularly when differences in size and power are aggravated by profound differences in culture. "By defining its own role in the world as anti-imperial," writes Jules Benjamin, "the United States has made difficult any self-understanding of its acts of domination. North American scholars need to begin their study of U.S. expansion from a position outside the sway of this aspect of their culture."[87] But by the same token, Cubans wrongly imputed evil intent to every American policy that had an ill effect, and failed to appreciate that the concerns animating American policy during the Eisenhower and Kennedy administrations—ill founded though they were—had nothing to do with America's quasi-imperial past and reflected a profound if paradoxical insecurity. Misunderstandings such as these are bound to affect the relations between states. They did so in 1962 because Fidel Castro—a product of a history the United States and Cuba shared but understood very differently—conceived his mission once and for all to overthrow the laws of political gravitation so that Cuba could achieve an independence he believed the United States would never willingly grant.

FIDEL CASTRO v. JOHN F. KENNEDY
"I've always believed . . . that we knew the Americans better than the Soviets"

In chapter 1, we briefly sketched the spiral of fear and hostility that led to the steady deterioration in relations between the fledgling Castro regime and the United States between 1959 and 1962. Each side saw the other as a threat, interpreted each other's actions in ways that seemed to confirm their fears and suspicions, and took steps to protect themselves from each other that succeeded only in provoking countermeasures worsening their respective perceived predicaments. Kennedy's policy of isolation, harassment, and intimidation, designed in

large measure to contain communism in Cuba and prevent Soviet penetration of the hemisphere, forced Castro to turn to the Soviet Union
for protection, ultimately in the form of nuclear weapons. Castro's
policy of supporting revolutionary movements in Latin America—
directed only against governments hostile to Cuba—was intended in
large part to demonstrate the vulnerability of those governments to
internal subversion, so as to make them reconsider their hostility. But
this policy provided both the need and the justification for the policy
of isolation, harassment, and intimidation coordinated and led by the
United States.[88]

With the benefit of hindsight—particularly now that the Cold
War is over—this spiral, a function of what Wayne Smith called in the
conference the "chicken and egg problem," would seem almost comical
had it not brought the world to the brink of nuclear war. But it had
two other notable and possibly paradoxical effects as well: it helped
Castro consolidate his revolution domestically, and it made any meaningful political rapprochement between the United States and Cuba
difficult if not impossible. "Once the source of political opposition was
transferred from within the island to abroad," writes Louis Pérez, "the
defense of the revolution became synonymous with the defense of
national sovereignty":

> And once the question of sovereignty was invoked, a deep wellspring
> of national sentiment was tapped in behalf of the revolution. Nothing
> was as central to the character of Cuban nationality as this notion of
> struggle for self-determination and sovereignty. The national memory
> was long. It could, and did, recall times before when the quest for
> nationality was thwarted or otherwise compromised and subdued.
> The revolution was thus transformed at one and the same time into
> the means and the end of a historic process. The hour of redemption
> of *patria* was at hand. The United States could not have adopted a
> more ill-conceived approach through which to attack the revolution.
> Ignorance of the backlog of Cuban historic grievances blinded the
> United States to the reality that it was challenging the revolution at
> its strongest point—the point at which the past and present con-
> verged in the defense of *patria*.[89]

But Castro's response—openly declaring his commitment to Marxism-
Leninism and aligning Cuba with the Soviet Union—completed, for
Americans, the process of his political diabolization that began with
the first expropriations of American property in May 1959. Castro is

so deeply loathed in the United States that it would be virtually impossible for any American administration even today—more than thirty years later—to take measures, such as lifting the economic embargo, that could be perceived as saving the Castro regime.

Castro's Predicament: The Nuclear Solution

By all accounts, Kennedy's policy succeeded in convincing the Cuban leadership in 1962 that the United States sought not merely to isolate the Castro regime, but to destroy it. Thus Castro turned to the Soviet Union for help. He claims that it never occurred to him to ask for help in the form of strategic nuclear missiles, but that when the Soviets made the offer, he and his colleagues accepted the offer enthusiastically.

Scholars of the crisis have long debated Khrushchev's primary motivation for seeking to deploy nuclear missiles in Cuba, suggesting that he may have done so to deter an American attack against Cuba; to shore up the strategic nuclear imbalance; to assuage his sense of outrage at the deployment of American nuclear missiles in Turkey, just across the Black Sea from the Soviet Union; to buttress his negotiating position in Berlin; to fend off the Chinese threat to Soviet leadership of the socialist bloc; or to salvage his domestic political program.[90] Our reading of the available evidence and testimony suggests that he was operating on some combination of the first three, and that the question of which motivation was "primary" may be irresolvable, since Khrushchev would not necessarily have asked the question of himself.[91] But whatever his real motives, he presented the idea to Castro—and to Aleksandr Alekseev, his newly appointed ambassador to Cuba (replacing Sergei Kudriatsev, whom Castro considered "even more boring than the American ambassador, Philip Bonsal"[92])—as solely intended to defend the Cuban Revolution.[93]

Castro claims today that he believes Khrushchev's real motivation in proposing the deployment was to repair his missile gap with the United States. "In the light of what we know today about the real balance of power, or correlation of forces, it is evident that repairing it was an imperative. I don't criticize Khrushchev for the fact that he tried to improve the balance of forces. I think this is something legal, something legitimate in terms of international law, and absolutely moral: that is, to try to improve the balance of forces between the socialist camp and the United States. And if what they really had was fifty or sixty ICBMs, it is clear that the presence of those forty-two missiles almost doubled their effective capacity."[94] Moreover, Castro claims that "[i]f we had known about that balance of power, which we ignored—I repeat, if the conversation had been framed in terms of improving the balance of power—we might have advised them to be prudent. Because I think if you've got fifty, you've got to be more prudent than if you've got three hundred. This is clear, of course. If we had been familiar with that information, and if it had been put to us in strategic terms, we would have advised prudence."[95] Nuclear missiles were not absolutely necessary to deter an American attack, Castro insists. "The USSR could have stated that an aggression against Cuba was the equivalent of an aggression against the USSR. We could have signed a military agreement, and we would have been able to achieve the objective of Cuba's defense without missiles."[96] Deploying nuclear missiles in Cuba "would imply a very high political cost" in Latin America, Castro maintains, "and, therefore, if the issue had been the defense of Cuba, we would have preferred not to have the missiles. Alejandro was right when he said . . . that we would not accept it because it was presented to us as being for the defense of Cuba. But as we immediately perceived it, the purpose was strategic, even though they emphasized the argument of defending Cuba."[97]

Why, then, did Castro accept Khrushchev's offer? "We analyzed the issue, and all of us had the same interpretation: that the real issue was strategic; that it was imperative to strengthen the socialist camp, and that if we expected the socialist countries to fight for us, we, for simple reasons of image, could not selfishly refuse that cooperation to the socialist camp."[98] This is the line Cuban officials have consistently taken in public. And it is possible, of course, that Castro's claims are sincere. But there is another interpretation toward which we incline: namely, that Castro and his colleagues found the idea of a nuclear deployment attractive for two reasons: first, by deterring an American invasion, it would guarantee the safety of the revolution; and second—perhaps no less importantly—because it would be supremely gratifying. At one stroke the deployment would raise Cuba, for the first time, onto a geopolitical plane with "imperialism."

Why are we inclined to doubt Castro's protestations? In the first place, knowledgeable Cubans close to Castro in 1962 have reported in interviews that they were personally attracted to the deployment primarily because of its deterrent value.[99] This undercuts Castro's claim that the Cuban leadership in 1962 was unanimous in its understanding of the situation. Second, there is an unmistakable hubris in the statements of Cuban officials in September and October 1962 that betrays a gloating excitement about the still-secret deployment.[100] Given the intensity of their revolutionary passions and the strength of their anti-American feelings in 1962, it would indeed be surprising if the proposed deployment had not conjured up powerful emotions, some of which would seem base, unseemly, or puerile in retrospect. To use a precise if inelegant locution, acquiring nuclear missiles would have enabled Cuba to say to the United States once and for all: "In your face." Third, precisely because this sentiment is so unbecoming, the defense of Cuba's dignity, in which Castro is ever vigilant, would not permit Castro to admit to it today. Fourth, Cuba's pride is better served by a reconstruction of events that emphasizes the mutuality of the deployment than one which highlights Cuba's vulnerability to the United States, and its dependence upon the Soviet Union. Fifth, and finally, if Cuba's leaders had been attracted to the deployment for emotional and symbolic reasons, there would be fewer gaps, puzzles, and contradictions in Castro's story, and those that remained would be easier to understand. The official version simply seems to us too full of holes to hold much water.

What are these gaps, puzzles, and contradictions to which we refer? One is that Castro's stated motivation makes no sense given his reconstruction of his thought processes. The purpose of the deployment, he maintains, was to bolster socialism on the world scale. But by his own admission, he did not know that socialism *needed* bolstering on the world scale. "Perhaps you should have told us the number of missiles the Soviets had," Castro said to Ray Cline. "That would have been very good. If the satellites that you placed in orbit had photographed the missiles that the Soviets had, you could have told us. You would have done well." Castro went on to say:

> I thought that the Soviets had several hundred intercontinental missiles. Later it was said that they had reached 800 or 1,000—this was said publicly in many conversations. But the figures that were read out here yesterday—forty, fifty, sixty—those are low figures, actually. We imagined thousands, even more, because that was the impression that was created. . . . If we had known that this was the correlation of forces, we would have advised prudence. "Don't bring that kind of missile," I would have said, "because under these conditions you can't do that. You shouldn't do that. That's what I think." As a friend, as a true friend of the Soviets—as a brother—I would have said, "Don't do that."[101]

If Castro truly believed the Soviets had "several hundred intercontinental missiles," surely he should have asked himself why Khrushchev wanted to deploy more missiles in Cuba, since the deployment—which he claims was unnecessary for the defense of Cuba—would only exacerbate his relations with Latin America?

To avoid this awkward conclusion, Castro appeals to his deference to the Soviets:

We were very confident in the experience of the Soviet Union. We had practically just won against the Batista army—it was just two years after the end of our war. The Soviets, on the other hand, had decades of experience in diplomatic, international, and military matters. The Soviets were our very powerful ally. You simply could not compare our power with theirs. . . . We had unlimited confidence in them. When we had an opinion on something, we expressed it; but always on the basis of the idea that they had more experience than we did, and that they knew how to do things better.

Secondly, we also based our position on the fact that only they knew what the correlation of forces was between them and the United States. You've got to go back to these times, the months before those days. The conquest of space—don't you remember Gagarin's flight? Don't you remember the great Soviet might, when they first put a man in space with colossal rockets? Don't you remember when Nikita said that the Soviet Union had missiles that could hit a fly in the air? I'll never forget that statement. But what we did not know was how many missiles the Soviets had, how many the Americans had, how many planes, how many bombs on each side and so on, because in Nikita's public rhetoric you could see—you could detect—confidence, certainty, and strength. You've got to go back to those times to be able to understand this.[102]

Yet U.S. deputy secretary of defense Roswell Gilpatric, in a speech in Hot Springs, Virginia, seven months earlier, had publicly revealed that the United States enjoyed significant strategic nuclear superiority over the Soviet Union.[103] How likely is it that Cuba would have missed this signal in view of its preoccupation, following the Bay of Pigs, with assessing the American threat?

Khrushchev was "very astute," Castro recalls. "He was capable of talking about an issue in one set of terms, while thinking about it in other terms."[104] It is therefore somewhat surprising that Castro was so deferential. If Castro suspected that Khrushchev was misrepresenting his true motivations by suggesting that the purpose of the deployment was to defend the Cuban Revolution, why did he not also suspect that Khrushchev was using him? Why did it not bother him that Khrushchev might be lying? Why was he later surprised and angered that Khrushchev proposed to resolve the crisis by trading Soviet missiles in Cuba for American missiles in Turkey? And how is his deference to Khrushchev, illustrated most dramatically by his willingness to let Khrushchev decide whether or not to go public with the deployment as the temperature rose in the United States throughout August and September 1962, consistent with Castro's emphatic claim that "we knew the Americans better than the Soviets: their psychology, their actions, what they do, their history"?[105]

Nevertheless, it is clear that Castro and his associates *did* defer to the Soviets throughout the period leading up to the crisis. No doubt they did their best to convince Khrushchev that they saw the deployment as an act of solidarity with socialism so that they could claim that they, too, were contributing to and making sacrifices for a cause. Castro's public story about his motivations for accepting the deployment preserves Cuba's dignity and honor. But it is much easier to explain and to understand Castro's behavior by focusing on the simple visceral attraction that nuclear missiles held for Cuba. They would at one stroke bring to an end a long epoch of Cuban vulnerability to, and dependence upon, the United States. They would put Cuba, in Edmundo Desnoes's phrase, "on the summit." They would represent a tactical victory over John F. Kennedy, and a strategic victory over History. With such goals apparently within reach, how could Castro possibly resist? Why would he demur? Why should he ask questions? And why should he not use Khrushchev, just as he suspected Khrushchev was using him?

Khrushchev's Predicament: The Nuclear Problem

Castro is undoubtedly correct to suspect that Khrushchev had more than merely the defense of the Cuban Revolution in mind. Gilpatric's speech had undercut the entire basis of Khrushchev's haughty Cold War policy, which he had tried to conduct on the cheap by claiming a measure of nuclear strength that he did not possess in order to devote precious resources to his ambitious program of domestic reform. According to his son Sergei Khrushchev—an engineer who worked on the Soviet Union's early missile programs—technical difficulties had delayed the development of reliable and accurate long-range missiles and bombers, and Khrushchev had no prospect of quickly increasing the numbers of these systems deployed.[106] By transferring to Cuba shorter-range weapons already operational in central Europe, Khrushchev could patch up his own missile gap until longer-range systems became available in quantity.

Khrushchev's desire to deploy to Cuba both a significant nuclear force (for purposes of deterrence) and a full combat-ready conventional force (to shore up Cuba's defensive capacity)—and to do so secretly—posed great difficulties for Gen. Anatoly Gribkov and his associates who were charged with drawing up plans for Operation Anadyr and overseeing its implementation. The logistical effort that the operation would require was unprecedented in the annals of either Soviet or Russian military history. And it very nearly succeeded. Had local commanders not failed to take the appropriate camouflage measures, the United States might not have discovered the missiles before Castro and Khrushchev revealed them to a stunned world in Havana in late November 1962.[107]

Castro professes that the Soviets did not keep him informed of the details or the progress of the deployment. At the Havana conference, he expressed surprise at various aspects of General Gribkov's presentation. By all indications, he was completely out of the decision-making loop, and the one occasion on which he attempted to insert himself into that loop—when he proposed through Che Guevara and Emilio Aragonés that Cuba and the Soviet Union go public with the deployment—he was rebuffed, and accepted the rebuff demurely. If indeed, as Castro claims, "we knew the Americans better than the Soviets," then Khrushchev erred in shutting Castro out of the decision-making process. Castro himself suggests that he could have helped the Soviets avoid some of their more egregious mistakes (Castro mentions two: not making the deployment public, and providing insufficient tactical nuclear weapons to the Soviet ground troops in Cuba).[108]

According to Alekseev, "Khrushchev was firmly convinced that the operation could be carried out secretly and that the Americans would not find out. The only thing he advised was, 'Do not rush. Do everything in such a way that U.S. public opinion will not be aware of this until November 4th or after November 4th. After that there won't be any great difficulties. The Americans are going to have to swallow this the same way we have had to swallow the pill of the missiles in Turkey. We are two sovereign states, and when everything is ready in November, I will travel to Cuba and we will tell the world about this operation.' Khrushchev was convinced that the operation would not be discovered until it was complete. So he insisted. He said, 'We can do the same thing the Americans do. We can use the same methods.' "[109] The legality and apparent symmetry of the deployment may have led to wishful thinking on Khrushchev's part; he may have had undue confidence in his military; he may have underestimated American intelligence capabilities; but whatever the reason, he was confident that the deployment would go through undetected.[110] And he was equally confident that, while the United States would be forced to accept a *fait accompli,* it was important not to give the United States forewarning of the deployment.

Castro disagreed. "Secrecy put us at a disadvantage," he recalled; "both at a political disadvantage, and at a practical disadvantage":

> Not only was it a mistake to deploy the missiles secretly, which was damaging to us, but it was a mistake to give Kennedy false informa-tion, having gotten into the game of the character of the weapons: whether they were offensive or defensive. No, in none of the Cuban statements was there ever any participation in this game of the charac-ter of the weapons. We refused to play that game, and in the public statements of the government, and then at the U.N., we always said that Cuba considered that it had the sovereign right to have the kind of weapons it considered convenient, and that no one had any right to establish what kind of weapons our country could or could not have. . . .
>
> On the other hand, you've got to admit this, given that Khru-shchev did get into the game of categorizing the weapons: his basis for categorizing the weapons was the intention behind their deploy-ment. Since he did not have the intention of using the weapons in an offensive operation, he considered them defensive. The intention de-fined the character of the weapons. But it became clear that Kennedy didn't understand it that way. He did not understand this question of intentions. He was looking at the *kind* of weapons—whether or not they were strategic weapons. That was the issue. And it's perfectly clear that Kennedy was convinced that strategic weapons were not going to be transferred to Cuba. So I would say that he saw more than just cunning in this; he saw deception. The secret of the military agreement, and the deception, were two realities that were very dam-aging. I think that there should have been a different approach, not this attempt at deception. This was very damaging because Kennedy had a lot at stake. He had already had the Bay of Pigs setback. He was going into his second year. There were going to be elections. Khru-

shchev didn't want to affect these elections. Perhaps this was one of the things Khrushchev considered in not publishing the agreement; he didn't want to do anything to damage Kennedy in those elections. But he did the worst possible thing, given that what was being done could be discovered.[111]

Kennedy indeed made a great deal of Khrushchev's deception in his diplomatic response to the discovery of the missiles. And Castro is correct to note that Khrushchev played a dangerous game of semantics by affirming that the Soviet Union was sending no "offensive" weapons to Cuba, knowing full well what kinds of weapons concerned Kennedy. But it is far from clear that Kennedy would have tolerated the deployment of nuclear missiles to Cuba if Khrushchev had announced his intention to do so in advance. We are inclined to suspect that he would not.[112] Khrushchev's insistence on secrecy and his policy of deception clearly look like mistakes in hindsight; it is engaging to speculate, but impossible to know, whether they would have been so regarded had his *fait accompli* succeeded.

The interesting point for our purposes, however, is that Khrushchev was so fully committed to his gambit that he was unable to reassess it in midstream, and he was sufficiently disdainful of the Cubans that he did not give their view the serious attention it deserved. Emilio Aragonés relates his conversation with Khrushchev in Moscow thus: "[H]e said to Che and me, with Malinovsky in the room, 'You don't have to worry; there will be no big reaction from the U.S. And if there is a problem, we will send the Baltic fleet.'" Aragonés insists that Khrushchev was "totally serious. When he said it, Che and I looked at each other with raised eyebrows."[113] If indeed there would be "no big reaction from the U.S.," and if indeed sending the Baltic fleet would suffice to address any problem that arose, then clearly there was no particular reason not to make the deployment public at the outset. Khrushchev was either engaging in defensive avoidance,[114] or he was toying with the Cubans. Perhaps both. The last time the Baltic fleet left Russian waters on a distant mission—in 1904—it traveled 18,000 miles over eight months only to be annihilated by the Imperial Japanese Navy at the battle of Tsushima.[115] In 1962, the mismatch in the Caribbean would have been even greater. The Soviet Baltic fleet would have been completely incapable of offering timely or effective assistance. It is difficult to resist the conclusion that Khrushchev was being flippant.

Several other aspects of the Soviet deployment cast doubt upon the judgment of Khrushchev and his Soviet planners. At the Havana conference, Gribkov revealed for the first time that "[w]e planned to deploy two [naval] squadrons to Cuba: one squadron of surface ships, comprising two cruisers and two destroyers; and a squadron of submarines, comprising eleven submarines. These two squadrons never went to Cuba. They were scheduled to be sent out later."[116] This in itself would have constituted a major provocation, given the United States' historic concern with controlling the waters of the Caribbean and the approaches to the Panama Canal. The reader will recall that it was the danger that France or Britain might establish a significant naval presence in Cuba that prompted Monroe to proclaim his famous doctrine in 1823. And it is no accident that the United States and Britain were able to improve their historically rocky relationship only after London conceded control of the Caribbean and Western Atlantic to the U.S. Navy in the early twentieth century. A significant permanent Soviet naval deployment to Cuba in 1962, more likely than not, would have precipitated a major crisis in its own right.

The conferees were even more intrigued when told that the tactical *Luna* missiles that the Soviets brought into Cuba were equipped with nuclear weapons. This is most puzzling. The purpose of equipping the *Luna*s with nuclear warheads does not seem to have been deterrent, since there is no indication that the Soviets intended to disclose their presence. It makes little sense to see them as defensive, since they were too few to assure the defeat of a full-scale American invasion. Castro, it seems, is quite right to conclude that "[n]ine was not a very logical number."[117] It cannot be that the Soviet units sent to Cuba merely took along their standard *Luna* complements unbeknownst to the civilian leadership, because Khrushchev issued explicit orders with respect to their use. He therefore clearly knew about the tactical nuclear weapons.[118] Had he consulted Castro on the matter, he might have thought through the tactical nuclear deployment in greater detail.

But the U.S. delegation at the Havana conference was even more fascinated by Gribkov's account of Khrushchev's standing orders. "When I traveled to Cuba," recalled Gribkov, "I received the instructions of Defense Minister Malinovsky. I want to repeat the order literally. He said, 'Tell Pliyev the view of the High Command. The Statsenko [strategic] missile division must only go into action'—we have this Russian saying, 'let it go into action'—'only on an authorization from the Commander-in-Chief to use the [strategic] weapons. If you use the tactical weapons, it must be in the face of an invasion, that is, a penetration into Cuban territory.' "[119] What astounded the

U.S. delegation was that Khrushchev would have *pre-delegated* authority to use nuclear weapons in Cuba under any circumstances. This seemed to contradict everything any of us had ever known about Khrushchev and his aversion to nuclear war. It seemed to contradict Castro's own assessment of Khrushchev's character: "I don't think Nikita wanted war. I think nothing could have been further from his mind than a nuclear war. He was very much aware of what a nuclear war meant for the Soviet Union."[120]

In the corridors of the Palace of Congresses, Gribkov's claim led to a heated debate about his trustworthiness. The debate spilled over into print shortly after the conference, when, in two separate articles, John Newhouse and Arthur Schlesinger took opposite sides of the issue.[121] "With America holding all the high cards," Newhouse asked, "why would Khrushchev have added greatly to the risk of nuclear war— a prospect he feared at least as much as the Americans did—by giving Soviet commanders in Cuba the authority to use nuclear weapons?"[122] One might ask in reply, why did Khrushchev send *any* nuclear weapons to Cuba at all in 1962? *That* certainly added greatly to the risk of nuclear war.[123] Moreover, the tactical weapons had insufficient range to reach the United States; they could only be used against American forces in the event of an invasion, in which case Soviet and American forces would already be at war. When Khrushchev originally formulated his standing orders, he may well have imagined that by investing Pliyev with authority to use them he was not appreciably adding to nuclear risk.

This is, of course, pure speculation. We cannot even be confident that Gribkov accurately reported Khrushchev's initial order, let alone reconstruct the chain of thought that might have led to it. But the issue became even more complicated in November 1992, when Gen. Leonid Garbuz, Pliyev's deputy in 1962, claimed that, when the crisis broke out—and unbeknownst to Gribkov—Malinovsky rescinded Pliyev's authority to use tactical nuclear weapons. At first Gribkov denied Garbuz's claim, but later, in interviews with us and then in print, reversed his position. He claimed that, on 22 October, Malinovsky sent Pliyev a message "absolutely forbidding" the use of Soviet nuclear weapons of any kind, and that he reiterated the message in a second cable on 27 October.[124] Gribkov's new line accorded with the recent recollections of Col. Nikolai Beloborodov, the commander of the "central nuclear base" in Cuba.[125]

Should we now believe that Khrushchev invested Pliyev with the authority to decide on his own whether or not to use tactical nuclear weapons in case of an American invasion? Gribkov's story as originally related at the Havana conference is less than fully compelling. We are concerned, for example, by discrepancies between his account of the number of nuclear warheads shipped to Cuba and the accounts of others (for example, Gen. Dimitry Volkogonov's at the 1989 Moscow conference, and Dokuchaev's in the 6 November 1992 issue of *Red Star*). We are also concerned by discrepancies between some of Gribkov's claims and information obtained by independent intelligence sources (in hallway discussions in Havana, for example, Gribkov seemed to deny that the Soviet merchant ship *Poltava* carried nuclear warheads to Cuba; but the CIA had independent evidence that the Soviets had loaded nuclear weapons aboard *Poltava* in Odessa).[126] But we are equally troubled by the revised story Gribkov embraced several months later. While Garbuz would have been in a position to know the details of Marshal Malinovsky's communications with Pliyev during the crisis itself (whereas Gribkov would not), and thus while his claim that Khrushchev rescinded Pliyev's pre-delegated authority on 22 October seems *prima facie* credible, we have not as yet seen any documentation supporting Garbuz's claim, nor is this the only revision to Gribkov's original story that we are now being asked to believe. We are now told that the Soviets shipped *102* tactical nuclear warheads to Cuba in 1962, not nine as Gribkov originally reported in Havana: twelve for the *Luna* missiles; eighty for tactical cruise missiles; four nuclear mines; and— most astoundingly—six for the Il-28 bombers. If this is so, then the Kennedy administration was certainly correct to insist upon the removal of the Il-28s, as they had sufficient range to reach the southeastern United States with a nuclear payload. But surely Gribkov, in his role as planner of Operation Anadyr, would have been aware of this information himself, and could have reported it to the conferees in Havana. It is curious that he did not. Moreover, throughout our investigation of the crisis, we have always been told—and Gribkov reiterated in Havana—that the Soviets never intended to provide the Il-28s with nuclear capability. We are also now told that on 26 October, Pliyev ordered Soviet nuclear warheads in Cuba dispersed and moved closer to their launch vehicles.[127] This claim is unprecedented. We have been unable to corroborate it, and we do not know what to make of it. It is difficult to understand why Khrushchev would have authorized such a move. Among other things, if U.S. intelligence had detected the movement of strategic nuclear warheads from storage sites toward missile bases, they would have interpreted it as a most threatening development, and President Kennedy would have faced considerable pressure to attack the strategic nuclear missile sites before the missiles could be armed.

In the course of seeking to resolve the uncertainty surrounding issues such as these, we sought further testimony—and supporting documentation—from Moscow. We do not consider them settled. Most of our efforts have been devoted to sorting out the confusion surrounding Pliyev's standing orders, and it is clear that the full story has yet to be told. To date, we have seen no original documentation or facsimiles of documents. The only precise quotations of, and citations to, documents in the General Staff archives that we have seen confirm Gribkov's original claim that Khrushchev invested Pliyev with pre-delegated authority to use tactical nuclear weapons in the event of a U.S. invasion of Cuba. We are therefore inclined to believe that aspect of Gribkov's account. However, it is plausible—and the weight of authoritative testimony now indeed suggests—that if Khrushchev did so, he rescinded it on 22 October. While we must await further documentation on Khrushchev's rescindment before we accept it as fact, it is worth noting that if Garbuz's modification to Gribkov's story is accurate, the implications for policy makers and students of decision making are both fascinating and disturbing. In essence, Garbuz and Gribkov now claim that Khrushchev perceived little risk in pre-delegating authority to use tactical nuclear weapons in the planning stages of the deployment, but perceived grave risks in the heat of the crisis itself. If a leader's judgments of risk depend critically upon the context in which those judgments are made, it would seem a difficult if not hopeless task to anticipate a leader's crisis behavior.[128]

Should the uncertainty surrounding Gribkov's testimony lead us to reconsider Robert McNamara's conclusion that the crisis was even more dangerous, and that the world came even closer to nuclear war in 1962, than we had previously thought? Yes and no. There are no serious grounds for questioning Gribkov's claim that there were tactical nuclear weapons for the *Luna* missiles in Cuba. No knowledgeable Soviet has ever denied it, and the fact that the CIA had independent evidence confirming the loading of warheads of some type aboard a ship bound for Cuba indicates that Khrushchev had been willing to send nuclear warheads of some type to Cuba; there was therefore no particular reason for him not to send tactical nuclear warheads. If the United States had invaded Cuba, the presence of Soviet tactical nuclear weapons most certainly would have increased the dangers of nuclear war, whether or not Khrushchev had pre-delegated authority to use them, because there was some finite probability that Soviet forces in Cuba would have taken the warheads from their storage sites, mated them to the *Luna* missiles, and fired them at American troops. We cannot know how large this probability would have been (intuitively, it would have been greater if Khrushchev had pre-delegated authority than if he had not); nor can we know the probability that a Soviet use of tactical nuclear weapons would have escalated to higher levels of nuclear destruction. But we *can* know that both of these probabilities would have been *zero* if there had been no tactical nuclear warheads on the island at all, and some probability is higher than none. On the other hand, if Kennedy refused to authorize an American invasion, the issue would have been moot. McNamara has consistently claimed that he thinks it highly unlikely Kennedy would have authorized an invasion of Cuba while the Soviet Union had conventional and nuclear forces stationed there. We agree.[129] "Highly unlikely" and "impossible" are two different things, however; logically, therefore, we are forced to conclude that the presence of tactical nuclear weapons in Cuba increased the risks of nuclear war between the superpowers, if perhaps only marginally.

Khrushchev believed the Cuban deployment would solve his predicament. On 22 October, when he received an advance copy of President Kennedy's speech, he learned that it had merely made it acute. Not only was the Soviet Union no better off strategically on 22 October than it had been before Operation Anadyr began—it was worse off. The missiles Khrushchev sought to install in Cuba secretly had been taken from deployed positions in the western Soviet Union, and were temporarily unavailable for service. Not only were Cuba's defenses still under construction, but the surprise discovery of the missiles had given Kennedy both the occasion and the excuse to attack. If Kennedy attacked, the Soviet forces in Cuba would have nowhere to run. They would be forced to fight or surrender. They had nuclear warheads. They might seek to use them before they were destroyed. If they did, Kennedy would face tremendous pressure to respond in kind. Even if they did not, Khrushchev would face tremendous pressure to respond somehow, somewhere in the world, to the American attack. He had grossly miscalculated. He had misjudged the Americans. He had overestimated his own military. He had stuck his neck out in Cuba, and it began to look as though he had caught it in an American noose. He should have listened to Troyanovsky. He should have listened to Castro.

But it was too late. His overriding concern now was to prevent a catastrophe.

The story of Khrushchev's handling of the crisis has been told before. The Havana conference added little to it, and we make no effort to recount it here.[130] Its salient features are Khrushchev's intense search for a face-saving solution and his strenuous effort to avoid provocative action. Gribkov reports that "[n]one of the missiles was placed in combat readiness. They had not yet been fueled, nor supplied with oxidating agents. The warheads were some 250 or 300 kilometers from the launch sites, and had not yet been released for use."[131] Troyanovsky recalls Kuznetsov suggesting to Khrushchev "that, in response to the pressure exerted by the Americans around Cuba, we had to respond by exerting pressure in some other place, preferably around Berlin," to which Khrushchev replied "quite harshly, saying that we did not need that kind of advice."[132] Raymond Garthoff reports that "[t]he United States later received information from a reliable Soviet source that the Soviet leadership had decided not to go to war over Cuba even if America invaded, and formalized that decision in a signed top secret Central Committee directive."[133] This would be consistent with the overall tenor of Khrushchev's behavior during the crisis.

The events of 27 October convinced Khrushchev to cut his losses and get out of the crisis with a public conditional American pledge not to invade Cuba and a secret American pledge to withdraw Jupiter missiles from Turkey, and possibly also from Italy. The relevant events included the unauthorized shoot-down of an American U-2 over Cuba; an incident over the Chukhotsk peninsula in eastern Siberia in which Soviet fighters intercepted (but did not shoot down) another U-2 that strayed off course while on a routine air-sampling mission; and messages from the Soviet ambassadors in Washington and Havana indicating that an American attack against Cuba was imminent.[134] Castro's cable of 26 October, which Khrushchev interpreted as a call for a preemptive nuclear strike, probably played a role as well.

According to Troyanovsky, Khrushchev and his advisers met at the climax of the crisis to assess their next move. General Ivanov was called to the phone, "and when he came back he said that a message had been received saying that Kennedy would once again speak at 1700 hours, Moscow time [28 October]. Everyone agreed that Kennedy intended to declare war, to launch an attack. A telegram was sent to the Embassy in Washington to verify this. . . . We had the feeling then that there was very little time to unravel what was taking place."[135] Khrushchev hurriedly drafted a message to Kennedy agreeing to withdraw Soviet missiles from Cuba. He did so without informing or consulting Fidel. He thereby solved his own predicament without regard for Castro's.

FIDEL CASTRO v. NIKITA KHRUSHCHEV
"You have to be resolute, or else you will be defeated"

In the heat of crisis, Khrushchev was no more inclined to bring Castro into the decision-making process than he had been beforehand. He sent Castro copies of his messages to Kennedy and U Thant in the early stages of the confrontation, but at no point did he actively seek Castro's advice on how to manage the crisis. Nor, as the crisis reached its crescendo, did Khrushchev keep Castro informed of the flurry of secret meetings between Anatoly Dobrynin and Robert Kennedy in Washington in which the U.S.-Soviet agreement bringing the crisis to an end gradually took shape.[136] Nor did Khrushchev forewarn Castro of his 27 October public missile-trade proposal, or of his agreement the following day to withdraw the missiles from Cuba.[137]

It is not surprising, in retrospect, that as tensions rose, Khrushchev played his cards close to his chest and jealously guarded his decision-making autonomy. Kennedy did the same. Only a few of the president's closest advisers—men whose views he knew and shared—were aware of the full details of the meetings between Robert Kennedy and Dobrynin, or of the president's decision on 27 October to prepare a contingency whereby, upon a further signal from the White House, Andrew Cordier, president of Columbia University, would prompt U Thant to propose a Turkish-Cuban missile trade, presented as a U.N. initiative, that Kennedy could quickly accept. In neither case did Kennedy inform or consult the ExComm as a whole.[138] At the height of the crisis, Kennedy and Khrushchev did not care to hear advice from, or waste precious time debating with, those whose views seemed to them dangerous and irresponsible. Only they bore ultimate responsibility for their nations and the world as the superpowers teetered on the brink; for that very reason—almost by definition, and certainly as a matter of psychological fact—no one else was qualified to judge what was to be done. Khrushchev expressed the sentiment best to Norman Cousins in a conversation several months after the crisis. The Soviet military had opposed the withdrawal of the missiles, Khrushchev said, and when he asked them whether they could guarantee that a refusal to withdraw the missiles would not lead to global nuclear war, they looked at him "as though I were out of my mind or, what was worse, a traitor. So I said to myself, 'To hell with these maniacs.' "[139]

From Khrushchev's perspective, Castro was clearly behaving like a maniac, first by opening fire on American aircraft as the crisis peaked, and then by issuing a call (as Khrushchev understood it) for a preemptive nuclear strike. In the confusion of the moment, Khrushchev also appears to have suspected that Castro was somehow responsible for the downing of Major Anderson's U-2 on 27 October.[140] It is hardly surprising that he kept Castro out of the decision-making process at the height of the crisis, when time was of the essence, not only because of the long delays they were experiencing in communicating with each other, but also because he knew that Castro would only complicate matters. Khrushchev was right. He was wise to exclude Castro. As Castro himself admits, if he had been a party to the negotiations he would have insisted, at a minimum, upon conditions that Kennedy most certainly could not have accepted, such as a withdrawal from Guantánamo Bay and an end to the economic embargo.[141]

Castro was, and clearly remains, furious at Khrushchev's handling of the crisis. "[J]udging by the letter Nikita sent me on the 23rd," Castro says, "I didn't see the slightest indication that he would solve the problem simply by caving in to American demands."[142]

> [W]e didn't know that Khrushchev had sent that message to Kennedy on the 26th, broaching the possibility of withdrawing the missiles in exchange for guarantees. We didn't know that the solution was already taking shape. When he sent the letter to Kennedy, he could have sent us a copy saying, "I've sent this letter to Kennedy." And then we would have at least been informed; if not consulted, at least informed. I believe that on the 27th, when he sent the Turkish letter, as I call it, he could have sent us a copy, and we would have been informed that Turkey was part of this negotiation. We didn't know anything about this.[143]

But Castro clearly would not have been satisfied with merely being informed of Khrushchev's proposals. He would have actively campaigned against them, and Khrushchev would have feared that Castro would do whatever he could to frustrate the delicate agreement that was taking shape.

Khrushchev's great fear, of course, was that Castro would succeed in somehow provoking an American attack on Cuba. Castro gives us no reason today to doubt that Khrushchev's fear was well founded. At the very least, if Khrushchev had followed Castro's wishes, the risks would have risen dramatically. "In Cuito Cuanavale, a crisis situation emerged which forced us to send an enormous amount of forces, and we did this resolutely," Castro recalls, delving, as he does so frequently, into historical analogy. "You have to be resolute, or else you will be defeated."[144] "[I]f this whole operation had been carried out with the same resolution [as the shooting down of the U-2], the outcome would have been different, and it would not have been war. The fact is that often it's hesitation that can lead to war, not firmness."[145] Firmness, at the height of the crisis, would have meant refusing to withdraw the missiles except under conditions that the United States simply would not have accepted. Khrushchev knew this. It is therefore curious that Castro insisted that the outcome "would not have been war," especially in view of the fact that in the very first sentence of his 26 October letter to Khrushchev, Castro said, "From an analysis of the situation and the reports in our possession, I consider that the aggression is almost imminent within the next 24 or 72 hours."[146] Castro continued by claiming that "[t]here are two possible variants: the first and likeliest one is an air attack against certain targets with the limited objective of destroying them; the second, less probable although possible, is invasion."[147] An invasion, Castro insists, would have meant nuclear war: "[W]e started from the assumption that if there was an invasion of Cuba, nuclear war would erupt. We were certain of that. If the invasion took place in the situation that had been created, nuclear war would have been the result. Everybody here was simply resigned to the fate that we would be forced to pay the price, that we would disappear."[148] Moreover, Castro admits, "I would have agreed to the use of nuclear weapons. Because, in any case, we took it for granted that it would become a nuclear war anyway, and that we were going to disappear. Before having the country occupied—totally occupied—we were ready to die in the defense of our country. I would have agreed, in the event of the invasion that you are talking about, with the use of tactical nuclear weapons. . . . I wish we had had the tactical nuclear weapons. It would have been wonderful."[149]

Resigned to his fate, Castro had no fear. "[I]f we are going to rely on fear," Castro said, "we would never be able to prevent a nuclear war. The danger of nuclear war has to be eliminated by other means; it cannot be prevented on the basis of fear of nuclear weapons, or that human beings are going to be deterred by the fear of nuclear weapons. We have lived through the very singular experience of becoming practically the first target of those nuclear weapons: no one lost their equanimity or their calm in the face of such a danger, despite the fact that the self-preservation instinct is supposed to have been more powerful."[150] But Khrushchev did not share Castro's fatalistic calm. His self-preservation instinct was alive and well. He completely disagreed with Castro's entire view of the confrontation, with two exceptions: he agreed that an American attack might be imminent, and he, too, strongly believed that an attack would lead to nuclear war.

It is therefore obvious in retrospect that Castro's letter to Khrushchev was bound to backfire. Castro spoke at length during the conference about his intentions in writing the letter:

We in Cuba had taken all the steps that were humanly possible. We had talked with the Soviet General Staff, we explained our views. There were other things I said that may come up sometime later. And when we finished all that, I asked myself, "What is still to be done? What remains to be done? What can I do? What is the last thing I can do?" And I dared to write a letter to Nikita, a letter aimed at encouraging him. That was my intention. The aim was to strengthen him morally, because I knew that he had to be suffering greatly, intensely. I thought I knew him well. I thought I knew what he was thinking and that he must have been at that time very anxious over the situation.

So I decided to write that letter—a letter, as I said, aimed at encouraging him. You see, I had other fears, really: I was afraid that there'd be mistakes, hesitations, because I was already seeing that mistakes were being made, and there were signs of hesitation. I proposed some ideas as to what should be done in the event, not of an air strike, but of an invasion of Cuba in an attempt to occupy it. . . . [I]f there was an invasion, and if war erupted, I thought that then the mistakes of the Second World War should not be repeated. I was very much concerned that, for either political or subjective reasons, the same mistake that they had made during the Second World War would be repeated. And this is what inspired my letter. I wanted to say, "If this happens, there shouldn't be any hesitation. We should not allow for a repetition of the events of the Second World War."[151]

Khrushchev's account is as follows:

Castro suggested that in order to prevent our own nuclear missiles from being destroyed, we should launch a preemptive strike against the United States. He concluded that an attack was unavoidable and that this attack had to be preempted. In other words, we needed to immediately deliver a nuclear missile strike against the United States. When we read this I, and all the others, looked at each other, and it became clear to us that Fidel totally failed to understand our purpose. Only then did I realize that our friend Castro, whom I respect for his honesty and directness, had failed to understand us correctly. We had installed the missiles not for the purpose of attacking the United States, but to keep the United States from attacking Cuba.[152]

Castro crafted the letter to address what he feared most at that moment: Khrushchev's weakness and irresolution. Khrushchev saw in Castro's letter what *he* feared most: warning of an imminent American attack,[153] and confirmation of Castro's recklessness. The letter intended to buttress Khrushchev's resolve helped to push Khrushchev in the other direction.

In chapter 1, we briefly described the reaction inside Cuba to the news on 28 October that Khrushchev had agreed to withdraw the missiles. Castro was absolutely stunned. He recalls feeling "humiliated."[154] His initial reply to Khrushchev, however, was surprisingly moderate. He justified his decision to authorize his air-defense forces to fire on American aircraft on 26 October by appealing to the importance of preventing a surprise attack, but he agreed not to open fire "for as long as the negotiations last and without revoking the declaration published yesterday about the decision to defend our airspace." He informed Khrushchev that he was "in principle opposed to an inspection of our territory," but expressed his appreciation for "the efforts you have made to keep the peace and we are absolutely in agreement with the need for struggling for that goal. If this is accomplished in a just, solid and definitive manner, it will be an inestimable service to humanity."[155] The sparks began to fly, however, when Castro received a long letter from Khrushchev on 30 October attempting to justify the decision to withdraw the missiles in return for what Castro, unaware of the Jupiter side-payment, regarded as an empty promise from Kennedy not to invade.

Khrushchev's letter pushed all the wrong buttons. Castro saw himself as one with the Cuban people in their revolutionary struggle; Khrushchev insisted that "we, political and government figures, are leaders of a people who doesn't know everything and can't readily comprehend all that we leaders must deal with." Castro fumed that Khrushchev had neither informed nor consulted him during his negotiations with Kennedy; Khrushchev wrote, "[W]e believe that we consulted with you, dear Comrade Fidel Castro, receiving the cables, each one more alarming than the next [sic], and finally your cable of October 27 [sic], saying you were nearly certain that an attack on Cuba would be launched. . . . Wasn't this consultation on your part with us? . . . If we had continued our consultations, we would have wasted time and this attack would have been carried out." Castro denies that he had called for a preemptive strike against the United States; Khrushchev's letter stated, "In your cable of October 27 you proposed that we be the first to launch a nuclear strike against the territory of the enemy. You, of course, realize where that would have led. Rather than a simple strike, it would have been the start of a thermonuclear world war. Dear Comrade Fidel Castro, I consider this proposal of yours incorrect, although I understand your motivation." Khrushchev had attempted to persuade Castro to accept the deployment of Soviet forces in Cuba in the first place on the ground that they were necessary for Cuba's defense; in his letter, Khrushchev now stated, "Even after the dismantling of the missile installations you will have powerful weapons to throw back the enemy, on land, in the air and on the sea, in the approaches to the island." By agreeing to dismantle the missiles, Castro felt Khrushchev had demonstrated his unwillingness to stand by Cuba in the face of a serious American threat; but in his letter, Khrushchev said, "we want to assure the Cuban people that we stand at their side and we will not forget our responsibility to help the Cuban people. It is clear to everyone that this is an extremely serious warning to the enemy on our part." Castro felt that Cuba could not rely for its security upon Kennedy's mere promise; Khrushchev did nothing to assuage this fear, essentially contradicting himself on the point: "You . . . stated during the rallies that the United States can't be trusted. That, of course, is correct. . . . The main thing we have secured is preventing aggression on the part of your foreign enemy at present. We feel that the aggressor came out the loser. He made preparations to attack Cuba but we stopped him and forced him to recognize before world public opinion that he won't do it at the current stage." Castro saw the withdrawal as a defeat; Khrushchev said, "We view this as a great victory." But the bitterest pill of all was that Khrushchev, who had ignored Castro's views at every stage, had the audacity to say, "We . . . view your statements on the conditions of the talks with the United States as correct. . . . Now, as the talks to settle the conflict get underway, I ask you to send me your considerations. For our part, we will continue to report to you on the developments of these talks and make all necessary consultations."[156]

In his reply the following day, Castro exploded:

> Countless eyes of Cuban and Soviet men who were willing to die with supreme dignity shed tears upon learning about the surprising, sudden and practically unconditional decision to withdraw the weapons. . . . We knew, and do not presume that we ignored it, that we would have been annihilated, as you insinuate in your letter, in the event of nuclear war. However, that didn't prompt us to ask you to withdraw the missiles, that didn't prompt us to ask you to yield.

Castro then savaged Khrushchev for his "misinterpretation" of his 26 October letter:

> I did not suggest, Comrade Khrushchev, that in the midst of this crisis the Soviet Union should attack, which is what your letter seems to say; rather, that following an imperialist attack, the USSR should act without vacillation and should never make the mistake of allowing circumstances to develop in which the enemy makes the first nuclear strike against the USSR. . . . You may be able to convince me that I am wrong, but you can't tell me that I am wrong without convincing me.

In other words, Castro called for a preemptive nuclear strike only *after* an American invasion had begun (a fine distinction from Khrushchev's perspective, when he feared that such an invasion was imminent).

On the subject of consultation, Castro merely said:

> I do not see how you can state that we were consulted in the decision you took.

And finally—in what must surely be one of the most tortured juxtapositions in the annals of diplomatic correspondence—Castro ended his broadside thus:

> There are not just a few Cubans, as has been reported to you, but in fact many Cubans who are experiencing at this moment unspeakable bitterness and sadness.
>
> The imperialists are talking once again of invading our country,

which is proof of how ephemeral and untrustworthy their promises are. Our people, however, maintain their indestructible will to resist the aggressors and perhaps more than ever need to trust in themselves and in that will to struggle.

We will struggle against adverse circumstances, we will overcome the current difficulties and we will come out ahead, and nothing can destroy the ties of friendship and the eternal gratitude we feel toward the USSR.[157]

Castro was furious; but he would not break with Khrushchev. As he told the conferees, he wanted "to avoid any further accumulation of bitterness in the relations between the Soviets and us. . . . [W]e had very close economic relations with the Soviets. The entire life of the country, the energy of the country, depended on the Soviets."[158] He simply could not afford to jeopardize Khrushchev's patronage, even if the crisis had demonstrated unambiguously that the Soviets would not jeopardize their security for the sake of Cuba.

Though unwilling to break with Khrushchev, Castro felt no obligation to make things easier for him, either. It seems he received some gratification from refusing to facilitate the conclusion of the U.S.-Soviet agreement, in particular by declining to allow U.N. inspectors to verify the removal of Soviet missiles from Cuban soil. "[W]e could not accept inspection," Castro insisted. "We could not. I think that would have diminished our sovereignty. The withdrawal of the missiles had already diminished our sovereignty, because the commitment never to reintroduce these weapons meant that we could not have them. That was a commitment we did not make. But the only country that could supply us those weapons was the Soviet Union; so, in fact, certain kinds of weapons were prohibited to us. We couldn't agree with that because we have a strong sense of sovereignty, a very deep-rooted sense; this is evident in all our materials and documents throughout our history, even those that are not public knowledge. We saw inspection as a humiliation of the country, because it wasn't necessary, in fact."[159]

It fell to First Deputy Premier Anastas Mikoyan to enlist Castro's cooperation in the resolution of the crisis, and Castro took additional gratification in making Mikoyan squirm—for instance, by giving him a frosty reception; by disappearing in the middle of negotiations for days on end; and by waxing allegorical at the Zapata swamps, likening the crocodiles to the superpowers, and the small fish they ate to countries like Cuba.[160] Castro seized every opportunity he could to let the Soviets know that they had let the Cuban Revolution down.

Every cloud has its silver lining, however. "[W]e did have one victory," Castro declares, "which was weapons free of charge. Before that, they were sold to us on credit. But because of the crisis—well, first, the weapons that were left here, we got those free. And then after that, for almost thirty years, we received our weapons and arms free from the Soviet Union. This was one of the positive aspects of the October crisis. So, we didn't want to make relations bitter. Who could profit from that? No one was going to profit from that. We simply had to control that anger."[161]

FIDEL CASTRO v. THE FUTURE
"Now, the United States is betting that we won't survive, and we are betting that we will"

Jorge Domínguez writes that in the wake of the Cuban missile crisis, the United States, the Soviet Union, and Cuba gradually established and refined a set of tacit norms, rules, and procedures, whose central purpose was to prevent a nuclear war, and which he collectively refers to as a "security regime."[162] This regime limited the numbers and types of weapons the Soviets could introduce to Cuba; committed the United States not to invade Cuba as long as the Soviet Union observed those limits (and as long as Cuba itself did not provide an independent *casus belli*); and committed all three countries to formal and informal communication and consultations so as to enhance security and build mutual confidence in the stability of the trilateral security relationship. On several occasions, as the three countries explored the boundaries of the regime, minor crises erupted or threatened to erupt: for example, when the Soviet Union probed the extent to which the United States would tolerate the presence of Soviet submarines in Cuban ports between 1970 and 1972; when the USSR provided Cuba with advanced MiG-23 aircraft in 1978; and when the United States "discovered" a Soviet combat brigade in Cuba in 1979.[163] All of these mini-crises were successfully resolved.

What the trilateral security regime did *not* do was regulate Cuban foreign policy in other respects. And for thirty years Castro sought to craft and pursue a foreign policy that would (in approximate order of importance) safeguard the Cuban Revolution, facilitate domestic development, and contribute to social justice abroad. It was important for Castro that Cuba be seen to have an *independent* foreign policy, for the sake of its national honor (something Castro has always felt acutely), even though Cuba depended heavily upon the generosity of the Soviet Union for its well-being and its safety. Thus Castro actively sought membership in, and at one point attained the leadership of, the so-called Non-Aligned Movement, which appeared to many observers to involve an obvious logical absurdity in view of Cuba's relationship with the Soviet Union.

In pursuit of this foreign policy, however, Castro repeatedly ran into opposition from *both* superpowers. That he ran into opposition from the United States is hardly surprising. Relations between Castro and successive American administrations were never cordial. The U.S. economic embargo remained firmly in place. For much of the post-crisis period, the two countries did not even exchange representatives. And, during the Reagan presidency, the two countries appeared more than once to be on the verge of open hostilities; for example, in October 1981, when Cuba mobilized in anticipation of an American attack, and in October 1983, when, during the U.S. invasion of Grenada, Cuban soldiers did battle with American troops.[164] Even today, in the depths of an acute economic crisis, Cuba devotes an astounding proportion of its resources to defense against an American attack. According to Castro, Cuba had only one respite from American hostility throughout the entire period: "We had a slight breathing space as a result of the Vietnam war. The United States was seriously committed in the Vietnam war. For several years, they had to send half a million men out there. They were involved in that war, and this was what you might call a breathing space for our country, because it was no longer the main objective of U.S. foreign policy."[165] During that war, Cuba did what it could for the North Vietnamese—and not merely out of empathy. As Che Guevara wrote in a 1967 letter to the Tricontinental Conference, "It is not a matter of wishing success to the victim of aggression, but of sharing his fate; one must accompany him to his death or to his victory."[166]

It is perhaps rather more surprising that Cuba has had such a difficult relationship with the Soviet Union. This was a function both of ideological differences and of national pride. "As important as Soviet aid was to Cuba's survival," writes Carla Anne Robbins, "the Cubans still did not hesitate to criticize their Soviet allies when Soviet policies appeared to diverge from Cuban ideals of internationalist behavior. The Cubans apparently saw themselves as the conscience of the socialist bloc."[167] Cuba promoted a theory of armed struggle, codified in Régis Debray's handbook for guerrilla warfare, *Revolution in the Revolution?*

(published in Havana in January 1967), which represented a direct challenge not only to the traditional Latin American communist parties' line, but also to the Soviet Union's position as leader in the revolutionary struggle.[168] Matters came to a head in 1968 when, in response to Castro's public criticisms of Soviet policy and doctrine, and in the wake of Castro's purge of a "microfaction" of the Cuban communist party with particularly close ties to Moscow, Soviet chairman Leonid Brezhnev reduced oil shipments to Cuba, and temporarily suspended military aid and technical assistance.[169] These measures—and the Soviet invasion of Czechoslovakia that same year—led Castro to mute his criticisms of the Soviet Union and, according to Domínguez, resulted in the reestablishment of Soviet "hegemony." Whether or not the word accurately describes the relationship between the two countries (it connotes a degree of control over Cuba that the Soviet Union probably never exerted), it did not take long for Cuba to learn that it would not find in Moscow's protection and patronage the freedom and respect that it had craved while under Washington's thumb.

The Soviet invasion of Czechoslovakia to crush its reformist government's liberalization program and reimpose socialist orthodoxy poignantly illustrated the constraints under which Castro operated as a Soviet client. The intervention pinned Castro on the horns of a dilemma. On the one hand, he found it difficult to approve the violation of a small state's sovereignty by a large state. This was the essence of his brief against American policy toward Cuba. On the other, he could neither afford to antagonize the Soviet Union at a time when relations between Havana and Moscow were already under severe strain, nor could he condemn the invasion too harshly without implicitly undercutting his claim that the Soviet Union had a duty to come to the defense of socialism wherever and whenever it was threatened.[170] On 23 August, Castro addressed the Cuban people on the subject. Noting that "some of the things we are about to say are in some cases in conflict with the emotions of many," he accepted "the bitter necessity that required sending those troops into Czechoslovakia."[171] There can be no question that that was a difficult statement for Castro to make. Had he been able to voice his true sentiments, no doubt he would have railed against the invasion in much the same tones as he railed against the American invasions of Grenada in 1983 and Panama in 1989. It was a hard lesson for Castro—that patronage has its price.

Though forced of necessity to suppress his objections to Brezhnev's foreign policy, Castro nonetheless managed to carve out something of an independent international role. From time to time the

Soviets would express their doubts and concerns about Castro's activities abroad—most notably, in Angola, Ethiopia, and Latin America.[172] "You can't imagine the reprimand the Soviets sent us because of our aid to the revolutionary movement in Venezuela," Castro remarks. "They were completely against our support for the revolutionary movement, and we were doing nothing on behalf of the Soviets. The Soviets had nothing to do with our aid for the revolutionary movement in Nicaragua, nor did they have anything to do with the force we sent to Angola in 1975. All we got from the Soviet Union was concern."[173] Nevertheless, there is little evidence that Castro felt constrained by Moscow's protestations. Cuba began to move one way, the Soviet Union another. The two countries were content to keep up the appearance of a happy marriage, but an increasing number of irreconcilable differences caused them inexorably to drift apart. In an interview with the Mexican newspaper *El Sol,* Raúl Castro recently revealed a major turning point: Brezhnev's flat refusal, following the election of Ronald Reagan in 1980, to accommodate Cuba's request to declare that the Soviet Union would not tolerate an American attack against Cuba. "We can't fight in Cuba because you are 11,000 kilometers away from us," the Soviets replied to Cuba's query. "Are we going to go all that way just to have our faces smashed?"[174] Nor would the Soviet Union demonstrate its support for Daniel Ortega's embattled Sandinista regime, the primary target of Reagan's effort to "roll back" communism on the periphery by creating, arming, and supporting revolutionary movements. Castro was so enraged at Constantin Chernenko's refusal even to send a flotilla to Nicaraguan waters to show the Soviet flag that, according to Nicola Miller, he refused both to attend Chernenko's March 1985 funeral and to sign the book of condolences at the Soviet embassy in Havana.[175]

The most serious rift, of course, followed in the wake of Mikhail Gorbachev's policies of perestroika (restructuring) and glasnost (openness). At the very moment when the Soviet Union turned to market incentives and political liberalization to solve its economic predicament, Castro turned the opposite way to solve his. His program of "rectification" reaffirmed socialist economic orthodoxy, and relied strictly on moral incentives.[176] Castro came to despise Gorbachev, although, at the Havana conference, he exercised notable restraint on the subject (perhaps because some members of the Russian delegation, such as Sergo Mikoyan and Sergei Khrushchev, were strong supporters of Gorbachev). Gorbachev was worse than a heretic, from Castro's perspective: he was a failure.

Castro clearly believes that the collapse of the Soviet Union vindicated his view that Gorbachev's reforms were ill conceived, and therefore doomed. Castro is clearly convinced of the wisdom of the path he has taken. Yet he knows that he is hardly in a position to gloat, for it is far from clear that Cuba will succeed, through its own efforts, in salvaging and safeguarding socialism at a time when socialism everywhere is in retreat. "[T]he United States is betting that we won't survive, and we are betting that we will," Castro says with a twinkle of defiance in his eye. "That's the gamble."[177] It is also, in a nutshell, Castro's central problem, and it may yet be his downfall. For the security regime that provided Cuba with the necessary breathing space to consolidate the revolution depended fundamentally upon the continuation of the rough balance of power between the United States and the Soviet Union. It was only the bipolar context, in which the threat of major nuclear war constrained and restrained the superpowers, that gave Cuba whatever measure of freedom and flexibility it had enjoyed. Che Guevara recognized this as early as 1960 when he wrote, "The present distribution of power in the world is what has permitted Cuba to take steps to cross the line between a colonial and a non-colonial country."[178]

As long as the United States and the Soviet Union continued to play out their geopolitical rivalry on the international chessboard, Cuba could collect the truly enormous subsidies from Moscow that permitted it to weather the American economic embargo and defy the forces of economic and political gravity that inexorably draw Cuba toward the United States. The missile crisis therefore played a crucial role in providing Castro with thirty years' worth of relative safety. The exceptionally frightening experience of standing on the brink of nuclear war and staring into the abyss was the single most powerful learning experience of the postwar era for the two superpowers. More than anything else, it was the missile crisis that led them to craft the modus vivendi upon which Cuba relied. Without the experience of the missile crisis, it is easy to imagine that Cuba itself would have been on the brink long before today, as the United States sought to topple the Castro regime and undo the damage to American interests that his revolution wrought. Now, with the Soviet Union no longer in the picture, the United States has no pressing interest in maintaining the security regime upon which Castro relied. It has no reason to fear that a local Caribbean conflict would escalate to global nuclear war.

Castro would like to portray the end of the Cold War as an opportunity for U.S.-Cuban rapprochement. "Everything has changed," he says, "but the United States has not changed its policy toward us."[179] He is mistaken. Not quite everything has changed. Americans still claim fair compensation for Cuban expropriations. They still abhor communism. Most importantly, they continue to detest Fidel Castro personally. Few Americans would shed tears if Castro died; many would rejoice if he were overthrown; virtually none would raise a finger to save him or Cuban socialism. But certain things *have* changed. Whereas in the United States of 1962 the overthrow of Castro was a *cause célèbre*, only a very few Americans today—primarily refugees from the Cuban Revolution whose hatred of Castro burns as intensely as ever—would support a military effort to oust him. Castro need no longer fear the United States Marines.

But the embargo remains. And it is clear that the American economic embargo has had a devastating effect on the island.[180] With the collapse of communism in eastern Europe, Cuba is only now feeling—for the very first time—the embargo's full weight: power outages are frequent and disruptive; once-bustling streets are now eerily empty of automobiles; basic foodstuffs are rationed. Castro is attempting to break free of it any way he can. He has started to open Cuba to foreign investment; he has structured barter deals with foreign countries to compensate for Cuba's shortages of hard currency; and he has invested heavily in industries such as biotechnology that are more intensive in human capital (of which Cuba has an abundance) than in plant and equipment. But some of these investments will not begin to bear fruit for many years. And Washington has thwarted many of Castro's efforts by subtly (and not so subtly) pressuring third countries not to bail him out.[181] The United States is enjoying Castro's predicament.

There are voices in the United States, of course, that are beginning to make the case that the end of the Cold War is an appropriate time to stop fighting its battles. They point to the hardships the Cuban people are now enduring and ask how in good conscience the United States can indulge its petty feud with Castro at their expense. But these voices are too few and too weak to be heard in Washington, whose ears are better attuned in any case to the many vested interests that favor the status quo.[182] The voices for change may grow stronger, particularly as farsighted Americans begin to realize that Europeans are taking the inside track on future investment opportunities in Cuba. But Castro cannot afford to rely upon them. And even if the United States were to lift the embargo, it would undoubtedly represent a defeat of sorts for Fidel Castro. The United States is unlikely to normalize political and economic relations in the absence of assurances that Americans would be free to invest in, and travel to, Cuba. If Castro were to open the doors, how long would it be before the laws of political and economic gravity enabled the United States to regain its economic—and perhaps political—dominance? And now that the Soviet Union no longer exists, who will answer when the ghost of José Martí asks, "[O]nce the United States is in Cuba, who will drive it out?"[183]

THE LEGACY OF THE BRINK: UNFINISHED BUSINESS OF THE HAVANA CONFERENCE

Fighting the United States—we're so small—might have a touch of greatness, but I reject that fate. I would rather go on underdeveloped. Not interested, a fate that must face death each minute is not for me. Revolutionaries are mystics of this century: willing to die for an implacable social justice. I'm a mediocre man, a modern man. . . . I don't want to die, there's always the hope of breaking through, of being happy some day.
—EDMUNDO DESNOES,
Memories of Underdevelopment

FIDEL CASTRO HAD CONCLUDED THE HAVANA CONFERENCE WITH a warning to the many participants who sought to move from a discussion of the missile crisis *directly* to a discussion of U.S.-Cuban rapprochement. Castro had said, in effect, that the issue had recently become more complex, and that, in his judgment, the considerable accomplishments of the conference might be swamped in verbal volleys of acrimony that would be wholly counterproductive. Many U.S. participants—though not all—breathed a sigh of relief when our host reached this conclusion.

Why? Why did it seem wise to stop with the successful conclusion of a primarily historical discussion when the exploration of U.S.-Cuban rapprochement was on the hidden agenda of virtually every American participant? Why did they not take advantage of the atmosphere of honesty, disclosure, and self-criticism to move into a discussion of the present situation and future prospects? Quite simply because almost everyone in the conference room knew that, for the foreseeable future, U.S.-Cuban rapprochement was impossible. The conditions under

which the United States and Castro's Cuba would be willing to nor-
malize relations and end their thirty-year feud are mutually exclusive.
Consider, for example, the following remarks by Presidents Bush and
Castro in the spring and summer of 1990:

> *Journalist:* Is there anything that Castro can do, other than abdicate,
> that would lead to a different U.S. attitude towards him, do you
> think?

> *President Bush:* Well, . . . free and fair elections and a recognition of
> the democratic changes that are taking place, and a shifting from a
> highly militarized island to something that would be more helpful to
> his own people . . . would all be helpful steps. . . . But instead . . . he's
> digging in. He's going against the tide. He's alone.[1]

> *Fidel Castro:* The more enemies socialism has, the more it is endan-
> gered, the more I love socialism.[2]

In short, the United States would consider rapprochement with Cuba
only if Castro renounced the Cuban Revolution. Castro could no more
do so than a leopard could change its spots. This is a simple impossibility. Historically, he was unwilling to accommodate the United
States when the "Cuban question" solely concerned security issues and
regional conflicts in Central America, the Caribbean, or Africa. Far
less willing is he now to accommodate the United States on matters
relating to Cuba's internal political and economic arrangements. To
Fidel Castro, U.S.-Cuban rapprochement may be possible if, one day,
the U.S. government could bring itself to accept a sovereign, independent, and socialist Cuba as a full member of the world community
of nations, and treat it with due respect. But this would require political
change in the United States, not Cuba. And the anti-Americanism
with which Castro secured his revolution at home has rendered politically impossible any American initiative that could be perceived in the
United States as bailing Castro out of his current predicament.

Most conference participants have keen enough political senses to
know that such change is not yet in the wind. Castro's decision to
conclude the Havana conference on a historical note was therefore wise.
As one relieved member of the U.S. delegation put it, "Good: he doesn't
ask us to get fitted out for green fatigues and combat boots; we don't
ask him to show up in a pin-striped suit and wing tips."

However, the Cubans had scheduled a press conference the afternoon following the conclusion of the conference (on Sunday, 12 January), without Fidel Castro present. Some of the conference participants who would address the media—and no doubt many of the reporters themselves—would raise the current state and future prospects of U.S.-Cuban relations. There having been virtually no discussion of the topic among the three delegations, there would obviously be little agreement to report to the press. Thus we worried about being trapped into a hopeless discussion of how best to normalize U.S.-Cuban relations in an entirely unsuitable forum. We therefore had serious misgivings that anything constructive could come from the exercise.

Our fears proved to be well founded: the result was a near fiasco, a "briefing" that at points strained civility and generated far more heat than light. Although the press conference begins on a congenial note, with McNamara's endorsement of normalized relations, the participants quickly become bogged down in an intractable debate about the status of Kennedy's non-invasion pledge. Ultimately agreeing to disagree, they move from the frying pan into the fire. Jorge Risquet blames the United States for the present impasse; Arthur Schlesinger deplores Cuba's lack of "civilized standards" in human rights; and Carlos Lechuga claims that all Cuban dissidents are CIA agents. By the time moderator Hector Argiles hastily calls the press conference to a close, none of the journalists in the room can quite believe the protestations of all three delegations that the closed-door sessions had been harmonious and productive.

HECTOR ARGILES: Good afternoon. The Tripartite Conference on the October Crisis of 1962 has concluded, and the participating delegations have agreed to hold this press conference. As usual, and in the interest of efficient organization, when the journalists want to speak, please, raise your hands, and press the button for the microphone. There are two wandering microphones; speak into the microphones, so that we can have translation. Those of you who need to listen to the translation will find earphones on the chairs, and you can find the language on the channels corresponding to those you see on the booth windows. When you ask your questions, take into account that there are three delegations, and that one question can imply the participation of three different answers.

To begin, Mr. Robert McNamara has asked to take the floor to make a brief introduction. I hereby recognize Mr. Robert McNamara.

McNamara: Good afternoon, ladies and gentlemen.

As I think you all realize, actions of the Soviet Union, Cuba and the United States in October 1962 brought our nations to the verge of military conflict, and brought the world to the brink of nuclear disaster. Not one of our nations intended by its actions to create such risks. To understand what caused this crisis, therefore—and, in particular, to learn how to avoid such events in the future—the parties have met together in a series of meetings, beginning some years ago. As a matter of fact, this is the fifth such meeting. We have sought, as I suggest, to learn why each of us behaved as we did, and based on that, to draw conclusions as to how changes in our behavior could avoid such crises in the future. We sought to place ourselves in each other's shoes. We began that, in particular, in Moscow, three years ago this month. We carried it on in Antigua last year, and I think we have made the greatest progress here in Havana.

Fear and hostility have characterized the relationships among our three nations for over thirty years. I think we in the U.S. now understand that Cuba did fear, throughout that period, a U.S. attack on the island. Cuba did fear invasion. I think we now understand how our actions contributed to that fear. And I think Cuba now understands that we in turn saw its actions as a threat to our security. Its alliance with the Soviet Union during the period of the Cold War, when—rightly or wrongly—we in the U.S. very much feared Soviet aggression and Cuba's support for revolutionary movements in the hemisphere—what we called "subversion"—we also saw as a threat to our security.

I think each of us has been very candid. In Moscow, I stated that, as secretary of defense in the Kennedy administration, I believe I knew exactly how the president thought, planned, and would have acted with respect to an invasion of Cuba. I said, "I want to tell you two things. The first point is that I can state categorically, without any equivocation whatsoever, that, excepting only the brief period from, say, October 15, 1962, after the discovery of the missiles, until the end of that crisis—however you wish to date the end; sometime in November—except for that brief period, at no time did the president ever intend to invade Cuba. I know that from my knowledge of his thoughts. I know as well that there couldn't have been any invasion of Cuba had it not come through me, and through the Joint Chiefs [of Staff]. Neither I nor the Chiefs ever had any intention during that period to invade Cuba."[3]

But secondly, I said in Moscow that, after listening to the Soviets and the Cubans explain their interpretation of our behavior, I now understood why each of them had a very clear basis for believing that we intended to invade Cuba. I thought that was clear, and I was prepared to state it; but I did not believe they then understood why we behaved as we did, and why we felt there was a threat to our security.

Now, in Moscow the Soviets made very clear their understanding of their actions' effect on us. And again they expanded on that in the meeting in Antigua, as I suggested, a year ago. We hadn't really had the kind of a discussion with the Cubans that indicated they were beginning to understand why we acted in ways which today appear reprehensible and irresponsible. I think here, in this meeting, we each increased our understanding of the other's behavior, and the roots of it. The Cubans were quite candid in saying that, yes, they did support revolutionary movements; they did carry out subversion in the hemisphere. They were equally candid in saying that they were not going to do it in the future. And they made what to me was a very perceptive and sophisticated statement when they said, "You know, there's much talk of political stability in the hemisphere today—political stability in Latin America. There's been a substantial movement forward with respect to political stability. But that stability, or apparent stability, rests on a foundation of very severe social and economic problems in many of the countries in the hemisphere." And by the way, I think they're entirely correct. The Cubans are entirely correct in coming to that judgment. They said that that may well lead to political instability in the future, and then they added a very significant statement: "Will we take advantage of it? No."

So I think, as I suggested, that in Moscow, in Antigua, and here in Havana, we've each learned much about why the others acted as they did. And based on that, I think we're in a much better position to ensure the next thirty years of relations amongst us—particularly between Cuba and the U.S.—now that there have been major changes ending the Cold War. I think we are in a much better position to ensure that the next thirty years of relations do not reflect the fear and the hostility that have shaped relations between us in the past.

There is no threat to U.S. security from Cuba today. I say that quite categorically, and I say it as one who spent seven years of my life worrying about such threats and believing, rightly or wrongly, that we were indeed endangered by the actions of the Cubans or the Soviets. That danger no longer exists for us. I'm positive of that. But I am equally positive that there is no threat to the security of Cuba today from the United States. I hope the Cubans are beginning to believe that. I know why they didn't believe it in the past. I hope our actions of the present, and particularly the future, will confirm in them a new evaluation of the potential of relations between our two countries. If one were to accept that the threats to our mutual security have dissolved—that they no longer exist—then is there not hope that we can recognize the divisive issues between us today? We in the U.S., for example, are concerned about what we consider to be restrictions on political freedom in Cuba. We are concerned about what we consider to be constraints on civil rights—and, by the way, when I am talking about civil rights, let me just clarify one possible misunderstanding. The term "human rights" is not equivalent to the term "civil rights." "Human rights" includes, as well, basic economic and social rights, the most basic of which, of course, is the right to live a productive life. And I want to say publicly that I admire immensely what Cuba has done to advance the welfare of its people in terms of health and education. It's truly an extraordinary accomplishment. I don't know any other Third World nation that has advanced this far. But I return to my point. There are major issues between the U.S. and Cuba, and they are not going to go away soon. But they are not issues of security. There is no basis for continuing to base our relationship on fear and hostility. The differences that remain—important as they are—are differences that the U.S. has with other countries in the world, and they are also differences that divide Cuba and other countries. So I think these types of issues, these differences of opinion, can be handled through—and I hope they will be handled through—normal diplomatic channels.

Now, so much for the major objective of our meeting, which was accomplished beyond my greatest hopes. There is one other matter I want to mention to you. Some of us believe there was great danger—possibly greater danger than our publics understood—to the events of October 1962. I think we've learned here that we greatly underestimated this danger. It was far more severe than I thought. One Saturday night—which would have been October 27th, a beautiful fall evening in Washington—when I was leaving the president's office at dusk to return to my office in the Pentagon, we were walking out of the Oval Office and we conversed on the veranda. I thought then that I might never live to see another Saturday night. Now, that is evidence of some apprehension. But I tell you I did not understand until the day before yesterday that I was understating the danger, rather than exaggerating it. We have learned here in Cuba that the Soviet forces—which at that time numbered 42,000, we have been told, although we then believed there were only 10,000—not only had thirty-six nuclear warheads for the missiles that were capable of striking the United States, at a time when we weren't certain but believed there were none on the island; we also learned here there were six launchers, which the Soviets called *Lunas*—our designation was FROGs—six *Luna* launchers, supported by nine missiles and nine nuclear warheads, which had a capability of being fired against the invasion force. And further, we learned that the command authority to utilize those warheads had been delegated— for reasons that seemed appropriate to the Soviets—to their field commanders.[4] The presumption is that they would have been used against the U.S. invasion force, the use of which, as many of you know, was an issue that had not been fully resolved on the 27th or the 28th. We can only speculate how the decision would have been made with respect to that force had not Khrushchev announced on the 28th that the missiles would be withdrawn. But what we do not need to speculate about is what would have happened had that force been launched, as many in the U.S. government—military and civilian alike—were recommending to the president on the 27th and the 28th. We don't need to speculate what would have happened. It would have been an *absolute disaster* for the world. Our force was not accompanied, and would not have been accompanied, by tactical nuclear warheads; but no one should believe that a U.S. force could have been attacked by tactical nuclear warheads without responding with nuclear warheads. And where would it have ended? In utter disaster.

So, it's been an absolutely fascinating meeting for me. Thank you, sir.

ARGILES: Having concluded the statement by Mr. McNamara, I would like to ask the Cuban and Soviet delegates if they care to add their brief introduction, or if we are going to go on to the questions and answers.

TROYANOVSKY: I wanted to make a brief statement on behalf of our Soviet delegation.

As you know, this is the fifth of these meetings devoted to the 1962 crisis. It might perhaps be correct to say that never in history has any historical event assumed such great importance in all of its aspects, and been studied in such depth. I believe this is fully understandable, because never before had humankind been so close to the brink of nuclear holocaust.

At the end of the analysis that we have been carrying out in this room over the past several days, we find that we have shed light on a number of aspects related to this incident—which was, I believe, much more than just an incident. I'd like to say that, as regards the leadership of the Soviet Union, we were moved, above all, by the massive amount of information which we had that led us to believe that an attack against Cuba was in fact possible. It may well be that part of that information was misinformation—diversionary—or that we misinterpreted some of the actions of the United States. But, in one way or another, the Soviet leadership was convinced that that attack was in fact possible. The goal of deploying missiles in Cuba was defensive. It never was our intention to use them, except in the event of an attack against Cuba. They would only have been used in the event of an attack against Cuba. The leaders of our three countries—the Soviet Union, the United States, and Cuba—found the political means by which to solve the crisis. This is a great lesson for future generations as I understand it.

As regards the debates that we have had here—as regards the level of those debates—I may say that they were raised to the highest possible level with the participation of Fidel Castro. It is my opinion that all the participants—the Americans and the Soviets—are aware of this fact, and we wish to express our appreciation to Comrade Castro for his participation, and for the great contribution that he made to our talks. Not only did he shed additional light on many aspects of the 1962 crisis, but in many respects he helped us better understand Cuba's policies.

Now, as regards what Mr. McNamara said, I would like to say that our debates took place in a very edifying atmosphere with the objective of arriving at an understanding, and I would like to express the hope that—perhaps not directly, but indirectly—this may be a contribution to the normalization of the situation in this part of the world.

ARGILES: I would like to thank Comrade Troyanovsky, and ask Comrade Risquet if he has something to add.

RISQUET: Esteemed friends: as Mr. McNamara said, this is the fifth meeting held to analyze the October crisis. The first was a U.S. initiative by scholars and leaders of the Kennedy administration that managed the crisis in the United States. The second was a meeting between Americans and Soviets. The third, which was held in Moscow, was actually the first tripartite analysis of the October crisis, and it was evident—and that's why we say we are so thankful for the invitation to participate—that one could not analyze all the angles of the October crisis without the participation of the three parties involved in it, and without the presence of the country where the missiles were deployed—that is, the site of the conflict.

At the Moscow symposium, we did make great progress, not only in clarifying the events that gave rise to the crisis—that is, its origins, its development, and its epilogue or solution—we also on that occasion attempted to draw lessons for the future. There, the Cuban delegation—the Cuban representatives—invited the others to participate in another meeting here in Havana. We did this for two reasons: first, because Cuba had been the theater of operations, the place where the missiles were that gave rise to, or that were the immediate cause of the crisis; and second, because of the three heads of state of the three countries involved in the crisis, two heads of state—Kennedy and Khrushchev—were no longer alive. The only living head of state of the three was Comandante Fidel Castro, and a meeting in Havana with his participation would obviously be of extraordinary value in clarifying policies, events, and motivations. That is how we arrived at this Havana meeting, although on the island of Antigua last year here in the Caribbean, we did have a preparatory meeting previous to this one.

As hosts, we should like to say that we are very satisfied with the American and Soviet participation. Their statements, their points of view, their sharp analyses—together with ours and the personal participation of Comrade Fidel—have helped us, as McNamara and Troyanovsky have said, make great strides forward in the clarification of the facts, and in the mutual understanding of causes, effects, and solutions.

In Moscow, at the end of the conference there, there was a brief joint communiqué containing the lessons to be derived from that joint analysis we performed.[5] In fact, I would say that the Havana conference could reaffirm, much more strongly and with much more data, that those conclusions arrived at jointly in Moscow were correct. Aside from trust among nations, aside from trying to avoid misinterpreting the policies of others, in Moscow we said that for the world never again to find itself on the brink of nuclear war, we had to continue struggling for the elimination of nuclear weapons in the world. The day that there are no longer nuclear weapons, or no longer any weapons of mass destruction, the world will be free of that danger. That was one of the conclusions which we arrived at in Moscow; and in the time since the Moscow meeting, I think we can all congratulate each other on the fact that great steps have been taken to eliminate the nuclear threat, first with the medium-range missiles, and subsequently, with thirty percent or so of the strategic weapons. Of course, new nuclear problems have arisen in the world, because the disappearance of the

Soviet Union has led to the fact that four former Soviet republics—Belarus, Kazakhstan, Ukraine, and Russia—are now, as I said, independent nations and nuclear powers. We also know that other nations of the former Soviet Union have tactical nuclear weapons, and this *de facto* proliferation is another source of danger. But, in general, we have moved along the road toward the step-by-step elimination of nuclear weapons, and the new independent republics that have become independent as a result of events in the Soviet Union have said that they subscribe to the agreements for the reduction of nuclear weapons.

Another conclusion arrived at in Moscow which should be underscored on this occasion is that it is not enough to eliminate nuclear weapons and weapons of mass destruction to bring peace to all nations, great and small, because the world in past centuries—that is, three quarters of the world—was colonized by powerful metropolitan nations with conventional weapons. This means that the elimination of nuclear weapons does not necessarily mean peace. What it means is the elimination of nuclear war. To bring peace to all nations, great and small, it is necessary to reject the use of violence, to reject interference in the internal affairs of states, and to have unlimited respect for the sovereignty of each nation, great or small, so that each country may freely choose, with no foreign interference, its own destiny and its own model of social and political development, as chosen by its own people. I am quoting, practically verbatim, the statement of the joint declaration in Moscow.

We also said in Moscow—and we have reaffirmed it at this conference—that the October crisis brought the world to the brink of nuclear war, and that while the outbreak of that war was avoided—and this was a positive development—what gave rise to the crisis was the tension between the United States and Cuba. Those causes had not disappeared. At that moment in Moscow, two or three years ago, they existed—and they exist today, when it is officially being declared that the Cold War has ended. For our country, the economic blockade has not ended; the possibility of aggression has not disappeared; and there are many actions that interfere in our internal affairs.

It has become perfectly clear to all that, at the present moment, all the necessary conditions exist for an open dialogue on an equal footing between Cuba and the United States which might help decrease these tensions. The U.S. delegation said through Mr. McNamara, now and during the conference, that they favor finding a road to dialogue that will end the present situation.

Cuba, a small and besieged nation, is not opposed to a debate or an equal footing, and with total respect for the sovereignty of both countries, on the questions that are being discussed, and which do not stem from the October crisis but from the end of the past century—from the struggle against Spanish colonialism, the U.S. intervention, and the signing of the peace treaty in Paris between the United States and Spain without the participation of the Cuban Liberation Army.

Therefore, I think we can congratulate each other on the success of our conference: on the climate of thought, respect and penetration into the issues of the crisis, its origins and development, and the lessons to be drawn for the future. We may say, in this connection, that our Havana meeting has in fact been a contribution, not only to the clarification of a historic event, but also to the quest for a solution to pending issues.

We should like to take this occasion to give our heartfelt thanks to all the members, to all the U.S. participants—these are not delegations; these are groups of individual personalities—we want to thank all the American participants in this conference, and all the Soviet participants in this conference. Thank you very much.

ARGILES: We are going to go on now to questions and answers. Who has the first question? Please identify yourself.

KAREN WALL (NBC-TV): For many years it was understood that one of the results of the missile crisis was a pledge by the United States not only that it would not launch an invasion of Cuba, but also, that it would restrain those anti-Castro Cuban exiles in the United States who wished to do so. With the recent increase in terrorist activities carried out by exiles who have been training more or less publicly in Florida, some observers are suggesting that with the demise of the Soviet threat, the United States no longer feels itself bound by this agreement.

I would like to ask Mr. McNamara if you have any reason to believe that the Bush administration is prepared to take action to stop or to prevent terrorist activities against Cuba from being prepared in, and launched from, the United States?

McNAMARA: Two points. First, I am not familiar with the level of terrorist activity, whatever it may be today. I don't know the source of it, and therefore, I can't comment on that element of your question. I want to make two statements, however, with respect to the assumptions underlying your question: namely, that the Kennedy administration gave a pledge, upon conclusion of the missile crisis, not to invade

Cuba. That is not correct. The exchange of correspondence with Khrushchev—between Khrushchev and Kennedy—related to the Soviets' proposal that they would withdraw the missiles, and the U.S. would pledge not to invade Cuba. The U.S. response stated, "If the Soviets would withdraw the missiles, the U.S. would pledge not to invade Cuba if there were U.N. inspection and surveillance of the withdrawal of the missiles, and of any potential further movement of missiles into Cuba." That condition, of course, was never met; and, therefore, there was no non-invasion pledge by the Kennedy administration.

However, I don't wish to leave the matter there. It implies that that was the end of it. It wasn't. And now I'm speaking in part from memory rather than first-hand acquaintance with the exchanges. I believe, if I recall correctly—and perhaps some of my associates may correct me if I am wrong—that in 1970, Secretary of State [Henry] Kissinger—prior to being secretary of state, national security adviser—did, speaking for the U.S. government, give a pledge of non-invasion.[6] And further—and please correct me, some of you, if I am wrong on this—I believe I recall reading that when President Bush was in Moscow last July, he in effect reiterated that pledge. If I'm mistaken, and any of my associates know it, please correct me. President Bush made in Moscow last July a pledge of non-aggression. So, as I said earlier, I do not believe there is a threat of a U.S. invasion of Cuba.

The specific incidents you refer to I have no knowledge of, and I'm not qualified to speak to.

ARGILES: Next question, please.

TROYANOVSKY: As far as I can recall, the commitment not to invade Cuba by the United States was made by, or ratified by, President Johnson immediately after the assassination of Kennedy.[7]

MCNAMARA: Mr. Ambassador, I don't believe that is the case.

SCHLESINGER: This is a historical question which needs a reference to the documents, and none of us has documents. I will say that as far as the Kennedy administration is concerned, and as to what Secretary McNamara correctly said, the non-invasion guarantee never went into effect because the condition of U.N. inspection of the missile sites never went into effect. What later administrations may have done, I don't know. I have no recollection of President Johnson ever stating that guarantee. Certainly Henry Kissinger did in 1970.

ARGILES: Comrade Lechuga has asked for the floor.

LECHUGA: I merely wanted to make a complementary remark to what has been said about Kennedy's promise not to invade Cuba. First of all, it must be said that no one has the right to invade any other country. This would be a violation of international law. Secondly, within the context of the crisis, everyone understood—and does understand—that, implicitly at least, there was a promise or guarantee not to invade Cuba; and not only not to invade directly, but also to keep other countries in the Western Hemisphere—that is, Latin America—from invading Cuba, whether they did so in agreement with the United States or not.

Then came what Mr. NcNamara referred to: Kissinger, in an official note issued by the U.S. government, ratified the promise of the Kennedy administration not to invade Cuba.

As regards Johnson, I don't recall the statement. I'm told that he did convey it through diplomatic channels to the Soviet Union. I didn't know about that. But what there is no doubt of is that, implicitly, during the crisis and in the exchange of correspondence between Khrushchev and Kennedy, a non-invasion pledge was made.[8] In fact, I recall that during the diplomatic negotiations in New York, when we were discussing the outcome of the crisis in the Security Council, the representative of the United States, the representative of the Soviet Union, and we understood that there was a promise not to invade Cuba. But, I repeat, such an invasion would, in any case, be a violation of international law. No country has the right to invade any other country.

ARGILES: Following the order on my list, I have a request from the U.S. delegation.

GARTHOFF: The assurances that President Kennedy in his letter of October 27 said would be provided were never formalized because, as has been mentioned, the conditions relating to them were never met. President Kennedy did give assurances that he had no *intention*—that the United States had no intention—to invade Cuba. He stated that to Soviet officials, and he stated it publicly. But there was no formal pledge of non-invasion, because the draft statement of such a possible pledge, taking into account the fact that not all the conditions had been met, was never agreed upon.

The United States, of course, understands that it is contrary to international law to invade any other country without just cause, and has no intention of doing so. The United States has not invaded Cuba in these thirty years. In that sense, there was an assurance which has been confirmed by history. But with respect to any formal pledge, the United States made clear at the time in the confidential negotiations that such an assurance was being given on the basis of existing conditions. If those conditions should change—for example, if Cuba should invade some other country in the region—the United States would not be bound by any pledge against the use of military action against Cuba. Other specific examples were mentioned; for example, if there were a Cuban attack on the American base at Guantánamo Bay.

So, there was a statement of the general American intention not to invade, but no juridical pledge for the future, because of this question of conditions.

Now, when President Johnson met briefly with First Deputy Prime Minister Anastas Mikoyan on the occasion of the funeral of President Kennedy, for which Mr. Mikoyan had come to Washington, the question was raised. I have read both the American and Soviet accounts of that meeting. There was, of course, no verbatim transcript, these are memoranda of conversations. There are nuances of difference between the two. The American account indicates that President Johnson reiterated that under his administration as well, the United States did not intend to invade Cuba. He did not say anything about reconfirming a pledge that did not exist, or giving it a new life.

It was a different situation in August 1970, when Mr. Kissinger, on President Nixon's instructions, did confirm—for the first time really—a mutual commitment tying the reaffirmed Soviet commitment not to introduce offensive weapons into Cuba with a statement that the United States would then, under those conditions, not invade Cuba. In these several later statements—oral comments by President Kennedy to Mr. Mikoyan at the end of November 1962; by President Johnson to Mr. Mikoyan in November 1963; and, formally, by the United States government in August 1970—there was no reference to the question of the United States seeking to inhibit any other party from invading Cuba, which had been mentioned in the initial letter sent by Mr. Khrushchev.

GRIBKOV: I wanted to explain here that when Mr. McNamara answered the first question, he expressed some sort of doubt about the possibility of one of these rockets having remained in Cuba.

McNAMARA: No, definitely not. I did not express any such doubt. I have complete confidence you removed them all.

ARGILES: Thank you very much, Mr. McNamara. Mr. Risquet?

RISQUET: To keep this conversation from following a single point—I mean, we have had one question, and what we are doing now is reproducing the meeting; the rest of the journalists are probably anxious to ask their questions—I'd like to wind up this point, if I can, as follows.

First of all, I want to state that Cuba has always based the defense of its territorial integrity and of its sovereignty on its own forces—on our armed forces and our people. Those are the foundations of the guarantee that Cuba will not be attacked, and that if it is attacked, the attack will be repelled and defeated. This is what we trust in, rather than any other commitment.

Second, Cuba believes that no country has the right to invade another. I think this is within international law, and Mr. McNamara and the Soviet delegation will certainly agree on that.

Third, on the issue that we are discussing, if there is no legal proof of that commitment, there is moral proof of that commitment. First of all, the commitment made by a government of a state is valid for successive administrations, because administrations pass but states remain. Otherwise, every time an administration changed, obligations to other states would change. Therefore, the commitment made at that time is valid for all U.S. administrations up to now, and future administrations.[9]

Now, if the commitment was not legal and juridical, it is nonetheless moral. The United States undertook the commitment not to invade Cuba and to keep other countries in the hemisphere from invading Cuba if the rockets were taken out of Cuba with their warheads, and if the Il-28s were taken out. They were taken out, and they have not been reintroduced. Cuba, of course, refused inspection, because it hadn't been consulted; but the withdrawal of the missiles was verified through inspection at sea. Thirty years have gone by, and Mr. McNamara has said very clearly—and with great common sense—that there are no longer any nuclear weapons in Cuba. Since there are not—even without inspection—that part of the commitment was fulfilled. There are no Il-28s. And who is going to give us nuclear weapons to install in Cuba? The possibility doesn't exist.

So, in fact, morally—whether or not juridically—we believe that the United States, besides complying with international laws against attacking any other country, has kept the specific commitment of not attacking Cuba, and of keeping other countries in the Western Hemisphere from doing so. This is a moral commitment. Would Mr. McNamara accept that definition? If so, then we can conclude the point and go on to another.

ARGILES: Thank you, Mr. Risquet. I must remind us all that we have one hour. The more time we take, the less we have for other questions. Would anyone else like to speak on this point? Can we go on to another one? Oleg wanted to say something.

DARUSENKOV: I wanted to add only the following: throughout seven U.S. administrations, I have been directly involved in this triangle of relations between Cuba, the United States, and the Soviet Union. I must say that all of these administrations have, at one time or another, reaffirmed this commitment to which we have referred.

ARGILES: Thank you, Oleg Darusenkov. The next question?

LOUIS AGUIRRE (GLOBE-TV): This question can either be addressed by Mr. McNamara or General Smith. It is my understanding that prior to this conference, you had suspicions but were not exactly sure that there were in fact tactical nuclear warheads—or any nuclear warheads—in Cuba. And second, should you have invaded Cuba, you were not going to use tactical nuclear weapons against Cuba during that invasion. Is that correct?

GENERAL SMITH: At the time the United States was preparing its forces to invade Cuba during the Cuban missile crisis, we had no evidence that there were nuclear weapons of any kind, even for the longer range missiles, in Cuba. We had to assume that they might be there, but we had no evidence that they were there. So, we proceeded on the assumption that although nuclear weapons might be in Cuba, we had no evidence. As a consequence of that, the U.S. forces that were preparing for the invasion of Cuba had no nuclear weapons with them. In fact, when Admiral Dennison, who was the commander of the forces at that time, learned that the Soviet Union had *Luna* rockets in Cuba, he sent a message to Secretary McNamara and the Joint Chiefs saying, "There are *Luna* rockets—which we call FROGs—in Cuba, that are nuclear capable. Since they are nuclear capable, I want my nuclear-capable forces to have some nuclear warheads, tactical nuclear warheads." The Joint Chiefs of Staff sent back instructions saying, "Since we have no evidence that the Russians have tactical nuclear weapons, you are not allowed to take with you tactical nuclear weapons at this time." We learned for the first time at this conference that there were, in fact, tactical nuclear warheads in Cuba that the Russians were prepared to use in the event of an invasion.

ARGILES: Thank you, General Smith. Next question? Please identify yourselves.

GONZALES DIAZ (ANSA, ITALY): At the beginning of this conference, it was said that the United States had not invaded Cuba because they had calculated that they would have had 100,000 casualties. Has any estimate been made of the possible casualties to the United States in an invasion against Cuba now? Could anyone, including the Cuban side, answer this question? Several assessments had been made at the time—assessments by the Soviets, by the Americans, and by the Cubans. Could any of the three sides now answer this question?

McNAMARA: I believe the statement made in association with the question is incorrect. (a) The U.S. did not refrain from an invasion because of an assessment of U.S. casualties; it did so for other reasons. (b) The assessment of U.S. casualties in the event of an invasion was not 100,000, but on the order of 18,000 to 20,000.[10]

ARGILES: Would someone on the Soviet or Cuban side care to add anything, or should we go on? Very well, we go on to the next question.

TASS: A question for any of the three delegations: Which, in your opinion, are the most important elements brought out here in this conference and never before broached in the previous four meetings? Thank you.

RISQUET: There are two essential elements. First, we had data on the number of rockets and nuclear warheads—this is a point that had been cloudy in previous conferences. Second was the extraordinary contribution made by the only living head of state of the three countries involved, Commander Fidel Castro, who gave a very clear and general explanation of the genesis and solution of the crisis.

ARGILES: Thank you, Risquet. Would the Soviet delegation care to add something? Mr. Troyanovsky.

TROYANOVSKY: I cannot say which was the most important new fact brought to light here, but I think the most important part of this meeting was, of course, the participation of President Fidel Castro, as has been said, his being the only living head of state of the three that participated.

MCNAMARA: There were two important points—I don't want to try to distinguish between them as to which was more important. The first is a repetition, but with greater emphasis and detail, of one of the conclusions that Mr. Risquet referred to from the Moscow meeting: namely, that human beings are fallible. We all make mistakes; we make them every day. In Moscow we identified the mistakes that each of us had made in coming to judgments that led to the crisis in 1962. Mistakes are costly in everyday affairs. They are costly in war—conventional war. They are beyond recognition of cost when they carry the risk of nuclear war. I think what we learned in this conference is that we made mistakes in appraising the potential cause and effect between our actions and an actual exchange of nuclear warheads. I have never seen a study that shows other than absolute disaster from an exchange of any significant number of nuclear warheads. And I've never seen a study that shows how to launch a small number of nuclear warheads without carrying the high probability of that escalating into an exchange of a large number. Therefore, what I'm suggesting to you is that this conference—more than any other single event I have ever been associated with—illustrated that there is no safety in a world in which there are thousands of nuclear warheads. We must learn how to avoid that risk. So that is one of the extraordinary and vivid conclusions I will take away from here.

And the other one—and it relates to this argument over invasion pledges, and so on—is that we are fighting an old war, the last war, when we are talking about that. The future does not involve threats to the security of Cuba or the U.S. We should move away from talk of invasions; we should find a way to normalize relations between our two countries, and to move to addressing the problems that we each have, and that the world has. I think President Castro stressed that in several of his interventions. We must get beyond the fear, the hostility, that have shaped our relations for the past thirty years. That's what I take away from this meeting.

ARGILES: Thank you, Mr. McNamara. Next question?

ARNALDO HERNÁNDEZ (RADIO HABANA CUBA): I want to address my question to the U.S. representatives here. I know you come as individuals and that you are not a delegation, but I think there is a consensus among all here present—not only the Americans, but also the representatives of the former Soviet Union—that this meeting can be very useful in contributing to the solution of the differences that still exist between the United States and Cuba. My question to any of the Americans here present is the following: Will you, in one way or another, carry back—Mr. McNamara himself has said that relations should be normalized by diplomatic means—I ask, will you in any way bring these opinions back to the U.S. administration?

McNAMARA: The Chief of the U.S. Interests Section was present during the discussions. There is no question in my mind that the points that you have alluded to, and others have alluded to, will be carried back to the State Department in Washington.

ARGILES: Next question.

MUÑOZ UNSAIN (AGENCE FRANCE PRESS): We have seen that the Soviet and Cuban sides have considered the participation of Cuban President Fidel Castro as one of the focal points of this meeting in Havana. But this is, in my opinion, a descriptive assessment. I would like to know exactly in which way Mr. Castro's statements clarified or provided new approaches to these questions that have been discussed for several years now.

The second question is this: Mr. Risquet has said that all conditions exist now for an open dialogue on an equal footing between Cuba and the United States to contribute to a decrease in the tensions that still exist. I ask myself, is this also descriptive merely, or is it what it appears to be—an invitation? The question was addressed to Mr. Risquet.

RISQUET: In the conference, the U.S. delegation said that it felt that, through dialogue, relations between Cuba and the United States should be normalized. Secondly, the U.S. side gave a number of examples of issues that were heretofore wielded to substantiate these differences, and which have disappeared. On the one hand, for instance, it was said that the alliance between Cuba and the USSR was a threat to the security of the United States. Mr. McNamara has said that the United States no longer considers relations between Cuba and the former Soviet Union a threat to the United States. Moreover, the Commonwealth of Independent States, formed on the basis of the former Soviet Union, was not a threat to the security of the United States.

Another issue which was used or considered an obstacle to relations between Cuba and the United States was the fact that Cuba aided revolutionary movements in Latin America, and, according to U.S. terminology, fostered subversion in Latin America. President Fidel Castro explained that we were convinced that revolutions cannot be exported; revolutions take place in countries depending on social and economic conditions, and so on. He explained that Cuba was not exporting revolution, and was against the export of counterrevolution. Furthermore, he said that, for Latin America, the time has come for integration, for mutual aid, and for cooperation. The era of military tyranny in Latin America has passed. The time when America joined the U.S. blockade against Cuba, leading to a hostility to which Cuba responded, has passed. The situation has changed, fully.

Furthermore, Comrade Fidel explained that now our internationalism was to defend the Cuban Revolution. The survival of the Cuban Revolution was the best contribution to the struggles of the peoples of the world. To keep this flag flying provides hope for the peoples of the world. Therefore, our internationalism will take place here. We have moved beyond the stage wherein Cuban soldiers were sent to other countries. Now, quite the contrary. We are ready to offer all countries of the world great aid in technicians, doctors, and teachers for their development. I am answering the first part and touching on some parts of the second aspect of your question.

This being so, if all the pretexts formerly used to explain bad relations between Cuba and the United States have disappeared, one would then suppose that conditions exist for a normalization of relations. Of course, Cuba's hope is to normalize relations; but this depends upon the political will of the U.S. government. The group of Americans here present have explained that they will work for that normalization.

Real obstacles do not exist. But new pretexts may become obstacles. I want to add that, because the first part of what I've said might give rise to unfounded hopes. Perhaps I wasn't as precise as I should have been the first time I spoke. Now, for example, new pretexts are used: the so-called human rights issue, the multiparty system, the market economy. Now the American complaint against Cuba has nothing to do with international affairs, and has nothing to do with bilateral issues: it has to do with domestic issues in Cuba. And of course, if a precondition to the normalization of relations is interference in the internal affairs of Cuba, dialogue cannot, under those conditions, take place. When I said that conditions for normalization existed, what I meant was that the old issues had disappeared. If new ones arise, or if new ones are invented, that's another matter.

ARGILES: Mr. Schlesinger?

SCHLESINGER: It has been noted that this is not a delegation. We are a collection of individuals. I speak only for myself. I speak as one who has advocated rapprochement with Cuba since President Kennedy initiated his exploration of that rapprochement towards the end of 1963. I am against the embargo, and for the restoration of diplomatic relations as quickly as possible. I do not think Cuba should be subject to more severe human rights tests than other countries with which we have relations, such as China. I subscribe to the traditional view that recognition of a country does not imply moral approval of all the internal arrangements in the country.

But, speaking as a practical matter, there is, as you know, a great political opposition to the restoration of relations with Cuba. And one reason for this fact, to state it bluntly, is that Cuba does not, in our view, observe civilized standards with regards to political, intellectual, and artistic freedom. I need not go into some of the cases where people who believe in nonviolent discussion have been subject to harassment, persecution, even sent to prison. I would say it would greatly facilitate the task of those like myself who favor rapprochement with Cuba if Cuba preserved a more generous and honorable course with regard to those who believe in peaceful debate, national dialogue, and peaceable dissent.

ARGILES: General Gribkov has asked for the floor.

GRIBKOV: The journalist asked whether the results of the conference are going to be conveyed to the corresponding administrations, and particularly to the U.S. administration. Thirty years have gone by since the October crisis, and the world has changed considerably. The Cold War is a thing of the past. The peoples and leaders of our countries hold different positions from the ones that existed in 1962 and after 1962. The participants in this conference, and in this press conference, have all changed considerably, in comparison with ourselves in 1962.

As I understand it, this is the fifth conference on the October crisis. We've had a frank debate. We have all come to the conclusion that all of this should have been analyzed before. I think we have all become more civilized. That is why I believe that the wisdom we have acquired should be reflected in a communiqué issued by the participants to the governments of the United States and Cuba calling for them to meet to hold negotiations and arrive at positive positions to take back to their peoples, and particularly to give the people of Cuba an opportunity to live in peace and free of fear.

However, we did not arrive at that conclusion, at that consensus. But I should like to reiterate here, in this press conference, that although all of us here have said that we are not official representatives, we can all do a great deal if we report back to our countries that the time has come to begin negotiations, and to do away with this lack of understanding that exists vis-à-vis Cuba, so that we can give the Cuban people an opportunity to live in peace.

ARGILES: I recognize the Cuban delegation.

LECHUGA: I merely wanted to refer to what historian Schlesinger has said in connection with cases of alleged violations of human rights. First of all, this is a domestic question. We are at a press conference to look at the things that were discussed at this seminar on the October crisis. Secondly, in Cuba we have laws, and laws must be respected. When a poet, an engineer, or a writer is punished, it is not because he is a poet, an engineer, or a writer, but because he has violated Cuban laws. In general, all those so-called "poets" that foreign propaganda considers human rights victims happen to be, in almost all cases, agents of a foreign intelligence service. I don't know if the CIA has a special Literature Department; but every time there is a sanction against a poet or a writer, it turns out that he is also a CIA agent.

But aside from that—and we are not going to talk about human rights in Cuba here—Mr. McNamara spoke about the right to life and education—which is the most essential right—and many other advantages that all foreign journalists here in Cuba know exist, whatever the ideological differences. We are not going to discuss those problems, because, I repeat, they are internal Cuban matters that have no place being discussed at a press conference of a different nature. Nor is it correct for there to be intervention in Cuba's internal affairs. Cuba should rather be analyzed according to its behavior and its record in the international arena, in international law, and so on. This doesn't mean that we are not ready to discuss this here; but I should like to reiterate that the press conference should not be diverted to internal Cuban issues. Thank you.

ARGILES: We have spent an hour and ten minutes on these issues, and we have no other alternative but to conclude the press conference. I want to thank the participants and the journalists here present. Thank you.

So much for a public attempt to extrapolate from a fruitful discussion of the missile crisis to a consideration of U.S.-Cuban rapprochement. What about a private attempt?

In the aftermath of the unfortunate press conference, Fidel Castro summoned four members of the U.S. delegation—Robert McNamara, Arthur Schlesinger, Robert Pastor, and James Blight—to meet him in a small room down the hallway, from which he had been watching the proceedings of the press conference via closed-circuit television. Present with Castro were Jorge Risquet, José Antonio Arbesú (then chief of the Cuban Interests Section in Washington, D.C.), and two young Politburo members: Carlos Lage, an economist; and Carlos Aldana, a foreign affairs specialist.

Much of the private discussion concerned the prospects for, and obstacles to, U.S.-Cuban rapprochement. Yet, though the subject was the same as that which Castro had refused to discuss openly toward the end of the conference and which had only moments earlier triggered a minor international crisis, the results produced far less heat and much more light than anything said thus far. What follows are excerpts from these discussions of the legacy of October 1962, the unfinished business on the hidden agendas of almost all the conference participants.*

———————————

MCNAMARA: . . . I am deeply impressed with your attempts at self-reliance. I admire that. I know you are trying to become totally self-reliant in the military area, but I hope to God you never need to test it. I hope you can shift soon from such a heavy emphasis on military preparedness to rebuilding your economy. . . .

I will be absolutely honest with you. There are severe constraints in the U.S. Congress and in the executive branch regarding what can be done to improve U.S.-Cuban relations. It is irrational, in my view, now that the Cold War is over, but there you are. My own personal view is that U.S. policy toward Cuba will not change dramatically any time soon. Some of us will report back to the State Department after the conference.[11] And of course, Mr. Flanigan, our Chief of Section, will send a report through official channels. But, to repeat, I would not expect a change any time soon. If I were you, I would move ahead, I would integrate Cuba as fast as possible into the world economy, and not wait for the U.S. to make a move.

CASTRO: I appreciate your honesty. I really do. Of course, we in Cuba want to improve our position, but we also want to retain so-

———————————

*These excerpts are reconstructed from James Blight's notes of the meeting.

cialism. We want to cooperate, not simply compete. Sometimes we call it "emulation." It is of course an open question whether we will be able, by means of methods compatible with socialism, to face up to, and conquer, our difficulties. But I must tell you: we believe firmly that capitalism will not solve our problems. We are convinced of this. Only a revolution can solve problems like ours, problems of a Third World country with modest resources. That is why we shall continue to try to keep Cuba separate from the herd. . . .

Look at what has happened to the Soviet Union. Anarchy, chaos, and disunion are everywhere. Are the people better off? Is there a reasonable prospect of the Soviet people—I mean *former* Soviet people, of course—becoming better off? It doesn't look good for our former allies and friends. We must look to their example, so to speak. We must maintain our cohesion. This is a life or death struggle and we do not believe Russian "shock therapy" can help us, any more than it is helping them.

Seeing my old friend Alejandro [Aleksandr Alekseev] brought tears to my eyes. Do you know what he told me? He said that his pension is 500 rubles a month. *500 rubles a month!* After all his service. These 500 rubles allow him to purchase one shoe or four kilograms of meat. He is well over seventy now, and is left without a penny. Millions are like this. And for what? Because of some experiment thought to be necessary by certain people in Moscow. It is a tragedy. Russian nihilism has prevailed once again. Everything was cast aside, so that they have destroyed the instruments, the infrastructure, that they might have used to improve their country. But now they have no country, no infrastructure. There is much discontent. Let us all hope that chaos and war can be avoided. If not, Cuba will not be alone in sharing first-hand the tragedy of the breakup of the former Soviet Union. We all need peace over there.

At first, Cuba welcomed Gorbachev's reforms. We too had embarked on an effort to rectify certain errors we had made along the way. But already on the 26th of July 1989, in—where was it, in Camagüey?

CARLOS LAGE: Yes, in Camagüey.

CASTRO: In Camagüey I said that even if the USSR ceased to exist Cuba will still be socialist. This seemed absolutely absurd at the time. But it disappeared, almost overnight. Gorbachev is now a sad case, a man without a country. You know, I got a cable only today—actually it was a press dispatch—and its title was, "Gorbachev in a Golden

Cage." We in Cuba, or some of us in Cuba, saw this two years and five months before it happened. And now the Cuban American National Foundation has, so to speak, "moved to Moscow"—they are bribing the new Russian leadership, trying to get them to isolate Cuba even further.

As for us, we believe the revolution must survive. That is our most important goal. Do you know that we now have direct elections to the National Assembly? This means if the majority opposes the revolution, well, then, the revolution loses power. It is as simple as that. You know, the conference on the October crisis got me to thinking. This crisis we are now in reminds me in certain ways of the October crisis. Our backs are to the wall. We are determined to fight for what we believe in.

You know, while we were discussing the October crisis, three guards were killed by people trying to get to the United States. These hijackings are becoming more frequent. It is very irritating to us when people like this are received as heroes when they get to the United States. This leads to more of the same behavior. It is a great invitation to certain malcontents here in Cuba to act out in anti-social ways.

PASTOR: I think we would all agree that a government has the right to defend itself from those who would try to overthrow it by violent means. But it seems to many in the U.S. that Cuba does not always make distinctions between those who advocate violence and those who merely seek by peaceful means to register some disagreement with established policy.

CASTRO: How are we to tell the difference between the so-called peaceful people and the violent ones? Do you know what it is like here, trying to fathom the many schemes and plans that are hatched from Miami? We have our own sources of information and one thing is clear: anyone in Cuba whom you might call a "dissident," regardless of personal motivation, will almost immediately fall under the influence of the counterrevolutionary groups in Miami. Almost immediately! They have no choice, it seems. And they talk about the lack of political freedom in Cuba? Hah! Well, in this difficult period in which Cuba is fighting for its survival, people try to take advantage of everything.

SCHLESINGER: Mr. President, I must tell you that by taking such a hard line on dissent, you pay a price. You tie the hands of people, like myself, who favor better relations with Cuba, who favor ending the embargo. Every time you beat up somebody or toss an intellectual into jail, you make it almost impossible for us to do what we want to do in the U.S.

CASTRO: Hard line? What hard line?

SCHLESINGER: Well, look, not all Cubans and not all Americans who are concerned by what we think are human rights abuses in Cuba are members of Alpha 66, or some other terrorist group.

CASTRO: As long as people do not engage in activities against the state, then fine. We have no problem with them. But you have seen how difficult is our situation just now in Cuba—economically, I mean. It is very difficult. We cannot allow the counterrevolution to get organized just now. We cannot, I'm afraid, be very flexible right now. Perhaps later, as conditions change, as people come to realize that Cuba will survive, that socialist Cuba will survive and even prosper.

SCHLESINGER: But jailing people, especially people whose only "crime" is having an opinion at variance with official views—Cuba pays a high price for this in the U.S. I am not trying to make a moralistic point. I am not trying to tell you how to run your business. But, as a matter of political fact, every time you throw someone like María Elena Cruz* or Elizardo Sánchez [Santacruz]† in jail, it sets back the cause of those in the U.S. who seek a more rational policy regarding Cuba. Do you understand that Cuba pays a price for this sort of thing?

CASTRO: You know, these people often call the international press in Miami and make outrageous claims.

SCHLESINGER: Why worry about that? Why not just *ignore* the people in Miami?

CASTRO: Because they dishonor our country. You know, Professor Schlesinger, you say we have taken a hard line, that we permit no dissent from some supposed "line" that must be followed. But let us take your

---

*On 19 November 1991, a crowd of government-sponsored demonstrators forced poet María Elena Cruz to swallow a declaration of principles she had written for the Cuban human rights group Criterio Alternativo. Subsequently, she was sentenced to two years in jail.

†Director of the Cuban Commission for Human Rights and National Reconciliation, Sánchez fell out of favor with Castro for his denunciation of the Warsaw Pact's 1968 invasion of Czechoslovakia, and recently spent 8½ years in jail—much of it in solitary confinement—for his political views. Shortly after the Havana conference—but not for the first time—Sánchez was the target of an officially inspired mob attack known as an "act of repudiation."

own case. We have not arrested you, in spite of what you have said. We have not mistreated you in any way, in spite of your having accused Cuba of being—I believe you said we are "uncivilized," or words to that effect. In fact, we are very tolerant here, very tolerant! We are often criticized for being *too* tolerant. Yes, too tolerant! So, yes, of course I realize Cuba must pay "a price," as you put it, for its policies. But, you see, Cuba pays a price, under the present situation, no matter what the policy. We are criticized by either the U.S. for being too tough, or by our own people for being too tolerant. Sometimes by both.

I wonder if you appreciate the conditions under which we must operate in this Special Period. Many forces seek to take advantage of Cuba, because of what some are now calling the "double blockade"— the U.S. embargo and the total collapse of the Soviet Union. There are embassies here in Havana openly plotting to humiliate us in some way. (Not the U.S. Interests Section, I am happy to say.) They do this with impunity and we must tolerate it, or else take measures and then pay the "price" in U.S. public opinion that you refer to. You mentioned the so-called poet María Elena Cruz. We said to certain Europeans, "Do you want her and her group? If you do, then take them." The U.S. said it would take them. Provocations were set up. Then Cruz distributed her manifesto. This led to serious conflicts with her neighbors who did not care for what she was doing. Well, you know the rest.[12] We get blamed for the most ridiculous things, like drugging Ochoa at his trial in 1989.[13] Wild stories. Don't most countries, even countries that are not under such extreme conditions as those in Cuba, punish such provocations? I think so.

SCHLESINGER: I take your point. But to reiterate: if you could find it possible to take it easy with people who do not actively try to overthrow the government, you would in turn make it easier for those of us in the U.S. who want what I believe you and Cuba want, which is rapprochement with the U.S. and the lifting of the anachronistic embargo.

CASTRO: Maybe the U.S. misses having its old enemy, the USSR. Perhaps Cuba must fill that role for a while, eh?

So the conversation ended. The unfinished business of the missile crisis—normalization of U.S.-Cuban relations—also remained, in the nature of things, the chief unfinished business of the Havana conference.

After the conversation with Castro, McNamara expressed frustration. "He'll never change," he said. "I see no movement whatsoever."

"I think the important thing is that he says he *will* change, if the U.S. takes the first step of removing the embargo," Schlesinger replied. "Now with the Russian problem out of the way, we should test him. I'm optimistic that if we'd change, he would too. And if he didn't, we'd have called his bluff."

On that half-hearted and hardly optimistic note, they parted. Schlesinger, Pastor, and several others went to visit Cuban dissident Elizardo Sánchez. McNamara strode back to his villa.

No one can doubt that Fidel Castro intends to stick by his social and political experiment, come what may. But we wonder at what point the point of the exercise will become obscure to Cubans other than those who, like Castro, cling to a point of view and a way of life discredited almost everywhere. The Cold War is over; whether or not the West "won," socialism clearly lost, and Cubans are now paying the price of that loss.

Perhaps as long as the remarkable Fidel Castro remains vigorously at the helm, the effects of having been on the wrong side of history can be repressed, or in some way controlled. Cuba is a "face-to-face" society, and Castro remains charismatic to many. But for how long? Will Castro survive the "Special Period in Time of Peace"? For that matter, will Cuba?

This is Castro's labyrinth. With the decline and fall of the Soviet Union, we have at last found it possible to discuss with Fidel Castro the historical origins of U.S.-Cuban hostility. But neither he nor we can transcend those origins or escape their implications. Fidel Castro has lived so that Cuba might wrest itself from the mercy of the United States. His tragic fate is to face the irony that, to escape his labyrinth, it is that very mercy for which he now must hope.

Notes

FOREWORD

1. Cuba's invisibility to scholars of the Cuban missile crisis is also part of the history of the project of which this book is the culmination. No Cuban, and no scholar of Cuba, was invited to the first two conferences of the missile crisis project.

2. Jorge I. Domínguez, *To Make a World Safe for Revolution: Cuba's Foreign Policy* (Cambridge, Mass.: Harvard University Press, 1989), chapter 2.

3. I had argued that the defense of Cuba had been, indeed, a Soviet motivation. Ibid., p. 39.

4. Ibid., p. 37.

5. Ibid., p. 41.

6. My book stated inaccurately that "most SAMs [surface to air missiles], perhaps all, were already owned by Cuba. . . ." In fact, at that time, Cuba did not own any SAMs. Ibid., p. 41.

7. On this general point, my earlier analysis was correct. Ibid., pp. 42–44.

8. See p. 242.

9. See pp. 344–48.

10. "Playboy Interview: Fidel Castro," *Playboy* 32, no. 8 (August 1985), 183.

11. Domínguez, *To Make a World Safe for Revolution,* pp. 251–52.

12. See p. 321.

INTRODUCTION: TOWARD THE BRINK

1. For the texts of Kennedy's 22 October speech and Khrushchev's 23 October reply, see David L. Larson, ed., *The "Cuban Crisis" of 1962: Selected Documents, Chronology, and Bibliography,* 2d ed. (Lanham, Md.: University Press of America, 1986), pp. 57–64, 67–68.

2. For the text of Khrushchev's message, see *Problems of Communism* 41, special issue (Spring 1992), 52–58.

3. James G. Blight and David A. Welch, *On the Brink: Americans and Soviets Reexamine the Cuban Missile Crisis,* 2d ed. (New York: Noonday, 1990), pp. 340–42.

4. Khrushchev to Kennedy, 26 October 1962; in *Problems of Communism* 41, special issue (Spring 1992), 37–45; 44.

5. These themes are elaborated in Blight and Welch, *On the Brink,* passim. See also James G. Blight, *The Shattered Crystal Ball: Fear and Learning in the Cuban Missile Crisis* (Savage, Md.: Rowman & Littlefield, 1990).

6. Khrushchev to Kennedy, 26 October 1962; in *Problems of Communism* 41, special issue (Spring 1992), 37–45; 38.

7. Robert F. Kennedy, *Thirteen Days: A Memoir of the Cuban Missile Crisis* (New York: Norton, 1969), pp. 127–28.

8. It is remarkable to note the unanimity on this point both within the Kennedy administration in 1962, and in American historiography of the crisis ever since. All of the best-known analyses of the event largely ignore the Cuban role in the genesis, management, or resolution of the crisis. See, e.g., Elie Abel, *The Missile Crisis* (Philadelphia: Lippincott, 1966); Graham T. Allison, *Essence of Decision: Explaining the Cuban Missile Crisis* (Boston: Little, Brown, 1971); David Detzer, *The Brink: Cuban Missile Crisis, 1962* (New York: Crowell, 1972); Herbert S. Dinerstein, *The Making of a Missile Crisis: October 1962* (Baltimore: Johns Hopkins University Press, 1976); Alexander L. George and Richard Smoke, *Deterrence in American Foreign Policy* (New York: Columbia University Press, 1974), pp. 447–99; Roger Hilsman, *To Move a Nation: The Politics of Foreign Policy in the Administration of John F. Kennedy* (New York: Doubleday, 1967), pp. 160–229; Robert F. Kennedy, *Thirteen Days;* Henry M. Pachter, *Collision Course: The Cuban Missile Crisis and Coexistence* (New York: Praeger, 1963); Arthur M. Schlesinger, Jr., *A Thousand Days: John F. Kennedy in the White House* (New York: Houghton Mifflin, 1965), pp. 726–69; Theodore C. Sorensen, *Kennedy* (New York: Harper & Row, 1965), pp. 667–718; and Albert and Roberta Wohlstetter, "Controlling the Risks in Cuba," Adelphi Paper no. 17 (London: International Institute for Strategic Studies, 1965).

9. See Blight and Welch, *On the Brink,* part 1.

10. At the time of the Hawk's Cay conference, existing Soviet treatments of the crisis were sparse and suspect on a number of accounts. The most detailed, Anatoly Gromyko's "The Caribbean Crisis," prosaically recapitulated the official line, and—since it was written after Khrushchev's ouster—masterfully succeeded in doing so without ever mentioning Khrushchev by name. In Ronald R. Pope, ed., *Soviet*

Views on the Cuban Missile Crisis: Myth and Reality in Foreign Policy Analysis (Lanham, Md.: University Press of America, 1982), pp. 161–226. (Pope's volume remains the best single resource for early Soviet writings on the crisis.) Other Soviet sources included Igor D. Statsenko, "On Some Military-Political Aspects of the Caribbean Crisis," *Latinskaya amerika* (November–December 1977), 108–17; Fyodor Burlatsky, "Black Saturday," *Literaturnaya gazeta*, 23 November 1983, 9–10; Anatoly Gromyko and Andrei Kokoshin, *Bratya Kennedi* (*The Kennedy Brothers*) (Moscow: Mysl', 1985); and Andrei Kokoshin and Sergei Rogov, *Serye kardinali belogo domo* (*Grey Cardinals of the White House*) (Moscow: Novosti, 1986).

11. Blight and Welch, *On the Brink*, part 3.

12. The best-known and most thorough analysis is Arnold L. Horelick, "The Cuban Missile Crisis: An Analysis of Soviet Calculations and Behavior," *World Politics* 16, no. 3 (April 1964), 363–89. In dismissing the defense-of-Cuba motivation, Horelick wrote, "To regard the outcome of the Cuban missile crisis as coinciding in any substantial way with Soviet intentions or interests is to mistake skillful salvage of a shipwreck for brilliant navigation." Ibid., p. 365. Horelick's analysis is largely deductive, and is instructive today primarily as an example of how an analyst's assumptions and concerns may powerfully influence interpretation under uncertainty.

13. For an analysis of how the Cambridge and Moscow conferences altered our angle of vision into the events of October 1962, see Bruce J. Allyn, James G. Blight, and David A. Welch, "Essence of Revision: Moscow, Havana, and the Cuban Missile Crisis," *International Security* 14, no. 3 (Winter 1989/90), 136–72 (which, with additions, forms the basis of the Afterword to the second edition of Blight and Welch, *On the Brink*). The complete transcript of the Moscow conference may be found in Bruce J. Allyn, James G. Blight, and David A. Welch, eds., *Back to the Brink: Proceedings of the Moscow Conference on the Cuban Missile Crisis, January 27–28, 1989* (Lanham, Md.: University Press of America, 1992).

14. The transcript of the Antigua conference is in James G. Blight, David Lewis, and David A. Welch, eds., *Cuba Between the Superpowers: The Antigua Conference on the Cuban Missile Crisis* (Savage, Md.: Rowman & Littlefield, forthcoming).

15. The Havana transcript repeatedly illustrates the mutual reciprocal conditioning of context and action before, during, and after the missile crisis. To borrow from the language of sociology, the agent-structure problem in the analysis of the crisis is acute. See Alexander Wendt, "The Agent-Structure Problem in International Relations Theory," *International Organization* 41, no. 3 (Summer 1987), 335–70; and David Dessler, "What's at Stake in the Agent-Structure Debate?" *International Organization* 43, no. 3 (Summer 1989), 441–74.

16. See the section entitled "Meta-lessons," in Blight and Welch, *On the Brink*, 2d ed., pp. 347–50. It should be noted that not all stages of our inquiry have equally satisfied the requirements of critical oral history. In particular, there remains an enormous "document gap." The National Security Archive in Washington, D.C., has a collection of literally thousands of declassified U.S. government documents relevant to the study of the Cuban missile crisis; to date, Moscow and Havana have released but a few. Consequently, in reconstructing the Soviet and Cuban stories, we have had to rely rather more heavily on recollections from the Soviet and Cuban sides, necessitating a somewhat higher degree of circumspection in the conclusions we draw from each.

17. The events of October 1962 have always been known in the United States as the "Cuban missile crisis"; in the Soviet Union as the "Caribbean crisis"; and in Cuba as the "October crisis." We will use "missile crisis," for the most part, unless the context seems to require one of the other two usages.

18. It is difficult to know how best to translate the title of the book into English. A translation by the author first appeared in the United States as *Inconsolable Memories*, with a foreword by Jack Gelber (New York: New American Library, 1967). But this title carries no meaning, and both the book and the popular film based on it (by Tomas Gutiérrez Alea) have always been known, in Cuba and the United States, by the title *Memories of Underdevelopment*. As the author dwells on this latter title at length, and as it bears considerable meaning in the context of the early days of the Cuban Revolution, we employ it throughout.

19. Gabriel García Márquez, *The General in His Labyrinth*, trans. Edith Grossman (New York: Knopf, 1990).

20. Ibid., pp. 255–56, 267.

1. CUBA ON THE BRINK, 1962

1. "Combat Alert," *Hoy*, 23 October 1962, 2. In *Chronology of Events in Cuba, January–December 1962* (Havana: Centro de Estudios sobre America [CEA], 1990), p. 32. Trans. David Lewis. Hereafter *CEA Chronology*. Under the direction of Deputy Director Rafael Hernández, the staff of CEA (a quasi-independent research arm of the Cuban Central Committee) compiled for our joint critical oral history a chronology from public sources of Cuban perceptions of the October crisis during 1962. While it contains no declassified material, it is an invaluable source for those seeking a running account of the approach, events, and denouement of the October crisis.

2. See Maurice Halperin, *The Rise and Decline of Fidel Castro* (Berkeley: University of California Press, 1972), esp. pp. 160–201. See also Oscar Lewis, Ruth M. Lewis, and Susan M. Rigdon, *Living the Revolution: An Oral History of Contemporary Cuba*, 3 vols. (Urbana: University of Illinois Press, 1977–78), esp. vol. 1, pp. 145–46, 487–88; vol. 2, pp. 189–90, 378–79; and vol. 3, pp. 141–42, 211–12, 355, 429; Philip Brenner, "Thirteen Months: Cuba's Perspective on the Missile Crisis," in James A. Nathan, ed., *The Cuban Missile Crisis Revisited* (New York: St. Martin's, 1992), pp. 187–217; and Philip Brenner, "Cuba and the Missile Crisis," *Journal of Latin American Studies* 22, no. 1 (February 1990), 115–42.

3. The best account in English of the U.S. invasion at Girón Beach is Peter Wyden, *Bay of Pigs: The Untold Story* (New York: Simon & Schuster, 1979). Though marvelously detailed, Wyden's study focuses almost entirely on the CIA's role in the event, and has little to say from the Cuban perspective. The same holds for Trumbull Higgins, *The Perfect Failure: Kennedy, Eisenhower and the CIA at the Bay of Pigs* (New York: Norton, 1987). Higgins's account complements Wyden's, however, by concentrating on decision making at the highest levels of the U.S. government. Higgins takes his title from the first line of an essay by Theodore Draper, "How *Not* to Overthrow Castro," in *Castro's Revolution: Myths and Realities* (New York: Praeger, 1962), pp. 59–113: "The ill-fated invasion of Cuba in April 1961 was one of those rare things in politico-military events—a perfect failure" (p. 59).

4. Jorge Risquet in Allyn, Blight, and Welch, *Back to the Brink*, p. 14.

5. Sergio del Valle in ibid., pp. 154–56. So confident were the Cubans of an American invasion that the "alert" order issued at 5:40 P.M. came an hour and twenty minutes *before* President Kennedy revealed that the topic of his television address would be Cuba.

6. Halperin, *Rise and Decline of Fidel Castro*, p. 76.

7. Three months later, Castro ended a speech to the Cuban Barbers' Union with the full version of the slogan: "patria o muerte, venceremos" ("fatherland or death, we shall overcome"). Ibid., pp. 76–77.

8. Eisenhower approved the plan on 17 March 1960. See Dwight D. Eisenhower, *Waging Peace, 1956–1961* (Garden City, N.Y.: Doubleday, 1965), p. 523. Wayne S. Smith, who was at the time serving in the U.S. embassy in Havana, agrees that the *La Coubre* explosion was pivotal. See *The Closest of Enemies: A Personal and Diplomatic Account of the Castro Years* (New York: Norton, 1987), p. 56. See also Tad Szulc, *Fidel: A Critical Portrait* (New York: Morrow, 1986), pp. 514–17.

9. The David and Goliath analogy is, as one might expect, popular in Cuba. Several billboards in Havana, for example, depict "David" (Cuba) looking fearlessly into the eyes of "Goliath" (the United States), slingshot in hand. The analogy also appears in the conclusion to an essay on the October crisis by Cuban scholar Rafael Hernández, "The October 1962 Crisis: Lesson and Legend," *Latinskaya amerika* (January 1988), 58–67.

10. Allyn, Blight, and Welch, *Back to the Brink*, pp. 14–18.

11. Ibid., pp. 16–17. While the CIA took operational responsibility for much of the activity associated with Operation Mongoose, the project was coordinated by Brig. Gen. Edward Lansdale, and had its headquarters in the Pentagon.

12. For the text of the resolution expelling Cuba from the OAS, see Halperin, *Rise and Decline of Fidel Castro*, p. 121. See also Jorge I. Domínguez, *To Make a World Safe for Revolution: Cuba's Foreign Policy* (Cambridge, Mass.: Harvard University Press, 1989), pp. 26–29.

13. On 1–2 December 1961, Castro concluded a speech by saying, "I am a Marxist-Leninist and shall remain one until the last day of my life." Halperin, *The Rise and Decline of Fidel Castro*, p. 137. Castro's escalation of rhetoric aided and abetted those in Washington who were pushing hardest for direct U.S. action against Cuba. In effect, Castro made their job much easier. One way he did so was to aid the cause of those who felt that Castro had been a communist all along, and that a Soviet-Cuban conspiracy had brought him to power in the first place. See Richard E. Welch, *Response to Revolution: The United States and the Cuban Revolution: 1959–1961* (Chapel Hill: University of North Carolina Press, 1985), pp. 87–99. The increased currency of this view was achieved at the expense of the view of Theodore Draper, who held that the essence of the Cuban Revolution was a betrayal of democracy by those who had once promised it, and probably believed in it, including Castro. See Draper, "The Two Revolutions," in *Castro's Revolution*, pp. 3–57. Draper's view found its way into the "white paper" issued by the Kennedy White House on 3 April 1961, drafted by Arthur Schlesinger, Jr. See U.S. Department of State, *Cuba*, Publication 7171, Inter-American series 66 (Washington, D.C.: Government Printing Office, 1961); and Welch, *Response to Revolution*, pp. 74–77.

14. Halperin, *Rise and Decline of Fidel Castro*, p. 138.

15. Domínguez, *To Make a World Safe for Revolution*, p. 116.

16. Brig. Gen. Edward Lansdale, Memorandum to the Special (5412) Group, "The Cuba Project," 20 February 1962 (Washington, D.C.: National Security

Archive). Thomas G. Paterson has synthesized much of the newly available documentation on U.S. covert actions against Cuba in "Fixation with Cuba: The Bay of Pigs, Missile Crisis and Covert War Against Castro," in Paterson, ed., *Kennedy's Quest for Victory: American Foreign Policy, 1961–1963* (New York: Oxford University Press, 1989), pp. 123–55.

17. See, e.g., Tad Szulc's interview with former Cuban interior minister Ramiro Valdés Menéndez, in *Fidel,* pp. 543–45, for insight into the way the Cuban intelligence service functioned in this period (chiefly via operatives in Miami, the hub of CIA activity directed against Cuba).

18. Allyn, Blight, and Welch, *Back to the Brink,* p. 18.

19. Ibid., p. 26. Fidel Castro also explained Cuban acceptance of the Soviet missiles to Herbert Matthews in 1967 as "an international proletarian duty in the interests of the Soviet bloc." Cited in Halperin, *Rise and Decline of Fidel Castro,* pp. 167–68.

20. See Blight and Welch, *On the Brink,* 2d ed., p. 328. For further discussion, see chapter 4, pp. 344–48.

21. "Fidel's Response to Kennedy's Insolent Comments," *Revolución,* 24 October 1962, 2 (*CEA Chronology,* p. 32).

22. *Revolución,* 24 October 1962, 8 (*CEA Chronology,* p. 32).

23. Sergio del Valle in Allyn, Blight, and Welch, *Back to the Brink,* pp. 155–56. During the crisis, del Valle was chief of staff of the Cuban army.

24. Interview, May 1991, New York City.

25. Halperin, *Rise and Decline of Fidel Castro,* p. 192.

26. Halperin reports that after virtually every speech Fidel Castro delivered, Cuban crowds would chant, "Fidel, Khru'cho/e'tamo' con lo' do' " ["We stand with both Fidel and Khrushchev"]. Ibid., p. 185.

27. Raúl Castro, quoted in *Revolución,* 13 September 1962, 1 (*CEA Chronology,* p. 24).

28. Fueling, arming, targeting, and firing an SS-4 medium-range ballistic missile are all processes that require coordinated action by a large number of skilled people, and which are made difficult when the launch sites themselves are the targets of an intense air attack. The CIA estimated that the fueling process, the warhead mating process, the targeting process, and the necessary countdown would take at least eight and possibly twenty hours. CIA memorandum on the construction of missile sites in Cuba, 19 October 1962 (Washington, D.C.: National Security Archive). General Gribkov's assertion that the warheads for these missiles were kept well away from the launch sites themselves (p. 61) suggests that this estimate is conservative. Given the proximity of American bases in Florida, it therefore seems virtually certain that American air strikes would have succeeded in destroying either the missiles themselves or the equipment necessary to prepare and fire them—provided, of course, Cuba did not have reliable advance warning of the attack. (Because of the instability of the SS-4's liquid fuel, the missiles could only be held on alert a maximum of five hours before the fuel had to be unloaded. Ibid.) For a detailed analysis, see Blight and Welch, *On the Brink,* pp. 209–12.

29. See the discussion in chapter 4, pp. 358–66.

30. See Bill Keller, " '62 Missile Crisis Yields New Puzzle," *New York Times,* 30 January 1989.

31. Allyn, Blight, and Welch, *Back to the Brink,* pp. 160–61. The denials came quickly and often. Aleksandr Alekseev, during the crisis the Soviet ambassador in Havana and the man who translated the cables between the Soviet Union and Cuba, told Bill Keller of the *New York Times,* "That's stupid. I wrote the telexes and there was nothing of the kind." Keller, " '62 Missile Crisis Yields New Puzzle." Sergei Khrushchev—having been told to do so by a person or persons unknown—denied the story on ABC's "Nightline" on 30 January, the day after the conference concluded. And Cuban scholar Rafael Hernández gave the official Cuban version in "Es ridículo pretender que teníamos la intención de provocar una guerra nuclear" (It is ridiculous to pretend that we wanted to provoke a nuclear war), *Granma,* 26 February 1989, 9.

32. Szulc, *Fidel,* p. 586.

33. Halperin, *Rise and Decline of Fidel Castro,* p. 82.

34. "Nikita mariquita—lo que se da no se quita, Pim pam fuera—abajo Caimanera!" ["Nikita, you little braggart—what one gives, one gives for keeps, Pim pam out—down with Caimanera!"] Caimanera is the Cuban town nearest U.S. headquarters in Guantánamo Bay. Cited in K. S. Karol, *Guerrillas in Power: The Course of the Cuban Revolution,* trans. Arnold Pomerans (New York: Hill and Wang, 1970), p. 272.

35. Halperin, *Rise and Decline of Fidel Castro,* pp. 189–90.

36. The terms were formalized in a letter from Castro to Acting Secretary General of the United Nations U Thant, 28 October 1962. In Larson, *The "Cuban Crisis" of 1962,* pp. 197–98.

37. See, e.g., Blight and Welch, *On the Brink,* 2d ed., p. 345.

38. See the letter from Fidel Castro and Cuban president Osvaldo Dorticós to U Thant, 25 November 1962, in Larson, *The "Cuban Crisis" of 1962,* pp. 214–19. "The United States Government demands that the United Nations should verify the withdrawal of strategic weapons. Cuba demands that the United Nations should verify in the territory of the United States . . . centers where subversion is prepared" (pp. 217–18).

39. "Kennedy Guarantees That He Will Not Invade Cuba and We Remember Girón Well; We Are More Alert Than Ever," *Revolución,* 29 October 1962, pp. 3, 13 (*CEA Chronology,* p. 36).

40. Interviews in Cuba with Central Committee and Foreign Ministry officials, May 1989 and April 1990.

41. See Karol, *Guerrillas in Power,* p. 274. Karol bases his report on the accounts of two eyewitnesses to the discussion: Saverio Tutino, *L'Ottobre Cubano* (Turin: Enaudi, 1968), pp. 46–47; and Andrés Suárez, *Cuba, Castroism and Communism, 1959–66* (Cambridge, Mass.: MIT Press, 1967), p. 175. On 1 November, at a joint press conference in Havana with U Thant, Castro declared, "In the course of the crisis . . . several disagreements between the Soviet and Cuban governments erupted. But . . . it is not here where it would be useful to discuss these differences, by merely inviting our enemies to profit from these discussions. . . . There will be no gulf between the Soviet Union and Cuba." "We Will Never Give in to the Position of the United States," *Revolución,* 2 November 1962, 4–5, 7 (*CEA Chronology,* p. 38).

42. Gianni Mina, *An Encounter with Fidel,* trans. Mary Todd (Melbourne: Ocean Press, 1991), p. 91.

43. Allyn, Blight, and Welch, *Back to the Brink,* pp. 70–73.

44. Ibid., p. 73.

2. USES OF THE BRINK

1. The American team was organized by Michael Cerre, head of Globe-TV of Sausalito, California, and included John Hessler, also of Globe-TV, and two staff members of WPLG-TV, the ABC affiliate in Miami: Jorge Pujol, a cameraman, and Louis Aguirre, an anchorman with WPLG Evening News. Both Pujol and Aguirre are Cuban-Americans, born in the United States. Their presence created intense, though brief, consternation among the Cuban organizers, who feared that the footage of the conference would return to Miami, only to be turned in some fashion into an anti-Castro diatribe. Yet the Cerre team adhered strictly to the rules laid down by the Cubans and, in turn, were taken to such out-of-the-way places as the Bay of Pigs and the San Cristóbal missile site. Cerre and his colleagues were the first Americans ever to visit a former Soviet missile site in Cuba. Aguirre later assembled a six-part evening news series from this material on WPLG in Miami—home to over a million Cuban-Americans—which emphasized, but went beyond, the conference. The series was notably fair and factual in its coverage. Moreover, when Jorge Pujol and Fidel Castro met at a reception given by Castro for all participants in the conference at the Presidential Palace, they discovered that Pujol's grandfather, a pediatrician, had actually cared for Castro and his mother when Castro was an infant.

In addition, the Cerre team was responsible for putting together lengthy special reports which aired shortly after the conference on "World News Tonight with Peter Jennings," and "Good Morning America." Cuban television produced a multipart special on the conference which aired in early February 1992.

2. See Bill Keller, "Rush Toward Disunion Spreads; Europe Embracing Baltic Independence; Purge of Military," *New York Times*, 25 August 1991, 1.

3. Nikita Khrushchev, *Khrushchev Remembers: The Glasnost Tapes*, trans. and ed. Jerrold L. Schecter, with Vyacheslav V. Luchkov (Boston: Little, Brown, 1990), p. 177.

4. Ibid., p. 183.

5. Fidel Castro, "Speech to the Committees for the Defense of the Revolution (CDRs) on the Thirtieth Anniversary of Their Founding, 28 September 1990," *Granma* (Cuban Communist Party Daily), 1 October 1990, 1 (trans. David Lewis).

6. Ibid.

7. Ibid.

8. The crisis correspondence between Castro and Khrushchev first appeared in *Granma* in late November 1990, and was reprinted in an official English translation in *Granma Weekly Review*, 2 December 1990, 1–4, with a long and interesting commentary on the crisis prepared under Castro's supervision. The timing of the release was only partly related to the publication of Khrushchev's remarks: Cuban officials informed us that the letters were released in time for their discussion at the Antigua conference, 3–7 January 1991, the transcript of which can be found in Blight, Lewis, and Welch, *Cuba Between the Superpowers*. For discussion and interpretation of the letters, see James G. Blight, janet M. Lang, and Aaron Belkin, "Why Castro Released the Armageddon Letters," *Miami Herald*, 20 January 1991, Sunday Supplement, 1; Aaron Belkin and James G. Blight, "Triangular Mutual Security: Why the Missile Crisis Matters in a World Beyond the Cold War," *Political Psychology* 12, no. 4 (December 1991), 727–45; and James G. Blight, Aaron Belkin, and David Lewis, "Havana Ground Rules: The Missile Crisis, Then and Now," in Wayne S. Smith, ed., *The Russians Aren't Coming: New Soviet Policy in Latin America* (Boulder, Colo.: Lynne Reinner, 1992), pp. 158–75.

9.   The letters were published in a special issue of the *Department of State Bulletin* 69 (1973).

10.   See Larry Rohter, "The Cold War of Cuba and the Miami Exiles Heats Up," *New York Times,* 26 January 1992, E-3; and Pamela Constable, "Cuba Giving Mixed Signals on U.S. Ties," *Boston Globe,* 15 January 1992, 2.

11.   A rare farcical moment occurred during the Miami stopover when a local TV anchorwoman and her camera crew appeared *inside* the charter after it had begun to pull away from the gate at Miami International Airport. Trapped in back of the plane, she yelled out, "Which one is the Khrushchev? Which one is the Khrushchev?" (referring to Sergei Khrushchev, son of Nikita) as she was ushered out. A voice full of helpfulness cried out: "The bald one on the left!" Unfortunately, several bald men happened to be sitting near Khrushchev, one of whom, an elderly Cuban exile on his way to visit family in Cuba, suddenly had a microphone shoved in his face. Unamused, he simply said, "*Gracias; no.*" Some of us wondered whether "the Khrushchev" appeared on the news that night anyway, seemingly disguised as a Cuban exile.

12.   See Saul Landau, "Killing the Wounded Beast: Economic War on Cuba," *The Nation,* 24 February 1992, 225–26; Arthur Schlesinger, Jr., "Four Days with Fidel: A Havana Diary," *New York Review of Books,* 26 March 1992, 22–29; and John Newhouse, "Socialism or Death," *New Yorker,* 27 April 1992, 52–83.

13.   On the Cuban style of deterrence, see Domínguez, *To Make a World Safe for Revolution,* esp. pp. 168–69, 251–53; and "Pipsqueak Power: The Centrality and Anomaly of Cuba," in Thomas G. Weiss and James G. Blight, eds., *The Suffering Grass: Superpowers and Conflict in Southern Africa and the Caribbean* (Boulder, Colo.: Lynne Rienner, 1992), pp. 57–78.

14.   Nikita S. Khrushchev to John F. Kennedy, 26 October 1962; in *Problems of Communism* 41, special issue (Spring 1992), 37–50; 48. This issue contains the complete Kennedy-Khrushchev correspondence under the title "Back from the Brink: The Correspondence Between President John F. Kennedy and Chairman Nikita S. Khrushchev on the Cuban Missile Crisis of Autumn 1962." Though the magazine is a publication of the U.S. Information Agency, this issue was a joint venture with the Russian Foreign Ministry. All letters between the leaders are printed in English and Russian, are carefully edited, and thus this source supersedes all previous anthologies.

15.   Ibid., p. 74.

16.   Castro returns to this point in chapter 3, pp. 223–25.

17.   The principal reason for the common equation of the "Cuban missile crisis" with "thirteen days" is the popularity of what remains by far the most riveting memoir of the crisis, Robert Kennedy's *Thirteen Days.* But all the U.S. memoirs reflect a common understanding of the time in the U.S. leadership: the Bay of Pigs invasion of 1961 was a U.S.-Cuban issue having nothing to do with the Soviet Union, and was a mistake; the Cuban missile crisis of 1962, on the other hand, was a U.S.-Soviet issue having nothing to do with Cuba, and had a successful outcome. Thus, none of the principal U.S. memoirists connect the missile crisis with the events of 1961 in a meaningful way, whereas from the Cuban perspective, they are two sides of the same coin: it was because of the Bay of Pigs and subsequent covert action that the Cubans turned to the Soviet Union for military assistance,

which came in the unexpected form of nuclear missiles. See George Ball, *The Past Has Another Pattern: Memoirs* (New York: Norton, 1982), pp. 286–310; Sorensen, *Kennedy,* pp. 667–718; and the recent synthesis by McGeorge Bundy, *Danger and Survival: Choices About the Bomb in the First Fifty Years* (New York: Random House, 1988), pp. 391–462.

18. Castro issued his "five points" on Cuban television on 28 October 1962, as well as in a letter to Acting Secretary General of the United Nations U Thant (dated 28 October 1962; reprinted in Larson, *The "Cuban Crisis" of 1962,* pp. 197–98).

19. The American delegation in Moscow contained not a single former official who dealt with Latin America, nor a single scholarly specialist on the area. Fortunately, Philip Brenner, a leading specialist on Cuba from American University in Washington, D.C., attended the Moscow conference as an observer, via his position as a member of the board of the National Security Archive, which provided the documents for use at the meeting. From the moment of our arrival, when we received confirmation of the presence of a Cuban delegation and the names of its members, Brenner was pressed into service giving briefings to the U.S. delegation and to the U.S. press corps covering the conference. He performed a very valuable service in what must have been the most active and strenuous "observer's" role in the history of conferences.

20. The subject of U.S. intentions regarding Cuba, in the period between the Bay of Pigs and October 1962, was scarcely mentioned at the first critical oral history conference in Hawk's Cay. The first time it entered the discussion was at the Cambridge conference, when it was raised by Sergo Mikoyan. See Blight and Welch, *On the Brink,* 2d ed., pp. 249–50.

21. For discussion and analysis of the question of Soviet motives, see ibid., pp. 116–21, 327–29.

22. Allyn, Blight, and Welch, *Back to the Brink,* pp. 16–17.

23. This was a source of controversy and some bitterness within the U.S. delegation. McNamara and Bundy had, during the Moscow conference, strenuously denied that the Kennedy administration had any intention of invading Cuba (except, perhaps, as a last resort to eliminate Soviet missiles during the crisis itself). But skeptics began voicing their doubts immediately thereafter. Among the first was Kennedy's former press secretary, Pierre Salinger. On 31 January, McNamara appeared on a special edition of ABC-TV's "Nightline," and Salinger, an ABC commentator, accused him of being less than candid. Salinger followed this with an op-ed piece in the *New York Times* less than a week later ("Gaps in the Cuban Missile Crisis Story," 5 February 1989, section 4, 16), which ran as leads, "Did the U.S. plan to invade a second time? McNamara's denial doesn't seem to wash." On the same day, Graham Allison of Harvard University—who, like Salinger, had been a member of the U.S. delegation to the Moscow conference—published a similar piece in the *Boston Globe,* "Avoiding Another Missile Crisis," in which he also doubted McNamara's and Bundy's denials in Moscow. Several days later, Bundy sought to set the record straight in an interview with the *Boston Globe*'s Charles Radin, "JFK Aide Downplays Report of U.S. Plan to Invade Cuba" (16 February 1989). Bundy's point was that while the United States surely had contingency plans to invade Cuba, there was never any intention to do so, and the matter was never even discussed in the circle close to Kennedy.

24. An excellent interpretive guide to issues of U.S. covert action against Cuba and other countries and groups is Gregory F. Treverton, *Covert Action: The Limits* *of Intervention in the Postwar World* (New York: Basic Books, 1987). Treverton worked for the so-called Church Committee, or the first Senate Select Committee on Intelligence, in 1975. He also worked on the Carter administration's National Security Council. His judgments are thus subject to considerations of what is right and legal, as well as what is effective and useful.

25. Fabian Escalante, in Blight, Lewis, and Welch, *Cuba Between the Superpowers,* p. 10.

26. Ibid., p. 46.

27. U.S. Department of State, *Cuba,* p. 1. For a useful appraisal of the white paper, see Richard E. Welch, *Response to Revolution,* pp. 74–75.

28. U.S. Department of State, *Cuba,* p. 35.

29. The material fell into two categories: what the Cubans *did,* and what they *said* about what they did. Some of the most useful secondary materials on the former were: Halperin, *The Rise and Decline of Fidel Castro,* esp. chapter 28 ("Cuban Subversion: A Major Card in Fidel's Hand"), and chapter 29 ("Intervention in Venezuela"). Also useful was Tad Szulc, "Exporting the Cuban Revolution," in John Plank, ed., *Cuba and the United States: Long Range Perspectives* (Washington, D.C.: Brookings, 1967), pp. 69–97. On the issue of Cuban rhetoric from the early period, we studied, in particular, Che Guevara's "The Real Meaning of the Alliance for Progress," his speech to a ministerial meeting of the OAS, 8 August 1961, in Punta del Este, Uruguay (in David Deutschmann, ed., *Che Guevara and the Cuban Revolution: Writings and Speeches of Ernesto Che Guevara* (Sydney: Pathfinder, 1987), pp. 265–98); and Fidel Castro's annual 26th of July address to the Cuban people in 1963, "The Road to Revolution in Latin America," in Jack Barnes, ed., *Twenty Years of the Cuban Revolution: Selected Speeches of Fidel Castro* (N.p.: Socialist Workers Party, 1979), pp. 77–86. In light of the evidence regarding Cuban covert action in Latin America, and especially in light of the way Castro and Guevara boasted about it and sought to justify it, Cuban refusal to admit any of this in Antigua seemed all the more perplexing and astonishing. At any rate, when we gave these materials to the Cuban organizers, we forewarned them that stonewalling would not be tolerated. Toward the end of the preparation for the Havana conference, we were also aided by having access to the manuscript of Edwin M. Martin, a member of the delegation and Kennedy's assistant secretary of state for Inter-American affairs: *Kennedy and Latin America.* This was especially useful in gaining perspective on the way the Kennedy administration viewed the problem of Castro's Cuba then, because of the many real-time documents contained in Martin's manuscript.

30. See, e.g., Central Intelligence Agency, "Soviet Military Buildup in Cuba" [briefing notes for Heads of Governments], 21 October 1962, p. 11 (Document 74 in *CIA Documents on the Cuban Missile Crisis,* ed. Mary S. McAuliffe [Washington, D.C.: CIA History Staff, 1992], p. 258), which stated, "Based on known voyages of ships, we believe at least 8,000 Soviet military and about 3,000 non-military personnel are now in Cuba."

31. Allyn, Blight, and Welch, *Back to the Brink,* pp. 6–9.

32. See generally Jules R. Benjamin, *The United States and the Origins of the Cuban Revolution: An Empire of Liberty in an Age of National Liberation* (Princeton: Princeton University Press, 1990).

33. John F. Kennedy, "Address in Miami Before the Inter-American Press Association," in *Public Papers of the Presidents,* 1963 (Washington, D.C.: Government Printing Office, 1964), pp. 872–77; 876.

34. Szulc, *Fidel,* p. 51.

35. At that time, the presence of really useful Soviets was thought to be an impossibility, so the "part" of the Russians was taken by Sovietologists Raymond Garthoff, Arnold Horelick, and William Taubman. Distinguished though these scholars are, they would be the first to admit that it is impossible for Westerners fully to "stand in" for Soviet leaders, as attested by the many faulty assumptions about Soviet motives, calculations, and behavior upon which Sovietologists had based their analyses of the crisis in the absence of informed and reliable Soviet testimony. See Blight and Welch, *On the Brink,* 2d ed., pp. 21–111, 225–90.

36. Accounts of Khrushchev's final days may be found in Roy A. Medvedev and Zhores Medvedev, *Khrushchev: The Years in Power,* trans. Andrew R. Durkin (New York: Norton, 1978), p. 178; and especially Roy Medvedev, *Khrushchev: A Biography,* trans. Brian Pearce (New York: Doubleday, 1984), pp. 256–60. The latter contains a very moving testament to Khrushchev in an account of the details of how his tombstone was chosen and sculpted by Ernst Niezvestny. The entire U.S. delegation to the Moscow conference was taken on a tour of the cemetery at Novodievechy Monastery, led by Sergei Khrushchev and Sergo Mikoyan, whose fathers are both buried therein.

37. Shakhnazarov, then one of six "personal aides" to President Gorbachev, was at that time heavily involved in foreign affairs, especially in relations with "friendly socialist countries." Hence his involvement with Cuba. Primakov was at that time the director of IMEMO, the Institute of World Economy and International Relations, having succeeded another Gorbachev adviser, Aleksandr Yakovlev, in that job. Both were part of an unusual group of intellectuals/politicians who at that moment were among Gorbachev's closest advisers.

38. The messages to the Moscow conference were published the following day on page 1 of *Pravda,* then the Communist Party daily.

39. Mikhail S. Gorbachev, in Allyn, Blight, and Welch, *Back to the Brink,* p. 2.

40. George Bush, in ibid., p. 3.

41. We had not known until arriving in Moscow that President Gorbachev would send a message to the Moscow conference, thus (according to our Soviet colleagues) requiring a reciprocal message from President Bush, who had just been inaugurated and, we assumed, must have had other business on his mind. But thanks to the good offices of Richard Gilbert, first secretary of the U.S. embassy in Moscow, we succeeded in contacting Lt. Gen. Brent Scowcroft, Bush's national security adviser, whose special assistant, Robert Blackwill, was instrumental in seeing to it that our unusual request was dealt with promptly. Jorge Risquet, leader of the Cuban delegation, confirmed to us later that, so far as he knew, President Castro had not been asked by the Soviets to submit a greeting to the conference.

42. The agenda of items related to lessons of the crisis was drafted in late December 1988 and early January 1989. Copies were made in Russian and in English and distributed to the members of the U.S. and Soviet delegations.

43. Mikhail S. Gorbachev, *Perestroika: New Thinking for Our Country and the World* (New York: Harper & Row, 1987).

44. Georgy Shakhnazarov, in Allyn, Blight, and Welch, *Back to the Brink,* p. 189.

45. On the Soviet departure from Cuba, see Andrés Oppenheimer, *Castro's Final Hour: The Secret Story Behind the Coming Downfall of Communist Cuba* (New York: Simon & Schuster, 1992), pp. 221–44. On the economic and political reasons

for the split, see James G. Blight, janet M. Lang, and Bruce J. Allyn, "Fidel Cornered: The Soviet Fear of Another Cuban Crisis," *Russia and the World* (Fall 1990), 21–25, 39–40. See also Sergo Mikoyan, "The Future of the Soviet-Cuban Relationship," in Smith, *The Russians Aren't Coming,* pp. 119–34.

46. Jorge I. Domínguez coined the phrase "managing the debris of the missile crisis." There is no better one-phrase introduction to Cuban-Soviet relations in the Castro period. As the Havana conference shows, both the Cubans and the Russians are still engaged in that process.

47. Georgy Kornienko was also to attend, but was kept from doing so because of a heart attack, for which he was hospitalized.

48. Shortly after the Moscow conference, the Cubans began to publish a series of articles in *Bastión,* the official magazine of the Revolutionary Armed Forces (MINFAR), emphasizing what was often called "the October crisis and a brotherly embrace," a romantic look back from a time, even in early 1989, when cracks were beginning to widen in the Cuban-Soviet relationship. The Cuban and Soviet military establishments both found the memory of the missile crisis a useful point of commonality. Dimitry Yazov, in 1962 a thirty-nine-year-old infantry commander in Oriente Province, Cuba, was portrayed in one such piece with the distinctly unsubtle title, "I have my uniform, ready to fight," which consisted of oral histories of Cubans who had known Yazov during the missile crisis. It was also published in *Granma Weekly Review,* 28 April 1989. The piece contains a marvelous picture of Raúl Castro and Sergio del Valle in fatigues, and Yazov, in what looks a bit like a golfing outfit—the "sport clothes" that were part of the Soviet attempt to camouflage the missile deployment.

49. The republics of the former Soviet Union and Cuba adopted an entirely hard-currency trade arrangement on 1 January 1992. While the Russian government has little or no interest in Cuba, the Russians *in Cuba* had a vested interest in remaining there, especially the military personnel—the motorized combat brigade of about 2,800 men and the Russian technicians at Lourdes, the giant intelligence-gathering facility outside Havana. The last members of the brigade departed in June 1993. See Oppenheimer, *Castro's Final Hour,* pp. 222–27, for an intimate look at the totally segregated way of life the Soviets have lived in Cuba over the past thirty years.

50. Andrei Kozyrev, "Foreword," *Problems of Communism* 41, special issue (Spring 1992), 3.

51. James A. Baker III, "Foreword," ibid., 2.

52. On Dulles's attitude toward nuclear risk, see John Lewis Gaddis, *The Long Peace: Inquiries into the History of the Cold War* (New York: Oxford University Press, 1987), pp. 104–46, esp. pp. 121–22.

3. CUBA ON THE BRINK, THEN AND NOW

1. The description of the Castro-Cline conversation is in J. Anthony Lukas, "Fidel Castro's Theater of Now," *New York Times,* 20 January 1992, E-17.

2. The memoir appeared in two parts, Anatoly Ivanovich Gribkov, "An der Schwelle zum Atomkrieg," *Der Spiegel,* 13 April 1992, 144ff.; and "Operation Anadyr," *Der Spiegel,* 20 April 1992, 196ff. The articles were two chapters from Gribkov's larger memoir, *I Served in the Soviet Army,* then in process.

3. McNamara told the *Washington Post* shortly after the Havana conference that if Soviet tactical nuclear weapons had been fired at invading U.S. troops in Cuba, the likelihood of U.S. nuclear retaliation was "99%" (Don Oberdorfer, "Small Missiles Heightened Peril in 1962 Cuban Crisis," *Washington Post*, 14 January 1992, A-6). McNamara also indicated on several other occasions after the conference that, in his view, President Kennedy would have had to consider seriously the option of resigning, so intense would have been the criticism from Congress and elsewhere for his having sent U.S. troops into battle without nuclear weapons, against Soviet forces which had them and had used them. This, according to McNamara, would have raised the odds that the American response would have been massive, in part because the United States would never have believed the Soviets had only a few tactical nuclear warheads on the island, and in part to compensate politically for having made a grave miscalculation at the outset of the invasion. As McNamara said at a Washington press conference the week following the Havana conference (carried live on C-SPAN), "We had tactical fighters that could carry tactical nuclear bombs available on the East Coast and those would have been in the air and dropping their bombs within an hour. And where would it have ended? You guess."

4. The question of Gribkov's veracity came up in a series of exchanges following the conference. Arthur Schlesinger reported Gribkov's testimony as received fact. See "Four Days with Fidel," pp. 22–29. John Newhouse, who attended the conference at the invitation of the U.S. organizers, took the opposite position, i.e., that Gribkov had been lying—in order to please Castro and in order to emphasize the centrality of his own position. See "Socialism or Death," pp. 52–83. Mark Kramer subsequently responded to Schlesinger's article, implying that Schlesinger, and indeed all members of the U.S. delegation who had believed Gribkov, were gullible and mistaken. Kramer thought it highly unlikely that the Soviets would have deployed tactical nuclear weapons in Cuba, especially taking into account Khrushchev's great caution in the matter of nuclear risks. See Kramer's letter to the editor of *New York Review of Books*, 28 May 1992, pp. 54–55. In the interval between the publication of his original article and his response to Kramer, however, Schlesinger obtained, via the U.S. organizers of the conference, a portion of a document from the Soviet General Staff Archives—a retrospective assessment of Operation Anadyr prepared shortly after the crisis—which largely confirmed what Gribkov had to say in Havana. See Schlesinger's letter, *New York Review of Books*, 28 May 1992, p. 56.

5. The Soviets originally proposed the title "Agreement Between the Government of the Republic of Cuba and the Government of the Union of Soviet Socialist Republics on the Deployment of Soviet Armed Forces on the Territory of the Republic of Cuba." The Cubans proposed three alternatives: the first is that reported by Gribkov here; the two others were "Agreement . . . on the Participation of Soviet Armed Forces in the Defense of the National Territory of Cuba in the Event of Aggression," and "Agreement . . . on Military Cooperation and Reciprocal Defense." Gribkov, "Operation Anadyr," trans. David Lewis.

6. A translation of the Spanish version of the draft agreement may be found in Laurence Chang and Peter Kornbluh, eds., *The Cuban Missile Crisis, 1962: A National Security Archive Documents Reader* (New York: New Press, 1992), pp 54–56.

7. In "Operation Anadyr," Gribkov lists eight ports: Kronstadt, Liepaja, Baltisk Sevastopol, Feodosiya, Nikolayev, Poti, and Murmansk.

8. In 1979, the United States announced the "discovery" of a Soviet motorize rifle brigade on the island of Cuba, precipitating a brief crisis. The brigade had in fact, been in Cuba since 1962. See Raymond L. Garthoff, *Détente and Confrontation: American-Soviet Relations from Nixon to Reagan* (Washington, D.C.: Brookings, 1985), pp. 828–48.

9. In his presentation at the Moscow conference, Volkogonov did not specify the number of warheads present in or in transit to Cuba; see Allyn, Blight, and Welch, *Back to the Brink,* pp. 27–29. The remarks to which McNamara refers were made in conversation during a break in the proceedings.

10. In his annual message to Congress on 2 December 1823, President James Monroe warned European states against any future attempts to colonize the Americas, declared that the United States would consider any attempt by the nations of Europe to extend their system into the hemisphere "dangerous to our peace and safety," and eschewed American participation in intra-European wars. See Ernest R. May, *The Making of the Monroe Doctrine* (Cambridge, Mass.: Belknap, 1975). While Khrushchev may have believed that American participation in World Wars I and II constituted a renunciation of the Monroe Doctrine, an informed observer of American affairs such as Troyanovsky would have known that it was not so considered in the United States.

11. While Troyanovsky is correct to note that messages sent from Moscow to Washington would be received the same day they were sent, owing to time zone differences, communications between Moscow and Washington were nonetheless difficult and tenuous, normally involving several hours' delay in transmission.

12. See Blight and Welch, *On the Brink,* 2d ed., pp. 312–14, for further discussion.

13. Khrushchev to Kennedy, 28 October 1962, in *Problems of Communism* 41, special issue (Spring 1992), 52–58; 53.

14. Gribkov is referring to Marshal S. S. Biryuzov, deputy defense minister and commander of the Strategic Rocket Forces, who traveled to Cuba in late May to assess the probability of deploying the missiles secretly. Anastas Mikoyan apparently considered him "a fool." See Blight and Welch, *On the Brink,* 2d ed., pp. 239, 332–33.

15. We are unaware of any such statement by Rusk. While it is difficult to know whom Mikoyan has in mind here, possibilities include Gen. Curtis LeMay, Richard Nixon, and Paul Nitze.

16. For further discussion, see Blight and Welch, *On the Brink,* 2d ed., pp. 333–34, and chapter 4, p. 351.

17. It remains an open question whether Soviet air defense forces could have shot down American U-2 aircraft prior to the discovery of the missiles even if Khrushchev had permitted (or ordered) them to do so. As of 18 October, the CIA deemed only nine of twenty-two known (and twenty-four planned) SA-2 sites operational, and on 21 October reported that "known radar emissions have thus far been very few." It is possible that the Soviets were experiencing difficulties readying their air defense system in Cuba. "Joint Evaluation of Soviet Missile Threat in Cuba," 18 October 1962, p. 2; and "Soviet Military Buildup in Cuba," 21 October 1962, p. 5; in McAuliffe, *CIA Documents on the Cuban Missile Crisis,* pp. 189, 252.

18. Interestingly, Castro says that he has not read the Szulc book, though this does not prevent him from criticizing it harshly. Actually, Szulc fills in the context of the use of U.S. planes and bombs, deriving from the U.S. base at Guantánamo,

in a manner very similar to that which Castro himself does in his remarks at the conference. See Szulc, *Fidel,* pp. 448–50. In addition, Castro seems to imply in his comments about Szulc that the journalist never spoke with him personally, which is not the case. Szulc had remarkably free access to Castro during a long stay on the island. Indeed, the back cover of the hardcover edition of Szulc's book shows a remarkable and ironic photograph: Szulc speaking and gesticulating, pipe in hand, while both Fidel and Raúl Castro listen intently.

19. Carlos Franqui, *Family Portrait with Fidel,* trans. Alfred MacAdam (New York: Vintage, 1985), p. 201.

20. Khrushchev oral message to Kennedy, 11 November 1962, in *Problems of Communism* 41, special issue (Spring 1992), 82–88; 85.

21. This remark seems somewhat inconsistent with the unqualified faith in Soviet judgment Castro expressed on pp. 82–83.

22. Castro wrote the letter in question to Celia Sánchez on 5 June 1958. Szulc quotes the following passage from the letter: "I have sworn that the Americans will pay very dearly for what they are doing. When this war has ended, a much bigger and greater war will start for me, a war I shall launch against them. I realize that this will be my true destiny." Szulc, *Fidel,* p. 51.

23. The incident to which Castro refers is described thus by Domínguez: "In May 1958, two Cuban government transport planes landed at the U.S. naval base at Guantánamo. Their mission was to exchange three hundred small rockets delivered mistakenly by the United States before the arms embargo; one of the planes was refueled. The rebels claimed the Batista Air Force was using this U.S. base to wage civil war. Although the charge was untrue, the facts were unclear at the time." Domínguez, *To Make a World Safe for Revolution,* p. 12. In fact, the United States provided arms to Batista on condition that they *not* be used to maintain internal order; moreover, on 14 March 1958, Secretary of State John Foster Dulles announced a total embargo of arms to Batista, and "apart from a few small deliveries of equipment that had already been paid for, the United States provided no more arms to the Batista government thereafter." Michael J. Mazarr, *Semper Fidel: America and Cuba 1776–1988* (Baltimore: Nautical & Aviation, 1988), p. 241; see also Smith, *The Closest of Enemies,* p. 16.

24. For further discussion, see Blight and Welch, *On the Brink,* 2d ed., pp. 344–46.

25. Some in the Kennedy administration felt that the Il-28s *did* represent a serious strategic threat, at least potentially. According to CIA director John McCone's memorandum of a meeting held in George Ball's conference room on the morning of 17 October, McNamara "feels that if nuclear warheads [are] supplied [for the MRBMs] the Soviet[s] will also supply nuclear bombs for bombers with offensive capability." McAuliffe, *CIA Documents on the Cuban Missile Crisis,* p. 159. Cf. chapter 4, p. 354.

26. Bundy made his statement on ABC's "Issues and Answers"; quoted in Allison, *Essence of Decision,* pp. 236–37.

27. Kennedy's 4 September 1962 statement supports Garthoff's conclusion: "There is no evidence of any organized combat force in Cuba from any Soviet bloc country; [or] of military bases provided to Russia. . . . Were it to be otherwise, the gravest issues would arise." Kennedy, in effect, had publicly committed the United States not to tolerate the presence of Soviet combat forces in Cuba. Larson, *The "Cuban Crisis" of 1962,* p. 17.

28. State Department memorandum, "Considerations in Defining Weapons Which Must Be Removed from Cuba," 29 October 1962, in Chang and Kornbluh, *The Cuban Missile Crisis, 1962,* p. 247.

29. In September 1962, the United States did not consider the Il-28s threatening because, given their obsolescence and extremely limited range, it was difficult to imagine that the Soviet Union would supply them with nuclear weapons. Recall, however, McNamara's judgment that if the Soviets supplied nuclear warheads for the strategic missiles deployed in Cuba, they would probably also supply nuclear bombs for the Il-28s (n. 25, above). Thus the Il-28s took on a more threatening complexion in the context of a strategic nuclear deployment.

30. Kennedy, *Thirteen Days,* p. 75. On the reactions of the Kennedy administration, see David A. Welch and James G. Blight, "The Eleventh Hour of the Cuban Missile Crisis: An Introduction to the ExComm Transcripts," *International Security* 12, no. 3 (Winter 1987/88), 5–29, 19–20; "October 27, 1962: The ExComm Transcripts," *International Security* 12, no. 3 (Winter 1987/88), 30–92, 62–72; Sorensen, *Kennedy,* p. 714; and Bundy, *Danger and Survival,* pp. 405–6.

31. Kennedy, *Thirteen Days,* p. 80.

32. Although the Museum of the Revolution is housed, for the most part, indoors, its last two exhibits are outside, in a sort of flower garden. The next-to-last is the U-2. The final stop is the yacht *Granma,* on which Castro and his colleagues arrived in Cuba from Mexico in 1956, and after which the Communist Party daily and a province in eastern Cuba have been named. The *Granma* is housed in a glass case, which is air-conditioned, to keep its wooden hull from deteriorating in the Caribbean humidity.

33. Castro makes this claim in Lee Lockwood, *Castro's Cuba, Cuba's Fidel* (Boulder, Colo.: Westview, 1990), p. 230. Lockwood's book was first published by Macmillan in 1967 and remains, in many ways, the most interesting interview of Castro ever done.

34. See Blight and Welch, *On the Brink,* 2d ed., pp. 338–40.

35. Franquí, *Family Portrait with Fidel,* p. 193.

36. The English version of Khrushchev's memoirs published in the West indicates that Khrushchev believed the Cubans had shot down the U-2. Khrushchev, *Khrushchev Remembers,* ed. Strobe Talbott (Boston: Little, Brown, 1970), p. 499. It appears that the original tapes Khrushchev dictated which formed the basis for his memoirs nowhere indicate that Cubans were responsible (Blight and Welch, *On the Brink,* 2d ed., p. 340); yet it also seems clear that, for some period of time, Khrushchev mistakenly believed that they were; see Castro's remarks and n. 37, below.

37. Paraphrased; Khrushchev to Castro, 28 October 1962; appendix 2, p. 483.

38. Castro makes no mention of the Second World War in his 26 October letter to Khrushchev. He does, however, in his letter of 31 October. See appendix 2, p. 491.

39. Castro concludes too much when he asserts that "the decision had already been made" and that his letter to Khrushchev "cannot have had any influence on that decision." Castro is correct to note that Khrushchev had already proposed to Kennedy the essential terms on which the crisis was publicly resolved well before his own letter reached Moscow, since Khrushchev, in his 26 October letter to

Kennedy, proposed withdrawing the missiles from Cuba in return for an American non-invasion pledge. However, Khrushchev subsequently toughened his terms in his 27 October letter to Kennedy, demanding as a condition for withdrawing missiles from Cuba that the United States withdraw its missiles from Turkey. Kennedy, in turn, offered to "accept" Khrushchev's 26 October offer in his 27 October letter to Khrushchev. Only on 28 October—*after* receiving Castro's 26 October letter—did Khrushchev agree, publicly announcing his decision to withdraw the missiles from Cuba in return for American guarantees. Khrushchev's decision to bring the confrontation to an end rather than to insist upon a Cuban-Turkish missile trade, therefore, could well have been influenced by Castro's 26 October letter. For the text of Khrushchev's 28 October letter to Kennedy, see *Problems of Communism* 41, special issue (Spring 1992), 52–58.

40. See n. 35, above.

41. See n. 37, above.

42. Khrushchev to Castro, 30 October 1962; in appendix 2, pp. 487–88.

43. Alekseev echoes Castro's error (see n. 39, above).

44. Radio Moscow broadcast the text of Khrushchev's 27 October letter to Kennedy, in which he proposed a Cuba-Turkey missile trade, at 5:00 P.M. Moscow time (9:00 A.M. Havana time, 27 October 1962). See *Problems of Communism* 41, special issue (Spring 1992), 45n. It is therefore curious that Castro did not receive word that Khrushchev had proposed a missile trade until the following morning.

45. Adela Estrada Juárez, "El General que Dió la Orden de: ¡Fuego!" *Bastión*, 30 March 1989, p. 4.

46. See Dino A. Brugioni, *Eyeball to Eyeball: The Inside Story of the Cuban Missile Crisis*, ed. Robert F. McCort (New York: Random House, 1991), pp. 63–70. For a reaction to Brugioni's book from a former close associate of Kennedy, see George Ball, "JFK's Big Moment," *New York Review of Books*, 13 February 1992, pp. 16–20.

47. In a characteristic self-congratulatory tone, for example, Khrushchev says: "Our goal was precisely . . . to keep the Americans from invading Cuba, and, to that end, we wanted to make them think twice by confronting them with our missiles. This goal we achieved. . . ." Khrushchev, *Khrushchev Remembers*, p. 496. Gromyko was equally terse at the Moscow conference in January 1989: "This action," he said, "was intended to strengthen the defensive capability of Cuba . . . that is all." Allyn, Blight, and Welch, *Back to the Brink*, p. 7. In his memoirs, however, Khrushchev was not always so precise and emphatic, noting that, "In addition to protecting Cuba, our missiles would have equalized what the West likes to call 'the balance of power.' " *Khrushchev Remembers*, p. 494.

48. N.B. that Cline's (and the CIA's) interpretation of Khrushchev's motive rested upon their knowledge that Soviet strategic nuclear capability was greatly inferior to that of the United States—a fact of which Castro claims he was unaware in 1962.

49. On the basis of inferences from the emplacement of SAMs in Cuba, McCone had concluded in late August and early September 1962—unlike Kennedy's closest advisers and the CIA's own Board of National Estimates—that the Soviets were planning to deploy strategic nuclear missiles in Cuba. See McAuliffe, *CIA Documents on the Cuban Missile Crisis*, pp. 13–17, 39–44, 51–52, 59, 67–68; and Brugioni, *Eyeball to Eyeball*, pp. 96–98. After the crisis, McCone went on the offensive, making speeches and testifying before Congress in a manner that struck some of his colleagues as having an unfortunate "I told you so" tone. The matter reached a crescendo in January/February 1963, when McNamara, and then McCone, testified before Congress. On 7 February, McCone told the Senate Preparedness Investigation Subcommittee of the Armed Services Committee, "I would be less than frank with you if I did not tell you that I have taken a more alarmed view of the developments in Cuba than others in official positions in Washington ever since the buildup started the first of August." Following this and other statements by McCone, Under Secretary of State George Ball asked for a report on how much damage McCone was doing to McNamara's credibility in Congress. Gerard Smith wrote to Ball in a memorandum dated 13 February 1963: "Mr. McCone is a very damaging witness" (p. 1). (Memorandum, and excerpt attached from McCone's testimony, available from National Security Archive, Washington, D.C.)

50. See Ray S. Cline, "Commentary: The Cuban Missile Crisis," *Foreign Affairs* 68, no. 4 (Summer 1989), 196. See also Cline, "Nuclear War Seemed Remote," *Washington Post,* 5 February 1989, p. D-8.

51. Cline, "Commentary," p. 190.

52. The distinction between so-called hawks and doves in the missile crisis is more complex than the usual saw that the hawks wanted to go to war and the doves wanted to avoid it. In fact, no one in the Kennedy administration desired a war with the Soviet Union under any circumstances. But the hawks tended to believe that the Soviets would not have responded to an American attack on Cuba, because of the reason mentioned by Cline: their tremendous nuclear inferiority (as well as their inferiority in conventional forces around Cuba). See James G. Blight, Joseph S. Nye, and David A. Welch, "The Cuban Missile Crisis Revisited," *Foreign Affairs* 66, no. 1 (Fall 1987), 170–89; and Blight and Welch, *On the Brink,* part 2 ("Hawks and Doves"). On "hawk" Paul Nitze's frustration with the doves— especially McNamara—see his memoir, *From Hiroshima to Glasnost: At the Center of Decision—A Memoir,* with Ann M. Smith and Steven L. Rearden (New York: Grove Weidenfeld, 1989), pp. 222–24.

To make the point that the hawks did not seek war, a senior aide to Cline during the crisis at CIA, William Hyland, once explained that he had made a bet with a terror-stricken neighbor in Washington during the missile crisis. If war broke out, Hyland would owe the neighbor dinner. If the Russians caved in and "nothing" happened, Hyland would collect. Hyland collected. He said he never had the slightest doubt that he would. (Personal communication.)

53. Khrushchev, *Khrushchev Remembers,* p. 493.

54. The weight of Soviet testimony plausibly suggests that Khrushchev considered Berlin wholly unrelated to the Cuban missile crisis. See Blight and Welch, *On the Brink,* 2d ed., p. 327.

55. See Adam B. Ulam, *Expansion and Coexistence: Soviet Foreign Policy, 1917– 73,* 2d ed. (New York: Praeger, 1974) pp. 588, 731. On Khrushchev's policy of strategic deception from 1958 to 1962, see generally Arnold Horelick and Myron Rush, *Strategic Power and Soviet Foreign Policy* (Chicago: University of Chicago Press, 1966).

56. See Sorensen, *Kennedy,* p. 667.

57. In two statements, on 4 and 13 September, Kennedy warned the Soviet Union that any deployment of "offensive" weapons to Cuba would precipitate a crisis. For the texts of these statements, see Larson, *The "Cuban Crisis" of 1962,* pp. 17–18, 31–32.

58. Kennedy met Gromyko at the White House on 18 October 1962, but did not ask him directly whether the Soviet Union was deploying nuclear missiles in Cuba. Neither, however, did Gromyko venture the information, asserting only that the Soviet Union was deploying "defensive" weapons to Cuba. From the Soviet perspective, of course, the missiles *were*, in a sense, "defensive"; therefore, it would be incorrect to suggest that Gromyko "clearly lied." Nevertheless, it is plain that Gromyko was attempting to preserve the secrecy of the deployment and was greatly relieved that Kennedy did not confront him with the matter directly. See Blight and Welch, *On the Brink,* pp. 304–5.

59. Raymond Garthoff, *Reflections on the Cuban Missile Crisis,* 1st ed. (Washington, D.C.: Brookings, 1987).

60. See Allyn, Blight, and Welch, *Back to the Brink,* p. 53.

61. Special National Intelligence Estimate 85-3-62, "The Military Buildup in Cuba," 19 September 1962, excerpted in McAuliffe, *CIA Documents on the Cuban Missile Crisis,* pp. 91–93.

62. In a letter from Kennedy to Khrushchev released just before the Havana conference, Kennedy was very explicit about the connection between verification in Cuba and the validity of the U.S. non-invasion pledge. Kennedy wrote: "You are, of course, aware that Premier Castro has announced his opposition to measures of verification on the territory of Cuba. If he maintains this position this would raise very serious problems." Kennedy to Khrushchev, 3 November 1962, in *Problems of Communism* 41, special issue (Spring 1992), 73–74.

63. The so-called New York documents could not be clearer about the firm connection made by U.S. officials at all levels between adequate verification and the validity of the non-invasion pledge. For example, in the "Codification of Instructions on Cuban Negotiations," President Kennedy told his negotiators on 5 November the following: "Finally, and most generally, the undertaking of the United States against invasion cannot take effect in any atmosphere of ambiguity or uncertainty such that the American government or the American people would lack assurance against the existence in Cuba now, or at any future time, of any Soviet military base or offensive weapons. The Soviet government must recognize that the events of the last three weeks have made it impossible for opinion in this hemisphere to be satisfied with Soviet assurances alone. Verification is essential if the governments of the Western Hemisphere are to be able to live with this situation without further action" (p. 4; document available from the National Security Archive, Washington, D.C.). In addition, see the memoranda by Assistant Secretary of Defense Paul H. Nitze, "How Can We Create the Optimum Environment for Continued Air Surveillance of Cuba?" (8 November 1962); and Deputy Under Secretary of State Jeffrey C. Kitchen, "Requirements for Pressure on USSR and Cuba" (7 November 1962), both also available from the National Security Archive. Their statements are completely consistent with Kennedy's instructions.

64. *Miami Herald,* 7 January 1992, p. 1.

65. This claim may be found in a release from the Cuban Foreign Ministry, 8 January 1992. The phrase "defend this bulwark to the last drop of blood" was used by Castro in his pivotal speech to the Federation of Cuban Women, 7 March 1990 (during the course of which he announced the onset of the "Special Period in time of peace"), reported in *Granma,* 10 March 1990, p. 1. Phrases like this derive from the dark days of the early 1960s, especially the missile crisis. For example, in a letter to U Thant on 15 November 1962, announcing that Cuba was resuming firing on low-level U.S. reconnaissance planes, Castro concluded as follows: "We believe in the right to defend the liberty, the sovereignty and the dignity of this country, and we shall continue to exercise that right to the last man, woman or child capable of holding a weapon in this territory." In Larson, *The "Cuban Crisis" of 1962*, p. 211.

66. See the Reuters News Agency release, "Cuba Siezes Three from Miami," in the *Boston Globe*, 9 January 1992, p. A-2; and Constable, "Cuba Giving Mixed Signals on U.S. Ties." A special report on the Havana conference by ABC-TV's Charlie Gibson, shown on "Good Morning America," 13 February 1992, included a film clip from the trial, released by Cuban television.

67. White House spokesman Marlin Fitzwater urged Cuban authorities to reconsider the death sentence originally given to all three men "out of concern for human life." Constable, "Cuba Giving Mixed Signals on U.S. Ties." See also Newhouse, "Socialism or Death," p. 56. U.S. officials in Havana privately expressed dismay at the State Department's handling of the episode, saying that such statements as Fitzwater's "make it very difficult for us to conduct business here in Cuba."

68. Raúl Castro, cited in Newhouse, "Socialism or Death," p. 72.

69. John F. Kennedy, quoted in Abel, *The Missile Crisis*, p. 200.

70. Personally, Raúl Castro could hardly have been more gracious to the U.S. participants. He even took several senior U.S. participants on an impromptu tour of the Cuban Defense Ministry Headquarters during a reception for all three delegations in the Palace of the Revolution. See Lukas, "Fidel Castro's Theater of Now"; Schlesinger, "Four Days with Fidel," p. 26; and Newhouse, "Socialism or Death," pp. 72–74.

71. Martin misleadingly implies that the United States took military action against European states to prevent European intervention in Latin America to collect debts. Only in the Spanish-American war (1898) did the United States engage a European state militarily, and then not to prevent the collection of debts but to halt Spanish atrocities in Cuba. The United States and Britain nearly came to blows in the Venezuelan boundary dispute (1895), but debts were not at issue. The United States did express its concerns about European attempts or threats to collect debts forcibly, e.g., when Britain temporarily occupied the Nicaraguan port of Corinto (1895) and when Germany and Britain repeatedly threatened military action against Venezuela (1901–1903); but the United States did not employ military force to prevent such actions. See generally Dexter Perkins, *A History of the Monroe Doctrine* (Boston: Little, Brown, 1955); and John A. S. Grenville and George Berkeley Young, *Politics, Strategy, and American Diplomacy: Studies in Foreign Policy, 1873–1917* (New Haven: Yale University Press, 1966).

72. 4 September 1962. See Larson, *The "Cuban Crisis" of 1962*, pp. 17–18.

73. The OAS foreign ministers declared, "The Soviet Union's intervention in Cuba threatens the unity of the Americas and of its democratic institutions . . . it is desirable to intensify individual and collective surveillance of the delivery of arms and implements of war and all other items of strategic importance to the Communist regime of Cuba, in order to prevent the secret accumulation in the island of arms . . . used for offensive purposes against the hemisphere." Quoted in ibid., p. 338.

74. The OAS meeting in Costa Rica led to the Declaration of San José, condemning "the intervention or the threat of intervention, even when conditional, by an extracontinental power in the affairs of the American Republics," and stating "no American state may intervene for the purpose of imposing upon another American state its ideologies or its political, economic or social principles," and "the inter-American system is incompatible with any form of totalitarianism." Four days later, Castro responded with his Declaration of Havana, his first formal call for hemispheric revolution. Domínguez, *To Make a World Safe for Revolution,* p. 27.

75. The Monroe Doctrine's bearing on the Falklands/Malvinas dispute is more complex than Risquet's remarks suggest. In his message to Congress of 2 December 1823, President James Monroe declared that American policy toward European involvement in the Western Hemisphere would be governed by two basic principles. The first of these would later become known as the "noncolonization principle." Monroe declared that "the American continents, by the free and independent condition which they have assumed and maintain, are henceforth not to be considered as subject for future colonization by any European power." The second would become known as the "non-interference principle": "With the existing colonies and dependencies of any European power we have not interfered and shall not interfere. But with the governments who have declared their independence and maintained it, and whose independence we have, on great consideration and just principles, acknowledged, we could not view any interposition for the purpose of oppressing them, or controlling in any other manner their destiny, by any European power in any other light than as the manifestation of an unfriendly disposition towards the United States." Perkins, *A History of the Monroe Doctrine,* p. 28. When Britain occupied the Falklands in 1833, the islands were occupied by a small number of Argentine settlers; but Argentina's title to the islands was in dispute. In fact, the islands had been controlled at various times by France, Britain, and (briefly) the United States. In any case, in no way did Britain's action constitute an "interposition for the purpose of oppressing" Argentina or "controlling" Argentina's destiny. It is therefore unclear whether Britain's action formally fit the class of acts that Monroe sought to deter. Moreover, the principle undergirding Monroe's declaration—the self-determination of peoples—was the very principle that Britain was defending in 1982 when it came to the rescue of the islands' British inhabitants in the wake of Argentina's invasion. Supporters of Argentina's claim correctly note that had Britain given the principle of self-determination weight in 1833, it would not have expelled the islands' Argentine settlers in the first place; but this does not undercut the sincerity of Britain's commitment to the principle in 1982. For further discussion, see David A. Welch, *Justice and the Genesis of War,* Cambridge Studies in International Relations 29 (Cambridge: Cambridge University Press, 1993), chapter 6, and citations therein.

76. "The U.S. objective is to help the Cubans overthrow the Communist regime from within Cuba and institute a new government with which the United States can live in peace." Program Review by Brig. Gen. E. G. Lansdale, Chief of Operations, "The Cuba Project," 18 January 1962, p. 1 (National Security Archive, Washington, D.C.).

77. Chang and Kornbluh, *The Cuban Missile Crisis, 1962,* p. 350.

78. See, e.g., McCone, Memorandum for the File, "Discussion in Secretary Rusk's Office at 12 o'clock, 21 August 1962," in McAuliffe, *CIA Documents on the Cuban Missile Crisis,* pp. 21–23, esp. p. 22: "McNamara expressed strong feelings that we should take every possible aggressive action in the fields of intelligence, sabotage and guerrilla warfare, utilizing Cubans and do such other things as might be indicated to divide the Castro regime."

79. Special Group (Augmented), "Guidelines for Operation Mongoose," 14 March 1962, in Chang and Kornbluh, *The Cuban Missile Crisis, 1962,* p. 38.

80. "Operation Mongoose," 28 January 1963 (National Security Archive, Washington, D.C.).

81. See Allyn, Blight, and Welch, *Back to the Brink,* pp. 16–17.

82. Lockwood, *Castro's Cuba, Cuba's Fidel,* p. viii. The phrase is from "The Second Declaration of Havana," 4 February 1962, following Cuba's expulsion from the OAS. The phrase also inspired the title for Domínguez, *To Make a World Safe for Revolution.*

83. On the issue of whether the U.S. leadership had an intention to invade Cuba in the six months or so leading up to the missile crisis, see Blight and Welch, *On the Brink,* pp. 329–31. There we take the view that if Kennedy and his associates had even the remotest idea of invading Cuba and ousting Castro, the subject would surely have come up in some fashion at the 16 October ExComm meeting in which the presence of the missiles in Cuba was discussed for the first time. But there is no hint of any such intent. Indeed, there is no hint of any awareness that the capability may soon be in place for such action, should it be deemed necessary. See "White House Tapes and Minutes of the Cuban Missile Crisis: ExComm Meetings, October 1962," *International Security* 10, no. 1 (Summer 1985), 164–203. Others disagree. See especially Thomas G. Paterson, "Fixation with Cuba: The Bay of Pigs, Missile Crisis and Covert War Against Castro," in Paterson, *Kennedy's Quest for Victory,* pp. 123–55; and James G. Hershberg, "Before 'The Missiles of October': Did Kennedy Plan a Military Strike Against Cuba?" *Diplomatic History* 14, no. 12 (Spring 1990), 163–99.

Since Paterson and Hershberg published their views, McNamara's summary instructions to the Joint Chiefs of Staff have been declassified. Whatever the "intentions" of Kennedy in this matter, there can be no doubt about military thinking about Cuba. In his "Memorandum for the Chairman, Joint Chiefs of Staff," 2 October 1962, McNamara lists ten contingencies "under which military action against Cuba may be necessary and toward which our planning should be oriented," only one of which is "positioning of bloc offensive weapons systems on Cuban soil, or in Cuban harbors" (p. 1). (Document available from National Security Archive, Washington, D.C.) The military clearly was ready to go in, even though Kennedy may not have been. But documents such as this one raise anew the question of why such matters were not discussed, or even alluded to, in the first day's discussions after the discovery of the missiles.

84. Mendoza became well known in the latter days of the Castro-led rebellion as the voice of the clandestine "Radio Rebelde" (Rebel Radio). He later became editor in chief of *Granma,* the Communist Party daily, after it was formed from the merger of two other newspapers, *Hoy* (*Today*) and *Revolución.* He has a reputation as a rather rigid ideologue, utterly loyal to Castro. See Szulc, *Fidel,* p. 73.

85. While waiting at Miami International Airport to board our charter for Havana, the U.S. organizers presented McNamara with a copy of Elmore Leonard's *Maximum Bob* (New York: Delacorte, 1991), a mystery thriller about a "hanging judge" in Florida who takes a very tough line. When McNamara received the book, he said that he ought not take it because he still firmly believed that the conference might well blow up in acrimony, and that he would be the one to lead the walkout if it did. He was reassured that this was precisely why the book was presented in Miami: we all wanted him to know before we got to Cuba that we appreciated the risk he was taking, come what may. We took to calling him "Maximum Bob" during the conference.

86. Schlesinger does not appear to be quoting precisely. General Taylor's original memorandum, "Guidelines for Operation Mongoose," dated 5 March 1962, stated: "The immediate objective of U.S. efforts during the ensuing months will be the acquisition of hard intelligence on the conditions inside Cuba. Concurrently, other actions generally political and economic in character may be taken provided that they are relatively inconspicuous and consistent with an overt policy of isolating Castro and of neutralizing his influence in the Western Hemisphere" (p. 1). (It is noteworthy that this paragraph follows, and seems to be in tension with, the statement of objectives quoted earlier by Escalante: "In undertaking to cause the overthrow of the Castro government, the U.S. will make maximum use of indigenous resources, internal and external, but recognizes that final success will require decisive U.S. military intervention.") John McCone, director of Central Intelligence, recommended the following change of wording: "The immediate priority objective of U.S. efforts during the coming months will be the acquisition of hard intelligence on Cuba. Concurrently, all other political, economic and covert actions will be undertaken short of those reasonably calculated to inspire a revolt within Cuba, or other development [*sic*] which would require U.S. armed intervention. These actions, insofar as possible, will be consistent with overt policies of isolating Castro and of neutralizing his influence in the Western Hemisphere." McCone, "Memorandum for the Special Group (Augmented)," 12 March 1962, p. 1 (National Security Archive, Washington, D.C.).

87. We have been unable to locate the source of Gribkov's quotation, in *Look*, or elsewhere.

88. Details of American contingency planning may be found in U.S. Navy, Atlantic Command, *CINCLANT Historical Account of Cuban Crisis—1963 (U)* (Norfolk, Va.: Headquarters of the Commander in Chief, 29 April 1963), available from the National Security Archive, Washington, D.C.

89. As Monroe's secretary of state (1817–25), John Quincy Adams advocated leaving Cuba on the Spanish vine until, like a "ripe fruit," it fell into the United States' lap. Mazarr, *Semper Fidel*, p. 26.

90. Martí posed the question in 1889. Philip S. Foner, ed., *Inside the Monster: Writings on the United States and American Imperialism by José Martí* (New York: Monthly Review Press, 1975), p. 45.

91. Philip S. Foner, *The Spanish-Cuban-American War and the Birth of American Imperialism, 1895–1902* (New York: Monthly Review Press, 1972), vol. 1, p. 13.

92. Exactly how White's statement constituted a threat to Cuban sovereignty is unclear, particularly in view of the fact that the 26th of July Movement had not yet formed a government in Cuba.

93. The best historical overview and analysis of the dynamics of U.S.-Cuban relations is Benjamin, *The United States and the Origins of the Cuban Revolution*.

94. See the discussion in n. 23, above.

95. Smith relates the tale in greater detail in *The Closest of Enemies*, pp. 54–57.

96. See Arthur M. Schlesinger, Jr., *Robert Kennedy and His Times* (New York: Ballantine, 1978), p. 523, and citations therein.

97. The most energetic espousal of this position was made by Philip Brenner, in remarks to a closed briefing of the Inter-American Dialogue and the Cuba Study Group, Carnegie Endowment for International Peace, Washington, D.C., 22 January 1992. See also, on this theme, the remarks of Jorge I. Domínguez, quoted in Constable, "Cuba Giving Mixed Signals on U.S. Ties"; John Tirman, "Cuba Still Awaits a Softer U.S. Line," *Chicago Tribune,* 1 February 1992, section 1, p. 19; Raymond L. Garthoff, "The Havana Conference on the Cuban Missile Crisis," *Cold War International History Project Bulletin,* no. 1 (Spring 1992), 3; and Wayne S. Smith, "Castro: To Fall or Not to Fall," *SAIS Review* 12, no. 2 (Summer–Fall 1992), 97–110; 106–7.

98. The exchange took place at a reception hosted by Fidel and Raúl Castro for all participants in the conference on 11 January at the Palace of the Revolution.

99. See p. 92.

100. In March 1901, the United States Congress passed the Platt Amendment, an attachment to the Army Appropriations Bill, authorizing the president to terminate the occupation of Cuba as soon as a Cuban government was organized under a constitution that (1) never permitted a "foreign power" to gain a foothold on Cuban soil; (2) restricted its foreign debt; (3) permitted American intervention to preserve Cuban independence or to maintain a government "adequate for the protection of life, property, and individual liberty"; and (4) leased or sold lands for American coaling stations or naval bases at points to be determined. Department of State, *Papers Relating to the Foreign Relations of the United States: 1902* (Washington, D.C.: Government Printing Office, 1903), p. 321.

101. Castro was in Washington 15–20 April 1959.

102. Contrary to Castro's implication, Nixon was not silent in their meeting. As Jules Benjamin remarks, "Nixon's interview with Castro reflected both the paternalistic attitude often taken toward Cuban leaders as well as a growing suspicion that the new Cuban prime minister bore close watching. Nixon unselfconsciously gave Castro a lecture on such subjects as democracy, capitalism, and the menace of communism. The vice president advised Castro to hold elections and attract foreign capital, suggesting Puerto Rico as an appropriate model. He concluded, in his own report of the meeting, that Castro had the makings of a strong leader and that 'he is either incredibly naive about communism or under communist discipline—my guess is the former. . . . But because he has the power to lead to which I have referred, we have no choice but at least to orient him in the right direction.'" Benjamin, *The United States and the Origins of the Cuban Revolution,* p. 178. See also Jeffrey Safford, "The Nixon-Castro Meeting of 19 April 1959," *Diplomatic History* 4, no. 4 (Fall 1980), 426–31.

103. For an overview of Castro's trip to Washington, see Szulc, *Fidel,* pp. 487–90.

104. On 26 July 1953, Castro and his associates attacked the Cuban army barracks and depot at Moncada, outside Santiago de Cuba. Most of his associates were killed, and the rest—Castro included—stood trial. In his concluding oration (he acted as his own lawyer), Castro laid out the "Moncada program" of reforms and proclaimed, "History will absolve me." Ibid., pp. 279–81.

105. On 8 July 1960, President Eisenhower suspended Cuba's sugar quota, eliminating 80 percent of Cuba's exports to the United States. On 9 July, the Soviet Union announced that it would buy the sugar Cuba would otherwise have sold to the United States.

106. For world prices and the prices the Soviet Union paid for Cuban sugar, see Domínguez, *To Make a World Safe for Revolution,* Table 4.1 (p. 83).

107. On 4 March 1960, the French freighter *La Coubre,* unloading ammunition and explosives from Antwerp, exploded in Havana harbor, killing eighty-one.

Castro's accusation that the explosion was the result of American sabotage has never been substantiated. See Szulc, *Fidel,* pp. 514–17.

108. The abortive expedition was planned for the late summer or early fall of 1947. For the story of Castro's role, see ibid., pp. 154–57.

109. See generally Carla Anne Robbins, *The Cuban Threat* (New York: McGraw-Hill, 1983).

110. Mazarr notes that Cuba's infant mortality rate is "comparable to many other Caribbean countries: Costa Rica (18.0), Grenada (15.4), Guadeloupe (15.5), Puerto Rico (16.0), Martinique (16.0), and so on. Cuba's rate of progress has again been similar to other countries, such as Chile." Mazarr, *Semper Fidel,* p. 414. But, citing the analysis of Nicholas Eberstadt, Mazarr goes on to note that, for methodological reasons, "the Cuban figures are of questionable validity (as indeed may be those of Chile and a few other countries)." Life tables, a more accurate measure of infant mortality than census data, suggest that in 1974 Cuba's infant mortality rate was 45 per 1,000 live births, 50 percent above the Cuban government's figure of 29. Moreover, during the early 1970s, Cuban statistics suggest that diseases commonly associated with infant mortality, such as acute diarrhea, respiratory infections, hepatitis, chicken pox, measles, and syphilis, increased five-fold. This would be highly unusual over a period in which infant mortality fell. Mazarr notes also that Cuba's low official infant mortality figures come directly from the Ministry of Health, "whose performance . . . they implicitly measure." Ibid., p. 414, citing Nicholas Eberstadt, "Did Fidel Fudge the Figures? Literacy and Health: The Cuban Model," *Caribbean Review* 15, no. 2 (Spring 1986), 5–7, 37–38.

111. Margaret Thatcher's 1990 poll tax proposal triggered widespread demonstrations in Britain, some of which were brutally dispersed by British police.

112. Two Argentine and two Venezuelan warships did serve on quarantine duty during the crisis with Task Force 137, based in Trinidad. The Dominican Republic offered two frigates to TF 137; these got as far as Puerto Rico, where they were deemed unfit for service. *CINCLANT Historical Account,* chapter 7, section 6 (pp. 126–31).

113. The anecdote by Raúl Roa is retold in Halperin, *The Rise and Decline of Fidel Castro,* p. 86.

114. On the trial of General Ochoa and his colleagues, see Julia Preston, "The Trial That Shook Cuba," *New York Review of Books,* 7 December 1989, pp. 29–31; and the definitive account by a *Miami Herald* journalist, Oppenheimer, *Castro's Final Hour,* pp. 17–129. Oppenheimer's access to Cuban officials, given his affiliation in Miami, is astonishing.

115. Liberal Democrat Arthur Schlesinger recalls hiring Ray Cline, then a young historian out of Harvard, to work with him in the Office of Strategic Services (OSS, forerunner of the CIA) during World War II. A Republican with decidedly hawkish views on American defense policy, Cline resigned from his post as deputy director of the CIA in 1966, frustrated by what he felt was McNamara's "no win" policy in Vietnam. It was obvious to many of us during the Havana meeting that both McNamara and Cline were straining to be civil with each other. They seemed to succeed.

116. Georgy Kornienko, later to become deputy chief of mission in Washington during the missile crisis and first deputy foreign minister under Brezhnev, reported to the Antigua conference that the identity of Castro's 26th of July Movement, and even of Castro himself, was unknown to anyone in Moscow official circles in January 1959, when Castro came to power. Khrushchev clearly was intrigued, reported Kornienko, but lacked even basic information. See Blight, Lewis, and Welch, *Cuba Between the Superpowers,* p. 29.

117. In the midst of a multifaceted dispute with the Soviet Union in early 1968, Fidel Castro called a special meeting of the Central Committee of the Cuban Communist Party and discussed the missile crisis with them for the better part of two days, 25–26 January 1968. One motive seems to have been to show younger Cuban officials how badly the Soviets had abandoned Cuba in October 1962. The Cuban delegation to Moscow in January 1989 used the transcript of this document to prepare for the conference, and referred to it extensively at the Havana conference. The context is the so-called microfaction controversy, in which Castro sought to purge a group of old-line Communists who had close ties to Moscow from the leadership. The group was led by Aníbal Escalante, the uncle of Gen. Fabian Escalante.

In the summer of 1992, Philip Brenner of American University obtained an official English translation of the document prepared by the Cuban government. With annotation and commentary, it forms the core of Philip Brenner and James G. Blight, *The October Crisis: Fidel Castro's 1968 "Secret Speech" and the Breach in Soviet-Cuban Relations* (Savage, Md.: Rowman & Littlefield, 1993). On the 1968 Cuban-Soviet crisis, see Domínguez, *To Make a World Safe for Revolution,* chapter 3; K. S. Karol, *Guerrillas in Power,* pp. 464–89; and Maurice Halperin, *The Taming of Fidel Castro* (Berkeley: University of California Press, 1981), chapters 33–35.

118. Rodríguez related the anecdote during an interview in his office at the Council of Ministers, Havana, 19 May 1991. Cf. Peter G. Bourne, *Fidel: A Biography of Fidel Castro* (New York: Dodd, Mead, 1987), p. 243, which quotes Rodríguez as follows: "That is the mistake. Fidel is not your son. Fidel is the leader of the Cuban Revolution and you have treated the Cuban revolution as a daughter of the Soviet revolution, which it is not, and Fidel as your son, which he is not. You have taken liberties that you can take with a son, but not with a leader."

119. Khrushchev, born 17 April 1894, was sixty-eight during the missile crisis. Castro, born 13 August 1926, was sixty-five at the time of the Havana conference.

120. Castro's speech before the U.N. General Assembly on 26 September 1960 is quoted in Halperin, *Rise and Decline of Fidel Castro,* p. 81.

121. Fidel Castro, "The Road to Revolution in Latin America," in Barnes, *Twenty Years of the Cuban Revolution,* pp. 77–86; 82. Castro delivered the speech in Havana, 26 July 1963.

122. Sorensen, *Kennedy,* p. 308n. For the text of Kennedy's address, see U.S. Department of State, *Bulletin 47,* no. 1230 (21 January 1963), 88–90; reprinted in Larson, *The "Cuban Crisis" of 1962,* pp. 227–30.

123. *Revolución,* 31 December 1962, p. 3; *CEA Chronology,* p. 47. "Worm"— or, in Spanish, *gusano*—is the term the Cubans have applied from the earliest days of the revolution to Cuban exiles involved in anti-Castro activities. Two recent fictional accounts of life among the *gusanos* (or "freedom fighters," depending on one's political orientation) are John Sayles, *Los Gusanos* (New York: HarperCollins, 1991), and Cristina García, *Dreaming in Cuban* (New York: Knopf, 1992). Both are bittersweet in their depiction of the life of the exiles, and especially of the generation gap that exists between those who fled from Castro, and their children, who are relatively indifferent toward the political passions of their elders.

124. The conversation took place over dinner on 31 August 1990 at a protocol house between Banes and Holguin, on the northeast coast of Cuba. It was notable in that the protagonists, Wayne Smith and Scott Armstrong (both of whom would be members of the U.S. delegations in Antigua and Havana), know a great deal about the Kennedy assassination, but they take opposite positions. Smith is a sophisticated conspiracy theorist who is working on a book on the subject. Armstrong is best described as an intellectual anarchist, who disbelieves in conspiracies, perhaps as a function of his work on the Watergate Committee's investigative staff. The Cubans present uniformly supported Smith's position, though Armstrong was unmoved. Essentially the same view as that espoused by Smith was given by Gen. Fabian Escalante at the Antigua conference in January 1991. "[W]e have always thought," said Escalante, "that Mongoose in the end became a boomerang that resulted in the murder." Blight, Lewis, and Welch, *Cuba Between the Superpowers*, p. 13.

125. The best book-length history of the Bay of Pigs operation is Wyden, *Bay of Pigs*.

126. Sorensen, *Kennedy*, p. 308.

127. The declassified U.S. memorandum of conversation between Kennedy and Khrushchev, reprinted in Chang and Kornbluh, *The Cuban Missile Crisis* (pp. 9–14), includes no such statement, although parts of the document have been deleted by the censors, and it is possible that the statement is in one of them.

128. For further discussion of the Soviet overture, see Blight and Welch, *On the Brink*, 2d ed., pp. 331–35.

129. In fact, Khrushchev's deterrent threats predated the Bay of Pigs operation. See, e.g., Khrushchev's speech of 7 July 1960, as reprinted in *Pravda* on 10 July 1960: "The socialist states and all peoples who stand for peace will lend support to the people of Cuba in their righteous struggle, and no one will succeed in enslaving the Cuban people. (Applause.) It should not be forgotten that the United States is not now at such an inaccessible distance from the Soviet Union as it used to be. Figuratively speaking, in case of need, Soviet artillerymen can support the Cuban people with their rocket fire if aggressive forces in the Pentagon dare to launch an intervention against Cuba. (Stormy applause.) And let them not forget in the Pentagon that, as the latest tests have shown, we have rockets capable of landing on a precalculated square at a distance of 13,000 kilometers. (Applause.) This, if you wish, is a warning to those who would like to settle international issues by force and not by reason." *Current Digest of the Soviet Press*, 10 August 1960, p. 5. The Kennedy administration's exposure of the "missile gap" myth in October 1961 undermined the credibility of such deterrent threats, and may have played some role in prompting the Soviet deployment.

130. Not all Cuban officials were quite so circumspect. President Osvaldo Dorticós, for example, broadly hinted at the deployment in early October in a speech to the United Nations. Dinerstein, *The Making of a Missile Crisis*, pp. 210–11.

131. Castro's letter to Khrushchev at the peak of the crisis on 26 October 1962 is particularly interesting when seen against the background of this remark. *Inter alia*, it suggests that Castro should have been sensitive to the possibility that Khrushchev would misinterpret the letter as a call for a nuclear first strike against the United States. See appendix 2, pp. 481–82.

132. While Castro may have approved the Soviet deployment primarily for geopolitical reasons, other high Cuban officials appear to have been attracted to the idea primarily because of its local deterrent value. This latter group included, for example, Sergio del Valle, a member of the Central Committee of the Cuban Communist Party and chief of staff of the Cuban army in 1962; and Emilio Aragonés, secretary of the Central Committee in 1962 and a former aide to Che Guevara. Blight and Welch, *On the Brink*, 2d ed., p. 328.

133. Operation Carlota began in October 1975. Castro's figure of 36,000 troops is more than twice as high as that given by Szulc, *Fidel*, p. 638. Domínguez, however, writes, "At the peak of the 1975–76 war, Cuba had 36,000 troops in Angola. . . . In relation to Cuba's population of 9.4 million, these troops were the equivalent of a U.S. deployment of over 800,000 troops, more than the United States had in Vietnam at the peak of that war." Domínguez, *To Make a World Safe for Revolution*, p. 152.

134. Castro's estimate is reasonable. For a detailed analysis of the extent to which the Soviet deployment would have increased Soviet strategic nuclear capability, see Blight and Welch, *On the Brink*, 2d ed., pp. 399–400, n. 15.

135. It is worth noting that there is no evidence that Castro's understanding of nuclear weapons and nuclear issues was as sophisticated and judicious in 1962 as it is today. Were it otherwise, his conduct during and after the crisis itself would be difficult to explain.

136. John F. Kennedy, Radio and Television Speech to the Nation, 22 October 1962; in Larson, *The "Cuban Crisis" of 1962*, pp. 60, 62. In a recently declassified letter from Kennedy to Khrushchev of 6 November 1962, Kennedy expressed his outrage at Khrushchev's deceit: "Secret action of this kind seems to me both hazardous and unjustified. But however one may judge that argument, what actually happened in this case was not simply that the action of your side was secret. Your government repeatedly gave us assurances of what it was *not* doing; these assurances were announced as coming from the highest levels, and they proved inaccurate. . . . Thus undeniable photographic evidence that offensive weapons were being installed was a deep and dangerous shock, first to this government and then to our whole people." *Problems of Communism* 41, special issue (Spring 1992), 79.

137. Blight and Welch, *On the Brink*, 2d ed., p. 247.

138. Ibid., pp. 333–34.

139. Allyn, Blight, and Welch, *Back to the Brink*, p. 20. We disagree with Castro that a public announcement of the Soviet Union's intention to deploy nuclear missiles to Cuba would have prevented a crisis. While it certainly would have put the United States in a difficult diplomatic position, it seems likely to us that such an announcement would have triggered *some* kind of crisis notwithstanding, given American sensitivities to Soviet encroachments in the Western Hemisphere and the domestic political pressures to prevent such a deployment that Kennedy would have faced. Moreover, even if the deployment had been public, the United States would have been able to rally the OAS by appealing to the very hemispheric threat that persuaded the organization to authorize the quarantine on 23 October 1962. It must also be noted that, had Khrushchev announced his intention to deploy missiles early enough, the United States would have been in a position to *deter* the deployment, a task significantly easier than that which Kennedy actually faced in October 1962—having to *compel* the withdrawal of missiles already deployed—because deterrence is less likely than compellence to require one's protagonist to suffer the public humiliation of backing down. We therefore suspect that there would still have been a Cuban missile crisis had the Soviets and Cubans announced their agreement beforehand—merely a significantly less dangerous one.

140. An English translation of the agreement may be found in Chang and Korn-bluh, *The Cuban Missile Crisis, 1962,* pp. 54–56.

141. On CIA intelligence gathering and analysis, see McAuliffe, *CIA Documents on the Cuban Missile Crisis,* pp. 1–147.

142. Certain members of the ExComm—such as Attorney General Robert Kennedy and Secretary of the Treasury C. Douglas Dillon—also felt that a surprise attack against Cuba would be immoral. Others, however—such as Chairman of the Joint Chiefs of Staff Gen. Maxwell Taylor and Assistant Secretary of Defense Paul Nitze—did not. See Blight and Welch, *On the Brink,* 2d. ed., pp. 50, 78, 141–42, 144, 152; see also Abel, *The Missile Crisis,* p. 64.

143. Ernesto "Che" Guevara to Fidel Castro, undated, but delivered to Castro on 1 April 1965, and read by Castro at a public ceremony in Havana on 3 October 1965, at which he introduced the newly created Central Committee of the Communist Party of Cuba. In Deutschmann, *Che Guevara and the Cuban Revolution,* pp. 374–75; 375. We are informed by our Cuban colleagues that the most common English translation of Guevara's phrase—"brilliant yet sad days of the Caribbean crisis"—is inaccurate.

144. For the text of Castro's letter, see Larson, *The "Cuban Crisis" of 1962,* pp. 197–98.

145. Fidel Castro, speech in Moscow, 23 May 1963. Quoted in *Fidel en la URSS* (Fidel in the USSR) (Havana, Cuba: Instituto del Libro, 1963), pp. 231–32. The staff at the Instituto de Historia de Cuba (Institute of the History of Cuba) compiled all the known public statements by Fidel Castro on the missile crisis, from 1962 until the present, as part of their own preparations for the conferences in Antigua and Havana, and made their compilation available to the U.S. organizers. We became aware of Castro's speech in Moscow thanks to their efforts.

146. For the full text of the letter (dated 26 October 1962), see *Problems of Communism* 41, special issue (Spring 1992), 37–45.

147. See ibid., pp. 45–50.

148. Our view is that Khrushchev's rage over the presence of American missiles in Turkey contributed to his decision to deploy missiles in Cuba. We doubt, however, whether this was either a necessary or sufficient condition for the deployment. For further discussion, see Blight and Welch, *On the Brink,* 2d ed., pp. 293–302, 327–29.

149. Castro's impression of the letters is at odds with our own. In our view, Khrushchev's letters evince growing exasperation with Kennedy's refusal to lift the quarantine or to commit to a broader cooperative agenda prior to full Soviet withdrawal of the missiles and bombers from Cuba. Khrushchev, in effect, begs Kennedy to help him smooth over relations with Castro, and to help him realize political gains from the crisis that are more useful publicly than a secret, tacit missile trade. Castro is correct to note Kennedy's inflexibility; his tone, however, is terse, businesslike, and faintly regal—far more noble than Khrushchev's. The sole exception to Kennedy's usual pattern is his letter dated 6 November 1962, which is Khrushchevesque almost to the point of mimicry. *Problems of Communism* 41, special issue (Spring 1992), 77–81.

150. Kennedy does not make such a strong claim, but he does suggest that Castro may have been seeking to undermine the U.S.-Soviet agreement. See ibid., pp. 92–96.

151. Khrushchev to Kennedy, 22 November 1962; in ibid., p. 108.

152. Khrushchev to Kennedy, 10 December 1962; in ibid., p. 116.

153. It remains unclear whether the Jupiter missiles in Italy were part of the secret arrangement between Kennedy and Khrushchev. By the end of April 1963, the United States dismantled the Jupiter missiles in Turkey and withdrew their warheads. On 1 April 1963 a Polaris submarine took up station in the Mediterranean, providing the nuclear umbrella for Turkey in the wake of the Jupiter withdrawal. Chang and Kornbluh, *The Cuban Missile Crisis, 1962,* pp. 395–96.

154. The interview was conducted on 28 and 29 June 1987, and published in Italy the following year. It did not appear in the United States, however, until late 1991.

155. Schlesinger, "Four Days with Fidel," p. 25.

156. Gabriel García Márquez, "Fidel—The Craft of the Word," introduction to Mina, *An Encounter with Fidel,* pp. 11, 14.

157. Fidel Castro, "The Road to Revolution in Latin America," in Barnes, *Twenty Years of the Cuban Revolution,* p. 80. See also Halperin, *Rise and Decline of Fidel Castro,* chapter 29 ("Intervention in Venezuela").

158. See, in particular, Blight, Lewis, and Welch, *Cuba Between the Superpowers,* pp. 46–49.

159. For background, see esp. Halperin, *The Rise and Decline of Fidel Castro,* pp. 318–46; and Szulc, "Exporting the Cuban Revolution," in Plank, *Cuba and the United States,* pp. 69–97.

160. Sorensen, *Kennedy,* p. 535.

161. See Carla Anne Robbins, "The 'Cuban Threat' in Central America," in Wolf Grabendorff, Heinrich W. Krumwiede, and Jörg Todt, eds., *Political Change in Central America: Internal and External Dimensions* (Boulder, Colo.: Westview, 1984), p. 218.

162. Castro's disdain for Prío did not prevent him from accepting Prío's financial support, which he used to buy the *Granma.* Mazarr, *Semper Fidel,* p. 227.

163. See Szulc, *Fidel,* pp. 154–57.

164. Carla Anne Robbins argues that while Castro and Betancourt had similar social goals, the two split primarily on tactical grounds (reform versus revolution). Given Castro's commitment to revolution, Betancourt came to represent a threat to the Castro way—all the more so because Venezuela was "the linchpin of Latin America." Robbins writes that "Venezuela was to Castro what Germany had been to Lenin: If the revolution was to succeed anywhere in the hemisphere, it would *have* to succeed in Venezuela." Robbins, *The Cuban Threat,* pp. 25–26.

165. See, for example, Schlesinger, *Robert Kennedy and His Times,* pp. 592–600.

166. Kennedy was shot at 12:30 P.M., 22 November 1963.

167. Kennedy delivered the speech to which Castro refers on the campus of American University in Washington, D.C., on 10 June 1963. While it stopped short of "praising" the Soviet Union, it certainly praised the Russian people and proffered a significant olive branch. "No government or social system is so evil," Kennedy said, "that its people must be considered lacking in virtue. As Americans, we find communism profoundly repugnant as a negation of personal freedom and dignity. But we can still hail the Russian people for their many achievements—in

science and space, in economic and industrial growth, in culture and in acts of courage." *Public Papers of the Presidents, 1963* (Washington, D.C.: Government Printing Office, 1964), pp. 459–64; 461.

168. In 1963, the CIA recruited Rolando Cubela Secades, a physician and former leader of the Students' Revolutionary Directorate forces in central Cuba during the war against Batista, to assassinate Castro. Cuban authorities discovered the plot and arrested Cubela Secades. Szulc, *Fidel*, pp. 56–57. See generally U.S. Senate, Select Committee to Study Government Operations with Respect to Intelligence Activities, *Alleged Assassination Plots Involving Foreign Leaders* (Washington, D.C.: Government Printing Office, 1975).

169. Jean Daniel, "Unofficial Envoy: An Historic Report from Two Capitals," *The New Republic*, 14 December 1963, 15–20.

170. William Attwood, *The Reds and the Blacks* (New York: Harper & Row, 1967), pp. 142–44.

171. Schlesinger, *Robert Kennedy and His Times*, pp. 594–97.

172. The official Cuban view of its intervention in Angola is amply represented in David Deutschmann, ed., *Angola and Namibia: Changing the History of Africa* (Melbourne: Ocean Press, 1989). It contains a long interview by the editor with Jorge Risquet, several speeches by Fidel Castro, and an interesting narrative of Operation Carlota (the massive lift to Angola in 1975) by novelist Gabriel García Márquez. For a more balanced assessment of Cuba in Angola, see the contributions by Jorge I. Domínguez, Newell M. Stultz, Gillian Gunn, and Fen Osler Hampson in Weiss and Blight, *The Suffering Grass*. On the performance of the Cubans' negotiating technique over the Angola/Namibia problem, see James G. Blight and Andrew W. Lynch, "Negotiation and the New World Disorder," *Negotiation Journal* 8, no. 4 (October 1992), 347–63.

173. For Emilio Aragonés's rather more colorful account, see Blight and Welch, *On the Brink*, 2d ed., p. 346.

174. Letter from President Dorticós and Prime Minister Castro to Acting Secretary General U Thant, 25 November 1962; in Larson, *The "Cuban Crisis" of 1962*, pp. 214–19; 218. See also Domínguez, *To Make a World Safe for Revolution*, pp. 43–44.

175. Kennedy to Khrushchev, 15 November 1962; in *Problems of Communism* 41, special issue (Spring 1992), 92–96; 95–96.

176. Blight and Welch, *On the Brink*, 2d ed., pp. 198–200.

177. On the peculiar "rationality" of the Cuban response to their situation in October 1962, see Aaron Belkin and James G. Blight, "Triangular Mutual Security," pp. 727–45; and Blight and Belkin, "Déjà Vu, '62?"

178. While it is difficult to know whether Castro is correct to surmise that the United States would have deployed a larger number of tactical nuclear weapons in an operation analogous to Operation Anadyr, it is interesting to note that American contingency plans for the invasion of Cuba in October 1962 did not call for such weapons. "Provisions of OPLAN 316 clearly stipulated that DAVY CROCKETT and other atomic delivery weapons were not to be taken into the objective area." The plan did provide, however, for bringing such weapons into the theater from their home bases on short notice. *CINCLANT Historical Account of the Cuban Crisis*, p. 72.

179. See appendix 2, p. 482.

180. Castro's remarks at this point are puzzling in view of his conviction that the *real* motive behind the Soviet deployment was strategic. If he believed in 1962 that the Soviet Union had assured destruction and second-strike capabilities, he ought to have wondered how the USSR stood to benefit strategically from a Cuban missile deployment. There is no evidence that he raised the question with Khrushchev, Biryuzov, or Alekseev.

181. McNamara seems to be mistaken in his recollection. American intelligence began receiving refugee reports of *Luna* missiles some time before October 19, and confirmed their presence through photography on 25 October. "Joint Evaluation of Soviet Missile Threat in Cuba, 19 October 1962," in McAuliffe, *CIA Documents on the Cuban Missile Crisis,* p. 208; "Supplement 7 to Joint Evaluation of Soviet Missile Threat in Cuba, 27 October 1962," in ibid., p. 325. No U.S. intelligence reports suggested that the *Lunas* were equipped with nuclear warheads, however. As General Smith notes in his remarks below (p. 261), Dennison requested authorization for equipping the American invasion force with nuclear weapons in anticipation of the *possibility* that Soviet forces in Cuba had tactical nuclear capability. See also Chang and Kornbluh, *The Cuban Missile Crisis, 1962,* pp. 175–76.

182. Paul H. Nitze, "Memorandum for the Executive Committee," 6 December 1962 (available from the National Security Archive, Washington, D.C.). This five-page memo consists of a summary of the views of Ernesto Betancourt, an anti-Castro Cuban who had been interviewed by a member of Nitze's staff, and whose views sufficiently impressed Nitze that he thought the Kennedy ExComm should know about them. During the first Reagan administration, Betancourt later became the head of Radio Martí. In a recent ironic twist, however, Betancourt resigned because of what he saw as a U.S. policy toward Cuba that is inappropriate in the post–Cold War era. See Ernesto F. Betancourt, "Let Cuba Be Cuba," *New York Times,* 6 September 1991, A-17, A-23.

183. Andrés Oppenheimer interviewed high-ranking Cuban officials of the new generation and asked them why they stuck with Castro, and why they still trusted his judgment. Oppenheimer writes: "In the mid-eighties, when almost everybody around Fidel had rushed to embrace Soviet Perestroika, Fidel had warned of the Soviet Union's coming disintegration. In Nicaragua, when Cuban reformists had applauded the Sandinistas' 1989 elections, Fidel predicted their defeat. In August 1991, while most Cuban officials celebrated the Soviet putsch, a worried Fidel had taken the news with prudent skepticism. 'Fidel has long headlights,' a member of the Politburo's new generation told me. 'He makes mistakes, but fewer than the rest of us. You can't dismiss his political genius.' " *Castro's Final Hour,* p. 404. From the outset, Castro has been suspicious of the kind of reforms tried by the Soviets and others in the Eastern bloc. He now sees their total failure as justifying his decision to stay the course.

184. Fidel Castro, "Moncada Barracks Anniversary Speech," 26 July 1988, Santiago de Cuba, *Foreign Broadcast Information Service,* LAT-88-145, pp. 1–18; 14, 15, 18.

185. Saul Landau, "Socialism on One Island?" *The Progressive,* June 1990, 18–20.

186. On 14 October 1991, Castro gave the closing speech at the Fourth Party Congress meeting in Santiago de Cuba, a speech which became known by Cubans as "Fidel's Ode to Death." It ended thus: "We're invincible! Because if all the members of the Politburo have to die, we will die, and we will not be weaker for it! If all members of the Central Committee have to die, we will die, and we will not be weaker for it! If all the delegates to the Congress have to die, all the delegates to-the Congress will die, and we will not be weaker for it! . . . If all the members of the Party have to die, all the members of the Party will die, and we will not weaken! If all the members of the Young Communist Union have to die, all the members of the Young Communist Union will die! And if, in order to crush the revolution, they have to kill all the people, the people, behind its leaders and its Party, will be willing to die! And even then we will not be weaker, because after us they would have to kill billions of people in the world who are not willing to be slaves, who are not willing to continue being exploited, who are not willing to keep going hungry!" Quoted in Oppenheimer, *Castro's Final Hour,* p. 400. It is easy to see why the pessimists, listening to speeches like this, expect a bloodbath in Cuba at some point; or why optimists, like a Cuban colleague who is a generation younger than Castro, say simply, "Fidel will always be a guy from the sixties."

187.   Fidel Castro, Speech to the Federation of Cuban Women, 7 March 1990; reported in *Granma,* 10 March 1990, p. 1.

188.   See, e.g., Susan Kaufmann Purcell, "Cuba's Cloudy Future," *Foreign Affairs* 69, no. 3 (Summer 1990), 113–30; Gillian Gunn, "Will Castro Fall?" *Foreign Policy,* no. 79 (Summer 1990), 132–50; Luis E. Aguilar, "Castro's Last Stand: Can Cuba Be Freed Without a Bloodbath?" *Policy Review,* no. 53 (Summer 1990), 74–77; Katherine Ellison, "Succeeding Castro: Will Cuba's Revolutionary Hero Share the Fate of Other Communist Leaders?" *The Atlantic,* June 1990, 34–38; and Tad Szulc, "Can Castro Last?" *New York Review of Books,* 31 May 1990, 12–15. In addition, Jacobo Timerman published *Cuba: A Journey* (New York: Knopf, 1990) at that time. It contains a seething criticism of intellectual decay in Cuba since the revolution, though one must understand Timerman's bias to understand the bitter vehemence of his attack.

189.   *Right v. Might: International Law and the Use of Force* (New York: Council on Foreign Relations, 1989).

190.   On Cuba's role in Ethiopia, see Mazarr, *Semper Fidel,* pp. 393–95; and Domínguez, *To Make a World Safe for Revolution,* pp. 159–62.

191.   The best analysis of the "Reagan Doctrine" is Fareed Zakaria, "The Reagan Strategy of Containment," *Political Science Quarterly* 105 (Fall 1990), 373–95.

192.   Khrushchev to Kennedy, 30 October 1962; in *Problems of Communism* 41, special issue (Spring 1992), 62–73; 69.

193.   Lockwood, *Castro's Cuba, Cuba's Fidel,* p. 209.

194.   García Márquez, "Fidel—The Craft of the Word," in Mina, *An Encounter with Fidel,* p. 16.

195.   The Committee of Santa Fe, a group of conservative political analysts interested in Latin America, met in the summer of 1980, in Santa Fe, New Mexico, to draw up a policy for the Caribbean Basin, in the event that Ronald Reagan was elected. One of the cornerstones of their statement was the rejection of any attempt to normalize relations with Cuba. Instead, the group proposed, though somewhat vaguely, to use threats of force and a tightening of the economic embargo to bring the Castro regime to its knees. One of the committee's principal drafters, Roger Fontaine, later became head of Latin American affairs in the first Reagan National Security Council. See Philip Brenner, *From Confrontation to Negotiation: U.S. Relations with Cuba* (Boulder, Colo: Westview, 1988), pp. 31–33.

196.   On the role Martí played in Castro's own political socialization, see Szulc, *Fidel,* esp. pp. 91–96.

197. For further discussion of the brigade and the crisis it provoked in 1979, see Garthoff, *Détente and Confrontation,* pp. 828–48.

198. Cf. Theodore Sorensen's remarks at the Moscow conference; Allyn, Blight, and Welch, *Back to the Brink,* pp. 91–93.

199. Most commentators doubt that the Cuban missile crisis *per se* figured heavily in Khrushchev's ouster, as it did not appear in the list of specific charges his colleagues leveled against him. While some of Khrushchev's associates, such as Mikhail Suslov, complained bitterly that Khrushchev had been indiscriminate and extravagant in his promises to other states, it seems that Khrushchev's greatest sin was unpredictability and recklessness, particularly in domestic policy. See, e.g., Edward Crankshaw, *Khrushchev: A Career* (New York: Viking, 1966), pp. 286–87; and Jonathan Steele, *World Power: Soviet Foreign Policy under Brezhnev and Andropov* (London: Michael Joseph, 1983), p. 163.

200. Castro's comments anticipate to a remarkable degree the argument presented in Richard Ned Lebow and Janice Gross Stein, *We All Lost the Cold War—Can We Win the Peace?* (Princeton: Princeton University Press, forthcoming).

201. Thompson died on 6 February 1972.

202. On 1 July 1991, the Warsaw Pact voted itself out of existence, and five days later NATO declared the Cold War over. "London Declaration on a Transformed North Atlantic Alliance," 6 July 1991 (NATO Press Service).

203. Castro's remarks here are implicitly contradicted by Nicola Miller, who writes that "Moscow has not succumbed to Cuban pressure to be admitted to the Warsaw Pact." Nicola Miller, *Soviet Relations with Latin America 1959–1987* (Cambridge: Cambridge University Press, 1989), p. 93. Miller, however, does not document the claim that Cuba sought membership. Nor does Garthoff, who echoes the claim; Garthoff, *Reflections on the Cuban Missile Crisis,* 1st ed., pp. 8n, 63.

204. Blight and Welch, *On the Brink,* 2d ed., p. 152.

205. Kennedy said, "There is no evidence of any organized combat force in Cuba from any Soviet bloc country; of military bases provided to Russia; of a violation of the 1934 treaty relating to Guantánamo; of the presence of offensive ground-to-ground missiles; or of other significant offensive capability, either in Cuban hands or under Soviet direction and guidance. Were it to be otherwise, the gravest issues would arise." Larson, *The "Cuban Crisis" of 1962,* pp. 17–18.

206. A 1967 study done for the House Foreign Affairs Committee concluded that there was conclusive evidence of only four "instances of direct Cuban support to insurgent groups" in Latin America. Quoted in Robbins, *The Cuban Threat,* p. 51.

207. The story is related in Szulc, *Fidel,* p. 638.

208. While Castro may well be correct to note that the U.S. government has changed its priorities vis-à-vis Cuba over the years, the rather stark sequence he paints is a gross oversimplification. The Carter administration, for example, simultaneously pressed Cuba on its activities in Africa, on its failure to compensate American firms and investors adequately for nationalizations after the revolution (a constant in American policy toward Cuba), and on its human rights record. Smith, *The Closest of Enemies,* p. 149. Some U.S. administrations, however, have not deemed Cuban domestic political issues barriers to improved relations. In 1971, for instance, Deputy Assistant Secretary of State Robert A. Hurwitch told

the Senate Foreign Relations Committee that "our concern is based upon the external, not internal, policies and activities of the Cuban government," and that the United States did not seek to overthrow the Cuban regime but to reduce "Cuba's capacity to export armed revolution" and to discourage "Soviet adventures in this hemisphere." U.S. Senate Foreign Relations Committee, *U.S. Policy Towards Cuba* (Washington, D.C.: Government Printing Office, 1971), p. 4.

209. See Smith, *The Closest of Enemies,* pp. 275–76.

4. CUBA AND THE BRINK

1. See chapter 3, p. 213.

2. Suárez, *Cuba, Castroism and Communism, 1959–66,* p. 169.

3. This does not mean, of course, that someone—like Saddam Hussein—who values survival above all else can always be successfully deterred. See Janice Gross Stein, "Deterrence and Compellence in the Gulf, 1990–91: A Failed or Impossible Task?" *International Security* 17, no. 2 (Fall 1992), 147–79.

4. Several of the American schemes to overthrow or to kill Castro are notable more for their hilarity than for their prospects of success. In one instance, the CIA's Technical Services Division (TSD) considered spraying the broadcast facilities from which Castro customarily delivered speeches with a chemical similar to LSD that produced erratic behavior, hoping that he would babble incoherently and lose his credibility; but the chemical proved to be unreliable and the plan had to be abandoned. In another scheme, the TSD succeeded in lacing a box of Castro's favorite cigars with a mind-altering drug, hoping that he would smoke one before he went on the air; but that plan, too, came to naught. The CIA contaminated another box of cigars with botulism toxin, but it is not known whether that particular box ever reached him. The CIA even tried to place a contract on Castro's life through two known mobsters in Florida, but negotiations fell through when the Mafia failed to find a suitable hired gun. The most creative plot of all involved waiting until Castro left his shoes outside a hotel door to be polished, and then dusting them with thallium salts—a powerful depilatory—so that his hair would fall out. *Sans* beard, the Agency surmised, Castro would have neither charisma nor popular support. But Castro canceled the trip on which the assault on his follicles was to take place. Wyden, *Bay of Pigs,* p. 40.

5. *Verde Olivo,* 10 October 1968; quoted in Robbins, *The Cuban Threat,* p. 47.

6. William Manchester, *American Caesar* (Boston: Little, Brown, 1978), pp. 335–36.

7. On the general form of the "hermeneutical circle" and its treatment by Heidegger and others, see Graeme Nicholson, *Seeing and Reading* (London: Macmillan, 1984).

8. Robert Jervis, "Perceiving and Coping with Threat," in Robert Jervis, Richard Ned Lebow, and Janice Gross Stein, with contributions by Patrick M. Morgan and Jack L. Snyder, *Psychology & Deterrence* (Baltimore: Johns Hopkins University Press, 1985), p. 23.

9. On the effects of the evoked set, see Robert Jervis, *Perception and Misperception in International Politics* (Princeton: Princeton University Press, 1976), pp. 203–16.

10. See, e.g., Bundy, *Danger and Survival,* chapter 8 ("Khrushchev, Berlin, and the West"), pp. 358–85.

11. See the early discussions in the White House immediately after the discovery of the missiles; "White House Tapes and Minutes of the Cuban Missile Crisis," *International Security* 10, no. 1 (Summer 1985), 164–203.

12. Even with the benefit of historical distance, it is difficult for American analysts to appreciate the defensive or deterrent motivations of the Soviet deployment. Thus Paul Huth and Bruce Russett do not even count the Soviet deployment as a case of attempted deterrence in the data set they created to explore the effectiveness of extended deterrence. Paul Huth and Bruce Russett, "What Makes Deterrence Work? Cases from 1900 to 1980," *World Politics* 36, no. 4 (July 1984), 496–526. While there is room for legitimate debate about the relative importance in Khrushchev's decision making of local deterrence vis-à-vis other motivations (defensive or otherwise), the suggestion that Khrushchev did not intend the deployment to serve *any* deterrent function seems definitively contradicted by the weight of evidence and testimony. See Blight and Welch, *On the Brink,* 2d ed., pp. 327–329.

13. See chapter 3, p. 174.

14. The story of American policy toward Cuba is long and complex. While we make no attempt here to examine the subject comprehensively, the following are particularly useful sources in this regard: Benjamin, *The United States and the Origins of the Cuban Revolution;* Louis A. Pérez, Jr., *Cuba and the United States: Ties of Singular Intimacy* (Athens, Ga.: University of Georgia Press, 1990); Basil Rauch, *American Interest in Cuba, 1848–1855* (New York: Columbia University Press, 1948); Walter LaFeber, *The New Empire: An Interpretation of American Expansion, 1860–1898* (Ithaca, N.Y.: Cornell University Press, 1963); Julius W. Pratt, *America's Colonial Experiment: How the United States Gained, Governed, and in Part Gave Away a Colonial Empire* (New York: Prentice-Hall, 1950); and Ernest R. May, *Imperial Democracy: The Emergence of America as a Great Power* (New York: Harcourt, Brace & World, 1961).

15. Adams to Hugh Nelson, 28 April 1823; quoted in Rauch, *American Interest in Cuba, 1848–1855,* pp. 24–25.

16. Ibid., p. 22.

17. See Samuel Flagg Bemis, *The Latin American Policy of the United States: An Historical Interpretation* (New York: Harcourt, Brace & Company, 1943), p. 95.

18. This concern antedates Adams's statement. The Jefferson administration, for example, expressly communicated to "influential persons in Cuba and Mexico" the following message: "If you remain under the dominion of the kingdom and family of Spain, we are contented; but we should be extremely unwilling to see you pass under the dominion or ascendancy of France or England. In the latter case, should you choose to declare independence, we cannot now commit ourselves by saying we would make common cause with you, but must reserve ourselves to act according to the then existing circumstances; but in our proceedings we shall be influenced by friendship to you, by a firm feeling that our interests are intimately connected, and by the strongest repugnance to see you under subordination to either France or England, either politically or commercially." Henry Adams, *History of the United States of America during the Administrations of Thomas Jefferson,* ed. Earl N. Harbert (New York: Library of America, 1986), p. 1161. Jefferson's message is a *Realpolitik* statement of American interests toward Cuba devoid of liberal sentiment or principle. That the author of the Declaration of Independence signed such a message speaks volumes of the prevailing attitude, for all but the small, aristocratic colonial class in Cuba were at least as oppressed by their mother country as the American colonists had been by Britain, and for most, political and economic hardships were significantly greater. Jefferson's message was not a message of hope or encouragement; it could only be read as an unwillingness or an inability to lend anticolonial movements the moral support they sought, offering nothing more than an undeveloped and seemingly hollow profession of "friendship." American interests would dictate American policy toward Cuba; those interests were to be defined in geopolitical terms. Cuban autonomy, on its merits, would count for little or nothing in the American calculus.

19. See chapter 3, n. 75, p. 422. The phrase "Monroe Doctrine" was not actually used until 1853. Perkins, *A History of the Monroe Doctrine,* p. 99. Ernest May argues that the Monroe Doctrine was almost entirely the result of the domestic political interests of the key players, especially Adams. See May, *The Making of the Monroe Doctrine.*

European leaders made no official response, but European commentators labeled the speech "blustering," "monstrous," "arrogant," "haughty," and "peremptory." Julius W. Pratt, Vincent P. DeSantis, and Joseph M. Siracusa, *A History of United States Foreign Policy,* 4th ed. (Englewood Cliffs, N.J.: Prentice-Hall, 1980), p. 70. The most accurate adjective would have been "immaterial." The policies of the European powers were generally unaffected by Monroe's pronouncement. Through much of the nineteenth century, the former Spanish colonies of Latin America looked primarily to Britain for defense of their independence, not to the United States; France intervened in Mexico, Argentina, and Uruguay in 1838 without so much as an American protest; Britain and France intervened with impunity in Argentina during the administration of President James K. Polk; Britain intervened in Central America in 1845 without any serious objection from the United States; and in what Perkins refers to as its "vindication" and "triumph"—the collapse of the French-supported Mexican regime of Emperor Maximilian in 1867—the United States objected vigorously to the establishment of a European monarch on Mexican soil without once invoking the Monroe Doctrine by name. Perkins, *A History of the Monroe Doctrine,* pp. 59, 68, 72–73, 85, 86, 132, 138. An ardent admirer of the doctrine, Perkins notes that by 1860, it had won neither "Latin American friendship, or European recognition" (p. 105), and describes the Venezuelan boundary dispute of 1895–99 as its only serious test (cf. p. 154). Although Britain accommodated the United States on this issue, it did so for the prudential reason of avoiding unnecessary strains in the two countries' relations at a time when its imperial commitments and European challenges were threatening to overwhelm its resources. Britain explicitly denied that the Monroe Doctrine had any legitimacy in international law and refused to recognize it in agreeing to arbitration of the boundary.

20. 27 April 1825; quoted in Rauch, *American Interest in Cuba,* p. 27.

21. Just seven years earlier (24 March 1818), Clay had this to say in the House of Representatives: "[It] is sometimes said that [Latin Americans] are too ignorant and too superstitious to admit of the existence of free government. This charge of ignorance is often urged by persons themselves actually ignorant of the real condition of that people. . . . They will, no doubt, adopt those kinds of governments which are best suited to their condition, best calculated for their happiness. Anxious as I am that they should be free governments, we have no right to prescribe for them." Quoted in Perkins, *A History of the Monroe Doctrine,* pp. 3–4.

22. Quoted in Rauch, *American Interest in Cuba,* p. 59.

23. Amos Aschbach Ettinger, *The Mission to Spain of Pierre Soulé, 1853–1855: A Study in the Cuban Diplomacy of the United States* (New Haven: Yale University Press, 1932), pp. 339–412.

24. See Grenville and Young, *Politics, Strategy, and American Diplomacy,* p. 3.

25. Perkins, *A History of the Monroe Doctrine,* pp. 155, 158; Bemis, *The Latin American Policy of the United States,* p. 130.

26. The public outcry against Weyler and Spanish atrocities, and how it pushed Cuba onto the American political agenda, is chronicled in May, *Imperial Democracy,* pp. 79–82. On the Cuban junta's success in supplying sensational stories to mainstream newspapers as well as to the yellow journals, see ibid., p. 71. Cf. Pratt, *America's Colonial Experiment,* pp. 40–41.

27. See LaFeber, *The New Empire,* p. 334; and Pratt, *America's Colonial Experiment,* p. 41.

28. May, *Imperial Democracy,* p. 85.

29. By the outbreak of the Spanish-American war, seventy-one filibustering expeditions were known to have been attempted from all sources; twenty-seven were successful. Spanish forces intercepted five on the coast of Cuba; the United States stopped thirty-three; Great Britain stopped two; and storms frustrated two. Bemis, *The Latin American Policy of the United States,* p. 131n, citing the Marquis de Olivart, "Le Différend entre l'Espagne et les États-Unis au Sujet de la Question Cubaine," in *Révue Générale de Droit International Public* 4 (1897), 577–620; 5 (1898), 358–422, 499–555; 7 (1900), 541–629; 9 (1902), 161–202.

30. Grenville and Young, *Politics, Strategy, and American Diplomacy,* p. 182.

31. Ibid., pp. 184, 189.

32. LaFeber, *The New Empire,* pp. 293–94.

33. Cleveland and his secretary of state, Richard Olney, opposed intervention not only because they feared it might result in annexation—which both of them opposed ("The administration already had enough problems without assuming those of the Cubans." Ibid., p. 286)—but also because it would lead to a war that either silver Democrats or Republicans would finish; and as Walter LaFeber notes, "such a thought was not comforting to the gold Democrats, who nursed hopes of regaining power in 1900." Ibid., p. 286.

34. Edward F. Atkins, a Cuban sugar grower and strong opponent of granting the rebels belligerent rights, was a close friend of Olney's. Ibid., p. 287.

35. Ibid., p. 292.

36. Grenville and Young, *Politics, Strategy, and American Diplomacy,* p. 192.

37. Ibid., pp. 196–97.

38. May, *Imperial Democracy,* p. 78.

39. Grenville and Young, *Politics, Strategy, and American Diplomacy,* pp. 244–45.

40. May, *Imperial Democracy,* p. 123.

41. "Against this deliberate infliction of suffering on innocent noncombatants . . . the President is constrained to protest, in the name of the American people and in the name of common humanity." The note was confidential. Ibid., p. 121.

42. See, e.g., LaFeber, *The New Empire,* p. 335.

43. May, *Imperial Democracy,* p. 135.

44. LaFeber, *The New Empire,* p. 344.

45. Pratt, *America's Colonial Experiment*, p. 47. A separate Spanish investigation concluded that the only explosion had been an internal one.

46. May, *Imperial Democracy*, pp. 139–47.

47. Grenville and Young, *Politics, Strategy, and American Diplomacy*, p. 255.

48. Pratt, DeSantis, and Siracusa, *A History of United States Foreign Policy*, p. 177.

49. Quoted in Bemis, *The Latin American Policy of the United States*, p. 138.

50. Pratt, for example, argues that the demand for intervention "arose primarily from humanitarian motives." Julius W. Pratt, "The Coming War with Spain," in Paolo E. Coletta, ed., *Threshold to American Internationalism: Essays on the Foreign Policies of William McKinley* (New York: Exposition Press, 1970), p. 39. LaFeber emphasizes economic motivations. *The New Empire*, passim.

51. Pratt, "The Coming War with Spain," p. 63.

52. Grenville and Young, *Politics, Strategy, and American Diplomacy*, pp. 180, 263.

53. Quoted in Pratt, *America's Colonial Experiment*, p. 119.

54. Theodore P. Wright, Jr., "United States Electoral Intervention in Cuba," *Inter-American Economic Affairs* 13, no. 3 (Winter 1959), 52.

55. Ibid., p. 52; from Department of State, *Papers Relating to the Foreign Relations of the United States: 1902*, p. 321.

56. Pratt, *America's Colonial Experiment*, p. 122.

57. David F. Healy, *The United States in Cuba, 1898–1902: Generals, Politicians, and the Search for Policy* (Madison: University of Wisconsin Press, 1963), p. 214. See also Perkins, *A History of the Monroe Doctrine*, pp. 228–29.

58. Perkins, *A History of the Monroe Doctrine*, p. 269.

59. Pratt, *America's Colonial Experiment*, p. 329.

60. See Bemis, *The Latin American Policy of the United States*, p. 203; and Perkins, *A History of the Monroe Doctrine*, p. 332.

61. Pratt, *America's Colonial Experiment*, p. 321.

62. Ibid., p. 317.

63. Bemis, *The Latin American Policy of the United States*, pp. 57–58. Irwin Gellman writes that "[t]here was a change in diplomacy under Roosevelt, but it was in mood only. The tactics were altered, not the strategy; the fundamental objectives of the United States in the Western Hemisphere remained constant. While the Good Neighbor Policy put a stop to use of United States troops to maintain order in the hemisphere, the United States continued to work for stability within Latin American states in order to protect American investments." Irwin F. Gellman, *Roosevelt and Batista: Good Neighbor Diplomacy in Cuba, 1933–1945* (Albuquerque: University of New Mexico Press, 1973), p. 5.

64. Ibid., p. 226; see also Bemis, *The Latin American Policy of the United States*, pp. 272–74.

65. Bemis, *The Latin American Policy of the United States*, pp. 281–82.

66. Gellman, *Roosevelt and Batista*, p. 232.

67. Ibid., p. 7.

68. Donald Marquand Dozer, *Are We Good Neighbors? Three Decades of Inter-American Relations, 1930–1960* (Gainesville: University of Florida Press, 1959), p. 110.

69. Ibid., p. 340.

70. Ibid., pp. 241, 355–56.

71. Quoted in ibid., p. 341.

72. Higgins, *The Perfect Failure,* p. 39.

73. Wyden, *Bay of Pigs,* p. 20.

74. Ibid., p. 160.

75. Ibid., p. 100.

76. Quoted in ibid., pp. 122–23.

77. Blight and Welch, *On the Brink,* 2d ed., p. 249.

78. Bemis, *The Latin American Policy of the United States,* pp. x, 386.

79. Ibid., p. 132.

80. Perkins, *A History of the Monroe Doctrine,* pp. 197–98. Not only did the McKinley administration consciously avoid referring to the Monroe Doctrine in its diplomacy with Spain, it seemingly ignored it altogether in the winter of 1897 when Germany sent two warships to neighboring Haiti and threatened to bombard the presidential palace to force the release of a German national from prison, extract a $30,000 indemnity, and secure an apology. The only official American response was a State Department declaration that the Germans were within their rights. Perkins, *A History of the Monroe Doctrine,* p. 196; May, *Imperial Democracy,* p. 128.

81. Bemis, *The Latin American Policy of the United States,* p. 138.

82. Ibid., p. 279.

83. Wright, "United States Electoral Intervention in Cuba," pp. 58–64.

84. See chapter 2, p. 43.

85. See chapter 3, pp. 175–77.

86. See generally R. G. Collingwood, *The Idea of History* (New York: Galaxy, 1956) and *Essays in the Philosophy of History* (New York: McGraw-Hill, 1966); and Raymond Aron, *Introduction à la Philosophie de l'Histoire: Essai sur les Limites de l'Objectivité Historique* (Paris: Gallimard, 1978).

87. Benjamin, *The United States and the Origins of the Cuban Revolution,* p. 3.

88. Carla Robbins explores Castro's early attempts to support revolutions in Latin America, and suggests that the United States overestimated Castro's threats of subversion. Robbins, *The Cuban Threat,* pp. 7–71, 130–31 (citing the report on the 1966 Tricontinental Conference prepared for the Internal Security Subcommittee of the Senate Judiciary Committee). For an analysis of Cuban support for revolutionary movements, see Domínguez, *To Make a World Safe for Revolution,* pp. 113–46.

89. Pérez, *Cuba and the United States,* pp. 247–48.

90. See Blight and Welch, *On the Brink,* 2d ed., pp. 116–17, and citations therein.

91. Ibid., pp. 296, 327–29.

92. Hugh Thomas, *The Cuban Revolution* (New York: Harper & Row, 1977), p. 603.

93. See chapter 3, pp. 77–78, 197–98, 242.

94. See chapter 3, p. 202.

95. See chapter 3, p. 203.

96. See chapter 3, p. 206.

97. See chapter 3, p. 242.

98. See chapter 3, p. 242.

99. Sergio del Valle and Emilio Aragonés, cited in Blight and Welch, *On the Brink,* 2d ed., p. 328.

100. E.g., Raúl Castro's statement of 11 September 1962, *Revolución,* 13 September 1962, 1 (*CEA Chronology,* p. 24); and Osvaldo Dorticós's statement to the U.N., 10 October 1962, cited in Dinerstein, *The Making of a Missile Crisis,* pp. 210–11.

101. See chapter 3, p. 254.

102. See chapter 3, pp. 82–83.

103. 21 October 1962. See Bundy, *Danger and Survival,* pp. 381–82.

104. See chapter 3, p. 203.

105. See chapter 3, p. 91.

106. Interviews and personal communications with the authors, 1989–93.

107. Western analysts have been tempted to blame organizational routines for this particular failure. Allison, *Essence of Decision,* pp. 110–11. But cf. David A. Welch, "The Organizational Process and Bureaucratic Politics Paradigms: Retrospect and Prospect," *International Security* 17, no. 2 (Fall 1992), 123–28, 135.

108. "I actually thought that there were *more* tactical nuclear weapons. . . . Nine was not a very logical number. If I had been consulted, I would have said that there was need for more tactical nuclear weapons." See chapter 3, p. 251. N.B. that, in making this statement, Castro both acknowledges his ignorance of the Soviet deployment and implicitly criticizes Gribkov, one of its primary architects.

109. See chapter 3, p. 79.

110. It is not unlikely that some combination of these led Khrushchev astray. Two other factors are clearly relevant, according to Troyanovsky's testimony: (1) Khrushchev failed to consult his Americanologists; and (2) he was not open to dissent. See chapter 3, pp. 71–72.

111. See chapter 3, pp. 207–8.

112. See chapter 3, n. 139.

113. Blight and Welch, *On the Brink,* 2d ed., p. 334.

114. Defensive avoidance is the tendency to deny the relevance of psychologically painful evidence. See Irving L. Janis and Leon Mann, *Decision Making: A Psychological Analysis of Conflict, Choice, and Commitment* (New York: Free Press, 1977), pp. 57–58, 107–33.

115. George Bruce, *Sea Battles of the 20th Century* (London: Hamlyn, 1975), pp. 7–21.

116. See chapter 3, p. 59.

117. See n. 108, above.

118. It remains possible, of course, that Khrushchev was not aware of the *number* of *Lunas* provided to Soviet forces in Cuba, and thus that the puzzling number was, in some sense, a function of standard operating procedures.

119. See chapter 3, p. 259. Elsewhere in chapter 3, Gribkov says, "I would like to quote Malinovsky when he gave me the order to convey Khrushchev's and the Defense Minister's instructions to Pliyev: 'The missile forces will fire only if authorized by Nikita Sergeievich Khrushchev'—it was repeated—'only if instructed by the Supreme Commander-in-Chief himself.' Comrade Pliyev was to remember that the missile division had been sent to Cuba to deter aggression. The tactical nuclear forces—the six *Luna* launchers I've mentioned—could be employed with nuclear weapons during a direct invasion by the aggressor. It was said that before arriving at a decision on employing the tactical missiles, the situation had to be very thoroughly and carefully assessed, and, in case of extreme need only, then could the decision be made" (pp. 60–61). In "Operation Anadyr," *Der Spiegel,* 20 April 1992, Gribkov relates the order thus: "The tactical *Luna* missiles can be used by Pliyev, using his own judgment, in the event of an attack by the USA and an imminent landing of troops on the coast. The *Luna* missiles must not be used rashly. Therefore, he must maintain a stable and reliable cable and radio communications with each missile unit. The missiles are not to be used without launch approval." (Trans. David Lewis.) There are no important differences in these three accounts.

120. See chapter 3, p. 204. Western analysts have long suspected that Soviet theater commanders in the early 1960s had authority to use tactical nuclear weapons in the event of war; see, e.g., Stephen M. Meyer, "Soviet Theater Nuclear Forces, Part II: Capabilities and Implications," Adelphi Paper no. 188 (London: International Institute for Strategic Studies, 1983), pp. 30–31. In this respect, such standing orders would not have been unusual. But the circumstances of the Cuban deployment were atypical for the Soviet armed forces, and one would expect Khrushchev to be sensitive to the unique escalatory dangers associated with pre-delegated authority to use tactical nuclear weapons in Cuba. What the U.S. delegation in Havana found difficult to credit was the idea that Khrushchev would not keep his forces in Cuba on a particularly tight leash.

121. Newhouse argued in "Socialism or Death" that Gribkov was lying; Schlesinger argued that he was telling the truth in "Four Days with Fidel," pp. 22ff. Cf. also Mark Kramer's critique of Schlesinger's article, and Schlesinger's reply, *New York Review of Books,* 28 May 1992, 54–55.

122. Newhouse, "Socialism or Death," p. 70.

123. Cf. Richard Ned Lebow, "Was Khrushchev Bluffing in Cuba?" *Bulletin of the Atomic Scientists* 44, no. 3 (April 1988), 38–42.

124. Anatoly I. Gribkov, "Karibskii krizis" (The Caribbean Crisis), part 3, *Voenno-istoricheskii zhurnal* (Military-Historical Journal), no. 12 (December 1992), 35.

125. Lt.-Col. Anatoly Dokuchaev, "100-dnevnyi yadernyi kruiz" (The 100-Day Nuclear Cruise), *Krasnaya zvezda* (Red Star), 6 November 1992, 2.

126. Blight and Welch, *On the Brink,* 2d ed., p. 276.

127. Dokuchaev, "100-dnevnyi yadernyi kruiz."

128. We do not mean to imply that this is an entirely new insight. Students of the July crisis of 1914, for example, have long been aware that the Kaiser was willing to take far greater risks early in the crisis, when the threat of a general European war seemed distant, than at the end, when war seemed imminent. Moreover, the historical record amply demonstrates that the Kaiser came to regret, at the beginning of August, that he had made strong commitments to Austria in a calmer time, and came to lament the fact that German military plans drawn up in peacetime severely reduced his diplomatic flexibility in the heat of crisis. But the theoretical implications of these observations have yet to be fully explored and it remains unclear whether they may be generalized. See, e.g., Richard Ned Lebow, *Between Peace and War: The Nature of International Crisis* (Baltimore: Johns Hopkins University Press, 1981), pp. 119–47; and Jack Snyder, *The Ideology of the Offensive: Military Decision Making and the Disasters of 1914* (Ithaca, N.Y.: Cornell University Press, 1984).

129. Welch and Blight, "The Eleventh Hour of the Cuban Missile Crisis," pp. 12–18.

130. See Blight and Welch, *On the Brink,* 2d ed., part 3 and Afterword; Raymond L. Garthoff, *Reflections on the Cuban Missile Crisis,* pp. 32–60; and Lebow and Stein, *We All Lost the Cold War,* chapter 6. The one piece of testimony introduced at the Havana conference dissonant with the story as it is currently understood came from Troyanovksy, who claimed that Khrushchev's initial reaction to Kennedy's speech was "quite calm, because what was talked about was a quarantine. The quarantine was something abstract. There was no real threat of aggression, or of strikes against Cuba, etc." Chapter 3, p. 73. All other accounts of Khrushchev's reaction uniformly suggest that he was enraged, as do his messages of 23 October to Castro (as read to the conferees) and to Kennedy. See *Problems of Communism* 41, special issue (Spring 1992), 31–32.

131. See chapter 3, p. 61.

132. See chapter 3, p. 73.

133. Garthoff, *Reflections on the Cuban Missile Crisis,* p. 51.

134. Blight and Welch, *On the Brink,* 2d ed., pp. 305–12, 336–44.

135. See chapter 3, p. 74.

136. For discussion of these negotiations, see Blight and Welch, *On the Brink,* 2d ed., pp. 337–38, 340–432. In interviews, Dobrynin has subsequently modified his testimony and now claims that he and Robert Kennedy did not meet on the night of 26 October. See Lebow and Stein, *We All Lost the Cold War,* chapter 6.

137. Khrushchev to Kennedy, 27 October 1962, 28 October 1962; in *Problems of Communism* 41, special issue (Spring 1992), 45–50, 52–58.

138. Blight and Welch, *On the Brink,* 2d ed., pp. 83–84, 113–15.

139. Editorial, *Saturday Review,* 10 October 1977, 4.

140. "[T]he Pentagon is searching for a pretext to frustrate this agreement. This is why it is organizing these provocative flights. Yesterday you shot down one of these, while earlier you didn't shoot them down when they overflew your territory." Khrushchev to Castro, 28 October 1962; in appendix 2, p. 483.

141. "It would have been enough for Nikita to say, 'We agree to withdraw the missiles if you give satisfactory guarantees for Cuba.' Cuba would not have blocked this; it would have helped in that negotiation. But the minimum guarantees we wanted were [the] five [conditions]—not just a guarantee of not invading." Chapter 3, p. 215.

142. See chapter 3, p. 121.

143. See chapter 3, p. 113.

144. See chapter 3, p. 202.

145. See chapter 3, p. 121.

146. Castro to Khrushchev, 26 October 1962; in appendix 2, p. 481.

147. Ibid. It is interesting that Castro regarded an air strike more likely than an invasion. The only reason he gives in the letter justifying this inference was that an invasion "would call for a large number of forces and it is, in addition, the most repulsive form of aggression, which might inhibit them." His reflections here on American sensibilities seem to us puzzling and incongruous. In any case, in the unlikely event that Kennedy had authorized an air strike, he would almost certainly also have authorized a follow-up invasion to ensure that all of the Soviet missiles were destroyed. "Inasmuch as the concept of a clean, swift strike has been abandoned as militarily impractical," wrote Theodore Sorensen on 20 October, "it is generally agreed that the more widespread air attack will inevitably lead to an invasion with all of its consequences." Sorensen, summary of objections to air strike option and advantages of blockade option, in Chang and Kornbluh, *The Cuban Missile Crisis, 1962,* p. 133.

148. See chapter 3, p. 251.

149. See chapter 3, p. 252.

150. See chapter 3, p. 252.

151. See chapter 3, pp. 109, 111.

152. Khrushchev, *Khrushchev Remembers: The Glasnost Tapes,* p. 177.

153. Troyanovsky noted that Castro's assessment "jibed with other reports and, also, bore some relation to the talks between Robert Kennedy and Dobrynin, where we were informed that the United States required an answer within twenty-four hours. There were a number of reports then coinciding, which helped accelerate the final decision to accept the Kennedy proposal." See chapter 3, p. 115.

154. See chapter 3, p. 214.

155. Castro to Khrushchev, 28 October 1962; in appendix 2, p. 484.

156. Khrushchev to Castro, 30 October 1962; in appendix 2, pp. 485–88.

157. Castro to Khrushchev, 31 October 1962; in appendix 2, pp. 489–91.

158. See chapter 3, p. 245.

159. See chapter 3, p. 243.

160. Sergo Mikoyan, interviews with the authors. See also Blight and Welch, *On the Brink,* 2d ed., pp. 268–69, 344–46.

161. See chapter 3, p. 245.

162. Domínguez, *To Make a World Safe for Revolution,* pp. 44–56. On the notion of security regimes, cf. Robert Jervis, "Security Regimes," *International Organization* 36, no. 2 (Spring 1982), 357–78; and Joseph S. Nye, Jr., "Nuclear Learning and U.S.-Soviet Security Regimes," *International Organization* 41, no. 3 (Summer 1987), 371–402.

163. See Garthoff, *Détente and Confrontation*, pp. 76–83, 300–304, 617–18, 828–48.

164. See Smith, *The Closest of Enemies*, pp. 238–77; 250, 272–75.

165. See chapter 3, p. 298.

166. Quoted in Robbins, *The Cuban Threat*, p. 49.

167. Ibid., p. 44.

168. Ibid., pp. 39–40. On Cuba's ideological challenge to the USSR in the 1960s, see also Domínguez, *To Make a World Safe for Revolution*, pp. 61–77.

169. Domínguez, *To Make a World Safe for Revolution*, pp. 72–77.

170. See the discussion in Miller, *Soviet Relations with Latin America 1959–1987*, pp. 104–105.

171. Domínguez, *To Make a World Safe for Revolution*, p. 76.

172. On the international dimension of Cuba's involvement in Africa, see, e.g., Garthoff, *Détente and Confrontation*, pp. 502–37 (and the sources therein, esp. p. 503n.); Mazarr, *Semper Fidel*, pp. 393–95; and Smith, *The Closest of Enemies*, pp. 128–42.

173. See chapter 3, pp. 271–72.

174. "End of a Beautiful Friendship," *The Globe & Mail* (Toronto), 23 April 1993, 1.

175. Miller, *Soviet Relations with Latin America 1959–1987*, p. 118.

176. "Rectification" began in April 1986. See the discussion in Miller, *Soviet Relations with Latin America 1959–1987*, pp. 122–25; and in Domínguez, *To Make a World Safe for Revolution*, pp. 109–11.

177. See chapter 3, p. 280.

178. *Revolución*, 20 July 1960, 16.

179. See chapter 3, p. 300.

180. Pérez, *Cuba and the United States*, pp. 250–52.

181. This is the intent of the "Cuban Democracy Act" of 1992, supported (reluctantly) by President Bush and endorsed by President Clinton.

182. Approximately 1 million Cubans—10 percent of the island's population—emigrated to the United States after the revolution, more than half of whom settled in southern Florida. They remain a powerful lobby and voting bloc against normalization. Other political forces in the United States who oppose rapprochement include sugar interests in Florida, Louisiana, and Hawaii, and the citrus industries of Florida, Texas, and California. These five states alone account for 126 Electoral College votes, or almost a quarter of the total (538). It is therefore hardly surprising that no presidential candidate of a major political party in the United States has ventured to call for improved relations with Cuba.

In addition to domestic constraints on normalization, there would also be international objections. If Cuba could trade freely with the United States, its exports would compete directly with those of Mexico, Central America, and the Caribbean. Cf. Pérez, *Cuba and the United States*, pp. 253, 258–59.

183. Foner, *Inside the Monster*, p. 45.

5. THE LEGACY OF THE BRINK

1. George Bush, "The President on Cuba," U.S. State Department Release (Office of Cuban Affairs), March 1990.

2. Fidel Castro, Speech in Havana on the anniversary of the attack on the Moncada Barracks, 26 July 1990. See *Miami Herald,* 27 July 1990, 1.

3. McNamara is not quoting precisely, but is paraphrasing his remarks. See Allyn, Blight, and Welch, *Back to the Brink,* pp. 7–9.

4. See the discussion in chapter 4, pp. 352–56.

5. Allyn, Blight, and Welch, *Back to the Brink,* pp. 215–16.

6. On 4 August 1970, Soviet chargé d'affaires Yuly M. Vorontsov raised with Kissinger the issue of reaffirming the 1962 Kennedy-Khrushchev understanding. Upon review, Kissinger decided the agreement was "never formally buttoned down" in 1962; but Nixon and Kissinger decided that it would be a good idea to "tie Moscow down" by "reaffirming" the deal, and so Kissinger informed Vorontsov on 7 August that the United States considered the agreement in effect and "noted with satisfaction" that the Soviets considered it "still in full force." Garthoff, *Détente and Confrontation,* p. 79; Henry Kissinger, *White House Years* (Boston: Little, Brown, 1979), pp. 632–35.

7. See the remarks by Raymond Garthoff, p. 386.

8. In their post-crisis correspondence, Khrushchev and Kennedy failed to agree on the issue of the non-invasion pledge. Khrushchev repeatedly attempted to nail down the American commitment, construed ambiguous remarks by Kennedy as confirmations of the pledge, and insisted that the verification condition had been met by aerial inspections of Soviet ships on the high seas. Kennedy, however, repeatedly insisted that the pledge was conditional upon inspections of Cuban territory. See, e.g., Khrushchev to Kennedy, 4 November 1962; Kennedy to Khrushchev, 6 November 1962; Khrushchev to Kennedy, 11 November 1962; Khrushchev to Kennedy, 13 November 1962; Kennedy to Khrushchev, 15 November 1962; Khrushchev to Kennedy, 19 November 1962; Khrushchev to Kennedy, 22 November 1962; Khrushchev to Kennedy, 10 December 1962; Kennedy to Khrushchev, 14 December 1962; in *Problems of Communism* 41, special issue (Spring 1992), 76, 80, 83, 90, 93, 98–105, 107, 113–14, 118.

9. Apparently, not even Khrushchev shared Risquet's view on this point. In the 1970 edition of his memoirs, Khrushchev cites a letter he wrote to Castro in late 1962: "Now that the climax of tension has passed and we have exchanged commitments with the American government, it will be very difficult for the Americans to interfere. If the United States should invade now, the Soviet Union will have the right to attack. Thus we have secured the existence of a socialist Cuba *for at least another two years while Kennedy is in the White House.*" Khrushchev, *Khrushchev Remembers,* p. 504 (emphasis added).

10. See *CINCLANT Historical Account,* pp. 55–56.

11. Upon their return to the United States, various members of the U.S. delegation briefed Deputy Secretary of State Lawrence Eagleburger, Assistant Secretary of State for Inter-American Affairs Bernard Aronson, National Security Adviser Brent Scowcroft, and Coordinator of Cuban Affairs Vicki Huddleston.

12. For summaries of the cases of María Elena Cruz and Elizardo Sánchez, see Schlesinger, "Four Days with Fidel: A Havana Diary," pp. 22, 27–29; and Newhouse, "Socialism or Death," pp. 74–75.

13. See Preston, "The Trial That Shook Cuba."

Bibliography

Abel, Elie. *The Missile Crisis*. Philadelphia: Lippincott, 1966.

Adams, Henry. *History of the United States of America during the Administrations of Thomas Jefferson*. Edited by Earl N. Harbert. New York: Library of America, 1986.

Aguilar, Luis E. "Castro's Last Stand: Can Cuba Be Freed Without a Bloodbath?" *Policy Review*, no. 53 (Summer 1990), 74–77.

Allison, Graham T. "Avoiding Another Missile Crisis." *Boston Globe,* 5 February 1989, 29–30.

——. *Essence of Decision: Explaining the Cuban Missile Crisis*. Boston: Little, Brown, 1971.

Allyn, Bruce J., James G. Blight, and David A. Welch. "Essence of Revision: Moscow, Havana, and the Cuban Missile Crisis." *International Security* 14, no. 3 (Winter 1989/90), 136–72.

——. eds. *Back to the Brink: Proceedings of the Moscow Conference on the Cuban Missile Crisis, January 27–28, 1989*. Lanham, Md.: University Press of America, 1992.

Aron, Raymond. *Introduction à la Philosophie de l'Histoire: Essai sur les Limites de l'Objectivité Historique*. Paris: Gallimard, 1978.

Attwood, William. *The Reds and the Blacks*. New York: Harper & Row, 1967.

"Back from the Brink: The Correspondence Between President John F. Kennedy and Chairman Nikita S. Khrushchev on the Cuban Missile Crisis of Autumn 1962." *Problems of Communism* 41, special issue (Spring 1992), 1–120.

Ball, George. "JFK's Big Moment." *New York Review of Books,* 13 February 1992, 16–20.

———. *The Past Has Another Pattern: Memoirs.* New York: Norton, 1982.

Barnes, Jack, ed. *Twenty Years of the Cuban Revolution: Selected Speeches of Fidel Castro.* N.p.: Socialist Workers Party, 1979.

Belkin, Aaron, and James G. Blight. "Triangular Mutual Security: Why the Missile Crisis Matters in a World Beyond the Cold War." *Political Psychology* 12, no. 4 (December 1991), 727–45.

Bemis, Samuel Flagg. *The Latin American Policy of the United States: An Historical Interpretation.* New York: Harcourt, Brace & Company, 1943.

Benjamin, Jules R. *The United States and the Origins of the Cuban Revolution: An Empire of Liberty in an Age of National Liberation.* Princeton: Princeton University Press, 1990.

Betancourt, Ernesto F. "Let Cuba Be Cuba." *New York Times,* 6 September 1991, A-17, A-23.

Blight, James G. *The Shattered Crystal Ball: Fear and Learning in the Cuban Missile Crisis.* Savage, Md.: Rowman & Littlefield, 1990.

Blight, James G., and Aaron Belkin. "Déjà Vu, '62? Deterring New World Desperation and Disorder." *Bulletin of Peace Psychology* 1, no. 3 (1992), 13–16.

Blight, James G., janet M. Lang, and Bruce J. Allyn. "Fidel Cornered: The Soviet Fear of Another Cuban Crisis." *Russia and the World* (Fall 1990), 21–25, 39–40.

Blight, James G., janet M. Lang, and Aaron Belkin. "Why Castro Released the Armageddon Letters." *Miami Herald,* 20 January 1991, Sunday Supplement, 1.

Blight, James G., David Lewis, and David A. Welch, eds. *Cuba Between the Superpowers: The Antigua Conference on the Cuban Missile Crisis.* Savage, Md.: Rowman & Littlefield, forthcoming.

Blight, James G., and Andrew W. Lynch. "Negotiation and the New World Disorder." *Negotiation Journal* 8, no. 4 (October 1992), 347–63.

Blight, James G., Joseph S. Nye, Jr., and David A. Welch. "The Cuban Missile Crisis Revisited." *Foreign Affairs* 66, no. 1 (Fall 1987), 170–89.

Blight, James G., and David A. Welch. *On the Brink: Americans and Soviets Reexamine the Cuban Missile Crisis.* 2d ed. New York: Noonday, 1990.

———. *On the Brink: Americans and Soviets Reexamine the Cuban Missile Crisis.* 1st ed. New York: Hill & Wang, 1989.

Bourne, Peter G. *Fidel: A Biography of Fidel Castro.* New York: Dodd, Mead, 1987.

Brenner, Philip. "Thirteen Months: Cuba's Perspective on the Missile Crisis." In *The Cuban Missile Crisis Revisited.* Edited by James A. Nathan. New York: St. Martin's, 1992, 187–217.

———. "Cuba and the Missile Crisis." *Journal of Latin American Studies* 22, no. 1 (February 1990), 115–42.

———. *From Confrontation to Negotiation: U.S. Relations with Cuba.* Boulder, Colo.: Westview, 1988.

Brenner, Philip, and James G. Blight. *The October Crisis: Fidel Castro's 1968 "Secret Speech" and the Breach in Soviet-Cuban Relations.* Savage, Md.: Rowman & Littlefield, 1993.

Bruce, George. *Sea Battles of the 20th Century.* London: Hamlyn, 1975.

Brugioni, Dino A. *Eyeball to Eyeball: The Inside Story of the Cuban Missile Crisis.* Edited by Robert F. McCort. New York: Random House, 1991.

Bundy, McGeorge. *Danger and Survival: Choices About the Bomb in the First Fifty Years.* New York: Random House, 1988.

Burlatsky, Fyodor. "Black Saturday." *Literaturnaya gazeta,* 23 November 1983, 9–10.

Bush, George. "The President on Cuba." U.S. State Department Release (Office of Cuban Affairs), March 1990.

Castro, Fidel. "Speech to the Committees for the Defense of the Revolution (CDRs) on the Thirtieth Anniversary of Their Founding, 28 September 1990." *Granma* (Cuban Communist Party Daily), 1 October 1990, 1.

———. "Moncada Barracks Anniversary Speech," 26 July 1988, Santiago de Cuba. *Foreign Broadcast Information Service,* LAT-88-145, 1–18.

CEA Chronology. See *Chronology of Events in Cuba, January–December 1962.*

Chang, Laurence, and Peter Kornbluh, eds. *The Cuban Missile Crisis, 1962: A National Security Archive Documents Reader.* New York: New Press, 1992.

Chronology of Events in Cuba, January–December 1962. Havana: Centro de Estudios sobre America [CEA], 1990.

Cline, Ray S. "Commentary: The Cuban Missile Crisis." *Foreign Affairs* 68, no. 4 (Summer 1989), 190–96.

———. "Nuclear War Seemed Remote." *Washington Post,* 5 February 1989, D-8.

Collingwood, R. G. *Essays in the Philosophy of History.* New York: McGraw-Hill, 1966.

———. *The Idea of History.* New York: Galaxy, 1956.

Constable, Pamela. "Cuba Giving Mixed Signals on U.S. Ties." *Boston Globe,* 15 January 1992, 2.

Cousins, Norman. Editorial. *Saturday Review,* 10 October 1977, 4.

Crankshaw, Edward. *Khrushchev: A Career.* New York: Viking, 1966.

Daniel, Jean. "Unofficial Envoy: An Historic Report from Two Capitals." *The New Republic,* 14 December 1963, 15–20.

Desnoes, Edmundo. *Inconsolable Memories* [Memories of Underdevelopment]. New York: New American Library, 1967.

Dessler, David. "What's at Stake in the Agent-Structure Debate?" *International Organization* 43, no. 3 (Summer 1989), 441–74.

Detzer, David. *The Brink: Cuban Missile Crisis, 1962.* New York: Crowell, 1972.

Deutschmann, David, ed. *Angola and Namibia: Changing the History of Africa.* Melbourne: Ocean Press, 1989.

———, ed. *Che Guevara and the Cuban Revolution: Writings and Speeches of Ernesto Che Guevara.* Sydney: Pathfinder, 1987.

Dinerstein, Herbert S. *The Making of a Missile Crisis: October 1962.* Baltimore: Johns Hopkins University Press, 1976.

Dokuchaev, Lt.-Col. Anatoly. "100-dnevnyi yadernyi kruiz" (The 100-Day Nuclear Cruise). *Krasnaya zvezda (Red Star)*, 6 November 1992, 2.

Domínguez, Jorge I. *To Make a World Safe for Revolution: Cuba's Foreign Policy.* Cambridge, Mass.: Harvard University Press, 1989.

Dozer, Donald Marquand. *Are We Good Neighbors? Three Decades of Inter-American Relations, 1930–1960.* Gainesville: University of Florida Press, 1959.

Draper, Theodore. "How *Not* to Overthrow Castro." In *Castro's Revolution: Myths and Realities.* Edited by Theodore Draper. New York: Praeger, 1962, 59–113.

Eberstadt, Nicholas. "Did Fidel Fudge the Figures? Literacy and Health: The Cuban Model." *Caribbean Review* 15, no. 2 (Spring 1986), 5–7, 37–38.

Eisenhower, Dwight D. *Waging Peace, 1956–1961.* Garden City, N.Y.: Doubleday, 1965.

Ellison, Katherine. "Succeeding Castro: Will Cuba's Revolutionary Hero Share the Fate of Other Communist Leaders?" *The Atlantic,* June 1990, 34–38.

Ettinger, Amos Aschbach. *The Mission to Spain of Pierre Soulé, 1853–1855: A Study in the Cuban Diplomacy of the United States.* New Haven: Yale University Press, 1932.

Fidel en la URSS (Fidel in the USSR). Havana, Cuba: Instituto del Libro, 1963.

Foner, Philip S., ed. *Inside the Monster: Writings on the United States and American Imperialism by José Martí.* New York: Monthly Review Press, 1975.

Foner, Philip S. *The Spanish-Cuban-American War and the Birth of American Imperialism, 1895–1902.* Vol. 1. New York: Monthly Review Press, 1972.

Franqui, Carlos. *Family Portrait with Fidel.* Translated by Alfred MacAdam. New York: Vintage, 1985.

Gaddis, John Lewis. *The Long Peace: Inquiries into the History of the Cold War.* New York: Oxford University Press, 1987.

García, Cristina. *Dreaming in Cuban.* New York: Knopf, 1992.

García Márquez, Gabriel. *The General in His Labyrinth.* Translated by Edith Grossman. New York: Knopf, 1990.

Garthoff, Raymond L. "The Havana Conference on the Cuban Missile Crisis." *Cold War International History Project Bulletin,* no. 1 (Spring 1992), 1, 3.

———. *Reflections on the Cuban Missile Crisis.* 1st ed. Washington, D.C.: Brookings, 1987.

———. *Détente and Confrontation: American-Soviet Relations from Nixon to Reagan.* Washington, D.C.: Brookings, 1985.

Gellman, Irwin F. *Roosevelt and Batista: Good Neighbor Diplomacy in Cuba, 1933–1945.* Albuquerque: University of New Mexico Press, 1973.

George, Alexander L., and Richard Smoke. *Deterrence in American Foreign Policy.* New York: Columbia University Press, 1974.

Gorbachev, Mikhail S. *Perestroika: New Thinking for Our Country and the World.* New York: Harper & Row, 1987.

Grabendorff, Wolf, Heinrich-W. Krumwiede, and Jörg Todt, eds. *Political Change in Central America: Internal and External Dimensions.* Boulder, Colo.: Westview, 1984.

Grenville, John A. S., and George Berkeley Young. *Politics, Strategy, and American Diplomacy: Studies in Foreign Policy, 1873–1917.* New Haven: Yale University Press, 1966.

Gribkov, Anatoly I. "Karibskii krizis (The Caribbean Crisis), Part 3." *Voenno-istoricheskii zhurnal (Military-Historical Journal)*, no. 12 (December 1992), 38–45.

———. "Operation Anadyr." *Der Spiegel,* 20 April 1992, 196ff.

———. "An der Schwelle zum Atomkrieg." *Der Spiegel,* 13 April 1992, 144ff.

Gromyko, Anatoly, and Andrei Kokoshin. *Bratya Kennedi* (The Kennedy Brothers). Moscow: Mysl', 1985.

Gunn, Gillian. "Will Castro Fall?" *Foreign Policy,* no. 79 (Summer 1990), 132–50.

Halperin, Maurice. *The Taming of Fidel Castro.* Berkeley: University of California Press, 1981.

———. *The Rise and Decline of Fidel Castro.* Berkeley: University of California Press, 1972.

Healy, David F. *The United States in Cuba, 1898–1902: Generals, Politicians, and the Search for Policy.* Madison: University of Wisconsin Press, 1963.

Heller, Mikhail, and Aleksandr M. Nekrich. *Utopia in Power: The History of the Soviet Union from 1917 to the Present.* Translated by Phyllis B. Carlos. New York: Summit, 1986.

Hernández, Rafael. "Es ridículo pretender que teníamos la intención de provocar una guerra nuclear" (It is ridiculous to pretend that we wanted to provoke a nuclear war). *Granma,* 26 February 1989, 9.

———. "The October 1962 Crisis: Lesson and Legend." *Latinskaya amerika* (January 1988), 58–67.

Hershberg, James G. "Before 'The Missiles of October': Did Kennedy Plan a Military Strike Against Cuba?" *Diplomatic History* 14, no. 12 (Spring 1990), 163–99.

Higgins, Trumbull. *The Perfect Failure: Kennedy, Eisenhower and the CIA at the Bay of Pigs.* New York: Norton, 1987.

Hilsman, Roger. *To Move a Nation: The Politics of Foreign Policy in the Administration of John F. Kennedy.* New York: Doubleday, 1967.

Horelick, Arnold L. "The Cuban Missile Crisis: An Analysis of Soviet Calculations and Behavior." *World Politics* 16, no. 3 (April 1964), 363–89.

Horelick, Arnold, and Myron Rush. *Strategic Power and Soviet Foreign Policy.* Chicago: University of Chicago Press, 1966.

Huth, Paul, and Bruce Russett. "What Makes Deterrence Work? Cases from 1900 to 1980." *World Politics* 36, no. 4 (July 1984), 496–526.

Janis, Irving L., and Leon Mann. *Decision Making: A Psychological Analysis of Conflict, Choice, and Commitment.* New York: Free Press, 1977.

Jervis, Robert. "Security Regimes." *International Organization* 36, no. 2 (Spring 1982), 357–78.

———. *Perception and Misperception in International Politics.* Princeton: Princeton University Press, 1976.

Jervis, Robert, Richard Ned Lebow, and Janice Gross Stein, with contributions by Patrick M. Morgan and Jack L. Snyder. *Psychology & Deterrence.* Baltimore: Johns Hopkins University Press, 1985.

Juárez, Adela Estrada. "El General que Dió la Orden de: ¡Fuego!" *Bastión,* 30 March 1989, 4.

Karol, K. S. *Guerrillas in Power: The Course of the Cuban Revolution.* Translated by Arnold Pomerans. New York: Hill and Wang, 1970.

Keller, Bill. "Rush Toward Disunion Spreads; Europe Embracing Baltic Independence; Purge of Military." *New York Times,* 25 August 1991, 1.

———. " '62 Missile Crisis Yields New Puzzle." *New York Times,* 30 January 1989, 1.

Kennedy, Robert F. *Thirteen Days: A Memoir of the Cuban Missile Crisis.* New York: Norton, 1969.

Khrushchev, Nikita S. *Khrushchev Remembers: The Glasnost Tapes.* Translated and edited by Jerrold L. Schecter, with Vyacheslav V. Luchkov. Boston: Little, Brown, 1990.

———. *Khrushchev Remembers.* Edited by Strobe Talbott. Boston: Little, Brown, 1970.

Kissinger, Henry. *White House Years.* Boston: Little, Brown, 1979.

Kokoshin, Andrei, and Sergei Rogov. *Serye kardinali belogo domo* (*Grey Cardinals of the White House*). Moscow: Novosti, 1986.

LaFeber, Walter. *The New Empire: An Interpretation of American Expansion, 1860–1898.* Ithaca, N.Y.: Cornell University Press, 1963.

Landau, Saul. "Killing the Wounded Beast: Economic War on Cuba." *The Nation,* 24 February 1992, 225–26.

———. "Socialism on One Island?" *The Progressive,* June 1990, 18–20.

Lansdale, Brig. Gen. Edward G. Memorandum to the Special (5412) Group, "The Cuba Project," 20 February 1962. Washington, D.C.: National Security Archive.

Larson, David L., ed. *The "Cuban Crisis" of 1962: Selected Documents, Chronology, and Bibliography.* 2d ed. Lanham, Md.: University Press of America, 1986.

Lebow, Richard Ned. "Was Khrushchev Bluffing in Cuba?" *Bulletin of the Atomic Scientists* 44, no. 3 (April 1988), 38–42.

———. *Between Peace and War: The Nature of International Crisis.* Baltimore: Johns Hopkins University Press, 1981.

Lebow, Richard Ned, and Janice Gross Stein. *We All Lost the Cold War—Can We Win the Peace?* Princeton: Princeton University Press, forthcoming.

Leonard, Elmore. *Maximum Bob.* New York: Delacorte, 1991.

Lewis, Oscar, Ruth M. Lewis, and Susan M. Rigdon. *Living the Revolution: An Oral History of Contemporary Cuba.* Vols. 1–3. Urbana: University of Illinois Press, 1977–78.

Lockwood, Lee. *Castro's Cuba, Cuba's Fidel.* Boulder, Colo.: Westview, 1990.

"London Declaration on a Transformed North Atlantic Alliance," 6 July 1991. NATO Press Service, 1991.

Lukas, J. Anthony. "Fidel Castro's Theater of Now." *New York Times,* 20 January 1992, E-17.

McAuliffe, Mary S., ed. *CIA Documents on the Cuban Missile Crisis.* Washington, D.C.: Central Intelligence Agency History Staff, 1992.

Manchester, William. *American Caesar.* Boston: Little, Brown, 1978.

May, Ernest R. *The Making of the Monroe Doctrine.* Cambridge, Mass.: Belknap, 1975.

———. *Imperial Democracy: The Emergence of America as a Great Power.* New York: Harcourt, Brace & World, 1961.

Mazarr, Michael J. *Semper Fidel: America and Cuba 1776–1988.* Baltimore: Nautical & Aviation, 1988.

Medvedev, Roy. *Khrushchev: A Biography.* Translated by Brian Pearce. New York: Doubleday, 1984.

Medvedev, Roy A., and Zhores Medvedev. *Khrushchev: The Years in Power.* Translated by Andrew R. Durkin. New York: Norton, 1978.

Meyer, Stephen M. "Soviet Theater Nuclear Forces, Part II: Capabilities and Implications." Adelphi Paper no. 188. London: International Institute for Strategic Studies, 1983.

Miller, Nicola. *Soviet Relations with Latin America 1959–1987.* Cambridge: Cambridge University Press, 1989.

Mina, Gianni. *An Encounter with Fidel.* Translated by Mary Todd. Melbourne: Ocean Press, 1991.

Newhouse, John. "Socialism or Death." *New Yorker,* 27 April 1992, 52–83.

Nicholson, Graeme. *Seeing and Reading.* London: Macmillan, 1984.

Nitze, Paul H., with Ann M. Smith and Steven L. Rearden. *From Hiroshima to Glasnost: At the Center of Decision—A Memoir.* New York: Grove Weidenfeld, 1989.

Nye, Joseph S., Jr. "Nuclear Learning and U.S.-Soviet Security Regimes." *International Organization* 41, no. 3 (Summer 1987), 371–402.

Oberdorfer, Don. "Small Missiles Heightened Peril in 1962 Cuban Crisis." *Washington Post*, 14 January 1992, A-6.

"October 27, 1962: The ExComm Transcripts." *International Security* 12, no. 3 (Winter 1987/88), 30–92.

Olivart, Marquis de. "Le Différend entre l'Espagne et les Etats-Unis au Sujet de la Question Cubaine. *Révue Générale de Droit International Public* 4, 5, 7, 9 (1897, 1898, 1900, 1902).

Oppenheimer, Andres. *Castro's Final Hour: The Secret Story Behind the Coming Downfall of Communist Cuba.* New York: Simon & Schuster, 1992.

Pachter, Henry M. *Collision Course: The Cuban Missile Crisis and Coexistence.* New York: Praeger, 1963.

Paterson, Thomas G. "Fixation with Cuba: The Bay of Pigs, Missile Crisis and Covert War Against Castro." In *Kennedy's Quest for Victory: American Foreign Policy, 1961–1963.* Edited by Thomas G. Paterson. New York: Oxford University Press, 1989, 123–55.

Pérez, Louis A., Jr. *Cuba and the United States: Ties of Singular Intimacy.* Athens, Ga.: University of Georgia Press, 1990.

Perkins, Dexter. *A History of the Monroe Doctrine.* Boston: Little, Brown, 1955.

Pope, Ronald R., ed. *Soviet Views on the Cuban Missile Crisis: Myth and Reality in Foreign Policy Analysis.* Lanham, Md.: University Press of America, 1982.

Pratt, Julius W. "The Coming War with Spain." In *Threshold to American Internationalism: Essays on the Foreign Policies of William McKinley.* Edited by Paolo E. Coletta. New York: Exposition Press, 1970, 35–76.

———. *America's Colonial Experiment: How the United States Gained, Governed, and in Part Gave Away a Colonial Empire.* New York: Prentice-Hall, 1950.

Pratt, Julius W., Vincent P. DeSantis, and Joseph M. Siracusa. *A History of United States Foreign Policy.* 4th ed. Englewood Cliffs, N.J.: Prentice-Hall, 1980.

Preston, Julia. "The Trial That Shook Cuba." *New York Review of Books*, 7 December 1989, 24–31.

Public Papers of the Presidents, 1963. Washington, D.C.: Government Printing Office, 1964.

Purcell, Susan Kaufmann. "Cuba's Cloudy Future." *Foreign Affairs* 69, no. 3 (Summer 1990), 113–30.

Radin, Charles. "JFK Aide Downplays Report of U.S. Plan to Invade Cuba." *Boston Globe*, 16 February 1989, 2.

Rauch, Basil. *American Interest in Cuba, 1848–1855.* New York: Columbia University Press, 1948.

Right v. Might: International Law and the Use of Force. New York: Council on Foreign Relations, 1989.

Robbins, Carla Anne. *The Cuban Threat.* New York: McGraw-Hill, 1983.

Rohter, Larry. "The Cold War of Cuba and the Miami Exiles Heats Up." *New York Times,* 26 January 1992, E-3.

Safford, Jeffrey. "The Nixon-Castro Meeting of 19 April, 1959." *Diplomatic History* 4, no. 4 (Fall 1980), 426–31.

Salinger, Pierre. "Gaps in the Cuban Missile Crisis Story." *New York Times,* 5 February 1989, section 4, 16.

Sayles, John. *Los Gusanos.* New York: HarperCollins, 1991.

Schecter, Jerrold L., and Peter S. Deriabin. *The Spy Who Saved the World: How a Soviet Colonel Changed the Course of the Cold War.* New York: Charles Scribner's Sons, 1992.

Schlesinger, Arthur M., Jr. "Four Days with Fidel: A Havana Diary." *New York Review of Books,* 26 March 1992, 22–29.

———. *Robert Kennedy and His Times.* New York: Ballantine, 1978.

———. *A Thousand Days: John F. Kennedy in the White House.* New York: Houghton Mifflin, 1965.

Smith, Wayne S. "Castro: To Fall or Not to Fall." *SAIS Review* 12, no. 2 (Summer–Fall 1992), 97–110.

———. *The Closest of Enemies: A Personal and Diplomatic Account of the Castro Years.* New York: Norton, 1987.

———. ed. *The Russians Aren't Coming: New Soviet Policy in Latin America.* Boulder, Colo.: Lynne Rienner, 1992.

Snyder, Jack. *The Ideology of the Offensive: Military Decision Making and the Disasters of 1914.* Ithaca, N.Y.: Cornell University Press, 1984.

Sorensen, Theodore C. *Kennedy.* New York: Harper & Row, 1965.

Statsenko, Igor D. "On Some Military-Political Aspects of the Caribbean Crisis." *Latinskaya amerika* (November–December 1977), 108–117.

Steele, Jonathan. *World Power: Soviet Foreign Policy Under Brezhnev and Andropov.* London: Michael Joseph, 1983.

Stein, Janice Gross. "Deterrence and Compellence in the Gulf, 1990–91: A Failed or Impossible Task?" *International Security* 17, no. 2 (Fall 1992), 147–79.

Suárez, Andrés. *Cuba, Castroism and Communism, 1959–66.* Cambridge, Mass.: MIT Press, 1967.

Szulc, Tad. "Can Castro Last?" *New York Review of Books,* 31 May 1990, 12–15.

———. "Exporting the Cuban Revolution." In *Cuba and the United States: Long Range Perspectives.* Edited by John Plank. Washington, D.C.: Brookings, 1967, 69–97.

———. *Fidel: A Critical Portrait.* New York: Morrow, 1986.

Thomas, Hugh. *The Cuban Revolution.* New York: Harper & Row, 1977.

Timerman, Jacobo. *Cuba: A Journey.* New York: Knopf, 1990.

Tirman, John. "Cuba Still Awaits a Softer U.S. Line." *Chicago Tribune,* 1 February 1992, section 1, 19.

Treverton, Gregory F. *Covert Action: The Limits of Intervention in the Postwar World.* New York: Basic Books, 1987.

Tutino, Saverio. *L'Ottobre Cubano.* Turin: Enaudi, 1968.

Ulam, Adam B. *Expansion and Coexistence: Soviet Foreign Policy, 1917–73.* 2d ed. New York: Praeger, 1974.

United States Department of State. *Foreign Relations of the United States: 1950.* Vol. 1. Washington, D.C.: Government Printing Office, 1977.

———. *Cuba.* Publication 7171, Inter-American series 66. Washington, D.C.: Government Printing Office, 1961.

———. *Papers Relating to the Foreign Relations of the United States: 1902.* Washington, D.C.: Government Printing Office, 1903.

United States Navy. Atlantic Command. *CINCLANT Historical Account of Cuban Crisis—1963 (U).* Norfolk, Va.: Headquarters of the Commander in Chief, 29 April 1963.

United States Senate. Select Committee to Study Government Operations with Respect to Intelligence Activities. *Alleged Assassination Plots Involving Foreign Leaders.* Washington, D.C.: Government Printing Office, 1975.

———. Foreign Relations Committee. *U.S. Policy Towards Cuba.* Washington, D.C.: Government Printing Office, 1971.

Weiss, Thomas G., and James G. Blight, eds. *The Suffering Grass: Superpowers and Conflict in Southern Africa and the Caribbean.* Boulder, Colo.: Lynne Rienner, 1992.

Welch, David A. *Justice and the Genesis of War.* Cambridge Studies in International Relations 29. Cambridge: Cambridge University Press, 1993.

———. "The Organizational Process and Bureaucratic Politics Paradigms: Retrospect and Prospect." *International Security* 17, no. 2 (Fall 1992), 112–46.

Welch, David A., and James G. Blight. "The Eleventh Hour of the Cuban Missile Crisis: An Introduction to the ExComm Transcripts." *International Security* 12, no. 3 (Winter 1987/88), 5–29.

Welch, Richard E. *Response to Revolution: The United States and the Cuban Revolution: 1959–1961.* Chapel Hill: University of North Carolina Press, 1985.

Wendt, Alexander. "The Agent-Structure Problem in International Relations Theory." *International Organization* 41, no. 3 (Summer 1987), 335–70.

"White House Tapes and Minutes of the Cuban Missile Crisis: ExComm Meetings, October 1962." *International Security* 10, no. 1 (Summer 1985), 164–203.

Wohlstetter, Albert, and Roberta Wohlstetter. "Controlling the Risks in Cuba." Adelphi Paper no. 17. London: International Institute for Strategic Studies, 1965.

Wright, Theodore P., Jr. "United States Electoral Intervention in Cuba." *Inter-American Economic Affairs* 13, no. 3 (Winter 1959), 50–71.

Wyden, Peter. *Bay of Pigs: The Untold Story.* New York: Simon & Schuster, 1979.

Zakaria, Fareed. "The Reagan Strategy of Containment." *Political Science Quarterly* 105 (Fall 1990), 373–95.

Appendix 1:
Chronology

(All times EDT unless otherwise noted)

1959

1 January
- The regime of Gen. Fulgencio Batista of Cuba falls; Fidel Castro assumes power.

17 May
- The revolutionary government of Cuba enacts an agrarian reform law. Shortly thereafter Cuba first expropriates U.S.-owned properties, promising compensation.

13 July
- President Manuel Urrutia of Cuba states on television that communism is not really concerned with the welfare of the people and that it constitutes a danger to the Cuban Revolution. On 17 July, Fidel Castro accuses President Urrutia of treason and resigns as prime minister. President Urrutia resigns, and is replaced by Osvaldo Dorticós. Castro resumes his post on 26 July.

19 October
- Major Huber Matos, military chief in Camagüey province, resigns, charging Communist penetration of the government. He is arrested and on 15 December he is sentenced to twenty years in prison for conspiracy, sedition, and treason.

26 October
- Fidel Castro accuses the United States of tolerating air incursions against Cuba and of threatening Cuba with economic strangulation.

1960

6 February
- First Deputy Premier Anastas I. Mikoyan of the Soviet Union arrives in Havana with a Soviet trade exhibition. He meets with the Cuban leadership and signs various agreements including, *inter alia,* $100 million in trade credits to help lessen Cuban dependence on the United States.

4 March
- The French steamer *La Coubre,* carrying a shipment of Belgian small arms, explodes in Havana harbor, killing dozens of workers and soldiers. Castro publicly accuses the CIA of sabotaging the ship. The United States protests the accusation.

10 March
- Apparently concluding that Castro is determined not to have good relations with the United States, President Dwight D. Eisenhower signs a National Security Council (NSC) directive to explore U.S. options for destabilizing the Castro regime.

19 April
- The first shipment of Soviet crude oil arrives in Cuba.

8 May
- Cuba and the Soviet Union establish diplomatic relations.

29 June
- Esso and Texaco refuse to refine Soviet oil in Cuba. The Cuban government nationalizes their refineries.

6 July
- The Cuban government passes a nationalization law providing for the expropriation of foreign holdings in Cuba.

8 July
- President Eisenhower reduces the Cuban sugar quota for the remainder of the year by 95 percent, thereby cutting off 80 percent of Cuban exports to the United States. The following day, the Soviet Union announces that it is willing to buy the sugar that had been destined for the United States.

6 October
- The Cuban government, using the powers granted in the Nationalization Law, expropriates without compensation all U.S. holdings, valued at over $1 billion.

19 December
- Cuba openly aligns itself with Soviet foreign policy and claims solidarity with the Sino-Soviet bloc, issuing a joint communiqué with the USSR.

1961

3 January
- In response to Cuban demands that the United States limit its embassy personnel to eleven, the United States terminates diplomatic and consular ties with Cuba; Cuba reciprocates.

31 March
- President John F. Kennedy (JFK) reduces the Cuban sugar quota to zero.

12 April
- JFK pledges the United States will not intervene militarily to overthrow Castro.

16 April
- Describing his regime as "socialist," Castro orders general mobilization and accuses the United States of scheming to invade Cuba.

17 April
- Backed by the United States, a group of Cuban exiles invades Cuba at the Bay of Pigs in an attempt to trigger an anti-Castro rebellion. By 19 April, the invasion has failed; more than a thousand Cuban rebels are captured by Castro's forces.

3–4 June
- Khrushchev and JFK meet in Vienna. Khrushchev announces a six-month deadline for a resolution of the Berlin situation.

12–13 August
- Soviet forces assist the East Germans in erecting the Berlin Wall.

7 September
- The U.S. Congress bars assistance to any country aiding Cuba, unless the president determines such aid to be in the American national interest.

11 September
- Former President Eisenhower announces that, during his presidency, no plan was ever made to invade Cuba.

21 October
- Deputy Secretary of Defense Roswell Gilpatric gives a speech in Hot Springs, Virginia, in which he publicly details the U.S.-Soviet strategic nuclear balance, revealing that the alleged "missile gap" in the Soviets' favor is a deception. Gilpatric acknowledges that the United States enjoys considerable nuclear superiority over the Soviet Union.

1962

19 January
- The Special Group (Augmented) of the National Security Council meets in the office of Attorney General Robert Kennedy (RFK) to consider Castro's ouster.

22–31 January
- The Organization of American States (OAS) meets in Punta del Este, Uruguay. U.S. Secretary of State Dean Rusk declares Cuba a threat to the Western Hemisphere and calls for its isolation. The OAS declares the Castro government

incompatible with the inter-American system, and expels Cuba from the organization. The organization agrees to prohibit its members from selling arms to Cuba, and agrees on collective measures against Cuba.

3 February
- JFK declares an embargo on all trade with Cuba, except for critical medical supplies.

20 February
- Brig. Gen. Edward G. Lansdale's "Cuba Project" program review details American covert activities in Cuba and specifies October 1962 as a target date for Castro's ouster.

19 April–11 May
- Exercise "Quick-Kick," a large-scale U.S. military maneuver, begins off the East Coast of the United States. Seventy-nine ships, 300 aircraft, and over 40,000 troops participate. Cuba denounces the exercise as a provocation and as proof that the United States intends to invade.

Late April
- Khrushchev first discusses the idea of deploying nuclear missiles to Cuba with Soviet First Deputy Premier Anastas I. Mikoyan. On 25 April, the Soviet press representative in Havana, Aleksandr Alekseev, receives an urgent cable to return to Moscow.

7 May
- Khrushchev informs Alekseev that he will be the new ambassador to Havana, effective 31 May.

8 May
- Exercise "Whip Lash" begins, designed to test contingency planning for military operations against Cuba. Another military exercise in the Caribbean, "Jupiter Springs," is planned for the spring or summer. The Cubans denounce these exercises as proof of hostile intentions.

14–20 May
- Khrushchev visits Bulgaria, where, according to his memoirs, "the idea of installing missiles with nuclear warheads in Cuba without letting the United States find out until it was too late to do anything about them" occurs to him for the first time. On the return flight to Moscow, Khrushchev first mentions the idea of the deployment to Foreign Minister Andrei Gromyko.

29 May
- A high-level Soviet delegation, including the commander of the Strategic Rocket Forces, Marshal S. S. Biryuzov, travels secretly to Havana to propose to Castro the deployment of nuclear weapons to Cuba. The Cuban leadership unanimously and enthusiastically gives its approval in principle.

10 June
- Biryuzov reports the results of the Soviet-Cuban negotiations to the Presidium, which then orders the Ministry of Defense to prepare detailed operational plans for the deployment. The plan is given the code name Operation Anadyr.

2–17 July
- A Cuban delegation led by Defense Minister Raúl Castro travels to Moscow to discuss Soviet military shipments to Cuba, including nuclear missiles

Khrushchev meets Raúl Castro on 3 and 8 July. Castro and Soviet Defense Minister Rodion Ya. Malinovsky initial a draft treaty governing the deployment of Soviet forces to Cuba.

Late July
- The first surface-to-air missiles (SAMs) and supporting equipment for the construction of nuclear missile sites leave the Soviet Union.

27 July
- Fidel Castro announces that Cuba is taking measures that would make any direct U.S. attack on Cuba the equivalent of a world war. He claims that the USSR is committed to helping Cuba resist further imperialist attacks.

10 August
- CIA director John McCone dictates a memo to JFK expressing his belief that Soviet medium-range ballistic missiles (MRBMs) will be deployed in Cuba.

23 August
- In National Security Action Memorandum (NSAM) 181, JFK calls for study and action "in light of the evidence of new [Soviet] bloc activity in Cuba." Highlights include: action toward potential removal of U.S. Jupiter missiles from Turkey; study of the probable military, political, and psychological impact of the establishment in Cuba of missiles capable of reaching the United States; and study of military alternatives should the United States decide to eliminate such missiles.

27 August–2 September
- A Cuban delegation led by Che Guevara and Emilio Aragonés travels to Moscow with Fidel Castro's revisions to the draft treaty. The Cubans propose that the deployment be made public to forestall an American overreaction; Khrushchev successfully argues for continued secrecy.

31 August
- Sen. Kenneth Keating (R-New York) tells the Senate that there is evidence of Soviet missile installations in Cuba. Keating urges JFK to take action and proposes that the OAS send an investigative team to Cuba.

4 September
- RFK meets with Soviet ambassador Anatoly Dobrynin and expresses JFK's concern over Soviet military equipment reaching Cuba. Dobrynin conveys a message from Khrushchev that no ground-to-ground or offensive weapons would be placed in Cuba, which RFK relays to Dean Rusk and to Secretary of Defense Robert McNamara. RFK suggests that a statement be issued declaring that the United States will not tolerate the introduction of offensive weapons in Cuba.
- JFK releases a statement, drafted by RFK and Assistant Attorney General Nicholas Katzenbach, revealing that SAMs and substantially more military personnel have been detected in Cuba by a reconnaissance flight on 29 August. The president reassures the American public that the Soviets have deployed no offensive weapons in Cuba and warns the Soviets against such a deployment.

6 September
- Theodore Sorensen, special counsel to the president, meets with Soviet ambassador Dobrynin at the Soviet embassy. Dobrynin reiterates his assurances that Soviet military assistance to Cuba was strictly defensive in nature and did

not represent a threat to American security. Dobrynin also delivers a message in which Khrushchev promises that the Soviets will refrain from any activities that "could complicate the international situation" before the American congressional elections in November. In a memorandum of conversation, Sorensen reports that Dobrynin repeatedly assured him that the Soviets "had done nothing new or extraordinary in Cuba—that the events causing all the excitement had been taking place somewhat gradually and quietly over a long period of time."

7 September
- JFK requests congressional authority to call up 150,000 reservists.
- Dobrynin assures U.S. Ambassador to the United Nations Adlai Stevenson that the USSR is supplying only defensive weapons to Cuba.
- The United States announces a major military exercise, PHIBRIGLEX-62, to begin in mid-October in the Caribbean. Cuba denounces this as a provocation, and proof of American plans to invade Cuba.

9 September
- Chinese communists shoot down a U-2 reconnaissance aircraft over mainland China.

11 September
- Soviet news agency TASS announces that the Soviet Union neither needs nor intends to introduce offensive nuclear weapons into Cuba.

13 September
- JFK announces that "if at any time the Communist buildup in Cuba were to endanger or interfere with our security in any way . . . or if Cuba should ever attempt to export its aggressive purposes by force or the threat of force against any nation of this hemisphere, or become an offensive military base of significant capacity for the Soviet Union, then this country will do whatever must be done to protect its own security and that of its allies." At the same time, JFK notes that no information to date suggests that military action would be necessary or justified.

15 September
- The first SS-4 MRBMs arrive in Cuba.

18 September
- Former Vice President Richard M. Nixon calls for a quarantine to stem the flow of Soviet arms to Cuba.

19 September
- A Special National Intelligence Estimate (SNIE) by the U.S. Intelligence Board, "The Military Buildup in Cuba," asserts that although the Soviets would gain considerable military advantage from establishing medium- and intermediate-range ballistic missiles in Cuba, Soviet policy does not support the establishment of nuclear forces on foreign soil and the Soviets are aware of the risks of U.S. retaliation. It therefore concludes that such a deployment is unlikely.
- The Senate Foreign Relations Committee and Armed Services Committee approve the text of a joint resolution on Cuba (no. 230, introduced by Sen. John Sparkman, D-Alabama) sanctioning the use of force if necessary to defend the Western Hemisphere against Cuban aggression or subversion.

20 September
- Resolution 230 passes the Senate by a vote of 86–1.

21 September
- In a speech to the U.N., Soviet foreign minister Andrei Gromyko warns that an American attack on Cuba would mean war with the Soviet Union.

26 September
- The House of Representatives passes the joint resolution on Cuba by a vote of 384–7.

28 September
- In Yugoslavia, Soviet president Leonid Brezhnev reiterates Gromyko's warning that an American attack on Cuba would mean war with the Soviet Union.

1 October
- McNamara and the Joint Chiefs of Staff (JCS) discuss contingency planning, ordering Adm. Robert L. Dennison, commander-in-chief of the Atlantic Fleet (CINCLANT), to make preparations for a blockade of Cuba if necessary.

4 October
- Congress passes a diluted version of the Joint Congressional Resolution on Cuba, introduced by Sen. Everett Dirksen (R-Illinois) and Rep. Charles Halleck (D-Indiana), sanctioning the use of American forces to defend the Western Hemisphere from aggression or subversion from Cuba, and pledging cooperation with the OAS and "freedom-loving Cubans" to achieve self-determination.

8 October
- In a speech to the U.N. General Assembly, Cuban president Osvaldo Dorticós declares: "If . . . we are attacked, we will defend ourselves. I repeat we have sufficient means with which to defend ourselves; we have indeed our inevitable weapons, the weapons which we would have preferred not to acquire and which we do not wish to employ."

9 October
- JFK approves a U-2 reconnaissance flight over western Cuba, delayed by bad weather until 14 October.

10 October
- Senator Keating charges that six intermediate-range ballistic missile bases are being constructed in Cuba.
- The Joint Chiefs of Staff request the transfer of the Fifth Marine Expeditionary Brigade from the Pacific to the Atlantic forces in order to support invasion plans of Cuba. The Chiefs justify their request "in view of the threat developing and the high level of national interest concerning Cuba."

13 October
- Former Under Secretary of State Chester Bowles questions Soviet ambassador Dobrynin on whether the Soviets plan to put "offensive weapons" in Cuba. Dobrynin denies any such intention.

14 October
- Presidential Assistant for National Security McGeorge Bundy appears on ABC's "Issues and Answers," denying any hard evidence of Soviet offensive weapons in Cuba.
- A U-2, piloted by Air Force Maj. Richard S. Heyser, flies over western Cuba.

15 October
- A readout team at the National Photographic Intelligence Center reviews photos taken during the 14 October U-2 flight, and identifies objects similar to

MRBM components observed in the USSR scattered about a meadow at San Cristóbal.

- (8:30 P.M.) CIA Deputy Director of Intelligence Ray S. Cline calls Bundy and Roger Hilsman, State Department director of research and intelligence, on a non-secure phone and, in cryptic language, informs them of the discovery of MRBMs in Cuba. Hilsman phones Dean Rusk, who in turn notifies Paul Nitze, assistant secretary of defense for international security affairs. Bundy decides to wait until morning to alert the president.
- (Midnight) McNamara is shown photographic evidence of the MRBMs at San Cristóbal.

16 October

- (8:45 A.M.) Bundy breaks the news to JFK, who calls an 11:45 A.M. meeting of his high-level advisers, a group later to become known as the Executive Committee ("ExComm").
- (6:30 P.M.) JFK and his advisers discuss possible diplomatic and military courses of action.

17 October

- Georgy Bolshakov, an official in the Soviet embassy in Washington, brings RFK a "personal message" from Khrushchev to JFK, assuring that "under no circumstances would surface-to-surface missiles be sent to Cuba."

18 October

- (Afternoon) Gromyko and JFK meet for two hours. Reading from notes, Gromyko assures JFK that the Soviet aid to Cuba "pursued solely the purpose of contributing to the defense capabilities of Cuba and to the development of its peaceful economy. . . ."

19 October

- JFK departs for scheduled campaign speeches in Cleveland and on the West Coast.
- Radio Moscow reports that U.S. naval maneuvers in the Caribbean are in preparation for an invasion of Cuba.

20 October

- (10:30 A.M.) White House Press Secretary Pierre Salinger announces in Chicago that the president is canceling the remainder of his campaign trip because of "a slight cold."
- The chief legal officers of the Departments of State, Defense, and Justice draft the quarantine proclamation prohibiting the shipment of offensive weapons to Cuba.
- (2:30 P.M.) JFK meets with his advisers and orders a defensive quarantine instituted as soon as possible. The group reviews and approves the full operation, and schedules the president's television address for Monday at 7:00 P.M. The group discusses and revises the president's speech.

21 October

- (11:30 A.M.) JFK, RFK, Gen. Maxwell Taylor (chairman of the JCS), and McNamara meet with Gen. Walter Sweeney, Jr., commander-in-chief of Tactical Air Command. Informed that an air strike could not guarantee the destruction of all Soviet missiles in Cuba, JFK confirms that the United States will impose a quarantine, rather than execute an air strike.
- JFK calls Orville Dryfoos of the *New York Times,* who cooperates in suppressing a story on the pending crisis. The morning edition of the *Washington Post,*

however, runs a story speculating about recent White House activity and surmising its focus might be Cuba, but mentions the possibility of Berlin.

22 October
- JFK signs NSAM 196, formally establishing the Executive Committee of the National Security Council (ExComm).
- (Noon) Salinger announces that JFK will make an important statement at 7:00 P.M. and requests air time from radio and television networks.
- (4:00 P.M.) Reacting to the announcement of the president's speech and to large-scale military movements in the Caribbean, Fidel Castro decrees a state of general mobilization and war alert throughout Cuba.
- (5:00 P.M.) Congressional leaders assemble at the White House for a meeting with JFK, who discloses the photographic evidence of missile sites and announces his quarantine plans. The congressional leaders express support, but many advocate stronger action. JFK resists.
- (6:00 P.M.) Rusk meets Dobrynin at the State Department and hands him an advance copy of JFK's forthcoming address, with a covering memo. According to reporters, Dobrynin is "ashen" when he leaves Dean Rusk's office. Virtually simultaneously, American ambassador Foy Kohler delivers a letter from JFK and the text of his speech to the Kremlin, but he does not meet with any high-ranking officials, and there is no immediate response. At the same time, American U.N. ambassador Adlai Stevenson informs Acting Secretary General U Thant of the president's speech, and announces that the United States will request a meeting of the Security Council.
- (7:00 P.M.) The president addresses the nation in a televised speech, announcing the presence of nuclear missile sites in Cuba.
- The alert level of American forces worldwide rises from Defense Condition (DefCon) 5 to DefCon 3, coincident with JFK's speech.
- The U.S. base at Guantánamo in southeastern Cuba is reinforced by three Marine battalions. Dependents are evacuated by the time JFK goes on the air.
- (10:40–11:25 P.M.) McNamara meets with Chief of Naval Operations Adm. George Anderson to discuss quarantine and surveillance procedures.
- The U.S. Air Force hands over the first of fifteen Jupiter intermediate-range ballistic missile launchers to the Turkish air force for maintenance and operation, signaling that they have become fully operational.
- Col. Oleg Penkovsky, a senior officer in Soviet Military Intelligence and a Western spy since 1961, is arrested in the Soviet Union.
- (Late evening) British philosopher and pacifist Bertrand Russell sends telegrams to Kennedy and Khrushchev calling on them to halt the courses of action they have undertaken which threaten to plunge the world into nuclear war.

23 October
- (2:41 A.M.) The State Department receives a telegram from Adlai Stevenson reporting Cuba's request for a U.N. Security Council meeting to discuss the unfolding crisis.
- (8:00 A.M.) TASS begins transmitting a Soviet government statement accusing the United States of piracy, violation of international law, and acts of provocation that might lead to nuclear war.
- (10:00 A.M.) The ExComm holds its first official meeting.
- The OAS Council meets to consider the proposed U.S. quarantine proclamation. The final vote is 20–0 in favor of condemning the Soviet missile deployment and endorsing the quarantine.
- The USSR requests a meeting of the Security Council to examine the "violation

of the Charter of the United Nations and threat to the peace on the part of the U.S."

- (11:56 A.M.) JFK receives a letter in which Khrushchev declares: "I should frankly say that the measures outlined in your statement represent a serious threat to peace and security of peoples. The United States has openly taken the path of gross violation of international norms of freedom of navigation on the high seas, a path of aggressive actions both against Cuba and against the Soviet Union." He adds: "We confirm that the armaments now in Cuba, regardless of the classification to which they belong, are destined exclusively for defensive purposes, in order to secure the Cuban republic from an aggressor's attack."
- (4:00 P.M.) Adlai Stevenson delivers his opening statement to the specially convened meeting of the Security Council, saying that Castro's regime "has aided and abetted an invasion of this hemisphere," making itself "an accomplice in the communist enterprise of world domination. . . . If the United States and other nations of the Western Hemisphere accept this new phase of aggression, we would be delinquent in our obligations to world peace."
- Soviet ambassador to the U.N. Valerian Zorin declares that Stevenson's charges are "completely false" and "a clumsy attempt to cover up aggressive actions" in Cuba.
- (6:00 P.M.) The ExComm meets. JFK reviews and signs the Proclamation of Interdiction.
- (7:30 P.M.) McNamara announces that he has taken the necessary steps to deploy American forces so that the quarantine may take effect at 10:00 the next morning.
- JFK agrees to preliminary talks with U Thant to explore the possibility of "satisfactory arrangements" for negotiations. Khrushchev agrees to U Thant's appeal for a moratorium on further action, and agrees that if the United States ends the quarantine, the USSR will suspend arms shipments to Cuba.

24 October

- (Early morning) Soviet ships en route to Cuba with questionable cargo either slow down or reverse their course; one tanker continues on.
- (10:00 A.M.) The ExComm meets. JFK's quarantine proclamation goes into effect.
- (2:00 P.M.) U Thant sends private appeals to Kennedy and Khrushchev to avoid any confrontation that will risk general war. He calls for voluntary suspensions of arms shipments to Cuba and for voluntary suspension of the quarantine for two to three weeks, so that a settlement may be negotiated. Khrushchev accepts U Thant's appeal; JFK rejects it.
- Bertrand Russell appeals to Khrushchev for caution and urges JFK to stop "the madness"; Khrushchev responds, stating that the USSR will make no "reckless decisions" and warning that if the United States carries out its planned "pirate action," the USSR will have no choice but to "make use of the means of defense against the aggressor."
- Gen. Thomas Power, commander-in-chief of the Strategic Air Command (CINCSAC), raises the alert level of the Strategic Air Command to DefCon 2, indicating full readiness for war. Unbeknownst to JFK, Power sends his alert message in the clear, rather than in code (as would have been standard procedure), to demonstrate to the Soviet Union his confidence in American nuclear superiority.
- The State Department cables Ankara, urgently requesting U.S. ambassador Raymond Hare's assessment of the political consequences of removing Turkish

Jupiter missiles outright, in conjunction with the deployment of a Polaris submarine in the area, or with some other significant military offset, such as a NATO seaborne multilateral nuclear force.

- Khrushchev summons American businessman William Knox to meet with him, rails against the quarantine, and threatens to order the sinking of quarantine vessels if Soviet ships are stopped. Khrushchev states that the United States will have to learn to live with Soviet missiles in Cuba, just as the USSR has learned to live with American missiles in Turkey. Khrushchev also claims that the SAMs and ballistic missiles in Cuba are under "strict Soviet control," and vaguely proposes a summit.

25 October

- (1:45 A.M.) JFK sends a letter to Khrushchev laying responsibility for the crisis on the Soviet Union. JFK draws Khrushchev's attention to his repeated warnings against the deployment of offensive weapons to Cuba, and to the Soviets' repeated statements that they had no need or intention to undertake such a deployment.
- After receiving various reports suggesting an imminent U.S. invasion of Cuba, and reacting to the U.S. DefCon 2 nuclear alert and President Kennedy's letter of 25 October, Khrushchev instructs his advisers to draft a letter containing the basis for a solution to the crisis. Initially the letter contains demands for a non-invasion pledge and for the withdrawal of U.S. missiles from Turkey and Italy. Later in the day, Khrushchev receives new reports suggesting that the invasion will begin shortly. Khrushchev re-dictates the letter, eliminating mention of the missiles in Turkey and Italy. The re-dictated letter is sent the next day.
- (10:00 A.M.) The ExComm meets.
- Foreign Minister Bruno Kreisky of Austria suggests that the Soviet Union withdraw its bases from Cuba in exchange for the withdrawal of American Jupiter bases from Turkey.
- Walter Lippmann advocates a Cuba-Turkey missile trade in his syndicated column.
- (11:45 A.M.) At a Defense Department news conference, Assistant Secretary of Defense for Public Affairs Arthur Sylvester states that at least a dozen Soviet vessels have turned back. He also announces that the tanker *Bucharest* has been intercepted and permitted to proceed without boarding.
- (5:00 P.M.) The ExComm meets and considers several political options for resolving the crisis, among them a proposal to withdraw U.S. missiles from Turkey in exchange for the withdrawal of Soviet missiles from Cuba; a proposal to send U.N. teams to Cuba and Turkey to take control of missiles there pending the outcome of negotiations; and a proposal for having a Latin American representative in Cuba approach Castro to convince him that the Soviets are merely exploiting Cuba.
- The State Department receives a cable from U.S. ambassador to NATO Thomas Finletter clarifying Turkey's position on the Jupiter missiles: the Turks deem the Jupiter missiles to be of great value, serving "as a symbol of the alliance's determination to use atomic weapons against Russian attack on Turkey whether by large conventional or nuclear forces; although the Turks have been most reluctant to admit the presence of IRBMs [intermediate-range ballistic missiles] publicly."

26 October

- (7:50 A.M.) A party from the USS *Pierce* and the USS *Kennedy* boards and inspects the Lebanese freighter *Marucla*, under charter to the Soviet Union.

Finding no prohibited material, the U.S. Navy permits the *Marucla* to proceed.

- (9:45 A.M.; 4:45 P.M. Moscow time) Khrushchev's letter agreeing to withdraw Soviet missiles from Cuba in return for an American pledge not to invade Cuba is delivered to the U.S. embassy in Moscow. A couple of hours earlier Georgy Kornienko, Dobrynin's deputy in Washington, reports that the information indicating an imminent invasion is faulty. Dobrynin and Kornienko choose not to report the information to Khrushchev, so as not to delay the delivery of the letter.
- (10:00 A.M.) The ExComm meets.
- (1:00 P.M.) ABC's State Department correspondent John Scali has lunch with Aleksandr Fomin, senior Soviet intelligence officer in Washington, at Fomin's request. Fomin asks Scali to determine from his "high-level friends in the State Department" whether the United States would be interested in resolving the crisis on the following terms: (1) The USSR would agree to dismantle and remove all offensive missiles from Cuba; (2) the United States would be allowed to verify the removal of these weapons; (3) the Soviets would promise never to introduce offensive weapons into Cuba again; (4) the United States would promise never to invade Cuba. Fomin suggests that if Stevenson were to propose this in the U.N., Zorin would be interested.
- (1:00 P.M.; 8:00 P.M. Moscow time) Khrushchev learns that Soviet intelligence reports of an imminent American invasion of Cuba are false and that the United States has not yet settled on that course of action. Khrushchev decides to reassert his demands on the Turkish missiles. Khrushchev inadvertently omits any mention of Jupiter missiles in Italy in the drafting of his next letter to Kennedy.
- (6:00 P.M.; 1:00 A.M., 27 October, Moscow time) Owing to delays in translation and transmission, Khrushchev's 26 October letter finally arrives in Washington. The letter proposes a solution along the lines suggested more explicitly by Fomin. ExComm mistakenly assumes Fomin's message to Scali was a precursor to Khrushchev's letter; Fomin, however, had no prior knowledge of Khrushchev's letter and had been acting on his own initiative.
- (Afternoon) Fidel Castro meets with the Soviet commander in Cuba, Gen. Issa Pliyev, who informs him that all units are "ready for combat." Fidel Castro then meets with the rest of the Cuban leadership to discuss the next course of action.
- Castro authorizes his air-defense forces, none of them equipped with SAMs, to fire on all American aircraft within range.
- Dean Rusk authorizes Scali to tell Fomin "that the highest levels in the government of the U.S." see real potential in his terms and that the U.S. and Soviet representatives "could work this matter out with U Thant and with each other."
- (7:35 P.M.) Scali meets Fomin to relay Rusk's message. Fomin assures him that the information will be relayed to the highest levels of the Kremlin and to Zorin at the U.N.
- U.S. ambassadors are directed to avoid public comments suggesting any symmetry between the presence of American Jupiter missiles in Turkey and Soviet missiles in Cuba.
- Khrushchev sends a letter to U Thant indicating that Soviet ships will stay away from the quarantine area temporarily.
- JFK sends a statement to the U.N. Security Council reporting that construction at the ballistic missile sites in Cuba is continuing at a rapid pace and that the sites will soon achieve full operational capability. JFK concludes that "there is no evidence to date indicating that there is any intention to dismantle or discontinue work on these missile sites. On the contrary, the Soviets are rapidly

continuing their construction of missile support and launch facilities and serious attempts are underway to camouflage their efforts."

27 October

- (2:00 A.M.) At the conclusion of his meeting with the Cuban leadership, Fidel Castro visits Alekseev at the Soviet embassy, where he stays until 7:00 A.M. Convinced that they have done all they can to prepare for a U.S. invasion, Castro dictates a letter to Khrushchev. Dated 26 October, the letter itself is sent at 6:40 A.M. (1:40 P.M. Moscow time) on 27 October. Alekseev sends a brief cable to Moscow summarizing his discussions with Castro and Castro's letter; it arrives in Moscow at 2:40 P.M. Moscow time.
- (10:00 A.M.) The ExComm meets.
- (10:17 A.M.) A new letter from Khrushchev arrives in Washington, proposing a public trade of Soviet missiles in Cuba for Jupiter missiles in Turkey. Moscow Radio carries Khrushchev's proposal, as well as his statement that Soviet missiles in Cuba are under strict Soviet control.
- (Morning) The SAM network in Cuba becomes operational. Soviet air defense forces shoot down an American U-2 over Banes in eastern Cuba, killing its pilot, Maj. Rudolf Anderson, Jr.
- A U-2 from SAC's Strategic Reconnaissance Wing at Eielson Air Force Base in Alaska, reportedly on a "routine air sampling mission," strays into Soviet airspace over the Chukhotsk Peninsula. Although Soviet fighters scramble to intercept it, the plane returns safely to base without drawing fire.
- The Soviet ambassador to Ankara attempts to persuade the Turks to agree to the missile-exchange deal proposed in Khrushchev's latest letter.
- U.S. and Canadian naval forces establish an anti-submarine barrier southeast of Newfoundland.
- The Fifth Marine Expeditionary Brigade sails from the West Coast.
- (4:00 P.M.) The ExComm meets.
- (4:15 P.M.) Scali and Fomin meet again. Scali has instructions from Rusk to determine what has happened to the previous proposal and why Khrushchev raised the idea of swapping Turkish for Cuban missiles. Fomin tells Scali he does not know and will attempt to find out.
- (6:10 P.M.; 1:10 A.M., 28 October, Moscow time) Gromyko orally relates to Khrushchev the contents of the Alekseev cable summarizing Castro's full letter of the previous day. Khrushchev interprets this as an appeal from Castro to launch a preemptive nuclear attack on the United States.
- (7:15 P.M.) RFK telephones Ambassador Dobrynin, requesting a meeting.
- (7:45 P.M.) Dobrynin and RFK meet. In his memoir, RFK recalls telling Dobrynin that the U.S. knew work on the missile bases in Cuba was continuing; that the shoot-down of the U-2 was a serious turn of events; that JFK did not want a military conflict but that his hand was being forced; that the U.S. needed a commitment "by tomorrow" that the Cuban missile bases would be removed by the Soviets, or the U.S. "would remove them"; and that the U.S. would not publicly trade missiles in Turkey for Soviet missiles in Cuba, though the Jupiters were scheduled to be removed in any case.
- (8:05 P.M.; 3:05 A.M., 28 October, Moscow time) Kennedy sends Khrushchev a carefully worded letter, potentially part of the contractual basis for a settlement. He writes: "(1) You would agree to remove these weapons systems from Cuba under appropriate United Nations observation and supervision; and undertake, with suitable safeguards, to halt the further introduction of such weapons systems into Cuba. (2) We, on our part, would agree, upon the

establishment of adequate arrangements through the United Nations, to ensure the carrying out and continuation of these commitments (a) to remove promptly the quarantine measures now in effect and (b) to give assurances against the invasion of Cuba."

- (9:00 P.M.) The ExComm meets. JFK reads a message from NATO commander-in-chief Gen. Lauris Norstad which presents the difficulty for NATO of any Cuban-Turkey missile trade. Also, JFK tells Stevenson to tell U Thant that a Soviet tanker is approaching the quarantine zone and to remind U Thant of the Soviet statement that their ships would not challenge the quarantine.

- (Late evening) JFK meets with Rusk, whom he asks to send a letter to President Andrew Cordier of Columbia University. Cordier is instructed, upon further signal from the White House, to give U Thant the letter, requesting him to propose the removal of both the Jupiters in Turkey and the Soviet missiles in Cuba. The contingency is never activated.

28 October

- (10:00 A.M. EST; 6:00 P.M. Moscow time) Radio Moscow announces that it will have the text of a new Khrushchev message when the ExComm convenes at 11:00. In part, it reads: "The Soviet Government, in addition to earlier instructions on the discontinuance of further work on construction sites, has given a new order to dismantle the weapons, which you describe as offensive, and to crate them and return them to the Soviet Union."

- JFK hails Khrushchev's decision as "an important and constructive contribution to peace."

- Khrushchev sends Fidel Castro a letter explaining his decision.

- Zorin informs U Thant that instructions to dismantle the missiles in Cuba arrived between 1:00 and 3:00 P.M. on 28 October, and that dismantling started at 5:00 P.M.

- American intelligence notices that troops in Cuban uniforms have taken up positions around the Soviet nuclear missile sites.

- In response to Khrushchev's message, Castro issues a five-point plan for the solution to the problems underlying tensions in the Caribbean, including an end to the U.S. economic embargo, an end to U.S. support for Cuban counterrevolutionary activities, and the return of the U.S. naval base at Guantánamo to Cuba. He steadfastly refuses to allow U.N. on-site inspections in Cuba.

29 October

- Adlai Stevenson and John McCloy meet with Vasily Kuznetsov in New York to work out details of the settlement.

30 October

- Khrushchev sends Fidel Castro a letter counseling patience and attempting to justify his lack of consultation prior to the decision to withdraw the missiles.

- U Thant travels to Cuba to secure Castro's cooperation in the settlement of the crisis.

31 October

- Castro replies to Khrushchev's letter of the day before and severely criticizes Khrushchev's handling of the crisis.

2 November

- Mikoyan travels to Cuba to smooth over relations with Castro. Mikoyan's instructions are to discuss verification procedures for the removal of the Soviet missiles, and to enlist Castro's cooperation in complying with the terms of the agreement, which include withdrawal of Il-28 bombers.

3 November
- Troops in Cuban uniform withdraw from the area of the Soviet nuclear missiles.

19 November
- Castro finally agrees to allow the withdrawal of the Il-28s.

20 November
- JFK announces at a press conference that Castro has agreed to permit the withdrawal of the Il-28 bombers within thirty days.
- U.S. forces return to their normal peacetime levels of alert.

21 November
- JFK issues a proclamation terminating the quarantine.

Appendix 2:
Letters Between Fidel Castro and Nikita Khrushchev

IN JANUARY 1989, DURING A U.S.–SOVIET–CUBAN CONFERENCE IN Moscow on the Cuban missile crisis, Sergei Khrushchev, son of former Soviet leader Nikita Khrushchev, said that during the crisis Fidel Castro had requested the preemptive launch of Soviet nuclear weapons in Cuba against the United States. Both Soviet and Cuban denials followed this revelation.

In September 1990, with the publication of *Khrushchev Remembers: The Glasnost Tapes,* Nikita Khrushchev's side of the story became clearer. In the book he recounts receiving a cable from Castro urging the Soviets to launch their nuclear weapons. According to Khrushchev, Castro had concluded that an attack was unavoidable and that Khrushchev should act to preempt it. But in a speech delivered on 28 September 1990, Castro again denied the reports, claiming "it did not happen like that." He promised that sometime soon Cuba would release the letters between himself and Khrushchev at the height of the missile crisis so that "present generations [might] learn the real positions of Cuba at that time." On 23 November 1990 the letters were published in full in *Granma,* the Cuban Communist Party daily, and subsequently in the *Granma* English weekly in early December.

Why did Castro publish the letters when he did? There are several possible reasons. First, he had good reasons for wanting to get the history right. The letters indeed show that his request for a Soviet nuclear strike did not spring from the mind of a suicidal madman. Instead, his request was contingent on a prior U.S. invasion of the island. Second, the context of the exchange is Cuba's most illustrious hour on the world stage. At the time of publication of the letters, Cuba was already slipping into irrelevance as an actor with worldwide aspirations, and revisiting 1962 was meant to be a stirring reminder to Cubans of Castro's generation of how it used to be. Third, the barely hidden message for the United States is that Cuba will fight to the death against any U.S. invasion and, if this is doubted, one may simply consult these letters, which show that Castro's Cuba was willing in 1962 to be martyred for socialism. The same message is intended for the majority of Cubans born since October 1962: to be Cuban is to act heroically, as in October 1962. Teaching the younger generation about the heroism of their elders is very important to Cuban leaders of Castro's generation.

The long introductory editorial that precedes the letters says all this and more about Cuban motives for publishing the letters in November 1990. Although the editorial is unsigned, it is the work of Fidel Castro himself.

WITH THE HISTORICAL TRUTH AND MORALE OF BARAGUÁ

In his farewell letter to Comrade Fidel Castro, Commander Ernesto Che Guevara said: "I felt at your side the pride of belonging to our people in the sad and luminous days of the Caribbean crisis. Seldom has a statesman been more brilliant than you in those days. I am also proud of having followed you without hesitation, identi-fied with your way of thinking and of seeing and appraising dangers and principles."

Nearly three decades later, "dangers" and "principles" are and will always be key words in an exact summary of those events.

More than half of the current Cuban population hadn't been born in those crucial days of October 22–28, 1962. In the testimony of their predecessors, in classrooms and history books and in some works of art and literature, the young people of today have learned about the circumstances and outcome of the crisis which placed humanity on the brink of nuclear war, more so than any time before or since, up to the present day.

But even most of those who lived through the events in the Soviet Union, the United States and Cuba, are unfamiliar with the messages exchanged between October 26 and October 31, 1962, between the then prime minister of the Soviet Union, Nikita S. Khrushchev, and the leader of the Cuban Revolution, Commander in Chief Fidel Castro, letters which had been unpublished to date.

Why publish them now?

The Cuban government has in its possession many documents, material evi-dence and testimonies that can shed light on the origin, development and outcome of the crisis. Furthermore, the main political and military leaders who determined the destiny of our country in that crucial period are still alive.

In the 28 years that have passed since then, on various occasions journalists, scholars and even political leaders involved in those events have sought to formulate theories about the experiences of the crisis, to shed light on the most controversial aspects and processes which led to the fundamental decisions, without asking for the Cuban view.

The Cuban government has been patient and careful. We haven't even rushed to refute the speculations about the Cuban position in those events.

Among the documents in our possession which are, of course, also in the archives of the Soviet Union, are these five letters we are publishing now. We really didn't plan to publish them now, so that we wouldn't force a debate, and we thought it would be possible to await a consensus of the three concerned parties to open their secret archives and reveal to the world all the details of the crisis. Of course, we always reserved the right to take any initiative in this field.

As far as Cuba is concerned, we have nothing to hide and have no fear of letting the historical truth be known.

Comrade Fidel Castro alluded to the intention to publish these five messages in full in his speech at the main ceremony marking the 30th anniversary of the Committees for the Defense of the Revolution on September 28. In that speech Comrade Fidel referred to Khrushchev's autobiographical notes that are included in the third part of his memoirs, in which he said that at the height of the crisis Comrade Fidel urged him to launch a preventive nuclear strike against the United States. This version was published in late September in *Time* magazine as part of the memoir excerpts.

This led to the decision, mentioned by Comrade Fidel in his speech, to publish these documents, and we took steps to have it coincide with the appearance in the United States and Europe of an edition of the memoirs entitled *Khrushchev Remembers: the Glasnost Tapes.*

Thus these letters are coming out in Europe on the same day as *Granma* daily published them. This decision has become unavoidable, because in a summary of the content of the tapes, *Time* says that among other things the author speaks of Fidel Castro's "apocalyptic temerity" during the 1962 Cuban missile crisis.

Khrushchev is alleged to have said the following:

"Then we received a telegram from our embassy in Cuba. It said Castro claimed to have reliable reports that the United States was preparing to attack Cuba within a few hours. Our own intelligence service had informed us that the invasion was probably inevitable, unless we quickly reached agreement with the President."

Then he added:

"Castro suggested that, in order to prevent the destruction of our missiles, we should launch a preventive strike against the United States. My comrades in the leadership and I realized that our friend Fidel had not understood our intention. We had deployed the missiles not with the goal of attacking the United States but to prevent the United States from attacking Cuba."

Anybody can easily see that the quote attributed to Khrushchev is intended to serve the sinister purpose of fanning anti-Cuban hysteria in the United States and around the world.

This comes at a time when the Bush administration is drunk with triumphalism as a result of the changes that have taken place in Eastern Europe and the complex internal situation in the USSR. The economic blockade against Cuba is being stepped up, as well as slander campaigns and all sorts of pressures with which they hope to isolate us from the rest of the world, and radio and television broadcasts are being used for aggression in a vain attempt to confuse our people and weaken us internally. The purpose of all this is to destroy our socialist revolution, for which military aggression cannot be ruled out.

An objective and calm reading of the letters to Khrushchev sent by Comrade Fidel on October 26, 28 and 31, 1962, shows precisely the real context in which a possible nuclear strike against the United States was discussed. There are no grounds for confusion in these writings, but without examining the circumstances in which these letters were exchanged we can't clarify the reasons which led Khrushchev to his interpretation, contained not just in the memoirs but also in his letter to Comrade Fidel on October 30.

Although a simple reading of the documents sheds light on the dramatic nature of the situation, we must briefly recapitulate to understand the situation which prevailed when Comrade Fidel sent his first message.

We must keep in mind that in the early '60s the Soviet Union still hadn't achieved nuclear parity with the United States. The information we now have, based on published data, shows that while the United States had some 5000 nuclear warheads and nearly 500 intercontinental missiles, the USSR had only about 300 warheads and a few dozen missiles of that type.

Furthermore, while Soviet military doctrine was defensive, that of the United States was offensive.

After the failure of the Playa Girón mercenary invasion, Cuba and the USSR were both convinced, and this was backed up by the facts and intelligence reports, that the United States was preparing to attack Cuba directly. Under these circumstances, the Soviet and Cuban sides signed a military agreement which strengthened the defenses of both the USSR and Cuba.

The agreement included the deployment in Cuba of medium- and intermediate-range missiles equipped with nuclear warheads and the presence of more than 40,000 Soviet soldiers on our soil.

The Soviets, when they suggested the deployment of the weapons, said they were intended to increase the deterrent power of the Cuban Revolution in the face of a real threat of aggression from the United States.

It is also true that the deployment of the missiles in Cuba increased the Soviet Union's ability to respond to a U.S. nuclear attack, both in terms of speed and effectiveness, and according to U.S. sources made 85 percent of the nuclear missile installations on U.S. territory vulnerable.

Comrade Fidel and the Cuban leadership realized from the start that the presence of Soviet missiles in our territory could affect our country's image in the political field and increase the dangers of confrontation of another sort with the United States.

Nor did they fail to understand the true nature of Khrushchev's proposals, which was to improve the balance of forces between the USSR and the socialist community on the one hand and imperialism on the other. But it would have been a cowardly act of national selfishness to have rejected them. As Comrade Fidel has often said in private conversations, he felt that if at the time we expected the USSR to struggle to defend Cuba in case of an attack by the United States, as Nikita Khrushchev himself had publicly proclaimed, then we were also unavoidably bound to take risks for the Soviet Union.

Also, Cuba acquired strategic protection in the face of the ever-present risk of conventional war waged by the United States against our country and if a world war broke out for any reason, we would be affected anyway.

Thus, 42 medium-range nuclear missiles arrived in Cuba, along with 43,000 Soviet soldiers, while at the time of the crisis there were 270,000 men in regular units and 150,000 troops in the people's defense, more than 400,000 fighting men and women altogether.

It was stipulated in the Soviet-Cuban agreement that once the atomic weapons were in Cuba the Cuban-Soviet agreement would be made public, along with the existence of the weapons, based on the inalienable right of the Cuban state to possess the means of deterrence which it deemed necessary to assure its national security, granting imperialism no right to decide what sort of weapons we should or should not have. Both countries had acted within the strictest principles of international law.

Watching the crisis develop, given the way the imperialists were dealing with the issue, as the military buildup of our country became evident and all sorts of confused rumors circulated on the international scene, Cuba proposed that the military agreement between Cuba and the USSR be made public. But Khrushchev persisted in the idea that the missile installation should be kept secret until the military agreement was made public during his visit to Cuba, set for the end of that year. Since Khrushchev was the only one who could know the exact balance of forces between the USSR and the United States, Cuba had no alternative but to accept this view.

The Soviet premier also stressed that the USSR was willing to go as far as necessary, even if the plan for the military buildup of the island was discovered before Cuba and the USSR made it public.

Recalling the huge military potential which Washington deployed as of October 22 around and in the area near Cuba, it is clear that the so-called "quarantine" was simply a prelude to an air attack on the missiles and other strategic points in Cuba, or a direct and large-scale invasion.

On October 26, after our country had adopted and implemented down to the slightest detail the defense plan that included protection with dozens of antiaircraft batteries of both nuclear and ground-to-air missiles, Comrade Fidel wrote a message and dictated it the same night in the Soviet embassy in Havana to Ambassador Aleksandr Alekseev. At that time the U.S. naval forces had encircled the island, a joint force of 250,000 Marines and ground troops [sic] plus more than 1,000 planes and 250 naval vessels were ready to attack our country, using one of the variants determined by the Pentagon. As Fidel has explained, when he asked himself what was left to do on that exhausting day, he decided to send a message to Khrushchev urging him to remain firm and not make irreparable errors in case war did in fact break out.

Basically, the content of this message to Comrade Khrushchev was that, according to our view and reports, an attack could come any moment and the most likely variant was "an air attack against certain targets with the limited objective of destroying them. . . ."

Our commander in chief handled the issue with such maturity, serenity and responsibility that he did not suggest that if the United States limited itself to a massive air strike, there should be a Soviet military response, notwithstanding the heavy loss of lives and property such aggression would have implied. Furthermore, Cuba was absolutely opposed to allowing overflights by enemy planes, something which had been happening since the start of the crisis, because this facilitated a U.S. surprise attack on the missile bases and other military targets. Therefore on October 27 the Cuban military command ordered its antiaircraft artillery to fire on planes which violated our airspace and that information was passed on to the Soviet military.

Comrade Fidel felt that an invasion was "less probable although possible." Such an invasion of Cuba, on whose soil there were 43,000 Soviet soldiers, all of whom were at risk, would have meant war against the Soviet Union and therefore, simultaneously or subsequently, a nuclear strike on Soviet territory. This and only this is the context in which Comrade Fidel saw as a rational development of the events that if the United States invaded Cuba it wouldn't stop to await a Soviet reaction and would launch a nuclear attack.

In view of that situation, Fidel warned the Soviet Union that it should never allow "circumstances in which the imperialists could strike the first nuclear blow against it," eliminating such a danger then and forever in an act of rightful defense.

So why did Khrushchev interpret and later reaffirm in his memoirs that Comrade Fidel advocated a preventive nuclear strike against the United States, when in reality this idea was never even suggested?

Perhaps he mistakenly but sincerely came to this conclusion, even though there is no room for confusion in the messages themselves.

No honest person can lose sight, in order to really understand these events, of the unprecedented tension facing humanity in those days, the tremendous responsibility that rested on the shoulders of the leaders who handled the crisis and the fact that 28 years ago the infrastructure, cadres, technical personnel and even translators were at incipient levels, at a time when we had only a small group of experts. The means of communication between the USSR and Cuba and the coding systems reflected the level of development reached by the Soviets in the early '60s, which can't even be compared with those of today.

In such a situation and regardless of the extreme care displayed in the process of consultation, nobody can rule out the possibility of there having been some error. A matter of life or death such as that involved in the concept that, given the course of events precipitated by the United States, the USSR should not leave itself open for a nuclear first strike might have been taken by Khrushchev to mean that Moscow was being urged to undertake a preventive first strike. Nor can we exclude the fact that Soviet representatives in Cuba could have unwittingly contributed to this perception by reporting the determination of the Cuban leadership and people not to yield in the face of a possible large-scale attack, even a nuclear strike.

The subsequent letters, as you will see, reflect the effort by Comrade Fidel to clear away this erroneous interpretation.

For many years, with no less sinister aims, the Western news agencies published the fictional report that the commander in chief himself had personally shot down the U-2 spy plane in Banes on October 27, 1962.

At the time, and we have been unable to ascertain how this confusion came about, Khrushchev also attributed this act to our forces, given that the Revolutionary Armed Forces command, in line with instructions from the political leadership of the country and the commander in chief, had issued the order to open fire on any enemy plane which violated Cuban airspace. That is, this was not a thoughtless reaction but rather a conscious act in keeping with the situation.

However, as it later became well known, during the days of the crisis Cuban antiaircraft artillery only had machine guns and cannons, while the antiaircraft missile groups were part of the Soviet military contingent sent to Cuba under the direct command of the Soviet Defense Ministry.

There is no doubt whatsoever that had we had the proper weaponry, Cuba would have shot down without hesitation the enemy spy planes which flew at great altitude, but the fact is that the plane was shot down by the Soviet antiaircraft missile groups headed by Lieutenant General G. A. Voronkov, since retired, to whom Cuba subsequently awarded the Ernesto Che Guevara Order, first degree.

In the case of the U-2 downing, Khrushchev was unaware of these details and, as can be seen from his memoirs, he probably never learned that the antiaircraft missiles were operated by Soviet personnel alone and that the Soviet forces in Cuba obeyed the order to fire on planes which violated our airspace. Regarding the key issue of a preventive nuclear strike, his subsequent conduct shows that down to the last minute he sincerely believed his version. According to what is contained in the U.S. edition of his memoirs, when Comrade Fidel visited the USSR in 1963 and the issue was allegedly discussed in the presence of Aleksandr Alekseev, to whom Fidel had dictated the message on October 26, Khrushchev, who didn't speak Spanish and based himself on the Russian text to uphold his notion, said that the text contained the words "war" and "strike."

The word "war" does not appear in the Cuban text, although "strike" does, but in a very clear and precise context and with an unequivocal qualification: "If the second variant is implemented and the imperialists invade Cuba with the goal of occupying it. . . ." Was there by some chance an error in the Russian translation done by the Soviet embassy? Anything is possible.

If the memoirs are not false and haven't been altered on this subject, then we must accept the evidence that many years after the events, when he wrote his memoirs, Khrushchev still clung to that completely mistaken interpretation, and continued to believe it until the end.

However, the main and historically important difference is contained in the letter of October 31, in which Comrade Fidel expressed sorrow and bitterness over the manner in which the USSR and the United States reached a settlement behind Cuba's back. In this letter, the explanation about the mistaken notion of a preventive strike is impeccable and constitutes an indispensable precedent for Cuban political leaders, both present and future, because of the masterful combination of wisdom, respect, courage and loyalty to principles.

In this same way we must review the historical record of Nikita S. Khrushchev, at the head of the USSR, in his attitudes toward the Cuban revolutionary process. Khrushchev can never be accused of lacking political courage. In the development of relations between our parties and governments at the time, which came to be exemplary, when we felt that the other party was mistaken we would say so in a sincere and fraternal manner.

Khrushchev was the pioneer of political, economic and commercial relations between the Soviet Union and the Cuban Revolution. He always represented the interests of the people and the state he headed in an honorable manner and displayed internationalist conduct.

Khrushchev will always have a place of honor and respect in the eternal gratitude of the Cuban people toward the Soviet Union.

He was convinced for the rest of his life that the main positive contribution resulting from the crisis was the U.S. pledge not to invade Cuba. Twenty-eight years later, we can say that, short of an invasion, the United States has done everything possible to destroy the Cuban Revolution and blot out its example.

Cuban security and sovereignty have been preserved, above all, because the eight U.S. administrations which have in one way or the other repeated the errors of their predecessors have been unable to make a dent or weak point in the unity and consciousness of the Cuban people.

Faced by threats and dangers, as Fidel told Khrushchev on October 30, our country has always responded in the same way: by going on a war footing.

If there is a contribution of historical value, not just for the destiny of Cuba but also for the experience of revolutionary movements all over the world, resulting from the outcome of the missile crisis, which was a world crisis, it can be summed up in the five demands made by Cuba as a guarantee against U.S. imperialism:

1. End the economic blockade and all other measures of trade and economic pressure exerted by the United States against Cuba all over the world.
2. Halt subversive activities, the infiltration of arms and explosives by air and sea, the organization of mercenary invasions, the infiltration of spies and saboteurs carried out from the territory of the United States and some nations which are its accomplices.
3. End the pirate attacks carried out from bases in the United States and Puerto Rico.
4. Halt all violations of our air and naval space by U.S. warships and planes.
5. Withdraw from the Guantánamo Naval Base and return that Cuban territory held by the United States.

In the pride of being Cuban aroused in Che by the sad and luminous days of October 1962 we find the historical truth and the morale displayed by Antonio Maceo in Baraguá. The greatest danger faced by our country at the time was not nuclear extermination but surrender. This time there was no Zanjón Pact, but the same intransigence and courage was needed to repulse those who wanted to humiliate us through the imposition of an inspection of our territory. The refusal to accept that, plus the five points, became a twentieth-century Baraguá.

That is the lesson that inspires us in the face of new challenges and which will live on in the immortal memory of our people.

LETTERS BETWEEN FIDEL CASTRO AND NIKITA KHRUSHCHEV

Havana, October 26, 1962

Dear Comrade Khrushchev:

From an analysis of the situation and the reports in our possession, I consider that the aggression is almost imminent within the next 24 or 72 hours.

There are two possible variants: the first and likeliest one is an air attack against certain targets with the limited objective of destroying them; the second, less probable although possible, is invasion. I understand that this variant would call for a large number of forces and it is, in addition, the most repulsive form of aggression, which might inhibit them.

You can rest assured that we will firmly and resolutely resist attack, whatever it may be.

The morale of the Cuban people is extremely high and the aggressor will be confronted heroically.

At this time I want to convey to you briefly my personal opinion.

If the second variant is implemented and the imperialists invade Cuba with the goal of occupying it, the danger that that aggressive policy poses for humanity is so great that following that event the Soviet Union must never allow the circumstances in which the imperialists could launch the first nuclear strike against it.

I tell you this because I believe that the imperialists' aggressiveness is extremely dangerous and if they actually carry out the brutal act of invading Cuba in violation of international law and morality, that would be the moment to eliminate such danger forever through an act of clear legitimate defense, however harsh and terrible the solution would be, for there is no other.

It has influenced my opinion to see how this aggressive policy is developing, how the imperialists, disregarding world public opinion and ignoring principles and the law, are blockading the seas, violating our airspace and preparing an invasion, while at the same time frustrating every possibility for talks, even though they are aware of the seriousness of the problem.

You have been and continue to be a tireless defender of peace and I realize how bitter these hours must be, when the outcome of your superhuman efforts is so seriously threatened. However, up to the last moment we will maintain the hope that peace will be safeguarded and we are willing to contribute to this as much as we can. But at the same time, we are ready to calmly confront a situation which we view as quite real and quite close.

Once more I convey to you the infinite gratitude and recognition of our people to the Soviet people who have been so generous and fraternal with us, as well as our profound gratitude and admiration for you, and wish you success in the huge task and serious responsibilities ahead of you.

Fraternally,

Fidel Castro

Dear Comrade Fidel Castro:

Our October 27 message to President Kennedy allows for the question to be settled in your favor, to defend Cuba from an invasion and prevent war from breaking out. Kennedy's reply, which you apparently also know, offers assurances that the United States will not invade Cuba with its own forces, nor will it permit its allies to carry out an invasion. In this way the president of the United States has positively answered my messages of October 26 and 27, 1962.

We have now finished drafting our reply to the president's message. I am not going to convey it here, for you surely know the text, which is now being broadcast, over the radio.

With this motive I would like to recommend to you now, at this moment of change in the crisis, not to be carried away by sentiment and to show firmness. I must say that I understand your feelings of indignation toward the aggressive actions and violations of elementary norms of international law on the part of the United States.

But now, rather than law, what prevails is the senselessness of the militarists at the Pentagon. Now that an agreement is within sight, the Pentagon is searching for a pretext to frustrate this agreement. This is why it is organizing the provocative flights. Yesterday you shot down one of these, while earlier you didn't shoot them down when they overflew your territory. The aggressors will take advantage of such a step for their own purposes.

Therefore, I would like to advise you in a friendly manner to show patience, firmness and even more firmness. Naturally, if there's an invasion it will be necessary to repulse it by every means. But we mustn't allow ourselves to be carried away by provocations, because the Pentagon's unbridled militarists, now that the solution to the conflict is in sight and apparently in your favor, creating a guarantee against the invasion of Cuba, are trying to frustrate the agreement and provoke you into actions that could be used against you. I ask you not to give them the pretext for doing that.

On our part, we will do everything possible to stabilize the situation in Cuba, defend Cuba against invasion and assure you the possibilities for peacefully building a socialist society.

I send you greetings, extensive to all your leadership group.

N. Khrushchev

October 28, 1962

Havana
October 28, 1962

Mr. Nikita Khrushchev
Prime Minister of the Union
of Soviet Socialist Republics
USSR

Dear Comrade Khrushchev:

I have just received your letter.

The position of our government concerning your communication to us is embodied in the statement formulated today, whose text you surely know.

I wish to clear up something concerning the antiaircraft measures we adopted. You say: "Yesterday you shot down one of these [planes], while earlier you didn't shoot them down when they overflew your territory."

Earlier isolated violations were committed without a determined military purpose or without a real danger stemming from those flights.

This time that wasn't the case. There was the danger of a surprise attack on certain military installations. We decided not to sit back and wait for a surprise attack, with our detection radar turned off, when the potentially aggressive planes flying with impunity over the targets could destroy them totally. We didn't think we should allow that after all the efforts and expenses incurred in and, in addition, because it would weaken us greatly, militarily and morally. For that reason, on October 24 the Cuban forces mobilized 50 antiaircraft batteries, our entire reserve then, to provide support to the Soviet forces' positions. If we sought to avoid the risks of a surprise attack, it was necessary for Cuban artillerymen to have orders to shoot. The Soviet command can furnish you with additional reports of what happened to the plane that was shot down.

Earlier, airspace violations were carried out de facto and furtively. Yesterday the American government tried to make official the privilege of violating our airspace at any hour of the day and night. We cannot accept that, as it would be tantamount to giving up a sovereign prerogative. However, we agree that we must avoid an incident at this precise moment that could seriously harm the negotiations, so we will instruct the Cuban batteries not to open fire, but only for as long as the negotiations last and without revoking the declaration published yesterday about the decision to defend our airspace. It should also be taken into account that under the current tense conditions incidents can take place accidentally.

I also wish to inform you that we are in principle opposed to an inspection of our territory.

I appreciate extraordinarily the efforts you have made to keep the peace and we are absolutely in agreement with the need for struggling for that goal. If this is accomplished in a just, solid and definitive manner, it will be an inestimable service to humanity.

Fraternally,

Fidel Castro

Dear Comrade Fidel Castro:

We have received your letter of October 28 and the reports on the talks that you as well as President Dorticós have had with our ambassador.

We understand your situation and take into account the difficulties you now have during the first transitional stage after the liquidation of maximum tension that arose due to the threat of attack on the part of the U.S. imperialists, which you expected would occur at any moment.

We understand that certain difficulties have been created for you as a result of our having promised the U.S. government to withdraw the missile base from Cuba, since it is viewed as an offensive weapon, in exchange for the U.S. commitment to abandon plans for an invasion of Cuba by U.S. troops or those of its allies in the western hemisphere, and lift the so-called "quarantine," that is, bring the blockade of Cuba to an end. This led to the liquidation of the conflict in the Caribbean zone which, as you well realize, was characterized by the clash of two superpowers and the possibility of it being transformed into a thermonuclear world war using missiles.

As we learned from our ambassador, some Cubans have the opinion that the Cuban people want a declaration of another nature rather than the declaration of the withdrawal of the missiles. It's possible that this kind of feeling exists among the people. But we, political and government figures, are leaders of a people who doesn't know everything and can't readily comprehend all that we leaders must deal with. Therefore, we should march at the head of the people and then the people will follow us and respect us.

Had we, yielding to the sentiments prevailing among the people, allowed ourselves to be carried away by certain passionate sectors of the population and refused to come to a reasonable agreement with the U.S. government, then a war could have broken out, in the course of which millions of people would have died and the survivors would have pinned the blame on the leaders for not having taken all the necessary measures to prevent that war of annihilation.

Preventing the war and an attack on Cuba depended not just on the measures adopted by our governments but also on an estimate of the actions of the enemy forces deployed near you. Accordingly, the overall situation had to be considered.

In addition, there are opinions that you and we, as they say, failed to engage in consultations concerning these questions before adopting the decision known to you.

For this reason we believe that we consulted with you, dear Comrade Fidel Castro, receiving the cables, each one more alarming than the next, and finally your cable of October 27, saying you were nearly certain that an attack on Cuba would be launched. You believed it was merely a question of time, that the attack would take place within the next 24 or 72 hours. Upon receiving this alarming cable from you and aware of your courage, we viewed it as a very well-founded alarm.

Wasn't this consultation on your part with us? I have viewed this cable as a signal of extreme alarm. Under the conditions created, also bearing in mind the information that the unabated warmongering group of U.S. militarists wanted to take advantage of the situation that had been created and launch an attack on Cuba, if we had continued our consultations, we would have wasted time and this attack would have been carried out.

We came to the conclusion that our strategic missiles in Cuba became an ominous force for the imperialists: they were frightened and because of their fear that our rockets could be launched, they could have dared to liquidate them by bombing them or launching an invasion of Cuba. And it must be said that they could have knocked them all out. Therefore, I repeat, your alarm was absolutely well-founded.

In your cable of October 27 you proposed that we be the first to launch a nuclear strike against the territory of the enemy. You, of course, realize where that would have led. Rather than a simple strike, it would have been the start of a thermonuclear world war.

Dear Comrade Fidel Castro, I consider this proposal of yours incorrect, although I understand your motivation.

We have lived through the most serious moment when a nuclear world war could have broken out. Obviously, in that case, the United States would have sustained huge losses, but the Soviet Union and the whole socialist camp would have also suffered greatly. As far as Cuba is concerned, it would have been difficult to say even in general terms what this would have meant for them. In the first place, Cuba would have been burned in the fire of war. There's no doubt that the Cuban people would have fought courageously or that they would have died heroically. But we are not struggling against imperialism in order to die, but to take advantage of all our possibilities, to lose less in the struggle and win more to overcome and achieve the victory of communism.

Now, as a result of the measures taken, we reached the goal sought when we agreed with you to send the missiles to Cuba. We have wrested from the United States the commitment not to invade Cuba and not to permit their Latin American allies to do so. We have wrested all this from them without a nuclear strike.

We consider that we must take advantage of all the possibilities to defend Cuba, strengthen its independence and sovereignty, defeat military aggression and prevent a nuclear world war in our time.

And we have accomplished that.

Of course, we made concessions, accepted a commitment, acting according to the principle that a concession on one side is answered by a concession on the other side. The United States also made a concession. It made the commitment before all the world not to attack Cuba.

That's why when we compare aggression on the part of the United States and thermonuclear war with the commitment of a concession in exchange for a concession, the upholding of the inviolability of the Republic of Cuba and the prevention of a world war, I think that the total outcome of this reckoning, of this comparison, is perfectly clear.

Naturally, in defending Cuba as well as the other socialist countries, we can't rely on a U.S. government veto. We have adopted and will continue to adopt in the future all the measures necessary to strengthen our defense and build up our forces, so that we can strike back if needed. At present, as a result of our weapons supplies, Cuba is stronger than ever. Even after the dismantling of the missile installations you will have powerful weapons to throw back the enemy, on land, in the air and on the sea, in the approaches to the island. At the same time, as you will recall, we have said in our message to the president of the United States dated October 28, that at the same time we want to assure the Cuban people that we stand at their side and we will not forget our responsibility to help the Cuban people. It is clear to everyone that this is an extremely serious warning to the enemy on our part.

You also stated during the rallies that the United States can't be trusted. That, of course, is correct. We also view your statements on the conditions of the talks with the United States as correct. The shooting down of a U.S. plane over Cuba turned out to be a useful measure because this operation ended without complications. Let it be a lesson for the imperialists.

Needless to say, our enemies will interpret the events in their own way. The Cuban counterrevolution will also try to raise its head. But we think you will completely dominate your domestic enemies without our assistance. The main thing we have secured is preventing aggression on the part of your foreign enemy at present.

We feel that the aggressor came out the loser. He made preparations to attack Cuba but we stopped him and forced him to recognize before world public opinion that he won't do it at the current stage. We view this as a great victory. The imperialists, of course, will not stop their struggle against communism. But we also have our plans and we are going to adopt our measures. This process of struggle will continue as long as there are two political and social systems in the world, until one of these—and we know it will be our communist system—wins and triumphs throughout the world.

Comrade Fidel Castro, I have decided to send this reply to you as soon as possible. A more detailed analysis of everything that has happened will be made in the letter I'll send you shortly. In that letter I will make the broadest analysis of the situation and give you my evaluation of the outcome of the end of the conflict.

Now, as the talks to settle the conflict get underway, I ask you to send me your considerations. For our part, we will continue to report to you on the development of these talks and make all necessary consultations.

I wish you success, Comrade Fidel Castro. You will no doubt have success. There will still be machinations against you, but together with you, we will adopt all the measures necessary to paralyze them and contribute to the strengthening and development of the Cuban Revolution.

October 30, 1962

N. Khrushchev

Havana
October 31, 1962

Mr. Nikita S. Khrushchev
Prime Minister of the Soviet Union
USSR

Dear Comrade Khrushchev:

I received your letter of October 30. You understand that we indeed were consulted before you adopted the decision to withdraw the strategic missiles. You base yourself on the alarming news that you say reached you from Cuba and, finally, my cable of October 27. I don't know what news you received; I can only respond for the message that I sent you the evening of October 26, which reached you the 27th.

What we did in the face of the events, Comrade Khrushchev, was to prepare ourselves and get ready to fight. In Cuba there was only one kind of alarm, that of battle stations.

When in our opinion the imperialist attack became imminent I deemed it appropriate to so advise you and alert both the Soviet government and command—since there were Soviet forces committed to fight at our side to defend the Republic of Cuba from foreign aggression—about the possibility of an attack which we could not prevent but could resist.

I told you that the morale of our people was very high and that the aggression would be heroically resisted. At the end of the message I reiterated to you that we awaited the events calmly.

Danger couldn't impress us, for danger has been hanging over our country for a long time now and in a certain way we have grown used to it.

The Soviet troops which have been at our side know how admirable the stand of our people was throughout this crisis and the profound brotherhood that was created among the troops from both peoples during the decisive hours. Countless eyes of Cuban and Soviet men who were willing to die with supreme dignity shed tears upon learning about the surprising, sudden and practically unconditional decision to withdraw the weapons.

Perhaps you don't know the degree to which the Cuban people was ready to do its duty toward the nation and humanity.

I realized when I wrote them that the words contained in my letter could be misinterpreted by you and that was what happened, perhaps because you didn't read them carefully, perhaps because of the translation, perhaps because I meant to say so much in too few lines. However, I didn't hesitate to do it. Do you believe, Comrade Khrushchev, that we were selfishly thinking of ourselves, of our generous people willing to sacrifice themselves, and not at all in an unconscious manner but fully assured of the risk they ran?

No, Comrade Khrushchev. Few times in history, and it could even be said that never before, because no people had ever faced such a tremendous danger, was a people so willing to fight and die with such a universal sense of duty.

We knew, and do not presume that we ignored it, that we would have been annihilated, as you insinuate in your letter, in the event of nuclear war. However, that didn't prompt us to ask you to withdraw the missiles, that didn't prompt us to ask you to yield. Do you believe that we wanted that war? But how could we prevent it if the invasion finally took place? The fact is that this event was possible, that imperialism was obstructing every solution and that its demands were, from our point of view, impossible for the USSR and Cuba to accept.

And if war had broken out, what could we do with the insane people who unleashed the war? You yourself have said that under current conditions such a war would inevitably have escalated quickly into a nuclear war.

I understand that once aggression is unleashed, one shouldn't concede to the aggressor the privilege of deciding, moreover, when to use nuclear weapons. The destructive power of this weaponry is so great and the speed of its delivery so great that the aggressor would have a considerable initial advantage.

And I did not suggest to you, Comrade Khrushchev, that the USSR should be the aggressor, because that would be more than incorrect, it would be immoral and contemptible on my part. But from the instant the imperialists attack Cuba and while there are Soviet armed forces stationed in Cuba to help in our defense in case of an attack from abroad, the imperialists would by this act become aggressors against Cuba and against the USSR, and we would respond with a strike that would annihilate them.

Everyone has his own opinions and I maintain mine about the dangerousness of the aggressive circles in the Pentagon and their preference for a preventive strike. I did not suggest, Comrade Khrushchev, that in the midst of this crisis the Soviet Union should attack, which is what your letter seems to say; rather, that following an imperialist attack, the USSR should act without vacillation and should never make the mistake of allowing circumstances to develop in which the enemy makes the first nuclear strike against the USSR. And in this sense, Comrade Khrushchev, I maintain my point of view, because I understand it to be a true and just evaluation of a specific situation. You may be able to convince me that I am wrong, but you can't tell me that I am wrong without convincing me.

I know that this is a delicate issue that can only be broached in circumstances such as these and in a very personal message.

You may wonder what right I have to broach this topic. I do so without worrying about how thorny it is, following the dictates of my conscience as a revolutionary duty and inspired by the most unselfish sentiments of admiration and affection for the USSR, for what she represents for the future of humanity and by the concern that she should never again be the victim of the perfidy and betrayal of aggressors, as she was in 1941, and which cost so many lives and so much destruction. Moreover, I spoke not as a troublemaker but as a combatant from the most endangered trenches.

I do not see how you can state that we were consulted in the decision you took.

I would like nothing more than to be proved wrong at this moment. I only wish that you were right.

There are not just a few Cubans, as has been reported to you, but in fact many Cubans who are experiencing at this moment un-speakable bitterness and sadness.

The imperialists are talking once again of invading our country, which is proof of how ephemeral and untrustworthy their promises are. Our people, however, maintain their indestructible will to resist the aggressors and perhaps more than ever need to trust in themselves and in that will to struggle.

We will struggle against adverse circumstances, we will overcome the current difficulties and we will come out ahead, and nothing can destroy the ties of friendship and the eternal gratitude we feel toward the USSR.

Fraternally,

Fidel Castro

Acknowledgments

ALTHOUGH WE HAVE NOW MOVED ON TO SEPARATE INSTITUTIONS, we owe a profound debt to those who first brought us together at Harvard's Kennedy School of Government a decade ago: to Graham Allison, Albert Carnesale, and Joseph S. Nye, Jr. In 1983, with the financial backing of the Carnegie Corporation of New York, they launched the Avoiding Nuclear War Project. During the following year, they asked us to join the project as research fellows: a psychologist (JGB), a specialist in Soviet affairs (BJA), and a political scientist (DAW). We remember them fondly from the days when, as the "troika," they created a marvelous atmosphere for research.

The Avoiding Nuclear War Project began all its efforts by posing the question: "How might a nuclear war begin?" The three-word answer we came up with again and again was: "in a crisis." That question and answer was the origin of the Cuban missile crisis project, launched in 1986. Graham, Al, and Joe challenged us to "get empirical" and we have endeavored to carry out their directive, perhaps further than any of us imagined back in 1986. We began to organize a series of conferences, beginning in March 1987, which would become the primary vehicle for the investigation of the most dangerous crisis of the nuclear age.

With the appearance of the Cuban delegation at the January 1989 Moscow conference, we recognized that we had virtually to re-invent the missile crisis project. None of us previously believed that Cuba had much, if anything, to do with the crisis. We knew next to nothing about Cuba. But it was clear that their perspective, in which the crisis is connected foremost to the checkered history of U.S.-Cuban relations, needed to be integrated with what we had already uncovered on the crisis. So we began, with a trip to Cuba in May 1989, an odyssey of which this book is the culmination.

In January 1990, the missile crisis project moved to the Center for Foreign Policy Development, of the Thomas J. Watson Jr. Institute for International Studies at Brown University (CFPD). From the headquarters at Brown, a multinational research team was assembled to tackle the difficult historical and contemporary issues that would be involved in any attempt to carry through on our intention to pursue the Cuban side of the crisis all the way to Havana, to President Fidel Castro, and to do so in an intellectually responsible way. The "team" and its members are as follows.

CFPD. The initial discussions about bringing the project to CFPD were with Mark Garrison, the director of CFPD, and the late Howard R. Swearer, the director of the Watson Institute. Mark and Howard, both trained as specialists on the Soviet Union and Eastern Europe, seemed genuinely excited about having the project at Brown, even though the primary subject matter—Cuba—was, to say the least, distant from their central interests. Via Mark and Howard, Thomas J. Watson Jr., the founder of both the center and institute, became interested in the project. All three attended the first conference in the series sponsored by CFPD, in Antigua, in January 1991. We are grateful to all three. And, with Mark and Tom, we miss Howard very much. Richard Smoke, CFPD research director, has been the most constructive of critics. Betty Garrison and Sheila Fournier have handled financial, logistical, and personnel issues so effectively that a rumor arose during the course of the project that they had cloned themselves. Timely assistance was also provided at various times by Melissa Phillips, Lori Fonseca, Richard Gann, Annie Prout, Anne Maloney, Brenda Menard and Protima Darynani. Research assistance and substantive stimulation were provided by Aaron Belkin and Andrew Lynch. Finally, a special word must be said about David Lewis. David, a quadrilingual wizard, searched, translated (especially translated), organized, called, answered—everything. Without David Lewis, the project and this book would not exist.

The National Security Archive (NSA). The rock-bottom requirements of critical oral history are declassified documents and an accurate chronology. In meeting such requirements, the NSA has no equal. Thanks, therefore, to NSA founder and former director Scott Armstrong, the original subversive, anarchist-archivist; and to current director Thomas Blanton, who carries on the NSA's tradition of deep respect for the First Amendment. Thanks, too, to NSA general counsel Sheryl Walter, research director Malcolm Byrne, and senior research analysts Laurence Chang and Peter Kornbluh.

The Cubanology Community. With the decision to pursue the Cuban story of the Cuban missile crisis, it was necessary for us to recruit the best available expertise on everything related to Cuban foreign policy and U.S.-Cuban relations. Philip Brenner blazed the trail when he attended the Moscow conference in January 1989, as our Cuba expert. Phil has done remarkable work with us and with the NSA in securing documents. Wayne S. Smith has made several unique contributions to the project: as former chief of the U.S. Interests Section in Havana, as a leading scholar on Cuban culture and history, and as a bon vivant in both Washington and Havana. Jorge I. Domínguez, in addition to making his thorough knowledge of Cuban foreign policy available to us, quickly became the project's most incisive conceptual critic. We are also grateful to him for agreeing to write the Foreword to this book. Robert A. Pastor contributed his experience as a former official in the Carter administration and his vast scholarly knowledge of the Caribbean basin, along with a relentless desire to see this project through to its conclusion. Bob also assumed primary responsibility for briefing (and re-briefing) Robert McNamara on Cuba and Latin American affairs. Bob McNamara's superb performance at the Havana conference is due in part to his ability to learn quickly, but also in part to Bob Pastor's ability to teach effectively. Finally, Gillian Gunn, conversant with all aspects of contemporary Cuba, was a valuable resource during the Havana conference, especially on issues connecting the missile crisis with current Cuban affairs.

Cuban collaborators. Our Cuban colleagues performed miracles before, during (especially during), and after the Havana conference. Chief among them was Jorge Pollo, an organizational genius and possibly the hardest worker on the island. His (then) boss, Politburo member Jorge Risquet, brought high enthusiasm and political clout to the project. Rafael Hernández, Cuba's finest scholar of the missile crisis, continually refined our own understanding of the Cuban perspective on the events of October 1962. José Ignacio Vasquez, conference director at the Palace of Congresses in Havana, and his staff were marvels of quiet efficiency throughout the conference. And Ariel Ricardo, from his post in Washington, was very helpful at critical moments during the approaches to both the Antigua and Havana conferences.

Facilitators. The Havana conference was the culmination of a process that could have faltered at many junctures, were it not for the timely intervention of several people. Margaret R. Dulany, at the Havana conference and thereafter, helped provide us with access to key people in Havana and Washington. Our editor, Linda Healey, prodded, quizzed, cajoled, and in other ways intervened many times to help shape the book for the better. She was the first to recognize that, with Fidel Castro's decision to participate in the entire Havana conference, the kind of book we were planning would have to be rethought, and so it was. Arthur Schlesinger, Jr., not once, but several times, permitted us the use of his bay window at "Mortimer's" to hold key discussions and, in other ways, lent his support to a project that seemed to many, at the outset, unlikely to succeed. Janet Shenk must be the most resourceful of foundation officials. From her post at the tiny Arca Foundation, she embraced this project and got several of her colleagues to do likewise—always, it seemed, at just the right moment. Finally, Kimberly Stanton seemed to understand critical oral history instinctively, especially its capacity to be used by political leaders, past and present. Without her tremendous enthusiasm, which she was able to impart to her colleagues, the Havana conference could not have occurred.

Foundations. Since January 1990, when the missile crisis project moved to Brown University, it has been supported by the following donors: The Arca Foundation, Carnegie Corporation of New York, The Ford Foundation, The General Service Foundation, The John D. and Catherine T. MacArthur Foundation, Ploughshares Fund, Rockefeller Family and Associates, The Rockefeller Foundation, The Alfred P. Sloan Foundation, and the Winston Foundation for World Peace. We are grateful to all of them. Obviously, the content of this book is our responsibility, not theirs, though we trust they will take well-earned pride in whatever may be judged to be its achievements.

Several people provided timely aid: Raymond L. Garthoff, Michael Kraus, janet M. Lang, Larry Leduc, Ana Margheritis, Timothy Prinz,

Stephen D. Shenfield, Allison Stanger, Katharin L. Welch, Stephen E. Welch, and Melissa Williams. We gratefully acknowledge their assistance.

Finally, we wish to say a word about three people who repeatedly and skillfully cleared away obstacles on our road to Havana. At bottom, the years of preparation for the Havana conference was a process with two main objectives: (1) to convince Robert McNamara, the unofficial leader of our team, to go to Cuba for the meeting; and (2) to convince ourselves that, if Bob did go, Fidel Castro would respond creatively and positively. Dozens of conversations that occurred on the "road" to Havana were focused on just these doubts. All involved janet Lang, Bob McNamara, and José Antonio Arbesú, then chief of the Cuban Interests Section in Washington. Thanks to them, solutions were found. The rest, as recounted in this book, is critical oral history.

JGB, BJA, and DAW

Index